The Theoretical and Philosophical Foundations of Criminal Law

The International Library of Essays on Criminal Law
Series Editor: Stephen Shute

Titles in the Series:

The Codification of Criminal Law
Michael Bohlander and Daley Birkett

The Theoretical and Philosophical Foundations of Criminal Law
David Dolinko

Criminal Law and Human Rights
P.H.P.H.M.C. van Kempen

Expert Evidence and Scientific Proof in Criminal Trials
Paul Roberts

Theoretical Foundations of Criminal Trial Procedure
Paul Roberts

The Structure and Limits of Criminal Law
Paul H. Robinson

The Theoretical and Philosophical Foundations of Criminal Law

Edited by

David Dolinko

UCLA School of Law, USA

ASHGATE

Published by
Ashgate Publishing Limited
Wey Court East
Union Road
Farnham
Surrey GU9 7PT
England

Ashgate Publishing Company
110 Cherry Street
Suite 3-1
Burlington, VT 05401-3818
USA

www.ashgate.com

British Library Cataloguing in Publication Data
A catalogue record for this book is available from the British Library.

The Library of Congress has cataloged the printed edition as follows: 2013954269

ISBN 9781409460992

MIX
Paper from responsible sources
FSC® C013985

Printed in the United Kingdom by Henry Ling Limited,
at the Dorset Press, Dorchester, DT1 1HD

Contents

Acknowledgements

Ashgate would like to thank our researchers and the contributing authors who provided copies, along with the following for their permission to reprint copyright material.

Buffalo Criminal Law Center for the essay: John Gardner (2007), 'The Gist of Excuses', in *Offences and Defences: Selected Essays in the Philosophy of Criminal Law*, Oxford: Oxford University Press, pp. 121–39. First published in the *Buffalo Criminal Law Review*, **1** (1998). Copyright © 1998 by The Regents of the University of California.

California Law Review for the essay: Larry Alexander (2000), 'Insufficient Concern: A Unified Conception of Criminal Culpability', *California Law Review*, **88**, pp. 931–54. Copyright © 2000 California Law Review, Inc. By permission of the California Law Review.

Cambridge University Press for the essays: Michael S. Moore (1990), 'Choice, Character, and Excuse', *Social Philosophy and Policy*, **7**, pp. 29–58. Copyright © 1990 Social Philosophy and Policy Foundation, published by Cambridge University Press, reproduced with permission; Jean Hampton (1988), 'The Retributive Idea' (partial), in J. Hampton and J. Murphy, *Forgiveness and Mercy*, Cambridge: Cambridge University Press, pp. 111–43. Copyright © 1988 Cambridge University Press, reproduced with permission; R.A. Duff (1986), 'Expression, Penance and Reform' and 'The Ideal and the Actual' (partial), in *Trials and Punishment*, Cambridge: Cambridge University Press, pp. 233–77. Copyright © 1986 Cambridge University Press, reproduced with permission.

The Canadian Journal of Law & Jurisprudence for the essay: S.E. Marshall and R.A. Duff (1998), 'Criminalization and Sharing Wrongs', *Canadian Journal of Law & Jurisprudence*, **11**, pp. 7–22.

Columbia Law Review Association for the essay: Kent Greenawalt (1984), 'The Perplexing Borders of Justification and Excuse', *Columbia Law Review*, **84**, pp. 1897–927.

Duke University School of Law for the essay: Henry M. Hart, Jr. (1958), 'The Aims of the Criminal Law', *Law and Contemporary Problems*, **23**, pp. 401–41.

Minnesota Law Review for the essay: Arnold N. Enker (1969), 'Impossibility in Criminal Attempts – Legality and the Legal Process', *Minnesota Law Review*, **53**, pp. 665–710.

The Monist for the essay: Joel Feinberg (1965), 'The Expressive Function of Punishment', *The Monist*, **49**, pp. 397–423. Copyright © 1965 *The Monist: An International Quarterly Journal of General Philosophical Inquiry*, The Hegeler Institute. Reprinted by permission.

Springer for the essays: Michael D. Bayles (1982), 'Character, Purpose, and Criminal Responsibility', *Law and Philosophy*, **1**, pp. 5–20. Copyright © 1982 by D. Reidel Publishing

Co., Dordrecht, the Netherlands, and Boston, USA; R.A. Duff (1993), 'Choice, Character, and Criminal Liability', *Law and Philosophy*, **12**, pp. 345–83. Copyright © 1993 Kluwer Academic Publishers.

Taylor & Francis Group for the essay: Douglas N. Husak (1989), 'Motive and Criminal Liability', *Criminal Justice Ethics*, **8**, pp. 3–14. Copyright © 1989 John Jay College of Criminal Justice of The City University of New York, reprinted by permission of Taylor & Francis Ltd (http://www.tandfonline.com) on behalf of John Jay College of Criminal Justice of The City University of New York.

UCLA Law Review for the essay: Paul H. Robinson (1975), 'A Theory of Justification: Societal Harm as a Prerequisite for Criminal Liability', *UCLA Law Review*, **23**, pp. 266–92.

University of Chicago Press for the essay: Mitchell N. Berman (2008), 'Punishment and Justification', *Ethics*, **118**, pp. 258–90. Copyright © 2008 by the University of Chicago Press.

John Wiley & Sons, Inc. for the essays: Lawrence C. Becker (1974), 'Criminal Attempt and the Theory of the Law of Crimes', *Philosophy & Public Affairs*, **3**, pp. 262–94. Reproduced with permission of Blackwell Publishing Ltd; Judith Jarvis Thomson (1991), 'Self-Defense', *Philosophy & Public Affairs*, **20**, pp. 283–310. Reproduced with permission of Blackwell Publishing Ltd; Jeff McMahan (2005), 'The Basis of Moral Liability to Defensive Killing', *Philosophical Issues*, **15**, pp. 386–405. Copyright © 2005, John Wiley & Sons; David Lewis (1989), 'The Punishment that Leaves Something to Chance', *Philosophy & Public Affairs*, **18**, pp. 53–67. Reproduced with permission of Blackwell Publishing Ltd.

Every effort has been made to trace all the copyright holders, but if any have been inadvertently overlooked the publishers will be pleased to make the necessary arrangement at the first opportunity.

Publisher's Note

The material in this volume has been reproduced using the facsimile method. This means we can retain the original pagination to facilitate easy and correct citation of the original essays. It also explains the variety of typefaces, page layouts and numbering.

Series Preface

This series, consisting of six volumes, brings together some of the most significant and influential writings to have been published in the field of criminal law, criminal procedure, and criminal justice in the last century or so. Individually, each volume illuminates many of the key debates that have ebbed and flowed in the field; collectively, they provide the conceptual, theoretical, and structural tools we need to understand how contemporary criminal law works. That understanding is further advanced by the fact that each volume begins with a synthetic introduction which places the selected essays in their context and explores the connections and contrasts between them.

The Theoretical and Philosophical Foundations of Criminal Law (David Dolinko) includes 19 path-breaking essays on criminal law theory. These essays consider demanding questions such as: What conduct should and should not be criminalised? What authority does the state have to respond to various criminal wrong doings by inflicting intentional harm on perpetrators in the form of criminal punishment? What role do the concepts of individual 'choice', 'capacity' and 'character' play in the ascription of moral and criminal responsibility? What is the relevance of mental state to culpability judgement and how should this judgement change when we have full information about the reasons someone had for acting as they did? What liability should be imposed on people for the crimes they seek to bring about but fail? and, more generally, What place should luck and happenstance have in the criminal law?

In *The Structure and Limits of Criminal Law* (Paul H. Robinson) a further 19 essays confront a series of important foundational questions regarding how we should best understand the architecture of the criminal law: Is it possible to construct a single, unified, conceptual framework into which all criminal law rules fit? if it is, What value does such a framework have? Can we identify a set of necessary and sufficient conditions for criminal liability? and, if we can, What are the proper limits of these doctrines and how should they be expressed?

In the volume on *The Codification of Criminal Law* (Michael Bohlander and Daley Birkett) issues concerning the development of criminal codes are considered by another 24 essayists. The apparently simple question 'What is a criminal code?' turns out to be frustratingly difficult to answer, as is the question whether it is sensible for every country to adopt one. Most authors in this volume, whether approaching the topic from a theoretical, historical, or comparative perspective, answer the latter question in the affirmative. But a few are more sceptical. For them, whatever approach is taken, the promised benefits of full codification – simplicity, accessibility and comprehensibility – will always remain tantalisingly out of reach or be undermined or negated by the likely loss of flexibility and responsiveness that codification brings.

Concern with human rights has been present in one form or another in all human societies since time immemorial. Yet, despite these deep roots, the notion that every human being is a rights-bearer by virtue of their humanity, and that certain of these rights are universal and inalienable, has been taken up in the last 100 or so years in a way that has no parallel in any previous historical period. This explosion of interest in human rights thinking raises difficult questions for the doctrines, rules, and principles of criminal law, criminal procedure, and criminal justice. It creates tensions between the instrumental aims of crime reduction and public safety embraced by all criminal justice systems and the protection and safeguards that human rights discourse seeks to achieve. So how are these tensions to be eased? This is the key question that lies at the heart of the 14 essays included in *Criminal Law and Human Rights* (P.H.P.H.M.C. van Kempen). Through the lens of human rights discourse, central criminal law conundrums are considered: What are the implications of the right to be presumed innocent? How should the conflict between the right to liberty and the use of preventive detention be resolved? How should the protection we offer to privacy affect the way criminal investigations are conducted? What is the impact of human rights protection on the scope of legitimate criminalisation? and What is its impact on the doctrines, principles, and rules of substantive criminal law, criminal procedure, and sentencing?

In *Theoretical Foundations of Criminal Trial Procedure* (Paul Roberts) 19 essays are gathered together with a focus on the criminal trial and its theoretical underpinnings. The reflection in these pieces embraces the detail of the trial process and the law of evidence as well as discussing the values that ought to be honoured in criminal trials, casting light on these issues through case analysis, the use of interdisciplinary methods, and insights drawn from international comparisons.

Finally, in the volume of essays on *Expert Evidence and Scientific Proof in Criminal Trials* (Paul Roberts), 26 essays focus on the role that science plays in the modern criminal trial. Here abstract discussions of the concepts of truth, fallibility, and authority nestle side by side with analyses of data collected from interviews and psychological experiments, including the use of mock juries, discussion of major decided cases, surveys of solutions found in other legal systems, and consideration of practical questions such as the admissibility of scientific evidence in criminal trials and issues regarding how expert evidence and scientific proof are portrayed in the media and on television.

Taken as a whole, the volumes in this series serve up more than 100 essays written by leading scholars in the field of criminal law, criminal procedure, and criminal justice. Reading or re-reading them will inform (and, I trust, entertain) both the novice reader and the expert alike. But, whatever their distinction and significance, no set of essays can - or should - mark the end of debate in these important areas. My hope, therefore, is that this series will spark yet more intellectual inquiry which will continue to advance our knowledge and understanding of these fields, something which becomes more of a necessity as each day passes.

STEPHEN SHUTE
Head of the School of Law, Politics and Sociology, University of Sussex, UK
Series Editor

Introduction

The nineteen essays reprinted in this volume address fundamental theoretical issues concerning criminal law. Philosophers have made criminal law the subject of reflection since at least the time of Plato, who had the eponymous sophist in his *Protagoras* endorse a deterrent theory of punishment. Yet most of the essays in this collection were published in the last forty years. For only in recent times have philosophically-minded criminal law scholars examined foundational issues beyond the perennial debate over the justification of punishment.

Older scholars had not ignored such matters as the meaning of 'mens rea' or the contours of attempt liability. They had addressed these matters, however, largely through traditional modes of legal analysis such as collating and harmonizing prior cases and extracting general principles from their holdings, and had made little or no use of any doctrines or techniques of moral or political philosophy. In the 1950s and 1960s, however, a pair of roughly simultaneous developments prompted efforts to apply the methods of analytic philosophy to issues concerning substantive criminal law – the evolution of the Model Penal Code in the United States and the criminal law scholarship of H.L.A. Hart in Britain.

In 1962 the American Law Institute completed its decade-long effort to draft a model code of criminal law that could stimulate and help state and federal lawmakers to rethink, revise and reorganize their generally chaotic and unsystematic bodies of criminal law. The resulting Model Penal Code (MPC) was in fact very influential in spurring state reform efforts. But the Code and its official commentaries had at least as great an impact on the legal academy, functioning as 'the first comprehensive treatise in this country [the US] devoted to rethinking the premises and principles of the criminal law' (Kadish, 1999, p. 950).

The Code embodied a utilitarian, instrumentalist perspective that approached criminal law as a means of advancing society's overall interests by deterring harmful conduct and incapacitating those dangerous persons who engaged in such conduct. It stimulated many authors to adopt the same perspective in their own work. Others, however, were inspired to pursue a different form of criminal law scholarship, often called 'criminal law theory', which studied blaming and punishing practices and the moral and philosophical features of such concepts as responsibility, culpability, excuse and justification.

Another stimulus for this new interest in theory came from the path-breaking essays that H.L.A. Hart published between 1957 and 1967 and collected in book form in 1968 (Hart, 1968). The essays included an influential 'hybrid' theory of punishment combining features of retributivism and utilitarianism. More importantly, Hart subjected such topics as responsibility, criminal negligence and the rationale of excuses to rigorous philosophical scrutiny, using then-novel methods of analytic philosophy.

The post-Code, post-Hart years witnessed an outpouring of work in criminal theory. One milestone was the appearance in 1978 of George Fletcher's *Rethinking Criminal Law*, which focused the attention of scholars on the significance of the concepts of wrongdoing and attribution (or culpability).[1]

The sheer volume of criminal law theory makes it impossible to compile a truly representative selection of particularly significant, influential work without vastly exceeding space limitations. Unavoidably, much outstanding work has been excluded, including essays readily available in prior anthologies or that are simply too long for this volume (examples include Dan-Cohen, 1984; Kelman, 1981; Morris, 1968; and Schulhofer, 1974).

The essays that are included address recurring topics in criminal law theory. The three essays in Part I deal with the proper scope of criminal law – what should be criminalized, and why? Part II presents competing views on the roles of a person's choices and character in determining liability for criminal acts. In Part III, two authors challenge, in different ways, prevailing views about the mental states relevant to criminal liability. Part IV presents different opinions on the bases of justification and excuse defences, on the significance of the distinction, and on what justifies self-defensive killings. The essays in Part V deal with perennially fascinating problems concerning criminal attempts – the problem of impossible attempts and the widespread practice of punishing attempts less than equally culpable completed crimes. Finally, Part VI focuses on the continuing controversy over the propriety of criminal punishment. Joel Feinberg's classic contribution to the characterization of punishment is followed by three recent efforts to justify punishment as an institution.

The Structure and Limits of Criminal Law

No question can be more fundamental for criminal law theorists than what conduct to criminalize. Are there articulable restrictions on the sorts of behaviour that may appropriately be made criminal, or should lawmakers be free to impose criminal sanctions whenever they deem it desirable? The question gains urgency from the relentless expansion that the criminal law has undergone. William Stuntz observed a dozen years ago that 'criminal codes have continually broadened throughout the past century and a half' (2001, p. 511). One (conservative) estimate found 4,000 federal offences carrying criminal penalties (Luna, 2005, p. 712) and state criminal codes have swelled similarly (Robinson and Cahill, 2003, p. 172 and n.16). England's criminal law has grown similarly, with an estimated 8,000 offences on the books when the current century began (Ashworth, 2000, p. 226).

Henry Hart's essay (Chapter 1) was a reaction to this trend, and especially to the proliferation of strict liability 'public welfare offences'. Hart famously declared that the crucial distinction between criminal and civil sanctions is that the former embody a judgment of community condemnation. The central theme of his essay is that because they necessarily imply blame, criminal sanctions are misused when applied to conduct that is not morally blameworthy. Hart's emphasis on the central role of *blaming* in criminal liability was later elaborated by Joel Feinberg (Chapter 16) and became a prominent theme in discussions of the justification of punishment.

---

[1] Other outstanding features of this book include its use of 'a wide range of interdisciplinary sources and methodologies', its influential presentation of 'a nonconsequentialist framework for understanding criminal law' and its path-breaking attention to comparative criminal law (Christopher, 2004, p. 738).

Hart wanted only conduct meriting the community's moral condemnation to be criminalized. Can any perspicuous account be given of what conduct *does* merit such condemnation? Some theorists answer 'no', including the prominent English criminal scholar Glanville Williams. He concluded that while the distinctive features of criminal *proceedings* could be described, one could define a *crime* only as 'an act capable of being followed by criminal proceedings having a criminal outcome' (Williams, 1955, p. 130). The essays by Lawrence Becker (Chapter 2) and by S.E. Marshall and R.A. Duff (Chapter 3), however, are more optimistic, presenting rival substantive accounts of what conduct may appropriately be criminalized.

These essays endorse the widely held view that crimes are, *in some sense*, public or social wrongs, but explain that sense differently. Becker contends that the distinctive kind of social harm wrought by the major sorts of crime is 'social volatility' – the potential for the disruption of fundamental social cooperation that is created when members of society fear aggression by their fellow citizens. Marshall and Duff, however, believe Becker's view minimizes or even ignores the specific harm that the criminal inflicts on his or her individual victim. Such a view, they think, stems from an 'atomistic' moral or political viewpoint that takes individuals as prior to and independent of society. Their own account rests instead on their communitarian premise that living in society is a precondition of one's development as a fully responsible, autonomous moral agent, and that one's identity and goods are bound up with relationships with one's fellow citizens. Accordingly, they conceive of crimes as those wrongs to individuals that amount to attacks on the community itself because they challenge values central to the community's identity and self-understanding.

Each of these essays offers only a sketch of a theory of criminality, leaving many details that call for further development. One problem they face confronts any search for features distinguishing criminal from civil wrongs – the enormous variety of behaviours that are treated as criminal. Can one realistically hope to find common features linking murder, rape and treason with minor vandalism, tax evasion, prostitution and bookmaking? Becker, convinced that no single principle can account for this entire range, explicitly limits his attention to the most serious criminal offences. Marshall and Duff, though less explicit, focus on crimes that directly wrong individual victims, and clearly only the most serious of these are plausibly seen as attacks on truly central community values. One is left wondering whether there is any way to explain why criminal law extends to so wide a spectrum of lesser offences.

Criminal Responsibility

After 'What should be criminal?' – what behaviours merit the censure and 'hard treatment' characteristic of criminal punishment – a natural question is what censure and punishment are imposed *for*. For what, exactly, is the criminal held responsible? The essays in Part II explore the rival answers that currently dominate the discussion.

The more traditional view is the 'choice theory' of criminal responsibility: the offender is held liable and punished for her free choice to act wrongfully. In H.L.A. Hart's canonical formulation: 'What is crucial is that those whom we punish should have had, when they acted, the normal capacities, physical and mental, for doing what the law requires and abstaining from what it forbids, and a fair opportunity to exercise those capacities' (1968, p. 152). A defendant lacking such capacities or opportunity – who 'could not have done otherwise' or 'had no real choice' – is excused for an otherwise criminal action.

The competing account, tracing back to Hume,[2] is the 'character theory' of responsibility. 'According to this conception, ascriptions of responsibility are based upon judgments about the *character* of the agent: actions for which we hold a person fully responsible are those in which her usual character is centrally expressed' (Lacey, 1988, pp. 65–66). A defendant is excused for an otherwise criminal action, on this theory, when features of the defendant or his situation block the ordinary inference from defendant's act to his character.

Hume stressed the role of character judgments in our *moral* evaluations of others, a notion developed in more detail by the contemporary philosopher Richard Brandt (1969) and subsequently extended to *legal* excuses (Brandt, 1985). Michael Bayles's essay (Chapter 4) played a leading role in prompting legal scholars to examine the character theory as an alternative to the reigning choice theory.[3]

Bayles sees socially undesirable character traits, rather than acts manifesting them, as the direct objects of blame and punishment. Only conduct disclosing such a trait is blameworthy and properly punished. He confronts two principal objections:

I If defective character traits rather than acts are what is punished, why require an actus reus at all – why not punish anyone in whom such traits are detected, even if they have committed no forbidden acts?

II Conversely, should punishment be proper only if *many* criminal acts have been committed? A single act is very weak evidence of a settled character trait: it could be completely 'out of character'.

Bayles dismisses (I) summarily by saying that abolishing the act requirement would so greatly expand the state's punishment power as to jeopardize 'freedom' or 'liberty' (which he leaves unanalysed). He counters (II) by arguing that the law's attention to a defendant's mental state (mens rea) greatly strengthens the inference of character from a single criminal act.

Bayles also contends that the character theory accounts nicely for such features of existing criminal law as accomplice liability and the treatment of mistakes. Though acknowledging that his theory differs radically from existing law by denying that mental abnormality can exculpate, he notes that punishment is not the only possible response to blameworthy character traits. Since punishing the mentally abnormal is unlikely to eliminate such traits, other, more effective alternatives (treatment? quarantine?) are appropriate instead.

Michael Moore (Chapter 5) and R.A. Duff (Chapter 6) are not persuaded. For Moore, as a retributivist, punishment is properly inflicted only on those who deserve it – those morally responsible for their wrongful acts. He therefore believes that defeating objection (I) requires a *moral* argument that punishment cannot be deserved without a criminal act. Bayles offers only the *prudential* claim that punishment for character alone would expand the state's power to a dangerous degree, which Moore finds irrelevant. Nor is he impressed by the character theory's good fit with current criminal law. The issue, for Moore, is whether the theory correctly

[2] 'If any *action* be either virtuous or vicious, 'tis only as a sign of some quality or character. It must depend upon durable principles of the mind, which extend over the whole conduct, and enter into the personal character' (Hume, 1888, p. 575 (Book III, Part III, section 1)).

[3] The character theory also benefitted from the growth of interest among moral philosophers in virtue ethics, with its focus on the character of agents rather than on their discrete actions (Finkelstein, 2002, p. 318).

describes moral responsibility for wrongful acts, so that the criminal law *should* conform to it, and Moore argues that it fares much worse in accounting for moral responsibility than the rival choice theory, which he therefore favours.

Duff endorses neither theory. He first argues that a choice theorist cannot account for such defences as duress and insanity without conceding that liability depends on how a putatively criminal action is related to the actor's attitudes, concerns and values – that is, his character. But when Duff then turns to the character theory, he concludes that its partisans will have to concede a major role for choice and action.

Duff rejects Bayles's contention that mentally disordered offenders should get no defence (but should receive some alternative to punishment). Duff objects that this makes diagnosing and treating mentally disordered offenders simply one way to deal with the *guilty*, thereby collapsing the vital distinction between punishing responsible wrongdoers and medically treating dangerous but irresponsible persons.

He also challenges Bayles's treatment of objections (I) and (II). In dealing with (I), Bayles presupposes that criminal acts are *evidence* of defective character traits. Duff insists, however, that such conduct is not mere evidence but an essential *constituent* of the relevant trait, and that recognizing this permits a defence of the act requirement much stronger than that which Bayles gives. As for (II), which turns on the possibility of a genuinely 'out of character' criminal act, Duff dismisses the appeal to mens rea in favour of a detailed discussion of when an act would truly be out of character. He concludes that out-of-character acts are precisely those that a choice theorist would consider 'not freely chosen'. This in turn leads him to label the entire choice-versus-character controversy spurious – each theory expresses, *in distorted form*, a truth about criminal responsibility, and, undistorted, those truths are perfectly compatible. Ultimately Duff suggests that the apparent controversy may reflect a clash between individualist and communitarian conceptions of criminal law.

Culpability

'Culpability' has different meanings. In a broad sense, it refers to criminal blameworthiness in general. The MPC, however, popularized a narrow sense: the particular mental state or states required by the definition of a crime. It recognized only four such states – purpose, knowledge, recklessness and negligence – and many legislatures followed suit, doing away with the bewildering proliferation of common law and statutory culpability terms. Critics like Simons (1992) and Michaels (1998) questioned whether these four culpability states were really sufficient. Larry Alexander (Chapter 7), however, contends that only *one* culpability state – recklessness – is needed, and that every instance of criminal conduct exhibits a single kind of moral vice.[4]

Alexander defines recklessness as the conscious imposition on others of risks not justified by the actor's reasons. This is essentially the MPC definition now standard in American

[4] In a recent book co-authored with Kimberly Ferzan, Alexander has developed and defended this and other ideas for revising criminal law doctrines (Alexander and Ferzan, 2009), but the essay reprinted here marked their initial presentation.

law,[5] though Alexander drops the Code's requirement of a 'substantial' risk and looks to the risk the actor believes exists rather than the actual, 'objective' risk (a concept he finds meaningless). He argues that purpose and knowledge are simply special cases of recklessness, while negligence should not be considered a form of criminal culpability at all. All criminal actions thus become instances of reckless risk creation and therefore violate the same moral injunction: do not impose unjustified risks on other persons. Criminal blameworthiness – culpability in the broad sense – is simply the imposition of such a risk.

Alexander contends that reducing all culpability to recklessness precludes several possible errors: (1) treating purposeful imposition of a risk as always more blameworthy than knowing creation of the same risk, (2) treating knowing imposition of a risk as always more blameworthy than reckless creation of the same risk, and (3) treating 'wilful blindness' as a form of knowledge. However, sweeping all crimes into the single category of 'insufficient concern for the interests of others' seems questionable. Suppose John occasionally blasts loud music into the wee hours, keeping his neighbours awake, while Jane enjoys setting homeless people on fire and watching their agonizing deaths. Have John and Jane really exhibited the *same* moral vice, insufficient concern for the interests of others?

Where Alexander advocates a single, unified form of culpability, Douglas Husak (Chapter 8) wants to recognize *more* culpability states than the MPC does. Because *motives* profoundly affect criminal blameworthiness, he argues, they should be treated as culpability factors in determining an actor's criminal liability.

In modern, MPC-influenced criminal codes, a defendant's motive plays no part in deciding whether he is criminally liable, but at most may affect his sentence if he is convicted. Husak rejects the reasons given for treating motives purely as sentencing factors. Many of these explanations simply make the irrelevance of motive to liability true by definition or stipulation. Others distinguish motive from intention without explaining why this distinction should affect the relevance of those factors to a defendant's liability. Moreover, Husak observes that many crimes are defined to include acts varying widely in blameworthiness, while the discretion traditionally accorded to sentencing courts has been significantly trimmed in recent years. In combination, these facts make it likely that defendants very different in blameworthiness (and hence desert) will receive identical sentences. Factoring motives into the liability decision would avoid this problem.

But *how*, exactly, should motives influence determinations of liability? Husak suggests that reference to motives could sometimes be incorporated into offence definitions, as current law does to a limited extent under the rubric of 'specific intent'. He cites three other ways in which motives already affect criminal liability. Some justification defences apply only if the defendant acted with the proper motive ('justificatory intent'). Likewise, motives bear on the availability of certain excuse defences. Finally, motives can exert a hidden influence, as when they sway a decision-maker to exempt an actor from liability by treating relevant conduct as an omission rather than an act.

Beyond the role of motives, Husak's essay opens up the broader question of the relationship, if any, that does or should exist between culpability in the broad sense of blameworthiness

[5] English law has been different since 1981, when the House of Lords held that a person who creates an 'obvious' unjustifiable risk is reckless not only if he is conscious of the risk but also if he has given no thought to the possibility that such a risk exists (Williams, 1983, p. 106).

and culpability in the narrow sense of the mental state requirements for particular crimes. Husak recognizes that we cannot incorporate every factor relevant to blameworthiness into our offence definitions. How, then, should we decide which factors to incorporate? What, other than its relevance to blameworthiness, makes *motive* itself such a factor?

Defences, Justifications and Excuses

One defence to a criminal charge is the claim that not every required element of the crime was satisfied. More conceptually interesting, however, are defences in which one does not deny – and may even concede – that one had satisfied the elements of the crime, but alleges that additional circumstances make criminal liability improper or inappropriate. Some such defences assert that the defendant faced special circumstances in which his ordinarily unlawful conduct was the right thing to do, or at least permissible. Other defences focus on unusual factors that are said to make it unfair to hold the defendant responsible or blameworthy for conduct that is admittedly wrongful. 'In the one defense, briefly, we accept responsibility but deny that it was bad; in the other, we admit that it was bad but don't accept full, or even any, responsibility' (Austin, 1979, p. 176). Defences of the first sort are *justifications*; those of the second sort are *excuses*.

In Blackstone's day the law sharply distinguished excused from justified homicides, treating their perpetrators differently. By the mid-twentieth century, however, defences of both types simply resulted in acquittals, leading H.L.A. Hart to conclude that 'this distinction has no longer any legal importance' (1968, p. 13). But there has subsequently been a dramatic surge of scholarly interest in the nature and implications of excuse and justification, sparked largely by the path-breaking work of George Fletcher (see Fletcher, 1973, 1974, 1975 and especially 1978).[6] The essays in Part IV showcase some of the issues involved.

Paul Robinson's essay (Chapter 9) dates from the outset of his prolific career. It sketches a theory of justification that challenges both prevailing law and many other scholars. From the near-universal consensus that criminal law targets harmful conduct and not evil thoughts alone, Robinson infers that justification must depend on how things actually are rather than on the actor's beliefs, reasonable or not. Two corollaries of this 'objective' theory of justification are particularly controversial. Robinson rejects the widely held view – which the MPC advocates – that *mistaken* beliefs, if reasonable, can justify one's actions, contending that at most they may excuse the actor. And he insists that conduct can be justified by circumstances of which the actor is unaware.[7] Robinson has continued to champion what he now calls the

---

[6] Note in particular that Fletcher argued that the legal consequences of excuses and justifications do differ. Third parties may lawfully assist a justified actor but not one merely excused, and the target of an excused action, but not one that is justified, may forcibly resist (Fletcher 1978, pp. 760–62). For a court that agrees, see *United States* v. *Lopez*, 662 F. Supp. 1083 (N.D. Cal. 1987).

[7] Robinson shares the first of these views with Fletcher (1978, pp. 762–69), but not the second (Fletcher, 1975), while many other scholars reject both. See, for example, Baron (2005), Corrado (1991) and Dressler (1984). Hurd (1999) defends views paralleling Robinson's. Others argue that the entire debate is misconceived – see Berman (2003) and Gardner (1996).

'deeds' theory of justification (Robinson, 1996a),[8] and the issues he pioneered are currently prominent in discussions of justification (Dressler, 1987, pp. 1161–63, n. 22).

Just as Robinson challenges prevailing views of justification, John Gardner (Chapter 10) presents an unorthodox account of excuses. These are often said to be 'predicated upon the presence of some disability or disabling condition affecting the actor' (Milhizer, 2004, p. 817; see also Kadish, 1987, p. 258). For Gardner, however, the 'gist' of excuses is that in acting, one lived up to the standards applicable to one's 'role' at that time. He thus rejects accounts of excuses that flow from the 'choice' and 'character' theories of criminal responsibility discussed in Part II. A character theorist, for example, would excuse a dishonest act too atypical to manifest a dishonest character. Gardner objects that any dishonest act, no matter how unprecedented, necessarily manifests at least the stirrings of dishonesty. It is not merely evidence of that trait, but *constitutive* of a dishonest character – a point on which he agrees with Duff (see Chapter 6). Gardner would excuse the actor only if the act is shown *not* to be really dishonest, and therefore denies that '[t]he distinguishing feature of excusing conditions is that they preclude an inference from the act to the actor's character' (Fletcher, 1978, p. 799). Rather, an excuse must come into play earlier, precluding the judgment that the act was dishonest at all.

Some choice theorists relativize the standards of character relevant to an excuse to the actor's capacities.[9] For example, they would excuse a defendant who yielded to coercion despite exerting all the courage he could, but not one who had the capacity to behave *more* courageously and resist the coercion. This presupposes that someone can have the capacity to live up to standards higher than those he does in fact meet. Gardner, however, argues that the defendant's capacity for courageous action at the time he was coerced is identical to the courage he actually displayed at that time. To excuse him if he'd exerted all the courage he was capable of would therefore be to excuse him if he'd exerted as much courage as he had exerted – an utterly vacuous 'standard'.[10] The degree of courage (or other virtue) we are entitled to expect of a person, Gardner asserts, should be relativized not to the person's capacities but to her *role*. If, at the relevant time, she was not acting in any special role, we should ask whether she met the normative expectations that apply to the role of 'member of a human community'.[11]

Interestingly, Gardner believes it erroneous to think that an excuse is a denial of one's responsibility for one's actions. Actually, one is responsible for one's actions if and only if those actions are in principle amenable to justification and excuse, because that means those actions have intelligible rational explanations. Someone whose actions lack such explanations – for example, a psychotic individual – is not responsible and is accordingly *exempt* from liability (*not* 'excused').

---

[8] 'Objective' and 'subjective', Robinson believes, have so many other uses that they are best avoided. The issue is whether justifications rest on *deeds* (what actually takes place, whether or not the actor is aware of it) or *reasons* (the beliefs motivating the actor).

[9] Hart, for example, discussing negligence liability, deplores 'conditions of liability … not adjusted to the capacities of the accused' (1968, p. 154).

[10] Note that Gardner's argument implies the highly counterintuitive proposition that no one is ever capable of exhibiting more courage than they do in fact exhibit.

[11] For objections to Gardner's position, see, for example, Horder (2004, pp. 108–18) and Tadros (2001).

Robinson and Gardner accept the distinction between excuse and justification. Kent Greenawalt, however, finds this distinction problematic (Chapter 11). Without denying its existence and its importance in the law, he contends it would be a mistake to seek to make the distinction fully precise and systematic.

Greenawalt argues that none of the suggested bases for drawing the distinction can achieve precision without doing violence to both existing law and our intuitions about specific cases. Moreover, legal actors who favour the same outcome, but on different grounds, may face pointless, time-wasting disputes if they must agree on the excuse or justification label. Similar difficulties, says Greenawalt, will plague any effort at a precise border between justification and excuse, because of the 'fuzziness' of these concepts themselves and the 'uneasy quality' of many of the moral judgments relied upon in deciding that conduct should not be criminal. Of course, many concepts have 'fuzzy' boundaries, and line-drawing problems are pervasive in both law and morals. But Greenawalt believes that what he is pointing to are not garden-variety line-drawing problems but consequences of fundamental differences in the moral views that people accept. These divergent ethical stances, he claims, preclude universal agreement on precise demarcations of excused and justified conduct.

The final essays in Part IV focus on one prominent form of justification – self-defence.[12] Many people would likely find this defence self-explanatory: 'A bad guy threatens to kill you, so you kill him. Enough said' (Grabczynska and Ferzan, 2009, p. 235). Actually self-defence, especially the lethal variety, poses difficult philosophical questions that have generated a sizable recent literature. Chapters 12 and 13 are expositions of the two accounts dominant today.

Judith Jarvis Thomson (Chapter 12) is the leading proponent of a *rights-based theory* of self-defence,[13] based on the belief that, other things being equal, every person has the right not to be killed by another. It is, however, permissible – justified, not merely excused – to kill another person if they *lack* the right not to be killed by you. And they do lack that right if, unless you kill them, they will violate *your* right not to be killed. Thus, you have the right to kill an aggressor who, without justification, threatens your own life.

Thomson extends the right to self-defence beyond such 'villainous aggressors', contending that whether someone posing an imminent threat to your life is at fault in doing so is *irrelevant* to your right of self-defence. Indeed, she claims it is equally irrelevant whether the threatening person is actually *doing* anything to create the threat. If a tornado hurls an unconscious fat man directly towards you so that his body threatens to crush and kill you, you may blow the man up if necessary to save yourself.

Not surprisingly, there are dissenters from this aspect of Thomson's theory (see, for example, Otsuka, 1994). One is Jeff McMahan, whose 'Responsibility Account' (Chapter 13) is the chief rival to Thomson's theory. For McMahan, one may permissibly kill in self-defence someone morally responsible, through objectively unjustified action, for an unjust threat of great harm to others. The threat is 'unjust' if the victim is not liable and has not consented.

McMahan denies that you may kill the fat man propelled by the tornado – he has not threatened you by engaging in any unjustified action (or *any* action at all). The Responsibility

[12] Self-defence is commonly categorized as a justification, although some dissenters believe it functions as an excuse.

[13] A similar view appears in Uniacke (1994).

Account does not permit the self-defensive killing of such 'non-responsible threats'. McMahan's account, though, like Thomson's, does not make culpability a requirement for liability to a defensive killing. Consequently it has debatable implications of its own. Consider, for example, a careful motorist whose car goes out of control because of freakishly unforeseeable events, and veers towards a pedestrian. McMahan thinks the pedestrian justified in blowing the car up if that is her only hope of stopping it. The motorist, he says, *did* engage in 'objectively unjustified action' that created the risk. That action was *driving* – an activity known to involve some risk to innocent lives, and 'objectively unjustified' because it is not justifiable to drive a car that will in fact go out of control. That the driver had no way to *know* this would happen negates his culpability, but is irrelevant to *objective* justification.

Attempts

Liability for unsuccessful attempts to commit crimes is a notorious source of philosophical conundrums. Part V deals with two of the most perplexing: whether some or all 'impossible attempts' should be exempt from punishment, and why attempts receive less punishment than equally culpable completed crimes.

Impossibility is the subject of Arnold Enker's essay (Chapter 14). Any attempt is by definition a failure to achieve the perpetrator's criminal goal, but only in some cases do circumstances exist that make failure inevitable. The would-be poisoner who mistakes sugar for cyanide and the deluded 'fence' who buys what he believes is stolen merchandise in a sting operation are classic examples. Traditionally, many courts and commentators thought impossibility should be a defence to an attempt prosecution in certain situations, although disagreement was rampant as to which situations, and why. Today a large number of states have followed the MPC's recommendation and abolished the defence. Enker's is a prominent dissenting voice, arguing that a properly circumscribed impossibility defence serves valuable goals.

Enker begins by laying out different patterns of attempt cases and singling out the category at issue, in which the defendant, neither interrupted nor foiled, apparently engages in the intended actions, but misses his goal due to the absence of some circumstance included in the definition of the intended crime. The would-be poisoner and deluded fence in the previous paragraph are examples. The MPC and modern criminal codes assess liability in such cases 'subjectively' – that is, in accordance with the situation the defendant *believed* existed – and would therefore convict in both of the examples.[14]

Enker argues that the 'subjective' approach creates an unacceptable risk of convictions based entirely on evidence of what was in the defendant's mind – evidence often derived from such unreliable sources as the testimony of accomplices and informants or proof of prior convictions. Given sufficient evidence of the defendant's beliefs, *anything* the defendant does can constitute the actus reus of attempt, opening the door to serious injustice and abuse (see

[14] The only 'impossibility' defence these codes recognize occurs in the rare case of a defendant aware of relevant circumstances but mistaken in believing the law prohibits his conduct.

Hasnas, 2012, pp. 765–66). Courts and commentators who favour an impossibility defence, or at least balk at wholly eliminating it, find this argument helpful.[15]

Enker has another, more problematic argument against treating attempts 'subjectively'. Where the legislature defines the completed, substantive crime to require a particular circumstance element, he finds no reason to empower courts to dispense with that requirement and convict for attempt a defendant who mistakenly believed the circumstance existed. If it wants such defendants punished, the legislature can simply redefine the substantive offence to require only *belief* that the circumstance exists, rather than creating serious issues of legality by allowing what amounts to judicial creation of newly defined crimes. Critics object that such redefinition would result in impractically convoluted statutory language. More tellingly, they observe that Enker's suggestion would compel an all-or-nothing choice between liability for the *completed* crime and no liability at all, eliminating the intermediate strategy of attempt liability (Weigend, 1977, p. 242).

Of course, what makes attempt liability an 'intermediate' strategy is that it is punished less severely than the completed crime – the traditional and still prevalent punishment differential. But scholars have difficulty explaining why, given two equally culpable actors who undertake identical crimes, the one who fails – even if by sheer bad luck – should be punished less than his successful counterpart. Most find this disparity unjustifiable (see, for example, Becker, Chapter 2 in this volume; Feinberg, 1995; Kadish, 1994; Schulhofer, 1974), although several prominent authors disagree (Fletcher, 1978, pp. 472–83; Katz, 2000; Moore, 1997, pp. 191–247). David Lewis (Chapter 15) has advanced a particularly ingenious and elegant defence of the punishment differential.

Lewis suggests that the practice of punishing attempts more severely if they succeed is a disguised form of *penal lottery*. A penal lottery is a system that subjects convicted offenders to a *risk* of punishment, with a lottery-like procedure determining who 'wins' (light punishment or none at all) and who 'loses' (severe punishment). At first glance the suggestion appears preposterous – making the success or failure of the criminal's attempt dictate the magnitude of her punishment seems completely different from determining punishment by drawing straws. And the lottery in itself looks seriously unjust. Lewis, however, first argues that none of the obvious objections to the lottery hold up. He then constructs a sequence of changes to his imagined lottery, none of which, he claims, affects the justice of the proceedings, with the end result being our actual practice.

To simplify his reasoning Lewis imagines a lottery limited to those who attempt murder, whether successfully or not, with the losers being executed. The initial lottery gives everyone the same chance of winning. The first modification makes the risk to each criminal equal the risk of death his homicidal conduct had imposed on the victim. Succeeding steps lead to a lottery where the risk to each criminal is determined by an exact re-enactment of his crime, which is then replaced by *enactment* – that is, the criminal is executed if his victim dies and given a moderate sentence if the victim survives. That, of course, is our actual practice – imposing harsher punishment on successful attempts than on failed ones.

Lewis does not claim that his defence of the punishment differential is successful, only that it is superior to previous efforts. Indeed, he doubts that a valid defence exists. Moreover, Lewis

[15] See, for example, Hasnas (2002, pp. 57–61) and *United States* v. *Oviedo*, 525 F.2d 881 (5th Cir. 1976).

acknowledges that, intuitively, a penal lottery seems unjust, although he cannot articulate *why*. In effect, readers who share his intuition are challenged to explain it.

The Justification of Punishment

Part VI is devoted to the justification of criminal punishment – the subject of centuries of debate, as noted at the outset of this introduction. Punishing lawbreakers means deliberately imposing 'hard treatment' – pain, suffering or another unpleasant regimen – on non-consenting adults. Such treatment, including deprivation of property, liberty or even life, would ordinarily be deemed to violate the rights of the persons affected. What needs explaining is why it is morally permissible – if it is – to subject offenders to treatment morally prohibited in most contexts.

For centuries, those who proffered explanations usually fell into one or the other of two broad camps. *Consequentialists* pointed to punishment's allegedly beneficial results, such as deterring potential offenders; *retributivists* viewed punishment as justified regardless of its consequences because it was what criminals deserved. The back-and-forth between these camps often appeared stale and predictable. Recently, however, various novel approaches have appeared – some of them versions of the traditional views and others fitting into neither of those categories. Three of the items in Part VI exemplify the influential idea that punishment can be seen and defended as an *expressive* or *communicative* practice. The final essay adopts an intriguing and original strategy.

Joel Feinberg's 1965 essay (Chapter 16) launched the proliferation of expressive theories by giving the expressive aspect of punishment the attention and emphasis it had rarely received previously. To be sure, Feinberg himself notes that many legal scholars (like Henry Hart in the first essay in this book) had described punishment as expressing communal condemnation of criminal conduct. Yet, as he also notes, the then-dominant definition of punishment said nothing about its reprobative function. Feinberg insists that an adequate definition must include not only 'hard treatment' but also punishment's symbolic role as a conventional method of expressing resentment, indignation and judgments of disapproval and reprobation. This expressive role, he believes, distinguishes genuine punishment from non-punitive sanctions, and can thus determine whether the use of certain penalties invokes constitutional protections. On the other hand, Feinberg emphasizes that a purported justification of punishment will have to justify not only its 'hard treatment' component but the judgments and attitudes it symbolizes.

Feinberg's claim that punishment has an expressive or communicative aspect has been widely accepted.[16] That claim is purely analytic, however, dealing with the definition of punishment but not its justification.[17] Two influential efforts to use the communicative aspect of punishment as the basis for its justification are those of Jean Hampton (Chapter 17) and

[16] For example, Falls (1987, p. 42: defining punishment to include expressing disapproval of criminal behavior); Lacey (1988, p. 193: 'symbolic or denunciatory element' is 'implicit in all punishment'); Matravers (1999, p. 108); Nozick (1981, p. 370: 'Retributive punishment is an act of communicative behavior').

[17] '[T]he fact that the institution we call "punishment" is essentially expressive hardly makes out the normative claim that punishment is justified in virtue of its expressive cast' (Adler, 2000, p. 1414).

R.A. Duff (Chapter 18). Chapter 17 is Hampton's initial and most thorough exposition and explanation of a view she subsequently reiterated and defended (see, for example, Hampton, 1992a, 1992b). It is a retributivist view but based on an expressive theory of punishment. Traditionally, retributivists asserted that punishment was morally legitimate because criminals deserved it, relying on unanalysed intuitions to explain why they deserved it and why that legitimated inflicting it. Hampton, however, like several other contemporary retributivists (for example, Fingarette, 1977; Murphy, 1971; Nozick, 1981, pp. 374–93), seeks to replace intuition by reasoned argument.

In Hampton's view, both crime and punishment express claims about the comparative worth or value of different persons. By his crime, the criminal asserts that he is superior in value – worth more – than his victim and may therefore use her for his own purposes. Punishment refutes this false moral claim and reaffirms the equal worth of victim and wrongdoer. The criminal's violation of the victim's rights is seeming evidence of the criminal's superiority, but punishment masters the criminal just as he mastered his victim and thereby nullifies the putative evidence of his superiority. Punishment, therefore, is the criminal's *defeat* by the victim or her agent, the state, symbolizing the moral truth that victim and criminal are of equal worth. Indeed, Hampton asserts that nothing else can vindicate the victim's value as well as punishment.

Thus Hampton replaces the traditional retributivist appeal to a bedrock intuition of the 'fittingness' of deserved punishment with a reasoned account of the role punishment plays. To Feinberg's expressive account of punishment she adds that crimes themselves are expressive, and that punishment responds to what the crime expresses by refuting the criminal's false assertion of superiority.[18] That idea offers a way of understanding Hegel's cryptic claim that punishment 'annuls' the crime.

Because she views punishment as a *means* to the goal of reaffirming moral truth, Hampton believes her theory is consequentialist as well as retributive – a 'teleological reduction' of retributivism to which hardcore retributivists may well object.[19] Antony Duff, like Hampton, presents an expressive theory of punishment that is retributive and yet ascribes a forward-looking purpose to punishment. Unlike Hampton, however, Duff rejects the consequentialist label, arguing that his theory gives punishment a goal to which it is related not contingently but logically. And where Hampton thinks punishment aims at refuting what the criminal has (implicitly) *said*, Duff believes it aims at changing what the criminal *is*, by inducing a reform.

For Hampton, punishment expresses the moral truth. For Duff it does more – it communicates to the wrongdoer society's condemnatory judgment of her actions and seeks to persuade

---

[18] These ideas have been influential. See Garvey (2003, p. 306: criminal's act '*says* something about his value or worth compared to mine' and this '*expressive* or *moral* injury' 'is what makes it a crime'); Kahan (1996, p. 606: 'punishment has an expressive dimension: it conveys a society's condemnation of the wrongdoer, and its affirmation of the values that his acts deny'); Robinson (1996b, p. 202: 'criminal sanctions signal moral condemnation' and 'a criminal system serves a communicative function in our society, separating and labelling certain behavior as morally condemnable').

[19] Michael Moore, for example, warns that retributivism is not 'to be confused with denunciatory theories of punishment', which hold punishment justified as 'the vehicle through which society can express its condemnation of the criminal's behavior. This is a utilitarian theory, not a retributivist one.' He thus implicitly rejects the possibility of a theory that is *both* retributive and 'utilitarian' (consequentialist) (Moore, 1987, p. 181).

her to accept that judgment, repent her crime and reform herself. In playing this role, Duff emphasizes, punishment respects the criminal, treating her as a rational moral agent rather than someone to manipulate or coerce. The goal is not simply to compel compliance, but to get the wrongdoer to understand and assent to the law's reprobative judgment and *therefore* to modify her future behaviour.

Duff believes that the biggest problem for this account is explaining why 'hard treatment' should be the vehicle for this communication and persuasion, rather than, say, a formal judgment of condemnation or a purely symbolic reprobative ritual. To dismiss such alternatives as less effective than hard treatment, Duff thinks, would mean accepting the consequentialist deterrence arguments that his theory is meant to supplant. And insisting that only hard treatment can adequately express society's condemnation of crime would, in his view, invoke the notion of inflicting deserved punishment, which his theory is designed to avoid. Duff deals with this dilemma by relying on his most disputed notion: hard treatment as a *compulsory penance*.

Duff believes that a crime injures not only the direct victim but the community itself because the criminal implicitly rejects the community's foundational values. Moreover, the criminal harms himself by damaging or destroying his relationships with other community members. Punishment that achieves its purpose – that brings the offender to understand and repent the wrongness of his crime and reform his conduct – will lead the offender to will his own 'hard treatment' and make of it a penance that can expiate his guilt and thereby reconcile himself to his community and to the Good.

Not surprisingly, this concept of punishment as a compulsory penance that one hopes the criminal will accept and convert into voluntary penance is the aspect of Duff's theory most frequently attacked by critics (for example, Baker, 1992, pp. 157–60; Harrison and Duff, 1988; Narayan, 1993, pp. 174–75; von Hirsch, 1993, pp. 72–77). Duff himself takes pains to emphasize that he is concerned only with what punishment *ought* to be – what it would be in an *ideal* society. Yet his view has not been without influence.[20]

Unlike Hampton and Duff, Mitchell Berman (Chapter 19) attempts to justify the practice of punishment by a strikingly novel argument that makes no reference to its expressive aspect. In one respect, though, he follows a well-worn path: his is a 'mixed' theory of punishment, combining retributive and consequentialist elements. He seeks, however, to avoid making the consequentialist component lopsidedly dominant, as hybrid theories have often done, and instead to devise an 'integrated dualist' justification of punishment.

Berman breaks new ground by dichotomizing punishment and by rigorously analysing the notion of justification. He divides punishment into *core* and *peripheral* cases. In core cases, defendants receive appropriate punishment for crimes they did in fact commit. Peripheral cases include those of wrongly convicted defendants and those where factually guilty defendants receive disproportionate punishment. Berman justifies core and peripheral punishment separately and differently.

As for justification, Berman argues that it is required only in response to some specific reasons to doubt the propriety of a practice or institution – a 'demand basis'. Justification

[20] Steve Garvey, for instance, believes that punishment in an ideal community would 'be a form of secular penance aimed at the expiation of the wrongdoer's guilt and his reconciliation with the victim and the community' (1999, p. 1802).

can be provided either by *cancelling considerations*, which show that the purported demand basis is inapplicable, or by *overriding reasons*, which outweigh the reasons forming the demand basis.[21] Punishment is commonly believed to need justification because it involves the intentional infliction of suffering, but Berman analyses this into a conjunction of two demand bases. First, punishment needs justification because it produces bad states of affairs – pain, suffering, loss of liberty and the like. Second, punishment needs justification because the intentional infliction of such evils infringes the rights of those punished.

Core cases of punishment, Berman contends, are justified by cancellation, on retributivist grounds. Retributivism maintains that wrongdoers experiencing deserved suffering is *not* a bad state of affairs, which cancels the alleged reason against it. More unconventionally, Berman asserts that the intentional *infliction* of deserved suffering does not infringe the wrongdoer's right against purposeful infliction of suffering because *there is no such right*. Rather, he argues, there is a more general, foundational right to be treated with the respect owed to persons. Although this general right usually entails that one ought not intentionally be made to suffer, that entailment fails when the suffering is deserved. Inflicting such suffering on a wrongdoer *does* treat her with proper respect – respect for her nature as an autonomous, responsible moral agent.

Berman then considers 'peripheral cases' of punishment – punishing someone who deserves either no punishment whatsoever or less than is inflicted. He claims that inflicting such punishment, and its attendant suffering, on persons who are *believed* to deserve it is no less respectful of their personhood than inflicting truly deserved punishment. Respect is a quality of one's attitudes towards others and thus depends on one's beliefs concerning 'brute facts' about their conduct. The infliction of peripheral punishment is thus justified *a posteriori* if infliction of deserved punishment is justified by cancellation. However, the *suffering* of wrongly punished persons is a bad state of affairs regardless of what one believes about them. But that 'bad' is outweighed – *overridden* – by the good consequences attributable to peripheral punishment. The only way to eliminate all cases of mistaken punishment is to eliminate *all* punishment, Berman argues, so that the relevant good consequences include all the good produced by the entire institution of punishment, core and peripheral.

Berman's reasoning draws on such familiar ideas as the intrinsic goodness of deserved suffering, the Razian notion of cancelling conditions, and the claim that inflicting deserved punishment respects the criminal's autonomy and personhood. But its overall shape and strategy are new and ingenious. Of course, it can be challenged on a number of grounds. Consider, as an example, the claim that the supposed individual right against the infliction of suffering is merely a generally valid consequence of the more abstract right to treatment that respects one's personhood. Clearly, this abstract rule is very abstract indeed. Which other supposed individual rights are likewise merely 'rules of thumb' derived from the right to respect – the right to life? to liberty? to own property? to free speech? to participate in choosing one's representatives? Berman tells us that no one aspect of personhood (including interests, preferences, sentience and the capacity to choose) is 'privileged' to trump the others in cases of conflict. Does this leave many generally accepted 'rights' to be overridden? Suppose a dictatorship satisfied people's important interests (health, livelihood, education and the like) but allowed them no voice in government; might it nevertheless perfectly well honour people's

[21] Canceling considerations and overriding reasons are defined in Raz (1975, pp. 25–27).

abstract right to respect? How could one decide? Nevertheless, Berman's is an unusually sophisticated theory of punishment that gives both retributivism and consequentialism indispensable roles.

The range of topics treated in the nineteen essays in this collection amply confirms the claim at the outset of this introduction that contemporary scholars are asking foundational questions about many aspects of criminal law beyond the traditional concentration on whether, and if so why, punishing lawbreakers is a morally legitimate practice. These questions invite attention to broader philosophical issues beyond those specific to criminal law, such as what rights we have, and where they come from; the nature and determinants of moral blameworthiness; the meaning of 'character' and its relation to a person's overt behaviour; and what is involved in justifying an institution or a social practice.

At the same time, however, one can view all the diverse questions that concern the authors represented in this volume as related more or less directly to the criminal law's central institution, punishment. What sort of conduct can rightfully justify criminal punishment, and what mental states of the actor need to be taken into account? Does such punishment target the choices or the character of the offender? Under what circumstances is punishment inappropriate despite the presence of the requisite conduct and mental state, because the actor is excused or his action justified? When should punishment be imposed for an unsuccessful attempt at crime – and how much punishment is proper? Investigations of the sort represented in this volume thus form a satisfying link between the details of criminal law on the one side, and the larger concerns of moral and political philosophy on the other.

David DOLINKO

References

Adler, Matthew (2000), 'Expressive Theories of Law: A Skeptical Overview', *University of Pennsylvania Law Review*, **148**, pp. 1363–594.

Alexander, Larry and Ferzan, Kimberly Kessler (2009), *Crime and Culpability*, New York: Cambridge University Press.

Ashworth, Andrew (2000), 'Is the Criminal Law a Lost Cause?', *Law Quarterly Review*, **116**, pp. 225–56.

Austin, J.L. (1979), *Philosophical Papers* (3rd edn), ed. J.O. Urmson and G.J. Warnock, Oxford: Oxford University Press.

Baker, Brenda M. (1992), 'Consequentialism, Punishment, and Autonomy', in Wesley Cragg (ed.), *Retributivism and Its Critics*, Stuttgart: Franz Steiner, pp. 149–61.

Baron, Marcia (2005), 'Justifications and Excuses', *Ohio State Journal of Criminal Law*, **2**, pp. 387–406.

Berman, Mitchell (2003), 'Justification and Excuse, Law and Morality', *Duke Law Journal*, **53**, pp. 1–77.

Brandt, Richard (1969), 'A Utilitarian Theory of Excuses', *Philosophical Review*, **78**, pp. 337–61.

Brandt, Richard (1985), 'A Motivational Theory of Excuses in the Criminal Law', *Nomos*, **27**, pp. 165–98.

Corrado, Michael (1991), 'Notes on the Structure of a Theory of Excuses', *Journal of Criminal Law & Criminology*, **82**, pp. 465–97.

Dan-Cohen, Meir (1984), 'Decision Rules and Conduct Rules: On Acoustic Separation in Criminal Law', *Harvard Law Review*, **97**, pp. 625–77.

Dressler, Joshua (1984), 'New Thoughts about the Concept of Justification in the Criminal Law: A Critique of Fletcher's Thinking and *Rethinking*', *UCLA Law Review*, **32**, pp. 61–99.
Dressler, Joshua (1987), 'Justifications and Excuses: A Brief Review of the Concepts and the Literature', *Wayne Law Review*, **33**, pp. 1155–75.
Falls, M. Margaret (1987), 'Retribution, Reciprocity, and Respect for Persons', *Law & Philosophy*, **6**, pp. 25–51.
Feinberg, Joel (1995), 'Equal Punishment for Failed Attempts: Some Bad but Instructive Arguments Against It', *Arizona Law Review*, **37**, pp. 117–33.
Fingarette, Herbert (1977), 'Punishment and Suffering', *Proceedings and Addresses of the American Philosophical Association*, **50**, pp. 499–525.
Finkelstein, Claire (2002), 'Excuses and Dispositions in Criminal Law', *Buffalo Criminal Law Review*, **6**, pp. 317–59.
Fletcher, George (1973), 'Proportionality and the Psychotic Aggressor: A Vignette in Comparative Criminal Law', *Israel Law Review*, **8**, pp. 367–90.
Fletcher, George (1974), 'The Individualization of Excusing Conditions', *Southern California Law Review*, 47, pp. 1269–309.
Fletcher, George (1975), 'The Right Deed for the Wrong Reason: A Reply to Mr. Robinson', *UCLA Law Review*, **23**, pp. 293–321.
Fletcher, George (1978), *Rethinking Criminal Law*, Boston: Little, Brown.
Gardner, John (1996), 'Justifications and Reasons', in A.P. Simester and A.T.H. Smith (eds), *Harm and Culpability*, Oxford: Clarendon Press, pp. 103–29.
Garvey, Stephen (1999), 'Punishment as Atonement', *UCLA Law Review*, **46**, pp. 1801–58.
Garvey, Stephen (2003), 'Restorative Justice, Punishment, and Atonement', *Utah Law Review*, **2003**, pp. 303–17.
Grabczynska, Arlette and Ferzan, Kimberly Kessler (2009), 'Justifying *Killing in Self-Defense*', *Journal of Criminal Law and Criminology*, **99**, pp. 235–54.
Hampton, Jean (1992a), 'An Expressive Theory of Retribution', in Wesley Cragg (ed.), *Retributivism and Its Critics*, Stuttgart: Franz Steiner, pp. 1–25.
Hampton, Jean (1992b), 'Correcting Harm versus Righting Wrongs: The Goal of Retribution', *UCLA Law Review*, **39**, pp. 1659–702.
Harrison, Ross and Duff, R.A. (1988), 'Punishment and Crime', *Proceedings of the Aristotelian Society (suppl.)*, **62**, pp. 139–51.
Hart, H.L.A. (1968), *Punishment and Responsibility*, Oxford: Oxford University Press.
Hasnas, John (2002), 'Once More unto the Breach: The Inherent Liberalism of the Criminal Law and Liability for Attempting the Impossible', *Hastings Law Journal*, **54**, pp. 1–77.
Hasnas, John (2012), 'Attempt, Preparation, and Harm: The Case of the Jealous Ex-Husband', *Ohio State Journal of Criminal Law*, **9**, pp. 761–70.
Horder, Jeremy (2004), *Excusing Crime*, Oxford: Oxford University Press.
Hume, David (1888), *A Treatise of Human Nature*, ed. L.A. Selby-Bigge, Oxford: Clarendon Press.
Hurd, Heidi (1999), 'Justification and Excuse, Wrongdoing and Culpability', *Notre Dame Law Review*, **74**, pp. 1551–73.
Kadish, Sanford (1987), *Blame and Punishment*, New York: Macmillan Publishing Co.
Kadish, Sanford (1994), 'The Criminal Law and the Luck of the Draw', *Journal of Criminal Law & Criminology*, **84**, pp. 679–702.
Kadish, Sanford, Schulhofer, Stephen, Steiker, Carol and Barkow, Rachel (eds) (2012), *Criminal Law and Its Processes* (9th edn), New York: Wolters Kluwer.
Kahan, Dan (1996), 'What Do Alternative Sanctions Mean?', *University of Chicago Law Review*, **63**, pp. 591–653.

Katz, Leo (2000), 'Why the Successful Assassin is More Wicked than the Unsuccessful One', *California Law Review*, **88**, pp. 791–812.

Kelman, Mark (1981), 'Interpretive Construction in the Substantive Criminal Law', *Stanford Law Review*, **33**, pp. 591–673.

Lacey, Nicola (1988), *State Punishment*, London: Routledge.

Luna, Erik (2005), 'The Overcriminalization Phenomenon', *American University Law Review*, **54**, pp. 703–43.

Matravers, Matt (1999), 'What to Say? The Communicative Element in Punishment and Moral Theory', in M. Matravers (ed.), *Punishment and Political Theory*, Oxford: Hart, pp. 108–32.

Michaels, Alan (1998), 'Acceptance: The Missing Mental State', *Southern California Law Review*, **71**, pp. 953–1035.

Milhizer, Eugene (2004), 'Justification and Excuse: What They Were, What They Are, and What They Ought to Be', *St. John's Law Review*, **78**, pp. 725–895.

Moore, Michael (1987), 'The Moral Worth of Retribution', in F. Schoeman (ed.), *Responsibility, Character, and the Emotions*, Cambridge: Cambridge University Press, pp. 179–219.

Moore, Michael (1997), *Placing Blame*, Oxford: Clarendon Press.

Morris, Herbert (1968), 'Persons and Punishment', *The Monist*, **52**, pp. 475–501.

Murphy, Jeffrie (1971), 'Three Mistakes About Retributivism', *Analysis*, **31**, pp. 166–69.

Narayan, Uma (1993), 'Appropriate Responses and Preventive Benefits: Justifying Censure and Hard Treatment in Criminal Punishment', *Oxford Journal of Legal Studies*, **13**, pp. 166–82.

Nozick, Robert (1981), *Philosophical Explanations*, Cambridge, MA: Harvard University Press.

Otsuka, Michael (1994), 'Killing the Innocent in Self-Defense', *Philosophy & Public Affairs*, 23, pp.74–94

Raz, Joseph (1975), *Practical Reason and Norms*, New York: Oxford University Press.

Robinson, Paul (1996a), 'Competing Theories of Justification: Deeds v. Reasons', in A.P. Simester and A.T.H. Smith (eds), *Harm and Culpability*, Oxford: Clarendon Press, pp. 103–29.

Robinson, Paul (1996b), 'The Criminal-Civil Distinction and the Utility of Desert', *Boston University Law Review*, **76**, pp. 201–12.

Robinson, Paul and Cahill, Michael (2003), 'Can a Model Penal Code Second Save the States From Themselves?', *Ohio State Journal of Criminal Law*, **1**, pp. 169–77.

Schulhofer, Stephen (1974), 'Harm and Punishment: A Critique of Emphasis on the Results of Conduct in the Criminal Law', *University of Pennsylvania Law Review*, **122**, pp. 1497–607.

Simons, Kenneth (1992), 'Rethinking Mental States', *Boston University Law Review*, **72**, pp. 463–554.

Stuntz, William (2001), 'The Pathological Politics of Criminal Law', *Michigan Law Review*, **100**, pp. 505–600.

Tadros, Victor (2001), 'The Characters of Excuses', *Oxford Journal of Legal Studies*, **21**, pp. 495–519.

Uniacke, Suzanne (1994), *Permissible Killing*, Cambridge: Cambridge University Press.

Von Hirsch, Andrew (1993), *Censure and Sanctions*, Oxford: Clarendon Press.

Weigend, Thomas (1977), 'Why Lady Eldon Should Be Acquitted: The Social Harm in Attempting the Impossible', *DePaul Law Review*, **27**, pp. 231–73.

Williams, Glanville (1955), 'The Definition of Crime', *Current Legal Problems*, **8**, pp. 107–30.

Williams, Glanville (1983), *Textbook of Criminal Law* (2nd edn), London: Stevens.

Part I
The Structure and Limits of Criminal Law

[1]

THE AIMS OF THE CRIMINAL LAW*

HENRY M. HART, JR.†

I

INTRODUCTION

In trying to formulate the aims of the criminal law, it is important to be aware both of the reasons for making the effort and of the nature of the problem it poses.

The statement has been made, as if in complaint, that "there is hardly a penal code that can be said to have a single basic principle running through it."[1] But it needs to be clearly seen that this is simply a fact, and not a misfortune. A penal code that reflected only a single basic principle would be a very bad one. Social purposes can never be single or simple, or held unqualifiedly to the exclusion of all other social purposes; and an effort to make them so can result only in the sacrifice of other values which also are important. Thus, to take only one example, the purpose of preventing any particular kind of crime, or crimes generally, is qualified always by the purposes of avoiding the conviction of the innocent and of enhancing that sense of security throughout the society which is one of the prime functions of the manifold safeguards of American criminal procedure. And the same thing would be true even if the dominant purpose of the criminal law were thought to be the rehabilitation of offenders rather than the prevention of offenses.

Examination of the purposes commonly suggested for the criminal law will show that each of them is complex and that none may be thought of as wholly excluding the others. Suppose, for example, that the deterrence of offenses is taken to be the chief end. It will still be necessary to recognize that the rehabilitation of offenders, the disablement of offenders, the sharpening of the community's sense of right and wrong, and the satisfaction of the community's sense of just retribution may all serve this end by contributing to an ultimate reduction in the number of crimes. Even socialized vengeance may be accorded a marginal role, if it is understood as the provision of an orderly alternative to mob violence.

The problem, accordingly, is one of the priority and relationship of purposes as well as of their legitimacy—of multivalued rather than of single-valued thinking.[2]

* This paper is a revision of a mimeographed note originally prepared for first-year law students to serve as a supplement to other materials on the basic purposes of the criminal law. It will be seen that it still bears the marks of this origin both in the respect of being elementary and in the respect of not attempting a comprehensive examination of competing views of the criminal law.

† A.B. 1926, LL.B. 1930, S.J.D. 1931, Harvard University. Professor of Law, Harvard University. Co-author [with Herbert Wechsler], THE FEDERAL COURTS AND THE FEDERAL SYSTEM (1953).

[1] LIVINGSTON HALL AND SHELDON GLUECK, CASES ON THE CRIMINAL LAW AND ITS ENFORCEMENT 15 (3d ed. 1958).

[2] See Wechsler and Michael, *A Rationale of the Law of Homicide II*, 37 COLUM. L. REV. 1261, 1262 (1937).

There is still another range of complications which are ignored if an effort is made to formulate any single "theory" or set of "principles" of criminal law. The purpose of having principles and theories is to help in organizing thought. In the law, the ultimate purpose of thought is to help in deciding upon a course of action. In the criminal law, as in all law, questions about the action to be taken do not present themselves for decision in an institutional vacuum. They arise rather in the context of some established and specific procedure of decision: in a constitutional convention; in a legislature; in a prosecuting attorney's office; in a court charged with the determination of guilt or innocence; in a sentencing court; before a parole board; and so on. This means that each agency of decision must take account always of its own place in the institutional system and of what is necessary to maintain the integrity and workability of the system as a whole. A complex of institutional ends must be served, in other words, as well as a complex of substantive social ends.[3]

The principal levels of decision in the criminal law are numerous. The institutional considerations involved at the various levels differ so markedly that it seems worth while to discuss the question of aims separately, from the point of view of each of the major agencies of decision.

II

THE PERSPECTIVE OF CONSTITUTION MAKERS

We can get our broadest view of the aims of the criminal law if we look at them from the point of view of the makers of a constitution—of those who are seeking to establish sound foundations for a tolerable and durable social order. From this point of view, these aims can be most readily seen, as they need to be seen, in their relation to the aims of the good society generally.

In this setting, the basic question emerges: Why should the good society make use of the method of the criminal law at all?

A. What the Method of the Criminal Law Is

The question posed raises preliminarily an even more fundamental inquiry: What do we mean by "crime" and "criminal"? Or, put more accurately, what should we understand to be "the method of the criminal law," the use of which is in question? This latter way of formulating the preliminary inquiry is more accurate, because it pictures the criminal law as a process, a way of doing something, which is what it is. A great deal of intellectual energy has been misspent in an effort to develop a concept of crime as "a natural and social phenomenon"[4] abstracted from the functioning system of institutions which make use of the concept and give it

[3] See *Note on Organized Societies and the Principle of Institutional Settlement*, in HENRY M. HART, JR. AND ALBERT M. SACKS, THE LEGAL PROCESS: BASIC PROBLEMS IN THE MAKING AND APPLICATION OF LAW 1 (mim. ed. 1957).

[4] See the discussion of the Italian positivists and their influence in American criminology in JEROME HALL, GENERAL PRINCIPLES OF CRIMINAL LAW 539-51 (1947), especially at p. 549.

impact and meaning.[5] But the criminal law, like all law, is concerned with the pursuit of human purposes through the forms and modes of social organization, and it needs always to be thought about in that context as a method or process of doing something.

What then are the characteristics of this method?

1. The method operates by means of a series of directions, or commands, formulated in general terms, telling people what they must or must not do. Mostly, the commands of the criminal law are "must-nots," or prohibitions, which can be satisfied by inaction. "Do not murder, rape, or rob." But some of them are "musts," or affirmative requirements, which can be satisfied only by taking a specifically, or relatively specifically, described kind of action. "Support your wife and children," and "File your income tax return."[6]

2. The commands are taken as valid and binding upon all those who fall within their terms when the time comes for complying with them, whether or not they have been formulated in advance in a single authoritative set of words.[7] They speak to members of the community, in other words, in the community's behalf, with all the power and prestige of the community behind them.

3. The commands are subject to one or more sanctions for disobedience which the community is prepared to enforce.

Thus far, it will be noticed, nothing has been said about the criminal law which is not true also of a large part of the noncriminal, or civil, law. The law of torts, the law of contracts, and almost every other branch of private law that can be mentioned operate, too, with general directions prohibiting or requiring described types of conduct, and the community's tribunals enforce these commands.[8] What, then, is distinctive about the method of the criminal law?

Can crimes be distinguished from civil wrongs on the ground that they constitute injuries to society generally which society is interested in preventing? The difficulty is that society is interested also in the due fulfillment of contracts and the avoidance of traffic accidents and most of the other stuff of civil litigation. The civil law is framed and interpreted and enforced with a constant eye to these social

[5] *Cf.* Llewellyn, *Law and the Social Sciences—Especially Sociology,* 62 HARV. L. REV. 1286, 1287 (1949): "When I was younger I used to hear smuggish assertions among my sociological friends, such as: 'I take the sociological, *not* the legal, approach to crime'; and I suspect an inquiring reporter could still hear much of the same (perhaps with 'psychiatric' often substituted for 'sociological')—though it is surely somewhat obvious that when you take 'the legal' out, you also take out 'crime'."

[6] For a discussion of types of legal duties generally, see HART AND SACKS, *op. cit. supra* note 3, at 121-23. Account should also be taken of a peculiar type of criminal prohibition, baffling analysis, which purports to forbid not conduct, but certain kinds of personal condition. See Lacey, *Vagrancy and Crimes of Personal Condition,* 66 HARV. L. REV. 1203 (1953); Foote, *Vagrancy-Type Law and Its Administration,* 104 U. PA. L. REV. 603 (1956). To the extent that these crimes are valid and enforceable, however, it seems that they reduce themselves to prohibitions of the conduct bringing about the condition.

[7] See HART AND SACKS, *op. cit. supra,* note 3, at 114-17.

[8] Many of the duties of the civil law, of course, are open-ended, the specific nature of what is to be done being privately determined, as in contracts, and wills. In the criminal law, in contrast, officials bear the whole burden of prescribing the details of private conduct. But the same thing is true, for the most part, in the law of torts and other areas of civil law. See *id.* at 108-10, 129-31.

interests. Does the distinction lie in the fact that proceedings to enforce the criminal law are instituted by public officials rather than private complainants? The difficulty is that public officers may also bring many kinds of "civil" enforcement actions—for an injunction, for the recovery of a "civil" penalty, or even for the detention of the defendant by public authority.[9] Is the distinction, then, in the peculiar character of what is done to people who are adjudged to be criminals? The difficulty is that, with the possible exception of death, exactly the same kinds of unpleasant consequences, objectively considered, can be and are visited upon unsuccessful defendants in civil proceedings.[10]

If one were to judge from the notions apparently underlying many judicial opinions, and the overt language even of some of them, the solution of the puzzle is simply that a crime is anything which is *called* a crime,[11] and a criminal penalty is simply the penalty provided for doing anything which has been given that name. So vacant a concept is a betrayal of intellectual bankruptcy. Certainly, it poses no intelligible issue for a constitution-maker concerned to decide whether to make use of "the method of the criminal law." Moreover, it is false to popular understanding, and false also to the understanding embodied in existing constitutions. By implicit assumptions that are more impressive than any explicit assertions, these constitutions proclaim that a conviction for crime is a distinctive and serious matter—a something, and not a nothing.[12] What is that something?

4. What distinguishes a criminal from a civil sanction and all that distinguishes it, it is ventured, is the judgment of community condemnation which accompanies and justifies its imposition. As Professor Gardner wrote not long ago, in a distinct but cognate connection:[13]

[9] In many legal systems, moreover, private persons may institute criminal proceedings, as, of course, they could in the English common law and still can in contemporary England.

[10] Thus, debtors were once imprisoned. Insane persons, aliens held for deportation, and recalcitrant witnesses still are. Juvenile delinquents are put on probation. A judgment for the payment of money, which objectively considered is all that a fine is, is, of course, the characteristic civil judgment. And the amount of the civil judgment may be "punitive," and not merely compensatory or restorative.

[11] See, *e.g.*, State v. Dobry, 217 Iowa 858, 861-62, 250 N.W. 702, 704 (1933): "In finding what shall constitute a crime, the legislature has unlimited power. In other words, they can make it include certain elements or omit certain elements therefrom as in their judgment seems best." See, further, the discussion in part four *infra*.

[12] See, *e.g.*, in the Constitution of the United States, art. I, § 3, para. 7 (preserving safeguards of criminal trial in matters of impeachment); art. I, § 9, para. 2 (habeas corpus); art. I, § 9, para. 3 (forbidding passage of bills of attainder and ex post facto laws by Congress); art. I, § 10, para. 1, cl. 6 and 7 (forbidding passage of bills of attainder and ex post facto laws by any state); art. III, § 2, para. 3 (jury trial and venue in federal criminal cases); art. III, § 3 (definition and regulation of conviction and punishment for treason); art. IV, § 2, para. 2 (extradition); amendment IV (unreasonable searches and seizures and search warrants); amendment V (indictment by grand jury, double jeopardy, self-incrimination, and due process clauses); amendment VI (rights in criminal cases of speedy and public trial, jury trial, local venue, knowledge of accusation, confrontation of witnesses, compulsory process for obtaining witnesses, and assistance of counsel); amendment VIII (prohibition of excessive bail, excessive fines, and cruel and unusual punishments); amendment XIII (recognition of involuntary servitude as punishment for crime); and amendment XIV (due process and equal protection of the laws in state action).

[13] Gardner, *Bailey v. Richardson and the Constitution of the United States*, 33 B.U.L. REV. 176, 193 (1953). It is, of course, to be understood that Professor Gardner's statement and the statements in the

The essence of punishment for moral delinquency lies in the criminal conviction itself. One may lose more money on the stock market than in a court-room; a prisoner of war camp may well provide a harsher environment than a state prison; death on the field of battle has the same physical characteristics as death by sentence of law. It is the expression of the community's hatred, fear, or contempt for the convict which alone characterizes physical hardship as punishment.

If this is what a "criminal" penalty is, then we can say readily enough what a "crime" is. It is not simply anything which a legislature chooses to call a "crime." It is not simply antisocial conduct which public officers are given a responsibility to suppress. It is not simply any conduct to which a legislature chooses to attach a "criminal" penalty. It is conduct which, if duly shown to have taken place, will incur a formal and solemn pronouncement of the moral condemnation of the community.

5. The method of the criminal law, of course, involves something more than the threat (and, on due occasion, the expression) of community condemnation of antisocial conduct. It involves, in addition, the threat (and, on due occasion, the imposition) of unpleasant physical consequences, commonly called punishment. But if Professor Gardner is right, these added consequences take their character as punishment from the condemnation which precedes them and serves as the warrant for their infliction. Indeed, the condemnation plus the added consequences may well be considered, compendiously, as constituting the punishment. Otherwise, it would be necessary to think of a convicted criminal as going unpunished if the imposition or execution of his sentence is suspended.

In traditional thought and speech, the ideas of crime and punishment have been inseparable; the consequences of conviction for crime have been described as a matter of course as "punishment." The Constitution of the United States and its amendments, for example, use this word or its verb form in relation to criminal offenses no less than six times.[14] Today, "treatment" has become a fashionable euphemism for the older, ugly word. This bowdlerizing of the Constitution and of conventional speech may serve a useful purpose in discouraging unduly harsh sentences and emphasizing that punishment is not an end in itself. But to the extent that it dissociates the treatment of criminals from the social condemnation of their conduct which is implicit in their conviction, there is danger that it will confuse thought and do a disservice.

At least under existing law, there is a vital difference between the situation of a patient who has been committed to a mental hospital and the situation of an inmate

text do not accurately describe the significance of a criminal conviction under many modern regulatory and other statutes which penalize people who have had no awareness nor reason for awareness of wrongdoing. The central thesis of this paper, to be developed below, is that a sanction which ineradicably imports blame, both traditionally and in most of its current applications, is misused when it is thus applied to conduct which is not blameworthy.

[14] Art. I, § 3, para. 7; art. I, § 8, cl. 6; art. I, § 8, cl. 10; art. III, § 3, para. 2; amendment VIII; and amendment XIII.

of a state penitentiary. The core of the difference is precisely that the patient has not incurred the moral condemnation of his community, whereas the convict has.[15]

B. The Utility of the Method

We are in a position now to restate the basic question confronting our hypothetical constitution-makers. The question is whether to make use, in the projected social order, of the method of discouraging undesired conduct and encouraging desired conduct by means of the threat—and, when necessary, the fulfillment of the threat—of the community's condemnation of an actor's violation of law and of punishment, or treatment, of the actor as blameworthy for having committed the violation.

The question, like most legal questions, is one of alternatives. Perhaps the leading alternative, to judge from contemporary criticism of the penal law, would be to provide that people who behave badly should simply be treated as sick people to be cured, rather than as bad people to be condemned and punished. A constitutional guarantee to accomplish this could be readily drafted: "No person shall be subjected to condemnation or punishment for violation of law, but only to curative-rehabilitative treatment." Would the establishment of this new constitutional liberty be well-advised?

Paradoxically, this suggested guarantee, put forward here as an abandonment of the method of the criminal law, is not far removed from a point of view that has been widely urged in recent years as a proper rationale of existing law. Professors Hall and Glueck express this point of view in their recent casebook, more moderately than some of its other exponents. They recognize that "no general formula respecting the relative proportions of the various ingredients of the general punitive-corrective aim can be worked out." But they then go on to say:[16]

> It is the opinion of many of those who have studied both the causes of crime and the results of its treatment by means of the death penalty and the usual forms of incarceration, that for the vast majority of the general rule of delinquents and criminals, the corrective theory, based upon a conception of multiple causation and curative-rehabilitative treatment, should clearly predominate in legislation and in judicial and administrative practices. No other single theory is as closely related to the actual conditions and mechanisms of crime causation; no other gives as much promise of returning the offender to society not with the negative vacuum of punishment-induced fear but with the affirmative and constructive equipment—physical, mental and moral—for law-abidingness. Thus, in the long run, no other theory and practice gives greater promise of protecting society.

This suggests the possibility of a modified version of the constitutional guarantee in question, directing that "The corrective theory of crime and criminal justice,

[15] For a convincing statement that the difference does not lie in the necessarily greater gentleness of the treatment administered in the hospital, see de Grazia, *The Distinction of Being Mad*, 22 U. CHI. L. REV. 339, 348-55 (1955). Of course, there are also differences in the legal provisions governing the possibility of release, but these are mostly corollaries of the basic difference in the nature of the judgment directing detention.

[16] HALL AND GLUECK, *op. cit. supra* note 1, at 19.

based upon a conception of multiple causation and curative-rehabilitative treatment, shall predominate in legislation and in judicial and administrative practices." Would such a provision be workable? Would it be wise?

Any theory of criminal justice which emphasizes the criminal rather than the crime encounters an initial and crucial difficulty when it is sought to be applied at the stage of legislative enactment, where the problem in the first instance is to define and grade the crime. How *can* a conception of multiple causation and curative-rehabilitative treatment predominate in the definition and grading of crimes, let alone serve as the sole guide?[17] But even if it were possible to gauge in advance the types of conduct to be forbidden by the expected need for reformation of those who will thereafter engage in them, would it be sensible to try to do so? Can the content of the law's commands be rationally determined with an eye singly or chiefly to the expected deficiencies of character of those who will violate them? Obviously not. The interests of society in having certain things not done or done are also involved.[18]

Precisely because of the difficulties of relating the content of the law's commands to the need for reformation of those who violate them, a curative-rehabilitative theory of criminal justice tends always to depreciate, if not to deny, the significance of these general formulations and to focus attention instead on the individual defendant at the time of his apprehension, trial, and sentence. This has in it always a double danger—to the individual and to society. The danger to the individual is that he will be punished, or treated, for what he is or is believed to be, rather than for what he has done. If his offense is minor but the possibility of his reformation is thought to be slight, the other side of the coin of mercy can become cruelty.[19] The danger

[17] Is the correlation between describable types of conduct (acts or omissions), on the one hand, and the need for cure and rehabilitation of those who engage in them, on the other hand, so close that the need can be taken as a reliable index of the types of conduct to be forbidden and the differentiation among offenses to be made? These determinations must be made in advance and in general terms. In making them, the extent of the depravity of character characteristically manifested by particular types of behavior ought, of course, to be taken into account so far as it can be. But this is a factor which is peculiarly difficult to appraise ahead of time by a generalized judgment. Depravity of character and the need of the individual for cure and rehabilitation are essentially personal matters, as the whole modern theory of the individualization of correctional treatment bears witness. A fortiori, the susceptibility of the individual to rehabilitation is personal.

[18] For the conclusion that the reformative principle has little that is distinctive to contribute in the substantive differentiation between criminal and noncriminal behavior, see Michael and Wechsler, *A Rationale of the Law of Homicide I*, 37 COLUM. L. REV. 701, 757-61 (1937). For a detailed and judicious appraisal of the respective roles of the deterrent and reformative principles in the *treatment* of criminals, including the legislative grading of offenses, see part two of the same article. *Id.* at 1261.

[19] So, two contemporary advocates of "a rational approach to crime repression" who urge reformation as the central objective in the treatment of criminals are led to follow out the apparent logic of their position by saying that "those who cannot be reformed . . . must be segregated for life—but not necessarily punished—*irrespective of the crimes they have committed.*" (Emphasis added.) HARRY E. BARNES AND NEGLEY K. TEETERS, NEW HORIZONS IN CRIMINOLOGY: THE AMERICAN CRIME PROBLEM 953 (rev. ed. 1945).

Speaking of the school of positivism which has dominated American criminology in recent years, Professor Jerome Hall says: "Its dogmas biased not only theories concerning prevention but also, combined with its determinism, stigmatized punishment as vengeance—at the same time opening the door to unmitigated cruelty in the name of 'measures of safety'." HALL, *op. cit. supra* note 4, at 551.

The rash of so-called "sexual psychopath" laws which disgrace the statute books of many states

to society is that the effectiveness of the general commands of the criminal law as instruments for influencing behavior so as to avoid the necessity for enforcement proceedings will be weakened.

This brings us to the crux of the issue confronting our supposed constitution-makers. The commands of the criminal law are commands which the public interest requires people to comply with. This being so, will the public interest be adequately protected if the legislature is allowed only to say to people, "If you do not comply with any of these commands, you will merely be considered to be sick and subjected to officially-imposed rehabiltative treatment in an effort to cure you"? Can it be adequately protected if the legislature is required to say, "If you do not comply, your own personal need for cure and rehabilitation will be the predominating factor in determining what happens to you"? Or should the legislature be enabled to say, "If you violate any of these laws and the violation is culpable, your conduct will receive the formal and solemn condemnation of the community as morally blameworthy, and you will be subjected to whatever punishment, or treatment, is appropriate to vindicate the law and to further its various purposes"?

On the sheerly pragmatic ground of the need for equipping the proposed social order with adequate tools to discourage undesired conduct, a responsible constitution-maker assuredly would hesitate long before rejecting the third of these possibilities in favor of either of the first two. To be sure, the efficacy of criminal punishment as a deterrent has often been doubted. But it is to be observed that the doubts are usually expressed by those who are thinking from the restrospective, sanction-imposing point of view.[20] From this point of view, it is natural to be impressed by the undoubted fact that many people do become criminals, and will continue to do so, in spite of all the threats of condemnation and of treatment-in-

illustrate the possibilities to which this streak of cruelty may lead. See Hacker and Frym, *The Sexual Psychopath Act in Practice: A Critical Discussion*, 43 CALIF. L. REV. 766 (1955); Guttmacher and Weihofen, *Sex Offenses*, 43 J. CRIM. L., C. & P.S. 153 (1952). For the shock of a concrete example of what may happen in the administration of such laws, until the courts correct it, read *In re Maddox*, 88 N.W.2d 470 (Mich. 1958), where the state hospital psychiatrist insisted on assuming the truth of unproved police charges in his treatment of one who had been civilly committed as a "sexual psychopath" and, when his victim kept protesting his innocence, had him transferred to state prison on the ground that this refusal to admit guilt made him "an adamant patient" lacking "the desire to get well" which was necessary to make him amenable to hospital care. Consider also the possibilities implicit in the Maryland Defective Delinquent Law, MD. ANN. CODE art. 31B (1951).

[20] See, *e.g.*, ADVISORY COUNCIL OF JUDGES, NPPA GUIDES FOR SENTENCING (1957). Almost the whole of what this handbook says about deterrence as a factor in sentencing is contained in the following paragraph:

"In some situations, knowledge of a penalty may deter an individual tempted to violate a law; on the whole, however, the deterrent force of severe penalty alone for major crimes has been highly overrated and belief in its value is unrealistic. A stubborn reliance on deterrence results in making sentences increasingly severe, and excessively severe sentences produce deteriorating effects on prisoners, without corresponding benefits to society." *Id.* at 2.

It will be observed that this confuses the question of the efficacy of the threat of criminal condemnation and punishment as a factor in controlling the conduct of the bulk of mankind with the question of the efficacy of severe punishments, a confusion which is not uncommon. Few people will deny that excessively severe sentences are undesirable, and many will agree that a large proportion of the sentences currently meted out *are* excessively severe.

consequence-of-condemnation that society can offer. But the people who do *not* commit crimes need to be taken into account, too. A constitution-maker, thinking from the prospective point of view of the primary, as distinguished from the remedial, law has especially to think of them, if he is to see his problem whole. So doing, he will be likely to regard the desire of the ordinary man to avoid the moral condemnation of his community, as well as the physical pains and inconveniences of punishment, as a powerful factor in influencing human behavior which can scarcely with safety be dispensed with.[21] Whether he is right or wrong in this conclusion, he will align himself, in reaching it, with the all but universal judgment, past and present, of mankind.

Moreover, there are other and larger considerations to be weighed in the balance. The case against a primarily rehabilitative theory of criminal justice is understated if it is rested solely on the need for the threat of criminal conviction as an instrument of deterrence of antisocial conduct. Deterrence, it is ventured, ought not to be thought of as the overriding and ultimate purpose of the criminal law, important though it is. For deterrence is negative, whereas the purposes of law are positive. And the practical fact must be faced that many crimes, as just recognized, are undeterrable. The grim negativism and the frequent seeming futility of the criminal law when it is considered simply as a means of preventing undesired behavior no doubt help to explain why sensitive people, working at close hand with criminals, tend so often to embrace the more hopeful and positive tenets of a curative-rehabilitative philosophy.

However, a different view is possible if an effort is made to fit the theory of criminal justice into a theory of social justice—to see the purposes of the criminal law in their relation to the purposes of law as a whole. Man is a social animal, and the function of law is to enable him to realize his potentialities as a human being through the forms and modes of social organization. It is important to consider how the criminal law serves this ultimate end.

Human beings, of course, realize their potentialities in part through enjoyment of the various satisfactions of human life, both tangible and intangible, which existing social resources and their own individual capacities make available to them. Yet, the social resources of the moment are always limited, and human capacities for enjoyment are limited also. Social resources for providing the satisfactions of life and

[21] *Cf.* RANYARD WEST, CONSCIENCE AND SOCIETY 165 (1945): "It is upon the fact of the potential criminal in every man that I would give to law its psychological grounding."

Compare the valuable analysis by a Norwegian scholar, Johs Andenaes, in *General Prevention—Illusion or Reality?*, 43 J. CRIM. L., C. & P.S. 176, 179-80 (1952). Professor Andenaes distinguishes between individual prevention ("the effect of punishment on the punished") and general prevention ("the ability of the criminal law and its enforcement to make citizens law-abiding"). He further distinguishes "three sorts of general-preventive effects": first, a "deterrent" effect (used in the narrow sense of "the mere frightening . . . effect of punishment—the risk of discovery outweighing the temptation to commit the crime"); second, a "moralizing" effect (punishment helping "to form and to strengthen the public's moral code" and so to create "conscious or unconscious inhibitions against committing crime"; and, third, a habit-forming effect (arousing "unconscious inhibitions against committing forbidden acts . . . without appealing to the individual's concepts of morality").

human capacities for enjoying them, however, are always susceptible of enlargement, so far as we know, without eventual limit.[22] Man realizes his potentialities most significantly in the very process of developing these resources and capacities—by making himself a functioning and participating member of his community, contributing to it as well as drawing from it.

What is crucial in this process is the enlargement of each individual's capacity for effectual and responsible decision. For it is only through personal, self-reliant participation, by trial and error, in the problems of existence, both personal and social, that the capacity to participate effectively can grow. Man learns wisdom in choosing by being confronted with choices and by being made aware that he must abide the consequences of his choice. In the training of a child in the small circle of the family, this principle is familiar enough. It has the same validity in the training of an adult in the larger circle of the community.

Seen in this light, the criminal law has an obviously significant and, indeed, a fundamental role to play in the effort to create the good society. For it is the criminal law which defines the minimum conditions of man's responsibility to his fellows and holds him to that responsibility. The assertion of social responsibility has value in the treatment even of those who have become criminals.[23] It has far greater value as a stimulus to the great bulk of mankind to abide by the law and to take pride in so abiding.

This, then, is the critical weakness of the two alternative constitutional provisions that have been discussed—more serious by far than losing or damaging a useful, even if imperfect, instrument of deterrence. The provisions would undermine the foundation of a free society's effort to build up each individual's sense of responsibility as a guide and a stimulus to the constructive development of his capacity for effectual and fruitful decision.[24]

If the argument which has been made is accepted and it is concluded that

[22] See HART AND SACKS, *op. cit. supra* note 3, at 10-16.

[23] WALTON HAMILTON MOBERLY, RESPONSIBILITY: THE CONCEPT IN PSYCHOLOGY, IN THE LAW, AND IN THE CHRISTIAN FAITH 23 (1956): "Recite a delinquent's disabilities and handicaps in front of him in open court and you are doing something to confirm them; you are impairing that self-respect and sense of responsibility which is the chief incentive to effort. Treat him as sane and responsible and as a whole man and you give him the best chance of rising to this level. In many circumstances to expect and to exact a high standard is the most likely way to get it."

See also the discussion of the problem of growth in responsibility in Katz, *Law, Psychiatry, and Free Will*, 22 U. CHI. L. REV. 397 (1955).

[24] See generally MOBERLY, *op. cit. supra* note 23, and especially the opening lecture on "The Concept [Of Responsibility] in Psychology and Law."

There are other agencies of social discipline, of course, than the criminal law. But the criminal law is the only one which speaks to the individual formally and solemnly in behalf of the whole society.

In what the criminal law says to the individual, moreover, much more is involved than training simply in the observance of the specific and mostly elementary standards of conduct which the law seeks directly to enforce. Limits of some kind upon the scope of permissible choice perform an indispensable psychological role in the development of personal capacity for successful social adjustment. By fixing even minimal limits, the law thus develops capacities which are transferable to the more complex problems of social existence. This is especially so to the extent that the individual is made conscious of the moral basis and social rationale of the law's commands, for the principles of social living underlying them have far wider relevance than the commands themselves.

explicit abandonment of the concept of moral condemnation of criminal conduct would be unsound, what then is to be said of the soundness of an interpretation of existing law which tries to achieve a similar result by indirection—treating the purpose of cure and rehabilitation as predominating, while sweeping under the rug the hard facts of the social need and the moral rightness of condemnation and of treatment which does not dilute the fact of condemnation?

C. Constitutional Limitations on the Use of the Method

It is evident that the view which the constitution-maker takes of the function of criminal law will be important in shaping his attitude on inclusion in the document of many of the traditional guarantees of fair procedure in criminal trials. Most of these, such, for example, as indictment by a grand jury or even trial by a petit jury, are largely or wholly irrelevant to the offender's need for, or his susceptibility to, curative-rehabilitative treatment.[25] Indeed, as already suggested,[26] even the basic concept that criminality must rest upon criminal conduct, duly proved to have taken place, would come into question under a purely rehabilitative theory. Present laws for the confinement and care of mentally-ill persons do not insist upon this requirement, and, if criminality were to be equated with sickness of personality generally, its rationale would not be readily apparent. But if what is in issue is the community's solemn condemnation of the accused as a defaulter in his obligations to the community, then the default to be condemned ought plainly to consist of overt conduct, and not simply of a condition of mind; and the fact of default should be proved with scrupulous care. The safeguards which now surround the procedure of proof of criminality or the essentials of them, in other words, will appear to be appropriate.

Should the constitution-makers go further and prescribe not only procedural safeguards, but substantive limitations on the kinds of conduct that can be declared criminal? For the most part, American constitution-makers have not done this.[27] They have relied, instead, primarily on the legislature's sense of justice. Secondarily, they have relied on the courts to understand what a crime is and, so, by appropriate invocation of the broad constitutional injunction of due process, to prevent an arbitrary application of the criminal sanction when the legislature's sense of justice has failed. Whether they have been wise in so doing is a question which can best be left to the reader's judgment, in the light of the examination which follows of the actual handling of the problems by legislatures and courts.

[25] Laws for the confinement of mentally-ill persons commonly dispense with these requirements, and with many others as well. See Note, *Analysis of Legal and Medical Considerations in Commitment of the Mentally Ill*, 56 YALE L. J. 1178, 1190-96 (1947). So also do the "sexual psychopath" laws referred to in note 19 *supra*.

[26] See note 19 *supra*.

[27] Ex post facto clauses are the only important express substantive limitation usually found in American constitutions. It should be noticed, however, that the principles of just punishment implicit in such clauses have relevance in other situations than that only of condemnation under an after-the-fact enactment—a wider relevance than courts have yet recognized.

III

THE PERSPECTIVE OF THE LEGISLATURE

A legislature deals with crimes always in advance of their commission (assuming the existence of constitutional prohibitions or practices excluding ex post facto laws and bills of attainder). It deals with them not by condemnation and punishment, but only by threat of condemnation and punishment, *to be imposed always by other agencies*. It deals with them always by directions formulated in *general terms*. The primary parts of the directions have always to be interpreted and applied by the private persons—the potential offenders—to whom they are initially addressed. In the event of a breach or claim of breach, both the primary and the remedial parts must be interpreted and applied by the various officials—police, prosecuting attorneys, trial judges and jurors, appellate judges, and probation, prison, and parole authorities —responsible for their enforcement. The attitudes, capacities, and practical conditions of work of these officials often put severe limits upon the ability of the legislature to accomplish what it sets out to accomplish.

If the primary parts of a general direction are to work successfully in any particular instance, otherwise than by fortunate accident, four conditions have always to be satisfied: (1) the primary addressee who is supposed to conform his conduct to the direction must know (a) of its existence, and (b) of its content in relevant respects; (2) he must know about the circumstances of fact which make the abstract terms of the direction applicable in the particular instance; (3) he must be able to comply with it; and (4) he must be willing to do so.

The difficulties of satisfying these conditions vitally affect the fairness and often even the feasibility of the effort to control the behavior of large numbers of people by means of general directions, subject only to an after-the-event sanction. This is so even when the sanction is civil, such as a judgment for compensatory damages or restoration of benefits. But the difficulties are especially acute when the sanction is criminal. For then, something more is involved than the simple necessity of getting the direction complied with in a sufficient proportion of instances to keep it in good working order—that is, to maintain respect for it and to avoid arbitrary discrimination in singling out individual violators as subjects of enforcement proceedings. If what was said in part two is correct, it is necessary to be able to say in good conscience in *each* instance in which a criminal sanction is imposed for a violation of law that the violation was blameworthy and, hence, deserving of the moral condemnation of the community.

This raises two closely related questions which lie at the heart of the problems of the criminal law: *First,* what *are* the ingredients of moral blameworthiness which warrant a judgment of community condemnation? *Second,* retracing the ground of part two, can the position be maintained that guilt in the sense of the criminal law is an individual matter and cannot justly be pronounced by the community if the individual's conduct affords no basis for a judgment of moral condemnation?

These questions present themselves in different guises in different types of criminal statutes. They can best be examined separately in relation to the various major types of purposes for which a legislature may seek to employ a criminal sanction.

A. The Statement of the Minimum Obligations of Responsible Citizenship: The Control of Purposeful Conduct

The core of a sound penal code in any view of the function of the criminal law is the statement of those minimum obligations of conduct which the conditions of community life impose upon every participating member if community life is to be maintained and to prosper—that is, of those obligations which result not from a discretionary and disputable judgment of the legislature, but from the objective facts of the interdependencies of the people who are living together in the community and of their awareness of the interdependencies.

In the mind of any legislator who recognizes this central and basic job as a distinct one and who is trying to do it faithfully and intelligently, a variety of aims will coalesce, to the point of becoming virtually indistinguishable. The inculcation of a sense of social responsibility throughout the society will be the dominant aim. But the stated obligations will, at the same time, represent desired standards of conduct and so will necessarily involve the aim of deterrence of undesired conduct. Since violators are to be condemned as defaulters in their duty to the community and treated accordingly, the aim can also be described as punitive. And if the conduct declared to be criminal does, indeed, evince a blameworthy lack of social responsibility, the declaration will also constitute an essential first step in identifying those members of the community whose behavior shows them to be in need of cure and rehabilitation, and this aim will likewise be included. So also, subordinately, will be the aim of temporary or permanent disablement of certain of the more serious offenders.

Returning now to the four conditions earlier stated for the successful operation of a general direction and to the problem of deciding when a failure of compliance due to a failure to satisfy one of the conditions is blameworthy, it will be seen that in this area of the criminal law, the difficulties are minimal, so long at least as the legislature is denouncing purposeful or knowing, as distinguished from reckless or merely negligent, conduct.[28]

If the legislature does a sound job of reflecting community attitudes and needs, actual knowledge of the wrongfulness of the prohibited conduct will usually exist. Thus, almost everyone is aware that murder and forcible rape and the obvious forms of theft are wrong. But in any event, knowledge of wrongfulness can fairly be assumed. For any member of the community who does these things without knowing that they are criminal is blameworthy, as much for his lack of knowledge as for his actual conduct. This seems to be the essential rationale of the maxim, *Ignorantia legis neminem excusat,* which has been so much misunderstood and abused in rela-

[28] On the special problems of control of reckless and negligent conduct, see subsection B of this part *infra.*

tion to regulatory crimes, involving conduct which is not intrinsically wrongful.[29]

Similarly, knowledge of the circumstances of fact which make the law's directions applicable will ordinarily exist when harms are inflicted or risks created of the elementary and obvious types sought to be prevented by these intrinsically wrongful crimes. But suppose that knowledge does not exist? The traditional criminal law, concerned almost exclusively with crimes of this kind, has ready to hand a solution in the traditional maxim that ignorance of fact excuses, as well as in cognate doctrines such as that of claim-of-right in the law of theft.[30] If the legislature can depend upon the courts to read these doctrines into its enactments, the requisite of blameworthiness as an element of criminality will be respected.

Obligations of conduct fixed by a fair appraisal of the minimum requirements for the maintenance and fostering of community life will, by hypothesis, be obligations which normal members of the community will be *able* to comply with, given the necessary awareness of the circumstances of fact calling for compliance. But suppose that in a particular case, this ability does not exist? Again, the traditional law provides materials for solution of the problem when inability negatives blameworthiness; and the only question is whether the legislature can count upon the courts to make use of the materials. The materials include doctrines with respect to duress, as well as doctrines providing for the exculpation of those individuals who because of mental disease or defect are to be deemed incapable of acting as responsible, participating members of society.[31]

There remains only the question of willingness to comply. In relation to direc-

[29] Compare the illuminating and much more subtle analysis of Jerome Hall in *Ignorance and Mistake in Criminal Law*, 33 IND. L. J. 1 (1957). Professor Hall points out the consideration here stressed: ". . . namely, that the criminal law represents certain moral principles; to recognize ignorance or mistake of the law as a defense would contradict those values." *Id.* at 20. But he is concerned to defend the application of the maxim not only in relation to crimes involving intrinsically wrongful conduct, but in relation to purely regulatory crimes which, if the views hereafter presented are correct, involve no other moral value than that of respect for constituted authority. This leads him into refinements which this paper passes by.

[30] See Hall, *Ignorance and Mistake in Criminal Law*, 33 IND. L. J. 1, 27-34 (1957). *Cf.* Morissette v. United States, 342 U.S. 246 (1952), where the Court invoked the whole broad tradition of criminal intent as a reason for giving a statute a restricted reading, although a reference to the specific doctrine of claim-of-right in theft would have been enough to do the trick.

[31] It is important to notice the extent to which the whole doctrine of irresponsibility by reason of mental disease or defect confirms the main thesis of this paper. The doctrine, to be sure, can be understood as a corollary of a coldly utilitarian deterrent theory which simply exculpates nondeterrables. And the *M'Naghten* test, on a narrow and literal reading, may be thought to bear out this view. But if nondeterrability were the sole basis of the doctrine, it would seem to follow that all doubts on that score should be resolved in favor of society. This is not the way in which the test is administered, even by courts which adhere to it most strictly. What the courts actually do, and even more plainly what the critics of the courts say, is eloquent testimony to the general understanding that something more is involved than a cold-blooded estimate of deterrability. The "something more" surely is not the defendant's personal need for cure and rehabilitation, for the greater the insanity, the greater the need. Nor can susceptibility to cure and rehabilitation be taken as the touchstone consistently with general principle, or else the more hardened the criminal, the better would be his claim to irresponsibility. What seems to be involved in general understanding, and certainly in any adequate analysis of the problem, is a reaching for criteria which will avoid attaching moral blame where blame cannot justly be attached, while, at the same time, avoiding a denial of moral responsibility where the denial would be personally and socially debilitating.

tions which make a reasonably grounded appeal to the citizen's sense of responsibility as a citizen, this willingness is likely to be at a maximum. Individuals who are able but unwilling to comply with such directions are precisely the ones who ought to be condemned as criminals.

In the sphere of conduct which is intrinsically wrongful, the legislature's task is further simplified by its ability (or the ability which it is entitled to suppose it has) to rely upon the courts for the elaboration of detail and the solution of unanticipated or peripheral problems. Indeed, this was a body of law which was largely built up by English judges without benefit of acts of Parliament and which in this country required the intervention of the legislature, on its primary side, only to satisfy the theoretical and emotional appeal of the maxim, *Nullum crimen sine lege.* Despite the maxim, most American legislatures have been content to make use of familiar words and phrases of the common law, relying upon the courts to fill in their meaning, and even leaving whole areas of doctrine, such as criminal intent and various phases of justification, entirely to the courts. So long as the courts are faithful in their reflection of the community's understanding of what is morally blameworthy, judgments of conviction are not subject to the reproach of being, even in spirit, ex post facto.

B. The Statement of the Minimum Obligations of Responsible Citizenship: The Control of Reckless and Negligent Conduct

Special difficulties are presented when the criminal law undertakes to state an obligation of conduct in a way which requires an addressee, if he is to comply with it, to have a certain kind of general knowledge or experience, or to exercise a certain degree of skill and attention, or to make an appraisal of the probable consequences of what he does or omits to do with a certain degree of accuracy. When can a criminal sanction be properly authorized in cases in which the addressee fails in one or another of these respects and harm results or a risk is created because of his failure?[32]

For example, one who undertakes to practice as a physician does not know that flannels saturated with kerosene will tend to produce severe burns if applied directly to the flesh of a patient.[33] A foreman of a railroad section gang misreads a timetable and orders railroad tracks to be taken up for replacement just before a train is due.[34] The owner of a night club fails to realize that the means of egress would be inadequate if a fire were to break out when the club was crowded.[35] Upon pre-

[32] Through use of the doctrine of conspiracy, attempt, and solicitation, and in other ways, the criminal law often condemns the deliberate planning of a blameworthy harm, even though no harm actually results. But even where it punishes the inadvertent creation of a risk which actually causes harm, Anglo-American law, wisely or unwisely, has developed no general principle condemning the same kind of risk-creating conduct in cases in which, by good fortune, no ultimate harm eventuates. Of course, however, there are a good many *ad hoc* statutes declaring specific forms of such conduct, such as speeding, to be criminal, regardless of their consequences.

[33] See Commonwealth v. Pierce, 138 Mass. 165 (1884).

[34] See Regina v. Benge, 4 F. & F. 504 (Kent Summer Assizes 1865).

[35] See Commonwealth v. Welansky, 316 Mass. 383, 55 N.E.2d 902 (1944).

cisely what kind of showing can a legislature justly provide that such people are to be condemned and punished as criminals?

If the legislature requires that an awareness of the risk be brought home to the actor and that the risk be one which, by the general standards of the community, is plainly excessive, a direction for criminal punishment creates no difficulty of principle, however trying may be the problems of application. For judgment about whether a given risk can justifiably be taken to promote a given end depends upon the evaluations implicit in community standards of right and wrong to which each member of the community can justly be expected to conform his conduct. If an individual knowingly takes a risk of a kind which the community condemns as plainly unjustifiable, then he is morally blameworthy and can properly be adjudged a criminal. He is criminally reckless in the traditional sense articulated with precision by the draftsmen of the American Law Institute's Model Penal Code.[86]

This concept of criminal recklessness may well embrace not only situations in which the actor adverts directly to the possibility of the ultimate harm, but those in which he adverts only to his own deficiencies in appraising the possibility of harm or preventing it from coming to pass and to the possible consequences of *those* deficiencies. Thus, the doctor who swathes his patient with kerosene-soaked rags, without even suspecting what is going to happen, may, nevertheless, know that special knowledge and training is generally needed in order to treat patients safely and successfully and that he does not have that knowledge and training. In any such situation, if the actor knows of his deficiency and of the risk which such a deficiency creates, and if *that* risk is one which in community understanding is plainly unjustifiable, there is a basis for legislative condemnation of the conduct as criminally reckless.

Moreover, as considered more fully under the next subheading, if the actor knowingly goes counter to a valid legislative determination that the risk he is taking is excessive, even though he himself does not believe it to be, there is an independent basis for moral condemnation in this deliberate defiance of law.

The question remains whether simple unawareness of risk, without awareness of any deficiency preventing appreciation or avoidance of it and without any element

[86] See MODEL PENAL CODE § 2.02(2)(c) and (d) (Tent. Draft No. 4, 1955):

"(c) Recklessly.

"A person acts recklessly with respect to a material element of an offense when he consciously disregards a substantial and unjustifiable risk that the material element exists or will result from his conduct. The risk must be of such a nature and degree that, considering the nature and purpose of the actor's conduct and the circumstances known to him, its disregard involves culpability of high degree. [Alternative: its disregard involves a gross deviation from proper standards of conduct.]

"(d) Negligently.

"A person acts negligently with respect to a material element of an offense when he should be aware of a substantial and unjustifiable risk that the material element exists or will result from his conduct. The risk must be of such a nature and degree that the actor's failure to perceive it, considering the nature and purpose of his conduct, the circumstances known to him and the care that would be exercised by a reasonable person in his situation, involves substantial culpability. [Alternative: considering the nature and purpose of his conduct and the circumstances known to him, involves a substantial deviation from the standard of care that would be exercised by a reasonable man in his situation.]"

of knowing disregard of a relevant legislative decision, can justly be declared to be culpable. The answer would seem clearly to be no, at least in those situations in which the actor lacks the ability either to refrain from the conduct which creates the risk or to correct the deficiency which makes engaging in the conduct dangerous, for otherwise, the third of the requisites above stated[37] for the successful operation of a general direction is impossible to satisfy. But suppose the actor has this ability? Guilt would, then, seem to depend upon whether he has been put upon notice of his duty to use his ability to a degree which makes his unawareness of the duty, in the understanding of the community, genuinely blameworthy. In exceptional situations of elementary and obvious danger, the circumstances of fact of which the actor is conscious may be sufficient in themselves to give this notice. But this can be true only when the significance of the circumstances of fact would be apparent to one who shares the community's general sense of right and wrong. If this is not so—if appreciation of the significance of the facts depends upon knowledge of what happens to be written in the statute books—then, the problem becomes one of the nature and extent of the moral obligation to know what is so written, which is discussed under the next subheading.

Criminal punishment of merely negligent behavior is commonly justified not on the ground that violators can be said to be individually blameworthy, but on the ground that the threat of such punishment will help to teach people generally to be more careful. This proposes, as legitimate, an aim for the legislature which is drastically different from that of inculcating minimum standards of personal responsibility to society. The issues it raises are examined under the subheading after the next.[38]

C. The Regulation of Conduct Which Is Not Intrinsically Wrongful: Bases of Blameworthiness

The statute books of the forty-nine states and the United States are filled with enactments carrying a criminal sanction which are obviously motivated by other ends, primarily, than that of training for responsible citizenship. The legislature simply wants certain things done and certain other things not done because it believes that the doing or the not doing of them will secure some ultimate social advantage, and not at all because it thinks the immediate conduct involved is either rightful or wrongful in itself. It employs the threat of criminal condemnation and punishment as an especially forceful way of saying that it really wants to be obeyed, or else simply from lack of enough imagination to think of a more appropriate sanction. Such enactments present problems which neither the courts nor the legislature of this country have yet succeeded in thinking through.[39]

[37] See p. 413 *supra.*

[38] For a valuable general discussion of problems of criminal negligence, see JEROME HALL, GENERAL PRINCIPLES OF CRIMINAL LAW c. 9 (1947).

[39] See generally Mr. Justice Jackson's review of the development in Morissette v. United States, 342 U.S. 246 (1952); Sayre, *Public Welfare Offenses*, 33 COLUM. L. REV. 55 (1933); JEROME HALL, GENERAL PRINCIPLES OF CRIMINAL LAW c. 10 (1947).

When a legislature undertakes to prohibit or require conduct theretofore untouched by the criminal law, what considerations *ought* to guide it in deciding whether to declare that noncompliance with its direction shall be a crime?

1. If the legislature can, in good conscience, conclude that the new direction embodies standards of behavior which have to be observed, under existing social conditions, if social life is to be maintained, then the use of a criminal sanction raises no difficulty. Obviously, there is room for growth, as conditions and attitudes in society change, in the central body of law earlier discussed which undertakes to state the minimum obligations of responsible citizenship. Obviously also, the legislature is an appropriate agency to settle debatable questions about the appropriate extent of growth, whether or not it is desirable for courts to have a share in the process.[40]

Statutes which make well-considered additions to the list of the citizen's basic obligations are not open to the objection of undue multiplication of crimes. Normal principles of culpability, moreover, can properly apply to such offenses, and should apply. Absent exceptional circumstances, in other words, ignorance of the criminality of the conduct (act or omission) which is forbidden ought not to be a defense. *Per contra,* ignorance of the facts ought to be. And, of course, the usual defenses based on inability to comply should be available.

2. If the legislature cannot, in good conscience, regard conduct which it wishes to forbid as wrongful in itself, then it has always the option of declaring the conduct to be criminal only when the actor knows of its criminality or recklessly disregards the possibility that it is criminal. For knowing or reckless disregard of legal obligation affords an independent basis of blameworthiness justifying the actor's condemnation as a criminal, even when his conduct was not intrinsically antisocial. It is convenient to use the word "wilful" to describe this mode of culpability, although the term is by no means regularly so limited in conventional usage.[41]

The inclusion in a new regulatory crime of the requirement of "wilfulness" avoids any difficulty of principle in the use of the criminal sanction—assuming that the requirement comprehends not only a culpable awareness (knowing or reckless) of the law, but a culpable awareness also of the facts making the law applicable, together with a sufficient ability to comply. The requirement, moreover, mitigates any objection on the score of undue multiplication of regulatory crimes, although it can hardly eliminate it entirely.[42]

3. Under what, if any, circumstances may a legislature properly direct the con-

[40] Obviously, the courts must have a share, whether it is desirable or not, in the interpretation of such enactments. See pp. 435-36 *infra.*

[41] See United States v. Murdock, 290 U.S. 389 (1933); Spies v. United States, 317 U.S. 492, 497-98 (1943); Wechsler, *The American Law Institute: Some Observations on Its Model Penal Code,* 42 A.B.A.J. 321, 324 (1956).

[42] The dominant objective of public education in the obligations of responsible citizenship is prejudiced if the public mind is confused by assertion of too many obligations. The force of the threat of criminal condemnation and punishment, moreover, is weakened if serious enforcement is impracticable, and there are, and seemingly must inevitably be, severe limitations upon the load which the machinery of criminal law enforcement can carry. See part four *infra.* Finally, the criminal law always loses face if things are declared to be crimes which people believe they ought to be free to do, even wilfully.

viction as a criminal of a person whose conduct is not wrongful in itself and who neither knows nor recklessly disregards the possibility that he is violating the law?

To engage knowingly or recklessly in conduct which is wrongful in itself and which has, in fact, been condemned as a crime is either to fail to comprehend the community's accepted moral values or else squarely to challenge them. The maxim, *Ignorantia legis neminem excusat,* expresses the wholly defensible and, indeed, essential principle that the action, in either event, is blameworthy.[43] If, however, the criminal law adheres to this maxim when it moves from the condemnation of those things which are *mala in se* to the condemnation of those things which are merely *mala prohibita,* it necessarily shifts its ground from a demand that every responsible member of the community understand and respect the community's moral values to a demand that everyone know and understand what is written in the statute books. Such a demand is *toto coelo* different. In no respect is contemporary law subject to greater reproach than for its obtuseness to this fact.

Granting that blame may, in some circumstances, attach to an actor's antecedent failure to determine the legality of his conduct, it is, in any event, blame of a very distinctive kind.

a. The blame in such a case is largely unrelated, in gravity or any other respect, to the external conduct itself, or its consequences, for which the actor is purportedly convicted. Indeed, all such instances of conduct in ignorance of laws enjoining *mala prohibita* might well be thought of as constituting a single type of crime, if they constitute any kind of crime at all—the crime of ignorance of the statutes or of their interpretation. Knowledge of the facts and ability to comply may be formal requisites of criminality, but in the absence of knowledge of the law, they are irrelevant, and willingness to comply remains untested. The whole weight of the law's effort to achieve its purpose has to be carried, in the first instance, by the effort to get people to know and understand its requirements.[44]

b. In such cases, the essential crime, if that is what it is, is always a crime of omission. If the purported crime is itself one of omission, as in the failure to take out a license, then the offense is doubly negative. As Professor Graham Hughes has recently abundantly demonstrated,[45]

> . . . a penal policy of omissions and a criminal jurisprudence of offenses of omission are overdue. . . . [W]here inaction is evidently socially harmful, no good reason appears for shrinking from penal prohibition. Any penal policy, however, must be linked with a consciousness of the need to promulgate and publicize offenses of omission and a recognition by the judiciary that conventional attitudes to *mens rea,* particularly with respect to ignorance of the law, are not adequate tools to achieve justice for those accused of inaction.

[43] See note 29 *supra.*

[44] *Cf.* Hughes, *Criminal Omissions,* 67 YALE L. J. 590, 603 (1958): "The conventional analyses of *mens rea* in omissions suffer either from a complete neglect of the aspect of ignorance of the law or a tendency to confuse the two separate issues of ignorance of the duty and ignorance of the circumstances which triggered the duty."

[45] Hughes, *supra* note 44, at 636.

Even when the nominal crime is one of commission rather than omission, the problem of promulgating and publicizing the offense, which Professor Hughes mentions, is likely to be serious if the nature of the affirmative conduct gives no warning of the possibility of an applicable criminal prohibition. But it is especally likely to be serious when the nominal crime is itself one of omisson, for mere inaction often gives no such warning whatever.[46]

c. The gist of a crime of statutory ignorance may lie not in the failure to inform oneself of the existence of an applicable statute, which is always in some sense a do-able thing if the statutes are published and there is a decent index to them, but in the failure to divine their meaning, which may be altogether non-do-able. All statutes are, of necessity, indeterminate in some of their applications. When a criminal enactment proscribes conduct which is *malum in se,* such as murder or manslaughter, however, the moral standards of the community are available always as a guide in the resolution of its indeterminacies, and there is a minimum of unfairness when doubt is resolved against a particular defendant. This guidance is missing when the proscribed conduct is merely *malum prohibitum*. The resolution of doubts must, thus, depend not upon a good human sense of moral values, but upon a sound grasp of technical doctrines and policies of statutory interpretation. Dean Pound has justly observed of American lawyers and judges that "we have no well-developed technique of developing legislative texts."[47] To condemn a layman as blameworthy for a default of technical judgment in a matter which causes trouble even for professional judges is, in many cases, so manifestly beyond reason that courts have developed various makeshift devices to avoid condemnation in particular situations.[48] And the draftsmen of the Model Penal Code have devised for such cases a generalized defense of limited scope.[49] Until the nature and dimensions of the

[46] See the discussion of the Supreme Court's recent decision in Lambert v. California, 355 U.S. 225 (1957), at pp. 433-34 *infra*.

[47] Pound, *Sources and Forms of Law,* 22 NOTRE DAME LAWYER 1, 76 (1946).

[48] The devices have generally dealt only with the extreme situation in which the defendant was misled by some form of official advice that his conduct was lawful. See, *e.g.,* State v. Jones, 44 N.M. 623, 107 P.2d 324 (1940), overruling a prior judicial interpretation of a statute now regarded as erroneous "with prospective effect only." See HART AND SACKS, *op. cit. supra* note 3, at 661-64. *Cf.* Long v. State, 44 Del. (5 Ter.) 462, 65 A.2d 489 (1949), allowing a defendant in a bigamy prosecution to show that he had acted in reliance on an attorney's advice that a prior divorce was valid.

[49] MODEL PENAL CODE § 2.04(3) and (4) (Tent. Draft. No. 4, 1955):

"(3) A reasonable belief that conduct does not legally constitute an offense is a defense to a prosecution for that offense based upon such conduct, when:

(a) the statute or other enactment defining the offense is not known to the actor and has not been published or otherwise reasonably made available to him prior to the conduct alleged; or

(b) he acts in reasonable reliance upon an official statement of the law, afterward determined to be invalid or erroneous, contained in (i) a statute or other enactment; (ii) a judicial decision, opinion or judgment; (iii) an administrative order or grant of permission; or (iv) an official interpretation of the public officer or body charged by law with responsibility for the interpretation, administration or enforcement of the law defining the offense.

"(4) A defense arising under paragraph (3) of this section constitutes an affirmative defense which the defendant is required to prove by a preponderance of evidence. The reasonableness of the belief claimed to constitute the defense shall be determined as a question of law by the Court."

problem have been more fully perceived, however, no genuinely satisfactory solution can be reached.

d. No doubt there are situations in which one who engages in a particular course of conduct assumes an obligation, in general community understanding, to know about the law applicable to that kind of conduct. Sometimes, this may be true in areas of statutory law affecting people generally, such as motor vehicle laws. It is most likely to be true of laws applicable to particular occupations. One cannot say categorically, therefore, that ignorance of a law creating a merely statutory crime never affords a basic for moral condemnation. What can be said, in general terms, is that (1) the criminal law as a device for getting people to know about statutes and interpret them correctly is a device of dubious and largely unproved effectiveness; (2) the indiscriminate use of the device dilutes the force of the threat of community condemnation as a means of influencing conduct in other situations where the basis for moral condemnation is clear; (3) the loss to society from this dilution is always unnecessary, since the legislature has always the alternatives of either permitting a good faith belief in the legality of one's conduct to be pleaded and proved as a defense,[50] or of providing a civil rather than a criminal sanction for nonwilful violations.

e. Under what, if any, circumstances may a legislature properly direct the conviction as a criminal of one who knows about the applicable law but who has been negligent, although not reckless, in ascertaining the facts which make the law applicable to his conduct—where the kind of conduct involved is morally neutral, both from the point of view of the actor and in actuality?

In the usual situation of assertedly criminal negligence earlier discussed,[51] the harm caused or threatened by failure of advertence is one which it would be morally wrongful to cause advertently. The assertion of a duty of attention is, thus, strengthened by the gravity of the risks actually involved. In the situation now under discussion, the facts are morally neutral, even to one who knows about them, save for the existence of an applicable statute. Thus, the basis of blame, if any, is inattention to one's duty as a citizen to see that the law gets complied with in all the situations to which it is supposed to apply. For example, manufactured food becomes adulterated or misbranded within the meaning of a statute, but in a way which involves no danger to health.

Condemning a person for lack of ordinary care in ascertaining facts at least does not involve the offense to justice sometimes involved in the ignorance-of-interpretation-of-statute cases of condemning him for failure to do the impossible. But otherwise, most of the points just made about ignorance of regulatory law apply: (1) the basis of moral blame will usually be thin and may be virtually nonexistent; (2) the likelihood of substantial social gain in stimulating greater care is dubious; (3) the social cost is a weakening of the moral force and, hence, the effectiveness of the

[50] See paragraph (4) of the Model Penal Code provision in note 49 *supra*.

[51] See subheading B of this part *supra*.

threat of criminal conviction; and (4) the cost is unnecessary, since the legislature has always the alternative of a civil sanction.

D. Strict Liability

A large body of modern law goes far beyond an insistence upon a duty of ordinary care in ascertaining facts, at the peril of being called a criminal. To an absolute duty to know about the existence of a regulatory statute and interpret it correctly, it adds an absolute duty to know about the facts. Thus, the porter who innocently carries the bag of a hotel guest not knowing that it contains a bottle of whisky is punished as a criminal for having transported intoxicating liquor.[52] The corporation president who signs a registration statement for a proposed securities issue not knowing that his accountants have made a mistake is guilty of the crime of making a "false" representation to the state blue-sky commissioner.[53] The president of a corporation whose employee introduces into interstate commerce a shipment of technically but harmlessly adulterated food is branded as a criminal solely because he was the president when the shipment was made.[54] And so on, *ad* almost *infinitum.*

In all such cases, it is possible, of course, that a basis of blameworthiness might have been found in the particular facts. Perhaps the company presidents actually *were* culpably careless in their supervision. Conceivably, even, the porter was culpably remiss in failing to ask the traveler about the contents of his bag, or at least in failing to shake it to see if he could hear a gurgle. But these possibilities are irrelevant. For the statutes in question, as interpreted, do not require any such defaults to be proved against a defendant, nor even permit him to show the absence of such a default in defense. The offenses fall within "the numerous class in which diligence, actual knowledge and bad motives are immaterial. . . ."[55] Thus, they squarely pose the question whether there can be any justification for condemning and punishing a human being as a criminal when he has done nothing which is blameworthy.

It is submitted that there can be no moral justification for this, and that there is not, indeed, even a rational, amoral justification.

1. People who do not know and cannot find out that they are supposed to comply with an applicable command are, by hypothesis, nondeterrable. So far as personal amenability to legal control is concerned, they stand in the same posture as the plainest lunatic under the *M'Naghten* test who "does not know the nature and quality of his act or, if he does know it, does not know that the act is wrong."

2. If it be said that most people will know of such commands and be able to comply with them, the answer, among others, is that nowhere else in the criminal law is the probable, or even the certain, guilt of nine men regarded as sufficient

[52] *Cf.* Commonwealth v. Mixer, 207 Mass. 141, 93 N.E. 249 (1910).
[53] State v. Dobry, 217 Iowa 858, 250 N.W. 702 (1933).
[54] United States v. Dotterweich, 320 U.S. 277 (1943).
[55] See City of Hays v. Schueler, 107 Kan. 635, 193 Pac. 311 (1920).

warrant for the conviction of a tenth. In the tradition of Anglo-American law, guilt of crime is personal. The main body of the criminal law, from the Constitution on down, makes sense on no other assumption.

3. If it be asserted that strict criminal liability is necessary in order to stimulate people to be diligent in learning the law and finding out when it applies, the answer, among others, is that this is wholly unproved and prima facie improbable. Studies to test the relative effectiveness of strict criminal liability and well-designed civil penalties are lacking and badly needed. Until such studies are forthcoming, however, judgment can only take into account (a) the inherent unlikelihood that people's behavior will be significantly affected by commands that are not brought definitely to their attention; (b) the long-understood tendency of disproportionate penalties to promote disrespect rather than respect for law, unless they are rigorously and uniformly enforced; (c) the inherent difficulties of rigorous and uniform enforcement of strict criminal liability and the impressive evidence that it is, in fact, spottily and unevenly enforced;[56] (d) the greater possibilities or flexible and imaginative adaptation of civil penalties to fit particular regulatory problems, the greater reasonableness of such penalties, and their more ready enforceability; and (e) most important of all, the shocking damage that is done to social morale by open and official admission that crime can be respectable and criminality a matter of ill chance, rather than blameworthy choice.[57]

4. If it be urged that strict criminal liability is necessary in order to simplify the investigation and prosecution of violations of statutes designed to control mass conduct, the answer, among others, is that (a) maximizing compliance with law, rather than successful prosecution of violators, is the primary aim of any regulatory statute; (b) the convenience of investigators and prosecutors is not, in any event, the prime consideration in determining what conduct is criminal; (c) a prosecutor, as a matter of common knowledge, always assumes a heavier burden in trying to secure a crim-

[56] There are more strict liability and other criminal statutes on the books than investigators and prosecutors, with their existing staffs, can hope to enforce. See part four *infra*. Nor is there any pretense that most of them are seriously enforced. Even with statutes which a genuine effort is made to enforce, only a relatively few cases of violation are selected for prosecution, and these are commonly chosen in accordance with standards quite different from the strict liability standards laid down by the legislature or judicially attributed to it. See, *e.g.*, Schwartz, *Federal Criminal Jurisdiction and Prosecutors' Discretion*, 13 LAW & CONTEMP. PROB. 64, 83-84 (1948); Developments in the Law, *The Federal Food, Drug, and Cosmetic Act*, 67 HARV. L. REV. 632, 694-97 (1954).

[57] Think, for example, about the implications of the language of an English court in rejecting as preposterous the suggestion that the defense of ignorance and good faith should be allowed in a prosecution for criminal conspiracy: "We demur to the notion that there is anything particularly wicked attached to the word 'conspiracy.' No doubt in common speech 'conspiracy' has a melodramatic and sinister implication, but it has been pointed out that it carries no such implications in law. . . . It does not matter how prosaic the unlawful act may be or how ignorant the conspirators may be of the fact that the act is prohibited by the statutory provision." Rex v. Clayton (Ct. Cr. App. 1943, unreported), reported in footnote to Rex v. Percy Dalton, 33 Cr. App. Rep. 102, 119 (1949). "There, there," says the court to the once sturdy-minded yeomen of old England, "no matter what your mothers and fathers may have told you, there is really nothing particularly wrong about being a criminal." The same overtones, though usually less baldly expressed, run through countless American opinions. See, *e.g.*, Mr. Justice Frankfurter, in United States v. Dotterweich, 320 U.S. 277, 280-81 (1943); and in Lambert v. California, 355 U.S. 225, 230-31 (1957).

inal conviction than a civil judgment; (d) in most situations of attempted control of mass conduct, the technique of a first warning, followed by criminal prosecution only of knowing violators, has not only obvious, but proved superiority; and (e) the common-sense advantages of using the criminal sanction only against deliberate violators is confirmed by the policies which prosecutors themselves tend always to follow when they are free to make their own selection of cases to prosecute.[58]

5. Moral, rather than crassly utilitarian, considerations re-enter the picture when the claim is made, as it sometimes is, that strict liability operates, in fact, only against people who are really blameworthy, because prosecutors only pick out the really guilty ones for criminal prosecution.[59] This argument reasserts the traditional position that a criminal conviction imports moral condemnation. To this, it adds the arrogant assertion that it is proper to visit the moral condemnation of the community upon one of its members on the basis solely of the private judgment of his prosecutors. Such a circumvention of the safeguards with which the law surrounds other determinations of criminality seems not only irrational, but immoral as well.

6. But moral considerations in a still larger dimension are the ultimately controlling ones. In its conventional and traditional applications, a criminal conviction carries with it an ineradicable connotation of moral condemnation and personal guilt. Society makes an essentially parasitic, and hence illegitimate, use of this instrument when it uses it as a means of deterrence (or compulsion) of conduct which is morally neutral. This would be true even if a statute were to be enacted proclaiming that no criminal conviction hereafter should ever be understood as casting any reflection on anybody. For statutes cannot change the meaning of words and make people stop thinking what they do think when they hear the words spoken. But it is doubly true—it is ten-fold, a hundred-fold, a thousand-fold true—when society continues to insist that some crimes *are* morally blameworthy and then tries to use the same epithet to describe conduct which is not.

7. To be sure, the traditional law recognizes gradations in the gravity of offenses, and so does the Constitution of the United States. But strict liability offenses have not been limited to the interpretively-developed constitutional category of "petty offenses," for which trial by jury is not required.[60] They include even some

[58] See note 56 *supra*.

[59] See, *e.g.*, the unconscionable proposal sanctioned by a commission of the American Bar Association, the leading association of lawyers in the United States, that in a Model Anti-Gambling Act, all forms of gambling, even purely social gambling, should be declared to be criminal, even while recognizing "that it is unrealistic to promulgate a law literally aimed at making a criminal offense of the friendly election bet, the private, social card game among friends, etc." The commission's reason for being thus "unrealistic" was that "it is imperative to confront the professional gambler with a statutory façade that is wholly devoid of loopholes." Its report indicated that pressure from prosecutors accounted for the proposal and that it was relying on prosecutors' discretion to avoid abuses. Approval of the proposition was mitigated by the fact that the commission, evidently uneasy about what it was doing, also reported an "optional" provision giving the social gambler a limited statutory protection. But the report gave no hint of awareness that basic issues of public morality were involved. 2 ABA COMM'N ON ORGANIZED CRIME, ORGANIZED CRIME AND LAW ENFORCEMENT 74-78 (1953).

[60] See Frankfurter and Corcoran, *Petty Federal Offenses and the Constitutional Guarantee of Trial by Jury*, 39 HARV. L. REV. 917 (1926); Callan v. Wilson, 127 U.S. 540 (1888); Schick v. United States,

crimes which the Constitution expressly recognizes as "infamous."[61] Thus, the excuse of the Scotch servant girl for her illegitimate baby, that "It was only such a leetle one," is not open to modern legislatures. And since a crime remains a crime, just as a baby is unalterably a baby, it would not be a good excuse if it were. Especially is this so since the legislature could avoid the taint of illegitimacy, much more surely than the servant girl, by simply saying that the "crime" is not a crime, but only a civil violation.[62]

E. The Problem of Providing for Treatment

In determining that described conduct shall constitute a crime, a legislature makes necessarily the first and the major decision about the appropriate sanction for a violation of its direction. For it decides then that community condemnation shall be visited upon adjudged violators. But there remain hosts of questions about the degree of the condemnation and the nature of the authorized punishment, or treatment-in-consequence-of-violation.

Entangled with the problems of the appropriate aims to be pursued which are involved in these questions are problems of the appropriate assignment of powers to

195 U.S. 65 (1904); District of Columbia v. Clawans, 300 U.S. 617 (1937). By the standards laid down in these cases, it will be seen, hosts of strict liability offenses are plainly not "petty."

[61] See *Ex parte* Wilson, 114 U.S. 417 (1885); *In re* Claasen, 140 U.S. 200 (1891); United States v. Moreland, 258 U.S. 433 (1922); Oppenheimer, *Infamous Crimes and the Moreland Case*, 36 HARV. L. REV. 299 (1923). By the standards of these cases, it will be seen, many a conviction for a strict liability offense carries infamy.

[62] The Model Penal Code, as tentatively drafted, recognizes, in large part, the moral indefensibility of strict liability and the lack of any real public necessity for it. See MODEL PENAL CODE § 2.05 (Tent. Draft No. 4, 1955). The draftsman's "comment" on this section, *id.* at 140, explains it as follows:

"1. This section makes a frontal attack on absolute or strict liability in penal law, whenever the offense carries a possibility of sentence of imprisonment. The method used is not to abrogate such liability but to provide that when conviction rests upon that basis the grade of the offense is reduced to a violation, which is not a "crime" and under Sections 1.04(5) and 6.02 may result in no other sentence than a fine or fine and forfeiture or other civil penalty. If, on the other hand, the culpable commission of the offense has been established, the reduction in grade does not occur. Negligence is, however, treated as sufficient culpability in cases of this kind.

"This position is affirmed not only with respect to offenses defined by the Penal Code; it is superimposed on the entire corpus of the law, so far as penal sanctions are involved. Since most strict liability offenses are involved in special, regulatory legislation, this superimposition is essential if the problem is to be attacked. We have no doubt that the attempt is one that should be made. The liabilities involved are indefensible in principle, unless reduced to terms that insulate conviction from the type of moral condemnation that is and ought to be implicit when a sentence of imprisonment may be imposed. In the absence of minimal culpability, the law has neither a deterrent nor corrective nor an incapacitative function to perform.

"It has been argued, and the argument undoubtedly will be repeated, that absolute liability is necessary for enforcement in a number of the areas where it obtains. But if practical enforcement cannot undertake to litigate the culpability of alleged deviation from legal requirements, we do not see how the enforcers rightly can demand the use of penal sanctions for the purpose. Crime does and should mean condemnation and no court should have to pass that judgment unless it can declare that the defendant's act was wrong. This is too fundamental to be compromised. The law goes far enough if it permits the imposition of a monetary penalty in cases where strict liability has been imposed."

The only shortcoming of the draft is that strict liability so far as concerns ignorance or mistake with respect to the existence or meaning of the applicable law is retained, subject only to the narrowly limited exceptions set forth in note 49 *supra*. In view of the magnitude of the reform actually urged by the Code, however, the decision to restrict the proposal reflects an understandable counsel of prudence.

make decisions in carrying out the aims. To what extent should the legislature undertake to give binding directions about treatment which will foreclose the exercise of any later discretion? To what extent should it depend, instead, upon the judgment and discretion either of the sentencing court or of the correctional authorities who will become responsible for defendants after they are sentenced?

It is axiomatic that each agency of decision ought to make those decisions which its position in the institutional structure best fits it to make. But this, as will be seen, depends in part upon the criteria which are to guide decision.

1. The traditional criminal law recognizes different grades of offenses, such as felony and misdemeanor, and modern statutes recognize different degrees within the grades. If the criminal law were concerned centrally with reforming criminals, this would scarcely be appropriate: a confirmed petty thief may have much greater need of reformation than a once-in-a-lifetime manslaughterer. If the thesis of this paper is accepted, however, it follows that grading is not only proper, but essential; that the legislature is the appropriate institution to do the grading; that the grading should be done with primary regard for the relative blameworthiness of offenses (a factor which, of course, will take into account the relative extent of the harm characteristically done or threatened to individuals and, thus, to the social order by each type of offense); and that the grading should be determinative of the relative severity of the treatment authorized for each offense.

2. Given such a ranking of offenses, the question remains: how far up or down the scale of possible severity or lenity of treatment should the whole array be moved? Are comparatively severe punishments to be favored or comparatively lenient ones? Here is a question of public policy which is pre-eminently for the legislature. On this question, its cardinal aims should be its cardinal guide. Punishments should be severe enough to impress not only upon the defendant's mind, but upon the public mind, the gravity of society's condemnation of irresponsible behavior. But the ultimate aim of condemning irresponsibility is training for responsibility. The treatment of criminals, therefore, should encourage, rather than foreclose, the development of their sense of responsibility. Allowance for the possibility of reformation, or formation, of character in the generality of cases becomes at this point, in other words, an overriding consideration. This consideration will point inexorably in the direction of eliminating capital punishment and minimizing both the occasions and the length of incarceration.

3. Should the legislature prescribe a single definite and unvarying form of treatment for each type of offense? The almost universal judgment of modern legal systems is that, ordinarily at least, it should not.[63] Two types of considerations seem to underlie this judgment. The first is the need of making the treatment fit the

[63] Notable exceptions, of course, are the mandatory death sentence and the mandatory life term for recidivists, both of which, however, have fallen into widespread disrepute and, one may hope, are on the way to complete abandonment.

crime. Statutory definitions of offenses are, of necessity, highly general categories covering a host of variant circumstances which are relevant to the blameworthiness of particular crimes. All the circumstances which are relevant in a particular case cannot be known until the case has been tried. The second type of consideration is the need of making the treatment fit the criminal, so as to take into account not only the kind of thing he did, but the kind of person he is. Only in this way can room be allowed for the effective play, on the basis of individualized judgment, of the criminal law's subordinate aims of reforming offenders or of disabling them where a special period of disablement seems to be needed. Both types of considerations indicate that discretion should be left to trial courts or correctional authorities, with respect both to the type of treatment—fine, imprisonment, probation, or the like—and to its extent or duration.

4. Should the legislature fix the maximum punishment, or the maximum severity of the treatment authorized, for particular types of crimes? Basic considerations of liberty as well as the logic of the aims of the criminal law dictate that it should. Men should not be put to death or imprisoned for a crime unless the legislature has sanctioned the penalty of death or imprisonment for that crime. Even with respect to penalties of an authorized type, the maximum of the permitted fine or term of imprisonment should be fixed by law. Only in this way can the integrity of the legislature's scheme of gradation of offenses and of the underlying principle that penalties should correspond in some fashion to the degree of blameworthiness of defendants' conduct be maintained. Only in this way can room be allowed for the beneficent operation of theories of reformation, while shutting the door to their tendencies toward cruelty.[64]

5. Should the legislature prescribe the *minimum* punishment, or the minimum severity of the treatment to be meted out, for particular types of crimes? The problem here is to make sure that society does not depreciate the gravity of its own judgments of condemnation through the imposition by sentencing judges of disproportionately trivial penalties. Yet, the virtues of individualization have their claims, too. Perhaps a suspended prison sentence, with probation, may be the best form of treatment even for a convicted murderer, as it certainly may be for a convicted manslaughterer. A society which entrusts its juries with power to bring in a verdict of acquittal in cases of undoubted guilt ought to be able to trust its judges to exercise the lesser discretion of leniency in sentencing.

6. In cases in which convicted persons are to be sentenced to a term of imprisonment, how should power be divided between the sentencing judge (or jury) and prison and parole authorities in determining the actual duration of the incarceration? This question can best be left to be considered when the problems of the criminal law are examined from the point of view of those agencies.

[64] See note 19 *supra*.

IV

THE PERSPECTIVE OF POLICE AND PROSECUTING ATTORNEYS

To shift from the perspective of the legislature to that of police and prosecuting attorneys is to shift from the point of view of formulation of general directions to that of their application. These law enforcement officers, moreover, have power only to determine how their own functions shall be carried out. Unlike the antecedent determinations of the legislature and the subsequent determinations of courts, their decisions carry no authority as general directions to others for the future. They have a lesser role to play, accordingly, in the conscious shaping of the aims of the criminal law.

Nevertheless, what enforcement officials do is obviously of crucial importance in determining how the criminal law actually works. Their problems and the policies they pursue in trying to solve them need to be studied for the purpose not only of learning how better to control their activities—familiar enough questions—but for the purpose also of a better understanding, which legislatures sadly need, of what responsibilities ought to be given them and of the consequences of unwise imposition of responsibility.

This is not the place to pursue these questions in detail. A few suggestions only will be ventured.

1. The breadth of discretion we entrust to the police and prosecuting attorneys in dealing with individuals is far greater than that entrusted to any other kinds of officials and less subject to effective control. This discretion presents obvious difficulties in securing the lawful and equal administration of law. It presents also less obvious, or less noticed, difficulties of transferring from the legislature to enforcement officials the *de facto* power of determining what the criminal law in action shall be.

2. To the extent that the activities of enforcement officials are confined to securing compliance with what have been described as the basic obligations of responsible citizenship, their discretion will tend to be reduced to the minimum which the necessities of the administration of law admit. If social morale is good, there will be community demand for enforcement of these obligations and community support of it, and it will be feasible to provide an enforcement staff reasonably adequate to its task. Under these circumstances, reliance upon enforcement only on private complaint or newspaper insistence will be minimized. The exercise of discretion by police and prosecutors will consist largely of making specifically professional, and inescapable, judgments concerning the sufficiency of the evidence to warrant further investigation or formal accusation, what charges to make, what pleas to accept, what penalties to ask for, and the like.

3. The stupidity and injustice of the thoughtless multiplication of minor crimes receives its most impressive demonstration in police stations and prosecutors' offices. Invariably, staffs are inadequate for enforcement of all the criminal statutes which

the legislature in its unwisdom chooses to enact. Accordingly, many of the statutes go largely unenforced. To this extent, their enactment is rendered futile. But it proves also to be worse than futile. For statutes usually do not become a complete dead letter. What happens is that they are enforced sporadically, either as a matter of deliberate policy to proceed only on private complaint, or as a matter of the accident of what comes to official attention or is forced upon it. Sporadic enforcement is an instrument of tyranny when enforcement officers are dishonest. It has an inescapable residuum of injustice in the hands even of the best-intentioned officers. A selection for prosecution among equally guilty violators entails not only inequality, but the exercise, necessarily, of an unguided and, hence, unprincipled discretion.

4. While the evils just described are common in the enforcement of most minor crimes, they are at their most acute in the sphere of regulation of conduct which is not intrinsically wrongful, and there a special phenomenon is likely to develop. Even though he ought not to seek the power in advance,[65] a conscientious prosecutor, faced with the fact of more violators than he can prosecute, is likely to single out for prosecution those whom he regards as morally blameworthy, in default of any better basis of selection.[66] Thus, he will negate the legislative judgment that all violators should be prosecuted, regardless of moral blame. But at the same time, he will create a *de facto* crime, the main element of which is withdrawn from proof or disproof by due process of law.

5. In the area of traditional crimes, enforcement officials have an opportunity to put the dominant aim of the criminal law to inculcate understanding of the obligations of responsible citizenship, and to secure compliance with them, into a meaningful relationship with its subsidiary aim of rehabilitating people who have proved themselves to be irresponsible. In the area of regulatory crimes, this is possible only if "wilfulness," as earlier defined,[67] is an ingredient of criminality. The whole concept of curative-rehabilitative treatment has otherwise no relevance in this area.

V

THE PERSPECTIVE OF COURTS IN THE ASCERTAINMENT OF GUILT

Courts look both backward and forward in the application of law. They look backward to the relevant general directions of the Constitution and the statutes, as interpreted and applied in prior judicial decisions. They look backward to the historical facts of the litigation. But when the facts raise issues with respect to which the existing general directions are indeterminate, they are bound to look forward to the ends which the law seeks to serve and to resolve the issues as best they can in a way which will serve them. This, of course, is the strength of the judicial process—that it permits principles to be worked pure and the details of implementing rules

[65] See note 59 *supra* and accompanying text.
[66] See note 56 *supra*.
[67] See note 41 *supra* and accompanying text.

and standards to be developed in the light of intensive examination of the interaction of the general with the particular. But it is a strength existing sometimes in the potentiality rather than in the realization. Notably has this been true in this country in the development of the substantive law of crimes.

The inherited criminal law was rich with principles and with potentialities for their reasoned and intelligible development. But the multiplication of statutory crimes and the inadequacy of judicial techniques of interpreting statutes, coupled with unimaginative and unintelligent use even of familiar common-law techniques, have shaken much of the law loose from these moorings.

It is possible to see the beginnings of this development in some unfortunate decisions in the area of customary crimes touching sensitive matters of sex and family law.

A well-known example is that of statutory rape and kindred offenses against immature girls. Here, the courts came widely to hold that when the legislature had specified a fixed age of consent, the man's belief in the girl's age, and even his utmost good faith and reasonableness in holding the belief, were irrelevant.[68] They pictured the legislature, in other words, as saying to mankind: "If you choose to have intercourse with a willing female who may be over or under the age of consent, you will be playing a game with the law as well as with her. If she is of age, you win the law's game. If she is under age, you lose it and will be condemned as a felon, regardless of what she may have told you and regardless of the good reasons you may have had for believing her." When account is taken of the long tradition that ignorance of the fact excuses, it is evident that this interpretation was not a necessary one, if, indeed, it was even plausible. But it seems to have had important influence in encouraging the modern trend toward strict liability.

Similarly, in prosecutions for bigamy, and particularly when the bigamy statute was coupled with a presumption of the death of a missing spouse after a fixed period of unexplained absence, the courts tended to hold that a man or woman who remarried within the statutory period did so at the peril of criminal conviction if the spouse were actually alive.[69] In effect, such courts said: "Good faith and reasonable inquiry have nothing to do with this. We read the legislature's presumption as not merely avoiding the necessity of specific proof of good faith when the presumption is applicable, but as barring such proof when it is inapplicable. We attribute to the legislature a purpose to discourage the remarriage of abandoned spouses as socially impolitic, by requiring those who attempt it to take a gambler's chance of becoming a criminal." Once again, obviously, the interpretation was not a necessary one. And once again, currency was given to the notion that people can commit crimes without really doing anything wrong at all.

Closely and vitally related to the failure of American courts to develop adequate

[68] The bellwether case is Regina v. Prince, L.R. 2 Cr. Cas. Res. 154 (1875).

[69] On this issue, Massachusetts led the way in Commonwealth v. Mash, 48 Mass. (7 Metc.) 472 (1844). A majority of the English judges, recoiling from Regina v. Prince, *supra* note 68, went the other way. Regina v. Tolson, 23 Q.B.D. 168 (1889).

principles of criminal liability and an adequate theory of the aims of the criminal law as guides in the interpretation of statutes has been their failure to come to grips with the underlying constitutional issues involved. This failure is the more surprising because of the obvious concern of the Constitution to safeguard the use of the method of the criminal law—especially, but not exclusively, on the procedural side—and the concern of the courts themselves, particularly in recent times, to give vitality to the procedural guarantees. What sense does it make to insist upon procedural safeguards in criminal prosecutions if anything whatever can be made a crime in the first place? What sense does it make to prohibit ex post facto laws (to take the one explicit guarantee of the Federal Constitution on the substantive side) if a man can, in any event, be convicted of an infamous crime for inadvertent violation of a prior law of the existence of which he had no reason to know and which he had no reason to believe he was violating, even if he had known of its existence?

Despite the unmistakable indications that the Constitution means something definite and something serious when it speaks of "crime," the Supreme Court of the United States has hardly got to first base in working out what that something is. From beginning to end, there is scarcely a single opinion by any member of the Court which confronts the question in a fashion which deserves intellectual respect.[70]

[70] A possible exception is Mr. Justice Jackson's spread-eagle dissertation in Morissette v. United States, 342 U.S. 246 (1952), involving the question whether a defendant charged with having "knowingly converted" government property consisting of rusty bomb casings dumped on a remote Air Force practice bombing range (which the defendant had openly appropriated and sold for junk) should have been allowed the defense that he believed in good faith that the casings had been abandoned. However, the opinion, which held the defense available, seems open to the objections indicated in the following imaginary concurring opinion, which is here reproduced to illustrate the main theme of the text of the importance of interpretative presumptions.

"Mr. Justice TENTHJUDGE, concurring in result.

"While I have an emotional sympathy with most of what is said in my brother Jackson's engaging opinion in this case, I should not wish to be understood as expressing judicial agreement with any part of it, except the very limited part which is necessary for decision of the narrow issue before us.

"We ought to refrain from writing discursive essays on the law, if only to spare law students the burden of reading them and law professors the pain of deciding whether to reproduce them in their casebooks. But there is a still more compelling reason for restraint. We cannot possibly apply our minds to all the considerations which are relevant to all the propositions which the Court's opinion advances. We cannot possibly be sure, therefore, that each proposition will stand up when it is tested in the crucible of a litigation squarely involving it. Thus, to the peccadillo of announcing too much law in this case, we add the cardinal sin of announcing law of dubious reliability.

"We have to deal here with a typical modern statute consolidating—with typical looseness of draftsmanship—the various forms of theft, so far as these crimes are of concern to the United States as a governmental entity. With respect to all these forms of theft—not only those which are of judicial origin, like trespassory larceny and larceny by trick, but those which have their origin in statutes, like obtaining property by false pretences and embezzlement—a 'claim of right' has traditionally been a defense. Morissette's claim falls comfortably within the types of claims which have traditionally been recognized as affording this defense. *E.g.*, People v. Shaunding, 268 Mich. 218, 255 N.W. 770 (1934); People v. Lapique, 120 Cal. 25, 52 Pac. 40 (1898); *cf.* Commonwealth v. Althause, 207 Mass. 32, 51, 93 N.E. 202 (1910). See generally ROLLIN M. PERKINS, CRIMINAL LAW 223 (1957).

"Hence the simple question before us is whether the vague and general language of the 'knowingly converts' clause of 62 STAT. 725 (1948), 18 U.S.C. § 641 (1952) should be read as incorporating this established element of the crime of theft or as eliminating it.

"There are a plethora of good reasons for the narrower reading.

The Court began with a few dicta suggesting that a crime is anything which the legislature chooses to say it is.[71] These were followed by a pair of narcotics cases,

"Statutes, generally, should be read in the light of the common law, save where they make plain a purpose to depart from it.

"This is doubly true of statutes defining crimes, which ancient learning tells us should be strictly construed, if a strict construction is sensible. McBoyle v. United States, 283 U.S. 25 (1931); United States v. Wiltberger, 18 U.S. (5 Wheat.) 76, 95-96 (1820).

"It is trebly true of statutes defining federal crimes, which are not readily to be given an expansive interpretation overlapping the criminal prohibitions of the states.

"It is quadruply true of a section which the statutory revisers tell us simply 'consolidates' previous provisions of the code, which provisions, as we know, had never been held to dispense with the common law defense.

"It is quintuply true when the section in question is contained in a recodification which, as the Court's opinion tells us (note 28), was generally 'not intended to create new crimes, but to recodify those then in existence.'

"It is sextuply true when the recodification in question—why not come right out and say it?—is one for which the spadework was done by the hired hands of three commercial law-book publishers, on delegation from a congressional committee desirous of escaping the responsibility of hiring and supervising its own staff.

"In these circumstances, the case against finding a major change of public policy in the interstices of this slovenly enactment is overwhelming.

"If the Court's opinion had chosen merely to add as a seventh reason that it is a general principle of our law that criminal condemnation imports moral blameworthiness and that the legislature ought not lightly to be taken as wishing to weaken this principle, I should have had no objection; indeed, I should have applauded.

"But I see no occasion for examination and labored distinction of the notorious instances in which Congress and this Court have sanctioned blatant defiance of this principle. In particular, whether United States v. Balint, 258 U.S. 250 (1922), United States v. Behrman, 258 U.S. 280 (1922), and United States v. Dotterweich, 320 U.S. 277 (1943), were soundly decided on their facts, and what, if any, the ramifications of their reasoning may be are questions which, I think, we ought to leave to the riper wisdom of another day.

"As an example of the need for such wisdom, it may not be inappropriate to call attention to the paradox in which my brother Jackson's ratiocinations have involved him.

"In relation to offenses of a traditional type, the Court's opinion seems to be saying, we must be much slower to dispense with a basis for genuine blameworthiness in criminal intent than in relation to modern regulatory offenses. But it is precisely in the area of traditional crimes that the nature of the act itself commonly gives some warning that there may be a problem about its propriety and so affords, without more, at least some slight basis of condemnation for doing it. Thus, Morissette knew perfectly well that he was taking property which, at least up to the moment of caption, did not belong to him.

"In the area of regulatory crimes, on the other hand, the moral quality of the act is often neutral; and on occasion, the offense may consist not of any act at all, but simply of an intrinsically innocent omission, so that there is no basis for moral condemnation whatever. Thus, in *Dotterweich*, the Court upheld a conviction of the president and general manager of a corporation doing a reputable business merely because the corporation had happened to ship an adulterated and misbranded drug in interstate commerce and Dotterweich happened to be its responsible executive.

"I think the Court is right in holding that Morissette should have been allowed to go to the jury on the question of his consciousness of wrongdoing. But it will take something more than the lucubrations of the present opinion to convince me that Morissette had a better title to do so than Dotterweich."

[71] The earliest discussion seems to be the elaborate and much cited dictum in Shevlin-Carpenter Co. v. Minnesota, 218 U.S. 57, 67-69 (1910). The case was a *civil* action for damages against a lumber company for trespass in cutting timber on state land after a permit to do so had expired. The state court had entered judgment for double damages against the company on the ground that the trespass was "wilful." Among the grounds of the company's appeal was the claim that the statute also made a "casual and involuntary trespasser" liable to the state in double damages, and that it included also a severe criminal penalty, "'and that declaring his act a felony violates the Fourteenth Amendment,' because those provisions 'eliminate altogether the question of intent,' and that the 'elimination of intent as an element of an offense is contrary to the requirements of due process of law.'" The Court's opinion made the obvious rejoinders that the company was in no position to advance this complaint, first, because

patently concerned with the evils of drugs rather than with the evil of disloyalty to a millennium of legal tradition.[72] Then came, only a few years ago, one of the most drastic of the Court's decisions, treating the whole matter as a *fait accompli.*[73] Not until the last term, in *Lambert v. California,*[74] did the Court discover that the due process clauses had anything to say about branding innocent people as criminals. But neither the majority nor the dissenting opinion in that case is persuasive of any need to qualify the second sentence in this paragraph.

The *Lambert* case involved a Los Angeles ordinance making it a criminal offense for any "convicted person," as defined, to be and remain in the city for more than five days without registering. The Court held that the application of

its action had been found to be "wilful" and, second, because in any event, the provisions for a criminal penalty were separable. But then, with impatience, and corresponding lack of hard thinking, it went on to say broadly that the argument with respect to the necessity of criminal intent was not any good anyway. It cited no authority whatever. Manifestly, the company had no claim of surprised innocence sufficiently plausible to draw the Court's real attention to the question.

Mr. Justice McKenna's *Shevlin-Carpenter* dictum was followed the next year by a dictum of Mr. Justice Holmes in United States v. Johnson, 221 U.S. 488, 497-98 (1911)—again, wholly nude of supporting authority. The case held that false claims of being a cure for cancer on the labels of plaintiff's patent medicine bottles did not make the bottles "misbranded" within the meaning of the Food and Drugs Act of 1906, because they constituted simply innocent puffing, rather than misstatements about the identity of the contents. For this shockingly narrow and distorting interpretation, the opinion gave the ironical reason that "the article may be misbranded without any conscious fraud at all," and that while "it was natural enough to throw this risk on shippers with regard to the identity of their wares," it was "a very different and unlikely step to make them answerable for mistaken praise." Morality and rationality alike, it is submitted, could hardly be more completely inverted.

[72] United States v. Balint, 258 U.S. 250 (1922); United States v. Behrman, 258 U.S. 280 (1922), both decided on the same black Monday. Both cases involved facts which, one may surmise, would have permitted conviction on orthodox principles. But Mr. Justice Holmes, dissenting in the *Behrman* case (although not in *Balint*), said that the indictment there had been framed "for the very purpose of raising the issue that divides the Court"; and the same thing seems to have been true of the *Balint* indictment. The *Balint* case held that a physician could be convicted of selling a certain opium derivative without the use of a required form, under a statute carrying a maximum penalty of five years imprisonment and a fine of $2,000, even though he had been without knowledge of the contents of the drug. The *Behrman* case made a similar holding with reference to the prescription of drugs.

Chief Justice Taft's *Balint* opinion said that the objection "that punishment of a person for an act in violation of law when ignorant of the facts making it so" had been "considered and overruled" in Shevlin-Carpenter Co. v. Minnesota, 218 U.S. 57 (1910), *supra* note 71, a manifestly cavalier use of dictum as controlling authority. For further authority, the opinion cited only some state court cases, some lower federal court cases, and two English cases. Mr. Justice Day's *Behrman* opinion cited only *Balint* and some lower federal court cases.

Chief Justice Taft said that the statute had the "manifest purpose" of requiring "every person dealing in drugs to ascertain, at his peril, whether that which he sells comes within the inhibition of the statute." It expressed its reasons for approving this in two sentences: "Congress weighed the possible injustice of subjecting an innocent seller to a penalty against the evil of exposing innocent purchasers to danger from the drug, and concluded that the latter was the result preferably to be avoided. Doubtless considerations as to the opportunity of the seller to find out the fact and the difficulty of proof of knowledge contributed to this conclusion." Exactly how the desired end of protecting innocent purchasers was served by convicting innocent sellers the opinion did not explain. Nor did it explore any of the other relevant considerations.

[73] United States v. Dotterweich, 320 U.S. 277 (1943). See the discussion of the case in note 70 *supra*. Mr. Justice Frankfurter's opinion disposes of the problem in a curt half paragraph, citing only the *Balint* case, *supra* note 72, and Holmes' dictum in United States v. Johnson, 221 U.S. 48 (1911), *supra* note 71. It pays no attention to the differences between the possibilities of protecting themselves which sellers of drugs have and those which corporation presidents have.

[74] 355 U.S. 225 (1957).

this ordinance to one who had no actual or "probable" knowledge of it violated the due process clause of the fourteenth amendment. Yet, four members of the Court dissented. They were led by so sensitive a judge as Mr. Justice Frankfurter, who, pointing to the large body of legislation which he believed to be put in question by the majority's reasoning, expressed his confidence "that the present decision will turn out to be an isolated deviation from the strong current of precedents—a derelict on the waters of the law."

The opinion of the Court by Mr. Justice Douglas pinned its holding upon the fact that the conduct condemned by the ordinance was "wholly passive" and "unlike the commission of acts, or the failure to act under circumstances that should alert the doer to the consequences of his deed." Yet, it made no effort to analyze the nature of crimes of omission, as distinguished from those of commission.[75] It spoke vaguely of "the requirement of notice" as "engrained in our concept of Due Process." But it cited only inapposite cases,[76] left the unexplained suggestion that notice making for "probable" personal knowledge would be enough, and wholly ignored the fact that the theretofore unqualified doctrine of Anglo-American law has been that notice by due promulgation and publication of a statute is all that is required.[77] On the issue of criminal intent, the opinion said that "we do not go with Blackstone in saying that 'a vicious will' is necessary to constitute a crime." More atrocious even than the rhetoric of this statement is its moral insensitivity and the intellectual inadequacy of the reasoning offered to support it. Why the views of Blackstone should be thus cavalierly overridden in interpreting a Constitution written by men who accepted his pronouncements as something approaching gospel was left unexplained. What the essential distinction is between those states of innocence which permit conviction of crime and those which do not was left to guesswork.

The dissenting opinion did not have the virtue even of the majority's muddy recognition that being a "criminal" must mean something. It contented itself with flat assertion that human beings may be convicted of crime under the Constitution of the United States even though they "may have had no awareness of what the law required or that what they did was wrongdoing." To this, one can say only, "Why? why? why?" The opinion gives only one answer, "So it has been decided. So it has been decided. So it has been decided." The replication has to be, "But this is wrong, wrong, wrong. And it will continue to be wrong so long as words have meaning and human beings have the capacity to recognize and the courage to resent bitter and unwarranted insult."[78]

[75] For the possibilities of such an analysis, see Hughes, *supra* note 44.

[76] The cases, as the Court said "involved only property interests in civil litigation."

[77] The analysis by Hughes, *supra* note 44, recognizes how crucial the question of the bearing of this doctrine is and comes to intellectual grips with it.

[78] It is true that the problem in *Lambert* was one of constitutionality under the fourteenth amendment and, so, of a kind which raises for Mr. Justice Frankfurter the ultimate problem of judicial self-restraint in the interpretation of the Constitution. That this is so, however, serves only to emphasize the casual way in which in United States v. Dotterweich, 320 U.S. 277 (1943), *supra* note 70, he disposed of an issue which was simply one of the just interpretation of a federal statute.

The importance of constitutional doctrine is not to be measured by the number of statutes formally invalidated pursuant to it or formally sustained against direct attack. Thinking in constitutional terms provides the points of reference which are necessary in building up a body of thought which is adequate to the task of statutory interpretation.[79] Correspondingly, the absence of such basic thinking is likely to result in a hiatus of thought when interpretive problems present themselves. Thus, the small handful of pre-*Lambert* decisions upholding the constitutionality of strict criminal liability helped to breed a multitude of other decisions blandly assuming, with no effort at ratiocination, that it was a matter of indifference whether ambiguous statutory language were to be read as importing a requirement of "criminal" intent or dispensing with it, and permitting slight evidence to tilt the scales in favor of dispensation. Correspondingly, what will be chiefly important to watch about the *Lambert* case will be the strength of the push it gives to interpretations insisting upon the necessity of a genuinely criminal intent. One may guess that the push would have been stronger if the majority opinion had been more muscularly written.

What are likely to be crucial in the development of any body of statutory law are the presumptions with which courts approach debatable issues of interpretation. For it is these presumptions which control decision when a legislature has failed to address itself to an issue and to express itself unmistakably about it. If the interpretive presumptions of the courts are founded on principles and policies rationally related to the ultimate purposes of the social order, then statutory law will tend to develop the coherence and intelligibility, and the susceptibility to being reasoned about, which a body of unwritten law tends always to have. Otherwise, it will tend to become a wasteland of arbitrary distinctions and meaningless detail.

Legislatures in our tradition have depended heavily upon the assistance of courts in giving statutory law this kind of in-built rationality. The articulation and use of interpretive presumptions by the courts is an essential means of providing this assistance. It involves no impairment of legislative prerogative, but, on the contrary, facilitates the legislature's work rather than hinders it. It serves to focus issues, to sharpen responsibilities, and to discourage buck-passing. It gives assurance that a legislature's departure from generally prevailing principles and policies will be a considered one. This, in turn, requires the courts to confront the resulting constitutional questions, if any, with recognition of the deliberateness of the legislature's determination and of the need for taking full account of the reasons for the determination before overturning it.

The need of some improvement in the shoddy and little-minded thinking of American legislatures about the problems of the criminal law is great. But adequate improvement cannot come from that source alone. Only if the courts acknowledge their obligation to collaborate with the legislature in discerning and expressing the

[79] See Book Review, 67 HARV. L. REV. 1456, 1485-86 (1954). See also the opinion in note 70 *supra*.

unifying principles and aims of the criminal law is it likely that a coherent and worthy body of penal law will ever be developed in this country. For the most part, American courts have, thus far, failed not only in the fulfillment, but even in the recognition of this obligation.

VI

THE PERSPECTIVE OF COURTS IN MAKING DECISIONS ABOUT TREATMENT

When an offender has been found guilty, the court's responsibility for the generalized statement of substantive legal doctrine is at an end. What ordinarily remains is only an individualized determination with respect to this particular defendant. This focus upon the defendant as an individual provides opportunities to be exploited. But it also points up tendencies to be resisted. For the defendant is a character in a much larger drama, and questions about his needs must not be allowed to push out of view questions about the effect of his treatment on other persons and on the well-being of society generally.

A. The Judgment of Conviction

If criminality is to be equated with antisocial conduct warranting the moral condemnation of society, then plainly the first and foremost function of the trial judge in every case, when a finding of guilt has been made, is to express to the defendant with all possible solemnity a judgment of condemnation of his conduct in society's behalf.

The trial judge, of course, can do this under existing law, as many do, when the defendant's offense is one which the community recognizes as blameworthy. But here we meet another of the hidden costs of the sacrifice of principle. For a conscientious judge who is called upon constantly to convict and to sentence defendants who have been guilty of bad luck more than anything else is forced to differentiate. Since he cannot, in honesty, tell such a defendant that his conduct is morally blameworthy, he is forced to draw a line among criminal defendants. This is not like drawing a line between genuinely criminal offenses of varying degrees of gravity. For this differentiation puts in question the very integrity and meaning of the concept of crime. The result may be that even the judge himself stops believing in the equation between criminality and blameworthiness.

A distinguished federal district judge said recently in private conversation that in entering judgments of conviction and passing sentence, he was careful always to refrain from expressing any view about the defendant's character or the morality of his conduct. One can respect the spirit of personal humility that lies behind this restraint. One can discern the main outlines of the supporting rationalization which the positivistic strain in American legal thought provides. One can understand why it is particularly easy for a federal judge, dealing with a considerably larger proportion of regulatory crimes than most state judges, to take such a view. Yet, it has still to be said that the practice described epitomizes the moral and intellectual debility of American criminal law. An able and sensitive judge does not consider that there is any difference between a criminal conviction and a civil judgment which it is worth while to try to communicate to the defendant. If this is so, what attention can ordinary people be expected to pay to the threat of a criminal as distinguished from a civil sanction?

The result, considered simply from the point of view of efficient social engineering, is a grievous waste. For all except the most hardened criminals, a judgment of community condemnation, solemnly and impersonally expressed, can be made a shaking and unforgettable experience. If legislatures had kept clean the concept of crime and sentencing judges were then enabled to tell a convicted criminal, in good conscience, that his conduct had been wrongful and deserved the condemnation of his fellow men, the very pronouncement of such a judgment would go far to serve the purposes of the criminal law by vindicating its threats and so to lessen the need for resort to other commonly less effective and invariably more expensive and oppressive forms of treatment.

B. The Sentence: Herein Also of the Perspective of Prison and Parole Authorities

A judgment of conviction having been entered, the trial judge must next face the harsh realities of imposition of sentence.

If what has been said is correct, the judge, in doing this, should be guided by two main, and interrelated, objectives. First, is the overriding necessity of a sentence which, taken together with the judgment of conviction itself, adequately expresses the community's view of the gravity of the defendant's misconduct. Second, is the necessity of a sentence which will be as favorable as possible, consistently with the first objective, to the defendant's rehabilitation as a responsible and functioning member of his community. The first objective stresses the interests of the community; but it does not ignore the interests of the defendant as an individual, since his rehabilitation requires his recognition of communty interests and of the obligations of community life. The second stresses the interests of the defendant as an individual; but it does not ignore those of the community, since the community is interested in the defendant's realization of his potentialities as a human being and in the contributions he can make to community life.[80]

The community's condemnation of the defendant's conduct can be expressed in four main ways: *first,* by the legislature's prior grading and characterization, in general terms, of the offense of which he has been found guilty; *second,* by the trial judge's formal expression of condemnation of the particular conduct, taking into

[80] The protection of society by disabling offenders who are likely to offend again is conventionally said to be one of the functions of the criminal law, and the statement in the text may be thought to be mistaken in ignoring this purpose. It is suggested, however, that there is serious danger in admitting so speculative a factor as a criterion in the exercise of general sentencing discretion. The existence of a special need for disablement of particularly dangerous individuals seems better taken into account either (1) by parole authorities, in the light of prison experience, in deciding whether to release a prisoner before his maximum term has expired; or (2) through statutory provisions for extended terms laying down carefully-stated criteria to be applied by the judge on the basis of special findings of fact. See MODEL PENAL CODE § 7.03 and accompanying comment (Tent. Draft No. 2, 1955).

account all the special circumstances of it; *third,* by a determination that the defendant shall be vulnerable to unpleasant consequences *in the future* if his behavior thereafter fails to conform to prescribed conditions; and, *fourth,* by a determination that the defendant shall *presently* and forthwith undergo unpleasant consequences, such as fine or imprisonment. Under modern statutes, the judge's exercise of discretion in sentencing will consist largely of choices about the use to be made of the third and fourth forms of condemnation.[81] This paper will not attempt a detailed analysis of the judge's problems in making these choices, but a few broad suggestions in line with the general thesis of the paper may be appropriately made.

1. It is first to be observed that the best possibilities of an imaginative and effective reconciliation of the community's interests and the individual's in fixing sentences will lie ordinarily in the use of the third of the forms of condemnation just described. To declare that the defendant is to be vulnerable to future punishment can be, in itself, an impressive expression of the community's moral disapproval. At the same time, the conditional suspension of the punishment, whether it be a fine or term of imprisonment, can provide an environment favorable to rehabilitation, both by conveying to the defendant a sense of the community's confidence in his ability to live responsibly and by giving him a special incentive to do so. It would seem to follow that a suspended sentence with probation should be the preferred form of treatment, to be chosen always unless the circumstances plainly call for greater severity.

2. Of all the forms of treatment of criminals, prison sentences are the most costly to the community not only because of the out-of-pocket expenses of prison care, but because of the danger that the effect on the defendant's character will be debilitating rather than rehabilitating. It would seem to follow that if some form of present punishment is called for, a fine should always be the preferred form of the penalty, unless the circumstances plainly call for a prison sentence.

3. Once it is decided that a defendant should be sent to prison, a problem arises about the division of authority and responsibility between the sentencing court and the parole authorities in deciding the time of the prisoner's release—assuming, that is, that the view earlier advanced is accepted that prison sentences ought not to be for a fixed term, neither more nor less.[82] The first aspect of this problem relates to the minimum length of the term. It was earlier urged that the legislature ought not to specify a fixed minimum term in such a way as to deprive the sentencing judge of power to give a suspended sentence.[83] But this was for the reason that the judge ought to have an opportunity to appraise the blameworthiness of the crime in

[81] As just suggested in subdivision A of this part, the judge has an important discretion also in deciding just what kind of ceremony he will make of the formal pronouncement of the judgment of conviction. In addition, the Model Penal Code, as presently drafted, proposes that he should have a discretion to reduce the grade of the offense for which the defendant is convicted in order to deal justly with those cases in which there are special ameliorating circumstances not taken into account in the general statutory definition of the crime. See *id.* § 6.11.

[82] See pp. 426-27 *supra.*

[83] See p. 427 *supra.*

the light of the particular circumstances of it. Should the judge, having made this appraisal, be empowered to fix a minimum prison term in such a way as to deprive the parole authorities of discretion to order an earlier release? Obviously, the judge is better qualified than the parole authorities to interpret the community's views of the blameworthiness of the defendant's conduct. Prima facie, therefore, it would seem that he ought to have the power to fix a minimum term, although the power should be used with caution, since its exercise will deprive the prisoner of an opportunity by his behavior in prison to justify an earlier parole.[84]

4. Should the sentencing judge also have power to fix a maximum term shorter than the statutory maximum so as to deprive the parole authorities of discretion to keep the prisoner in confinement for the full statutory term? Undoubtedly there will be cases in which extenuating circumstances make the conduct of a guilty defendant less blameworthy than that of the general run of those who commit the same type of crime. This suggests that the judge, as the community's representative, should have the power to recognize these special circumstances in some fashion, either in his judgment of conviction or in his sentence.[85] Yet, it will be observed that whereas the minimum term has the sole function of seeing that the community's condemnation of the defendant's conduct is adequately expressed, different, or at least additional, considerations enter into the fixing of the maximum term. The statutory maximum has as its prime function the fixing of a limit upon the period during which the prisoner may be subjected to administrative control.[86] Judicial power to lower this maximum may be less essential than judicial power to see to the adequate expression of community disapproval.

5. In relation to both of the two points last made, a further and vitally important aspect of the problem of sentencing needs to be taken into account—namely, the necessity of avoiding anarchical inequality in the sentences handed down by different sentencing judges. The achievement of the purposes of the criminal law can never be satisfactorily approximated until this intractable problem is in some fashion reduced to minor, instead of major, proportions. The very ideal of justice is offended by seriously unequal penalties for substantially similar crimes, and the most immediate of its practical purposes are obstructed. Grievous inequalities in sentences are ruinous to prison discipline. And they destroy the prisoner's sense of having been justly dealt with, which is the first prerequisite of his personal reformation. Experience seems to show that large numbers of sentencing judges with power to fix both individualized minimum terms and individualized maximum terms will inevitably produce an indefensible heterogeneity of result. How can a reasonable degree of order be brought into this chaos?

6. Legal experience gives a relatively precise answer to the question just put.

[84] The Model Penal Code proposes that the trial judge should be given the authority to fix a minimum prison term of not less than one year—the theory of the one-year minimum for the judicially-fixed minimum term being that it is "an institutional necessity" for effective treatment. See MODEL PENAL CODE § 6.06 and accompanying comment (Tent. Draft No. 3, 1955).

[85] For an alternative form of power to give this recognition, see note 81 *supra*.

[86] See p. 427 *supra*.

Consistency of result in similar cases can be secured either by the laying down of quite precise rules of decision (which here seems impossible), or by subjecting heterogeneous discretionary decisions to review and revision by a single tribunal, or in both ways. Appellate courts seem ill-adapted to the function of reviewing and revising the sentences of trial judges, besides being too preoccupied with other functions. The creation of a new authority, with the single responsibility of equalizing sentences initially imposed, to the end of assuring that they reflect uniform concepts of degrees of blameworthiness, is a tempting possibility. Short of this expedient, the only institutional machinery presently available in most American legal systems is the parole board.

7. In an ideal system, perhaps, prison and parole authorities would receive prisoners from trial courts with sentences for predetermined, individualized maximum and, when appropriate, minimum terms. The correctional authorities would then have the sole responsibility of custody and treatment of each prisoner, with an eye single to determining, within those limits, first, what kind of custodial treatment would best promote the individual prisoner's growth in responsibility; and, second, when, after the minimum sentence, if any, had been served, growth had progressed to a point which made it proper to permit the prisoner to resume, on parole, the effort at responsible living. But if such a regime is to work effectively, prisoners must have some sense of reasonable equality, and hence justice, in the terms under which they are asked to work out their salvation. In the existing institutional structure, and in any alternative structure which seems feasible, parole boards seem to be the agency best qualified to take responsibility for bringing about this sense of equality. Occasional minimum sentences, which have the special justification already indicated, would not seriously interfere with the discharge of this responsibility. But regular, judicially-tailored maximum sentences would.[87]

VII

CONCLUSION

The views expressed in this paper are somewhat, but not widely, at variance with the statement of purposes and principles of construction contained in the present tentative draft of the American Law Institute's Model Penal Code. That statement would approximate these views more closely if it were revised to read as follows (new matter being in italics):

Section 1.02. PURPOSES: PRINCIPLES OF CONSTRUCTION.

(1) The general purposes of the provisions governing the definition of offenses are:

(a) *To foster the development of personal capacity for responsible decision to the end that every individual may realize his potentialities as a participating and contributing member of his community:*

(b) *To declare the obligation of every competent person to comply with* (1)

[87] The Model Penal Code denies the judge the power to fix an individualized maximum term which is less than the statutory term, except in the special case where sentence for an extended term is imposed. See MODEL PENAL CODE § 6.06 and accompanying comment (Tent. Draft. No. 2, 1955).

those standards of behavior which a responsible individual should know are imposed by the conditions of community life if the benefits of community living are to be realized, and (2) those further obligations of conduct, specially declared by the legislature, which the individual either in fact knows or has good reason to know he is supposed to comply with, and to prevent violations of these basic obligations of good citizenship by providing for public condemnation of the violations and appropriate treatment of the violators;[88]

(c) To safeguard conduct that is *not blameworthy*[89] from condemnation as criminal;

(d) To give fair warning of the nature of the conduct declared to constitute an offense; *and*

(e) To differentiate on reasonable grounds between serious crimes and minor offenses.

(2) The general purposes of the provisions governing the conviction, sentencing, and treatment of offenders are:

(a) *To further the purposes of the provisions governing the definition of offenses;*[90]

(b) To promote the correction and rehabilitation of offenders;

(c) *To subject to a special public control those persons whose conduct indicates that they are disposed to commit crimes;*[91]

(d) To safeguard offenders against excessive, disproportionate, or arbitrary punishment;

(e) To give fair warning of the nature of the sentences that may be imposed on conviction of an offense;

(f) To differentiate among offenders with a view to a just individualization in their treatment;

(g) To define, co-ordinate, and harmonize the powers, duties, and functions of the courts and administrative officers and agencies responsible for dealing with offenders;

(h) To advance the use of generally accepted methods and knowledge in the sentencing and treatment of offenders; and

(i) To integrate responsibility for the administration of the correctional system in a State Department of Correction (or other single department or agency).

(3) The provisions of the Code shall be construed according to the fair import of their terms but when the language is susceptible of differing constructions it shall be interpreted particular provision involved. The discretionary powers conferred by the Code shall be to further the general purposes stated in this section and the special purposes of the exercised in accordance with the criteria stated in the Code and, in so far as they are not decisive, to further the general purposes stated in this section.

[88] The provisions of the MODEL PENAL CODE (Tent. Draft No. 2, 1954) which the italicized paragraphs (a) and (b) replace are as follows:

"(a) To forbid and prevent conduct that unjustifiably and inexcusably inflicts or threatens substantial harm to individual and public interests;

"(b) To subject to public control persons whose conduct indicates that they are disposed to commit crimes";

In the suggested revision, the latter paragraph is transferred to subsection (2) of the section dealing with sentencing and treatment.

[89] The words "not blameworthy" are substituted for "without fault."

[90] The language is substituted for the clause, "To prevent the commission of offenses."

[91] See note 88 *supra*.

[2]

Criminal Attempt and the Theory of the Law of Crimes

LAWRENCE C. BECKER

The fundamental problem addressed in this paper is that of getting an adequate rational justification for the distinction the law draws between criminal and noncriminal wrongs. But because theorizing about the law is not only vacuous but likely to be positively misguided apart from a consideration of concrete issues in the law, I want to frame the discussion of theory with an example of its application.

I have chosen, as the example, a proposal for reforming the law of criminal attempt–specifically the proposal that, at least in many cases, successful crimes and (the corresponding) attempted crimes should be punished equally. I have chosen this example both because it has intrinsic interest and because the current status of attempt law, as well as discussion of it, directly reflects what I will argue is a mistaken theory of the law of crimes, and thus is a convenient way of introducing my own view. Due to the fact that the law of attempts has several complex elements, much of what follows will be about those elements. But this should not be allowed to mask the fact that the philosophical crux of the paper is in its discussion of the fundamental aims of criminal law.

There are two additional remarks to be made as preliminaries.

I am indebted to Joseph Raz, Thomas T. Lawson, Theodore Long, Lewis H. La Rue, and the members of the Hollins College Seminar in Philosophy for help with an early draft of this paper. Jesse Zeldin and Roscoe Hill gave me useful bibliographical material at the same stage. A shortened version was read to the Virginia Philosophical Association in October 1973. Valuable criticism from that group, from Charles A. Fried, and from the editors of *Philosophy & Public Affairs*, have gone into the current version of the paper.

263 *Criminal Attempt and the Theory of the Law of Crimes*

First, I will speak throughout of *punishment* for crimes, because that is the traditional way of speaking. But my argument is independent of the question of whether we should "punish" criminals, in the usual sense, at all. Everything argued for here is perfectly compatible with less retributivistic ways of speaking. Further, the proposal for *equal* penalization of attempts and successes is independent of the question of whether one should equalize the penalties by raising those for attempt or by lowering those for success.

Second, and more importantly, it must be noted that there is general agreement that no adequate single principle can be found which will provide a rational basis for the full variety of wrongs currently involved in the criminal/noncriminal distinction. The law has grown in too random a fashion for that, and we shall, I suppose, never be able to find a plausible theory of the law of crimes which justifies both treating pilfering petty cash as criminal and certain sorts of highly harmful breaches of contract as noncriminal. An historical explanation is one thing; no doubt we can get that. But a single justifying principle is quite another matter. This is the difficulty which has led some writers to do little more than state the problem and then give up,[1] and has caused others simply to ignore the problem for more promising pursuits.[2]

But while it may not be possible—or even important—to get an adequate single distinguishing principle, it is possible, I think, and quite important to get clear on what is *fundamentally* at stake here: that is, why it is that we mark off the major sorts of criminal wrongs from others and make them part of public, rather than private, law. This is an important task because there is general consensus in the legal profession on this more limited version of the problem, and I am convinced that the consensus has latched onto a mistaken theory—a theory which is reflected in the treatment of attempted crimes, and which has contributed to the quite unnecessary overestimate of just how far from rational consistency the criminal law as a whole is.

1. See P. J. Fitzgerald, *Criminal Law and Punishment* (Oxford, 1962), p. 7.

2. Glanville Williams, for example, in his enormous textbook on English criminal law, *Criminal Law: The General Part*, 2nd ed. (London, 1961), does not devote so much as a sentence to an attempt to define his subject in a general way.

I

The common law was late in recognizing attempts as criminal. Early English law started from the principle that an attempt to do harm was no offense.[3] Of course, if a man wounded another in an attempt to kill him (or to steal from him, etc.), he could be punished for the wounding. But that was not punishment for an attempt at the more serious crime, and, apparently, if no physical damage was done by an attempt, no prosecution was possible, nor thought to be proper.[4] It was not until the sixteenth century, in the Court of the Star Chamber, that the criminal law was consistently extended to attempts, and then it was apparently only extended to attempted felonies.[5]

The modern doctrine of criminal attempt had to wait until 1801 for its formulation. The case was *Rex* v. *Higgins*, a prosecution for the

3. Pollock and Maitland, *History of English Law* (2nd ed. 1898: in the 1952 reprint by Cambridge University Press) II, p. 475 remark that the principle in English law at the end of the middle ages was "where there is no harm done, no crime is committed; an attempt to commit a crime is no crime." At page 509, they remark that this is true "as a general rule" of ancient (English) law.

The situation was somewhat different on the Continent. Attempts were apparently punished there all through the middle ages, though scholars have had little success in uncovering any theoretical discussion of the practice from that time. By the sixteenth century, attempt was included in recognized Continental criminal codes. See Jerome Hall, "Criminal Attempt: A Study of Foundations of Criminal Liability," *Yale Law Journal* 49 (1940): 789-791.

4. See Henrici de Bracton, *De Legibus et Consuetudinibus Angliae* (Twiss, ed. 1878) vol. II, p. 337, where Bracton quotes as "well known" [*illud*] a phrase refusing penalties for attempts: "for what harm did the attempt cause, since the injury took no effect?" There was, however, an early English law against unlawful assembly, rout, and riot which held that any assembly of three or more persons for an illegal purpose, involving action toward that purpose, was punishable as a rout. As with the many acts held to constitute treason (e.g., writing letters denouncing the King, or making a bet that he would not live long), it is a fairly small conceptual step from such laws to the notion of criminal attempt. There are three early cases, in addition, which are sometimes cited as deviations from the usual practice. In one, reported in 27 Ass. pl. 38 (1353), Shardlowe, J. said, "One who is taken in the act of robbery or burglary even though he does not carry it out, will be hanged according to the law." The other two cases concern attempted murder, and in both cases, the culprits were hanged, the judges citing the maxim *volantas reputabitur pro facto* [the will is to be taken for the deed]. This particular excursion into Latin maxims quickly proved embarrassing and was not pursued in subsequent decisions. See, for a review of these matters, Jerome Hall, *op. cit.*

5. See Hall, *op. cit.*, pp. 796-797.

misdemeanor of solicitation. Higgins had asked a man's servant to steal a quantity of rope from the servant's master. The servant did nothing, but the plot was discovered and Higgins was brought to trial. His counsel argued that although an attempted *felony* was a crime, an attempt at a misdemeanor was not, and Higgins' act had clearly been no more than an abortive attempt at the misdemeanor of solicitation. He was, however, convicted and the Court said in part: "every attempt to commit a crime, whether felony or misdemeanor, is itself a misdemeanor and indictable."[6] This piece of judicial legislation was a success, and has been followed faithfully since.

The situation at present is that, in England, criminal attempts remain punishable as common-law misdemeanors, with life imprisonment as a theoretical maximum. In practice, however, courts normally award lighter sentences for attempts than they do for complete offenses, and in some cases, statutes require this.[7] In the U.S., "the usual punishment grading system for attempt involves making [attempt] punishable by a reduced factor of the punishment for the completed crime. In California [for example] attempt carries a maximum term of not more than one-half of the highest maximum term authorized for the completed crime."[8] In a small number of states–e.g., Illinois and Mississippi–most attempts are punished equally with successes. But even here, attempts at first degree felonies are punished less severely than the completed crimes. We can say, then, that the current practice generally treats attempted crimes more leniently than completed ones.[9]

6. *R.* v. *Higgins* [1801] 2 East 5 at 11; 102 E.R. 269 at 272.

7. Fitzgerald, *Criminal Law and Punishment*, p. 98.

8. Sanford H. Kadish and Monrad G. Paulsen, *Criminal Law and Its Processes*, 2nd ed. (Boston, 1969), p. 368.

9. The Model Penal Code, however, recommends the following sort of law: "Except as otherwise provided in this Section, attempt . . . [is a crime] of the same grade and degree as the most serious offense which is attempted. . . . An attempt . . . to commit a [capital crime or a] felony of the first degree is a felony of the second degree" (American Law Institute, *Model Penal Code* (1962), §5.05(1)). Earlier cultures in the West have also tended toward the more stringent approach. The Romans punished attempts, and though for "ordinary" crimes an attempt got a lighter penalty than a success, for "atrocious" crimes attempts were apparently punished just as severely as completed crimes, at least

The standard arguments in support of current practice make the following points:[10]

(1) The Reform Argument. They acknowledge that, in terms of the reformative aims of penal sanctions, there is probably no point in distinguishing between attempts and successes. One who tries and fails is not likely (merely from that fact) to be in less need of reform than one who tries and succeeds. Thus we have some reason for punishing attempts and successes *equally*.

(2) The Deterrence Argument. On the other hand, they hold that lesser penalties for attempts do not reduce the *deterrent* effect of the law, for at the stage when a person is contemplating a crime, the penalty which has deterrent force for him (if any) is the one for what he *intends* to do. On the assumption that the criminal does not intend

---

as long as the result of the attempt was not insignificant. See Hall, "Criminal Attempt," p. 790. And Plato has this to say about attempted murder:

> If anyone has a purpose and intention to slay another who is not his enemy, and whom the law does not permit him to slay, and he wounds him, but is unable to kill him, he who had the intent and has wounded him is not to be pitied—he deserves no consideration, but should be regarded as a murderer and be tried for murder. Still having respect to the fortune which in a manner has favored him, and to the providence which in pity to him and to the wounded man saved the one from a fatal blow, and the other from an accursed fate and calamity—as a thank-offering to this deity, and in order not to oppose his will—in such a case the law will remit the punishment of death, and only compel the offender to emigrate to a neighboring city for the rest of his life, where he shall remain in the enjoyment of all of his possessions. But if he have injured the wounded man, he shall make such compensation for the injury as the court deciding the case assess . . . (Plato, *Laws*, Book IX: 877; trans. Jowett, Modern Library Editions, vol. 2, p. 621).

In all these instances, however, from the earliest to the latest, there has been hesitation, if not flat refusal, to treat attempt and success alike for all crimes, and ever to impose the death penalty for an attempt.

Pollock and Maitland, *History of English Law* II, p. 497 n. 2, say, however, "It is further to be remembered that among some barbarous folks, which are not utterly lawless, successful theft is regarded with tolerance, if not admiration, and gives rise to a mere claim for the restoration of the goods, while 'manifest theft' is unsuccessful theft and exposes the thief to a beating."

10. Examples of such arguments may be found in P. J. Fitzgerald, *Criminal Law and Punishment*, p. 98; Waite, John Barker, *The Prevention of Repeated Crime* (Ann Arbor, 1943), pp. 8-9; Hall, "Criminal Attempt," p. 817 n. 130; and American Law Institute, *Model Penal Code, Tent. Draft No. 10* (1960), comment to §5.05.

merely to attempt, but rather to succeed, it follows that the severity of the penalty for attempt has little or no force as a deterrent. In accordance with the principle of minimizing pain, then, we have some reason for giving *lesser* penalties for attempts than for successes.

(3) The Unequal Harm Argument. The conflict between (1) and (2) is resolved, or so the arguments go, by noting that since attempts do less actual harm than successes, the principles of proportionality and similar treatment for similar cases combine on the side of (2) to require the lesser penalties. We are committed, for good reason, to making the severity of punishments roughly proportionate to the gravity of the wrongs done. (Consider, for example, the injunctions against "cruel and unusual punishments"–ordinarily interpreted to mean excessive or disproportionate punishments.) We are also committed, of course, as a part of a general commitment to rational decision-making, to treating similar wrongs similarly. If attempts do less harm than successes, the latter principle requires us to class them, on that basis at least, with crimes of similar gravity–i.e., not with successes. And if the penalty is to be proportional to the gravity of the offense, the lesser wrongs should get lesser penalties.

I shall not deal with all the issues raised by such arguments. Specifically, I shall not attack the deterrence argument (2), even though I think it is contestable. I shall, rather, challenge the theory of criminal wrongs implicit in the unequal harm argument (3). If that argument falls, as it may when the theory of criminal wrongs is revised, and it is replaced with an *equal* harm argument (3)', the principles of proportionality and similar treatment for similar cases will combine on the side of the reform argument (1)–which I assume is uncontestable–to support equal punishment for attempts and successes.

II

A leading characteristic of the criminal law is that it is *public law*–a region in which society itself takes the initiative for prosecution and itself exacts the penalty. The major sorts of wrongs we classify as criminal are as old as law itself (murder, mayhem, theft . . .), but primitive law typically treated such matters, along with what we now call torts and breaches of contract, as private law problems.[11] It was

11. B. Nicholas, *An Introduction to Roman Law* (Oxford, 1962), p. 208.

not that people were then unaware of the distinction between murder and accidental death through negligence (or at least it would be odd to suppose so). They merely treated the two wrongs–legally–in the same way: by using the legal process to establish who the wrongdoer was, and to see to it that he made amends to the injured party. Thus indemnities were often acceptable penalties for killings of both sorts, and when they were not, they were replaced with Solomon-like provisions which emphasized the private law nature of the system: e.g., if *X* falls from a tree and kills *Y*, *Y*'s kinsman, if he insists on vengeance, is entitled to climb a tree and fall on *X*.[12]

It is characteristic of private law that the initiative for prosecution rests with the injured party (or his representatives), and that the issue at stake is the satisfaction of his grievance. At some point (it is not clear just when) certain wrongs began to get special treatment. Prosecution in these cases no longer depended on the initiative of the injured party; and the penalties assessed the wrongdoer were less and less designed to "satisfy" the victim. The thief was imprisoned rather than forced to make restitution.

The historical explanation for this shift (which, of course, was a gradual process) is no doubt complex. Political utility was quite likely a large part of the cause, both in terms of the administration of the thickets of laws drawn up to protect and strengthen monarchs, and in terms of handling public outrage and public safety in the case of particularly vicious wrongdoers. Further, it is reasonable to suppose that as governments grew in strength, and sought popular support in terms of the stability and protection they could afford to citizens, the development of a public law response to particularly "visible" and unsettling wrongs would follow. In addition, there were doubtless some moral demands which found expression in the growth of public law–particularly the principles of equity and desert in cases where no injured party remained to initiate an action (as in the murder of a destitute and "relationless" person), and probably convictions about Divine Law as well in cases where the government put itself forward as a servant of such.

12. Pollock and Maitland, *op. cit.* II, p. 471, quote Leges Henrici at 90.§7 as saying that "if by mischance you fall from a tree upon me and kill me, then, if my kinsman must needs have vengeance, he may climb a tree and fall upon you."

But an historical explanation is one thing, and a rational justification is another. It is the public law character of the whole criminal law as it now exists—from whatever historical causes—which must be justified, and it is clear that the hodgepodge of reasons one can assemble from the causes listed above will not even begin to produce a justification. Why should the law take over the prosecution of fraud but not intentional breach of contract? Why should the prosecution of motor vehicle homicide be a matter for public initiative (and the penalty be imprisonment, even when the wrongdoer is uninsured) when deaths caused by the negligence of one's employer are not? Why, in general, is the amount of damage done to the victim, or the amount of suffering he endures, or his capacity to initiate and carry through a prosecution not even a relevant factor in deciding which wrongs will be publicly prosecuted? (After all, one can die just as horrible a death by someone's noncriminal negligence as by intentional criminal conduct. And one can be just as incapable, financially or otherwise, of carrying through a lawsuit for breach of contract as one may be in carrying through a criminal prosecution.) And why are the penalties of the criminal law not directed toward recompense of the victim, at least where possible?

When jurisprudents have reached for an answer to such questions—or rather, to the general question of what is fundamentally at stake in distinguishing criminal from noncriminal wrongs—they have typically said two things: first, that the relevant distinguishing characteristic of the major sorts of wrongs defined as criminal is that they are social or public harms; and second, that no single distinguishing principle can be found for the full range of criminal wrongs.

The former point has become virtually an uncontested definition in the law.[13] Its rational appeal is obvious. If some harms are harms to

13. "A crime may be described as an act, default or conduct prejudicial to the community, the commission of which by law renders the person responsible liable to punishment . . ." (P. G. Osborn, *A Concise Law Dictionary*, 5th ed. [London, 1964], p. 97). "The distinction between a *crime* and a *tort* or civil injury is that the former is a breach and violation of the public right and of duties due to the whole community considered as such, and in its social and aggregate capacity; whereas the latter is an infringement or privation of the civil rights of individuals merely." Or again, "A crime, as opposed to a civil injury, is the violation of a right, considered in reference to the evil tendency of such violation, as regards the community at large" (*Black's Law Dictionary*,

the community as a whole, then it is only fitting that the community itself, through its legal officers, take the initiative for prosecution. And it is likewise fitting that the sanctions imposed for these harms should be designed to get the necessary community benefits (e.g., reform and deterrence). Indeed, it is hard to see what other theory could account for both public initiative and public-regarding sanctions for anything like the list of wrongs we now define as criminal.

One can, of course, argue for public initiative as a way of spreading the cost of (personally) important prosecutions, but then one cannot draw the public/private law distinction between crimes on the one hand and torts and contract on the other. Moreover, one has no ground, on that account, for public-regarding sanctions. Any argument adequate to establish the justifiability of such sanctions—even if it is expressed in terms of the state's duty to enforce morality or Divine Law—will, it seems, be some version of a social harm argument. Similarly for straight social utility arguments. They either concern rectifying or preventing *dis*utility consequent to the wrongs done, in which case they are social harm arguments; or else they concern simple expediency for the political/legal process, in which case both the list of crimes we have and the public-regarding sanctions we have appear bizarre.

So if there is a rational justification for the public law response to what we call crimes, it appears that it must be some version of the standard legal thesis that crimes are social harms. I say "some version" of the thesis because just anything which harms the community cannot plausibly be a candidate for the crime category. In general, the law restricts the social harms involved to those produced by intentional, malicious conduct which is aimed at doing (or tends to do)

4th ed. revised [St. Paul, 1968], p. 443). See also pp. 1-14 of the standard hornbook on the substantive criminal law, LaFave and Scott, *Handbook on Criminal Law* (St. Paul, 1972).

Such definitions are also commonplace in the cases: "All such acts or attempts as tend to the prejudice of the community are indictable" (*R.* v. *Higgins* [1801] 2 East 5). "The common law is sufficiently broad to punish as a misdemeanor . . . any act which directly injures or tends to injure the public to such an extent as to require the state to interfere . . ." (*Commonwealth* v. *Mochan* 177 Pa. Super. 454, 110 A. 2nd 788). There has been much judicial discussion of the proper scope of such pronouncements, but that this approach to what makes an act criminal is the correct one does not seem to be in dispute.

physical or financial damage to persons or property, and "wanton" or "willful" negligence which shows a "reckless or indifferent disregard" of the health and safety of others.[14] The explication of the social harm argument must account for why these sorts of social harm—and not those produced by "lesser" negligence, for example—justify a public law response. As noted previously, it is not likely that the whole list of things the law currently defines as criminal can be justified on some such ground. The law has grown too randomly to make such an expectation reasonable.[15] This need not destroy the importance of the point, however, that the main body of criminal wrongs can be understood in terms of a social harm principle.

What makes all this interesting in the case of criminal attempt is that jurisprudents in favor of lesser penalties for attempts appear to forget their own theory of criminal wrongs when they make the unequal harm argument [(3) above]. When they argue for the lesser penalty on the basis of penalties proportional to the harm done, they are clearly referring to the harm done to the individual victims, since they treat the point about lesser harm resulting from attempts as an obvious one—as a truism requiring no argument. The issue of whether less *social* (i.e., *criminal*) harm is done by attempts than by completed crimes is of course not nearly so clear. It is not clear partly because the *sort* of social harm at stake in the distinction between criminal and tortious wrongs is rarely made explicit. I intend to make it explicit below, but the first correction to be made to arguments about criminal attempt is simply this: that they must show that attempts produce less specifically *criminal* harm than do completed crimes.

But is this true of attempts? I think not, even though an affirmative answer has some plausibility. The plausibility rests on a mistaken notion of the sort of social harm the criminal law is specifically aimed at. Consider the following (erroneous) line of argument: A mere attempt on the life of Robert Kennedy during his campaign (even if, like the

14. See the definition of criminal negligence in *Bell* v. *Commonwealth*, 170 Va. 597; 195 S.E. 675 at 681.

15. In fact, as Fitzgerald actually argues, to "explain" the *whole* list we are forced to say simply that "whether or not any conduct constitutes a crime . . . depends solely on whether or not such conduct has been proscribed as criminal by the law. The hallmark of criminality is that it is a breach of the criminal law" (Fitzgerald, *Criminal Law and Punishment*, p. 7).

attempt on George Wallace, its effect had been to cripple him and stop his candidacy) would have been much less socially damaging than what actually happened. Indeed, the differences in the public responses to both actual events are, in part, an example of the ways in which we may say that a killing does more social damage than a crippling. In the former case there was a great deal more public turmoil (desire for revenge, dislocation of the political structure, violation of expectations, frustration of desires) which had to be dealt with than in the latter. The reasons for this are no doubt to be found in people's reactions to the amount of harm suffered by the victims (and in their attitudes toward the victims). Furthermore, of course, in the former case, the victim was lost to society forever, while in the latter case, he can still contribute, even if at a reduced level. In short, since an attempt does less social (criminal) harm than a completed crime, it can reasonably be punished less severely.

This sort of argument will not do, however. After all, if we are to determine the severity of the penalty on the basis of the sorts of social harm this argument refers to, then we must distinguish *among* attempts as well as between attempts and successes, for some attempts do much more of the sort of social damage referred to than do others. And we would be forced to distinguish various attempts on a basis which violates one of the most firmly justified controlling principles of law. After all, an attempt on the life of a gangster will presumably do less social damage than the same sort of attempt on the life of a beloved public figure. To distinguish them on that basis would put us in the untenable position of having to decide, perhaps as a matter of statute, how much to punish an offender on the basis of how "popular" and socially useful his victim happened to be. Clearly this would violate, at a minimum, one of our most deeply felt and thoroughly justified moral and legal principles: that of equal protection under the law. For if anyone who is contemplating murdering me knows that his penalty will be next to nothing compared to that of someone who kills, or tries to kill, Martin Luther King (because, in terms of the sorts of social value at issue here, I am next to nothing compared to Martin Luther King), then the law hardly protects me at all, let alone equally. The initial plausibility of this interpretation of criminal harm, then, falls away sharply when its consequences are made plain.

273

Criminal Attempt and the Theory of the Law of Crimes

There is, however, a sort of social harm which is at the root of criminality and which argues strongly for treating not only all "attempters" alike (regardless of the status of their victims and the amount of harm done to them) but also argues for treating at least some attempts with the same severity as completions. This is the social harm done, the social volatility, if you like, consequent to the *process* of doing the major sorts of conduct we punish criminally.[16]

To explain: when a person is killed by accident, we respond very differently than we do to a premeditated murder or to voluntary or involuntary manslaughter. More exactly, our normal responses to accidents, regardless of intensity, regardless of the amount of damage done to victims or to society at large, are not socially volatile. That is, they do not have the potential for destructive disturbance of fundamental social structures to be found in our responses to intentional, malicious harms, or even to extreme negligence. What calls forth a socially volatile response to the latter sorts of acts is their relation to what might be called socially unstable character traits. To wit:

Let us define perfect social stability as that state of affairs in which everyone always acts in ways which are "socially justifiable" (i.e., in ways which are at least consistent with the maintenance of social coherence, social institutions and the systems of mutual expectations necessary for the productivity of the members of society). Perfect social stability is no doubt only approachable as a limit, and indeed may not even be a desirable achievement. But it is clear that it is not even approachable unless each of us can have assurance that his person and activities will not be unjustifiably interfered with by others. For insofar as I do not possess such assurance, my own criteria for decision-making will (only rationally) include the prospect of abandoning my own socially stable behavior in self-defense. This is what I describe

16. While unconventional, the approach developed here is anticipated by some remarks of Pollock and Maitland, *History of English Law* II, p. 503, with regard to the law of treason. In discussing treason law prior to its crystallization into an elaborate statute in 1352 (25 Edw. III, stat. 5, cap. 2), and specifically those parts of it which penalize conspiracies, "compassing" the king's death, and the like, they say: ". . . in marked contrast to the general drift of our old criminal law, the crime was in this case found, not in a harmful result, but in the *endeavour to produce it* . . ." (emphasis added).

as a volatile response, and its community-wide occurrence is social volatility.

Assurance about the justifiable behavior of others depends upon beliefs or assumptions about, and consequent trust in, their dispositions to behave in justifiable ways—that is, on belief in their not having socially unstable character traits. There are, of course, many kinds of such traits. The disposition to break one's promise whenever it is convenient is one, and a harmful one. Promise-breaking can do social as well as personal damage, and its spread community-wide would certainly create a socially volatile situation. But individual instances of promise-breaking are not, at least in our society, typically productive of social volatility. X may break his promise to Y, and Y may kill him for it (surely a personally volatile response), but it is typically the killing, and not the breaking of the promise, which produces the *community-wide* volatility. The most malicious, deceitful dealing imaginable may turn a family out in the cold, but the typical public response is an affirmation of socially *stable* behavior (through, for example, public support for the family and scorn for the wrongdoer), and not a chain reaction breakdown of such behavior in self-defense.[17]

Some unstable traits, thus, get a socially volatile response while others do not. And social volatility is to be regarded as a disvalue in itself, the creation of which, by acts produced by an individual's socially unstable character traits, is a social harm. It is this sort of social harm, I want to argue, which justifies the public law response we make by defining the acts involved as criminal. And it is the absence of such harm, together with the other arguments which support *mens rea* and *actus reus* requirements, which justifiably excludes some wrongs from the category of a crime. Similarly, it is the (supposed) absence of such harm which alone could justify leaving intentional, but yet personally and socially harmful, breaches of contract to private law.

17. The law sometimes recognizes this in a big way in its handling of rescue cases. See, for example, the incredible case of *Yania* v. *Bigan* 347 Pa. 316; 155 A. 2nd 343 (1959) in which Bigan "enticed, taunted and inveigled" Yania to jump into a trench ten feet deep in water, and then stood by doing nothing while Yania drowned. Bigan was not even held *civilly* liable, let alone criminally liable.

The interpretation of criminal harm as the harm consequent to the social volatility of conduct thus makes a good deal of sense out of the current list of things defined as criminal, the list of things defined as noncriminal, and the insistence of jurisprudents that social harm is the issue at stake in justifying the two lists as they (mostly) stand.[18] It also, of course, gives some rationale (however inadequate) for the general absence of reparation-to-the-victim in criminal sanctions. Reparation for the amount of harm done to the victims is not a part of the logic of opting for a *public* law response at all. Thus the criminal penalties for murder and for negligent manslaughter may justifiably be *different*, even though the harm to the victims is the *same*. And the penalties for attempts and completed crimes need *not* be different, merely on the ground of a difference in the amount of harm to the victims.

Two things are important to keep in mind, however, about this line of argument. First, the sorts of socially unstable character traits which produce a socially volatile response probably vary considerably from culture to culture. Which traits produce such a response in any given time and place is an empirical issue, and one to be taken seriously by any proposal for law reform. Second, the amount of social volatility (and consequent harm) produced by various types of crimes is also an empirical issue, though I want to argue that there is no reason *in general* for thinking it to be less for attempts than for successes.

With these two cautions in mind, we may proceed. The argument against the *general* conclusion that attempts should be punished less severely than successes may be put briefly as follows. Once we acknowledge that it is social harm which is specifically criminal, then we must recognize that the sort of social harm involved is precisely the harm consequent to the social volatility of the conduct at issue. It is this sort of social harm for which we punish a person's *successful*

18. There are notable exceptions. There are, for example, regions of both strict and vicarious liability in the criminal law. The concept of criminality developed here will not apply to them. But I think these cases may be safely ignored for present purposes. They do not represent the major thrust of the criminal law, and there is nearly continuous, vigorous debate over the justifiability of such laws (as one would expect, were the theory proposed here the correct explication of the distinction).

criminal conduct. And it is the same sort of social harm for which we punish criminal attempts. Now it seems plausible to suppose that, at least for many sorts of crimes, no less of such harm is done by attempts then by successes, for the breakdown of the assurance of social stability (i.e., of one agent's contribution toward it) is complete once the attempt has been made, and made known. A rash of public shootings, successful or not, are socially volatile. I see no reason to suppose that attempts are, in general, any less "public," and thus less productive of social harm, than successes. Some attempts, such as the one on George Wallace's life, are more public than nearly all successful murders, while some murders are never discovered by anyone and thus cannot do any of the sort of social harm at issue here. These vagaries, and others like them, must be ignored for present purposes. Just as it is unjustifiable to make the severity of the penalty depend on the prominence or social usefulness of the victim, so it would be unjustifiable to make the penalty depend on the amount of subsequent publicity produced at the discretion of news agencies; or, indeed, to make it depend on the degree of success a criminal has in keeping things quiet. Once we have decided on a public law response to certain wrongs, and decided roughly how much social harm (conditions of public information being equal) each type of wrongdoing causes, principles of equal treatment and advance notice require the sort of variables mentioned above to be disregarded. When this is done, there is no difficulty in seeing that the killer who fails because his bullet accidently hits his victim's belt buckle is no less a social menace in the requisite sense than one who succeeds because his victim happens to be wearing suspenders.

The usual rationale for treating attempts, in general, less severely than successes thus breaks down: attempts are seen as presumptively equal in social harm to successes; the principles of proportionality and similar treatment for similar cases thus require that, unless the presumption is rebutted, attempts be treated equally with successes, and combined with the admittedly equal needs of the attempters and the successful for reform [the reform argument (1) above], the deterrence argument [(2) above] is overwhelmed.

III

As a convenient way of advancing additional arguments for it, I want now to consider a set of objections to the theory of criminal wrongs just presented.

A. *Confusion of General Justifying Principle with Regulative Principles*. It might be urged that the construction of an elaborate theory of social volatility to supplant a perfectly straightforward theory of social harm suggested by the Kennedy-Wallace example is based on a simple confusion. It might be maintained that the general justification for treating X as a public law matter is indeed its potential for social harm of the "usual" sort (e.g., the "costs" to society, etc.), but what controls the *grading* of the particular *sort* of offense is the amount of harm done to the victim, just as what controls the amount of punishment meted out to a particular offender is (or ought to be) its utility for reform and deterrence. Thus there is no problem with differential punishments depending on how "popular" one's victim happens to be. The *general* principle controls only the public-law/private-law decision; other principles regulate the grading of offenses and sentencing.

There is much that could be said in response to such an objection, but it will suffice to produce the sort of counterexample which can be generalized. On the theory advanced by this objection, premeditated murder and motor vehicle homicide must be graded at the same level. We typically think (for good reasons, I believe) not only that both offenses are properly public law matters (as this theory also would have it), but that they are *not* offenses of equal "criminal" gravity. But if offenses are to be graded on the basis of the amount of harm done to the victim(s), then the two forms of homicide cannot, on that basis, be distinguished. This counterexample has a structure which can be filled in many ways. Generally speaking, it shows that the objection ignores what we typically take (quite justifiably, I believe) to be a crucial element in the grading of crimes—*mens rea*. It cannot be repaired by importing intent into the grading process, for that simply raises the question of why intent is a crucial factor—and that question leads directly to the sort of social harm argument I propose. How can intent be the factor which controls our decision to classify a given act as criminal?

Only, it seems, if intentional wrongdoing is socially damaging in a way that other sorts are not. What could such a way be, if not through social volatility?

B. *Having It Both Ways.* It might also be urged, however, that the "usual" sort of social harm was faulted for violating a cherished principle of justice (equal protection) while a similar failing of the new interpretation of social harm was passed over smoothly. If the new interpretation can be shored up by introducing a principle which "holds" publicity equal for instances of a given crime (in order to meet the requirements of justice), then surely the "usual" interpretation can be shored up in a similar way. So what reason is there for opting for one interpretation over the other?

The reply here may also be brief. The equal protection problem is a *difficulty* for the usual interpretation of the social harm argument, but alone it is not decisive. What is decisive is that in addition to this difficulty, the usual interpretation—just as is so, ultimately, for objection A above—cannot give an account of why *mens rea* is a crucial element in the grading of crimes. To do so it would have to invoke a theory of social volatility, and once that is done (and the harm consequent to the status of the victim is held constant for reasons of equal protection), one doesn't have the "usual" interpretation at all, but in effect at least, the one I propose. To see this clearly, one need only ask how one could account, on the usual theory, for treating injuries produced negligently differently than the same injuries intentionally and maliciously produced.[19]

C. *Oversimplification.* The theory of criminal wrong presented here may also be attacked as oversimplified. Even granting that the rationale for the public law response to certain wrongs may have to be elab-

19. It might be noted that in tort law, as well as criminal law, intentional wrongs are distinguished in important ways from negligent ones. For one thing, victims of intentional torts are able to collect punitive or exemplary damages. In addition they need not always be able to show actual injury from the wrong, whereas such a showing is a necessary part of an action for negligence. And in some cases, time limitations on the initiation of an action are more generous to victims of intentional torts than to victims of negligence. See Charles O. Gregory and Harry Kalven, Jr., *Cases and Materials on Torts*, 2nd ed. (Boston, 1969) p. 23. Whether the rationale for this difference is in any way related to the concept of social volatility is unclear.

orated along those lines, it surely is obvious that the criminal law—even for intentional and malicious injuries—has a much more complex social function than that. We take the administration of justice out of the hands of injured parties to prevent blood feuds and the vicious self perpetuating cycles of revenge they spawn. This we find socially necessary, just as we find it necessary to go further and make prosecutions a matter of public initiative. But we must recognize the tendency these necessary steps have to impart a sense of frustration and alienation to the injured parties and to the sympathetic public at large. A vicious crime is committed, and immediately upon the capture of the culprit the engines of justice start to grind in virtual isolation from those most profoundly concerned. The outraged public is an impotent spectator; the victim is at best a mere source of evidence. Yet precisely in terms of the sort of social volatility described above, this sense of frustration and alienation can be the source of significant social instability. So we punish to reform and to deter, certainly. But we also must punish to satisfy the desire for retaliation felt by victims of crime and to satisfy the public outrage generated by those crimes. Thus, the logic of reparation and retaliation must remain very much a part of the criminal law. The severity of penalties must reflect that logic. Does this not mean, then, that equal penalties for attempts and successes would be viewed as excessive—and perhaps further aggravate the sense that the criminal law is something alien and unresponsive to the needs of those most directly concerned?[20]

The answer to the question must be, I think, no. The places where the logic of retaliation becomes a factor in the grading of crimes are (i) where the penalties dictated by the grading are less than what is needed for retributive satisfaction; and (ii) where the penalties dictated by the grading are felt to be excessive. In either of those cases, one can imagine social instability arising. But clearly neither of those cases obtain for attempts if the analysis I propose is correct. In terms of reform, a penalty equal to that for success is indicated, and the proposed analysis of criminal harm supports equalization in general. Unless the penalty for *success* is too low for retributive satisfaction,

20. For a similar argument in favor of lesser penalties for attempts, see Wechsler and Michael, "A Rationale of the Law of Homicide II," *Columbia Law Review* 37 (1937): 1290-1298.

there is no way the proposal for equalization could result in damage under (i) above. Further, the proposed analysis of criminal harm argues against the view that the equalization of penalties is excessive by providing grounds for a presumptive claim of the equal social harm of attempts and successes. It is true that if one considers only the physical harm done to the victims, the equalization proposal may seem excessive. But we need not suppose that people are so unsophisticated as to believe that that is the only harm crimes do. And once it is shown that in terms of specifically *criminal* harm attempts and successes do equal damage, what ground is there for supposing that there would be any social outcry from retributivists for giving the two crimes equal criminal penalties? We may, I think, lay this objection aside with the others.

D. *The Need for Evidence.* It may be objected, however, that throughout the whole discussion of social harm, social volatility and the like, a number of crucial issues have been settled a priori which really stand in need of empirical evidence. This, it may be urged, is especially true of the claim that attempts are no less socially volatile than successful crimes. How can one know such a thing a priori? And until one knows it, mustn't the whole proposal for reform of attempt law stand in abeyance?

This is an objection to be taken seriously, and indeed it does weaken the proposal regarding criminal attempt. It does not, of course, strike at the analysis of what is at stake in justifying the criminal/noncriminal distinction, but that does not allow one to bypass it in a discussion of the applicability of the analysis to this region of the criminal law.

Two things need to be said. First, the amount of social harm done by attempts as opposed to successes *is* an empirical issue, and it is plausible to suppose that attempts at certain sorts of minor crimes might well be a significantly lesser source of the requisite sort of social harm than successes. I do not deny this, and would not dispute a decision to grade such attempts a notch (or several notches) below the corresponding successes. I have merely argued that there is no reason to suppose that, *in general*, attempts do less criminal harm than successes, and that we may thus establish a rebuttable presumption in favor of equal penalties.

Even so, it may asked whether this is not based on an indefensibly a priori judgment. This leads to the second point which must be made. I do not think the difficulty raised here must be regarded as decisive, when one notices that some issues which are nominally empirical really present no discoverable *need* for empirical investigation. A good case in point is the contention that attempters stand no less in need of reform than successful criminals (at least if their failure is due to ineptness or intervening circumstances). For it is reform of dispositions, behavior patterns, motivation and the like which is at stake, and what reason is there for supposing that there is a significant difference in such factors between attempters and the successful? Likewise (though I admit, less conclusively) there seems to be little discoverable need for empirical confirmation of the point that an attempted armed robbery on a downtown street is just as disconcerting to passersby as a successful one, and that an increase in the number of such attempts would cause just as much apprehensiveness in people as would a corresponding increase in successes. One may imagine a bizarre society in which practically no attempts at *any* crime ever succeeded or did any harm to anyone, and so people were more bemused by such happenings than alarmed by them. But that is certainly not our situation. And so I think this objection, too, can be laid aside.

IV

The analysis of social harm, its adequacy as a principle for making the criminal/noncriminal distinction, and its applicability *in principle* to the reform of criminal attempt law have probably been discussed sufficiently for present purposes. No actual application of such an analysis to the law, however, can end with such an abstract discussion. So in this section and the next, I want to take up a number of objections which might be raised, not about the applicability of the analysis "in the abstract," but about its relation to a whole set of concrete problems in the law—especially, but not exclusively, in the area of criminal attempts.

A. *The Difficulty of Distinguishing Attempt from Mere Preparation.* It is notoriously difficult to draw a hard and fast line between acts merely *preparatory* to the commission of a crime and an actual attempt. It may be urged that to exact the same penalties for attempt as for completion thus puts too much strain on decisions which are often shaky anyway, and the result might be both a significant amount of injustice (the very severe penalization of people who could reasonably have been held to be merely *preparing* to commit a crime, and thus innocent of any criminal offense), and–to borrow a phrase from Justice Frankfurter–the consequent sensationalization of the judicial process with respect to trials for attempt. This is a serious enough argument to require an extended examination.

Mere preparation, of course, is not an offense in either the common law or the penal codes which have sprung from it. This is so, apparently, for two reasons, both similar to the reasons for not punishing mere intent: first, the difficulty, in most merely preparatory stages, of proving that the actions involved were really directed toward fulfilling a criminal intent (after all, one may buy poison for any number of reasons); and second, the fact that one may always abandon his criminal purpose during the preparatory stage, thus correcting his own behavior and rendering punishment unjustifiable, while once he has *attempted* the crime, it seems by definition too late to claim renunciation of the intent as an excuse–no more than one can claim renunciation as an excuse upon *completion* of the crime.

The problem is, however, in deciding at what point, in the series of steps leading towards the completion of the crime, an actual attempt has been made. Some cases are clear: firing a gun at a man's head with intent to murder is surely an attempt at murder. Going to a gunshop to choose a weapon for murder is clearly still at the stage of preparation. But consider:

(a) A man met a fourteen-year-old boy in a park, took him to a cafe and bought him ice cream. They then walked back to the park, where the man sat with the boy on a bench, put his arm around him, made indecent gestures to him, and engaged in indecent conversation with him. He suggested to the boy that they sleep out together in the park, and although he did not actually suggest participating in indecent conduct, asked the boy to meet him in the park the next night and promised him money, a walk and a movie if he did so. The next night the boy met him and was told it was too late for the movie but that they should take a walk together. At this point the man was arrested and charged with attempting to procure the boy to commit an act of gross indecency. He argued that his conduct did not constitute an attempt, but at most merely preparation.[21]

(b) A man was talking with his employer about getting a raise, and in the course of the conversation, began to pull a revolver from his pocket. Before he could raise his arm, however, the employer grabbed him. During the struggle, in which he was eventually disarmed without having fired, he said several times to the employer, "You've got to die." He was charged with attempting to discharge a loaded revolver with intent to do grievous bodily harm. It was objected on his behalf that his acts did not constitute evidence of attempt.[22]

(c) A jeweler who had insured his stock against theft concealed some of it in a recess under his safe, then tied himself up and called for help. When the police came, he told them he had locked up, gone upstairs and been knocked down and tied up by someone. The safe was found open and empty. The police were not satisfied with the story, and after searching the store, found the hidden merchandise. Told of this, the jeweler confessed to having hoped to get insurance money for the "stolen" goods. He was charged with attempting to obtain money under false pretenses. He argued that at most his conduct was preparatory.[23]

(d) A man constructed and arranged combustibles in a building with intent to commit arson in order to "injure the insurers" of the building and its contents. The combustibles were ready to be lighted, but on his way back to the building to do it—when he was some quarter of a mile away—he changed his mind and drove away. He was arrested for attempting to burn the building and injure the insurers. He argued that his acts were merely preparatory.[24]

21. *R.* v. *Miskell* (1953) 37 Cr. App. R. 214. He was convicted and his appeal dismissed.

22. *R.* v. *Linneker* [1906] 2 K.B. 99. He was convicted, and the conviction was affirmed on appeal.

23. *R.* v. *Robinson* (1915) 11 Cr. App. R. 124. He was convicted, but on appeal it was held that his acts were not enough to constitute an attempt and his conviction was quashed.

24. *Commonwealth of Mass.* v. *Peaslee* 177 Mass. 267; 59 N.E. 55 (1901). He was convicted, and on appeal the court suggested, but declined to decide, that

(e) A group of armed men cruised the streets of an area of New York City, looking for a particular payroll clerk whom they intended to rob of about $1200. Their futile efforts to find the clerk led to their surveillance and arrest by the police. They were charged with attempted robbery. They argued that their acts did not constitute attempt.[25]

These cases illustrate adequately, I think, the difficulty courts have had in drawing the line between preparation and attempt. From time to time there have been attempts to enunciate a general principle for making the distinction, and there has been some progress in the sense that a number of obvious candidates for a distinguishing principle have been found inadequate. At least it may be said that the definitions of attempt now offered are a good deal more sophisticated than, for example, the untenably narrow principle that the accused must have done all that was necessary to actually commit the crime to be guilty of an attempt.[26] Even Salmond failed to provide an adequate formulation:

> An act done with intent to commit a crime is not a criminal attempt unless it is of such a nature as to be in itself sufficient evidence of the criminal intent with which it is done. A criminal attempt is an act which shows criminal intent on the face of it. The case must be one in which *res ipsa loquitur*. An act, on the other hand, which is in its own nature and on the face of it innocent is not a criminal attempt.[27]

Clearly, though, it is not so much what we see (i.e., the act) as what we know (about the intent) which determines whether we regard something as an attempt, and information on that can come from sources other than the act—for example, from a confession. The act

---

the evidence was sufficient for a conviction for attempt. Instead it reversed the conviction on an unrelated procedural ground.

25. *People* v. *Rizzo* 246 N.Y. 334; 158 N.E. 888 (1927). They were convicted, but on appeal the conviction was reversed on the ground that their acts constituted mere preparation.

26. Enunciated by Parke, B. in *R.* v. *Eagleton* 6 Cox C.C. 559. This was thrown out in *R.* v. *White* [1910] 2 K.B. 124 where it was held that the giving of the first dose of poison in series intended to cause death was attempted murder.

27. In *R.* v. *Barker* [1924] N.Z.L.R. 865.

of turning the wheel which opens the sluice gates of a dam is ambiguous. Did the actor think he was *opening* the gates (thus intending to let the water out)? Or did he think he was making sure the gates were *closed*? We cannot determine criminal intent merely from this act. Yet if the actor later confessed an intent to open the gates to flood the town, it would surely be odd to have to say that because *res ipsa loquitur non*, he was not guilty of attempt.

As a result of the failures of general formulas, statutory definitions of attempt have had to rely on vague formulations–for example, to the effect that the criminal intent must be clear and the act toward accomplishing the crime must be a "substantial step" toward the commission of the crime which is "strongly corroborative of the actor's criminal purpose."[28] One then relies on examples–drawn, naturally enough, from the cases–to illustrate the meaning of "substantial step" and "strongly corroborative."[29] But it must be admitted that such "definitions" of attempt are no more than guidelines; they are by no means an exhaustive statement of the necessary and sufficient conditions for attempts.

In the face of this difficulty, then, the argument may be pressed that increasing the penalties for attempts to the level of the penalties for completed crimes–especially in the case of first degree felonies, for which the most severe penalties are exacted–demands a level of certainty in distinguishing preparation from attempt which simply cannot be achieved.

The reply to this argument must be made in several stages. First, it should be noted that preparation/attempt is not the only distinction in the criminal law which it is difficult to draw with precision. And if we were to step down the penalties for crimes on the basis of the "degree of difficulty" involved in determining whether they have been committed, a number of unfortunate things would result. For one thing, all crimes involving proof of intent would *per se* be subject to a similar argument concerning "strain on a difficult distinction,"

28. See American Law Institute, *Model Penal Code, Tent. Draft No. 10* (1960) §5.01(1).

29. For example, from the Model Penal Code, *op. cit.*, §5.01(2): examples of "substantial steps": "(a) lying in wait, searching for or following the contemplated victim of the crime; (b) enticing or seeking to entice the contemplated victim of the crime to go to the place contemplated for its commission. . . ."

for it is clear that if preparation vs. attempt is a difficult distinction for the law to draw, conceptually, the existence/nonexistence of *mens rea* is an even more difficult one, if not to draw, then at least to apply. Yet that distinction is utterly fundamental to nearly all major criminal proceedings.

Further, and closer to the subject at hand, the distinction between attempt and completion itself–upon which the present law depends for deciding the level of penalties to be assigned–is sometimes the subject of dispute. Suppose X hits Y on the head with an ax, intending to murder him. Thinking Y dead (which he is not), X then throws him off a cliff, or down an ant-bear hole, or into a river, in order to hide his body. The second act is what actually kills Y. Now, X claims that his *intent* to kill Y was extant only during the *first* act (hitting Y on the head), and since that did not succeed, he can only be charged with attempted murder. After all, the act that actually killed Y was not *intended* to kill him at all, hence not itself an attempt at–or rather success at–murder.[30]

Difficulties in distinction-making are pervasive in the law, and while we should not needlessly add to the list of difficulties, the reform of the law of attempt suggested here is not such a needless addition. If it is agreed for any class of crimes, in accord with the argument in II above, that attempts and successes are equivalent criminal wrongs, then the extension of equal treatment to both is hardly "needless." On the contrary, it–and it alone–satisfies one of the most fundamental principles of justice: that of equal treatment for relevantly similar cases. And while it may "add" to a problem of proof, it also "subtracts" from one: it eliminates the importance of making the sort of discrimination between attempt and success striven for in the cases just mentioned.

Borderline cases of attempt would, under the reform suggested, be dealt with much as borderline cases of intent are presently dealt with. If there is reasonable doubt that the act constitutes an attempt (com-

30. There are at least four such cases on the books. In one, *Thabo Meli et al.* v. *R.* [1954] 1 W.L.R. 228; 1 All E.R. 373, the accused was convicted of murder. In the other three (*R.* v. *Khandu* [1890] T.L.R. 15 Bom. 194; *R.* v. *Shorty* [1950] S.R. 280; *R.* v. *Chiswibo* [1961] 2 S.A. 714) the accused were convicted only of attempt.

pare: an intended, malicious injury), then it is treated as mere preparation (compare: mere accident) and not punished criminally. If this has the effect of acquitting some reprehensible people who would otherwise–under the lighter penalty for attempt–have been punished at least a little bit, then so be it. This is perfectly consistent with the fundamental principles of the standards of proof required in criminal cases.[31]

In fact, it would be distressing to think that standards of proof can justifiably be lowered in the case of attempt as long as the penalties are kept significantly lower than those for successful crimes. And this is really what, underneath it all, the argument being discussed here is saying: that we need not be worried about making the wrong decisions on borderline preparation/attempt cases as long as the penalties for attempts are kept low. Such feelings may be justified in some cases of distinction-making in the criminal law (the reverse–the *increased* concern about getting things right–is surely warranted in the case of capital crimes). But where the issue is one of conviction as opposed to acquittal, as it is in the preparation/attempt cases, we cannot allow

31. It has been suggested by at least one eminent legal writer that we might do well to make certain unambiguous preparations (which clearly fall short of attempts) criminal in themselves. See Glanville Williams, "Police Control of Intending Criminals," *Criminal Law Review* 66 (1965); and by the same author, in *Criminal Law: The General Part*, pp. 632-633. And it may be noted that Soviet law does just that. See Article 15 of *Fundamentals of Criminal Legislation for the USSR* (official text in translation) (Moscow, 1960). This is a much more radical change than that suggested here for the law of attempt, however, and I am very sceptical, to say the least, about its justifiability. It would, no doubt, allow us to deal more adequately with some frustrating cases (e.g., *People* v. *Rizzo*, cited above). But the danger is, of course, that it would reach too far back toward mere intent. Everyone will doubtless agree that mere imaginative rehearsals (as distinct from intent) ought not to be made criminal. And punishment for mere intent is held by most to be similarly incompatible with the principles of a free society. But it may also be that if we are to treat our fellows as free, moral agents, we need to allow them more latitude in the process of deciding right from wrong than that. It may be that we need to respect the possibility of renunciation of criminal purpose enough not to reach back further than an actual attempt. Merely making renunciation of intent an affirmative defense (as Soviet law does: see Article 16 of the *Fundamentals*) does not answer this objection. It is the widest possible *opportunity* for renunciation which is at stake, and it is clear that persons who could not have gone through with even an attempt might well be caught before they had "had a chance" to change their minds.

ourselves the comfort of thinking that the problem can be minimized by keeping the penalties for attempt one notch lower than those for success. If there is reasonable doubt as to whether an act is criminal *at all* (i.e., in this case, should count as preparation or attempt), the benefit should fall to the accused, just as it does when there is reasonable doubt that he actually intended to harm his victim. And if there is no reasonable doubt as to whether the act is an attempt or not, the decision will be obvious. In either case, the severity of the penalty for attempt is not at issue. The reasons which justify the reasonable doubt rule for criminal cases are well enough known not to require repetition here.

In short, then, we may confidently dismiss the objection resting on the difficulty of distinguishing attempt from preparation. There are, however, some further objections to consider.

B. *The Half-hearted Attempt.* It may be argued that, just as some attempts at suicide are really not attempts at all, but calls for help, so some attempts at crimes are properly regarded as "something else": for example, as the working out of a desire, for whatever reason, to be *caught.* Some criminals are caught in attempts so often that it is hard for those intimately connected with them to interpret their behavior in any other way. It would be wrong, this argument goes, to punish such "attempts" equally with successful crimes, since the actor was not really trying to commit the crime so much as to get attention.

The reply to this, of course, is that if a distinction in penalties is to be made for those who *attempt* crimes for such motives, then it should also be made for those whose attempts (for those motives) just happen to succeed. If there are half-hearted attempts, there are half-hearted successes as well. They should be treated alike. Whether, then, the category of "half-hearted crimes" should receive lesser penalties than "whole-hearted" ones is a separate issue, and does not affect the outcome of the proposal for reforming attempt law put forward here.

C. *The Encouragement of Second Thoughts.* Another objection which might be raised against the proposal, however, is that having lesser penalties for attempt encourages "second thoughts" during the commission of some crimes. Equalizing the penalties for attempts and completions eliminates one motive a person may have for stopping in the middle of an attempt, should he suddenly change his mind about the wisdom of what he is doing. Thus the lesser penalty may be a better deterrent in this case than the greater one.

A fairly straightforward response to this is that if we want to encourage second thoughts (i.e., abandonment of criminal purpose before the crime has been completed), we can do this directly, without regard to the relative severity of penalties for attempts and completed crimes, by making renunciation of intent an affirmative defense and/or an admissible ground for mitigation. This is surely a much more rational way of dealing with the problem than by simply excusing from the heavier penalty all whose attempts fail to come off–for whatever reason. As it stands now, the person who gives up in the middle of the attempt merely out of fatigue, or because he is interrupted by the arrival of the police, is given the same penalty as one who has given up because he has come to see the wrongfulness of his behavior. Certainly in terms of the reformative aims of criminal sanctions, as well as in terms of the amount of specifically criminal harm (social volatility) produced, the genuine repentance must be distinguished from attempts which fail for other reasons.[32]

32. Making renunciation of intent an affirmative defense has its difficulties, of course. Authorities are clear that "involuntary" abandonment of attempt (as when a police patrol spots the activity and moves in, forcing the attempters to run) cannot reasonably be a defense. But although voluntary abandonment is also often said to fail as a defense, there are cases in which it has been accepted. See, for example, *People* v. *von Hecht* 133 Cal. App. 2d 25; 282 P.2d 764 (1953); and *Weaver* v. *State* (*of Georgia*) 116 Ga. 550; 42 S.E. 745 (1902). For a review of the authorities, see *Model Penal Code, Tent. Draft No. 10* (1960), §5.01.

The Model Penal Code, *op. cit.*, §5.01(4) recommends that renunciation of intent be an affirmative defense if it is "complete and voluntary." On the meaning of "complete and voluntary," it says: "renunciation of criminal purpose is not voluntary if it is motivated, in whole or in part, by circumstances, not present or apparent at the inception of the actor's course of conduct, which increase the probability of detection or apprehension or which make more difficult the accomplishment of the criminal purpose. Renunciation is not complete if it is motivated by a decision to postpone the criminal conduct until a more advantageous time or to transfer the criminal effort to another but similar objective or victim." In 1967, New York adopted a similar version of this doctrine: New York Penal Law §34.45.

Not all cases are easy to evaluate on such grounds, however. Consider *Le Baron* v. *State* (*of Wisconsin*) 32 Wisc. 294; 145 N.E.2d 79 in which the defend-

Still, in all fairness, one must recognize the possibility that penalizing attempts and completions equally might in some cases weaken the motive for giving up before completion. This would not, of course, be so for anyone who is prepared to renounce his criminal purpose as a matter of moral principle. But one who is merely in personal turmoil about the rightness of advisability of his conduct, or one who has come to believe it is simply highly unlikely that he will be able to succeed anyway, may well reflect that he might as well go ahead. After all, convincing a jury that he gave up due to a renunciation of intent is an uncertain business at best. Yet if he cannot convince them of that, thus getting a lesser penalty, it really does not matter whether he finishes the crime or not. He will get the same penalty in either case if he is caught. As Huck Finn puts it: "... what's the use of learning to do right when it's troublesome to do right and it ain't no trouble to do wrong, and the wages is just the same?"[33]

Even acknowledging this problem, however, the gains to be gotten for the reformative aims of penal sanctions by equalizing the penalties for attempt and success seem to me to outweigh the possible disadvantages noted. Once again, then, an objection to the proposed reform seems to be met adequately.

D. *Impossible Attempts*. The proposal may, nevertheless, be attacked on yet another ground. In cases in which the crime attempted was *impossible* of accomplishment, one may argue that it is unfair to treat the offender even on a par with other attempters, let alone those who are successful. Consider: a man who, as it turns out in the course of the event, is impotent, seizes a woman and tries to rape her. It was physically impossible for him to have achieved his purpose. Can he be guilty of attempted rape?[34] Or consider a man who "places an il-

---

ant forced a woman into a shack and up against the wall and made further moves in preparation to rape her. The woman was finally able to convince him that she was pregnant and that he would hurt her baby if he proceeded. He gave up the attempt, warning her that if she screamed or went to the police after he left, he would kill her. It is uncertain whether this would fall within the meaning of "complete and voluntary" renunciation as defined above.

33. Mark Twain, *Huckleberry Finn* in *The Complete Works of Mark Twain* (Garden City, 1964), chap. 16, p. 810.

34. *Preddy* v. *Commonwealth* (*of Virginia*) 184 Va. 765; 36 S.E.2d 349 (1946). He was found guilty of attempt.

legal bet" on a horse which, as it turns out, has been scratched from the race an hour before. Is he guilty of an attempt to place an illegal bet?[35] Or consider a man who attempts to buy what he thinks are stolen goods. They are not. Can he be convicted of an attempt to receive stolen property?[36]

As can be seen, there has been some conflict among the cases as to the legitimacy of the defense of impossibility. More often than not, the courts have rejected the defense, as have academic writers.[37] But whatever the resolution of the conflict turns out to be, we may safely argue that whatever is to be done with "impossible attempts" should be done on the issue of whether they are to be regarded as attempts at all. If they are, then one can see no reason for treating them differently than other attempts. If they are not, then the question does not arise.

E. *Generosity*. Finally, it may be wise to comment on the sort of objection suggested by Plato's remarks (above, note 9). The suggestion is that when the attempt does not come off, it is only gracious of us to exercise the virtue of generosity, to reduce the penalty as a way of marking the proper human response (i.e., joy, relief . . .) to fortuitous and happy turns of fate which prevented the completion of the crime. Such an objection is not in the least frivolous (though I have not given it the development it deserves). Benevolence and related virtues are of the first importance in the moral life, and there is every reason to believe, at least in terms of moral theory, that considerations of what conduct would be virtuous with respect to criminal attempts ought to carry as much weight as considerations of what duties we have toward society and what values are involved in various sorts of policies on criminal attempt.[38] Unfortunately for this objection, however, while spontaneous generosity "for no good reason" is

35. *O'Sullivan* v. *Peters* (1951) SR (South Australia) 54. He was convicted.

36. *People* (*of New York*) v. *Jaffe* 184 N.Y.497; 78 N.E. 169 (1906). It was held, on appeal, that since the crime he intended to commit could not possibly have been consummated even if he had succeeded in buying the goods, he could not be found guilty of an attempt.

37. For a good overview of the problem, see Kadish and Paulsen, *Criminal Law and Its Processes*, pp. 393-410.

38. I have argued for this thesis at length in *On Justifying Moral Judgments* (London and New York, 1973).

something without which life would hardly be bearable, its ossification into a policy (such as punishing all attempts less severely than successes) eliminates its spontaneity, and hence, a necessary feature of what makes it virtuous to begin with. So again, the proposal for treating attempts on a par with successes must stand.

V

Some concern, however, may understandably be directed toward the question of the ramifications of this reform. In particular, the analysis of the nature of criminality given above has two rather startling consequences which deserve mention, not to say further study.

A. *Criminal Negligence.* If criminal harms come not from the consequences of the victim's injuries, but rather from the consequences of the ways in which those harms come about, then an argument analogous to the one for treating criminal attempt and success equally suggests itself for cases of what might be called "uneventful" and "eventful" criminal negligence. Take the case of reckless driving. Suppose two men are driving in equally reckless ways—at night, perhaps, in cars whose brakes and steering could not pass inspection standards, and through a residential section at high speed. One is unlucky enough to hit and kill a pedestrian who unwittingly steps into the street. The other had passed by the same spot, "uneventfully," in the same criminally reckless manner, several moments earlier. The criminality of the acts is, it seems, equal, and the acts therefore ought to be punished equally. Yet we charge the one with only reckless driving, a relatively minor offense, and the other with negligent manslaughter. The difference in the two offenses is one of mere chance, just as is the difference between the assassin whose bullet hits the belt buckle and the one whose bullet finds its target. To be consistent with the analysis of criminal attempt given here, then, it seems we should equalize the penalties for both "uneventful" and "eventful" negligence.

Resistance to any such proposal would doubtless be strong—and based on a complex of factors, not the least of which is the difficulty of determining degrees of negligence *prospectively*. Just as occasionally we may use the very fact that an injury resulted from some sort of unusual conduct as evidence that the conduct was negligent, so too it may happen that we cannot determine *whether* an act was negligent, or *how* negligent it was, in the absence of some physical damage done. This proof problem, it may be argued, militates against extending the attempt argument analogously to uneventful negligence. But it is clear that the issue needs careful analysis.

As to whether such a startling consequence casts a question mark over the adequacy of the whole analysis of criminal wrongs proposed here, I can only remark that it is not at all unusual for the law to have to depart from even the clearest and most thoroughly grounded rules, principles or conceptualizations for reasons of equity or even practicality. If that is so in this case, it need not destroy the value of the analysis for other parts of the criminal law.

B. *Motive vs. Intent.* Another consequence suggested by the account of criminality given here is the reform of the criminal law's traditional refusal to differentiate offenses on the ground of motive, as opposed to intent. If, again, criminal harms come from the consequence of the way in which the victim's injuries (or the social harms) are accomplished, then it seems irrational to exclude a consideration of motive in grading offenses. We respond very differently (and in ways which alter the social harms done) to violations of the law done as a matter of civil disobedience than we do to the same violations done for purely personal and antisocial motives. Yet the law as it stands does not allow a consideration of motive to enter the judicial process in determining the seriousness of the crime (except as a matter of discretionary prosecution or as a matter of judicial discretion in sentencing).[39] It might be argued, then, that the reform of attempt law proposed here should be extended to include a reform of the law with regard to motive. Like the extension with regard to criminal negligence, however, I suspect that a rather extensive inquiry would be needed to assess such a suggestion.

39. See, for example, *Chandler* v. *DPP* [1962] 3 W.L.R. 694 in which protesters at a Royal Air Force base were not permitted to defend their illegal acts in terms of their motives of civil disobedience. For an argument in favor of exercising prosecutorial and sentencing discretion with respect to some forms of civil disobedience, see Ronald Dworkin, "On Not Prosecuting Civil Disobedience," reprinted in Murphy, *Civil Disobedience and Violence* (Belmont, Calif., 1971), pp. 112-130.

C. *Transferred Intent.* Finally, in addition to these somewhat problematic extrapolations, the theory of criminality given here has at least one rather straightforward extension: it renders the transferred malice (or intent) rule easily intelligible. The rule is, oversimply, that when X is trying to murder Y, but misses and accidentally kills Z, his malice or intent toward Y "transfers" to Z and he may be charged with murder.

On the basis of the usual theory of crimes, the rule is a bit problematical, for it looks as though the criminal is punished either for the unintended result (the accidental harm done a bystander) or the mere intent toward the intended victim. One alternative is uncomfortable in terms of standard accounts of the rationale for the *mens rea* requirement; the other is uncomfortable in terms of the principle of not punishing mere intent. Clearly, understanding criminal wrong as the social instability created by the process of doing certain things provides a ready and easily intelligible rationale for the transferred malice rule.[40]

Perhaps enough has been said, then, to establish the main points: that reform of the theory of the law of crimes, and the consequent reform of the law of criminal attempt, are clearly indicated as part of the continuing process of rationalizing the criminal law. The analogous extensions of these reforms will, of course, have to be subjected to further study. But the lines of inquiry look promising, and it appears that they will confirm rather than disconfirm the results reached here.

40. For a clear statement of the difficulties in the traditional justification for transferred malice, see Glanville Williams, *Criminal Law: The General Part*, §49. And on the U.S. version, see LaFave and Scott, *Handbook on Criminal Law*, pp. 252-255.

[3]

Criminalization and Sharing Wrongs

S.E. Marshall and R.A. Duff

Introduction

In colloquial speech the terms 'crime' and 'criminal' have a use which, though connected to the strictly legal notion of criminality, goes well beyond it. It is a way of indicating a serious condemnation of an activity or action. Similarly, when people say of something 'There ought to be a law against it,' they are not necessarily speaking literally, though they might be. Nonetheless, even when they are speaking colloquially and figuratively in using this expression, it is clear that the 'law' here is the criminal law and not the civil law. The sense that 'something ought to be done' expressed in these usages reflects the idea that there is a kind of wrong which demands a collective response rather than just an individual one. The figurative, colloquial use trades, of course, on the literal one. However, *pace* Devlin,[1] it requires more than a general feeling of outrage to characterise just what kinds of wrongs are appropriately categorised as crimes. The enduring debates concerning the distinction between crime and tort bear witness to the fact that such a characterisation is far from easy.[2]

These academic debates can be situated against the background of wider philosophical discussions about the relationship between the individual and the collective, the private and the public, and the way in which these pairs of concepts map onto one another. We might agree with George Fletcher that "Blackstone had a point in identifying crimes as public wrongs and torts as private wrongs":[3] the criminal law should deal with those kinds of wrong which are matters of public concern, and which therefore require a collective response from the whole community; wrongs which are, by contrast, properly the concern only of the private or individual victim should be dealt with under the civil law. What is far less clear, however, is how we should characterise that distinction.

Public wrongs are not simply 'collective' wrongs, if by that we mean wrongs which are directed at a collective; nor are private wrongs simply 'individual' wrongs, if by that we mean wrongs which are directed at individuals. Indeed, if asked for examples of paradigmatic crimes, people tend to cite the kinds of actions

---

This paper began life as a response to an unpublished paper by Andrew von Hirsch and Andrew Ashworth, at a workshop on criminalization which was generously funded by the Fulbright Commission and by the Fund for the Study of Criminal Jurisprudence, School of Criminal Justice, Rutgers University. We are grateful to the participants in that workshop, and especially to Andrew von Hirsch and Andrew Ashworth, whose views (as they were then) form the basis of the account we sketch and criticise in s.1 of this paper.

1. See, notoriously, P. Devlin, 'Morals and the Criminal Law' in P. Devlin, *The Enforcement of Morals* (Oxford: Oxford University Press 1968) 1.
2. See the recent symposium in (1996) 76 Boston U. L. Rev. 1. Public policy debates concerning the possible decriminalization of a whole range of activities including drug-taking, prostitution and insider trading display the complexities of the concept of crime—though rarely do participants in those public debates address that complexity head on.
3. G. Fletcher, 'Domination in Wrongdoing' (1996) 76 Boston U. L. Rev. 347 at 347.

which are directed at individuals: thus, murder, rape, theft and burglary are the kinds of crimes that naturally spring to mind. If we focus on these, we might then be tempted to think that the real difference between crimes and torts is a matter of seriousness. But while the law might in particular contexts attend to the issue of seriousness in distinguishing criminal from civil wrongs,[4] it is certainly not in general the case that the wrongs which our existing law counts as crimes are typically more serious than those which count as torts. For just one example, a breach of contract could be far more serious in both its wrongfulness and its harmful consequences than a minor act of vandalism: but the former remains a matter of civil law, whilst the latter is a case of criminal damage.

However, we think that the idea of the 'seriousness' of a wrong cannot be characterised independently of the distinction between 'public' and 'private' wrongs, which is our central concern in this paper: the difference lies not in the degree of seriousness but in its *character*.

So, supposing that we accept that crimes are 'public' wrongs, how are we to characterise that sense of a 'public' dimension to certain kinds of wrongs against individuals? How, that is, are we to give an account of the individual, seen as a member of a collective, in a way which does not either eliminate the individual altogether, or reduce to the kind of individualism which ultimately eliminates all sense of the collective and the public. Our main concern in this paper is, therefore, the concept of crime, and we do not directly engage in the debate about the distinction between crime and tort. Nonetheless, what we say about crime will have some implications for that debate: for we aim to identify a central feature of certain kinds of wrongdoing which gives a community reason to count them as 'public' rather than merely as 'private' wrongs, and thus as matters for the criminal law rather than merely for the civil law.

1. Individual and Public Goods

We noted above that what figure in public consciousness as paradigmatic crimes tend to be crimes which directly victimise individuals. Such crimes might seem to be not only in fact salient in public perception, but also *normatively* paradigmatic: surely any system of criminal law must at least proscribe and punish such wrongs as these.

If we take such crimes as our initial focus, one way of expressing the nature of criminal law might be this: the criminal law should proscribe intrusions into important individual '*Rechtsgüter*' such as life, liberty, property and health.[5] It might seem

4. Thus part of the definition of the rarely prosecuted crime of 'defamatory libel' in English law is that the libel must be 'serious'—more serious than it would need to be to be the subject of a civil suit: see J. C. Smith & B. Hogan, *Criminal Law*, 8th ed. (London: Butterworths, 1996) at 735-36.

5. The German term '*Rechtsgut*,' which figures prominently in German discussions of the proper aims and functions of the criminal law, is convenient here, as capturing the notion of a significant legally protected interest: see U. Ebert, *Strafrecht Allgemeiner Teil*, 2nd ed. (Heidelberg: C. F. Müller, 1994) at 1-4; and C. Roxin, *Strafrecht Allgemeiner Teil*, 3rd ed. (Warszawa: C. H. Beck, 1997) at 10-30.

uncontroversial that the criminal law should also proscribe conduct which directly endangers such individual *Rechtsgüter*; and beyond that it might also be argued that a limited category of crimes of 'abstract endangerment' (conduct, like dangerous driving, which threatens such *Rechtsgüter*, but individual instances of which might not in fact endanger any individual) can be justified.[6]

This kind of perspective makes wrongs done to individual victims central to the concerns of the criminal law. If we ask *why* such wrongs as murder, rape, and theft should be crimes, the natural answer is not that such actions threaten 'the social order' or 'the public interest': for such answers seem to ignore, and thus to denigrate, what the individual victim has suffered, and to (mis)portray crimes simply as acts of bad citizenship. The answer is, rather, that such wrongs injure important *Rechtsgüter*: the state has a duty to use the criminal law to promote respect for such significant individual rights. Such a perspective can also ground the demands, which have become more strident in recent years, that victims of crime should be allowed a more prominent, personal role in the criminal process, particularly in sentencing: since the offender's punishment is owed primarily, if not only, to those he has wronged, they should surely have a voice in determining that punishment.

This perspective also finds room for at least some 'public' or 'collective' goods that the criminal law should protect. By proscribing and punishing attacks on individual *Rechtsgüter*, it serves at the same time to assure *all* citizens that such wrongs against them will not go unpunished, and thus to foster collective security;[7] and if it includes crimes of 'abstract endangerment' (dangerous or drunken driving, for instance, or crimes to do with safety at work or with dangerously toxic materials), these can be seen as protecting collective interests in public safety. However, such 'public' or 'collective' goods are not, as so far understood, *irreducibly* public or collective: they may be understood simply as aggregates of individual goods, whose protection is thus still the basic aim of the criminal law.

Now one objection to this perspective on the criminal law is that it does not do justice to the idea of genuinely public or collective goods, which cannot be reduced to aggregates of individual goods: goods belonging to a 'we' which cannot be adequately understood as a collection of discrete and individual 'I's; goods which matter to us not as aspects of our merely individual well-being, but as members of a community; goods which are goods *of* that community. This objection rests on two related claims of a communitarian kind, although we do not have space to develop either of them in detail here.

The first claim is that even if *some* 'public' goods *could* be analysed as aggregates of individual goods, others resist such reductive analysis: consider, for just one instance, the idea of a thriving culture as a 'public' or common good. The

6. The distinction between crimes of 'concrete' and of 'abstract' endangerment is important in the German literature (see Ebert, *ibid.* at 38; Roxin, *ibid* at 351-60): we cannot take up here the question of just how broad the category of crimes of 'abstract' endangerment should properly be: see A. von Hirsch, 'Extending the Harm Principle: "Remote" Harms and Fair Imputation' in A. P. Simester & A. T. H. Smith, eds., *Harm and Culpability* (Oxford: Oxford University Press, 1996) 259; R. A. Duff, *Criminal Attempts* (Oxford: Oxford University Press, 1996) at 134-35.
7. Compare J. Braithwaite & P. Pettit, *Not Just Deserts* (Oxford: Oxford University Press, 1990) at chs. 4-5, on 'dominion,' as including the 'assurance' of liberty, as the central aim of the law.

second, and for our purposes more significant, claim is that we cannot adequately understand even individual goods in purely individualist terms, since we cannot identify or understand merely as individuals the persons whose goods they are. We draw here on the communitarian conception of the self as 'constitutive':[8] as constituted in essential part by its intersubjective relations and its location in a particular community, and thus as identifiable only in terms of those relations and location. For citizens of a polity (citizens whose goods the law is to protect), therefore, "community describes not just what they *have* as fellow citizens but also what they *are*, not a relationship they choose (as in voluntary association) but an attachment they discover, not merely an attribute but a constituent of their identity.'"[9] What this conception suggests is not, of course, that individuals and their goods do not matter, but rather that both they and their goods must be identified and understood as (the goods of) members of a community. We will argue later that this can help us to see why the criminal law should be used to protect certain individual *Rechtsgüter* as in a significant sense 'public' or shared goods—why actions which attack such *Rechtsgüter* should be seen as 'public' or shared wrongs.

A second objection, related to the first, is that this perspective does not do enough to show why attacks on individual *Rechtsgüter* should be a matter for the criminal rather than for the civil law. If the wrong done by such crimes as rape or theft is understood as essentially a wrong done to the individual victim, why should the state 'steal' this 'conflict' from the victim,[10] by making it a matter of criminal law: why should it not rather be for the victim to seek redress by bringing a civil case?[11] Of course, we might expect the state to provide public assistance (investigative resources, legal advice, funding) for those who wish to pursue such cases; and there would be cases which, in the absence of any individual victim who could bring a suit, would need to be pursued by a public authority (homicide cases in which the victim is dead, for instance, and cases of abstract endangerment): but why should the presumptive or default position not be that it is for the person or persons directly victimised by the wrongdoing to bring a civil case against the wrongdoer?

Such a suggestion has obvious resonances with the views of some 'abolitionists,' who argue that we should 'civilize' our responses to 'crime.' The state should not 'steal' 'conflicts' from the individuals (both 'victims' and 'offenders') to whom they properly belong, by making them matters of criminal law to be dealt with by the state and its courts; it should rather offer an orderly forum in which the individuals concerned—with the help of fellow members of their community—can resolve their conflicts for themselves.[12]

---

8. In particular, our argument here is related to Charles Taylor's distinction between 'convergent' and 'common' goods: see C. Taylor, 'Cross-Purposes: The Liberal-Communitarian Debate' in N. L. Rosenblum, ed., *Liberalism and the Moral Life* (Cambridge, MA: Harvard University Press, 1989) 159.
9. M. Sandel, *Liberalism and the Limits of Justice* (New York: Cambridge University Press, 1982) at 150.
10. See N. Christie, 'Conflicts as Property' (1977) 17 British J. of Criminology 1.
11. On the 'civil' model in some systems of ancient law, see J. Lindgren, 'Why the Ancients May Not Have Needed a System of Criminal Law' (1996) 76 Boston U. L. Rev. 29.
12. See, e.g., *supra* note 10; L. Hulsman, 'Penal Reform in the Netherlands II' (1982) 21 Howard J. 35, and L. Hulsman, 'The Abolitionist Case: Alternative Crime Policies' (1991) 25 Israel L. Rev. 681 [hereinafter 'Abolitionist'].

We might wonder just where this abolitionist path would ultimately lead us: in particular whether the state would in the end be left with even this role in 'conflict-resolution,' or whether we would be led towards even more radically informal modes of community-based justice.[13] We might also wonder about the tension which is discernible in some such versions of abolitionism: between a libertarian individualism which insists that 'crimes' must be seen as conflicts between and belonging to the individuals directly involved (and denies to anyone else the right to condemn either party's conduct as 'wrong'); and a more communitarian view which portrays such 'conflicts' as matters that properly concern, and that must be resolved by and within, the community to which those individuals belong. Such issues are not, however, our present concern: our point is simply that an account of the proper aims of the criminal law which begins with the protection of individual *Rechtsgüter* will find it hard to explain why this should be a matter for a criminal rather than for a civil law, and to resist the abolitionist argument that we should 'civilize' our conceptions of, and responses to, 'crime.'

The obvious alternative starting point lies in the idea of public, common or collective goods—goods which, we have suggested, cannot always be analysed as aggregates of individual goods. That is, rather than starting with infringements of individual *Rechtsgüter* as our paradigm of criminality, and then asking whether and why the criminal law should also protect public or common goods, we begin with the idea that the criminal law should protect common or collective goods, and then ask whether any (and if so which) individual goods should also count as 'common' goods which the criminal law should protect.

By starting from this point we can at once explain (as we cannot so readily explain if we begin with individual *Rechtsgüter*) why criminal cases are, typically, brought by the 'State,' or the 'People,' or the 'Commonwealth,' or 'Regina' against the defendant, whilst civil cases are, typically, brought by individual plaintiffs. For apart from the fact that, in the case of genuinely common goods, there is no distinct individual victim who could be the plaintiff, it is clearly appropriate that injuries to common goods should be pursued by the whole community (as represented by the 'State' or the 'People') whose goods they are: by contrast, as we have noted, it is not yet obvious why injuries to individual *Rechtsgüter* should not be pursued (with assistance from the state) by the individuals concerned.

Such a starting point also accords, of course, with the roughly communitarian perspective implicit in our earlier comments on common goods. But it also faces an obvious problem, one which we have already gestured. If we are going to say that such actions as murder, rape and theft should be criminal because they injure or threaten some *common* good, are we not then ignoring, and thus denigrating, the wrong done to the individual victims of such actions—a wrong which surely should be central to the law's concerns?

Such a criticism is certainly apposite in response to some kinds of account of 'crimes' as 'public' wrongs: if it is said, for instance, that attacks on individual

13. On which see R. Abel, ed., *The Politics of Informal Justice* (New York: Academic Press, 1982); M. Cain, 'Beyond Informal Justice' (1985) 9 Contemporary Crises 335; R. Matthews, ed., *Informal Justice* (London: Sage 1988).

Rechtsgüter should be criminal if and because they 'threaten the social order'; or if and because they cause 'social volatility'; [14] or because such attackers must be punished in order to incapacitate them from further such attacks or in order to deter other potential attackers; or because the attacker takes an unfair advantage over all law-abiding citizens (he accepts the benefits of their law-abiding self-restraint, whilst avoiding the burden of self-restraint himself).[15] For such accounts do seem to subordinate the individual victim (a concern for their good, or for the wrong done to them) to some supposedly larger social good. The offender's conduct is counted as criminal, and he is to be punished, for the sake of that larger good: to which it is appropriate to object that his conduct should be criminalised because of, and he should be punished for, the wrong he does to the individual victim. We do not criminalise rape, and punish rapists, because rape causes social volatility; or because the rapist takes an unfair advantage over his law-abiding fellow citizens: but because of the nature of the wrong that the rapist does to his victims.

However, our argument in the following sections will be that we can provide a more plausible and adequate account of the idea that crimes should be understood as 'public' wrongs against a 'common' good (i.e. that conduct should be criminalised if and because it injures or threatens such a 'common' good): an account that shows why attacks on individual *Rechtsgüter* should be the concern of the criminal law, as attacks on a common good, *without* thereby ignoring or denigrating the wrong done to the individual victim.

As an essential prelude to that argument, however, we should try to make clearer the very notion of 'criminalization': what is it to say that a certain kind of conduct should be criminal? In the following we will identify features of the criminal process which bear on our account of crimes as common or shared wrongs.

2. Crime and the Criminal Process

If we could just take for granted the structures characteristic of our Western systems of criminal justice, the question of what it means to say that certain kinds of conduct should be criminalized might seem unproblematic. To criminalize a type of conduct is to prohibit it by statute or common law, and to render those who breach that prohibition liable to prosecution and punishment; to say that a certain type of conduct should be criminalized is therefore to say that it should be thus prohibited, prosecuted and punished.

However, quite apart from the dangers of ethnocentricity involved in defining 'crime' or 'criminalization' purely in terms of our own local systems of law, we need to be more sensitive to the different aspects or dimensions of the concept(ion) of crime as it figures within our own systems. If these different aspects are (as we will suggest they are) to some degree separable, the question of what it is to

14. L. Becker, 'Criminal Attempts and the Theory of the Law of Crimes' (1974) 3 Phil. & Publ. Affairs 262.
15. See e.g. J. G. Murphy, 'Marxism and Retribution' (1973) 2 Phil. & Publ. Affairs 217; W. Sadurski, 'Distributive Justice and the Theory of Punishment' (1985) 5 Oxford J. of Legal Stud. 47.

'criminalize' something becomes less straightforward. For we will be able to imagine legal institutions and practices which share some but not all of those aspects—to which we can ascribe a concept in some respects like, but in other respects unlike, our concept(ion) of 'crime'; and we will thus realise that to 'criminalize' something could, given different institutional structures, mean rather different things—in which case to ask what kinds of conduct should be criminalized, or what principles or considerations should guide decisions about criminalization, could be to ask not one question, but a set of distinct questions.

A further benefit of such a discriminating approach is that it might assist discussion between those who are, by and large, willing to work within the framework of our existing institutions of criminal justice, and more radical critics who argue that those institutions are fundamentally flawed (and who may thus not be happy to discuss the appropriate normative criteria of criminalization if 'criminalization' entails subjection to those institutions). It might turn out, for example, that even those who count themselves or are counted as 'abolitionists,' some of whom reject the very concept of 'crime' as it figures in our existing institutions,[16] would be willing to say that some kinds of conduct should be, in *some* sense, criminalized; and we can at least hope that such an approach will enable us to identify more clearly what common ground (if any) there is between the reformers and the radicals, and what divides them.

We therefore try here to pick out what we take to be the central features of the concept of crime, as it is embodied in our existing criminal justice systems: that is, the different things that are said, implied or presupposed in declaring that conduct is (or should be) criminal. This is not intended as a definition of 'crime,' or as a set of necessary and sufficient conditions for the normative identification of conduct as criminal; indeed, it will follow from our argument that we could articulate concept(ion)s of crime that lack some of these features. It is, rather, intended as a way of providing a clearer focus for the kinds of discussion which are needed if we are to ask what kinds of conduct should be 'criminalized.'

First, crime involves wrongdoing: what we may call socially proscribed wrongdoing. Crime, that is to say, is not just conduct which is inconsistent with values held by other members of the community—we may disapprove of many kinds of conduct, without thinking that we have the right, or the standing, to declare that others ought not to engage in them. But to believe that a certain kind of conduct should be criminal is to believe, at least, that it is conduct which should be declared wrong by the community: that it is a matter on which the community should take a shared and public view, and claim normative authority over its members.[17] This is one dimension of the distinction between the 'public' and the 'private.' Some kinds of conduct belong in the private sphere, as matters of private life or private

16. See e.g. *supra* note 10; L. Hulsman, 'Critical Criminology and the Concept of Crime' (1986) 10 Contemp. Crises 63.

17. This feature of crime, that it must involve conduct which is not merely wrong, but wrong in a way which gives the community the standing to prohibit and condemn it, raises important questions about the notion of 'standing' which we cannot pursue here: see R. A. Duff, 'Law, Language and Community: Some Preconditions of Criminal Liability' (1998) 18 Oxford J. of Legal Stud. (forthcoming).

conscience on which I might accept advice or criticism from my friends or family, but in which the larger community to which I belong does not have the right to tell me what I ought to do. Other kinds of conduct, including conduct that may take place 'in private,' such as beating up my spouse, are not private matters: the community claims the right, for instance, to declare that spouse-beating is wrong.[18]

Such public social values need not be expressed in institutionalized rules—there might be no need for such institutionalization in small communities with a fair degree of normative consensus. But they can be expressed in the kind of formal rule which figure in a legal system, and this is then one basic aspect of the criminal law: that it declares norms which claim authority over all members of the community whose law it is. Such norms may concern *mala in se* (actions which can be shown to be wrong independently of such a social norm), or *mala prohibita* (actions which are wrongful because they breach a social rule which is accepted as serving some common good).

Second, insofar as crime involves wrongdoing (leaving aside here issues about what counts as 'doing' and about whether all crime must or should involve a 'doing'), it also involves a wrongdoer—someone who does the wrong and can be held responsible for it. The wrongdoer need not be an individual: we can see corporations, for instance, as agents, (and should perhaps be more prepared) to see them thus).[19] But a crime requires a criminal agent, who is (and can be held) responsible for it: who can properly be called, by the community, to answer for that wrong.

To say that crime involves wrongdoing by a (putatively) responsible agent may not seem to get us very far: but it already picks out certain important points. It reminds us that crimes are not just undesirable *occurrences* which a community might wish to prevent; nor are they just 'conflicts' which must be resolved.[20] To believe that we should have a criminal law is, at least, to believe that there are some kinds of conduct that the community should declare authoritatively to be *wrong* (such declarations helping to cement, as it were, those normative relations which bind the members of the community together);[21] and that they are kinds of wrongful conduct whose agents can properly be held responsible for them.

But how should the community respond to breaches of such norms?[22] That there should be *some* response follows from the nature of crime as a breach of an

18. We talk here and elsewhere of 'the community' rather than of 'the state', on the (ideal) assumption that the state should represent and serve the community: an assumption that clearly raises large issues both about the nature of the state and about the conditions for the existence of a community which the state could serve.

19. See C. Wells, *Corporations and Criminal Responsibility* (Oxford: Oxford University Press, 1993).

20. See *supra* note 10; 'Abolitionist,' *supra* note 12.

21. Contrast some abolitionists who object to any such 'imposition' of values: see e.g. H. Bianchi, 'Abolition: Assensus and Sanctuary' in H. Bianchi & R. van Swaaningen, eds., *Abolitionism: Towards a Non-Repressive Approach to Crime* (Amsterdam: Free University Press, 1986) 113; we have also heard Christie and Hulsman talk in such terms.

22. Another identifying feature of crime is that the law may allow the use of force to prevent crime—but not to prevent merely civil wrongs (see, e.g., *Criminal Law Act 1967* (U.K.), 1967, c. 58, s.3(1); American Law Institute, *Model Penal Code*, s.3; Canadian *Criminal Code*, R.S.C. 1985, c. C-34, s.27). We will not discuss this here, save to note that the question of which kinds of conduct should be criminalized is then also partly the question of which kinds of conduct can legitimately be prevented by force.

authoritative community norm: to take such norms seriously, to believe that conduct which breaches them is wrong, is to be ready to respond to it; simply to ignore breaches is to say that we do not take the norm or its breach seriously. But two further kinds of question now arise. One focuses on outcomes: should the wrongdoer be liable to censure; to pay compensation to those s/he has wronged; to punishment (however that is to be understood)? The other focuses on processes: by what kinds of process should such outcomes be determined? This raises the issue of 'informal' as against 'formal' justice;[23] it also, and for our present purposes more crucially, raises the issue of 'criminal' as against 'civil' processes. What we want to focus on here is the question of who controls the process—is it the individual victim, or the community?

A 'civil' model puts the victim in charge. She is the complainant who initiates the proceedings against the person who (allegedly) wronged her; it is for her to carry the case through, or to drop it. This is not to say that the community has no role. It declared those norms to which she appeals in claiming that she was wronged; it provides the institutional structure through which her case is decided, and the arbitrator or judge who will assist in resolving the case or produce an authoritative decision, as well as enforcement mechanisms to ensure that the alleged wrongdoer complies with the decision; it could also provide advice and resources to assist the complainant in pursuing her case. But she is still in charge: it is for her to decide whether the case is brought and pursued, and whether the decision is enforced; there is no thought that she has a *duty* to bring a case. Moreover, the reasons why she might decide not to bring the case will remain private and could be quite arbitrary.

A 'criminal' model puts the community (the state) in charge. The case is investigated by the police; the charge is brought by Regina, the People or the State;[24] whether it is brought, and how far it proceeds, is up to the prosecuting authority; it is not for the victim to decide whether any decision it produces is enforced. In practice, it might be the case that wrongdoing is investigated only if the victim first complains to the police. A charge might be brought, and the case pursued only if she is willing that it should be; if she is unwilling, the prosecuting authority might drop the case—out of deference to her feelings perhaps, or because it could not practicably be pursued without her willing co-operation. (In such cases, unlike the 'civil' case, there is room to argue that she *ought* to co-operate, that she has a duty to do so. We do not have space here to discuss this claim of duty, but such an argument would require a foundation in ideas of citizenship and responsibility to the community). Even when a case is dropped for the kinds of reason just indicated, however, it is still not hers: the community takes it over, and may pursue it or drop it against her will. So there are two aspects to the criminal model. On the one hand, the victim receives more support from the community than she might under the

23. See *supra* note 13.

24. The 'People' or the 'State' (or the 'Commonwealth', as in some American states) might seem to be a more appropriate way of expressing the community's role in bringing the case than 'Regina': though we cannot discuss this point here, we would certainly argue that those who want to see themselves as citizens of a polity rather than (merely) as subjects of a sovereign should indeed prefer some such alternative to 'Regina.'

civil model: she is not left to bring the case by herself. But, on the other hand, she loses control of it: it is no longer hers to pursue or not as she see fit.

The question of what kinds of outcome the process might lead to is, to a degree, distinct from that of who controls it. A 'civil' process could lead to censure as well as compensation; it can also lead to (a kind of) punishment, insofar as it allows for the award of explicitly 'punitive' damages, which exceed what is thought to be required by way of direct compensation for the wrongful harm done to the plaintiff. A 'criminal' process need not lead to 'punishment,' insofar as that is something distinct from censure and compensation. It does seem natural that a 'civil' process should lead to victim-directed compensation rather than to punishment. Insofar as punishment is rationalised as a matter of deterrence, incapacitation, reform, or rehabilitation; insofar as it is imposed for the sake of (as well as in the name of) the community: the victim might reasonably argue that it should not be up to her to bring the case to achieve goods for the community—it should be up to the community to pursue such goods. But it is not, we think, so 'natural' that a criminal process must lead to punishment: whether it should depends on our understanding of punishment, and on why we think that the 'criminal' process is appropriate for certain kinds of case.

That a response to socially prescribed wrongdoing should involve censure seems obvious enough. We owe it to the victim to take seriously the wrong she has suffered, as a wrong; we also owe it to the wrongdoer, as a fellow member of the community to respond honestly and seriously to her wrongdoing.[25] But even if it is appropriate that, given the social character and the seriousness of the norms she has breached, such censure should be justified by, and administered through, some more or less formal process (rather than being left to the individual reactions of the victim and others), this is not yet to say either that it must be administered through a 'criminal' process, or that it should be expressed by punishment. It could be administered through a 'civil' process; and while one could argue that censure itself is a kind of punishment, the kind of 'hard treatment' punishments imposed by our existing legal systems cannot (we would argue) be justified purely on the grounds that this is the only way to ensure that censure is effectively communicated.[26]

That victims who have been harmed by wrongdoing should, when possible, receive some form of compensation may also seem obvious enough, at least when the compensation can be seen as genuinely reparative or restorative—although this leaves to some degree open the questions of what kinds of wrong *can* be compensated;[27] of what modes of compensation are appropriate to what kinds of wrong

25. On the significance and importance of censure, see A. von Hirsch, *Censure and Sanctions* (Oxford: Oxford University Press, 1993), especially ch. 2; and R. A. Duff, 'Penal Communications: Recent Work in the Philosophy of Punishment' (1996) 20 Crime and Justice 1 at 31-57.

26. On 'hard treatment' see J. Feinberg, 'The Expressive Function of Punishment' in J. Feinberg, *Doing and Deserving* (Princeton, NJ: Princeton University Press, 1970) 95: for two different accounts of how it can be justified within an account of punishment as serving (primarily) to communicate censure, see A. von Hirsch, *ibid.* at ch. 2; Duff, *ibid.* at 45-57.

27. See R. E. Goodin, 'Theories of Compensation' in R. Frey & C. Morris, eds., *Liability and Responsibility* (Cambridge: Cambridge University Press, 1991) 257.

(are monetary damages really appropriate for libel, for example?); and of whether that compensation should be paid, either directly or indirectly, by the wrongdoer. But compensation could be the outcome of a 'criminal' as well as of a 'civil' process (English courts can make compensation orders following a criminal conviction);[28] and punishment is distinct from compensation (even though criminal courts can make compensation orders,[29] and even though civil courts can award punitive damages), since as well as expressing censure, it is designedly onerous or painful (whereas compensation is only contingently onerous).

The final, but separable, implication of criminalization is thus that crimes are punished: to ask what kinds of conduct should be criminalized is to ask, in part, what kinds of conduct should attract punishment rather than merely formal censure or liability to pay compensation (though any answer to that question must also depend on our understanding of the rationale of punishment).

Now it might be tempting to take the question of punishment as the central (if not the only) question about criminalization: to suppose that the essential distinction between criminal and merely civil wrongs is that the former attract punishment, and that to ask what kinds of conduct should be criminalized is thus essentially to ask what kinds of conduct should be threatened and visited with punishment. But our discussion of the different aspects of the concept of crime should have shown that this would be a mistake.

To hold that a certain kind of conduct should be criminalized is to hold at least some of the following: that it should be proscribed and condemned by a socially authoritative norm, as a type of wrongdoing for which we can identify a responsible, culpable agent; that it thus merits the censure of the community; that it is appropriately responded to or dealt with by a 'criminal' rather than a 'civil' process; that it should render the agent liable to punishment rather than to merely formal censure or a duty to compensate. But whilst to hold that a certain kind of conduct should be be criminalized by our existing legal systems is in effect to make all these claims about it, part of our point in separating these aspects of the concept of crime is to show that one could make some of these claims without making them all. Our aim has also been to show that the different aspects of the concept raise different questions. We need to ask what kinds of conduct merit social proscription; a 'criminal' process; punishment—and we cannot suppose in advance either that the answers to these questions will be just the same, or that the considerations relevant to answering each of them will be just the same.

In the following section we focus on the distinction between a 'civil' and a 'criminal' process, since we think that this raises one central question about criminalization: we will argue that by asking why certain kinds of conduct should be dealt with by a 'criminal' rather than by a 'civil' process, we can see why some notion of the 'common' or 'public' good is crucial to the criminalization even of attacks on individual *Rechtsgüter*.

---

28. See A. J. Ashworth, *Sentencing and Criminal Justice* (London: Weidenfeld & Nicolson 1992) at 249-52.

29. See generally A. J. Ashworth, 'Punishment and Compensation: Victims, Offenders and the State' (1986) 6 Oxford J. of Legal Stud. 86.

3. Sharing Wrongs

Consider rape as an example. Why should rape be a crime? We can agree that it should be socially proscribed and condemned. It is not a 'private' matter in which the community has no proper interest (and English law has, at last, recognised that this is true even of intra-marital rape);[30] nor is the rape victim simply involved in a 'conflict' with her attacker, which they need to 'negotiate' and resolve: leaving aside problem cases on the borderlines of rape, we should say that rape is a non-negotiable wrong which the community should declare to be so. This has to do in part with the seriousness of the harm wrought by rape—both the harm contingently consequent upon rape, and the harm intrinsic to it. It also has to do, we suppose, with the idea that it is not difficult for a 'reasonable' man to refrain from rape (indeed, that any 'reasonable' man should not need to *refrain* from rape); and that any woman ought to be able confidently to expect not to be thus attacked as she goes about her normal life. To say that rape should be criminal is also to say that rapists are (presumptively) responsible for what they do, and can properly be held answerable, and be censured, for it: whatever we may say about the kinds of social structure and attitude which encourage men to see women as mere sexual objects and may thus be said to encourage rape, this does not negate the individual rapist's responsible, culpable agency.

But why should rape be dealt with by a 'criminal' rather than by a 'civil' process? Why should rape not be defined simply as a civil wrong, so that it is for the victim to bring a case herself (if but only if she wishes) against her attacker? Part of the answer will be that the rapist should be punished, rather than being liable only to pay compensation to his victim—and we must ask why we should think that. But there is, we think, more to it than that; and that 'more' has to do with the kind of interest the community as a whole should take in such wrongdoing—with, we will argue, the sense in which the community should see the wrong done to her as a wrong done to 'us.'

Of course even if we envisaged rape as only a civil wrong, there are different possibilities. At one extreme it would be for the victim to find the resources herself to bring and pursue the case: the community provides the structure (the civil court) through which she can do so, declares the norms to which she appeals, and will enforce the decision; but no further help is offered. The first step towards some greater community involvement is then to say that the community should at least also offer her resources (advice, help in identifying her assailant and collecting evidence, legal counsel...) to help her bring the case. If we ask why this should be so, we might refer again to the seriousness of the injury she has suffered. We may also say that there is a stronger case for offering such help to citizens when the wrong or harm they have suffered is not one they should be seen as having voluntarily risked suffering, or one that they should be willing to risk suffering (subject to a right to compensation if it is actualised) as a part of their ordinary lives. That is to say, there are certain kinds of wrongful harm which we should be able to expect,

30. See *R* v. *R*, [1991] 4 All ER 481; *supra* note 4 at 452-53.

categorically, to be safe from; and if we suffer such a harm we should at least be able to expect the community to help us pursue its perpetrator.

Perhaps it is the categorical nature of this requirement which makes the difference here, and points us towards a 'criminal,' rather than a 'civil,' process. In a civil case, there is room for the idea of 'contributory negligence': the defendant can admit that he caused the harm, culpably, but argue that the plaintiff was also at fault—and should thus bear part of the cost. Now judges have, notoriously, sometimes talked explicitly of, or (more often) appealed implicitly to, a rape victim's 'contributory negligence': the rapist's culpability (and so his sentence) is thought to be properly reduced by the fact that his victim put herself in danger, or acted in a way which increased the risk of being raped. It is also clearly true that some kinds of conduct—how she dresses, where she goes, how she behaves—in fact create or increase the risk that a woman will be raped; and friends might tell her that she is stupid to behave like that, or criticise her morally if her conduct is intended to stimulate sexual desire or to encourage the prospects of sexual intercourse in a man with whom she has no intention of having sexual intercourse. We might analogously criticise householders who 'encourage' burglary by leaving their houses obviously insecure, or a car owner who 'encourages' theft by leaving valuables in view in an unlocked car. But we do not think that this reduces the culpability of the thief, burglar or rapist: for we think that people should categorically refrain (and should be able to refrain, even if they are tempted) from such wrongs, even if the victim has in fact made it possible or tempting for them to commit such a wrong.

But there is more to the 'criminal' process than this. We still need to ask why the community should not merely offer assistance to a victim who wants to pursue a civil case against her assailant, but also take that case over. Does this amount to 'stealing' her 'conflict' from her;[31] or are there reasons why the case should become the community's ('ours') rather than just hers? We have noted the inadequacy of some answers to this question: answers which appeal to a 'public' good distinct from the victim's own individual good, and which thus fail to do justice to the wrong that *she* has suffered:[32] that wrong must, surely, be integral to the rationale for criminalising rape and for subjecting the rapist to a criminal process.

But we can offer a more plausible account of the sense in which rape is a wrong against the community, which does not involve ignoring or denigrating the wrong done to the individual victim. Consider how a group of women might respond to a sexual attack on one of them (or how a self-conscious racial group might respond to a racial attack on one of them). They may see it as a collective, not merely an individual, wrong (as an attack on *them*), insofar as they associate and identify themselves with the individual victim. For they define themselves as a group, in terms of a certain shared identity, shared values, mutual concern—and shared dangers which threaten them: an attack on a member of the group is thus an attack on the group—on their shared values and their common good. The wrong does not cease to be 'her' wrong: but it is also 'our' wrong insofar as we identify ourselves with

31. See *supra* note 10 and accompanying text.
32. See *supra* notes 14-15 and accompanying text.

her. The point is not just that we realise that other members of the group are also vulnerable to such attacks, or that we want to warn other potential assailants that they cannot attack members of the group with impunity (although the thought that any of us could be attacked and the desire to defend all members of the group are clearly involved): it is that the attack on this individual victim is itself also an attack on us—on her as a member of the group and on us as fellow members.

A group can in this way 'share' the wrongs done to its individual members, insofar as it defines and identifies itself as a community united by mutual concern, by genuinely shared (as distinct from contingently coincident) values and interests, and by the shared recognition that its members' goods (and their identity) are bound up with their membership of the community. Wrongs done to individual members of the community are then wrongs against the whole community—injuries to a common or shared, not merely to an individual, good. This, we suggest, provides an appropriate perspective from which we can understand the point and significance of a 'criminal' rather than a 'civil' process. For suppose we understand a political society not merely as a collection of discrete and separate individuals bound to each other by an imagined social contract, but as a community in this sense (which is what is implied by the communitarian framework of our argument): suppose, that is, that citizens see (or should see) each other as bound together in a way analogous to the way in which members of the women's group or the racial group mentioned in the previous paragraph see each other as bound together see (even if those bonds may be somewhat less intimate). We can then also see how wrongs against individual citizens can be understood as shared wrongs, as wrongs against the whole community, insofar as the individual goods which are attacked are goods in terms of which the community identifies and understands itself.

We can from this perspective begin to see both why the community should bring the case 'on behalf of' the individual victim—rather than leaving her to bring it for herself; and why it might sometimes *insist* on bringing the case even if she is unwilling to do so. For, just as we may say that we owe it to her to associate ourselves with her in this way (to take her wrong as also our wrong), so we may say that she owes it to us to recognise that the wrong was done to us as well as to her. This is not yet to say that the outcome of the case should be *punishment*—rather than censure, apology, or compensation to the individual victim; and we noted earlier that to justify a 'criminal' rather than 'civil' process need not be to justify a punitive outcome of that procedure: but we would also suggest that punishment should be understood in terms of the wrongdoer's relationship to the community as well as to the individual victim.[33]

If this is right, it suggests that crimes (as distinct from civil wrongs) must indeed be portrayed as 'public' wrongs, against the community (for if they are not public wrongs it is not clear why they should be dealt with by a criminal rather than a civil process). But it also shows how wrongs done to individuals, attacks on their *Rechtsgüter*, can be understood as being at the same time, and in virtue of their character as wrongs against individuals, wrongs against the community to which

---

33. See Duff, *supra* note 25.

the individual belongs. In making the wrong done to the rape victim 'ours,' rather than merely 'hers'; in thus understanding it as an attack on 'our' good, not merely on her individual good: we do not turn our attention *away* from the wrong that she has suffered, towards some distinct 'public' good. Rather, we share *in* the very wrong that she has suffered: it is not 'our' wrong *instead of* hers; it is 'our' wrong *because* it is a wrong done to her, as one of us—as a fellow member of our community whose identity and whose good is found within that community.

It might be objected that the contents of the individual *Rechtsgüter* which (it seems clear) the criminal law should protect—of such goods as life, liberty, property and health—resist our attempt to 'collectivise' such goods: for the contents of those goods are, surely, irreducibly *individual* interests. But we do not want to deny that these are the interests, and goods, of individuals; nor do we deny that individuals and their goods and interests are important: quite the reverse. Our argument concerns rather the way in which that 'importance' should be understood, if it is to provide one ground for a distinction between 'criminal' and 'civil' law, and one reason for subjecting certain kinds of wrong to individuals to a 'criminal' process; it thus also concerns the way in which we should understand the 'individual' in relation to, and as a member of, the larger community.

What we want to resist here is an atomistic moral or political ontology which takes 'individuals' and their individual goods as basic—as prior to their place in a community—in favour of a more holistic view of individuals as finding their identities and their goods within their relationships to others; in particular, in the context of discussions of the criminal law, in their relationships with each other as citizens of a political community. Any account of the concept of crime and of the proper scope and aims of the criminal law must, we assume, be informed by a political theory (understood in its broadest sense). The political theory to which we would appeal, and on which the idea of community involved in our argument depends, is some version of the 'civic republicanism' sketched by Charles Taylor.

> [T]he bond of solidarity with my compatriots in a functioning republic is based on a sense of shared fate, where the sharing itself is of value. This is what gives this bond its special importance, what makes my ties with these people and so this enterprise particularly binding, what animates my 'virtue,' or patriotism.[34]

Fellow citizens of such a republic will find their individual goods within that republican community, and will see attacks on the central goods of their fellows as attacks on that community; they will share the wrongs which such attacks involve.

To say this is not, of course, to begin to show just what kinds of conduct ought to be criminalized: but it is to show, we hope, what kinds of question we must ask in asking what kinds of conduct should be criminalized. We must ask, in part, what kinds of wrongs should be seen as wrongs against 'us'; and this is to ask which values are (which should be) so central to a community's identity and self-understanding, to its conception of its members' good, that actions which attack or flout

34. Taylor, *supra* note 8 at 170.

those values are not merely individual matters which the individual victim should pursue for herself, but attacks on the community.

4. Final Remarks

The argument of this paper is intended as a prolegomenon. We have not tried to say what kinds of conduct should be criminalized—and we deliberately chose as our central example in the previous section an obvious, paradigmatic, example of something which should surely be criminal if anything should be. There is clearly a very long way to go before we could begin to draw any determinate conclusions from what we have suggested here.

We hope, however, that this discussion can help to show the direction in which more concrete discussions about criminalization should proceed, and to provide a framework within such discussions should be set, by making clearer the kinds of question we must ask. Instead of asking directly and simply what kinds of conduct may or should be criminalized, we can more usefully ask the more particular kinds of question indicated above, focused on more particular aspects of the concept of crime; and a central question, we suggest, should be that of what kinds of wrong should be seen as 'public' or 'shared' wrongs in the sense indicated above.

One final comment about methodology. Discussions of criminalization—like other normative discussions—often proceed by searching for principles: articulated, general criteria by reference to which we can decide individual cases (which is not to say that they assume that we will be able to find just *one* principle by which we can determine what kinds of conduct should be criminalized, or even one set of coherent principles). What we have said here is certainly a long way from articulating any such principles: but we are not sure that that is what the aim should be. We might do better to take seriously John Wisdom's comment that "at the bar of reason, always the final appeal is to cases."[35] That is to say, we should found our discussion not on the search for general principles, but on examples which we can suppose to be paradigmatic, or non-controversial as examples of conduct which should, or should not, be criminalized. By looking carefully at such examples, at the resemblances (and the differences) between them which we can come to see to be relevant, we might be able gradually to build up a plausible conception of crime: it will be messy and untidy—but that is not something that should surprise or alarm us.

35. J. Wisdom, 'A Feature of Wittgenstein's Technique' in J. Wisdom, *Paradox and Discovery* (Oxford: Blackwell, 1965) 90 at 102; see also J. Wisdom, 'Philosophy, Metaphysics and Psycho-Analysis' in J. Wisdom, *Philosophy and Psycho-Analysis* (Oxford: Blackwell 1953) 248 at 248-54.

Part II
Criminal Responsibility

[4]

CHARACTER, PURPOSE, AND CRIMINAL RESPONSIBILITY

MICHAEL D. BAYLES

ABSTRACT. This paper explores analyzing criminal responsibility from the Humean position that blame is for character traits. If untoward acts indicate undesirable character traits, then the agent is blameworthy; if they do not, then the actor is not blameworthy – he has an excuse. A distinctive feature of this approach is that the voluntariness of acts is irrelevant to determining blameworthiness.

This analysis is then applied to a variety of issues in criminal law. Mens rea supports inferences to character traits, and the Humean approach provides a reason for rejcting strict criminal liability. The Humean approach also helps resolve a number of issues about attempts, such as punishment for impossible attempts and the defense of abandonment. It also supports the broad outlines of the defense of mistake and provides a third alternative in the Wooton-Hart debate over punishment and treatment.

This paper explores criminal responsibility – mens rea and excuses – from a perspective quite different from that in most recent writing. Philosophical literature provides three general theories of blame and excuses largely stemming from Bentham, Kant, and Hume. The Kantian type of view predominates in recent literature, with the utilitarian view being the only other one usually considered. This paper explores a Humean theory of blame and excuses for criminal responsibility. Although a more detailed analysis would be necessary for a complete justification of the Humean approach, this paper argues for its plausibility and general compatibility with the current law.

The utilitarian theory of criminal responsibility stems from Bentham. His rationale for excuses, as opposed to other reasons for not punishing, is that punishment would be inefficacious, that is, could not deter.[1] This general rationale, he thought, would

---

[1] Jeremy Bentham, *An Introduction to the Principles of Morals and Legislation* (New York: Hafner Publishing Co., 1948), chap. 13, sec. 3, pp. 172–75.

support several sets of excuses. Ignorance of insufficiently promulgated laws, infancy, insanity and intoxication excuse, because the penal law could not haye an effect on persons committing crimes in such conditions. Excuses of lack of mens rea and mistake are justified, because the law could not deter the individual act. Finally, because the penal law is not the dominant influence on the actor, duress excuses. Bentham's utilitarian theory of criminal excuses has been rejected by a number of contemporary writers, because even though punishment may have no deterrent effect on the punished individual (specific deterrence), it may have a deterrent effect on others (general deterrence).[2] For example, although punishing an insane person might not deter him, it might deter others who would otherwise think they could feign insanity or who would not interpret the case as one of punishing an insane person.

The predominant theory of criminal responsibility is a form of Kantian theory. People should be excused if they could not have avoided performing a criminal act. This claim is reminiscent of Kant's dictum that 'ought' implies 'can'. The Kantian dictum does not, however, apply to excuses. Excuses differ from justifications precisely in that with them what a person did was wrong (ought not to have been done) even though he is excused from blame or punishment, whereas if a person has a justification, what he did was not wrong. Excuses defeat blame or punishment of the particular individual but not the wrongness of his conduct. Nevertheless, the underlying moral force is the same, namely, that a person should not be punished if he could not have reasonably avoided violating the law.

H. L.A. Hart is the most prominent recent exponent of this type of view. To punish someone is unjust and unfair, he claims,

---

[2] H. L. A. Hart, *Punishment and Responsibility* (New York: Oxford University Press, 1968), pp. 40–43; George P. Fletcher, *Rethinking Criminal Law* (Toronto: Little, Brown and Co., 1978), pp. 813–17. See also Hyman Gross, *A Theory of Criminal Justice* (New York: Oxford University Press, 1979), pp. 302–04.

unless the person had the capacity and a fair opportunity to conform to the law.[3] Although Hart's argument for this principle is perhaps more utilitarian than Kantian, the principle remains one stemming from the Kantian retributivist tradition. This principle of responsibility is also adopted by Hyman Gross in his recent book on criminal law.[4] It grounds excuses such as mental abnormality, compulsion, ignorance of the law, and a lack of mens rea. Individuals who act in these conditions either cannot conform to the law or do not have a fair opportunity to do so.

Although the arguments for the dominant Kantian view of criminal responsibility are strong, it is worth exploring an alternative stemming from David Hume.[5] This theory is based on character. Blame and punishment are not directly for acts but for character traits. On this view, 'character trait' is not, as in the Aristotelian view,[6] restricted to traits which people can voluntarily control possessing or manifesting in behaviour. Instead, it refers to any socially desirable or undesirable disposition of a person. Acts may or may not indicate character traits. If an act does indicate an undesirable character trait, then blame is appropriate; if it does not, then blame is inappropriate although measures to prevent such conduct in the future might be taken. For example, if a person accidentally kills another, his conduct does not indicate an undesirable character trait. However, to try to prevent similar accidents in the future, one might take measures such as keeping guns away from people.

One must distinguish blame, expressions of blame, and punishment. Blame is a negative attitude towards a person for a character

---

[3] Hart, *Punishment and Responsibility*, pp. 181–82, 201, and 22–23.

[4] Gross, *Criminal Justice*, p. 137.

[5] *Treatise of Human Nature*, ed. L. A. Selby-Bigge (Oxford: Clarendon Press, 1888), pp. 477, 575; see also Michael D. Bayles, 'Hume on Blame and Excuse,' *Hume Studies* 2, 1 (1976): 17–35.

[6] The Aristotelian view emphasizes that one is responsible for one's character traits because one could have avoided developing them. For an application of this view to the criminal law, see Edmund L. Pincoffs, 'Legal Responsibility and Moral Character,' *Wayne Law Review* 19 (1973): 905–23.

trait; it is appropriate if the person is blameworthy. Even if a person is blameworthy, one may or may not express blame verbally. Finally, punishment is more than an individual expression of blame; it is a particular social response to blameworthy conduct – that exhibiting an undesirable character trait. Because legal punishment is a particular social response, it is not always appropriate for blameworthy conduct. Considerations other than blameworthiness are needed to justify punishment. However, the assumptions in this paper are that blameworthiness (or blame) is a necessary condition for justifiable punishment and that justified excuses render individuals blameless and thus punishment inappropriate.

1. MENS REA AND CHARACTER

At the outset, this character trait view confronts a powerful objection. Single acts do not necessarily indicate dispositions. As Gross puts it, from a single dangerous act one cannot infer that the actor is a dangerous person.[7] This objection may be defeated if other elements of criminal law aid in making the inference from an act to a disposition. In particular, the law's emphasis upon mens rea – whether an act is committed purposely, knowingly, recklessly, or negligently – may greatly strengthen the warrant for inferring an undesirable character trait. If a person kills purposely, his act reflects more undesirably on his character than if he merely kills another negligently. Even this line of thought, however, confronts Gross's further claim that the distinctions among degrees (or kinds) of mens rea are based on dangerousness rather than a particular mental element. Thus, an analysis of the various states of mens rea is necessary.

The distinction between purposely and knowingly bringing about a harm cannot be made simply by the dangerousness of the acts. Gross contends that acting purposely involves a harmful act in which the occurrence of harm is imminent and avoided only by

[7] Gross, *Criminal Justice*, pp. 340, 386.

chance.[8] Acting knowingly involves only an imminently dangerous act in which the harm will almost certainly occur in the normal course of events and failure to take steps to avoid it is irrational. This basis for the distinction will not suffice, however, for a purposeful act may not create as great a risk of harm as one done knowingly. Gross fails to see this because he always uses examples of the same type of conduct, such as fumigating a ship with a sailor below deck. If one compares different forms of conduct, then it is clear that some purposeful acts are not as dangerous as some done knowingly. Sticking to homicide, in which the harm is the death of another person, purposely cutting the brake hose on someone's car in the hope that it will cause a fatal accident is not as dangerous as blowing up a building knowing someone is inside it. To act knowingly with respect to some harm is to be practically certain that the harm will result, yet purposely to try to bring about a harm, one need not be practically certain, or even very sure at all, that one will succeed.

In contrast, the distinction between acting knowingly and recklessly does require a difference in the risk of a harm's occurrence. Whereas to act knowingly, the actor must be practically certain a result will occur, to act recklessly, he need only consciously disregard a substantial and unjustifiable risk of its occurrence.[9] The major difference is thus the degree – practical certainty or substantial – of risk.

Nevertheless, each of these distinctions indicates something about an actor's character which is plausibly the reason for distinguishing them. They each indicate something about an actor's attitude toward the occurrence of a harm. A person who acts purposely desires or wants a harm to occur. A person who acts knowingly displays a less undesirable attitude towards a harm, because although he does not care whether it occurs, he does not desire its occurrence. Nevertheless, he displays a more undesirable

---

[8] Ibid., pp. 84, 87, 429.

[9] *Model Penal Code: Proposed Official Draft* (Philadelphia: American Law Institute, 1962), sec. 2.02 (2) (b) and (c).

attitude than one who acts recklessly. Indifference to a substantial risk of a harm is different from indifference to its practical certainty. A person who operates a factory recklessly, indifferent to a substantial risk of pollution, does not have as undesirable an attitude as one who is practically certain his factory pollutes but does not care. A reckless person, such as a reckless driver, will usually try to avoid a harm at the last moment, whereas someone who knowingly causes harm, simply not caring, will not.

The requirement of one of these mental elements supports the inference of an undesirable character trait and conforms to the Humean analysis of blame and excuses. The claim that a dangerous act may not indicate a dangerous person sounds plausible because it does not consider these mental conditions. Discharging a gun in a crowded room is a dangerous act, but it may not indicate a dangerous or undesirable character trait. If the discharge was accidental, then it does not. But if the gun was discharged purposely, knowingly, or recklessly, then, a justification being absent, the act does warrant inferring an undesirable character trait. The various mental states indicate different attitudes towards harm. Blame is greater the more undesirable the attitude. The behaviour plus the attitude evidence an undesirable disposition. While attitudes may be fleeting, the law uses a general presumption that the combination of behaviour and attitude indicates an undesirable character trait, and excuses are designed to show that the normal inference is not warranted.

Considering negligence only strengthens this analysis. One who acts negligently is unaware, but should be aware, of a substantial and unjustifiable risk of harm.[10] On the predominant Kantian view, negligence is punishable only if the actor had a fair opportunity to become aware of the risk. On the Humean character view, all that matters is whether the conduct indicates an undesirable character trait. As the actor is unaware of the harm, the act does not indicate as undesirable a trait as the other mental states. Moreover, on the basis of one careless act, the inference to a careless

[10] Ibid., sec. 2.02 (2) (d).

attitude is less valid. Failure to conform to a standard of care on one occasion does not indicate an attitude of indifference to standards of care. Consequently, the basis for blame is much less sure. This may account for the qualms most people have about punishing negligent conduct. On the predominant view, these qualms do not find a purchase, because even though an actor was unaware of the risk of harm, he may have had as great a capacity and as fair an opportunity to become so as one who was aware of the risk and disregard it – acted recklessly. One might try to avoid this criticism by claiming that awareness of a risk is part of the degree of opportunity to avoid harm. However, this conflates avoidable and unavoidable ignorance the distinction in which depends upon the opportunity to know, and it also rewards carelessness.

Finally, the Humean view provides a reason for rejecting strict criminal liability. With strict liability, no inquiry is made into an actor's state of mind. As no attitude to the harm is shown, the basis for inferring an undesirable character trait is undermined. Thus, blame and punishment become inappropriate. This conclusion does not, however, rule out an alternative rationale and method for dealing with strict liability offences, but it does support the widespread judgment that punishment for them is inappropriate.

2. ATTEMPTS

If a Humean character approach draws strength from the mens rea requirements for criminal acts making inferences to undesirable character traits more reliable, then it may provide a good account of liability for criminal attempts. It is widely recognized that the contemporary law of attempts emphasizes the intent to commit a crime over the dangerousness of acts, and certainly over the occurrence of harm. Less widely recognized is that the law of attempts requires acting purposely, not merely knowingly. (The failure to realize the significance of this requirement of purpose may stem either from the fact that much criminal law fails to distinguish between knowingly and purposely – lumping them together as intentionally – or the obviousness of the point.) To attempt a crime involves more than simply knowing that harm will result; it involves striving to bring it about, making its occurrence an aim in acting.

If punishment is a response to undesirable character traits rather than dangerous acts, then punishment for impossible attempts seems to make more sense. One may approach this point by considering the now classic hypothetical umbrella examples.[11] In the first case, *D* finds an umbrella left in his house after a party. Thinking it belongs to someone else and hoping to keep it for himself, he puts it away. However, the umbrella was left by one of his guests as a gift, with a note inside to that effect. Presumably *D* is not guilty of an attempt. In the second case, *D* sees a celebrity put his umbrella in a stand at a club. When no one is looking, *D* goes to the stand and takes the umbrella in the rack where the celebrity has left his. However, someone has since moved the umbrellas, and *D* in fact takes his own. Presumbly *D* is guilty of an attempt.

In both cases, *D* takes his own umbrella and, therefore, does not take possession of anyone else's and so cannot commit theft. In each case, however, he mistakenly believes he is taking possession of someone else's umbrella. Consequently, the questions arise whether these cases should be treated differently, and if so, why they should. At bottom is the question of when mistakes are relevant to attempt liability.

George Fletcher persuasively argues for the thesis that "mistaken beliefs are relevant to what the actor is trying to do if they affect his incentive in acting. They affect his incentive if knowing of the mistake would give him a good reason for changing his course of conduct."[12] This he calls the rational motivation test. If this test is applied to the umbrella cases, then the presumed results can be justified. In the first case, if *D* knew that the umbrella was left as

---

[11] See Gross, *Criminal Justice*, pp. 204–7.

[12] Fletcher, *Rethinking Criminal Law*, p. 161.

a gift, he would still have kept it. In the second case, had *D* known he was taking his own umbrella rather than the celebrity's, he would have not taken it but would have tried to find the celebrity's.

As the rational motivation test determines whether a fact was relevant to an actor's motivation, it picks out elements of an actor's purpose. In the first case, the actor was not purposely but, had the facts been as he supposed, only knowingly taking or keeping another's umbrella. In the second case, his purpose was to take another's umbrella; he wanted it *because* it belonged to someone else. Thus, his conduct gives evidence of a more undesirable character trait than does the conduct in the first case.

As Fletcher recognizes, the rational motivation test has difficulty with one class of cases, namely, those in which the attempt is obviously impossible, such as trying to kill someone by sticking pins in a doll replica of him.[13] As only part of a Humean character approach, the rational motivation test fares better in these cases. Punishment is a social response to undesirable character traits and requires more for its justification than mere blameworthiness. Although people who hope to kill others by sticking pins in dolls may not have admirable characters, they are more a nuisance than a harm. For punishment, one must look not simply to whether their intent or purpose indicates an undesirable trait, but also to whether this trait is likely to produce criminal harm. The criminal law should be restricted to those undesirable dispositions which may result in criminal harm. As long as the person's disposition is manifested only in ways which obviously cannot produce harm, such as sticking pins in dolls, the character trait is not one with which the criminal law should be concerned, and a social response is not appropriate. However, should the person be disposed to change methods in light of the ineffectiveness of his current one, then a social response is appropriate.

The Humean character trait approach also fits well with the

---

[13] Ibid., pp. 165–66.

affirmative defense of abandonment. This defense requires a voluntary and sincere renunciation of an attempt.[14] Ceasing the attempt for fear of being apprehended will not suffice. Most discussion of the voluntariness of abandonment is concerned with factors other than coercive threats and only brought under the rubric of 'voluntariness' by a weak analogy. In some borderline cases, such as the intended victim of a potential robbery not having enough money[15] or that of a potential victim of rape being pregnant, desisting has been held insufficient to provide a defense of abandonment. A character approach may help explain these cases. If a person ceases an attempt only because the circumstances make it appear less desirable than it did, then there is no rebuttal of his having a disposition to commit the crime should the circumstances be more attractive, e.g., he espies an attractive woman who is not pregnant. What is needed is proof that the defendant gave up his purpose in such a way as to prevent the inference of an undesirable character trait. As long as that evidence is forthcoming, how abandonment is brought about does not matter. Thus, if two people on probation desist from breaking and entering, as long as the change of purpose is evident, it is irrelevant that one talked the other one out of it.[16]

3. MISTAKE

The defense of mistake is another one in which purpose and inferences of character play an important role. In general, to excuse, a mistake must be about part of the definition of the criminal act.[17] For example, a mistaken belief about the day of the week is irrelevant to a charge of unlicensed sales of liquor, but it is relevant to a charge of selling liquor on Sunday or election day. If a mistake is not relevant to the definition of a criminal

---

[14] *Model Penal Code*, sec. 5.01 (4).
[15] Fletcher, *Rethinking Criminal Law*, p. 191.
[16] Ibid., p. 194.
[17] Ibid., pp. 696–97; Gross, *Criminal Justice*, pp. 259–62.

offense, it does not prevent inference of an undesirable character trait, for the person still intends to do a wrongful act and thus evidences a disregard for the harm involved.

As long as a mistake blocks inference of an undesirable character trait, it makes no difference how unreasonable the mistaken belief may be. However, should the crime be one for which there is a lesser offense of doing the act negligently, then an unreasonable mistake should not prevent conviction for the lesser offense. A mistake is unreasonable if it may be avoided by the exercise of reasonable care, so an unreasonable mistake constitutes negligence.

Finally, an actor's purpose may define the crime of which he is guilty. Suppose a defendant breaks and enters a business mistakenly believing it to be a dwelling. As his purpose is to burglarize a house, he is guilty of an attempt at that rather than burglary of a business. His act manifests a desire and disposition to burglarize a dwelling rather than a business.

The excuse of mistake of law indicates a special feature of several affirmative defenses. These defenses require more than evidence to block the inference of an undesirable character trait; they require evidence that the conduct manifested a desirable character trait. Except for a small class of cases, the defense of mistake of law requires that one acted upon an authoritative opinion of the law.[18] The advice of one's lawyer does not count; the authority required is that of an official, of someone who is in authority, not merely of someone who is an authority upon the law. For example, consider the case of a minister who checked with the attorney general's office before placing a sign to aid in soliciting couples for marriage.[19] When charged with violating a regulation about the placement of such signs, his unsuccessful defense was that he relied upon an authoritative opinion of the law. In this case, as in many others, both the predominant view and the Humean character view imply that the unfortunate minister should have been excused. On the predominant view, he

---

[18] See *Model Penal Code*, sec. 2.04 (3); Gross, *Criminal Justice*, pp. 271–72.
[19] Hopkins v. State, 193 Md. 489, 69 A. 2d 456 (1950).

lacked a fair opportunity to discover the law. On the Humean view, his conduct exhibited a desirable character trait, namely, of being disposed to discover the law and conform to it.

These two rationales give differing results in other cases. If the excuse of mistake rests on a person lacking a fair opportunity to conform to the law, then a person's attempt to discover the law should be irrelevant. Thus, were it not possible to discover the law on a matter, a person should be excused even if he made no attempt to discover the law. On the Humean character view, however, such a person would not have manifested the desirable character trait of trying to conform to the law; one could instead infer an attitude of indifference to the legality of his conduct. Consequently, no excuse but blame and punishment would be appropriate.

This general pattern applies to all defenses which are justifications. As exceptions to general laws prohibiting certain conduct, a person's conduct must not merely be such that it is justified, but he must have acted for the reason specified by the justification. Only if a defendant proves that he acted for that reason can one infer a desirable character trait. Otherwise, room is left to infer that he was at least negligent with respect to the harm. Suppose that *D* shoots his mortal enemy *V* as *V* approaches him. Further suppose that unbeknownst to *D*, *V* was carrying a pistol in his pocket and was about to shoot *D* with it had *D* not killed him first. *D*'s purpose was to kill *V*, regardless of self-defense. Consequently, one may still infer the undesirable character trait of being disposed to kill one's enemies.

Unlike mistakes about the elements of the definition of crimes which may be unreasonable, the law usually requires that mistakes relevant to justifications be reasonable. On the character view, the reason may be to make sure the person was actually acting for the reason the justification provides. Suppose *V* approaches *D* with a hot dog in plain view in his hand and *D* shoots him. At trial, *D* claims that he thought the hot dog was a piece of lead pipe and that *V* intended to beat him with it, so he killed *V* in self-defense. The unreasonableness of the mistake makes it possible that *D* had the undesirable character trait of killing enemies or at least of a careless disregard for their lives. In some areas, the law may simply declare that no mistake can be plausible enough to evidence a desirable character trait. For example, the *Model Penal Code* does not allow a defense of mistake of age for rape of a person under the age of ten years.[20] It is simply not plausible that a person who committed such an act had the permissible disposition to have intercourse only with mature consenting persons.

4. MENTAL ABNORMALITY

The Humean character view of criminal responsibility most differs from the current law with respect to its treatment of mental abnormality excuses. Given the current problems with mental abnormality defenses in the criminal law, this divergence does not automatically signify a defect in the theory. Three central points may be made about the general approach of the Humean character view. First, whether the accused could have helped doing what he did, whether he had the capacity to conform to the law, is itself irrelevant to an excuse. Second, it is irrelevant because the conduct of a mentally abnormal person may be good evidence of an undesirable character trait justifying a social response. Consider, for example, a psychopath who is fascinated by the sounds people make as they take their last breaths while being strangled to death.[21] If he goes around strangling people so he can hear this sound, then he obviously has an undesirable character trait and a social response is appropriate. Hence, he has no excuse. Third, although psychological disorders enduring to the time of trial do not excuse, temporary ones disappearing before trial almost always do so. Temporary insanity prevents the conduct from indicating a character trait – un undesirable disposition the actor still has.

---

[20] Sec. 213.6 (1).

[21] Richard B. Brandt, *Ethical Theory* (Englewood Cliffs, N.J.: Prentice-Hall, 1959), p. 522.

Many people would reply that convicting and punishing the mentally abnormal would be unjust. However, the Humean character view does not necessarily require that the mentally abnormal be punished. Indeed, if punishment would not be effective in correcting or eliminating the undesirable character traits, then punishment would not be an appropriate social response. For many persons who commit wrong acts, punishment is an appropriate response because it corrects their character trait or prevents the development or expression of similar character traits of others. For some people, among them many of the mentally abnormal, another form of social response may be more effective and appropriate. The general point is that social response to an undesirable character trait need not be of only one kind. It need not be fixed by the method for determining an undesirable character trait, for example, by violation of the criminal law.

The most interesting aspect of the Humean character view is that it offers a third approach in the current debate about punishment and treatment. The issue has generally been framed as between (1) a thoroughgoing attempt to treat dangerous persons without any consideration of excuses at the conviction stage and (2) a punishment system incorporating the predominant view's requirement that those who are punished have had the capacity and a fair opportunity to conform to the law.[22] The Humean character view is concerned to respond to undesirable character traits, but it does not eliminate excuses. As indicated above, defenses of lack of mens rea, accident, mistake, abandonment of attempts, and justifications would still have a place in the criminal law, along with others not discussed, such as duress. Nonetheless, some forms of mental abnormality and perhaps other conditions which do not prevent the inference of an undesirable character trait would no longer excuse. The choice of social response would then be determined by its effectiveness in correcting or pre-

[22] See generally, Barbara Wooton, *Crime and the Criminal Law* (London: Stevens & Sons, 1963); Hart, *Punishment and Responsibility*, chap. 8.

venting the undesirable trait as well as other considerations, such as the cure not being worse than the disease.

Nonetheless, it might be claimed that the Humean view, like the treatment view, would support punishment or treatment without the requirement of an overt act. That is, were it possible to diagnose undesirable character traits before people commit criminal acts, then they are blameworthy and a social response appropriate. This criticism ignores the previous distinction between blame or blameworthiness, expressing blame, and punishment or other organized social responses. Blameworthiness is only a necessary, not a sufficient, condition for punishment. To grant political or legal authorities the power to punish for mere undesirable character traits, which may or may not ever be manifested in overt socially harmful behaviour, unreasonably risks freedom for security. Less drastic measures which do not restrict liberty, as are often provided by school and social counseling, may help people remove such traits before social harm eventuates.

The concern of the criminal law with social harm also explains why, even on a Humean view, the law is not ordinarily concerned with motives. Criminal harm may spring from good or bad motives. A desire for wealth, even greed, is acceptable provided it is pursued in nonharmful ways, e.g., business. The criminal law is concerned with more specific dispositions which produce social harms. Hence, motives are not usually relevant, at least to conviction. At least as the law currently is, a generous disposition to alleviate pain does not justify killing people in pain – euthanasia – although it may be relevant to sentencing.

This paper has not attempted a complete justification of the Humean character view of criminal responsibility but only to argue for its plausibility and general compatibility with the current criminal law. However, it indicates that the Humean character view is worthy of more serious consideration than it has received. It is not only compatible with the emphasis upon mens rea and the distincions between acting purposely, knowingly, recklessly, and negligently, but these elements are important for warranting the inference of an undesirable character trait and distinguishing between the undesirability of the character traits inferred. It seems more compatible with the law of attempts than approaches to criminal law based on producing harm or the dangerousness of acts. It provides a rationale for conviction and punishment for impossible attempts as well as the broad outlines of a basis for the excuse of mistake. It further explains the burdens upon defendants and the requirement of reasonableness in defenses of mistake of law and justifications. It provides a third approach between recognizing the excuse of mental abnormality and abandoning all excuses in a thoroughgoing treatment system without implying punishment or treatment if undesirable character traits may be detected without a person having committed a criminal act. A view with all these strengths is certainly worth being taken more seriously than it has been.

Westminster Institute, London, Canada

[5]

CHOICE, CHARACTER, AND EXCUSE*

By Michael S. Moore

Introduction

Freud justified his extensive theorizing about dreams by the observation that they were "the royal road" to something much more general: namely, our unconscious mental life. The current preoccupation with the theory of excuse in criminal law scholarship (including my own) can be given a similar justification, for the excuses are the royal road to theories of responsibility generally. The thought is that if we understand why we excuse in certain situations but not others, we will have also gained a much more general insight into the nature of responsibility itself. Nowhere has this thought been more evident than in the century-old focus of criminal law theoreticians on the excuse of insanity, a focus that could not be justified by the importance of the excuse itself.

In this paper I wish to isolate two theories of excuse, each of which instantiates its own distinctive theory of responsibility. One is what I shall call *the choice theory of excuse*, according to which one is excused for the doing of a wrongful action because and only because at the moment of such action's performance, one did not have sufficient capacity or opportunity to make the choice to do otherwise. Such a choice theory of excuse instantiates a more general theory of responsibility, according to which we are responsible for wrongs we freely choose to do, and not responsible for wrongs we lacked the freedom (capacity and opportunity) to avoid doing. The second I shall call *the character theory of excuse*, according to which one is excused for the doing of a wrongful action because and only because such action is not determined by (or in some other way expressive of) those enduring attributes of ourselves we call our characters. Such a character theory of excuse instantiates a more general theory of responsibility, according to which the primary object of our responsibility is our own character, and responsibility for wrongful action is derivative of this primary responsibility, our actions being proxies for the characters such actions express.

These abbreviated formulae require much clarification, some of which I undertake in the succeeding parts of this paper (sections I and II). I then compare the merits of the two theories in section III, concluding that the choice theory is correct. Before undertaking any of these tasks, however, something needs to be said about what the excuses are and what a theory of the excuses should look like. The balance of this introduction is devoted to these questions.

* This essay has benefited greatly from the comments and suggestions made by the contributors to this volume. My attention was drawn to the character theory by Peter Arenella's work, and my reasons for rejecting that theory were sharpened by my long-term discussions with Larry Alexander, Heidi Hurd, Sandy Kadish, Herbert Morris, Stephen Morse, and Jeremy Waldron.

First, what are the excuses? Do we seek a theory of moral excuse or one of some distinctively legal excuse? My interest is in the moral excuses, although my ultimate interest is in developing a theory of what ought to be our legal excuses. The connection between the moral excuses and what ought to be the legal excuses is a very tight one on the punishment theories I shall here presuppose to be correct. If one is either a retributivist or a holder of the mixed theory of punishment (of the side-constraint type), so that in either case moral responsibility is at least a necessary condition to legal liability to punishment, then wherever there is a moral excuse (and thus an absence of moral responsibility), there should also be a legal excuse (and thus an absence of legal liability).[1] The substantive criminal law of England and America by and large reflects this dependence of legal excuse upon moral excuse, so that where there is a moral excuse there not only ought to be, but often *is*, a legal excuse as well; however, defending this last, doctrinal proposition is no part of the present undertaking.

Even focusing immediately on moral excuse leaves an ambiguity that requires clarification. The most obvious kinds of moral excuse are the excuses we have for violating moral norms. I also intend to include another kind of moral excuse, however: namely, the excuses morality requires for violating legal norms. Often a condition is an excuse in both these senses, such as insanity or duress. Sometimes, however, morality contains excuses that make sense only in relation to legal norms. Mistake of law is one such moral excuse, for although it is morality that demands that actors without a fair opportunity to acquaint themselves with the laws of their jurisdiction be excused, such an excuse makes sense only in relation to a legal norm.

I have elsewhere classified the moral excuses – and correspondingly, what ought to be legal excuses – into three groups.[2] (1) The first consists of those excuses that show some actor not to have violated some moral or legal norm. This may be because (for instance) although it was movements of his body that were part of the causal sequence that brought about the harm, he didn't will such movements; it may be because, although he did will the movements of his body that allowed the wrong to take place, he didn't himself do the wrong because someone else did; or it may be because we think moral norms to prohibit certain intentions, not certain actions, and he lacked the mental state such norms prohibit, even though his

[1] A retributivist about punishment believes that moral responsibility is not only a necessary condition of state punishment, but that it is a sufficient condition as well. The moral responsibility of an actor makes it not only not unfair to punish him; it also gives everyone else the duty to see that he is punished. A mixed theorist of the side constraint type, by contrast, believes that the moral responsibility of an actor is necessary to state punishment, but not sufficient. On the mixed theory, we neither have a duty to punish the guilty nor is their guilt a sufficient justification for punishment. Some other rationale, such as crime-prevention, typically is used by mixed theorists to complete their justification of punishment. I have defended the retributivist theory of punishment in Michael S. Moore, *Law and Psychiatry: Rethinking the Relationship* (Cambridge: Cambridge University Press, 1984), pp. 233–43, and in Michael S. Moore, "The Moral Worth of Retribution," ed. F. Schoeman, *Responsibility, Character, and the Emotions* (Cambridge: Cambridge University Press, 1987), pp. 179–219. For a discussion of the mixed theory of punishment where moral innocence acts as a side constraint on the pursuit of the utilitarian goal of crime-prevention, see *Law and Psychiatry*, pp. 237–38, 240–42.

[2] Michael S. Moore, "Causation and the Excuses," *California Law Review*, vol. 73, no. 4 (July 1985), pp. 1091–1149.

behavior would have been the appropriate means to satisfying such an intention had he possessed it.[3]

(2) Other excuses admit that the actor did the wrongful act, but deny his responsibility anyway. On the view that moral and legal norms prohibit actions, not intentions, then mistake and ignorance belong here.[4] These are often called "cognitive" excuses, because it is cognition, not volition, that is defective. The other branch of this class of excuses are volitional, in the sense that the actor knew what he was doing but didn't have the willpower to stop himself from doing it. Duress, necessity, provocation, and addiction are common examples of this branch of excuse.

(3) The last category of excuses consists of those excuses in which it is unclear whether moral norms were violated or not. These I call the status excuses, because it is the general condition of the agent (his status) that determines whether or not he is excused. Infancy, insanity, diminished capacity, and intoxication[5] are the main examples. What such conditions commonly betoken is that the individuals in them do not and cannot function well enough for us to confidently liken their "actions" and "intentions" to the actions and intentions of sober, sane adults.

A *theory* of this heterogenous range of excusing conditions should be a general statement that accurately describes all or most of the particular conditions we are confident morally excuse, and that itself has some intuitive plausibility to it in light of some yet more general theory of moral responsibility we think to be true. The two competing theories of excuse I wish to examine make both of these claims for themselves, and it is to these theories that I turn.

I. The Choice Theory of Excuse

What I call the choice theory of excuse is also called the "capacity conception of responsibility," the "responsibility principle," the "voluntarism principle," the "Kantian theory of responsibility," the "value of choice" theory of excuses, the "voluntariness principle," the "personhood principle," and my own earlier label, the "disturbed practical reason" theory of excuse.[6] An early expression of the

[3] The moralist who adopts the Catholic doctrine of double effect will take the view that those norms of morality we think of as "absolutes" – deontological constraints – generalize over intentional actions and not simply over actions. See, e.g., Thomas Nagel, *The View From Nowhere* (New York: Oxford University Press, 1986), p. 179.

[4] Argued for in Moore, "Causation and the Excuses," p. 1097, and in R.B. Brandt, "A Motivational Theory of Excuses in the Criminal Law," eds. R. Pennock and J. Chapman, *Nomos XXVII: Criminal Justice* (New York: New York University Press, 1985), pp. 165–98, at pp. 166–67.

[5] I classify intoxication on a particular occasion differently than addiction (a tendency to become intoxicated) on the following assumption: that being addicted, if it excuses, excuses because of a compelling desire that operates within an otherwise undisturbed mind; whereas being intoxicated, if it excuses, excuses because the intoxicated subject is generally incapacitated from reasoning. On this view intoxication, but not addiction, operates like insanity and infancy – as an excuse of general incapacity (status).

[6] See, respectively, to the labels used in the text: Nicola Lacey, *State Punishment* (London: Routledge, 1988), p. 62; Hyman Gross, *A Theory of Criminal Justice* (New York: Oxford University Press, 1979), p. 137; Sandord H. Kadish, "Excusing Crime," in his *Blame and Punishment* (New York: MacMillan, 1987), pp. 81–106, at p. 88; Michael D. Bayles, "Character, Purpose, and Criminal Responsibility," *Law and Philosophy*, vol. 1, no. 1 (April 1982), pp. 5–20, at p. 6; T.M. Scanlon, Jr., "Quality of Will and the Value of Choice" (unpublished manuscript, 1988), p. 42; George Fletcher, *Rethinking Criminal Law* (Boston: Little, Brown,

theory can be found in Blackstone[7] when he said that the legal excuses of his time could be "reduced to this single consideration, the want or defect of *will.* An involuntary act, as it has no claim to merit, so neither can it induce any guilt: the concurrence of the will, when it has its choice either to do or avoid the act in question, being the only thing that renders human actions praiseworthy or culpable."

Despite its long history and its many current adherents, the choice theory's classical modern expression is to be found in the writings of Herbert Hart.[8] In examining legal excusing conditions, Hart thought:

> What is crucial is that those whom we punish should have had, when they acted, the normal capacities, physical and mental, for abstaining from what it forbids, and a fair opportunity to exercise these capacities. Where these capacities and opportunities are absent, as they are in different ways in the varied cases of accident, mistake, paralysis, reflex action, coercion, insanity, etc., the moral protest is that it is morally wrong to punish because 'he could not have helped it' or 'he could not have done otherwise' or 'he had no real choice.'[9]

Such a theory of excuse is itself but an instance of a more general principle of moral responsibility: "what the law has done here is to reflect, albeit imperfectly, a fundamental principle of morality that a person is not to be blamed for what he has done if he could not help doing it."[10]

This theory of excuse, and its accompanying, more general theory of responsibility, was given two quite different justifications by Hart. Hart's early justification, found in his seminal 1957 paper, "Legal Responsibility and Excuses,"[11] arguably was a kind of rule-utilitarianism. The function or value of having duress, insanity, automatism, etc., be excuses to criminal liability was to maximize "the efficacy of the individual's informed and considered choice . . ."[12] Hart more fully described the good that excuses achieved in the criminal law:

> On this view excusing conditions are accepted as something that may conflict with the social utility of the law's threats; they are regarded as of moral importance because they provide for all individuals alike the satisfactions of a choosing system. Recognition of excusing conditions is

1978), p. 804; Joshua Dressler, *Understanding Criminal Law* (New York: Mathew Bender, 1987), at p. 185; Joshua Dressler, "Reflections on Excusing Wrongdoers: Moral Theory, New Excuses, and The Model Penal Code," *Rutgers Law Journal*, vol. 19, no. 3 (Spring 1988), pp. 671–716, at p. 701; Moore, "Causation and Excuse," pp. 1148–49; Moore, *Law and Psychiatry*, pp. 85–90.

[7] Sir William Blackstone, *Commentaries on the Laws of England*, Chitty ed., vol. IV (London, 1826), p. 20.

[8] See the essays collected in H.L.A. Hart, *Punishment and Responsibility* (Oxford: Oxford University Press, 1968).

[9] *ibid.*, p. 152.

[10] *ibid.*, p. 174.

[11] H.L.A. Hart, "Legal Responsibility and Excuses," ed. S. Hook, *Determinism and Freedom* (New York: New York University Press, 1958), and reprinted in *Punishment and Responsibility*, pp. 28–53. (Subsequent references to this essay are to the reprinted version.)

[12] *ibid.*, p. 46.

> therefore seen as a matter of protection of the individual against the claims of society from the highest measure of protection from crime that can be obtained from a system of threats. In this way the criminal law respects the claims of the individual as such, or at least as a *choosing being*, and distributes its coercive sanctions in a way that reflects this respect for the individual.[13]

Hart's idea here was that choice is a power that people prefer and whose exercise provides substantial satisfactions. It is therefore a good that competes with the good that is crime-prevention. The goodness of choice to people is largely due to the power we all want to predict the future.[14] As Scanlon puts Hart's point here: "The most obvious reason why choice has value for me ... is simply instrumental: I would like what happens (e.g., what appears on my plate) to conform to my preferences..."[15] The way that the excuses of the criminal law further the good that is choice is by protecting unfree, unimpeded choice from criminal sanction; only my free choices will be sanctioned, and knowing that, I can maximally predict what will follow upon my decisions. As Scanlon puts it, if I can "believe that if what happens depends on my subjective response under given conditions then the result is likely to coincide with what I want."[16]

This rationale for having the excuses we do is arguably utilitarian, for it balances off the maximization of one good most people prefer, crime-prevention, against the maximization of another such good, the good that is free choice. It becomes a *rule*-utilitarian rationale once one says, as Hart did, that the attainment of the goodness of choice is not balanced against the attainment of the goodness of crime-prevention in one overall calculation of the good; rather, such calculations are assigned their own "levels" of appropriate domain. The doctrines necessary to achieve a satisfactory level of free choice (once set by separate calculation) then operate as a constraint on the maximization of the good that is crime-prevention.

Hart's second and later justification for the choice theory of excuse – and the way he is usually read today – grounds it in considerations of fairness and justice that are not themselves products of utilitarian calculation. That is, the excuses and the "could have done otherwise" principle they instantiate are seen as deontological, or non-consequentialist, side constraints that constrain the maximization of any utilitarian goals, crime-prevention and choice-maximization included. As Hart himself later recognized, there are constraints "which civilized moral thought places on the pursuit of the utilitarian goal by the demand that punishment should not be applied to the innocent ..."[17] One of those constraints is "that out of considerations of fairness or justice to individuals we should restrict even punishment designed as a 'preventative' [i.e., utilitarian punishment] to those who had a normal capacity and a fair opportunity to obey."[18]

[13] *ibid.*, p. 49 (emphasis in original).
[14] *ibid.*, p. 49.
[15] Scanlon, "Quality of Will," p. 25.
[16] *ibid.*
[17] Hart, *Punishment and Responsibility*, p. 80.
[18] *ibid.*, p. 201.

As important for our purposes as the justification of the choice theory of excuse is the meaning of the theory. What does it mean to say, "one is responsible only for *free* choice," or that "one is responsible if he *could* have done otherwise"? Although Hart made fruitful beginnings in the unpacking of these terms, more detail than he himself provided is needed if we are to understand the choice theory of excuse.

Take the word "could" in the "could have done otherwise" principle. There are three readings of "could," only one of which is intended by the principle. The first is the weak, or behavioral, sense of "could." On this reading, our abilities (what we *can* do, or, counterfactually, what we *could* have done) are measured by what we actually do. If on some occasion we do run a mile in under four minutes, then on that occasion we *could* run a mile in under four minutes; if on some occasion we run a mile in over four minutes, then on that occasion we *could not* run a mile in under four minutes. This weak or behavioral sense of "could" is obviously not what is wanted in the principle, because it trivializes our abilities into merely alternative descriptions of our behavior. In this sense of "could," a broken clock *could* tell the correct time twice every 24 hours (because it did so); a mechanically perfect clock that was set too fast *could not* tell the correct time (because it did not do so). These are not only not idiomatic usages of "could"; they are nonsensical, because they eliminate the idea of general ability presupposed by "can" and "could." Put simply: it has to be possible that I *can* do some things I do not in fact do.

The second reading of "could" is the strong, or incompatibilist, sense of the word. On this reading, we *can* do some action A only if A is not caused by factors exernal to the will of the actor. On this view, "I could have run a mile in four minutes" means not only that there were no causes sufficient to prevent me from doing it, but also, had I done it, that there would have been no causes of that doing of it (other than my willing to do it, which itself must be uncaused).

I doubt that this is an ordinary or idiomatic sense of the word "could," despite a defense of this sense of the word by no less an ordinary language philosopher than J.L. Austin.[19] Notice that to use this sense of the word in the statement about an accurately set, perfectly functioning clock, "it can tell the correct time," attributes free wwll to the clock. In any case, the issue here is not a question of linguistic usage but of morals:[20] is the incompatibilist sense the right sense to be plugged into the "could have done otherwise" principle in order to make that principle true? I have elsewhere argued in some detail that it is not.[21] Not wanting to devote this essay to another defense of my compatibilist metaphysics, let me therefore only mention the incompatibilist sense of "could" in order to put it aside. The choice theory of excuse as Hart and I have construed it does not require any libertarian metaphysics in order to make it true.[22]

[19] J.L. Austin, "Ifs and Cans," ed. H. Morris, *Freedom and Responsibility* (Stanford: Stanford University Press, 1961).

[20] Argued for in Moore, "Causation and the Excuses," pp. 1143–44.

[21] *ibid.*

[22] A libertarian in metaphysics (as opposed to political theory) believes that human actions are uncaused by any factors external to the will of the actor. A compatibilist, as I am here using the word, believes that choice and causation are compatible, so that the statements "he chose to do that" and "his choice was caused by factors themselves unchosen by him" can both be true of some actor and his action. Correspondingly, an

What is required is a third, compatibilist, reading of the principle, which is this: "he could have done otherwise" is elliptical for "he could have done otherwise if he had chosen to." His choice, in other words, was not made *impossible* by factors over which he had no control; his choice was a cause of his behavior (even if it itself was caused). Moreover, his choice was not made *very difficult* by factors over which he had no control; his choice was what lawyers call an *intervening cause*, intervening between the factors that caused it and the action it caused.[23]

We arrive, then, at the crux of the interpretation of the choice theory of excuse. What makes choices impossible or very difficult? Notice the implausibility of the incompatibilist answer to this question (just to give my favorite dead horse a few more lashes): the incompatibilist thinks that the factors that *cause* choice, being themselves unchosen, *preclude* choice. Discover, for example, that will (choice) is caused by certain complex sorts of brain states,[24] and, presto, you have really discovered that choice was impossible or very difficult: i.e., that either there is no choice (idiomatically, "really no choice") or that all choices are hard choices (idiomatically, "no real choice"). This seems about as plausible to me as saying that once you discover the causes for Lake Michigan (glaciation, etc.), the lake disappears.

Be that as it may, I said we were putting aside incompatibilist views, for (when coupled with deterministic metaphysics) they make *all* choices impossible and thus all actions excused on the choice theory of excuse. Hart's answer was different. What makes choices impossible or very difficult is either an incapacity in the agent or the lack of fair opportunity to use a non-defective capacity. Hart thus subdivides the ability presupposed by his sense of "could" into two components. One relates to the equipment of the actor: does he have sufficient choosing capacity to be responsible? The other relates to the situation in which the actor finds himself: does that situation present him with a fair chance to use his capacities for choice so as to give effect to his decision?

An example perhaps is helpful here. Imagine that someone who is accused of stealing in order to get money with which to purchase heroin proffers his addiction to heroin as an excuse. There are two versions of his excuse that are relevant on the choice theory as Hart construes it. One would be defective capacity: at the time of stealing, his reason was overcome by the compelling desire (construed as a reason-unhinging emotional storm) for heroin. The other would be lack of fair opportunity: at the time of stealing, he was not in the grip of any compelling desire

incompatibilist believes that choice and causation are incompatible in the sense that the two statements just mentioned cannot both be true. (Notice that, on the choice theory of responsibility, a compatibilist about choice and causation will also be a compatibilist about responsibility and causation.)

[23] For an analysis of the notion of an intervening cause, see H.L.A. Hart and A.M. Honoré, *Causation in the Law* (Oxford: Oxford University Press, 2nd ed. 1985). As Hart and Honoré analyse it, for a human action to be an intervening cause it must be "voluntary" in their extended sense of that word, which means not done in ignorance, not done in compulsion, not done while insane, etc.

[24] On the neurophysiology of willing, choice, and self-directed action, see Benjamin Libet, "Unconscious Cerebral Initiative and the Role of Conscious Will in Voluntary Action," *The Behavioral and Brain Sciences*, vol. 8, no. 4 (Fall 1985), pp. 529–66. See also Myles Brand, *Intending and Acting* (Cambridge: MIT Press, 1984).

or other emotion; rather, he coolly foresaw that if he did not get money for heroin, he would not get heroin, and that if he did not get heroin, he would eventually suffer the extremely unpleasant consequences of withdrawal symptoms. His opportunity to avoid stealing was thus less than for the rest of us, for (unlike the rest of us) not stealing had extremely unpleasant consequences for him.

If addiction were an excuse for stealing, on the choice theory of excuse one or other of these variants would have to be true. That addiction is so implausible as an excuse for stealing is due to the implausibility of either of these claims being true. The defective capacity version depends on what many now regard as an implausible psychological story,[25] and the lack of fair opportunity version depends on a morally implausible view of how diminished our opportunities must be in order to excuse choices made in such circumstances. Thus, that addiction is a poor candidate for an excuse to stealing is something the choice theory of excuse can explain as well as it can explain why it is a candidate for an excuse at all.

Consider duress as a second example of excuse that allows us to delve more deeply into the nature of the choice theory of excuse. One is legally and morally excused for doing an illegal and wrongful act if the doing of it was caused by the threat of a third party to do something unpleasant to the actor unless he complied with the threat. For example, D_1 is threatened with being shot in the knees unless he drives an IRA gunman to the location of a policeman whom the gunman intends to kill.[26]

Put aside any justificatory readings of duress; assume that being shot in the knees is a lesser evil than is the evil of making possible the death of an innocent. D_1's claim can then only be excuse, not justification. There are two readings of D_1's excuse claim on the choice theory. He can tell a psychological story about how hard it was to even think about resisting the threat because his consciousness was flooded by a fear of being shot and a revulsion at the thought of seeing his own blood. Or he can tell a story of how unfair the gunman's threat made D_1's situation of choice, because the threat attached a consequence to D_1's choosing not to help the gunman that is not commonly attached to the choice of the rest of us not to aid terrorists. His first claim is defective capacity; his second, diminished opportunity.

A reason for favoring the opportunity version over the incapacity version of duress can be seen from the following example.[27] D_2 unjustifiably hates another, X, who is in fact an exemplary individual. Much to D_2's delight, X is dying. He can be saved, however, by a rare drug known to T. T threatens D_2 with T's giving the drug to X, and thereby saving X's life, unless D_2 robs a bank with T. D_2 is not otherwise inclined to rob the bank – he does not need the money – yet the thought of X being given the drug and not dying is more than he can stand. After days of not being able to keep the picture of X's happy, smiling, healthy face out of his mind, D_2 reluctantly agrees to rob the bank with T.

[25] See, e.g., Herbert Fingarette, *Heavy Drinking: The Myth of Alcoholism as a Disease* (Berkeley: University of California Press, 1988), reviewed by me in *Ethics*, vol. 99, no. 3 (April 1989), pp. 660–61.

[26] Cf. Lynch v. Director of Public Prosecutions, [1975–1] All Eng. Rep. 913.

[27] Other reasons for favoring the opportunity versus the capacity version of the duress excuse as it is reflected in current criminal law doctrine are given by Dressler, "Some Reflections," pp. 708–12.

Common intuition – at least if a decade-full of criminal law students is any guide – tells us that D_2 is not excused for the bank robbery. Yet, on the capacity version of the duress defense, why not? D_2 was seemingly as incapacitated by his hatred of X as D_1 was by his fear of his own injury. D_2's faculty of reason apparently did not have the same capacity to make choices as does the reason of those not under such emotional distraction.

To reject D_2's proffered excuse is to reject the idea that this kind of (internal) incapacity can, by itself, excuse. The intuition that guides this rejection is the intuition that people like D_2 are responsible. This intuition of a larger responsibility has apparently motivated both Sandy Kadish's recent favoring of the opportunity version of excuses[28] and Stephen Morse's disfavoring of what he calls the "internal compulsion" type of excuses.[29] Kadish and Morse, like Aristotle before them,[30] are worried that recognizing fears, cravings, instinctual desires, strong passions, or other internal states as excuses unduly reduces one's true responsibility. The child's "something made me do it" is taken to be a bad imitation of an excuse, not the general form of an internally incapacitating excuse.

Freud had a similar insight about the proper extent of one's responsibility in the face of fears like those of my hypothetical D_1 and D_2. In discussing the responsibility of each of us for the content of one's dreams, Freud recognized the temptation to subdivide the self and to attribute the bad stuff to a "not-me," an it or id within me but not identical to me. Freud rejected such a narrow notion of responsibility, disdainfully leaving "it to the jurist to construct for social purposes a responsibility that is artificially limited to the metapsychological ego."[31]

Freud had his finger on what I take to be bothering Kadish, Morse, and Aristotle: D_1's and D_2's responsibility are too circumscribed on the capacity version of the duress excuse because the *self* who is being held responsible (or excused) is itself too narrow. We – the persons or selves who are the subjects of responsibility – are more than the faculty of reason that does battle with the faculty of emotion; we are our emotions as much as we are our reason.

Resolving this worry about internal factors operating as incapacitating excuses thus involves us in some deep questions that go to the heart of the choice theory of excuse. One is the question already mentioned: what self-boundaries does the theory presuppose? Does the responsible self who chooses include any emotions, or is the responsible self who chooses only to be identified with the conscious will, against which all emotions are alien and potentially disturbing (incapacitating) factors? The example of D_2 should incline the choice theorist strongly towards Freud's view: some emotions, at least, have to be included within the self who

[28] Kadish, "Excusing Crime," pp. 101–2, 104–6.

[29] Stephen Morse, "Psychology, Determinism, and Legal Responsibility," ed. G. Melton, *Nebraska Symposium on Motivation 1985: Volume 33* (Lincoln: University of Nebraska Press, 1986), pp. 35–85.

[30] Aristotle, *Nichomachean Ethics*, bk. III, ch. 1, in Richard McKeon, *Introduction to Aristotle* (Chicago: University of Chicago Press, 1973), pp. 387–88.

[31] Sigmund Freud, "Moral Responsibility for the Content of Dreams," in *Standard Edition of the Works of Sigmund Freud*, ed. James Strachey (London: Hogarth Press, 1961), vol. 19, pp. 131–34. I discuss this passage from Freud and others on responsibility in Moore, *Law and Psychiatry*, pp. 343–48.

chooses. D_2's hatred of X is part of him; it cannot be seen as an alien factor that incapacitates *him* from deciding whether or not to rob the bank.

Such an extended view of self may seen unavailable on the choice theory of responsibility, for it may seem that to hold people like D_2 responsible for their actions requires a prior judgement holding them responsible for being who they are (viz., people with these kinds of emotions). This would mean that we are ultimately judging D_2 for his bad character, and – only in light of that judgment – then judging the culpability of his choice.

Whether this is so depends on a second fundamental question the choice theorist about responsibility and excuse must answer: does our choosing agency, the will, include those of our emotions that are part of our self, or are such emotions not part of such agency even though they are part of us? Such a question makes sense because our subpersonal agencies (of perception, cognition, etc.) are not coextensive with our personal selves;[32] it is thus possible that an emotion can be part of us and yet not part of our processes of choice. If this possibility is in fact realized in a case such as D_2, then when we hold D_2 responsible, it is not for his choice to do evil (for his choice was a hard one, given the emotion alien to it), but for the fact that he is evil in his emotional makeup.

If we think through what choosing to act (willing) is, we will find it difficult to keep emotions like D_2's hatred of X separate from D_2's choice to help T with the bank robbery. In its narrowest sense, willing is the initiation of those motor responses we call basic actions – acts like moving one's finger, raising one's arm, and the like.[33] Yet the choice that is the touchstone of responsibility for the choice theorist includes much more than this. It includes the deliberative processes that lead up to the initiation of bodily movements. It is here that intentions and plans are formed in light of the actor's desires and beliefs. It is here that the actor chooses his actions under more complex descriptions than simply "moving my body": descriptions such as "taking my revenge on X" or "eliminating that hateful X." Choice, to be morally interesting, must include not only the initiation of basic actions but also the formation of the intentions and beliefs that guide and motivate the doing of basic actions. We choose our plans (complex actions), and not simply the (basic) actions that execute them.

If this is what is meant by "choice," then some emotions will necessarily have a place in this process. As Sabini and Silver observe: "the emotions are connected to cognition, connected to desires and plans . . ."[34] On this view, the emotions are not invaders of our processes of reasoned deliberation, nor are they preemptors of such

[32] I discuss Dan Dennett's distinction between personal versus subpersonal levels of explanation in *Law and Psychiatry*, pp. 274–75. By "subpersonal agency," I mean those centers of functioning posited to exist at the subpersonal level by the approach to mind known as "homuncular functionalism." A homuncular functionalist believes that the nature of a person's actions and thoughts are best approached by subdividing them into the "actions" and "thoughts" of subpersonal agencies each of who "do" only a part of what the whole person does. See *ibid.*, 414–45; see also Michael Moore, "Mind, Brain, and Unconscious," eds. C. Wright and P. Clark, *Mind, Psychoanalysis and Science*, (Oxford: Basil Blackwell, 1988), pp. 141–166.

[33] On the distinction between basic and complex actions, see Moore, *Law and Psychiatry*, pp. 67–77.

[34] John Sabini and Maury Silver, "Emotions, Responsibility, and Character," ed. F. Schoeman, *Responsibility, Character, and the Emotions* (Cambridge: Cambridge University Press, 1987), pp. 164–75, at p. 168.

processes. Rather, our emotions are both products and causes of the judgements we make as we decide what to do. When we get angry, for example, our anger can itself be caused by judgment: e.g., that an innocent person has just suffered undeserved punishment. Such anger reflects our judgment that something immoral has just taken place.[35] Further, such anger at unjust treatment need not make reasoned choice more difficult. It may instead make choice easier by highlighting what we otherwise might have missed. Anger at injustice is at least as effective as reciting Kant when keeping the priority of justice before one's mind as one decides how to respond.

If all of this is true, then it may seem that Kadish and Morse are right: internal factors like emotions cannot be said to incapacitate our choices, except by an impermissibly narrow view either of who we are or of what our choosing agency consists.

As much as I agree with this in cases like D_2 – where the emotion in question clearly seems both part of him and part of his choice to allow X to die – if all emotions are treated in this way, then there is no incapacitation of choice story to be told about D_1 either. True, D_1 may invoke the 'lack of fair opportunity' branch of excuse, whereby he is excused by his comparative lack of opportunity to avoid doing evil. Yet the diminished opportunity branch excuses D_1 without regard to how hard he found the choice; doesn't the D_1 who is "overcome" by his fear of being shot and his revulsion at the thought of his own blood have some excuse in addition to diminished opportunity?

I don't know the answer to this question. It doesn't matter much in cases of duress, because the diminished opportunity branch of the excuse is available in any event. The answer matters a lot to alleged excuses such as provocation, pathological gambling, or obsessional neurosis, where there is no plausible diminished opportunity story to be told. Common-sense morality seems to reflect the idea that some emotions incapacitate choice, and thus excuse. Such an idea is based on a psychological view that holds that some emotions are not "judgment-connected" in the two ways described before: (1) such emotions are not caused by judgments and so do not take intentional objects (these emotions are decribed as "blind rage" or "free-floating anxiety"), and (2) such emotions cause behavior in the way that anger or fear causes our heartbeats to increase: namely, not by motivating a choice to act but by causing action directly without the mediation of choice and judgment.

My doubts about common-sense morality here stem from my doubts about its psychological suppositions. Are any emotions truly free of corresponding judgments that justify them to the agent whose emotions they are? Is any rage truly blind, or any anxiety without its object? Do the emotions that allegedly cause action by "short-circuiting" choice ever proceed except by a chosen letting go, a chosen self-indulgence?

[35] Being caused by judgment, such emotions obey laws of proportionality, keeping feeling proportional, both in type and intensity, to its object. (Grieve over a dead goose too long and it won't take a Freudian to surmise that the real object of your feeling is something else, something more appropriate to the nature and depth of your feelings.)

A complete exposition of the incapacity branch of the choice theory of excuse would have to answer these questions. Since my purpose is merely to sketch the choice theory for purposes of contrasting it to the character theory, I fortunately can leave them open. We still need to clarify the diminished opportunity branch of the theory before we turn to the character theory of excuse. Think again of my example of the unjustifiably hateful bank robber (D_2). Why cannot such a bank robber make out the diminished opportunity version of the duress excuse? After all, his opportunity not to rob the bank was less than ours: if he did not rob it, this would have had the consequence that his old enemy X would have survived.

What this brings out is the sense of "unfair opportunity" being used in the opportunity branch of the theory. Our opportunities to avoid wrongful action are not *unfairly* diminished simply because they are diminished. The "cost" to D_2 of not robbing the bank should not have been regarded as a cost at all; in reality, it was a benefit that X not die. That D_2 did not so regard it made it psychologically harder for him (the narrow "him") to refrain from robbing the bank. But D_2's *fair* opportunity is not measured by his psychological difficulties, but rather by the objective facts of the matter. Objectively D_2 had a fair opportunity not to rob the bank, even if subjectively he experienced it as a hard choice.[36]

This may raise a doubt about the opportunity branch of the choice theory of excuse: namely, how it differs from justification.[37] For to lack a *fair* opportunity to avoid doing wrong, there must be some (objectively regarded) evil that one is avoiding, and that may seem to imply that one is justified in doing wrong. Yet the opportunity branch of excuse does not collapse into justification in this way. The fair opportunity idea could be called the "failed justification" idea of excuse. Even though an actor does more bad than good in his action (and is thus not justified), he nonetheless may have lacked a fair opportunity to avoid doing wrong if he acted to prevent some substantial evil. Loss of one's bodily integrity by being shot in the knees is such a substantial evil; the survival of a good person is not such a substantial evil, explaining why D_1 but not D_2 may avail himself of the excuse of duress on the fair opportunity construal of it.

II. The Character Theory of Excuse

The choice theory just examined has come to be regarded as the traditional or orthodox view of excuse. There has recently arisen something of a chorus that is critical of the choice theory and instead puts forward a character theory of excuse.[38] This excuse theory is grounded in a general view of moral responsibility. On this general view, the ultimate object of our responsibility is our own character. Our responsibility for actions is derivative of our more fundamental responsibility for character.

[36] Just as D_1 has a diminished opportunity sort of excuse, even if he experienced his choice as an easy one.

[37] I owe the thought to Jeremy Waldron.

[38] The character theory of excuse is normally attributed to David Hume, who held that "actions are objects of our moral sentiment, so far only as they are indications of the internal character." David Hume, *An Enquiry Concerning Human Understanding* (LaSalle: Open Court, 1949), p. 108. Perhaps the foremost modern exponent of the character theory of excuse has been Richard Brandt. See Richard Brandt, *Ethical Theory* (Englewood Cliffs: Prentice-Hall, 1959), pp. 465–74; Brandt, "Blameworthiness and Obligation," ed. A.

On this view, the excuses, in both law and morality, serve a kind of filtering function. We are *prima facie* morally responsible and legally liable for wrongful and illegal acts, but we are only *prima facie* responsible and liable because we do not yet know whether such wrongful acts were truly expressive of our characters. If they are, we are actually responsible and liable; if they are not, we are neither. The excuses, in such a case, serve to filter out wrongful actions for which we are not responsible because they are not expressive of our character. In such a way the excuses reconcile the ultimate nature of moral responsibility – it is for character, not action – with the surface features of our moral and legal ascriptions: namely, that they are for actions and not character.

This theory of excuse, and the conception of responsibility that stands behind it, are both in considerable need of clarification. Let us begin with the more general conception of responsibility and work towards the filtering function of the excuses. First of all, what is it we are responsible for when we are said to be responsible for our *characters*?[39] The most initially tempting answer may be what I shall call the backward-looking behavioral answer. On this view, the character traits we ascribe to people are simply general descriptions of past actions. To be courageous is to have acted courageously in the past, to be honest is to have acted honestly in the past, etc.

One might also call this the verificationist idea of character, because it takes usual evidence of character – past behavior – to be character itself, in the usual reductionist style of verificationism. What's wrong with this idea of character is what is wrong with verificationism generally: such reductions eliminate what they were supposed to explain. Take Michael Dummett's famous question about courage: can X have been a courageous man, when he is now dead and in his entire life no occasion ever arose that called for courageous behavior?[40] Unlike Dummett, I think the answer to this question to be rather obviously "yes,"[41] showing that character is not *identical* to past behavior (conceding that character is often *evidenced* by past behavior).

Melden, *Essays in Moral Philosophy* (Seattle: University of Washington, 1958), pp. 1*ff.*; Brandt, "The Ultilitarian Theory of Excuse," *Philosophical Review*, vol. 78, no. 3 (July 1969), pp. 337–61; and Brandt, *A Motivational Theory of Excuse*. For other defenses of the theory, see also Fletcher, *Rethinking Criminal Law*, pp. 799–802; Robert Nozick, *Philosophical Explanations* (Cambridge: Harvard University Press, 1981), pp. 387–84, 394–96; Bayles, "Character, Purpose, and Criminal Responsibility"; George Vuoso, "Background, Responsibility, and Excuse," *Yale Law Journal*, vol. 96, no. 7 (June 1987), pp. 1661–86; Lacey, *State Punishment*, pp. 67–78; and the as yet unpublished work of Tim Scanlon ("Quality of Will") and Peter Arenella ("In Praise of Blaming: The Centrality of Character," 1989). As Scanlon discusses ("Quality of Will," p. 13), the theory is implicit in Peter Strawson's general analysis of responsibility in terms of our reactive attitudes "not simply at what happens to us or to others as a result of what is done, but at the attitudes of agents towards ourselves or others as revealed [in] their actions." See P.F. Strawson, "Freedom and Resentment," ed. G. Watson, *Free Will* (Oxford: Oxford University Press, 1982), pp. 59–80. Gary Watson also explores this aspect of Strawson's thought in Watson, "Responsibility and the Limits of Evil," ed. F. Schoeman, *Responsibility, Character, and the Emotions* (Cambridge: Cambridge University Press, 1987), pp. 256–86, particularly at p. 265.

[39] For discussion of character, see particularly Brandt, *Ethical Theory*, "Blameworthiness and Obligation," and "The Utilitarian Theory of Excuse." See also Brandt, "Traits of Character: A Conceptual Analysis," *American Philosophical Quarterly*, vol. 7, no. 1 (January, 1970), pp. 23–37.

[40] Michael Dummett, *Truth and Other Enigmas* (Cambridge: Harvard University Press, 1978), pp. 14–16.

[41] See Brandt, "Traits of Character," p. 26.

This suggests a second sense of character; I shall call it the forward-looking behavioral sense. On this view, our traits of character name dispositions to future behavior. Such traits thus can sensibly be attributed to persons whose behavior never realizes them, because such persons can be *disposed* to act in certain ways even if they never do so act because the occasion never arises.

Gilbert Ryle held this dispositional view of character traits.[42] Ryle thought that persons as well as other objects possessed dispositions in his sense: namely, that certain predictions were true of them. A greedy person will (or would), in certain circumstances, act greedily; a soluble object will (or would), in certain circumstances, dissolve in water. But such dispositions are mere behavioral constructs, a part of an agent only in the sense that such predictive and counterfactual statements are true of that agent.

The problem with this view of character is that it is still too exclusively behavioral. Character, on this view, still doesn't say much about the person whose character it is. To remedy this, why not say, as Quine did against Ryle,[43] that every disposition like greediness requires there to be a dispositional *state* of greediness? Further, that the nature of this state may be physiological, so that certain brain states always underlie greedy behavior; and/or the nature of this state may be reflected in our mental experiences, so that greediness involves certain characteristic emotional experiences and attitudes.[44] We don't adopt a purely behavioral view of solubility or brittleness (Ryle's example of dispositions in natural objects), seeking a physical nature to the *states* such dispositions require; so why be so parsimonious about the physical or phenomenological nature of the states that the character traits of persons require?

Character, on this enriched dispositional view, then becomes logically independent of both the past behavior that typically evidences it and the future (or counterfactual) behavior that will (or would) typically manifest it. Unlike the characters conceived of by Dummett and Ryle, character as I conceive it can *cause* the past behavior that evidences it and will or could cause the future or hypothetical behavior that manifests it – just because character so conceived is logically independent of such behaviors.

We now need to examine more carefully the nature of states of character like greediness, honesty, etc., in order to reveal an ambiguity on which the character theorist about responsibility needs to take a position. We know little of the physiology of character, so let us stick with its phenomenology. Freud and contemporary Freudians such as Morris Eagle[45] and Herbert Fingarette[46] have studied the ways in which we constitute our sense of ourselves through owning up

[42] Gilbert Ryle, *The Concept of Mind* (London: Hutcheson, 1949).

[43] Willard Van Orman Quine, *Word and Object* (Cambridge, Mass.: MIT Press, 1960), pp. 222–25. See also David Papineau, *Theory and Meaning* (Oxford: Clarendon Press, 1979), p. 182.

[44] For my general views on how phenomenology interacts with physiology and behavior to get at the deep nature of mental states, see Michael S. Moore, "Mind, Brain, and the Unconscious."

[45] Morris Eagle, "Anatomy of the Self in Psychoanalytic Theory," ed. M. Ruse, *Nature Animated* (Dordrecht: Reidel, 1983), pp. 133–61. For a commentary on Eagle, see Michael S. Moore, "The Unity of Self," pp. 163–202 of the same volume.

[46] Herbert Fingarette, *Self-Deception* (London: Routledge and Kegan-Paul, 1969).

to, or disowning, various emotions, desires, or behaviors. The phenomenological sense of the id is of the "not-me," the ego-alien emotions, thoughts, etc., that (1) come unbidden by my will; (2) are experienced as not-me; and (3) cohere neither with the other emotions, etc., that we have nor with the picture we have of what we are like. Sometimes we repress such ego-alien entities into unconsciousness, and sometimes we defend our view of ourselves through other defense mechanisms like projection. In any case, "we" select some subset of all the traits "we" in some sense possess, and cohere that subset into a view of who "we" are. (The scare quotes are there because one 'we' is arguably different from another.)

One of Freud's persistent theses about this kind of self-inflicted division of self was that the items typically experienced as ego-alien were instinctual desires and emotions such as sex and aggression. This same tendency can be seen in Gary Watson's discussion of character as well, dividing character into appetitive versus evaluational character.[47] Appetitive character is not what we identify as ourselves, but rather as what intrudes upon or potentially disturbs our selves; our self is to be found in that reflective, evaluative self that picks and chooses which of the desires, emotions, thoughts, etc., are worth being considered part of the self.

The choice faced by the character theorist is this: how broadly does he wish to identify character? Does the character of a person include only that which he reflectively identifies as "me"? This would be a narrow and subjective view of character, for it excludes those actions, thoughts, and feelings that the person himself subjectively experiences as ego-alien. Or does the character of a person include not only those items *he* identifies as part of his sense of self, but also those he experiences as an *id*? This we shall call the broad and objective view of character, since it includes more items and does so on a nonsubjective basis.

As we saw earlier, the choice theorist had to decide whether an emotion such as the hatred of D_2 for X was part of D_2's self, and if it was, whether such emotion was part of that part of D_2 that I called D_2's choosing agency. The character theorist faces a similar decision. If his intuition also is that people like D_2 are responsible, then the character theorist must argue that, no matter how ego-alien may be D_2's experience of his hatred for X, nonetheless (1) D_2's hatred is part of his self, and (2) the character trait that D_2's hatred instantiates is part of D_2's character (so that D_2's action can be expressive of D_2's character and thus not excused on the character theory of excuse). This would commit the character theorist to the broad, objective view of character whereby a person's character includes more than that with which he identifies. This allows the character theorist to say (quite plausibly, to my mind) that someone such as Bulstrode in George Eliot's *Middlemarch* has a character marred by greediness, even though Bulstrode's sense of who he is excludes greediness.

Aside from clarifying what character theorists should mean by "character," one thing the discussion thus far reveals is that a commonly perceived difference between the character and the choice theories does not exist. It is commonly thought that the choice theorist cannot hold a person responsible for those of his

[47] Gary Watson, "Free Agency," *Journal of Philosophy*, vol. 72, no. 8 (April 1975), pp. 205–20.

actions that stem from strong emotions because such emotions impede choice (and should thus excuse on the choice theory of excuse), whereas the character theorist can easily hold such persons responsible for such actions because (on the character theory) responsibility for actions is only a proxy for responsibility for the emotional makeup such actions express. Yet, as we have seen, this difference can only exist if we make asymmetrical assumptions about the two theories: namely, we stick the choice theorist with a narrow view of choosing agency while we allow the character theorist the broad view of character. Whereas if we allow each theorist the most plausible assumptions about what choosing and character include, this difference disappears.

One last nuance in our usage of "character" needs attention here in order to keep clear the real differences that do exist between the two theories. Sometimes our talk of character is not about character *traits* or *attributes*; indeed, such talk does not use "character" to name universals of any kind. Rather, we talk of characters doing things, and what we mean to designate is some particular agency. When we speak of characters in novels, we think in this way of character as a particular – in this case, the whole person in the novel. Sometimes we even speak of characters as particular agencies within the person. Bernard Williams notes this usage in his discussion of multiple-personalitied persons.[48] What we seem to mean when we talk of different characters (personalities) operating within one person is that character names a particular, an agency within one person that itself chooses actions. Such a character (as a particular) can itself have a character (as a set of universals).

There is nothing wrong with this usage of "character." I come neither to praise nor to condemn such usage; only to bury it for purposes of this enquiry. For this cannot be what the character theorist on responsibility can mean by "character," on pain of collapsing his theory into the choice theory. If "character" simply names our choosing agency, then responsibility for character is simply responsibility for choice, and there is no debate to have about which is the correct theory of responsibility. For the two theories to be as different as they seem to be, there must be a metaphysical difference between that aspect of our selves we call our character and that part we call our agency of choice. One can heighten the difference between the two theories by claiming that either character or will *constitutes* the self exclusive of the other; to maintain any difference at all between the two theories, however, one must see a metaphysical difference between character and will.

If we are clear about what character is, we next need to inquire whether and in what sense we can be *responsible* for our characters. One debate a choice theorist could have with a character theorist about the excuses is whether there is a responsibility for character at all.[49] If there is not, if there is only responsibility for actions, then the excuses cannot have as their function the isolation of actions expressing bad character; if one is not responsible for one's character, then responsibility for action cannot be derivative of that responsibility.

[48] Bernard Williams, *Problems of the Self* (Cambridge: Cambridge University Press, 1973), pp. 15–18.

[49] This appears to be the point at which Nicola Lacey believes the two theories of excuse diverge. See Lacey, *State Punishment*, p. 68.

This route to denying the character theory of excuse (by denying the character conception of responsibility that lies behind it) is not one I adopt. For I think it is obvious that, in some sense, we are responsible for being the kind of people that we are – i.e., for our characters. This includes responsibility for traits like greediness and honesty, emotions like love, gratitude, guilt, and envy, desires and ambitions, etc. There is a morality of virtue versus vice, not only for academic ethicists but also reflected in the common judgments of daily life. We morally judge our own and others' general moral worthiness all the time.[50]

There is room for disagreement as to exactly how, and in what sense, we are each responsible for our characters. With regard to the "how" question, there are two possibilities: (1) we are responsible for our characters because we *chose* to become persons with such character, or (2) we are responsible for our characters because we *are* (at least in part) our characters. The first possibility, of course, collapses the character conception of responsibility back into a choice conception of responsibility; on this view, the character theory of excuse becomes the idea that we hold persons responsible only for those choices (actions) expressive of their character, *and* we hold persons responsible only for those attributes of character that are themselves freely chosen. Choice ultimately is what matters on such a view, even if character mediately explains why we are responsible for some of our choices.

Despite the distinguished lineage of this first view in Aristotle,[51] there are two reasons to doubt its correctness. One is an empirical worry: do we really have much capacity to mold our characters? We do have some such capacity. We do form "second-order desires"[52] or "ego-ideals" about what kind of person we would like to become, and we have some causal power to effect changes in ourselves in conformity with such desires or ideals. Yet the social science on this issue gives little encouragement to thinking we have much of this power.[53]

Secondly, there is a conceptual worry: who is the "he" who is choosing character? Does he himself have any character, and, if so, was it chosen too? To the character theorist who grounds responsibility for choice and action in responsibility for character, a characterless chooser is an odd legitimator of responsibility for the character he chooses; yet a chooser of character who already possesses character before he chooses invites an infinite regress.[54]

[50] Consider but one example: the moral judgment Morgan Forster invited us to make of Henry Wilcox in Forster's novel, *Howard's End*. Forster persuasively presents Henry as having a fatally flawed character because of his failure "to connect," which defect was itself due to Henry's having a mind like "an unweeded garden." We rightly blame Henry for his flawed character, quite independently of the fact that that character leads him to do actions that are themselves clumsily hurtful to himself and others.

[51] Aristotle, *Nichomachean Ethics*, pp. 395–99. For explications of the Aristotelian view, see Charles Taylor, "Responsibility for Self," ed. A. Rorty, *The Identities of Persons* (Berkeley: University of California Press, 1976), pp. 281–99.

[52] Harry Frankfurt's description of our power to mold our own characters. Harry Frankfurt, "Freedom of the Will and the Concept of a Person," *Journal of Philosophy*, vol. 68, no. 1 (January 1971), pp. 5–20; Frankfurt, "Identification and Wholeheartedness," ed. F. Schoeman, *Responsibility, Character, and the Emotions* (Cambridge: Cambridge University Press, 1987), pp. 27–45.

[53] See Dressler, "Some Reflections," pp. 695–96 for doubts on these grounds.

[54] Seen clearly by Vuoso, "Background, Responsibility, and Excuse," p. 1676; Susan Wolf, "Sanity and the Metaphysics of Responsibility," ed. F. Schoeman, *Responsibility, Character, and the Emotions*, pp. 46–62; and Gary Watson, "Responsibility and the Limits of Evil," p. 281.

One might attempt to alleviate both these worries by what might be called the weak Aristotelian view.[55] This view concedes that our characters are formed initially by processes over which we have little choice or control; however, our responsibility for character comes from our later choices to *maintain* these already formed character traits. Patty Hearst, for example, may have had little choice in the processes that caused her to have the beliefs, desires, emotions, and dispositions that she had on emerging from the Symbionese Liberation Army's closet.[56] Responsibility for that character became hers, however, by the passage of time during which she maintained and/or failed to change those attributes of character. After some period of time, "Tania" was the character for whom Patty was responsible.[57]

The weak Aristotelian view at least sounds empirically more plausible. Even so, the weak view cannot accommodate all the attributes of self that intuitively are the proper subject of moral judgement. Take the emotions, for example. There seems very little that we can do about willing our emotions into or out of being. (Thus the oddness of questions like "why don't you love me?", as if not loving someone was a choice for which one was responsible.) Yet we do hold people responsible for their emotional makeup, including the presence or absence of particular emotions on particular occasions.[58] This inclines me to think that it is the second possibility that captures our responsibility for our character: we are responsible for our character because we are, in part, constituted by our characters.

Since we by-and-large do not choose to become or remain who we are, the sense in which we are *responsible* for our character no doubt differs from the sense in which we are responsible for our actions, which we do choose. "Responsibility" may not even be the right word here, for it is a kind of aesthetic morality that governs our assessments of character. Someone who lacks good character is poorly made, a defective being for a being of his or her kind. Unlike most aesthetic judgments, however, our judgments of character have moral overtones. We shun those with bad characters, avoid their friendship, and disadvantage them in various ways. Moreover, we feel entitled to so treat them because they deserve no better. To the extent that such persons did not choose their character, they are to that extent morally unlucky in being the defective creatures they are. The morality of the virtues, like that governing actions, has a good deal of moral luck built into it.

All of this should be a welcome conclusion to a character theorist about excuse, for if he avoids the conclusion that we are responsible for our character only insofar as we choose our character, then he has conceded nothing to the priority of choice

[55] See, e.g., Nozick, *Philosophical Explanations*, p. 396.

[56] For those too young to remember the Patty Hearst story, the 18-year-old Ms. Hearst was kidnapped by a group of would-be revolutionaries who subjected her to physical abuse, isolation, and indoctrination. At some point it appeared that this heiress to the conservative Hearst family empire succumbed to this indoctrination and believed in the justice of the revolutionary cause. She renamed herself "Tania" and appeared (complete with commando garb and assault rifle) in bank films as a voluntary participant in the revolutionary group's bank robbery.

[57] So argued by Dan Dennett, "Mechanism and Responsibility," ed. T. Honderich, *Essays on Freedom of Action* (London: Routledge and Kegan Paul, 1973), pp. 175–80.

[58] See the discussions of this in Moore, *Law and Psychiatry*, pp. 343–47, in Bernard Williams, "Morality and the Emotions," in his *Problems of the Self*, pp. 207–229, and in Sabini and Silver.

over character as the touchstone of responsibility. We should also be clear that such an answer also concedes nothing to the priority of character over choice, however. Thus far, all that has been established is that we have two different sorts of moral judgments that we appropriately make about persons: we hold them responsible for the actions they choose to do, and we hold them responsible for being the sort of people that they are. Although I have just rejected the claim that moral judgments about character are merely a disguised form of moral judgments about choice, that rejection says nothing in favor of the claim that moral judgments about choice are merely a disguised form of moral judgments about character. And it is this latter claim that the character theorist about excuse must establish.

Before we assess this crucial claim of the character theorist on its moral merits, we have one last clarificatory question to explore about the claim itself. This is the question of the sort of relationship that the character theorist asserts to exist between character and action that makes an actor responsible for action. The character theory of excuse variously asserts that we are excused from responsibility for our actions when those actions do not *manifest*, *express*, *reveal*, or *indicate* bad character; when such actions are not the *result* of, not *determined by*, *explained by*, or are not *attributed to* bad characters; when such actions are not an *exercise* of a character defect; or when such actions are not *evidentiary of* bad character.[59] We need to be clearer about what is meant by these expressions.

Three different sorts of relations might be meant by them. The first would be a logical relation between character and actions that are "in character." On this view, the relation between someone's greedy action on a particular occasion and his greedy character is the logical relation between a particular and the universal that it instantiates. Such a view of the relation commits one to a behavioral view of what character is, and that is sufficient reason for the character theorist to avoid it.

Preferable on this ground is a second view of the relation, which is that it is a causal relation. A greedy action, on this view, is in character for a person only if that action was caused by that person's greedy character. This view of the relation presupposes a nonbehavioral view of what character is, but that is a virtue – not a defect – of this relational view. There is a problem with this second view, however; it stems from the non-discriminating nature of the causal relation. Greedy character in a person can cause any number of behaviors besides greedy actions. My greed can cause my heart rate to go up (e.g., I get excited when I see large amounts of money). It can cause overtly generous behavior (e.g., Bulstrode in *Middlemarch*, who compensates for his greediness by overtly generous behavior). Indeed, any given character trait can probably cause virtually any kind of behavior on a given occasion. For example, suppose Van Gogh was greedy; his greed could have caused him to cut off his ear (e.g., by way of punishment of himself for not being paid enough for a picture).

George Vuoso, who sees the problem, attempts to contain the promiscuity of the causal relation by the pragmatics of explanatory utterance.[60] Vuoso attempts to

[59] All such expressions may be found in Nozick, *Philosophical Explanations*, p. 383; Bayles, "Character, Purpose, and Criminal Responsibility," p. 7; Brandt, "A Motivational Theory of Excuse," pp. 165, 169, 170, 171; Lacey, *State Punishment*, p. 66; Fletcher, *Rethinking Criminal Law*, pp. 799, 801.

[60] Vuoso, "Background, Responsibility, and Excuse," pp. 1672–73.

limit the causal relation to those instances when it would be appropriate to say "that character trait explains the action." Yet we might well say that about any of the foregoing examples, and I doubt that a character theorist holds them to be examples of actions "in character" for the greedy person.

If not, the character theorist has need of a more discriminating relation. The evidentiary relation is his best bet. Some act A will evidence some trait C if and only if not only C causes A, but also states of type C typically cause events of type A. Effects are evidence of their causes only when there is some general connection between the *class* of events that includes the effect and the *class* of events that includes the cause. Evidentiary inference is the more discriminating relation sought by the character theorist. Then acts of refusing to give to charities, forcing poor debtors to pay, paying employees as little as possible, etc., are acts "in character" for the greedy person; lopping off one's ear, or giving away all of one's money, are not acts "in character" for some greedy person even if they happen on some occasion to be caused by his greed.

This last clarification allows us to pinpoint what are and are not the differences between the two theories of excuse. One difference that does not exist is the difference between "historical" and "mesh" theories.[61] That is, one cannot contrast the character theory to the choice theory on the ground that the first is concerned only with the "mesh" (or logical fit) of action with the actor's character and not with any historical inquiry into an action's genesis. The nonbehaviorist account of character, and the evidentiary account of the relation between character and actions "in character" makes the character theory focus on an action's genesis too.

The difference between the two theories has to be in the kinds of causes of action they each find to be the touchstone of responsibility: character or choice. Whether there is any difference between the two theories boils down to the question of whether there is any difference between a person's character and his choices. On the assumption that choices are possible only if a person has and exercises a choosing agency (will), the question is whether there is a difference between a person having a character and a person having a will. The evidentiary relation just discussed seems to isolate just such a difference: any action evidences the possession of a will, because a will can typically will anything and still be a will. But as we have seen, while a character *can* cause any action, to be possessed of a character precludes the possibility that one's character can *typically* cause any class of actions equally well. Characters, to be characters, can only typically cause some classes of actions, but not others. Character in this sense is inherently general, requiring typical causal connections to classes of actions; will and the choices that issue from it are in this sense particular, being equally capable of causing any particular act and not being tied to any general class of actions.

[61] For the contrast between "historical" versus "mesh" theories of responsibility, see John Martin Fischer, "Responsiveness and Moral Responsibility," ed. F. Schoeman, *Responsibility, Character, and the Emotions*, pp. 81–100, at 103–5. Fischer is a choice theorist (his "reasons-responsiveness" test being his way of measuring free choice) who criticizes certain character theorists (Frankfurt, Watson) for being ahistorical in the sense indicated in the text.

III. Character versus Choice as the Touchstone of Responsibility and Excuse

Perhaps the place to start in assessing the moral merits of the two theories of excuse is with the main arguments put forward by the character theorists in favor of their theory. Unfortunately, of the five main arguments, four are irrelevant to the moral issue I wish to raise. Let me mention them, if only to put them aside.

One is the argument that proceeds from utilitarian (or, more broadly, consequentialist) theories of punishment. Richard Brandt[62] and Nicola Lacey[63] both make arguments of this type in favor of the character theory of excuse, Brandt from his rule-utilitarian theory of punishment and Lacey from her non-utilitarian but consequentialist theory of punishment. Briefly, the argument is that the preventive goals of punishment do not require its infliction on those whose actions have not manifested bad character, because such persons are not dangerous nor can their punishment have any significant deterrent effect. It is not clear to me that the character theory of excuse would better serve crime-prevention goals than would the choice theory. But in any case, the argument for me is a non-starter since it proceeds from an unacceptable theory of punishment. At the very least, moral innocence should operate as a side constraint on the pursuit of goals like crime prevention; what we need is a theory of excuse that tells us when someone is morally innocent. These utilitarian and consequentialist arguments do not tell us that, so we may put them aside.

A second argument, one that also does not address the moral issue about excuses focused for us by the mixed and retributivist theories of punishment, is the argument of Michael Bayles and others which is designed to show how well the character theory fits the legal excuses that presently exist in American law.[64] This is an exercise in doctrinal exegesis that is relevant to deciding what theory of excuse our present law comes closest to instantiating. It is not an exercise capable of answering the normative question of which theory of excuse our law ought to recognize.

A third argument in favor of the character theory is by far the major consideration which in fact motivates character theorists to adopt their theory.[65] This is the argument that proceeds from hard determinist premises. The assumption is that the choice conception of responsibility is in trouble because it is hostage to the questionable truth of libertarian (Strawson: "panicky") metaphysics; if determinism turns out to be true, the choice conception is assumed to have the unhappy implication that no one is responsible for anything. Whereas, the

[62] See particularly Brandt, "A Motivational Theory of Excuses," pp. 184–94.

[63] Lacey, *State Punishment*, pp. 65–72.

[64] Bayles, "Character, Purpose, and Criminal Responsibility."

[65] See Lacey, *State Punishment*, pp. 65, 73; Vuoso, "Background, Responsibility, and Excuse"; Strawson, "Freedom and Resentment"; Scanlon, "Quality of Will"; Watson, "Responsibility and the Limits of Evil"; Fletcher, *Rethinking Criminal Law*, pp. 801–2; Nozick, *Philosophical Explanations*, pp. 393–96. Of the character theorists, only Richard Brandt and Peter Arenella see clearly that a characterological conception of responsibility has no advantage over a choice conception in answering the hard determinist. See Brandt, "A Motivational Theory of Excuse," p. 172; Arenella, "Character, Choice, and Moral Agency," *Social Philosophy & Policy*, vol. 7, no. 2 (Spring 1990).

character theorist thinks, responsibility can be preserved by his theory even in the face of determinism. So long as he rejects Aristotle's notion that we are responsible for our characters because we choose them, and sticks to the idea that we are responsible for our characters because we are our characters, he escapes any threat from determinism. For his idea of responsibility does not depend on an actor's choices being free. Rather, he can happily admit that responsible choices are caused by character, and that character in turn is caused by factors not themselves chosen by the actor. By *his* idea of responsibility, the actor is responsible for any actions in character just because he is his character. This is known in the trade as the "character-stop" answer to determinism.[66]

There is nothing wrong with the character-stop strategy. This is why that part of morality known as the theory of the virtues is not hostage to the falsity of determinism. However, the character theorist overlooks the fact that the choice conception of responsibility has an answer just as good to the hard determinist: we are at least in part the agency that chooses whether to act or not; that agency's choices can themselves exist even if caused by factors external to the will; it would make choice a very peculiar event if it has to be uncaused in order to exist; there is no persuasive argument showing that choices have this peculiar feature; and the fact that some people find such arguments persuasive can be explained in ways having nothing to do with the truth of the arguments in question. I and others have sought to draw this argument out in detail, and the conclusion – that compatibilism between choice and causation is true – is far from being problematic and worrisome within philosophy, but is now a kind of philosophical orthodoxy. As one not very sympathetic philosopher has recently observed, "compatiblism, as a philosophical position, has become complacent."[67]

Any argument for the character theory proceeding from that theory's supposed advantage in answering hard determinism had better first show why the philosophical orthodoxy about compatibilism is false. Since none of the character theorists undertake this uphill struggle, we should ignore arguments for the character theory built on this shaky metaphysical base.

A fourth argument for the character theory proceeds from a very general intellectual fashion prevalent today. This I have elsewhere called "interpretivism."[68] Briefly, the idea is that moral questions (if not the explanatory questions of social and even natural science) are interpretive questions, questions that seek the best interpretation of various social practices. To ask what responsibility is, or when a person is responsible, is to ask what the best interpretation of the "blaming stories" prevalent in our society might be. The character theory of excuse appears to be favored by interpretivists because such a theory requires "more story" than

[66] For a contemporary use of the character-stop argument, see Nozick, *Philosophical Explanations*, pp. 395. The character-stop argument has not been without its critics. See, e.g., John Hospers, "Meaning and Free Will," *Philosophy and Phenomenological Research*, vol. 10 (1950), pp. 307–30.

[67] Ferdinand Schoeman, "Introduction," *Responsibility, Character, and the Emotions*, p. 5. Schoeman appears to favor the character theory of excuse (see *ibid.*, pp. 2–3), perhaps because he is not so convinced of the truth of compatibilism.

[68] Moore, "The Interpretive Turn in Modern Theory: A Turn for the Worse?," *Stanford Law Review*, vol. 41, no. 4 (April 1989), pp. 871–957.

does the choice theory. That is, to see whether an action expresses the agent's character requires a longer, more complete narration of what sort of person, in general, he is; whereas to see whether an action was freely chosen by an agent seemingly requires a more limited enquiry into his capacities and opportunities at the moment of acting.

It is hard to get a handle on just what this argument comes to. Even if one's metaethics commits one to viewing moral reasoning as storytelling and -retelling, why should one prefer "more story"? Are not "short stories" an appropriate genre? The interpretivists here sound like the psychiatrists of the 1950s who criticized the M'Naughten definition of insanity on the ground that it did not allow them to tell their psychiatric stories.[69] In both cases, we should like to know why the stories someone wants to tell are better because they are closer to some relevant truth.

It is a fifth kind of argument in favor of the character theory of excuse that raises the relevant issues. Consider George Fletcher's nonutilitarian appreciation of the need for this kind of argument:

> An inference from the wrongful act to the actor's character is essential to a retributive theory of punishment. A fuller statement of the argument would go like this: (1) punishing wrongful conduct is just only if punishment is measured by the desert of the offender, (2) the desert of the offender is gauged by his character – i.e., the kind of person he is, (3) and therefore, a judgment about character is essential to the just distribution of punishment.[70]

It is the second premise, of course, that the character theorist must defend.

Despite her consequentialist leanings (and her resulting disavowals of any intent to answer the question of moral blameworthiness), Nicolas Lacey presents some defense of this essential premise. She defends the moral view that "it is unfair to hold people responsible for actions which are out of character . . . fair to hold them so for actions in which their settled dispositions are centrally expressed."[71] In order to test the moral correctness of these conclusions, we should construct examples of two kinds: (1) an actor freely chooses to do wrong (i.e., he had the capacity and a fair opportunity not to so choose), and yet the action is "out of character" for that actor; (2) an actor's behavior is good evidence for a settled disposition (character) of a bad kind, and yet he has not (yet) chosen to act on that disposition. If Lacy is right, we ought to find it fair to punish the second but not the first, because the first but not the second has a moral excuse. However, I shall contend that we rightly find it fair to punish the first but not the second, because we rightly think the second but not the first to have a moral excuse.

[69] See the discussion in Moore, *Law and Psychiatry*, p. 228. Because the M'Naughten test required that a defendant be unable to know either the nature and quality of his action or that it was wrong in order to be excused by reason of insanity, many psychiastrists were frustrated by the lack of fit of their "stories" (psychiatric explanations) and the story the law required them to tell. In criticizing the M'Naughten test on this ground, what they overlooked was why the law should care that their story didn't fit the law's concerns about responsibility and blame.

[70] Fletcher, *Rethinking Criminal Law*, p. 800.

[71] Lacey, *State Punishment*, p. 68.

As an example of the first kind, consider the well-publicized killing of Bonnie Garland by her jilted boyfriend, Richard Herrin.[72] Bonnie was an undergraduate at Yale; Richard was a graduate student there. Richard had not had much experience with women, and he found Yale a lonely and alien place. He had grown up in the *barrio* of East Los Angeles, but had succeeded at getting good grades and was, by all accounts, a stunning success. He early and heavily committed himself emotionally to Bonnie once a romance had begun between them. Before too long, she found his neediness off-putting and sought to break off the relationship. Like many people whose kindness makes them weak and unintentionally cruel, she couldn't bring herself to break it off with Richard cleanly. He accordingly felt misled, hurt, and frustrated by her attempt to let him down gradually.

Staying over at her parents' house one night, Richard decided he couldn't stand it any more. He went down to the basement, looking around for something with which to kill her. He found a claw hammer and proceeded upstairs to her room with it. Finding her asleep, he beat her to death with the hammer. He had planned to commit suicide after the act, but found he could not bring himself to do it and instead sought out some Christian counseling.

Richard had the capacity not to choose to kill Bonnie, and he had a fair opportunity to exercise that capacity. Nonetheless, he chose to kill her. For that, to my mind, he fully deserved the eight to twenty-five year sentence he received for Bonnie's killing. Yet a character theorist should find this conviction unfair, for the act was out of character for Richard. Richard himself felt that way about his sentence:

> Herrin: I feel the sentence was excessive.
>
> Gaylin (a psychiastrist interviewing Herrin in prison): Let's talk about that a little.
>
> Herrin: Well, I feel that way now ... Considering all the factors that I feel the judge should have considered: prior history of arrest, my personality background, my capacity for a productive life in society – you know, those kinds of things – I don't think he took those into consideration. He looked at the crime itself ... This being my first arrest and considering the circumstances, I don't think I should have been given eight to twenty-five years.[73]

Richard wanted credit for an otherwise good – even, in some ways, exemplary – life. He felt it was unfair to have eight years of his life taken from him because of a momentary choice that was at odds with who he really was and how he both had lived and would live his life. His choice to kill Bonnie in the middle of a sleepless night must have looked, in retrospect, like an unbelievable action for him.

Yet is there any doubt at all that Richard Herrin was seriously culpable for his choice? No matter how out of character this act was for him behaviorally, no matter how alien it seemed to him phenomenologically, *he* horribly violated another's

[72] The facts below are taken from William Gaylin, *The Killing of Bonnie Garland* (New York: Penguin Books, 1983).

[73] *ibid.*, p. 325.

rights at a single point in time. His generally good character puzzles us, because we don't understand very well how a generally kind, non-violent (if somewhat weak) individual could do what he did. But such explanatory puzzlement is not accompanied by a similar puzzlement about his responsibility: his clear choice to do evil is sufficient to make him very culpable.

Character theorists have two responses to such examples. They might deny that someone like Herrin is culpable. Or they could deny that Herrin's action was really out of character. I shall first deal with the second kind of response.

A character theorist might think that Richard Herrin really did have bad character that was evidenced by his choice to kill Bonnie – but it was a *hidden* character defect. Yet the character theorist has to be careful here, lest "hidden character defect" become her label for "free choice." "Character," as we have seen, has to mean something considerably more general than merely a disposition to do the particular act done – on pain of this kind of collapse of the character theory into the choice theory. By "bad character," Lacey (for example) means a settled hostility to, rejection of, or indifference to the values of the community that the criminal law exists to protect and foster.[74] Richard Herrin had no such settled hostility, indifference, or rejection, so presumably he would be included by Lacey in the category of those excused: "To punish those who have exhibited no such hostility [to the values protected by the criminal law] would be to fly directly in the face of those values themselves. . . ."[75]

Any theory of excuse that has an implication that people like Richard Herrin ought to be excused is a bad theory of excuse. Those character theorists opting for the first response above (denying that Herrin was responsible) obviously disagree. Their disagreement seems to me to be motivated by two intuitions, one metaphysical and the other moral. The metaphysical intuition is that it wasn't really Richard that did the killing, because who Richard is is guided by his character so that an act truly out of character was no act of Richard's. Lacey appears to adopt this idea when she holds that the criminal law should "respond punitively only to actions which are in a real sense [the actor's] *own* . . ."[76] She appears to equate this with actions centrally expressive of settled features of the actor's character. Elsewhere, Lacey elaborates that the criminal law should "treat seriously the individuality and sense of identity of each citizen by responding punitively only to actions which are genuinely expressive of the actor's relevant disposition: with which the agent truly identifies, and can call her own."[77] If this means what it seems to mean – what I have called the metaphysical intuition that actions we do are not *our* actions unless they are in character for us – then it is hostage to a very problematic theory of personal identity. This is the theory that holds character to swamp both spatiotemporal contiguity and unified consciousness as the touchstone of personal identity.[78] On this theory, we are only our

[74] Lacey, *State Punishment*, pp. 189–90.

[75] *ibid.*, p. 189.

[76] *ibid.*, p. 71.

[77] *ibid.*, p. 77.

[78] For a discussion of these three factors as determining personal identity, see Michael Moore, "The Unity of the Self," ed. M. Ruse, *Nature Animated* (Dordrecht: Reidel, 1982), revised and reprinted as chapters 3 and 11 of Moore, *Law and Psychiatry*.

character, a conclusion that has two startling implications. First, when "we" radically change our character over time, we literally become someone else – not just another kind of person, but a different person. Second, multiple-personalitied persons are not single persons with multiple characters; they are rather many persons with one character each. This allowance of the possibility that many persons can inhabit one body – either over time or even at one time – raises havoc with some basic metaphysical, moral, and legal ideas that are difficult to imagine giving up.[79] One of those ideas is just the sort of thing Lacey is apparently willing to abandon: namely, how we individuate and attribute basic actions to persons. Normally we do this by the body involved in the action: one movement by one body, one basic action. Yet multiple persons (characters) acting through one body could yield a variety of possibilities: several actions, if the movement was in character for several characters; one action, but by "someone" other than the person at home at the time the action was performed; or no action, if the action was not in character for any of the characters sharing one human body. These implications are so unacceptable that we should not think of character as exclusively constituting the identity of persons – and if we do not think this, then we cannot think that an action out of character is no action of ours.[80]

The moral intuition that may motivate denials of culpability like Herrin's is a kind of "there but for the grace of God go I" intuition, for isolated acts of violence like Herrin's may well seem possible for any of us in the right circumstances. Yet it would still be us, even if we slipped like Herrin slipped... We are all basically good, we hope. Yet if we think about how we would view ourselves in this circumstance, would it in fact be excusing of ourselves, as Richard excused himself? Wouldn't it rather be that we felt guilty unto death for our horrible violation of another? Far from leading to conclusions of excuse, for me this thought-experiment yields a judgment of very heavy culpability when someone like Herrin steps out of his otherwise good character to perform a wrongful act.[81]

I said that there were two kinds of examples with which to test the choice versus character theory of excuse on moral grounds. I now turn to the second kind of example, where there is behavior revealing bad character, but no free choice to do wrong. Virtually any preventive detention example will do – e.g., Dallas Williams, in whom psychiastrists detected violent character traits even though Williams had not yet acted upon them.[82] May someone like Williams fairly be punished even though he has done nothing wrong?

[79] I explore some of these in *Law and Psychiatry*, pp. 147–52.

[80] Perhaps Lacey intends a less metaphysical defense here. To speak of a "sense of identity" is not necessarily to speak of personal identity, for who we *think* we are need not coincide with who we are in fact. Yet then Lacey has no basis for saying that an action out of character is not our action. Rather, such a phenomenological observation can only generate the conclusion that we have disowned (not identified with) one of *our* own actions.

[81] I pursue this thought-experiment in the context of justifying a retributive theory of punishment in Moore, "The Moral Worth of Retribution," pp. 212–16.

[82] See Jay Katz, Joseph Goldstein, and Alan Dershowitz, *Psychoanalysis, Psychiatry, and Law* (New York: Free Press, 1967), pp. 526–35 for the history of the real Dallas Williams.

The question is a hard one for the character theorist. After all, he thinks that we are ultimately responsible for our characters and that action-responsibility is only a derivative of this more basic character-responsibility. If this is true, then why not punish people directly for bad character, since that is the locus of their just deserts? Why punish bad character indirectly, only through punishing actions expressive of it? George Fletcher seeks to answer this question in terms of a value distinct from the justice of the guilty getting their just deserts: namely, privacy.

> The limitation of the inquiry to a single wrongful act follows not from the theory of desert, but from the principle of legality. We accept the artificiality of inferring character from a single deed as the price of maintaining the suspect's privacy ... Disciplining the inquiry in this way ... secures the individual against a free-ranging enquiry of the state into his moral worth.[83]

I mention Fletcher's argument because it illustrates a kind of argument that cannot establish what the character theorist needs to establish here. Much of the literature on "punishment for thoughts alone" is persuasive on why it would be undesirable for various reasons to dispense with the *actus reus* requirement of the criminal law.[84] But our moral question has only to do with the *fairness* of dispensing with the *actus reus* requirement. That punishment would be *deserved* because of bad character alone is something the character theorist seems committed to, however much other values prevent punishment of this class of deserving persons.

Nozick sees the need to escape this seeming implication of the character theory – namely, that people with bad character do deserve punishment directly for their character and not for actions, if any, expressing that character.[85] Yet Nozick's escape is only a statement of the conclusion needed by him: "It is through actions that correct values are flouted; the actions constitute the flouting. ... Since it is flouting that is to be punished, actions are required."[86] Stated this tersely, Nozick's argument says little more than his conclusion. If flouting is a kind of action, then Nozick is by definition correct that only actions can constitute flouting: but why is the action of flouting required for a just punishment? Alternatively, if flouting is not necessarily a kind of action, why isn't the possession of bad character a flouting of the values that show it to be bad?

If the character theory were correct, the answer given to Moliere's Robespierre (when the latter asks why he is being condemned to death) should not be jarring: you are being condemned, Robespierre is told, "because you lack grace." Yet the answer is jarring precisely because no one deserves to be punished for being a poor specimen of humanity. The aesthetic kind of responsibility that we admittedly do have for so much of our characters as are unchosen cannot fairly lead to

[83] Fletcher, *Rethinking*, pp. 800–801.

[84] For example, Lacey's argument in *State Punishment*, p. 199. The criminal law's "*actus reus* requirement" forbids punishment for bad states of mind or bad character; it is necessary for punishment that the defendant performed a forbidden action.

[85] Nozick sees the question clearly (*Philosophical Explanations*, pp. 380–82) before giving his own answer (*ibid.*, pp. 383–84).

[86] *ibid.*, p. 384.

punishment, because we could not have avoided possessing these aspects of ourselves. A choice theorist – even one such as myself who admits that there is such a think as responsibility for unchosen character – can readily say this, because he conceives of the existence of two independent kinds of (and bases for) responsibility. I have yet to see how the character theorist can deny that character-responsibility alone makes it fair to punish, given his notion that character-responsibility is basic and act-responsibility only derivative.

Both kinds of examples point to the choice theory of excuse, for only it excuses where there is no choice, no matter how much bad character may be exhibited (the second kind of example); it doesn't excuse where there is a free choice, however much out of character it may be (the first kind of example). I accordingly reject the character theory of excuse on these moral grounds.

While I find these moral thought-experiments to be conclusive against the character theorist, the latter is not without her own troublesome counterexamples. Her best stem from our apparent responsibility for negligence. The character theorist may think that people who negligently cause harm are morally responsible. Taking that judgment to be secure, she then claims (1) that such responsibility for negligent conduct cannot be squared with the choice theory, and (2) that such responsibility is just what one should expect on the character theory.[87] I shall address each of these two claims separately before returning to the underlying assumption that negligence generates responsibility.

Responsibility for negligence *is* difficult to square with the choice conception of responsibility for the obvious reason that a negligent actor does not choose to do the complex act (such as killing) that is forbidden. True, such an actor does choose to do some basic action, such as moving his finger on the trigger of his gun; and it also may be true that he chooses to do more complex acts (such as hitting a target) through his doing of the basic act of moving his finger. But in the sense of choice earlier described, he does not choose to do the complex action forbidden by morality and law (such as killing the man standing behind the target) because his mind was not adverting to that aspect of his action.[88]

Herbert Hart's attempt to reconcile responsibility for negligence with the choice conception of responsibility results in a considerable alteration of the choice conception. Hart argued that although the negligent actor did not choose to do a

[87] Lacey makes both of these points: she concludes that "negligence liability ... sits unhappily with traditional conceptions of responsibility in the criminal law" (*State Punishment*, pp. 105-6), and that "the link with a possible rationale for negligence liability is obvious" (*ibid*, p. 66) on the character theory of responsibility.

[88] A choice theorist who rejects my notion of choice might deny that we ever do hold people responsible for unchosen actions. Negligence, he might say, is not a *mens rea* requirement like knowledge or recklessness; rather, it is a criterion of wrongful action. As such, the injunction "don't kill negligently" is a shorthand for all the injunctions aimed at more particular actions, such as "don't shoot at a target without first ascertaining whether someone is behind it or not." And those latter acts, he might conclude, are chosen under every aspect that makes them wrongful. The lesser responsibility for negligent (as opposed to intentional) killing is not due to the differential presence of choice, but the differential wrongness of the acts chosen.

Tempting as this line may be, it slurs over the crucial fact that someone who only negligently kills (e.g., by shooting at a paper target without checking for persons behind it) does not choose just that feature of his action that makes it wrongful; in the example given, he does not make a choice one way or the other about checking. It simply doesn't occur to him to check, although it should have.

wrongful act, he had the capacity and a fair opportunity to have chosen not to do it, and is therefore fairly blamable for his non-exercise of that capacity.[89] So long as we individualize the standard by which we judge an actor's behavior so that we can say of him, "he could have done otherwise, given his capacities,"[90] then, Hart urges, we may blame negligent actors with as much confidence as we do intentional wrongdoers.[91]

In accommodating responsibility for negligence in this way, Hart, as he recognized, shifted the touchstone of responsibility from choice to capacity.[92] A choice to do a wrongful act then becomes only one way in which the actor's capacity to avoid evil goes unexercised; inadvertence is another. My objection to this shift is a moral one: it relegates choice to a subsidiary role in our responsibility assessments that our judgments won't support. What makes the intentional or reckless wrongdoer so culpable is not unexercised capacity – although that is necessary – but the way such capacity to avoid evil goes unexercised; such wrongdoers are not even trying to get it right. Their capacity goes unexercised because that is what they choose. Choice is essential to their culpability, not one way among others that they could have been seriously culpable.

Does this mean that when we blame for negligence we blame for character (the second of the character theorist's two claims here)? Interestingly enough, although the choice theorist cannot easily accommodate responsibility for negligence, neither can the character theorist. For the character theorist must bridge two gaps in order to link her theory with responsibility for negligence. The first is the gap between the failure of a negligent actor to advert to the risk that made his action negligent *at the time of that action*, on the one hand, and the *general tendency* of such an actor to be inadvertent about such risks, on the other. Thus, Lacey (for example) urges that we may infer of the actor who makes an unreasonable mistake of fact that "this is a person who systematically, characteristically makes unreasonable mistakes causing danger to the interests of others ..."[93] This may indeed be an inference we may sometimes draw, but the fact is ignored that we hold negligent actors responsible irrespective of whether one can draw such an inference or not. Put simply, judgments of negligence don't depend on any general traits of carelessness; an isolated act of negligence suffices for responsibility for the harm that act causes.

The second gap is between the actor who does "systematically, characteristically make unreasonable mistakes" and the bad character of such an actor. Lacey thinks we can infer from the presence of such mistake-proneness in a person that that person had a "genuine practical indifference to the interests protected by the criminal law," such as the interests of others in their bodily integrity.[94] Again, this

[89] H.L.A. Hart, "Negligence, *Mens Rea*, and Criminal Responsibility," in *Punishment and Responsibility*, pp. 136–57. I earlier adopted Hart's view in *Law and Psychiatry*, pp. 81–84.

[90] A point on which Hart's view of the moral idea of negligence diverges considerably from present law on the subject. See "Negligence, *Mens Rea*, and Criminal Responsibility," pp. 152–57.

[91] *ibid.*, p. 152.

[92] *ibid.*, p. 140.

[93] Lacey, *State Punishment*, p. 66.

[94] *ibid.*

is indeed sometimes an inference we can draw about a careless person, because a general attitude of indifference to others does sometimes explain such carelessness. But one can be careless – even characteristically so – without having a bad character in this sense. Such carelessness can be due to awkwardness and stupidity as easily as indifference. And, again, we blame for carelessness irrespective of *why* one is careless.[95]

Thus responsibility for negligence fits poorly with either conception of responsibility. When we attribute moral responsibility to someone for a negligent act, we cannot base such attribution either on a judgment of culpable choice or of culpable character. Negligent actors may often have both, but to be negligent they need have neither. What this suggests to me is that perhaps negligence by itself does not merit any moral blame,[96] and that its presence in the law has to be explained on purely utilitarian grounds.

Negligence does not exhaust the kinds of moral thought–experiments the character theorist might use to support her theory. The criminal law we have suggests several others.[97] All of such thought–experiments will be of one of the two kinds I earlier distinguished, where bad choice is present but bad character is not or where bad character is present but bad choice is not. (The latter is where negligence allegedly falls.) Unlike my own thought–experiments, of course, the character theorist's will assume there is responsibility in the second sort of situation but not in the first.

In thinking through such thought–experiments, two things should be borne in mind. One is that it is not enough to show that *usually* an inference of bad character can (or cannot) be drawn when moral excuse fails (or succeeds). A theory of excuse has to do better than this, and tell us what it is that always makes us responsible and, in its absence, always excuses us. Secondly, it is not enough to show the presence or absence of bad character whenever an excuse fails or succeeds; one must also show that the presence or absence of bad choice does not stand in that same relation to the excuse in question. After all, bad choices are usually made by bad people, and bad people usually make a lot of bad choices, so it shouldn't be surprising if the two theories overlap greatly when they excuse. Still, they do not always excuse in the same situations. Moreover, even when both theories yield the same conclusions about responsibility, it is important that we understand the reasons on which these conclusions are based. If I am right in this essay, we excuse because culpable choice is lacking, not because the action fails to manifest bad character.

Law, University of Pennsylvania

[95] The extent to which this last statement is true depends upon the degree to which we individualize the standard of care by virtue of which we judge an actor negligent. If morality is like Anglo-American law here, ignoring the different degrees to which people are hasty, awkward, and stupid, then our judgments of carelessness are blind to these different explanations of carelessness.

[96] A conclusion that should be agreed to by character theorists too. See Bayles, "Character, Purpose, and Criminal Responsibility," pp. 10–11, who sees that "on the basis of one careless act, the inference to a careless attitude is less valid," sees that such carelessness "does not indicate an attitude of indifference to standards of care," and concludes that, on the character theory, "the basis for blame [for negligence] is much less sure."

[97] See Dressler, "Reflections," p. 693, n.107, for a partial list of where the law appears to take character into account. See also Bayles, "Character, Purpose, and Criminal Responsibility."

[6]

CHOICE, CHARACTER, AND CRIMINAL LIABILITY

R. A. DUFF

The criminal law appears to focus on actions. It defines certain kinds of action (killing a human being, damaging another's property, driving dangerously . . .) as crimes; a defendant is accused of committing such an action; it is for such an action that she is convicted and punished. Legal theorists, however, often want to search behind these appearances for the "real" or ultimate focus of ascriptions of criminal liability: that for which defendants are really held liable and punished. Criminal liability must, they think, ultimately depend on something deeper than action: on what lies behind or produces the actions for which defendants are formally convicted and punished. In particular, some argue, it must be founded either on "choice", or on "character": what justifies conviction and punishment must, that is, be either the defendant's wrongful choice, or some defect of character that her criminal conduct revealed.[1]

[1] Recent contributions to this debate include: E. L. Pincoffs, 'Legal Responsibility and Moral Character', *Wayne Law Review* **19** (1973): 905–23; G. Fletcher, *Rethinking Criminal Law* (Boston: Little, Brown, 1978), ch. 10.3; M. D. Bayles, 'Character, Purpose, and Criminal Responsibility', *Law & Philosophy* **1** (1982): 5–20; R. B. Brandt, 'A Motivational Theory of Excuses in the Criminal Law', in J. Pennock & J. Chapman, eds., *Criminal Justice, Nomos* **27** (New York: New York University Press, 1985): 165–98; S. Kadish, 'Excusing Crime', in Kadish, *Blame and Punishment* (New York: Macmillan, 1987): 81–106; G. Vuoso, 'Background, Responsibility and Excuse', *Yale Law Journal* **96** (1987): 1661–686; N. Lacey, *State Punishment* (London: Routledge, 1988), ch. 3; J. Dressler, 'Reflections on Excusing Wrongdoers: Moral Theory, New Excuses and the Model Penal Code', *Rutgers Law Journal* **19** (1988): 671–716; M. S. Moore, 'Choice, Character, and Excuse', *Social Philosophy & Policy* **7** (1990): 29–58; P. Arenella, 'Character, Choice and Moral Agency', *Social Philosophy & Policy* **7** (1990): 59–83; S. H. Pillsbury, 'The Meaning of Deserved Punishment: An Essay on Choice, Character and Responsibility', *Indiana Law Journal* **67** (1992): 719–52. I refer to these hereafter by italicised author's name.

I will argue that this "choice or character" controversy, as it figures in contemporary debates, is misleading, since it rests on a false dichotomy. Once each of these apparently competing conceptions of the foundation of criminal liability is appropriately explicated and refined, we will see that they converge towards each other – or towards an account of liability as grounded in actions. I will also suggest, however, that the controversy does reflect a real tension between two different political conceptions of law and the state.

I. RESPONSIBILITY AND CHOICE

I begin with the "choice" conception. This is sometimes related to Kant's view of the "will" as the locus of moral worth, and as the focus of moral appraisal. The moral worth of my action depends, not on its actual outcome (which may be a matter of chance); nor on such "inclinations" as may help to motivate it (which, since they belong to my heteronomous rather than my autonomous self, are not within my direct control), but on whether my "will", which alone is truly mine as a rational agent, accords with the moral law. We might dislike or regret other aspects of a person's character, but only his will is a proper object of moral criticism. A contemporary "choice" theorist, however, though perhaps finding inspiration in Kant, should not rely upon the dubious metaphysical distinction between the "noumenal" and the "phenomenal" self (between the rational will, and other aspects of the self which bear contingently on our actions) upon which Kant himself relied.

Some find a modern Kantianism in Hart's principle that a person is justly punished only if he had the capacity, and a fair opportunity, to obey the law.[2] Now this principle does not found liability on actual choice: indeed, it permits liability for negligence, which does not

[2] See H. L. A. Hart, 'Prolegomenon to the Principles of Punishment', pp. 21–24; 'Legal Responsibility and Excuses'; 'Punishment and the Elimination of Responsibility', pp. 181–83; 'Responsibility and Retribution', pp. 227–30: all in *Punishment and Responsibility* (Oxford: Clarendon Press, 1968).

involve choosing to break the law.[3] Rather, it specifies a minimal condition of liability, which is satisfied alike by a wilful murderer and by one who negligently causes death. That minimal condition could, however, be taken to require the possibility of effective choice: a person has the capacity to obey the law, we can say, only if she would obey the law if she chose to do so, and has a fair opportunity to obey only if she has a real choice of whether to obey or not. Hart also offers a stronger principle which founds liability on actual choice: a person is justly punished only if "he broke the law by an action which was the outcome of his free choice".[4]

Why should criminal liability thus depend on choice? Hart offers one answer. The law is "a *choosing* system" that aims "to guide individuals' choices as to behaviour by presenting them with reasons for exercising choice in the direction of obedience, but leaving them to choose";[5] such a system maximises "the efficacy of the individual's informed and considered choice in determining the future" by making his choice "one of the operative factors determining whether or not" he is punished.[6] Another answer is that choice is the central condition of responsibility.[7] I am properly held responsible, and so can properly be convicted and punished, only for my choices: for what I choose to do, for my action qua chosen. Only these are properly mine as a responsible agent, since only they are within my control.[8] What happens independently of my choice lies without my control: it might be caused by what I do, as when an action has some unforeseen consequence, but it cannot be ascribed to me as its responsible agent.

But what is "choice"? What is it to choose to do *X*, or to bring *x* about? Sometimes, choice involves a deliberative process preceding

---

3 See Hart, 'Negligence, *Mens Rea*, and Criminal Responsibility', in *Punishment and Responsibility*, p. 136.

4 'Prolegomenon to the Principles of Punishment', p. 22.

5 'Legal Responsibility and Excuses', p. 44.

6 Ibid., pp. 46–47.

7 See, Moore: 29, J. C. Smith, 'Some Problems of the Reform of the Law of Offences Against the Person', *Current Legal Problems* **31** (1978): 15–29, 19.

8 See, for instance, A. J. Ashworth, 'Criminal Attempts and the Role of Resulting Harm', *Rutgers Law Journal* **19** (1988): 725–72, 742.

action, producing a conscious decision: I consider my alternatives, and decide to do *X*. But choice as a condition of responsibility cannot require this. Voluntary, intentional, and responsible actions are not always preceded by any such process of deliberation or decision; nor does a claim that someone "chose to do *X*" assert the occurrence of any such mental process.[9] I realise that by lighting my bonfire I might well damage a neighbour's property. If I nonetheless light it, I can properly be said to have "chosen to endanger her property":[10] but that "choice" need not have involved any mental process of deliberation, or any mental act of choosing.

What then does choice involve? A minimal notion of choice can be found in the orthodox "subjectivist" account of criminal fault. Liability requires intention (either direct or oblique) or recklessness (defined as conscious risk-taking) as to every non-fault element of the offence.[11] For, we might say, only given such a "fault element" did the defendant choose to commit, or to take an unreasonable risk of committing, the crime: I choose to bring about, or to take a risk of bringing about, a result that renders my conduct criminal (damage to another's property, for instance) only if I intend, or expect, to bring that result about, or at least realise that my action creates a real risk of its occurrence. If I do not realise even that I might bring a result about, I do not choose even to take a risk of bringing it about: however unreasonable my failure to notice that risk, I am therefore not reckless as to the possible occurrence of that result, and should not be held criminally liable for it if it occurs.[12]

---

[9] See my *Intention, Agency and Criminal Liability* (Oxford: Blackwell, 1990), ch. 3.2, ch. 6.

[10] See Smith, op. cit., n. 7 above.

[11] As in Law Commission No. 177, *A Criminal Code for England and Wales* (London: HMSO, 1989), Draft Criminal Code Bill, cl. 19 (and 18(c)); American Law Institute, *Model Penal Code* (Philadelphia: American Law Institute, 1985) s. 2.02(3) (and 2.02(2)(c)).

[12] See A. J. Ashworth, 'Belief, Intent and Criminal Liability', in J. Eekelaar & J. Bell, eds., *Oxford Essays in Jurisprudence*, third series (Oxford: Clarendon Press, 1987), 1–31, on the "belief" and "intent" principles; Smith, op. cit., n. 7 above: 19.

Knowledge is therefore a necessary condition of choice. I choose to do (to take a risk of doing) *X* only if I know that my action will (or might) amount to doing *X*. But knowledge is not a sufficient condition of choice: if I am to be said to have chosen to do *X*, it must also be true that I could have avoided doing *X* – that I "could have acted differently".[13] We might initially say, however, that a person could have acted differently if she would have acted differently had she chosen to do so,[14] and see this requirement as being implicit in the requirement for a "voluntary act" as a condition of liability.[15]

To claim that choice, in this minimal sense, is even a *necessary* condition of criminal liability is already controversial. That claim precludes liability for negligence. While some theorists accept this implication, however,[16] and others portray negligence liability as a pragmatic exception to the general principle that liability requires fault,[17] we could define negligence as a lesser species of fault: we could say that an agent was negligent if she should have taken care, and would have taken care had she chosen to do so; by portraying it, that is, as a failure to make a choice which she should have made.[18]

That claim also involves an arguable conception of recklessness, as conscious risk-taking. It requires us, for instance, to acquit of rape a man who acted in the wholly unreasonable and mistaken belief that his victim consented;[19] to acquit of murder a man who fails to notice the obvious risk to life which his violent and actually fatal attack creates, even if that failure manifested a callous disregard for his

[13] More precisely what matters is my belief that my action will amount to doing *X*, and that I could avoid doing *X*: I can be said to choose to do *X* even if such beliefs are mistaken. See H. Frankfurt, 'Alternate Possibilities and Moral Responsibility', *Journal of Philosophy* **46** (1969): 829–39.

[14] See Moore: 35; and A. J. Ayer, 'Freedom and Necessity', in his *Philosophical Essays* (London: Macmillan, 1965), pp. 271–84.

[15] See, for instance, *Model Penal Code*, n. 11 above, s. 2.01(1).

[16] For instance Moore: 56–58.

[17] See G. Williams, *Textbook of Criminal Law* (2nd ed.; London: Stevens, 1983), pp. 88–94.

[18] See Hart, op. cit., n. 3 above.

[19] See *Morgan* [1976] A.C. 182; *Cogan* [1976] Q.B. 217.

victim's life.[20] This is, I have argued elsewhere, an inadequate account of recklessness. We should rather explain recklessness as a species of "practical indifference" to the interests of others: an indifference which can be manifested not only in the agent's conscious risk-taking, but also in his very failure to notice a risk he is creating, or in his readiness to form and act on a wholly unreasonable belief.[21]

I will not repeat that argument here. If it is sound, it points away from "choice" as the essential basis of criminal liability, towards the attitudes (the character-traits, one might say) which the agent's conduct manifests. We should focus now, however, on the fact that choice in this minimal sense is clearly not a *sufficient* condition of criminal liability. We should not be held criminally liable for all that we "choose" in this minimal sense to do: for everything that we do knowingly and not involuntarily. "Choice" theorists do of course recognise this point: the question is, however, whether they can explain what more is required for liability without, ultimately, founding liability on "character" rather than "choice". I will argue that they cannot.

II. CHOICE, OPPORTUNITY, AND CAPACITY

Some excuses, such as ignorance or mistake of fact, negate liability by negating "choice" in the minimal sense. But others negate liability for actions which were in the minimal sense chosen: which satisfy the normal requirements of mens rea.

Consider first duress.[22] Duress can justify what would otherwise have been a criminal action: the defendant admits responsibility for what she did (chose to do), and claims that her action was right, or at least permissible. But duress can also excuse: someone who acted

[20] See Miller & Denovan 1960; described in G. H. Gordon, *The Criminal Law of Scotland*, 2nd ed. (Edinburgh: W. Green & Son, 1978), p. 741.

[21] Op. cit., n. 9 above, ch. 7.

[22] See *Draft Criminal Code* (n. 11 above) cl. 42; *Model Penal Code* (n. 11 above) s. 2.09. J. C. Smith & B. Hogan, *Criminal Law*, 6th ed. (London: Butterworths, 1988), pp. 230–38.

under duress can be properly acquitted though his action was neither right nor permissible. One who is excused on grounds of duress, however, surely "chooses", in the minimal sense, to act as he does. One who commits perjury under a threat of serious injury if she refuses to do so[23] knows that she is giving false evidence, nor is her conduct strictly involuntary – she "chooses" to commit perjury. How then can a "choice" theorist explain why she should be excused?

She (and we) might say that she "had no choice": but what would this mean? It sometimes means that there was no rational or acceptable alternative; it would have been wrong or stupid to resist such a threat. For to choose to do *X* is to do *X rather than* some *Y* which is a genuine alternative; and *Y* can be a genuine alternative only if there is some reason to do *Y* rather than *X*. I do not choose to throw a lifebelt to a drowning person, or to move out of the way of an oncoming bus, since there is "every reason" to do such things, and no reason not to; "there is no alternative".[24] If the reason I have for doing *X* is overwhelmingly stronger than any reason there is to do *Y*, we might then naturally say that I "had no choice". A bank clerk who hands over money at gunpoint might thus say that he "had no choice": meaning that it would have been folly to endanger his life in order to protect the money. In these kinds of context, however, "I had no choice" functions as a justification: we must ask what it could mean as an excuse.

Or consider mental disorder as an excuse. In cases which satisfy the

---

[23] See *Hudson & Taylor* [1971] 2 Q.B. 202.

[24] "*A* chose to do *X*" implies that there *was* a genuine alternative, but not necessarily that he saw it as such. Someone indifferent to the interests of others might not see the fact that his action will endanger them as a reason for acting differently: but if *we* see some other, safer action as a genuine alternative which he had reason to do, *we* can properly say that he chose to endanger them (see op. cit., n. 9 above, ch. 4.2–3). This feature of the concept of choice is missing from the minimal notion of choice as requiring only awareness of the probable results of my voluntary actions, but is implicit in the "choice" conception of criminal liability. For if the *X* that I do is criminal, and I could do some non-criminal act instead, that act is in the law's eyes a genuine alternative: thus, given the conditions of knowledge and voluntariness, I choose to do *X*.

M'Naghten Rules as interpreted by English courts, the defendant did not even "choose" in the minimal sense to break the law: someone who does not know the empirical "nature and quality" of his act does not choose it under the description under which it is criminal; one who does not know that it is "wrong", i.e., illegal, does not choose "to break the law".[25] But if the defence extends beyond these narrow limits, it acquits some who did in the minimal sense choose to break the law. Someone who is acquitted because he lacked a "substantial capacity either to appreciate the criminality [wrongfulness] of his conduct or to conform his conduct to the requirements of law",[26] or because his offence was "attributable to the severe mental illness or severe mental handicap" that he was then suffering[27] might well have known the facts that rendered his conduct criminal; it might be true too that he would not have acted thus had he chosen not to: he is thus to be acquitted though he might have chosen, in the minimal sense, to act as he did. How can a "choice" theorist explain this?

Two kinds of account seem possible. First, we might suggest that excusable actions done under duress, or under the influence of mental disorder, are not really "chosen": someone acting under duress, for instance, acts from terror, not from choice.[28] Now we might well say this. But it applies a richer concept of choice than the minimal notion sketched above: so what could this richer concept be?

One possibility is this. To say that a person "chose to do *X*" is to say not merely that she knew that she was doing *X* and did not act involuntarily; nor merely that she in some sense "wanted" to act as she did (for that much is true of one who acts under duress or while seriously disordered): but also that her action reflected a rational judgment that *X* was, if not the best, at least a good or reasonable

---

[25] *M'Naghten* [1843] 10 Cl&F 200, 209: *Codere* [1916] 12 Cr.App.R. 21; *Windle* [1952] 2 Q.B. 826; Smith & Hogan, op. cit., n. 22 above, 192–3.

[26] *Model Penal Code* s. 4.01(1).

[27] See *Draft Criminal Code* (n. 11 above) cl. 35.

[28] Compare Fletcher, p. 811, on "morally involuntary responses to danger": "when individuals merely react rather than choose to do wrong, they cannot fairly be held accountable".

thing to do under those circumstances, given the available alternatives. That is why we might not talk of "choice" if the agent acted out of sheer terror at some immediate threat: we would not take his action to reflect any rational judgment or weighing of alternatives. Likewise, we might not ascribe "choice" to the seriously disordered agent, if we think that his actions reflected no such rational judgment: if, that is, we suppose that he was unable either to engage in such practical reasoning or to conform his conduct to any judgments he might make.

If we were to follow this line, we would need to ask whether the "rational judgments" that choice is now said to involve can be separated from what we might properly call the agent's character. This richer conception of choice might, for example, lead us towards Aristotle's concept of *prohairesis* (usually translated as "choice"). An action flows from *prohairesis* only if it flows from the agent's conception of the good, only if it is done for what he sees to be good reason, because it serves values to which he is committed.[29] Not all actions done knowingly and not involuntarily are "chosen": an impulsive act done from immediate fear or anger is not "chosen"; a weak-willed person "acts with appetite but not with choice".[30] But such an account cannot help the "choice" theorist, since it relates "choice" to the agent's character – to that structure of attitudes, concerns, and values from which the particular action flows: whether an action is "chosen", that is, depends on its relationship to central aspects of the agent's character.

However, it could not anyway be plausibly claimed that we should be criminally liable only for what we choose, in this richer sense, to do. For my criminal act might reflect, not some rational judgment of value, but my weakness of will: I commit an act of vandalism or a petty theft, not because I really think this is worth doing (I might regret the action as soon as it is done), but because I give in to a momentary impulse or temptation.[31] I am still surely, on any plausible

[29] See Aristotle, *Nicomachean Ethics* III.2–4, VI–VII.

[30] Ibid. III.2, 1111b13–14; see more generally VII.1–10.

[31] I do not suggest that every kind of crime could be plausibly or coherently ascribed to "weakness of will", only that some can.

account, criminally liable for what I do: but I did not choose, in this richer sense, to do it.

The second possible account of how duress or mental disorder can excuse would be that such agents should be excused if they *could not have chosen* to act otherwise than they did. It is a necessary condition of responsibility, and so also of justified criminal liability, that the agent "could have acted differently", not only in the sense that he would have acted otherwise had he chosen to, but also in the sense that he could have chosen to act differently.[32] A weak-willed agent could, we suppose, have chosen to obey the law; that is why he is justly punished for what he did (for what he "chose", in the minimal sense, to do). But a mentally disordered agent, or one who acts under duress, should be excused if and because this condition is not satisfied.

But what does it mean to say that a person can or cannot choose, could or could not have chosen, to act differently? We might draw on Hart again here, and say that a person can choose to act differently only if she has the capacity and a fair opportunity to do so.[33] But these notions themselves need explanation.

The idea of "fair opportunity" need not detain us. Moore thinks we should understand duress as an excuse in this way. One who breaks the law under threat of a genuine, substantive evil has his opportunity to obey the law unfairly diminished: he is unfairly deprived of the opportunity to obey the law without suffering undesirable consequences of that kind.[34] But this does not show why duress should be an excuse. When duress is an excuse rather than a justification, the threatened harm is not so severe, relative to the seriousness of the crime committed, that the agent is permitted to commit that crime in order to advert that harm: for only then does he need an excuse. But

---

[32] Contrast the simple Humean Compatibilism according to which we act freely so long as we would act differently if we chose or wanted to (D. Hume, *An Enquiry Concerning Human Understanding* s. VIII; see Ayer, op. cit., n. 14 above): to which the obvious objection is that it also matters whether we could choose to act differently (see for instance A. C. MacIntyre, 'Determinism', *Mind* **66** (1957): 28–41).

[33] See at n. 2 above; and Moore: 35–40.

[34] Moore: 36–40.

in such cases the law in effect declares that, even allowing for the unfair limitation of opportunities which the agent suffers, he ought not to commit that offence. If he is then excused for committing the offence, this cannot be because of his unfairly diminished opportunities (since that possible ground for acquittal has been allowed for already): if his excuse is that he "could not have obeyed" or "could not have chosen to obey" the law, his claim must be that he suffered some impairment of his capacity to (choose to) obey the law.

We turn then to the idea of capacity: an agent should be excused if she lacked the capacity to (choose to) obey the law.[35] This might seem to offer the "choice" theorist a secure position. For, she can argue, people are of course properly convicted and punished for what they choose to do only if they could have chosen (and chosen effectively) to obey the law: only if, that is, they are rational agents who possess, and can exercise, the capacities necessary for choice. But, first, the possession of such capacities is a presupposition of moral responsibility and criminal liability, not the object of moral criticism or legal condemnation: what we condemn and punish is still her wrongful choice – the way in which she exercised her capacities. Second, we can explain what those capacities involve, what it is to be able or unable to choose, without reference to the agent's character. For the possession and exercise of those capacities is not a function of having any particular kind of character (they are exercised by people of very different characters): we can thus condemn a person's choices, her exercise of those capacities, without attending to or making any judgment on her character.[36]

---

[35] We might say of this agent too that she does not really "choose" to break the law (see at n. 28 above): if choice involves the availability of genuine alternatives amongst which the agent can choose, one who could make no other choice has not made a real choice.

[36] See especially Pillsbury for this argument. Arenella argues too that we are justly condemned and punished for our choices or actions only if we have the requisite capacities: but on his account those capacities belong to a "character-based conception of moral agency" which includes the capacity to reflect upon and modify the aspects of our characters that determine our choices and actions; see n. 46 and text at n. 61 below.

The success of this argument depends on what account we can give of these "capacities". Some can be defined in purely cognitive terms that do not threaten the attempt to retain a clear distinction between "choice" and "character". Someone who is to be held responsible for his choices must at least be capable of recognising the relevant empirical aspects of his action and its circumstances, and of foreseeing its consequences; he must also have the kind of "instrumental rationality" which enables him to determine which actions will serve whatever ends he has.[37] But the possession of such capacities is not a feature of what we would normally call the agent's character; thus, in holding that a person is criminally liable only if he had and was able to exercise these capacities, we are not founding liability on "character".

But liability cannot depend on the possession of only such capacities as these. Someone who is terrified by a threat might, indeed, suffer some impairment of such capacities: he might be so frightened that he is less able than usual (and less able than people of normal capacities normally are) to assess the plausibility of the threat or to work out whether and how he could protect himself against it. But someone who acts excusably under duress might suffer no such impairment as this. She realises the consequences of giving in, or of not giving in, to this threat; she makes no mistake about whether or how she could protect herself against it; she displays her capacity for instrumental reasoning in seeing, and doing, what she needs to do to avoid suffering the threatened harm: all this could surely be true, while we would still insist that she should be excused, because she "could not have resisted" that threat.

Similar points apply, though far more controversially, to mental disorder as an excuse. Some mentally disordered agents do manifest a lack or impairment of such basic cognitive capacities. But in other cases we would want to talk, instead, of his inability to appreciate the normative aspects of his actions, as with a psychopath;[38] of the way in

---

[37] See Arenella: 63–65 (he argues that such a purely instrumental conception of practical rationality is inadequate).

[38] See the *Model Penal Code* definition, quoted at n. 26 above. For conflicting views on the responsibility of the psychopath see Arenella: 65–69; and Pillsbury:

which his normative understanding is distorted by some pathological emotional state, as with a psychotic depression (whose role as an excusing condition does not depend essentially on any factual delusions it might involve);[39] of his inability to conform his conduct to what he sees to be right, as with a so-called "irresistible impulse" or compulsive behaviour.[40]

How can we explain these kinds of (in)capacity? I can here only sketch what I think is the most plausible kind of account, but it is an account which undermines the "choice" theorist's attempt to keep "choice" and "character" distinct.

What does it mean to say that duress provides an excuse only "if the will of the accused has been overborne by threats"?[41] What must be resisted here is the temptation to hypostatise "the will" as some distinct power or faculty that might (like a spiritual limb) be weak or strong; or to portray it as an adjunct of "reason", which is set against (and might have to resist) "desire" or "impulse". For if we populate the mind with these distinct faculties, and ascribe "force" or "strength" to them in quasi-mechanistic terms, we will be unable to explain how we can decide whether a person's failure to resist a threat or temptation was due to the "weakness" of her will or to the "strength" of the impulse which led her to act. We will also find it hard to make sense of the idea that it is the person herself who is "compelled" to act as she does: why should we identify her with the "will" which is "overborne", rather than with the impulse or emotion which "overbears" it?

English law holds that duress can excuse only if "a sober person of reasonable firmness sharing the characteristics of the defendant" would

---

744–47. I have argued elsewhere that psychopathy, properly understood, should be seen as negating responsibility: in 'Psychopathy and Moral Understanding', *American Philosophical Quarterly* **14** (1977): 189–200.

[39] See my 'Mental Disorder and Criminal Responsibility', in R. A. Duff and N. E. Simmonds, eds., *Philosophy and the Criminal Law* (Wiesbaden: Franz Steiner, 1984), pp. 31–48.

[40] His lack of capacity "to conform his conduct to the requirements of law": *Model Penal Code* s. 4.01(1); see at n. 26 above.

[41] *Hudson & Taylor* [1971] 2 Q.B. 202, 206 (Lord Widgery CJ); see Smith & Hogan, op. cit., n. 22 above, p. 230.

have acted as the defendant did in response to that threat.[42] Essentially the same doctrine is also expressed by holding that the threat must be "one which in all the circumstances (including any of his personal circumstances that affect its gravity) he cannot reasonably be expected to resist";[43] or one that "human nature could not be expected to resist".[44] Such a doctrine must seem quite unreasonable if we try to interpret the notion of "capacity" here in purely factual terms. For if it is a matter of fact about a defendant that he had or lacked the "capacity" to resist the threat (that he could or could not resist it), the figure of the "reasonable person" must, surely, play only an *evidential* role: that a reasonable person would have resisted the threat can provide nothing more than (rebuttable) evidence that this person could have resisted it. Now this doctrine gives the "reasonable person" a *criterial* role: even if this person could not have resisted the threat, he must be convicted if a "reasonable person" would have resisted it. But how can this be just, if he really could not resist the threat?

The answer must be that the idea of "capacity", of what a person "could" do, is in this context not purely factual, but normative. We should take the "reasonable person" to be someone with a reasonable or proper regard for the law and the values it protects, and having a reasonable or proper degree of courage: what is "reasonable" here is what we can reasonably expect or demand of citizens. To say that the "reasonable person" would have resisted a particular threat is thus to say simply that anyone with a proper regard for the law and the values it protects, and having a proper degree of courage, would have resisted it: from which it follows that someone who gives in to that threat lacks either a proper regard for the law and its values, or a proper

---

42 *Graham* [1982] 74 Cr.App.R. 235, 241 (Lord Lane L.C.J.): see Smith & Hogan, op. cit., n. 22 above, pp. 235–6, and *Model Penal Code* s. 2.09(1).

43 *Draft Criminal Code* (n. 11 above) cl. 42(3)(b).

44 *Stratton* [1779] 1 Doug. K.B. 239 (Lord Mansfield). And see Aristotle, *Nicomachean Ethics* III.1, 1110a23–6: duress or necessity (which are normally would-be justifications, portraying the action as "worthy of choice" in the circumstances) can make "pardon" legitimate for a "wrongful act" which is done "under pressure which overstrains human nature and which no one could withstand".

degree of courage, and is thus justly condemned. To say, on the other hand, that a "reasonable person" would have given in is to say that (even) someone with a proper regard for the law and its values, and with a proper degree of courage, would have given in: in which case this person's giving in did not display a lack or failing for which she can properly be condemned.[45]

We must, of course, ask whether a "reasonable person *sharing the characteristics of the defendant*" would have withstood that threat; we must thus determine which of this defendant's characteristics we should ascribe to the "reasonable person". But the analysis sketched here shows at least how we should approach that task: we should give the reasonable person any of this defendant's actual characteristics that affected his response to the threat, other than characteristics which involve or reveal a lack of proper regard for the law and its values, or a lack of proper courage. So we ascribe to the reasonable person, for instance, this defendant's pathological fear of spiders, but not his unusual (but non-pathological) lack of concern for the property-rights of others.

If this is how we should understand duress as an excuse, it suggests that criminal liability does depend on "character" rather than purely on "choice". For we must look behind the defendant's immediate choice to give in to the threat, to those attitudes or concerns, (a disregard for the law and its values, an excess concern for one's own safety, cowardice) which her choice did or did not manifest: but these are surely aspects of a person's character.[46]

A similar conclusion would, I think, also emerge from any plausible

---

[45] The normative character of such judgments about what a person could resist is visible in Aristotle's comment that "some acts, perhaps, we cannot be forced to do, but ought rather to face death after the most fearful sufferings" (*Nicomachean Ethics*, III.1, 1110a26–28): some wrongs are so terrible (his example is matricide) that to commit them, under whatever threat, displays a serious moral deficiency (this bears on the controversy over duress as a defence to murder).

[46] Note that we have not yet asked whether she was responsible for such character-traits. Arenella (see n. 36) argues that she is justly convicted only if she was responsible for them (only if she could have avoided acquiring them or could have modified them): but my argument does not require this claim.

account of mental disorder as an excuse. A defendant should be excused if his offence must be ascribed to his disorder, because to ascribe it to his disorder is precisely to say that it did not manifest some attitude, or a lack of proper concern, which could render his conduct culpable. To explain his conduct in terms of the radical distortion of thought and feeling which psychotic states involve; or in terms of some pathological, compulsive "impulse" which is utterly alien to his own understanding of what is good (of what can provide reasons for action); or in terms of his inability even to understand the kinds of value and concern which underpin the law's prohibition on his conduct: this is precisely to insist that his conduct did not manifest the kind of commitment to intelligible but improper values, or the kind of disregard for, or lack of appropriate commitment to, norms and values which he could nonetheless understand, that renders an agent culpable.[47]

What is the difference between a sane person who kills for monetary gain, and someone in the grip of a paranoid delusion who kills the person he believes is persecuting him, such that the latter, but not the former, should be acquitted of murder? The former's action, we suppose, flowed from an intelligible motive for whose sake he was prepared to flout a basic legal and moral value which he could nonetheless understand: the latter's action, by contrast, displayed neither his excessive concern for an intelligible end, nor a disregard for values that he could understand; it rather reflected the radical distortion of his thoughts and emotions from which he was suffering. But this is surely to say that what makes the former person culpable is that his action flowed from an intelligible set of attitudes and concerns (from, that is, certain character-traits) which renders the action both intelligible and culpable.

---

[47] There is of course deep controversy about just how far the insanity defence should extend: should it exempt psychopaths, for example, or so-called "irresistible impulses"? Although I think it should extend further than many would allow (see my articles cited in nn. 38–39), my present argument requires only the plausible claim that it ought to extend beyond the very narrow range of purely cognitive incapacities specified by the M'Naghten Rules.

We cannot explain such excuses as duress and mental disorder if we insist that criminal liability should depend on "choice" as distinct from "character". These excuses show that liability depends on the relationship between the agent's action and her attitudes, concerns, and values: on whether or not her action displayed an improper indifference or lack of commitment to others' rights and interests, or to the law and its values. Similarly, I suggested above, an agent who does not notice the risk that her action creates can properly be condemned as "reckless" if that action, and her very failure to notice the risk, displayed a gross practical indifference to the rights or interests which she threatened.[48] But to talk of an agent's attitudes or concerns, of her (lack of) commitment to certain values, is precisely to talk of aspects of her character.

III. CULPABILITY AND CHARACTER

Should we then see criminal liability as founded on "character", rather than on "choice"? But just what would this involve?

One ancestor of the "character" conception of criminal liability is Hume's argument that character is the proper object of moral appraisal. "If any *action* be either virtuous or vicious, it is only as a sign of some quality or character. It must depend upon durable principles of the mind, which extend over the whole conduct, and enter into the personal character".[49] Now this argument depends on Hume's particular account of the sentiments of approval and disapproval that produce our moral judgments: those sentiments are aroused, through the mechanism of sympathy, by qualities of character which tend "to the good [or ill] of mankind" or society. But we need not be Humeans to think that moral appraisal is properly focused on "character" rather than (purely) on "choice".

The objections to a simple "choice" theory discussed in the last section showed, we could say, that such a theory is inadequate as an

---

48 See at nn. 19–21 above.

49 David Hume, *A Treatise of Human Nature*, III.iii.1.

account of what it is to be a responsible agent. For to see what it is to be a responsible agent, we must explain what it is to be responsible for my choices, which involves explaining what it is for a choice or action to be truly "mine" in a sense richer than that provided by the simple "choice" theory, which makes an action "mine" so long as it was done knowingly and not involuntarily. We can do that, however, only by examining the way in which my "choices" are related to my attitudes and concerns, my conceptions of value and of reasons for action: but these are aspects of my character.[50] This objection fits with more general objections to the Kantian conception of moral agency and moral worth as residing purely in "the will".[51] The moral character of a person's actions, the critic argues, and so her moral condition as the agent of those actions, depends not primarily upon what she "chooses" to do, but upon the motives, concerns, and values which inform her action, on the structures of attitudes and feeling from which action and choice flow – on, that is, the character which her actions manifest.

But what kind of account of criminal liability could emerge from such anti-Kantian thoughts about moral agency and worth? It is easy enough to sketch a "character" conception of criminal liability, but harder to explain it in sufficiently clear detail.

The proper focus of the criminal process is not, the "character" theorist argues, on the particular actions for which a defendant is formally convicted and sentenced, but on some character-trait that

---

[50] See especially Vuoso. For some useful discussions of what makes an action "mine", see H. Frankfurt, 'Freedom of the Will and the Concept of a Person', *Journal of Philosophy* **68** (1971): 5–20; G. Watson, 'Free Agency', *Journal of Philosophy* **72** (1975): 205–20; and C. Taylor, 'Responsibility for Self', in A. Rorty, ed., *The Identities of Persons* (Berkeley: University of California Press, 1976), 281–99. All three are reprinted in G. Watson, ed., *Free Will* (Oxford: Oxford University Press, 1982).

[51] See, for instance, I. Murdoch, *The Sovereignty of Good* (London: Routledge, 1970); L. Blum, *Friendship, Altruism and Morality* (London: Routledge, 1980); B. Williams, 'Persons, Character and Morality', in his *Moral Luck* (Cambridge: Cambridge University Press, 1981), 1–19; S. D. Hudson, *Human Character and Morality* (London: Routledge, 1986); J. Kupperman, *Character* (Oxford: Oxford University Press, 1991).

his criminal act revealed. He is convicted if and because his action warranted an inference to an undesirable character-trait; it is that character-trait which the law condemns and punishes. If on the other hand he is acquitted because he lacked the requisite mens rea or had some further defence or excuse, this is because that inference from criminal act (from the commission of the actus reus of the crime, or from its commission with the requisite mens rea) to character-trait is then blocked.

D is charged with criminal damage, and it is proved that he did break a window of *V*'s house. If it is also proved that he broke the window intentionally or recklessly, and without lawful excuse,[52] he is properly convicted: for we can then infer from his conduct an undesirable character-trait which merits condemnation and punishment. That trait might be described as, for instance, an indifference to, or a lack of proper regard for, the property-rights of others – the "absence of an adequate aversion" to infringing those rights;[53] or as a "practical attitude" of "hostility or indifference towards, or rejection of, either that particular norm [against damaging others' property] or the standards of the criminal law in general".[54]

If, however, the prosecution fail to prove that *D* acted with the mens rea required for the offence, he is not guilty, since no inference to a relevant undesirable character-trait is then warranted: if he thought it was his own property, for example, or (reasonably) did not realise that he might damage anyone's property, we cannot infer from his conduct any such undesirable character-trait. Likewise, if he broke the window intentionally but under duress (he was plausibly threatened with immediate and serious injury if he refused to break it), he should be acquitted. We can infer something about his character from his conduct: that he values his own physical safety more highly than another's property; or that he is the kind of person who breaks down to that extent under that kind of threat. But if we suppose it to be

52 *Criminal Damage Act* 1971 s. 1(1).

53 See Brandt, p. 174.

54 Lacey, p. 76.

right (or at least permissible) to set such value upon one's own physical safety, or that a person of "reasonable firmness" would have thus given in to such a threat, we cannot infer a defective character-trait: we cannot infer that *D* had less regard for the property-rights of others or for the law's norms, or less courage in relation to such rights and norms, than we can reasonably expect any citizen to have.

Choice is thus neither a necessary nor a sufficient condition of criminal liability. It is not necessary, since I might manifest some defective character-trait (such as gross indifference to the rights of others) in my very failure to notice the risk to which I subject them – and to which I therefore do not choose to subject them.[55] It is not sufficient, since one who "chooses" to break the law might be able nonetheless to plead a defence which blocks the usual inference from conduct to defective character-trait.

Various questions are raised by this sketch. Why should the law focus on "character", rather than on action or choice? What kinds of character-trait should make a person criminally liable, and what is a "character-trait"? What is the connection between action and character; what kind of inference are we to make from one to the other? How can one criminal act warrant any inference to a character-trait (why is action sufficient for liability)? Why should we require action at all (why is action necessary for liability)?

We should begin by clarifying the notion of a "character-trait". Obvious examples of character-traits which may be relevant to criminal liability are virtues and vices: honesty and dishonesty, courage and cowardice, generosity and meanness, compassion and callousness. But we need to know more about what a character-trait is.

A point that "character" theorists emphasise is that character-traits are lasting or stable.[56] This is part of the very concept of "character": a purely momentary feeling or impulse is no part of the person's character; for characters and character-traits are extended both diachronically and synchronically. A character-trait, that is, involves a pattern of

---

55 See at nn. 19—21 above.

56 See, for instance, Pincoffs, Bayles, Brandt, and Lacey.

thought, feeling and action, extending through time: it is not the kind of attribute which can be suddenly acquired and as suddenly lost, or which has just one single manifestation. My character consists in the continuing structures of thought and conduct which constitute my unity as a person, both at a given time and through time.

This suggests one reason, related to the purposes of punishment, why the criminal law might focus on character. If we take punishment to have any reformative or corrective aim, what justifies punishment must be something about the offender that requires reform or correction; this cannot be simply the particular past action or choice for which she has been convicted, but must presumably be some underlying and continuing character-trait which that action manifested. Or, if we focus instead on the condemnatory aspect of criminal convictions and punishments, we might say that what is condemned is not (merely) the past action, but the defendant as the author of that action: but what makes that action "hers" is precisely its relationship to those settled dispositions which constitute her character – and constitute her as an agent.[57]

Character-traits are analysed dispositionally. To have a certain character-trait is to be disposed to . . .: but to be disposed to *what*? Character-traits are clearly related to action: to be generous is to be disposed to give (money, or other goods such as time), especially to those in need, and even when the gift involves real deprivation; to be cowardly is to be disposed to flee or avoid dangers or threats that should be faced. But character-traits are not merely dispositions to behave in particular ways. They are also dispositions to be motivated in certain ways, by certain kinds of consideration: a generous person is

[57] By contrast, "choice" theorists may prefer to see punishment either as a system of rational deterrence, which aims to guide the choices of rational agents by giving them prudential incentives to choose to obey the law (see Hart on the law as a "choosing system", at nn. 5–6 above); or as a system which inflicts retribution on past wrongful acts – perhaps aiming to restore that fair balance of benefits and burdens which crime disturbs (J. G. Murphy, 'Marxism and Retribution', *Philosophy & Public Affairs* **2** (1973): 217–43; H. Morris, 'Persons and Punishment', *Monist* **52** (1968): 475–501).

disposed not just to give to those in need, but to be motivated by their need – rather than by a desire for reward or because she enjoys the sense of power.[58] They are also and relatedly dispositions to be affected in certain ways: a generous person is moved to sympathy by the needs of others; she is happy to help them, and sad if she cannot help them.[59]

Nor do such behavioural, motivational, and affective dispositions exhaust the content of a character-trait: it also typically involves a disposition to think in certain ways, to notice certain things, to see certain considerations as reasons for action, and to see (or not to see) certain actions as options. Someone's generosity is shown in the fact that she thinks about, and attends to, the needs of others; that she notices their needs, and sees them as providing reasons for her to act; that she does not, if the need is urgent, see not helping as an open option. By contrast, a person's meanness is shown in his failure even to notice the needs of others, as possible reasons for him to act; in the way in which his thoughts, his attention, his deliberations are focused on, and structured by, the preservation of his own money or goods.

(Some character-traits, of course, must be understood largely in negative terms: not as dispositions to think, feel, or act in certain ways, but as the absence of such dispositions. Thus callousness, for instance, might be best described as the absence of even the modest kind of concern for the interests of others that we expect of each other.)

A person's character-traits embody her settled values, concerns, and attitudes – what she cares about, what matters to her. We can now note two more reasons for suggesting that the criminal law should be concerned with character. First, what the law demands of us is not a set of particular and discrete acts, but certain patterns of action: patterns of obedience to the general rules which constitute the law, and of respect for the values that the law protects. But this is to demand certain character-traits: dispositions to act in appropriate ways, and those dispositions of thought and attitude that enable us to under-

---

58 Contrast Hobbes, *Human Nature*, ch. IX, s. 17.

59 See Blum, op. cit., n. 51 above, pp. 146–49.

stand the law's demands and respond to them appropriately.[60] Second, since actions flow from and are determined by character, our characters can be seen as the locus of our responsibility as agents: we are responsible for our actions, and are justly blamed for them, insofar as they do indeed reflect or flow from our characters. Some would say that we are responsible for what we do only if we are also responsible for our characters,[61] but I am not sure that we should, or sensibly can, ask if someone is responsible for his character: we can more plausibly say that we are our characters, and are for that reason responsible for the actions which flow from them.[62]

But can it really be the proper business of the criminal law to inquire into the deep and subtle structures of the citizen's character? Might not a "choice" theorist reasonably respond that, even if such dispositions of thought, feeling, and motivation are the proper focus of moral appraisal, they are not the business of the criminal law? For the law's proper concern is not to appraise or improve our moral characters, but to declare and enforce those minimal standards of conduct towards each other that are necessary for any tolerable social life – and which leave individuals free to develop their own lives and relationships, and to pursue their own conceptions of the good. My moral character properly concerns me, and those with whom I enter into those various personal relationships that constitute my private life. The law can properly demand that I conform my conduct to its requirements, and can condemn and punish me if I fail (voluntarily) to do so, but it should not pry into the inner reaches of my character (of my soul).

This response embodies a familiar liberal conception of the role of the state and the criminal law, which I will say a bit more about later.[63] It presents the "character" theorist with an opposite problem to that faced by the "choice" theorist in the last section. The problem for

[60] See Pincoffs.

[61] See for instance Aristotle, *Nicomachean Ethics* III.5; and Pincoffs: 919–23; Arenella (see n. 36 above).

[62] See Vuoso: 1679–81; Lacey, pp. 67–8; Moore: 44–6.

[63] See s. 5 below.

a simple "choice" theorist is that she offers too skimpy an account of the conditions of criminal liability: there is more to being a criminally responsible agent than she can allow. The problem for the "character" theorist, by contrast, is that if she founds her account on the *moral* significance of character, it is surely far too rich as an account of *criminal* responsibility. There is surely *less* to being a criminally responsible agent than this: the criminal process is radically ill-suited to serve as an inquiry into the subtler depths of a defendant's moral character; nor is such an inquiry the law's proper business.

A "character" theorist could, of course, reply that the criminal law *should* be more interested in character: it should inquire, more deeply and in more detail than it now does, into the citizen's moral character; its aim should be to improve, to reform, those aspects of the citizen's character which are damaging to or destructive of his relationships with his fellows.[64] This would demand a radical transformation of the criminal process, towards something much more like the kind of critical moral examination that occurs between friends, or within close-knit communities; it is one possible implication of a communitarian, rather than liberal, conception of the state, which I will again say a little more about later. It is not, however, the route that "character" theorists usually take. Their aim is, rather, to rationalise something more like our existing systems of criminal law and punishment; and to do that they must set stricter limits on the extent and depth of the criminal law's interest in character.

This can be done by insisting that the criminal law is properly interested only in those kinds of defective character-trait that are liable to issue in familiar types of criminal conduct: conduct which infringes or threatens to infringe the basic rights and interests of others (a "character" theorist might agree with the "choice" theorist that the criminal law's proper aim is to declare and enforce the minimal standards of conduct which make social life possible). It is concerned with such defective character-traits only insofar as they are liable to produce such criminal conduct: it is interested not in those deeper or

[64] I have explored an account of punishment which embodies this view in *Trials and Punishments* (Cambridge: Cambridge University Press, 1986).

subtler aspects of the person's character that are often the object of moral appraisal, but purely in the fact that he has a character-trait that disposes him to break the law.

The notion of "character" which is on this view relevant to the criminal law is thus narrower than that which figures in moral appraisal: but it still requires further explication. There are psychological attributes which might lead those who have them to behave in ways that are *prima facie* criminal, but which surely do not justify the ascription of criminal liability: the "character" theorist must explain why these are not defective "character-traits" that warrant criminal liability.

Consider stupidity, as might be exhibited by a person who "systematically, characteristically makes unreasonable mistakes, causing danger to the interests of others".[65] Now such mistakes might manifest "a genuine practical indifference to the interests protected by the criminal law":[66] but they could surely, instead, manifest a cognitive deficiency which does not merit conviction or punishment. The "character" theorist could accept this possibility, however, and say that defects of character are defects of attitude or motivation: so stupidity is non-culpable insofar as it involves, not an attitude of indifference or any lack of appropriate motivation, but a cognitive incapacity that inhibits the effective actualisation of the respect for the interests of others which the well-meaning but stupid person does have (as is shown in part by his distress when he realises what he has done).

More problematic, however, is the case of mental disorder as an excuse. Once we move beyond the realm of purely cognitive disorders, must we not say that the mentally disordered criminal (a pathologically depressed person who kills his family, the "compulsive" thief, the psychopath) manifests some radical defect in attitude and motivation:[67] a defect which, since it leads to criminal conduct, should on the "character" conception make the person criminally liable?

Bayles holds that such disordered criminals should be convicted,

---

65 Lacey, p. 66.

66 Ibid.; and see at n. 19–21 above.

67 See at nn. 26–7, 38–40 above.

because their conduct is "good evidence of an undesirable character trait justifying a social response": that social response need not, however, take the form of punishment, since another kind of response "may be more effective and appropriate".[68] But if this is the shape that the "character" theory takes, it is no longer a theory of *criminal liability*: for it destroys the distinction, vital to any system of law and punishment, between condemning and punishing responsible wrongdoers for their crimes, and diagnosing and treating those who are dangerous to themselves or to others. Now there are, of course, still those who would indeed like to destroy that distinction. But a "character" theorist aims to rationalise something like our existing systems of criminal law and punishment: she must, therefore, be able to rationalise this central distinction.[69]

She can do this, however, by arguing that mental disorder is not the kind of "defective character-trait" that merits condemnation and punishment. For character, as an object of moral or legal criticism, consists in the person's rational dispositions – of thought, feeling and motivation; "rational" here means roughly that his dispositions reflect an intelligible conception of reality and value. Now insofar as this is not true of a mentally disordered person (and I think it is a defining feature of mental disorder that it involves rationally unintelligible patterns of thought, feeling, and motivation), we cannot explain his actions in terms of any intelligible set of beliefs and values; we cannot engage with him in any critical discussion of the propriety or impropriety of his conduct or of what motivated it. But it follows from this that we cannot hold him morally responsible or criminally liable: for moral criticism and criminal condemnation are (that is, should be) modes of communication with a rational agent about her intelligible actions.[70]

---

[68] Bayles: 17–18 – a purely temporary disorder excuses, however, since it is not "an undesirable disposition the actor still has".

[69] I will not try here to justify the claim that we *should* look for an account of criminal liability, rather than merely an account of the kinds of dangerous condition which warrant a "social response": but see my op. cit., n. 64 above.

[70] See my op. cit., n. 39 above; and Lacey, p. 76.

IV. CHARACTER AND ACTION

We are now clearer about the kinds of character-trait which are, on this account, the proper concern of the criminal law: but we need still to know more about the relation between such character-traits and the criminal actions which are the immediate focus of the criminal process. In particular, why should action be required at all for criminal liability; and why should just one criminal act suffice?

If the aim of the criminal process is to identify, condemn, and punish character-traits that are liable to lead to criminal conduct, why should conviction and punishment require proof of such conduct: why should we not convict and punish those who can be shown to have such a character-trait, even if they have not yet acted criminally?

One answer to this question gives criminal conduct an evidential significance.[71] The criminal act provides the safest evidence of the defective character-trait: evidence, that is, which is both strong enough, and obtainable by acceptable means. It would be very difficult to be (reasonably) certain that someone really has a defective character-trait which would lead to criminal conduct, if she has not yet provably engaged in any such conduct; whilst the investigative methods required to establish the existence of such character-traits in the absence of proven criminal conduct would be grossly intrusive on individual privacy and freedom.[72]

This answer portrays the connection between character and action as contingent and causal: the character-trait is a disposition that causes action; the inference from action to character is from effect to cause, analogous to a doctor's diagnostic inference from spots to the virus which caused them. One implication of this view is that it is conceivable, though perhaps empirically very unlikely, that someone should have a particular character-trait, but never manifest it in action: the disposition to action is never actualised, because he never finds

[71] See, for instance, Bayles: 19; Brandt, p. 189.

[72] Compare the common evidential rationale for the "act" requirement in criminal attempts: the requisite act provides the safest evidence of that firm criminal intent which is the law's primary concern.

himself in a situation that would activate it. Some have indeed argued this: someone could be courageous, for example, though he has never acted courageously – since he has never faced a situation calling for courage.[73]

Now one problem in discussing this issue is that it is difficult to imagine a human life in which there is no occasion for the active manifestation of the kinds of character-trait which concern us here. This is true even of courage and cowardice. Someone might be fortunate enough never to face a situation of physical danger that calls for courage: but our courage or cowardice is also manifested in our responses to other kinds of threat, in our willingness or unwillingness to confront uncomfortable truths and difficult situations; and it would be hard to imagine a human life in which there were no such occasions for the manifestation of one's courage or cowardice.

I suggest, however, that the possession of such character-traits does necessarily involve their manifestation in action. A courageous person is not just someone who would respond courageously to danger, but someone who does respond thus; a coward is not just a person who would flee dangers which he should face, but a person who does flee. The point about someone who has not yet faced a situation that calls for courage is not that we do not yet know whether he is courageous: rather, there is as yet no fact of the matter to be known. Criminal conduct is not merely evidence for the distinct character-trait that causes it. Rather, the conduct is itself an essential aspect of the character-trait; and the "inference" from action to character-trait is not a matter of inferring a cause from its effect, but of setting the action in the wider and deeper context of thought, attitudes, and motivation that gives it its meaning. The action completes a picture that is incomplete without it; whereas on the evidential view, the relevant picture is already complete (though perhaps not completely known by us) without the action from which it is inferred.

---

[73] For instance, R. Brandt, 'Traits of Character: A Conceptual Analysis', *American Philosophical Quarterly* 7 (1970): 23–37, 26; Moore: 41: for the opposing view see M. Dummett, *Truth and Other Enigmas* (Cambridge, Massachusetts: Harvard University Press, 1978), pp. 14–16.

Consider dishonesty. Only certain kinds of dishonesty are criminal: most obviously, those involved in theft and fraud. Now someone can be dishonest without ever breaking the law: she may be dishonest in dealings and in ways that do not concern the law; she can display a kind of dishonesty in contemplating committing or being tempted to commit theft or fraud. But her dishonesty concerns the criminal law only if it involves an actual disposition to break the law; and such a disposition, I am suggesting, is constituted by, and only by, some actual breach of the law (which includes an attempted crime). We may predict with some confidence that a person who has displayed certain kinds of dishonest disposition, but has not yet committed any crime, will or would commit a crime of dishonesty if given the chance: that would be to predict, however, not merely a further manifestation of a character-trait which she already and fully has, but rather a development of her character into criminality. It is by and only by her actions that she constitutes herself as a thief or as a fraud, and constitutes her character as criminally dishonest.

This argument depends on the assumption that there is some substantive difference between those kinds of action which are criminal and those which are not: only given that assumption can I claim that a manifested disposition to some pattern of non-criminal thought and action is not yet a disposition to criminal conduct. But that is an assumption which, I think, we should be able to make of a tolerable legal system. That substantive difference might consist (in the case of *mala prohibita*) in the very fact of illegality: for if the law's demands have any normative significance for the agent (and we cannot assume, without criminal conduct, that they do not) a disposition to engage in non-criminal conduct is not yet a disposition to break the law.[74] Or it might consist (in the case of *mala in se*) in some moral difference between criminal and non-criminal conduct, independent of (and

[74] This is strictly true only if the agent knows whether her conduct is criminal, and is thus problematic if ignorance of the law is not an excuse: but the claim that (excusable) ignorance of the law ought to be an excuse seems to me persuasive in the case of *mala prohibita*.

presumably underpinning) the fact that the former is criminal: in this case too, a disposition to engage in non-criminal conduct is not yet a disposition to engage in criminal conduct.

A "character" theorist can thus argue that criminal conduct is a necessary condition of liability: only by breaking the law does anyone constitute himself as a person with some undesirable character-trait of a kind which concerns the law. But why is just one criminal action a sufficient condition for liability? Liability requires the manifestation of a settled disposition:[75] how can one single action warrant an inference to that?

Some "character" theorists recognise a problem here. Thus Bayles admits that the "attitudes" that constitute the various species of mens rea "may be fleeting": but he then suggests that "the law uses a general presumption that the combination of behaviour and attitude indicates an undesirable character trait", without showing how that "presumption" is justified.[76] Lacey argues that we would often need "to look more broadly at the defendant's attitudes as manifested in other relevant areas of behaviour" to establish "the inference from action to disposition":[77] but she does not tell us how "broadly" we must look. Fletcher notes "the artificiality of inferring character from a single deed", but argues that this artificiality is the price we pay to protect "the individual against a free-ranging inquiry of the state into his moral worth".[78]

To see whether there really is a problem here, we should look at the supposed difficulty presented by "out of character" actions. The "character" theorist might argue that we should not punish a person whose admitted criminal action was "out of character", since it did not then manifest the kind of settled disposition which concerns the criminal law;[79] and a critic might object to the theory just because it commits us to excusing or acquitting one whose crime was "out of

75 See at n. 56 above.

76 Bayles: 10.

77 Lacey, p. 75.

78 Fletcher, pp. 800–1: he does not, however, finally favour a "character" theory.

79 See for instance Lacey: 68.

character".[80] We must ask more carefully, however, just what it is for a crime to be "out of character".

A trusted employee steals a large sum from his employer; this is his first and only act of criminal dishonesty. What might lead us to count this action as "out of character"? Would it also incline us to acquit him of theft?

The mere fact that he has not previously stolen does not render his action out of character. Perhaps he was waiting for a chance to steal; or perhaps, although he had no such prior plan, this was the first chance he actually had to steal without (as he thought) being detected. In taking that chance, he showed himself to be criminally dishonest: he was disposed to steal if a chance presented itself.

But suppose he had hitherto refrained from stealing, and for the appropriate moral reasons, even when he had opportunities to do so. Perhaps he had been tempted before: he had noticed opportunities to steal (which a more honest person would not even have noticed); but had resisted the temptation which they presented. Suppose also that he now bitterly repents his crime. We might now see that crime as a case of giving in, tragically, to a kind of temptation which he had hitherto resisted. We might also accept that his remorseful recognition of his crime is so deep and genuine that he would not now steal even if he had a chance to do so. His remorse might secure him some mitigation of sentence: for it changes his relationship to his past crime, and shows that he has done for himself some of the work that punishment should aim to do. It also renders his crime out of tune with his present character. But it does not show that his crime was out of character (a persistent offender might equally come to repent her past crimes), nor that he should not be convicted and punished: indeed, he might himself insist that he should be.

We must also ask why he gave in to temptation on that occasion. Suppose there had been no significant change in his situation: there was nothing which gave him a stronger motive to steal on that occasion. We might then see his act as manifesting weakness of will. He recognised the importance of honesty, though he was also tempted by

80 See for instance Moore: 51–54; Dressler: 697.

dishonesty, but that balance between duty and temptation was a fine one, which on this occasion tipped the other way. Now one could so define "character" that weak-willed actions are "out of character", by counting as parts of my "character" only those dispositions with which I wholeheartedly identify myself. For weak-willed actions flow from motives which I reject or disown: motives that tempt me to do what I think is wrong, that are inconsistent with my conception of the good, and external to the "character" with which I identify myself. Such a definition is implicit in Lacey's remark that the state should respond "punitively only to actions which are genuinely expressive of the agent's relevant disposition: with which the agent truly identifies, and can call her own".[81]

Now the difference between weak-willed action, and action with which the person wholeheartedly identifies herself, is indeed significant for our understanding of the action and its agent. But a "character" theorist cannot plausibly portray weak-willed actions as being "out of character" in a sense that should preclude criminal liability. It would be absurd to argue that we should not be morally or criminally liable for our weak-willed actions; and such actions surely reflect relevant character-traits. They show something about the nature and depth of our commitment to the values they flout; they show that we lack the moral strength to resist temptations that a more virtuous person would resist — or would not even be tempted by.[82]

Weak-willed action is thus in the relevant sense "in character". But suppose something had changed in the employee's situation, which helps to explain why he committed the crime. He was suddenly in need of money (for himself, or his family); or he found that his employer had been exploiting him; or she refused him a raise he thought his due. Depending on the particular facts (and our knowledge of the person) we might now describe the case in various ways. We might say that the theft was still "in character", as being continuous and consistent with his already existing attitudes and values: his commitment to honesty was never that strong; it was no surprise

---

[81] Lacey, p. 77; contrast Moore: 42–43 on the "narrow" and "broad" views of character.

[82] See Aristotle, *Nicomachean Ethics* I.13, II–III, VI–VII.

that he reacted in that way to that situation. Or we might talk of a change in his attitudes and values: when faced by that situation he came to think and feel (as he had not thought or felt before) that theft was permissible in this context; or at least he was now prepared, as he would not have been prepared before, to steal (though neither he nor we might know whether this will be a lasting change). Now it may be hard to decide which kind of story is more appropriate. But even if we do talk of a change in his character, and could thus say that his action was "out of [*previous*] character", he should surely still be criminally liable. And his action was in another way still "in character", not just because it manifested what had become his attitudes and values, but because those attitudes and values marked an intelligible modification or development of his existing character.

But we might tell a different story. We might talk of the devastating effect on an honest person of some sudden and acute need (he was desperate to raise money to get treatment for his seriously ill spouse), or of some perceived injustice (after twenty years of devoted service he was made redundant, for no good reason that he could see, from the job with which he had identified himself). This story would ascribe his theft, not to some rational conception of values (of the importance of honesty, of what could count as a good reason for such dishonesty), but to emotional disturbance: his desperate anxiety and fear, or his indignant rage, was such that it distorted his grasp of the values to which he was truly committed; it impaired his capacity to think in any rational way about what he should do. We might even talk now of a kind of temporary insanity. His action still of course shows something about him – trivially, that he is a person who breaks down in that way under that kind of pressure. But if we feel that in this kind of case he should perhaps be excused (a feeling that is, at least, more plausible in this case than in the previous ones), we might express that view by saying that his action was "out of character": for it did not show him to be truly dishonest, or manifest a culpably dishonest character.[83]

Now I think that some story like this must be told, if we are to

[83] We might say too that anyone would have reacted as he did to such pressure: compare the discussion of duress at nn. 42–46 above.

portray his crime as "out of character" in any sense that could bear on his criminal liability, but then it could never be the case that an agent "freely chooses to do wrong (i.e., he has the capacity and a fair opportunity not to so choose), and yet the action is 'out of character' for that actor".[84] A "freely chosen" action is determined by some intelligible conception of the good, but that is not true of an action which is "out of character" in the sense indicated here. This suggests that the controversy between "choice" and "character" theorists over "out of character" actions is illusory, for the cases in which a "character" theorist could plausibly argue that an action was excusable because "out of character" are precisely the cases in which a "choice" theorist would say that it was excusable because it was not "freely chosen".

This also shows, however, that there is something spurious about the general controversy between "choice" and "character" theorists.

What makes a person's action "out of character" in the relevant sense is not its inconsistency with what he has shown in other contexts to be his settled dispositions, but that it does not manifest "character" at all: it does not, that is, manifest the kind of valuational and motivational structure of attitudes and practical reasoning in which a person's "character", as an object of moral or criminal appraisal, consists. By contrast, we condemn and punish the agent of previously "good character" who steals, but who can cite no special factor (such as emotional disturbance) to explain and excuse his action, because his action did manifest the kind of attitude (a dishonest willingness to infringe the property rights of others, for his own profit) that makes it a criminally dishonest action.

Such attitudes, such structures of value and motivation, cannot, of course, be merely fleeting aspects of a person's psychology. This is the element of truth in the "character" theory: that the actions for which a person is convicted and punished must be "hers", in that they must be appropriately related to attitudes or motives that are necessarily aspects of her continuing identity as a person. But this is not to say that the law condemns and punishes offenders for those character-traits rather than for the actions in which they are manifested (which is what "character" theorists seem to claim). I argued earlier that criminal

---

[84] Moore: 51.

action is logically necessary to the kinds of "character-trait" which concern the criminal law: an act of theft is not merely strong evidence of the distinct and underlying character-trait, but partly constitutive of the particular kind of dishonesty that concerns the law. But a criminal action is also, as we can now see, logically sufficient for liability: a single act of unjustified theft committed by one who is neither mentally disordered nor acting under a kind of pressure which could excuse the action, suffices to define him as a criminally dishonest thief. The action does not provide empirically adequate evidence of a settled disposition likely to issue in such conduct again (for it suffices to convict a weak-willed thief, even if we are confident that he will never steal again): it is, rather, constitutive of his criminal dishonesty.

But if a non-disordered, uncoerced criminal action is logically necessary and logically sufficient for criminal liability, we should surely conclude that it is for our criminal actions that we are convicted and punished, rather than for those lasting character-traits that may underlie them. This is the element of truth in the "choice" theory – that criminal action is not merely evidence from which guilt (some undesirable disposition) is inferred, but *constitutes* criminal guilt, although "choice" theorists wrongly suppose that an action's criminal character is determined purely by what the agent "chose" to do.[85]

What we should really conclude, however, is that the controversy between "choice" and "character" theorists rests on the shared, but mistaken, assumption that we must see either "choice" or "character" as the true foundation of criminal liability, and the true focus of criminal convictions and punishments. "A person is good or bad", one "character" theorist says, "directly because of what he *is*, and *not* directly because of what he *does*":[86] to which "choice" theorists may reply that he is (if not morally good or bad) criminally innocent or guilty "because of what he *does*", not "because of what he *is*". But I suggest that each assertion embodies a spurious distinction between what a person "is" and what she "does". In the eyes of the criminal law, what a person "is" is constituted precisely by what she "does": her "character" is constituted by the character of her actions.

---

[85] See at nn. 19–21 above.

[86] Vuoso: 1673.

A "character" theory expresses, but also distorts, a significant truth about who can be properly blamed, convicted, and punished. Only moral agents, whose lives and actions exhibit the continuing structures of thought, attitude, and motivation that constitute character, should be blamed and punished. Only such agents are responsible for, as the authors of, their actions; only they can be called to answer for their actions through the criminal process of trial, conviction, and punishment – to accept those actions as their own, and to repent them.[87] The "choice" theory expresses, but also distorts, a significant truth about what we can properly convict and punish people for. We convict and punish them for their willful actions – for a wrongful theft, for instance: it is that for which the defendant must answer, and that for which he is convicted and punished. What makes a person criminally liable is thus not "choice" as distinct from "character"; nor "character" as distinct from "choice" or action: but a wrongful action which, as the action of a responsible moral agent, manifests in and by itself some inappropriate attitude towards the law and the values it protects.

V. FRIENDS AND STRANGERS

I have argued that anyone who begins with "choice" as supposedly definitive of criminal liability is forced to move from "choice" toward "character" by the need to explain such excuses as duress and insanity, and to accept that criminal recklessness need not involve choosing to take a risk. I have also argued that one who begins with "character" as the focus of criminal liability is forced to move from "character" (as consisting in settled dispositions) towards action, since criminal action is both a necessary and a sufficient condition of criminal liability. The controversy between "choice" and "character" theorists might also, however, reflect a deeper tension between individualist and communitarian conceptions of the criminal law.

A "choice" conception of criminal liability sits happily with a familiar species of liberal individualism that adopts a contractual

[87] For the communicative conception of the criminal process that underpins these remarks, see my op. cit., n. 64 above.

model of law and the state. The social contract structures the relationships of discrete individuals: it specifies those fairly modest constraints on conduct whose observance will enable the citizens to live their own lives, pursuing their own goods. Breaches of the contract are punishable so long as they are "voluntary"; and one might then see punishment either as a system of rational (choice-guiding) deterrence, or as a retributive practice that deprives criminals of the unfair advantages they gained in breaking the law.[88]

Such contractarians may agree that in our personal relationships we are not so exclusively interested in choice and overt conduct: we are also interested in those structures of thought and feeling that lie behind overt action, and that determine the deeper character or spirit of such actions. But, they will insist, such interests belong to our private lives: they are not relevant to the criminal law as a system of rules which regulates our public lives.

Now this distinction between public choice and private character could be clearly drawn if we could appeal to a Kantian conception of moral agency: if, that is, we could identify and appraise a person's "choices" without reference to the deeper structures of thought and feeling which constitute her "character". I have argued that we cannot do this, but a liberal contractarian might still insist that the criminal process must strictly limit the extent of any such inquiry into the defendant's character, to avoid improper intrusion into her private sphere: what matters, essentially, is still the chosen conduct which infringed the social contract.

One could say that on this liberal view the social contract, and the criminal law as an aspect of that contract, regulates our dealings with each other as strangers: as individuals who are not bound to each other by any of those shared concerns, affections, projects, and values which structure our personal relationships, but who find themselves thrown together in a situation that requires them to work out some modus vivendi if they are to be able to live their own separate and individual lives. The contract does not of course preclude the development of closer, more personal relationships, but it does not require or presuppose them. One communitarian objection to this individualist contrac-

---

[88] See n. 57 above.

tarian view is that we cannot portray a society of (nor, accordingly, a social contract between) strangers: our very existence and identity as agents, and thus as citizens who are subject to the law, depends on the affective social relationships which the liberal individualist relegates to the "private" sphere. Such a communitarian's guiding image of society is not that of a collection of strangers who agree to respect each others' rights, but of a community of friends who care for each others' "weal and woe".[89]

Now friendship is of course precisely a context in which we take an interest in each others' characters. What matters to me about my friends (about lovers, siblings, colleagues . . .) is not merely their overt conduct towards me, but the deeper and more complex character-traits from which that conduct flows: these determine the nature of our relationship; these are the focus of the kind of moral criticism appropriate between friends.

This is one possible source of a "character" conception of criminal liability. If our interest in each other as fellow citizens is not just the interest that strangers might have in the mutual observance of the limited terms of a social contract, but rather the kind of interest that fellow members of a community have in each other as friends, that interest must extend beyond overt conduct or "choice", to character; and the criminal law, as expressing the moral demands we make of each other as fellow members of the community, must also take such an interest in the citizen's character. Our life together, as a community, requires us to develop and sustain appropriate attitudes towards and concerns for each other – appropriate dispositions of thought, feeling and motivation. The criminal law, which embodies the values central and essential to that communal life, should thus be concerned

[89] I draw here on an unpublished paper by Sandra Marshall, 'The Community of Friends'; see also Blum, op. cit., n. 51 above, on friendship as involving a mutual concern for each other's "weal and woe". The concept of friendship here is that captured by the Greek term "*philia*", which covers a wider range of familial and social relationships than "friendship" usually covers: see Aristotle, *Nicomachean Ethics* VIII–IX; J. M. Cooper, 'Aristotle on Friendship', in A. Rorty, ed., *Essays on Aristotle's Ethics* (Berkeley: University of California Press, 1980), 301–40.

with failures or defects in such dispositions, and with the criticism and correction of such failures or defects.[90]

But should the state or the criminal law really take the kind of interest that friends may properly take in our characters? A liberal contractarian favours a minimalist conception of the proper scope of the criminal law: it should concern itself only with those kinds of conduct which harm, or threaten, interests that must be protected if social life is to be possible; it should inquire into the characters of those who break the law only so far as that is strictly necessary to decide whether they can be justly held liable for their conduct. Such a communitarian view, by contrast, seems to favour a maximalist account of the scope of the criminal law: by denying the distinction between the public and the private on which the liberal insists, it would permit official intrusion by the law into every aspect of our lives. But surely even whole-hearted communitarians should shy away from this.

If the communitarian is to avoid this implication, she must draw her own distinction between the "public" realm that properly concerns the criminal law, and a "private" realm which is not the law's business. This might lead her down the route that I sketched for the "character" theorist in the last section, to an account which makes certain kinds of action both necessary and sufficient for liability: but I cannot fill out this suggestion here.[91]

Department of Philosophy,
University of Stirling,
Stirling FK9 4LA,
Scotland

[90] I do not suggest that such a communitarian perspective underlies all versions of the "character" conception; many indeed flow from a more limited and pragmatic view of punishment as a technique for correcting defective behavioural dispositions, whose focus is still simply on preventing harmful conduct.

[91] An earlier version of this paper was read at the 1992 University of Southern California/Oxford Legal Theory Workshop; I am grateful for the criticisms and suggestions made by participants in the Workshop.

Part III
Culpability

[7]

Insufficient Concern: A Unified Conception of Criminal Culpability

Larry Alexander†

Introduction

Most criminal law theorists and the criminal codes on which they comment posit four distinct forms of criminal culpability: purpose, knowledge, recklessness, and negligence.[1] Negligence as a form of criminal culpability is somewhat controversial,[2] but the other three are not. What controversy there is concerns how the lines between them should be drawn[3] and whether there should be additional forms of criminal culpability besides these four.[4]

My purpose in this Essay is to make the case for fewer, not more, forms of criminal culpability. Indeed, I shall try to demonstrate that purpose and knowledge can be reduced to recklessness because, like recklessness, they exhibit the basic moral vice of insufficient concern for the interests of others. I shall also argue that additional forms of criminal culpability are either unnecessary, because they too can be subsumed within recklessness as insufficient concern, or undesirable, because they punish a character trait or disposition rather than an occurrent mental state.

---

† Warren Distinguished Professor of Law, University of San Diego. I wish to thank all the participants at the Symposium on The Morality of Criminal Law and its honoree, Sandy Kadish, for their comments and criticisms, particularly Leo Katz and Stephen Morse, who gave me comments prior to the event, and Joshua Dressler, whose formal Response was generous, thoughtful, incisive, and prompt. I also want to thank my colleague Kevin Cole, who also gave me comments prior to the Symposium. On the remote chance that any errors remain, these people are responsible for not having spotted them.

1. *See* MODEL PENAL CODE § 2.02 (1985); JOSHUA DRESSLER, UNDERSTANDING CRIMINAL LAW ch. 10 (1995).

2. *See, e.g.*, Larry Alexander, *Reconsidering the Relationship Among Voluntary Acts, Strict Liability, and Negligence in Criminal Law*, 7 SOC. PHIL. & POL'Y 84 (1990); Jerome Hall, *Negligent Behavior Should Be Excluded from Penal Liability*, 63 COLUM. L. REV. 632 (1963); *see also* authorities cited *infra* notes 55, 57, and 59.

3. *See, e.g.*, Michael S. Moore, *Intentions and Mens Rea*, *in* ISSUES IN CONTEMPORARY LEGAL PHILOSOPHY 245 (R. Gavison ed., 1987) (chronicling the debate over "oblique intention").

4. *See, e.g.*, Alan C. Michaels, *Acceptance: The Missing Mental State*, 71 S. CAL. L. REV. 953 (1998); Kenneth W. Simons, *Rethinking Mental States*, 72 B.U. L. REV. 463 (1992).

Finally, I shall argue that negligence cannot be subsumed within the single form of criminal culpability that can encompass all the other forms, but that is because negligence does not reliably track the moral vice of insufficient concern that all the other legitimate forms of criminal culpability display.[5] Although one who is negligent on a particular occasion may in fact be one who would act recklessly when given the opportunity, only when he does act recklessly can we deem him to have acted culpably.

With respect to this last point, however, let me be clear: Although I continue to argue that negligence be dropped as a form of criminal culpability, that issue is not the focus of this Essay. Rather, my purpose here is to argue that purpose and knowledge can be reduced to forms of recklessness, and that, leaving negligence to one side, no form of criminal culpability other than recklessness is necessary or desirable.

My plan of attack is as follows: In Part I, I describe recklessness as a form of criminal culpability and then address some interesting features of its standard formulation. I first point out that although recklessness is generally described as acting with conscious disregard of a substantial and unjustifiable risk (of harm to a potential victim or victims),[6] it is the unjustifiability of the risk, not its substantiality, that should and probably does do all the work. I then turn to the question of whether one acts recklessly or only attempts to act recklessly if he incorrectly believes a risk to be more substantial than it actually is. Finally, I consider and reject Ken Simons's proposal to amend the formulation of recklessness.[7]

Having set forth and somewhat reshaped the contours of recklessness, I turn in Part II to the task of demonstrating how the culpable mental states of knowledge and purpose can be folded into recklessness as I have reshaped it. The resulting unified form of criminal culpability is not only theoretically elegant, but it also has practical advantages over the current tripartite division of purpose, knowledge, and recklessness. Such advantages include its ability to handle the variety of "wilful blindness" cases and to avoid the straitjacket of deeming all cases of purpose with respect to a given harm to be more culpable than all cases of recklessness with respect to the same harm.

In Part III, I turn to some difficulties with the unified approach I have proposed. Complicity, solicitation, and conspiracy typically require a mens rea of purpose regarding the conduct aided, solicited, or agreed upon.[8] I argue that recklessness can replace purpose for these forms of criminality without creating huge difficulties. With respect to incomplete attempts, which also require purpose, and which cannot be deemed reckless, I urge

---

5. *See* Alexander, *supra* note 2; *infra* Part III.C.
6. *See* MODEL PENAL CODE § 2.02(2)(c).
7. *See* Simons, *supra* note 4.
8. *See* MODEL PENAL CODE §§ 2.06(3), 5.02(1), 5.03(1).

that they be eliminated as crimes.[9] Finally, I reprise arguments I have made elsewhere that negligence should be dropped as a form of criminal culpability.[10]

I
Recklessness and Its Problems

The Model Penal Code describes criminal recklessness as follows: "A person acts recklessly with respect to a material element of an offense when he consciously disregards a substantial and unjustifiable risk that the material element exists or will result from his conduct."[11] This formulation is substantially the same as the formulations of recklessness in federal and state criminal codes and judicial decisions.[12] As I shall explain below, however, this formulation is misleading in one important respect and ambiguous in another.

A. *The Dependence of the Substantiality of Risk on Its Unjustifiability*

The standard formulation of recklessness makes it appear that a defendant, to be deemed reckless, must consciously disregard a risk that satisfies two independent criteria: (1) the risk must be "substantial"; and (2) the risk must be "unjustifiable." I believe that this appearance is mistaken both with respect to the purpose behind the formulation and with respect to a normatively attractive conception of the culpability displayed through recklessness.

Consider the following cases:

(1) Driver is accompanied by Passenger, who suddenly displays the symptoms of a severe heart attack. Driver speeds down city streets in order to get Passenger to a hospital in time to save his life. In doing so, Driver creates risks to bystanders' lives, limbs, and property of magnitude R.

(2) Daniel loves to set off dynamite on city streets just for the thrill of it. In doing so, he creates risks to bystanders' lives, limbs, and property of magnitude R/100.

(3) Deborah likes to take Sunday drives. Although she is a very careful driver, in taking Sunday drives she creates risks to bystanders' lives, limbs, and property of magnitude R/10,000.

---

9. *See also* Larry Alexander & Kimberly D. Kessler, *Mens Rea and Inchoate Crimes*, 87 J. Crim. L. & Criminology 1138 (1997).

10. *See* Alexander, *supra* note 2.

11. Model Penal Code § 2.02(2)(c).

12. *See* U.S. Sentencing Guidelines Manual § 2A1.4 cmt. 1 (1998); Ariz. Rev. Stat. Ann. § 13-105(9)(c) (West 1998); Cal. Penal Code § 450(f) (1998); N.Y. Penal Law § 15.05(3) (McKinney 1999); *In re* Steven S., 31 Cal. Rptr. 644, 652 (1994); Dressler, *supra* note 1, at 116.

(4) Demented likes to expose others to risk. He has concocted his own version of Russian roulette in which, when he pulls a switch, he creates a risk of magnitude R/100,000 that an innocent person will die or be severely injured.[13]

Now if the substantiality criterion is truly independent of the justifiability criterion, then there must be some level of risk imposition below which the actor cannot be reckless. Suppose that level is just above R/100. In Case 1, Driver does satisfy the substantiality criterion but may escape the judgment of recklessness by failing to satisfy the justification criterion. In other words, Driver may have justifiably imposed risk R on bystanders because his purpose in doing so was to save the life of Passenger. Deborah, the Sunday driver in Case 3, also escapes the judgment of recklessness, in this case because R/10,000 is below the risk threshold.

The problem with the independent criteria approach, however, surfaces with Cases 2 and 4. Both Daniel and Demented have imposed risks that by hypothesis fail the substantiality criterion, yet the intuition is virtually unshakable that they are being culpably reckless toward bystanders. This is perhaps clearer in the case of Demented, who subjects others to risk simply because he enjoys it. Imposing Russian roulette on others, no matter how high the ratio of empty to loaded chambers, seems a clear case of criminally culpable conduct.[14] What is doing all the work here is, of course, the justifiability criterion, which also explains the intuition about Daniel, namely, that the mere thrill of a dynamite blast does not justify imposing more than a de minimis risk on others.

What emerges from consideration of these cases is the proposition that the level of risk that one may permissibly impose on others is dependent on the reasons one has for imposing that risk. The reason Driver has for imposing risks on bystanders is a weightier one than the reason Deborah, the Sunday driver, has for doing so. Thus, we deem it permissible for Driver to impose a higher risk on bystanders than Deborah may impose. Daniel's reason—the thrill of explosions—may justify even less risk-imposition than Deborah is permitted. And Demented's reason—imposing risks on others for its own sake—cannot justify even the slightest increase in risk.

The conclusion that one should draw from these examples is that recklessness consists of imposing unjustifiable risks on others. The level of risk imposed will bear on its justifiability but is not itself an independent criterion of recklessness. Even very tiny risk-impositions can be reckless if

13. *See* Larry Alexander, *Are Procedural Rights Derivative Substantive Rights?*, 17 L. & Phil. 19, 20 (1998); David McCarthy, *Rights, Explanation, and Risks*, 107 Ethics 205, 211 (1997).

14. *See* McCarthy, *supra* note 13.

imposed for insufficient or misanthropic reasons, just as very large risk-impositions can be nonculpable if supported by weighty reasons.[15]

If recklessness consists of imposing unjustifiable risks on others, then it can be characterized as displaying the central moral vice of insufficient concern. It is my contention in this Essay that all recognized forms of criminal mens rea other than negligence display this single moral vice, and that they do so in ways that establish their unity rather than their separateness.

B. Does Recklessness Require "Objective" Risk?

Consider the following case: David wants to get home in time to watch the Lakers game on television. He accelerates until his speedometer reads ninety miles per hour, a speed that he believes creates a very substantial risk of death, serious bodily injury, or property damage to other drivers, passengers, and pedestrians. In fact, his speedometer is broken, and he is only going fifty-five miles per hour, a reasonable speed given the road and traffic conditions. Is David acting recklessly?

There are two approaches one might take to this case. One might say that David is not acting recklessly because the actual risk he is imposing is reasonable, even given his fairly unimportant reason for imposing that risk. In other words, on this view, recklessness requires that an actor actually impose an unjustifiable risk, and it is not sufficient that he merely believes he is imposing a risk that would be unjustifiable were it to exist. David is culpable in that he is attempting to act recklessly, but he is not reckless.

Let us call this approach the objective approach. Essentially, under the objective approach, one is reckless when one adverts to an actual risk of a magnitude that would render one negligent if imposed inadvertently. If one believes a risk exists that would render one negligent if imposed inadvertently, but the actual risk is below that level, then one has attempted but failed to act recklessly.

The other approach is the subjective one: An actor is reckless if he believes he is imposing a level of risk that would be unjustifiable regardless of the actual risk he is imposing. On this approach, David is driving recklessly at fifty-five miles per hour based on his belief that he is driving ninety miles per hour.

For one who shares my belief that attempts and successes should be regarded not only as equally culpable, but also as equally blameworthy and punishable, it ultimately matters little whether the objective or the subjective approach to recklessness is chosen. On either approach, David is equally culpable, and therefore equally blameworthy and punishable.

15. For a discussion of the complex morality of risk-imposition, see Kenneth W. Simons, *Negligence*, 16 SOC. PHIL. & POL'Y 52 (1999).

Nonetheless, I believe the correct approach is the subjective one because it avoids the troubling notion of an objective risk. Risk is an essentially epistemic concept. Risk is always relative to someone's perspective, a perspective that is defined by possession of certain information but not other information. For God—who possesses complete information about everything—risk does not exist. For God, all events have a probability of either one or zero.

The objective approach to recklessness requires us to be able to assign a risk to an activity that is different from both whatever risk the actor perceives and the risk God perceives (one or zero). Thus, this approach requires that we construct an artificial perspective containing some but not all information. There are obviously an indefinite number of such possible perspectives, each one generating a different risk. I maintain that there is no nonarbitrary way for us to construct such a perspective. Nor, if we are not bothered by treating "attempted recklessness" the same as recklessness, is there any motivation for us to construct such a perspective.

Imagine that in our hypothetical case, David, actually driving fifty-five but believing that he is going ninety, hits and kills a child who darts out in the road. If David had been driving more slowly, he could have averted the tragedy. It turns out then that the actual risk of death he was imposing had a probability of one, which is even higher than the unjustifiable risk he thought he was imposing. Of course, someone who knew David's actual speed but who, like David, was unaware of the presence and movements of the child, would not have deemed David's speed to be an unjustifiable risk-imposition. But why should we privilege that hypothetical perspective over either David's perspective or the perspective of someone aware of the child?

My quarrel with the notion of objective risk, and the reason I favor the subjective approach, is part of my quarrel with negligence as a form of criminal culpability.[16] I should point out that not only is the law against me on the issue of negligence, but it also appears to be against me on the issue of objective versus subjective approach to recklessness.[17] As I have said, the latter issue is only of practical importance if attempts are punished less severely than successes. Nevertheless, even if attempts and successes were equated, I think it is important to expunge from the law the notion of objective risk, and with it the objective approach to recklessness. That

16. *See* Larry Alexander, *Crime and Culpability*, 5 J. CONTEMP. LEGAL ISSUES 1, 17-20 (1994); Alexander, *supra* note 2, at 98-103.

17. The Model Penal Code's formulation of recklessness as a form of criminal liability is consistent with either the objective or the subjective approach. *See supra* notes 11-12 and accompanying text. However, one important commentator assumes that the Code adopts the objective approach. *See* Paul H. Robinson, *Competing Theories of Justification: Deeds v. Reasons*, *in* HARM AND CULPABILITY 45, 57-58 (A.P. Simester & A.T.H. Smith eds., 1996).

done, the distinction between recklessness and attempted recklessness would be completely effaced.

C. *Recklessness as Callousness*

Recently, Ken Simons has proposed "rethinking" the traditional criminal mental states of purpose, knowledge, recklessness, and negligence, and adding a new one to the existing four.[18] Simons divides criminally culpable mental states into two categories: states of belief and states of desire. In the former he places knowledge, recklessness, and negligent ignorance or mistake. In the latter he places purpose. According to Simons, this division omits recklessness as callousness or indifference, which Simons places under states of desire as a lesser form of culpability than purpose. Thus, Simons ends up proposing five criminal mental states, namely, the traditional four plus the desire-state form of recklessness.

Simons's crucial assumption is that traditional recklessness is culpable solely because of the cognitive state of the actor and not because of the conative state it reflects. He therefore proposes a second form of recklessness to cover culpability based on conative vices, such as callousness or indifference toward others' interests. But Simons's assumption is incorrect, and his proposal is either unnecessary—because it is already covered by recklessness—or troubling.

As I argued in the previous section, recklessness turns on whether it is unjustifiable for the actor to impose the risk on others he perceives to be present. The justifiability of his taking that risk is in turn a function of (1) the level of risk he perceives and (2) the reasons he has for taking that risk. Actors who impose risks on others that are not justified by their reasons are aptly characterized as "callous" or "indifferent," but that characterization is merely another way of saying that they have acted recklessly. There is no culpability lacuna that recklessness *qua* callousness or indifference is needed to fill.

Simons argues that the categories of belief-states and desire-states are independent of one another, and that there is a hierarchy of culpable belief-states and a separate hierarchy of culpable desire-states.[19] But this is quite misleading. As I have shown, recklessness is a function of both belief (in the level of risk) and desire (reasons for acting). And in Part Two, I shall argue that purpose and knowledge are included within recklessness. No act is culpable solely because of the belief-state of the actor, nor is any act culpable solely because of the actor's desire-state.

Simons's view that desire-states can be culpable apart from belief-states suggests a troubling, as opposed to redundant, interpretation of his proposal. There is some evidence in his article that Simons would punish

18. *See* Simons, *supra* note 4.

19. *See id.* at 477.

an actor solely for acting with a callous or indifferent attitude towards others' interests.[20] Suppose, for example, that Deborah is engaging in her Sunday driving within the speed limit and believes she is creating a low level of risk to others. And suppose that the pleasures of Sunday driving are sufficient to justify imposing that low level of risk on others. But suppose also that Deborah is callous towards the risks she imposes on others, and that even if she were to come to believe that the risks imposed by her Sunday driving were much higher than she actually believes them to be, she would continue to drive notwithstanding that belief. On my account and the law's, Deborah is not acting recklessly at this moment and is therefore not culpable. She has an undesirable character trait, one that might dispose her to act recklessly if the circumstances were right, but her counterfactual culpability does not translate into present culpability.

Does Simons believe that because of her callousness, Deborah is now acting culpably, even though the risk level she perceives is justified by her reason for acting? Expanding criminal liability to include callous Deborah would convert criminal liability from being act-focused to being character-focused. Deborah has not acted wrongly; rather, she has a character trait that at most makes her a counterfactual wrongdoer.

I doubt that Simons intends for us to punish callous Deborah. Indeed, I prefer to read Simons's proposal to focus more attention on desire-states as consistent with my contention that the justifiability criterion for recklessness is dominant, and that the level of risk-imposition permitted is a function of the actor's reasons for acting. Thus interpreted, Simons's argument can be turned, not into a brief for more culpable mental states, but rather into a brief for a single conception of criminal culpability.

II

A Unified Theory of Criminal Culpability: Recklessness as Comprehending Knowledge, Purpose, and Wilful Blindness

Morality enjoins us to be concerned with others' interests. On some views, such as utilitarianism, that injunction is quite demanding. On other views, such as libertarianism, it is less so. But on all views, we are enjoined at a minimum not to inflict certain harms on others.

From the basic moral injunction to have due regard for others' interests, we can derive injunctions for how to act in situations of epistemic uncertainty, situations in which we do not know for certain how our acts will affect others. One basic injunction is that we should not choose an act in order to bring about harms (of certain types) to others, unless, that is, certain greater interests (of ours or of third parties) require such harms to

20. The evidence is Simons's insistence that recklessness as callousness be viewed as separate from recklessness as acting in the face of a perceived substantial risk of harm.

others. In other words, we are enjoined *ceteris paribus* not to act with the conscious object of harming others.

A second basic moral injunction is that we not choose an act that creates what we believe is a risk of harm to others, again unless that act is required to vindicate the greater interests of ours or third parties. Because it is impossible to act at all without creating risks of harms of various degrees and kinds, this injunction boils down to an injunction to impose only justifiable risks on others. These two moral injunctions can be easily consolidated into a single one if we deem trying to bring about harm to others as presumptively making any risk imposed on others an unjustifiable one. We end up with a single moral injunction for how to choose when one is uncertain about the consequences his acts will cause: choose only those acts for which the risks to others' interests—as you estimate those risks—are sufficiently low to be outweighed by the interests, to yourself and others, that you are attempting to advance (discounted by the probability of advancing those interests).[21]

This single moral injunction can serve as the basis for a unified conception of criminal culpability. In other words, all cases of criminal culpability represent failures to comply with this injunction. Because, as I have shown, recklessness consists of imposing risks on others not justified by the actor's reasons—no matter the level of the risks—recklessness fits squarely within this moral injunction. In this Part, I shall show how two of the remaining forms of criminal culpability, knowledge and purpose, fit within the same injunction. Indeed, I shall argue that the single moral injunction is no more than an injunction against criminal recklessness, and that knowingly harming others and acting for the purpose of harming others are forms of criminal recklessness.

Another way of thinking about the ways in which knowledge and purpose fit within a conception of recklessness is to visualize recklessness as an area on a graph, where risk is the x-axis and justification is the y-axis. As I shall explain below, knowledge is the limiting case of recklessness on the risk axis; purpose is the limiting case of recklessness on the justification axis.

A. *Knowledge*

A person acts with criminal "knowledge" with regard to an element of a crime when he believes to a practical certainty that his conduct is of a particular nature, that an attendant circumstance exists, or that his conduct will bring about a particular result.[22] Unlike recklessness, which focuses on

21. The parenthetical phrase is necessary because imposing even a moderate risk of harm on others cannot be justified by even very compelling interests of the actor or third parties if the chance of the act's succeeding in advancing those interests is quite remote.

22. *See* MODEL PENAL CODE § 2.02(2)(b) (1985).

both the risk imposed and the actor's justification for imposing it, at first glance knowledge appears to focus only on risk.

One might think from a superficial comparison between the formulation of knowledge and the formulation of recklessness that when an actor is practically certain that his act will be harmful to others, he is forbidden from undertaking it regardless of his reasons for doing so, whereas if he believes the risk is less than that of practical certainty, he may act if his reasons are sufficiently weighty. But it is not the case that knowingly imposing harm is always unjustified. For example, one may justifiably impose a practical certainty of harm on another to defend oneself or others, or in some cases where worse harm to another or a similar harm to many others can only be averted thereby.[23]

"Knowledge"—acting with the belief that it is practically certain that one's act will be harmful to others—is merely a limiting case of recklessness along the axis of degree of perceived risk of harm. The other recklessness axis, the axis of the actor's reasons, remains fully operative. The only real distinction between knowledge and recklessness in the criminal law is that at some point as the risk of harm approaches a practical certainty, the burden of proof (or production)[24] on the issue of whether the defendant's reasons for acting justified the risk of harm he created shifts from the prosecution to the defendant. That shift in the burden of proof (or production) makes sense both in terms of the probability that the act is or is not justified and the relative access to the justifying circumstances, if any. But the difference in the allocation of burdens does not reflect any substantive distinction between knowledge and recklessness.

Seeing knowledge as just a species of recklessness enables us to avoid two errors. First, it allows us to avoid the error of deeming all cases of knowledge to be more culpable than all cases of recklessness, even where the harm risked is the same. For example, someone who imposes a very high risk of harm on another—a risk just short of practical certainty—for a very frivolous reason, such as a thrill, is surely more culpable than one who imposes a practically certain harm for a quite weighty, but ultimately insufficient, reason. For example, if I knowingly inflict severe bodily injury on another to prevent him from accidentally destroying my entire life's work, I may be culpable; but I am surely less culpable than if I impose a slightly lower risk of the same harm on him just to satisfy my urge to drive like a madman.

---

23. *See, e.g., id.* §§ 3.02, 3.04, 3.05.

24. The Model Penal Code regards (the absence of) justification as part of the prosecutor's burden of proof. *See id.* § 1.12(2). In most jurisdictions, the defendant has the burden of proving the justifying facts. *See, e.g.*, Commonwealth v. Markum, 541 A.2d 347 (Pa. Super. Ct. 1988); Commonwealth v. T.J.R., Inc., 548 A.2d 390 (Pa. Cmmw. Ct. 1988).

The second error averted by seeing knowledge as just a species of recklessness is the misclassification of cases of wilful blindness. A typical such case is one where the defendant is asked by someone at an airport in a drug-producing country to carry a package on the plane and give it to a specific person when he arrives in the United States. Where the applicable statute punishes only "knowing" drug smuggling, courts have struggled to find the defendant—whom they rightly regard as culpable—guilty by deeming his wilful blindness to be tantamount to knowledge.[25] Yet wilful blindness is not knowledge; it is an attempt to avoid knowledge, and it frequently achieves that goal in that defendants who engage in wilful blindness do not believe to a practical certainty that their conduct is harmful.

The prototypical wilfully blind defendant is, of course, reckless. The risk he is taking of, say, smuggling drugs is an unjustifiable one. The unjustifiability of the risk cannot, however, convert his recklessness into knowledge without absurd results. For example, suppose a drug smuggler employs 100 "mules" to do his smuggling.[26] His modus operandi is to give each mule a suitcase to carry into the target country. In ninety-nine of the suitcases he places only innocent items, such as clothes. In one he places drugs. The mules are not told which suitcase holds the drugs, and they do not open the suitcases. In such a situation, it would be absurd to deem the mule with the drugs to have "knowingly" smuggled them. What he has done is take a one in a hundred chance of smuggling drugs for no legally sufficient reason.[27] If a similar risk-imposition would not be deemed "knowing" if undertaken for good reasons—say, for example, you are visiting a foreign country and a person whom you greatly admire asks you to carry a gift to a friend in the United States, and you entertain the thought that there is a tiny but real chance that the person you admire is a drug smuggler—then it is misguided to deem the risk-imposition "knowing" merely because one disapproves of the reasons for undertaking it.

In some sense, all risk-imposition is wilful blindness in that the actor could always seek more information about the risk before acting, although the act thereafter undertaken would be different temporally and circumstantially from the act undertaken without gathering more information.

25. *See, e.g.*, Mattingly v. United States, 924 F.2d 785, 792 (8th Cir. 1991) ("[T]he element of knowledge may be inferred from deliberate acts amounting to willful blindness . . . ."); State v. LaFreniere, 481 N.W.2d 412 (Neb. 1992); *see also* United States v. Whittington, 26 F.3d 456 (4th Cir. 1994); United States v. Mancuso, 42 F.3d 836 (4th Cir. 1994); United States v. Jewell, 532 F.2d 697 (9th Cir. 1976); United States v. Incorporated Village of Island Park, 888 F. Supp. 419 (E.D.N.Y. 1995).

26. This example is, I discovered, very similar to one used elsewhere by Douglas Husak and Craig Callender. *See* Douglas N. Husak & Craig A. Callender, *Wilful Ignorance, Knowledge, and the "Equal Culpability" Thesis: A Study of the Deeper Significance of the Principle of Legality*, 1994 WIS. L. REV. 29, 37.

27. Note how this example ties into the earlier argument that the actor's reasons can render taking even small risks "reckless." *See infra* Part II.A.

Moreover, in ordinary recklessness cases, when we assess the actor's reasons for imposing the risk, we are also implicitly assessing his reasons for not investigating the danger further. Viewing recklessness as the all-encompassing conception of criminal culpability, rather than as different from and less culpable than knowledge, allows us to evaluate correctly the wilful blindness cases and does not tempt us to distort them into cases of knowledge.[28]

B. *Purpose*

A person acts with criminal purpose with respect to the conduct or result elements of an offense if "it is his conscious object to engage in conduct of [the required] . . . nature or to cause [the required] . . . result."[29] Unlike knowledge, which at first glance appears to focus only on the actor's assessment of the risk of harm, purpose at first glance appears to focus only on the actor's desires regarding the possibility that his conduct will prove harmful, while ignoring his beliefs about this possibility. But as with knowledge, this initial appearance proves to be misleading.

The crucial point is that in order to act with criminal purpose, the actor must believe that his conduct increases the risk of harm, even if the increase is very slight. Consider the Jackal, who fires a shot at deGaulle from the Eiffel Tower believing his chance of success to be one in a million. If he does succeed, he will have shot deGaulle "purposely," given that it is his "conscious object" in shooting that deGaulle be killed (that is how he collects his assassin's reward). But characterizing this act as purposeful assumes that the Jackal believes that although firing the gun produces only a one in a million chance of killing deGaulle, firing the gun does increase the probability of deGaulle's being killed over the probability of deGaulle's being killed if the Jackal refrains from firing the gun. If the Jackal does not believe his firing the gun increases the probability of killing deGaulle—if he believes deGaulle has no worse chance of surviving if he fires the gun than if he does not—then were the shot to kill deGaulle, it would not be a purposeful killing. For in such a case, the Jackal would not have fired the gun for the purpose of killing, given that he did not believe firing the gun produced any increased chance of killing deGaulle.

If, in order for an act to be criminally purposeful, the actor must believe that he is increasing to some extent the risk of harm, then criminal purpose has the same structure as recklessness. It has an axis for the actor's

28. Recklessness, because it is sensitive to both risks and reasons, allows us to distinguish between those whom David Luban calls *ostriches*, who merely do not want to know, and those whom he calls *foxes*, who contrive deniability. *See* David Luban, *Contrived Ignorance*, 87 GEO. L.J. 957, 968-75 (1999). Ostriches and foxes may take the same risks, but they have different reasons for doing so. Both may be culpably reckless, but foxes are more culpable than ostriches given the same level of risk and the same harm.

29. MODEL PENAL CODE § 2.02(2)(a)(i).

belief in risk and an axis for the actor's reasons for imposing it, the latter in the case of purpose being the actor's desire to bring about the prohibited result or conduct. And as with knowledge, the possibility of justification is not eliminated but rather the burden of proof (or production) is shifted to the defendant. In other words, just as knowledge can be viewed as a special case of recklessness, in which the defendant's belief regarding risk (that it is very high) creates a presumption of sorts that his reasons are inadequate to justify his conduct, so too can purpose be viewed as a special case of recklessness, in which the defendant's reason is presumptively unjustifying.

I say that the conscious object to engage in harmful conduct or produce harmful results is only presumptively unjustifying because there are cases in which purposeful criminal conduct can be justified. Having harm to others as one's conscious object is not the same thing as having that harm be one's ultimate object. Nor is it the same thing as appropriating others' bodies, talents, or labor, something some deontologists might claim can never be justified.[30] Thus, for example, it might be my conscious object to wound a homicidal maniac who otherwise will kill an innocent party. My wounding him sufficiently to foil his attack will be a purposeful battery. Nonetheless, I may be acting justifiably in defending others against his attack.

Or consider the case of the trapped spelunceans.[31] Suppose that they kill one of their party because they calculate that his continued breathing will deprive the rest of the oxygen they need to survive until the rescue party can reach them. Whether or not they are ultimately deemed to have been justified in killing the one member, they have not "appropriated" him to benefit themselves. Rather, they have merely prevented him from harming them.[32]

If purposeful criminal conduct is not always unjustified, neither is it always more culpable than knowledge or recklessness. One may well believe that the spelunceans lack a justification for homicide without believing they are more culpable than those who impose high risks of death on others for the mere thrill of it but who do not have others' deaths as their conscious object. One may also conclude that a purposeful criminal actor who imposes a very tiny risk—for example, my hypothetical Jackal—is less culpable than a nonpurposeful actor who imposes huge risks for weak reasons. Thus, as we saw for knowledge, a unified

30. *See* Larry Alexander, *Is Morality Like the Tax Code?*, 95 MICH. L. REV. 1839, 1845-47 (1997).

31. *See* Lon L. Fuller, *The Case of the Speluncean Explorers*, 62 HARV. L. REV. 616 (1949).

32. *Compare* Regina v. Dudley and Stephens, 14 Q.B.D. 273 (1884) (sailors appropriated a cabin boy's flesh for food), *with* United States v. Holmes, 26 F. Cas. 360 (C.C.E.D. Pa. 1842) (No. 15,383) (sailors threw overboard lifeboat passengers threatening to capsize the boat).

conception of criminal culpability may actually avoid the potential problems that arise within the existing category of purpose.

III
PROBLEM CASES FOR THE UNIFIED CONCEPTION

A. *Complicity*

To be deemed complicit in a crime, most criminal codes require that one have aided, attempted to aid, or encouraged the crime with the purpose that the crime be committed.[33] It is not enough to suspect that the person aided or encouraged will commit the crime, or even to be practically certain that the person aided or encouraged will do so. To be deemed a criminal accomplice, one must have the conscious object that the person aided or encouraged commit the crime.

The drafters of the Model Penal Code, in requiring purpose for complicity, recognized that such a standard would be controversial. However, they were afraid that allowing knowledge, much less recklessness, to suffice for complicity would create severe difficulties, particularly for merchants.[34] Suppose, for example, the owner of a hardware store strongly suspects that the purchaser of a crowbar intends to use it in a burglary. If knowledge or recklessness sufficed for complicity, the owner would fear possible criminal liability if he allowed the sale. On the other hand, if he did not allow the sale, and he turned out to be mistaken about the purchaser, he would face embarrassment and possible liability. And interrogating the purchaser would hardly be better than just denying the sale outright. Therefore, to avoid placing merchants in this dilemma, the Code retained the common law requirement of purpose for complicity.

Moreover, there is a broader policy concern beyond freeing the merchants from this dilemma. If knowledge or recklessness were sufficient for accomplice liability, people's actions would be burdened "with doubts and worries about what someone else might culpably do as a consequence . . . [, which] would tend to create an undesirable insecurity in the conduct of ordinary affairs."[35]

I believe that a unified mens rea of recklessness—insufficient concern—is capable of serving as the mens rea for complicity. To show this I shall first argue that the purpose requirement fails to criminalize too many instances of conduct that should be criminalized (and probably are

33. *See, e.g.*, MODEL PENAL CODE §§ 2.06, 5.02; People v. Beeman, 674 P.2d 1318 (Cal. 1984). Note that some states have a form of criminal complicity called criminal facilitation that requires only knowledge. *See, e.g.*, ARIZ. REV. STAT. ANN. § 13-1004 (West 1989); KY. REV. STAT. ANN. § 506.080 (Michie 1990); N.D. CENT. CODE § 12.1-06-02 (1997);N.Y. PENAL LAW § 115 (McKinney 1998); United States v. Fountain, 768 F.2d 790 (7th Cir. 1985).

34. *See* MODEL PENAL CODE § 2.06 cmt. 6(c).

35. Sanford H. Kadish, *Reckless Complicity*, 87 J. CRIM. L. & CRIMINOLOGY 369, 371 (1997).

criminalized, despite the formal requirement of purpose). I shall then describe how a unified conception of criminal culpability can address the concerns that led the drafters of the Model Penal Code to retain the purpose requirement.

Here is a scenario that is probably not unusual. Godfather announces to Soldier that Godfather wants to whack Vinnie, who has insulted him, and that Godfather wants Soldier to bring him a gun with a silencer. Soldier brings Godfather such a gun, and Godfather uses it to kill Vinnie. Soldier is tried for complicity in the murder.

Suppose that at his trial, Soldier testifies, and the jury believes him, that he did not care whether Godfather killed Vinnie with the gun, although he was pretty sure that Godfather would do so. Indeed, suppose Soldier testifies, and the jury believes him, that he liked Vinnie and hoped that Godfather would not kill him. Soldier's sole motive in complying with Godfather's request was loyalty to Godfather, not any desire that Vinnie be killed. Should the jury acquit Soldier? According to the law, the answer is "yes." Soldier lacked purpose, and purpose is required for conviction.

But should Soldier be off the hook? Here, I believe, most would answer "no." Moreover, regardless of the law's formal requirement of purpose, I suspect that most juries and even judges would deem Soldier to be an accomplice in Vinnie's murder. To find otherwise would open the door to vast numbers of those who assist the commission of crimes to argue, often credibly, that they assisted for reasons other than their desire to see the crime committed.

Indeed, Soldier should be criminally liable even if he was not certain that Godfather would kill Vinnie but only thought there was a sufficient probability of that outcome.[36] For example, consider the case of Mule, who, solely out of friendship to Cartagena Carl, agrees to pick up a suitcase Carl has shipped into the United States, knowing that such suitcases frequently contain drugs. Mule is acting recklessly with respect to aiding drug smuggling—not knowingly or purposely—but we may well believe that Mule should be deemed an accomplice in drug smuggling.

Or consider an example provided by Sanford Kadish.[37] Defendant reveals the combination of his employer's safe to someone he knows to be a career burglar. He does so because he is bedridden and needs some papers from the employer's safe. He realizes that there is a very high risk that the burglar will steal the employer's cash, but he believes that his need for the papers is worth that risk. Of course, he fervently hopes that the cash

36. The level of probability estimated by Soldier, to be sufficient for complicity purposes, should be that at which the risk to Vinnie outweighs whatever value attaches to Soldier's loyalty to Godfather—probably a very low level of risk.

37. *See* Kadisb, *supra* note 35, at 371.

will be left untouched. If the burglar does steal the cash, defendant is not an accomplice in the burglary under the law as it stands.[38]

Some commentators have argued that the basis of criminal liability for complicity is that criminal associations increase the risk that successful crimes will occur. In the words of Daniel Yeager, an accomplice is guilty of a crime not because he necessarily causes the crime to occur, but because he is "an excessive risk-taker" with respect to the crime's occurring.[39]

It is but a short step from Yeager's position that aiding crimes is a form of risk-taking to my position that the mens rea for complicity should be recklessness rather than purpose. Although, as I have argued, purpose is a form of recklessness, recklessness includes more than acting with harm as one's conscious object. And complicity should not be limited to those who assist with harm as their conscious object; rather, it should extend to all whose assistance involves risk imposition that is excessive relative to their reasons for so acting.

Indeed, Kadish points out that recklessness has already become the mens rea for complicity in a class of cases, namely, those in which the defendant purposely assists someone else in the commission of one crime, and it is foreseeable that the latter, in committing that crime, will commit some further crimes.[40] Even if the defendant has no purpose that those further crimes be committed—indeed, even if he lacks the mens rea required for those crimes—if the parties he assists go ahead and commit those further crimes, most jurisdictions deem him to be an accomplice in those crimes.[41]

Kadish, like me, approves of such examples of reckless complicity, except that, again like me, he would deem the defendant guilty only of the crimes for which recklessness is a sufficient mens rea.[42] Because I would make recklessness the only mens rea for criminal liability, the question for me becomes a simpler one: Did the defendant take an unjustifiable risk that the parties he assisted or encouraged would bring about the specific harm they did? (Indeed, because I would not distinguish between "attempts" and "successes," it would not matter whether the parties assisted committed either the crime the defendant intended or the further

38. Kadish argues against this result. He also provides additional examples of cases where recklessness should suffice for complicity. *See id.* at 386-87.

39. Daniel Yeager, *Helping, Doing, and the Grammar of Complicity*, 15 CRIM. JUST. ETHICS 25, 31 (1996).

40. *See* Kadish, *supra* note 35, at 373-78.

41. *See id.* at 375-76. Kadish also points out that recklessness *or less* as to circumstances—for example, a girl's age in a statutory rape prosecution—is sufficient for accomplice liability. *See id.* at 285-86.

42. *See id.* at 378-79.

crimes the defendant foresaw; all that would matter is what harms the defendant unjustifiably risked.)[43]

What about the concerns for merchants that led the drafters of the Model Penal Code to adopt the more restrictive mens rea of purpose for complicity? I believe that a provision that exculpates all merchants who sell at the market price or who offer services at their customary rate should alleviate the merchant's dilemma. No matter how suspicious a merchant is of a customer's intentions, he may deal with the customer with no fear of prosecution so long as he does not discriminate in the customer's favor, say, by "selling" him a $300 gun for 10 cents. This safe harbor for merchants, however, is not so large that Soldier and Mule can avail themselves of it, unlike the existing restriction to purpose.

A second kind of safe harbor can be created for persons who are not merchants but whose "aid," even when accompanied by awareness of the criminal propensities of the one aided, should not rise to the level of recklessness. Consider Kadish's example of someone who knows that another intends to commit arson but who helps the arsonist fix his car's seat belt, or shows him where to wait for a taxi.[44] Kadish believes, and I concur, that such cases of everyday, ordinary assistance should not rise to the level of recklessness, perhaps because such assistance is usually so readily available from others, or because in the absence of such assistance, the one aided would probably still proceed with his criminal project.

Finally, Kadish attributes much uneasiness about extending complicity to include reckless assistance to an ethic of individualism that makes us responsible for our own acts but not responsible for acts of those whom we may assist or influence but who remain free moral agents.[45] Even if we can predict another's freely chosen act, we may still feel that such an act is not our responsibility, even if we have facilitated and encouraged it.

This ethic of individualism would be grounds for objecting to reckless complicity. But more importantly, the objection it raises is not to the recklessness side of the equation. Rather, it is an objection to liability for complicity *tout court.* For according to this view, even purposeful aid should not implicate one in the criminal choices of another. In the end, then, even those who buy this objection should favor dropping complicity from the criminal law rather than retaining complicity but restricting it to purposeful aiding.

B. *Inchoate Crimes*

Attempts typically require a mens rea of purpose regarding either the proscribed conduct or the proscribed result, although the Model Penal

43. *See* Alexander, *Crime and Culpability, supra* note 16.

44. *See* Kadish, *supra* note 35, at 388.

45. *See id.* at 393.

Code allows knowledge regarding results to suffice for result crimes.[46] On the other hand, the Code and most jurisdictions recognize a crime of reckless endangerment that covers conduct that is reckless regarding certain proscribed results.[47] The latter crime could easily be expanded so that it covers anyone who acts recklessly regarding any proscribed conduct—that is, anyone who takes an unjustifiable risk that he is engaging or will, without further action, engage in proscribed conduct—or anyone who acts recklessly regarding any proscribed result. Such a person would be guilty of what essentially would be an omnibus attempt, with punishment geared to the conduct or result risked, the degree of risk estimated by the actor, and the actor's reasons for taking the risk. Ordinary completed attempts—those in which the actor takes the last step he believes necessary to engage in proscribed conduct or bring about a proscribed result, and in which the actor has as his conscious object the proscribed conduct or result—would be an included subgroup within this expanded class of reckless "attempts."

What would not fit within this reconceptualization of attempts qua recklessness are incomplete attempts. Incomplete attempts are those in which the actor has taken "substantial steps" toward commission of a crime but has not taken the last step he believes is necessary.[48] Incomplete attempts require purpose—the purpose to engage in what will be a complete attempt (which, under the law as it presently stands, itself requires purpose regarding proscribed conduct or results). If complete attempts are replaced by recklessness along the lines I suggest, incomplete attempts would consist of taking substantial steps toward acting recklessly with the purpose of acting recklessly. The purpose requirement would have to remain, however, for it makes no sense to deem someone to be recklessly approaching acting recklessly. At any given moment, one is either reckless with respect to proscribed conduct or results, or one is not. If one is not in the act of creating a substantial risk of proscribed conduct or results, then even if one intends to act recklessly in the immediate future, one is not reckless at that particular moment. One's future freely chosen acts are not the kind of thing about which one can now act in a risky way.[49]

Kimberly Kessler and I have elsewhere argued at length for dropping incomplete attempts from the criminal law,[50] and I shall not repeat those arguments here. I should point out, however, that the implications of our

46. *See* Model Penal Code § 5.01(1)(b) (1985). Result crimes are those, such as homicide, in which the conduct, to be criminal, must bring about some further event, such as death.

47. *See id.* § 211.2 (recklessly endangering another person); *id.* § 220.2(2) (risking catastrophe); N.Y. Penal Law § 120.25 (West 1998) (reckless endangerment); Wash. Rev. Code Ann. § 9A.36.050 (West Supp. 1988) (reckless endangerment).

48. *See* Model Penal Code § 5.01(1)(c).

49. Leo Katz raises some interesting possible counter-examples to this claim, however. *See* Leo Katz, Ill-Gotten Gains: Evasion, Blackmail, Fraud, and Kindred Puzzles of the Law (1996).

50. *See* Alexander & Kessler, *supra* note 9, at 1168-73.

argument extend beyond the pure substantial step attempt and encompass a whole host of substantive crimes such as burglary that include an incomplete attempt as an element of the offense.[51] The argument also implies that the crime of conspiracy should be eliminated and replaced in part by the crime of criminal solicitation, expanded along the lines suggested in the previous subsection to include recklessness regarding whether one has encouraged others to commit crimes.[52]

C. *Negligence*

Negligence involves inadvertence to a risk that, if adverted to, would render the actor reckless. I have argued elsewhere that negligence as inadvertent risk-taking is not culpable conduct.[53] I have further argued that because such negligence is nonculpable, it cannot be defined nonarbitrarily, nor can it be distinguished from cases of strict liability or involuntariness. For these reasons, I have urged that negligence be dropped from criminal codes as a form of criminal culpability.

I have no new arguments to deploy in favor of this conclusion, so I shall sketch the old arguments briefly and leave it to my prior efforts to pull the laboring oar on this point.

1. *The Moral Immateriality of Failure to Advert to Risk*

The world is full of risks to which we are oblivious. Or more accurately, because risk is an epistemic, not ontic, notion,[54] we frequently believe we are creating a certain level of risk when someone in an epistemically superior position to ours would assess the risk to be higher or lower than we have estimated. Sometimes the epistemically superior position is the product of better information: For example, the doctor knows that what we believe is just a mole is in fact a life-threatening melanoma. At other times we have failed to notice something that another might have noticed, or we have forgotten something that another might have remembered. And once in a while, our lack of information, failure to notice, or forgetfulness results in our underestimating the riskiness of our conduct and causing harm.

We are not morally culpable for taking risks of which we are unaware, or so I contend. At any point in time we are failing to notice a great many things, we have forgotten a great many things, and we are misinformed or uninformed about many things. An injunction to notice, remember, and be fully informed about anything that bears on risks to others is an injunction no human being can comply with, so violating this

51. *See id.* at 1193.
52. *See id.* at 1178-81.
53. *See* Alexander, *supra* note 2.
54. *See supra* Part I.B (discussing objective risk).

injunction reflects no moral defect. Even those most concerned with the well-being of others will violate this injunction constantly.

Of course, inadvertence to risk may reflect moral culpability in the sense that it is the product of a prior reckless act.[55] I may have failed to take the free course on medical problems of children, realizing at the time that I was taking a substantial risk that I might someday fail to recognize a child's serious medical problem. I may have failed to take the course on Japanese for sailors, realizing at the time that I was taking a substantial risk that I might someday cause harm because of a misunderstanding.[56] I may have failed to write a note to myself to get the brakes fixed, realizing at the time that I was taking a substantial risk of forgetting. Or I may have engaged in a heated discussion with the passenger in my car, realizing at the time the discussion began that I was taking a substantial risk of having my attention diverted from my driving. In all of these examples I might be acting recklessly toward others, and hence culpably, by taking a risk that I would later fail to advert to a risk to others.

Even if inadvertence to risk is sometimes the product of a culpable act, it is still not culpable. It is merely the nonculpable product of some prior culpable act. And most often, inadvertent risk imposition cannot be traced to any prior act that we would deem morally culpable.

I realize that both the criminal law and most people's intuitions run against me on the issue of whether inadvertent negligence is culpable, so I would like to construct what I believe is the strongest example on the side of majority opinion. Sam and Ruth are a self-absorbed yuppie couple with a small child. They are throwing a dinner party for some socially prominent people who can help both Sam's and Ruth's careers and their social standing, and they are quite obsessed with making sure the party is a success. They put their child in the bathtub and begin drawing bathwater, but just then the first guests begin to arrive. Sam and Ruth both go downstairs to greet the guests, both realizing that the child would be in grave danger if they failed to return and turn off the water, but both believing correctly that at the rate the tub is filling, they will have plenty of time to return to the child after they have welcomed the guests. Of course, when they greet their guests they become so absorbed with making the right impression that both forget about the child, with tragic consequences.

If there is ever a case of culpable negligence, this is it. Sam and Ruth are not morally attractive people. And their moral shortcomings have

55. *See* Alexander, *supra* note 2; Holly Smith, *Culpable Ignorance*, 92 PHIL. STUD. 543 (1983); Michael J. Zimmerman, *Negligence and Moral Responsibility*, 20 NOUS 199 (1986).

56. *Cf.* United States v. Short, 4 C.M.A. 437, 16 C.M.R. 11 (1954) (discussing prosecution for assault with intent to rape where American defendant claimcd he believed Japanese victim was expressing consent).

played a role in their child's death.[57] Still, I would argue, they did not act culpably. When they went downstairs they did not believe they were taking any substantial risk with their child, perhaps no more substantial a risk than we believe we are taking (for the sake of our careers) when we attend a workshop and leave our children with a sitter. Of course, once Sam and Ruth became engaged with their guests, the child's situation slipped out of their minds. And once the thought was out of their minds, they had no power to retrieve it. They were at the mercy of its popping back into mind, which it did not.

As Michael Zimmerman and Ishtijaque Haji have recently written, one is culpable only for acts over which one has control.[58] If one is unaware that, say, someone has replaced the sugar on the table with poison, then one is not culpable for placing that poison in another's coffee and thereby killing her. For although one is in control of the conduct of placing the white substance in the coffee, the mistaken belief that it is sugar deprives one of the kind of control necessary for culpability. And what holds true for conduct taken in ignorance of its nature or likely consequences also holds true for the ignorance itself. One is not culpable for one's ignorance unless one is in control of it. And one can be in control of

57. The fact that character defects play a role in agents' not adverting to risks leads Steven Sverdlik to reject what he calls the Aristotelian Strategy of linking the culpability of negligence to a past reckless act, the strategy favored by the authors in note 55 *supra*. *See* Steven Sverdlik, *Pure Negligence*, 30 AM. PHIL. Q. 137 (1993). The problem, however, is that it is impossible to prove the counterfactual proposition that an agent who forgets something important would have remembered it had he not had a particular character defect. And in the absence of such a showing, all that the agent can be blamed for is the character defect itself, not the inadvertence and risk-imposition that may or may not have been its product.

Sverdlik at one point implies that the burden should be on the negligent actor to show why he could not have adverted to the risk prior to the risk-imposition. *See id.* at 146. In other words, the actor needs to show the presence of a causally relevant excuse rather than the absence of a causally relevant character defect. The mere fact that it did not cross one's mind that there is something that should be attended to is not, for Sverdlik, such an excuse. But Sverdlik fails to give a convincing explanation for why it is not.

Jeremy Horder maintains that failing to advert to a high risk can be symptomatic of what he calls *weak indifference*. *See* Jeremy Horder, *Gross Negligence and Criminal Culpability*, 47 U. TORONTO L.J. 495 (1997). The weakly indifferent actor would not impose a high risk were he aware of it. Sam and Ruth in my example are weakly indifferent in Horder's terms. Horder deems such people criminally culpable, but, like Sverdlik, he fails to demonstrate how his position avoids punishment based on a character defect rather than a choice.

Finally, James Montmarquet argues that the negligent actor is culpable when his incorrect beliefs about risk are the result of an arrogant overconfident attitude. *See* James A. Montmarquet, *Culpable Ignorance and Excuses*, 80 PHIL. STUD. 41 (1995). Although arrogance is surely an unattractive characteristic, Montmarquet does not adequately distinguish cases of certainty of one's beliefs from cases of beliefs held arrogantly. Are we "arrogant" in believing that the Earth revolves around the Sun? Were pre-Copernicans "arrogant" in believing otherwise?

58. *See* Ishtiyaque Haji, *An Epistemic Dimension of Blameworthiness*, 57 PHIL. & PHENOMENOLOGICAL RES. 523 (1997); Michael J. Zimmerman, *Moral Responsibility and Ignorance*, 107 ETHICS 410 (1997). For an attempt to rebut Zimmerman, see James Montmarquet, *Zimmerman on Culpable Ignorance*, 109 ETHICS 842 (1999).

one's ignorance only indirectly, say, by deliberately refraining from learning something while being aware that one is running an unjustifiable risk of dangerous ignorance.

Because the actor who fails to advert to a risk acts in ignorance of that risk, he is not culpable for taking it. He may or may not be culpable for some earlier act that he realized at the time could result in further ignorance of the kind that did result. But even if he were culpable, he would be culpable only for the earlier recklessness, not the consequential negligence.[59]

2. *The Arbitrariness of the Definition of Negligence and the Lines Between Negligence, Strict Liability, and Involuntariness*

If one accepts my argument in the previous subsection that negligence is nonculpable, then the very concept of negligence, in contradistinction to strict liability and involuntariness, collapses. The "reasonable actor," the construct by which negligence is gauged, is supposed to be somewhere between God, who knows with certainty whether conduct will cause harm, and the negligent defendant, who underestimated a particular risk. That is, the reasonable actor is supposed to be aware of more than the negligent actor but less than God.

There is, however, no way to construct the reasonable person nonarbitrarily. All of us are ignorant of many risks. When is that ignorance the kind that the reasonable person would possess, when is it not, and why? If negligence were culpable, then we could give an answer: The reasonable person would not be ignorant of those risks the ignorance of which would render him culpable. But if ignorance is never culpable because we lack direct control over it,[60] then we have no materials from which to construct a nonarbitrary "reasonable person."

For the very same reason, negligence must collapse into strict liability and involuntariness. Take the person who drives a new car off the lot, sets the cruise control at the speed limit, and then, when the speed limit

59. It is sometimes suggested that negligence, though nonculpable, especially when it is "gross," is strong evidence that the putatively negligent defendant was really reckless. That is, gross negligence serves as a convenient proxy for advertence to risk because it is rare that someone engages in the highly risky conduct that gross negligence involves without adverting to the risk. If this is the case, then perhaps criminal liability for gross negligence can be justified along the same lines as strict liability is sometimes defended, namely, as a means of ensuring that the truly culpable do not escape punishment without at the same time ensnaring too many of the truly nonculpable. (The courts routinely permit such implicit "conclusive presumptions" of culpability even while rejceting explicit conclusive presumptions. *Compare* DRESSLER, *supra* note 1, at 126-28, *with id.* at 64-65.) I take no position here on this argument for criminal liability based on negligence, either regarding its empirical premise or regarding its normative one.

60. *See* Zimmerman, *supra* note 58.

changes, cannot disengage the cruise control in time to avoid speeding.[61] If he were deemed guilty of a traffic offense and punished, would this represent punishment for involuntary conduct, strict liability punishment, or punishment for negligence? The case for involuntariness is that for the period the cruise control was stuck, the defendant was a passenger in a runaway vehicle and had no control over its movement. On the other hand, he did voluntarily bring the car to its original speed and engage the cruise control, which from that standpoint makes his case seem like one of strict liability. In other words, depending on the point in time from which we begin to tell the story of the crime—the time at which the driver engages the cruise control versus the time at which he tries to slow down—his conduct can appear to be either one thing or the other. Without a culpable act to mark the beginning of the story of the crime, the choice of when to begin it, and thus whether it is a case of strict liability or a case of involuntariness, is purely arbitrary.

For the very same reason, given that negligence is nonculpable, the case could also be characterized as one of negligence. The defendant failed to advert to the condition of his cruise control that would cause it to malfunction. The risk of malfunction was high—in fact, one. His failure so to advert—his ignorance—was nonculpable; but so is all ignorance.

Conclusion

If negligence is not a type of culpability, then recklessness can serve as a comprehensive, unified conception of criminal culpability. It can encompass knowledge, purpose, and wilful blindness. And it can serve as the mens rea for complicity as well as for completed "attempts." Criminal culpability is always a function of what the actor believes regarding the nature and consequences of his conduct and what the actor's reasons are for acting as he does in light of those beliefs. Recklessness, minus its substantiality of risk requirement, perfectly expresses these two dimensions of culpability.[62]

61. *See* Alexander, *supra* note 2, at 90-92 (discussing State v. Baker, 571 P.2d 65 (Kan. Ct. App. 1977)).

62. I should mention and respond briefly to several points brought up during the discussion of this Essay at the conference on The Morality of Criminal Law.

First, Joshua Dressler in his Response to my Essay urges that the "substantiality" component of recklessness be retained but applied, not to the degree of risk that the actor believes he is imposing, but rather to the degree of unjustifiability that such risk imposition represents. *See* Joshua Dressler, *Does One Mens Rea Fit All? Thoughts on Alexander's Unified Conception of Criminal Culpability*, 88 Calif. L. Rev. 955, 957-958 (2000). In other words, Dressler would restrict recklessness to those conscious risk impositions that are not only unjustifiable, but substantially so.

I am uncertain whether Dressler's recommendation should be adopted. It is true that without it, my proposal would make one who commits even a very petty crime reckless regarding all the risks committing that crime creates. Thus, for example, if one were accidentally to kill in the commission of a petty crime, and one were aware that committing that crime increased the risk of such an accidental death, albeit only infinitesimally, one would have committed a reckless homicide. That result would not bother me, however, because I reject the materiality of results. *See supra* text accompanying note 43. One's culpability is the same as one's degree of recklessness, which is fixed at the point one commits the petty crime and does not turn on what harm occurs.

I should add here that an actor's mistaken belief that his risk-imposition is legally justifiable is, like mistakes of criminal law generally, nonexculpatory, unless, that is, the mistake is one regarding the necessity of the risk-imposition as opposed to the worthiness of the actor's goal. Thus, if someone mistakenly believes that imposing risks of serious harm on others is legally justified by the large thrill the actor receives from doing so, the actor is reckless. On the other hand, if the actor mistakenly believes that imposing a risk of serious harm on others is legally justifiable because it is the only way to avert a greater harm, or so he mistakenly believes, then unless his mistaken belief is recklessly held, he is not reckless in imposing the risk.

Second, several participants pressed me on the doctrinal implications of my thesis. In particular, they were concerned about the discretion and potential for its abuse that courts and juries would possess if their task was to find degrees of a single scalar form of culpability rather than to employ the current imperfect categories of purpose, knowledge, and recklessness. That is surely a point worth considering, and one I have not considered. However, I am doubtful that the current categories work as well as those pressing this objection assume. For example, the line between knowledge and recklessness is surely not a bright one. And the wilful blindness area is a morass. But the argument that the current doctrinal categories provide more and better guidance than a single scalar category of recklessness may nevertheless be correct, in which case my thesis has fewer doctrinal implications than it might otherwise have.

Third, Michael Moore, in private conversation, pressed me on what kind of consciousness or awareness of risk I require for recklessness. In particular, can a defendant be reckless if he "believes" that a risk exists, in the sense that he is disposed to act responsively to it, but is not fully conscious of that risk? We have often had the experience of driving successfully down a road for several minutes without being able to recall anything about our driving. We obviously adverted to the risks along the way and responded to them, but we were not fully conscious of them at the time and later cannot recall them. Aspects of riding a bicycle and other habitual activities frequently fall below the level of full consciousness. I am inclined to deem such low-level consciousness of risk to be sufficient for recklessness culpability, although I would want to consider the issue more fully than I have. My principal reservation about deeming low-level consciousness of risk sufficient for recklessness is that the actor may not have an adequate sense of the risk's magnitude, as opposed to its presence, to regard him as culpably indifferent.

Finally, several participants expressed reservations about having recklessness serve as the mens rea for inchoate crimes. Because a satisfactory response to this concern requires a complete reexamination of inchoate criminality, which space precludes in this Essay, I can only refer the reader to the article by Kim Kessler and me, which undertakes precisely that task. *See* Alexander & Kessler, *supra* note 9.

[8]

Motive and Criminal Liability

DOUGLAS N. HUSAK

According to Jerome Hall, "Hardly any part of penal law is more definitely settled than that motive is irrelevant."[1] This thesis is endorsed, sometimes with minor qualifications, by almost all leading criminal theorists. Hall and these commentators must be understood to mean that motive is and ought to be immaterial to *liability*. Roughly, criminal justice is dispensed in two stages: first it is decided whether the defendant is liable; if so, it is next determined to what extent he is to be punished. It is beyond dispute that motive is relevant to the latter inquiry. Thus a bad motive might aggravate, or a good motive might mitigate, the severity of the defendant's punishment -- but the goodness or badness of his motive does not bear on the prior issue of his liability.

Commentators should have been more critical of the thesis that motives are and ought to be material to sentencing, but not to liability. A defense of this thesis requires a theory about why a given factor that reflects on a defendant's blameworthiness should be assessed at the sentencing rather than at the liability stage of the criminal justice system. It is true that Anglo-American criminal theory has been relatively clear about whether to assign a particular issue to one stage or the other. Modern penal codes typically identify only four culpable states (purpose, knowledge, recklessness, and negligence) that are relevant to the defendant's liability. All other "mentalistic" factors that bear on his blameworthiness are consigned to the sentencing stage. Foremost (but not alone) among these is his motive. But there is no good reason why the *mens rea* component of liability should be construed so narrowly as to include only these four "mental states." No satisfactory explanation supports the decision to relegate a factor to one stage or the other. Why are such issues as whether the defendant succeeds in killing his victim, as opposed to failing in his attempt, material to his liability but not to his punishment? Why are such issues as his stress, economic background, ignorance of law, inherited character, education, amount of temptation, or degree of complicity in the offense, material to his punishment but not to his liability? The writings of orthodox criminal theorists provide no principled answers to these questions.[2]

In the absence of a theory to identify why a factor is properly assigned to the first or the second stage of the criminal justice system, one would expect disputes about where a given issue should be assessed. These disagreements are surprisingly rare, although they surface occasionally. Commentators have recently debated whether a "cultural defense" should be permitted to defeat liability, as opposed to merely mitigate punishment, for an alien whose otherwise illegal act would have been acceptable in his native land.[3] Provocation and intoxication provide additional instances in which the law is ambivalent about the stage at which a factor should enter into the judicial process. Typically, provocation is pertinent to liability in the law of homicide, but is material only to sentencing for all other offenses. In most jurisdictions, gross intoxication precludes liability for crimes of "specific intent," but is relevant only to sentencing for crimes of general intent. The principles on which these doctrines rest remain obscure.

Commentators should have been more critical of the thesis that motives are and ought to be material to sentencing, but not to liability.

Lately, however, this traditional (but largely unprincipled) consensus to relegate a consideration of motives

Douglas N. Husak, author of Philosophy of Criminal Law, *is Associate Professor of Philosophy at Rutgers University.*

to the sentencing stage of the criminal justice system has been eroding. Impetus for change has come not from theoreticians of liability, but from advocates of sentencing reform. The traditional treatment of motives is at odds with recent (and welcome) trends in sentencing theory. Perhaps the most noteworthy aspect of the revival of retributivism (or "just deserts") is the reduction of discretion among sentencing authorities. If the severity of the defendant's punishment is to be proportionate to his desert and not responsive to the need to deter or to rehabilitate him, there is almost no reason to allow sentencing authorities the wide discretion they have generally exercised in the last several decades. But any effective strategy to lessen discretion in sentencing will prove draconian in implementation without revising the substantive criminal law.[4] Penal codes typically create broad offenses, encompassing a diverse spectrum of conduct that merits a wide range of punishment. A single offense of robbery or rape, for example, includes behavior of varying degrees of blameworthiness. It is morally obtuse to suppose that each instance of robbery or rape warrants an equivalent punishment. Particular characteristics of offenders or offenses that justify especially severe or lenient penalties must be taken into account *somewhere* in the criminal justice system. If the discretion to take account of these characteristics is withdrawn from sentencing authorities, a viable solution is to make them relevant to liability. This proposal, however, requires a redrafting of criminal codes.

Consider an extreme example in which the incorporation of motives into the substantive criminal law would be sensible. Suppose Smith deliberately kills in order to relieve the suffering of his incurable wife, while Jones is hired to kill a stranger for money. The range of available punishments for a purposeful killing would have to be incredibly vast if guidelines allowed both Smith and Jones to be punished in proportion to their desert. Here the difficulty does not arise because the latitude available to sentencing authorities to tailor the severity of the punishment to the gravity of the offense is too narrow. The source of the problem is that Smith and Jones are guilty *of the same offense.* No sentencing guidelines can realistically hope to correct the injustice that results from convicting Smith and Jones of the same crime. And the most obvious means to differentiate between the conduct of Smith and Jones is to incorporate reference to motives into their respective offenses.

Several advantages would follow if motives were sometimes considered to be relevant to liability.[5] The incorporation of motives into the substantive criminal law would publicize whatever significance motives are thought to have. For example, if an assault motivated by racial hatred is believed to be more reprehensible than an assault motivated by sexual jealousy, this judgment should be explicitly included in a criminal code.[6] A properly drafted criminal code should provide effective notice. Statutes not only should identify objectionable conduct, but also should draw whatever distinctions are necessary to indicate the extent to which conduct is blameworthy. The public is less likely to be informed of the relevance of such judgments as long as the evaluation of motives is reserved to the less visible decision of sentencing authorities.

The incorporation of motives into the substantive criminal law would publicize whatever significance motives are thought to have.

On the other hand, there are obvious limits to the number of variables that a criminal code can effectively include. Offenses would become horribly complex if all (or even most) factors relevant to blameworthiness were incorporated into statutes. It is unclear exactly when this limit is exceeded. Perhaps draftsmen of criminal codes should proceed cautiously by explicitly identifying only a few especially benevolent or malevolent motives, leaving finer distinctions to sentencing authorities.

Even this modest experiment, however, runs afoul of Hall's thesis. We cannot begin to undertake the more ambitious project of identifying the precise conditions under which motives should be relevant to criminal liability without first addressing the more general reservations about whether motives should *ever* be relevant. In short, if Hall's thesis is sound, criminal justice reformers must resist any inclination to incorporate a consideration of motives into the substantive criminal law. In this paper I will argue that Hall's thesis is neither descriptively nor prescriptively accurate. His contention that motives are *in fact* immaterial to liability cannot withstand critical scrutiny. Nor are there compelling reasons to believe that motives *should* be treated as irrelevant. But I am not merely interested in refuting Hall's thesis. I am equally concerned to indicate the several respects in which the pretense that motives are and ought to be immaterial to liability has had a pernicious impact on Anglo-American criminal theory.

The Concept of Motive

It is tempting to believe that these conclusions about the significance of motive cannot be defended without first engaging in conceptual analysis. To what extent does uncertainty about the relevance of motive to criminal liability derive from disagreement about the concept of motive itself? The answer, I believe, is hardly at all. This answer should be surprising. The concept of motive, I concede, *is* unclear and imprecise. Insofar as commentators have sought to analyze the concept of motive, they have defended radically different conceptions. One might expect this difference of opinion to be reflected in debates about the importance of motive to criminal liability, just as, for example, unclarity and imprecision about the concept of free will are reflected in disputes about whether persons are responsible for their behavior. But I believe that the same is not true of debates about the concept of motive. I will argue that motive is relevant to criminal liability according to virtually *any* conception of motive that satisfies the most minimal criteria of adequacy.

One of the most minimal constraints on an adequate analysis of motives is that the account not be circular. Yet this obvious constraint disqualifies a number of attempts to defend Hall's thesis. Many commentators have explicated the concept of motive in order to preserve, rather than to test, the inviolability of Hall's thesis. The most effective (but least satisfactory) means to guarantee the accuracy of this thesis is to construe it as a necessary truth. Conceptions have been rejected for no better reason than that they are incompatible with the claim that motives are irrelevant to liability.[7] But Hall's thesis is substantive, and is trivialized when construed as a tautology. Nothing in the *concept* of motive (or of criminal liability) requires its irrelevance. It should be *possible* to construct a theory of criminal liability that renders motives important. Hall's thesis should be understood not to deny the coherence of such an alternative, but rather to affirm that the Anglo-American tradition does not (and ought not to) conform to this possibility.

> *I will argue that motive is relevant to criminal liability according to virtually* any *conception of motive that satisfies the most minimal criteria of adequacy.*

It is disappointing that criminal theorists have embraced Hall's thesis while expending so little effort to understand the nature of motives. Some commentators simply offer examples of motives; others seem content with metaphors. Perhaps the most colorful illustration is provided by Hyman Gross: "If a rich man has an ugly daughter, he is concerned about her suitor's motives. But a poor man with a beautiful daughter is concerned about her suitor's intentions."[8]

As Gross's example suggests, most of the (few) attempts by criminal theorists to analyze the concept of motive begin (but too frequently end) by emphasizing the similarities and differences between motive and intention. It is not surprising that accounts of motive focus on intention. The exceptional significance Anglo-American criminal law attaches to intention stands in stark contrast to its (alleged) complete disregard of motive. This disparate treatment demands attention. Perhaps an explanation is to be found in whatever distinguishes intention from motive. Alleged differences and similarities between these concepts provide a useful means to introduce the two most familiar attempts of criminal theorists to analyze motives. According to the first school of thought, motives are one species of the genus intention. According to the second, motives and intentions are logically separate types.

Neither account is altogether satisfactory. The correct view, I believe, is that some but not all motives are intentions; motives and intentions are not separate types, but not all motives can be subsumed under the broader category of intentions.[9] But I am less interested to defend the philosophically correct account of motives than to argue that motives are relevant to criminal liability according to *any* plausible conception. Nonetheless, it will prove instructive to provide a brief critical evaluation of these competing accounts.

Glanville Williams defends a version of the first kind of definition, according to which motives are a species of the genus intention. He writes: "Motive is ulterior intention – the intention with which an intentional act is done. Intention, when distinguished from motive, relates to the means, motive to the end."[10] Of course, the end of one action may be the means toward another. Williams continues: "Much of what men do involves a chain of intention (D pulls the trigger of his revolver in order to make the bullet enter P's body in order to kill P in order to get him out of the way, etc.), and each intention is a motive for that preceding it."[11] This account relativizes the distinction between intention and motive to moments of time. Since "each intention is a motive for that preceding it," the only intention that is *not* (also) a motive is that currently entertained by the defendant. An intention ceases to remain a motive only when it becomes immediate. Williams concludes: "It is only the immediate physical act that can never be called a motive."[12]

Although Williams's view has been extensively criticized, it is seldom noticed that it does not readily lend itself to support for Hall's thesis. For if Williams is correct, Hall's thesis is false, or at least extraordinarily misleading. Since a determination of liability always includes an examination of conduct that has already taken place, such inquiries must be interested in those intentions that are also motives. In other words, insofar as the criminal law is concerned with past intentions, it *must* also be concerned with motives, since each past intention *is* a motive. If Hall's thesis is to be salvaged, it must be reinterpreted to mean that although the criminal law *is* concerned with motives, it is only concerned with them *qua* intentions, and not *qua* motives. I am puzzled to understand what could be meant by claiming that, although the criminal law *is* concerned with motives, it is not concerned with them *qua* motives. Even if sense can be made of this reinterpretation, Hall's thesis is rendered much less interesting, to say the least.[13]

Insofar as the criminal law is concerned with past intentions, it must *also be concerned with motives since each past intention* is *a motive.*

Moreover, any number of offenses include an "ulterior intention" as an element. Common law burglary, to cite one of several examples, includes within its definition a breaking and entering "with the intent to commit a felony." If "ulterior intentions" *are* motives, as Williams claims, how can the existence of these offenses be reconciled with Hall's thesis? The sensible approach is simply to renounce the thesis and affirm the importance of motives to criminal liability.[14] Curiously, however, Williams is unwilling to take this step. His "solution" is simply to redescribe any "ulterior intention" that comprises an element of an offense not as a motive but as a "specific intent." He writes: "In short, whenever an intention to commit another crime is involved in the definition of a crime, it is generally referred to as an intention and not as motive."[15] In other words, if what (otherwise) satisfies the definition of motive is relevant to criminal liability, it cannot (for this reason alone) be deemed a motive.[16]

It is lamentable that scholars willfully embrace such a strategy. Perhaps the major obstacle to the development of Anglo-American criminal theory is the tendency among commentators to advance principles that are initially defended as important substantive insights, but become embellished as vacuous tautologies.[17] The fundamental principles of criminal theory should be falsifiable. Hall's thesis hardly qualifies as an important claim if no conceivable instance of liability could possibly contravene it.

Those who embrace versions of the second account of motives, and construe them as conceptually distinct from intentions, typically regard motives as "springs" or "originators" of actions. Differences between theorists of this school derive largely from disagreements about the nature of practical reasoning. Some accept the Humean account according to which reason is inert in producing action, and thereby liken motives to urges or desires. Others reject the Humean account, and allow that motives *can* function as *reasons* for action. But whatever the nature of reason in influencing behavior, the contrast between motive and intention is expressed by the principle that motives *explain why* a person acted, while intentions *describe what* action was performed. The principle that motives explain while intentions describe is affirmed by all theorists who regard motives and intentions as logically distinct.[18] Gross writes: "A motive can be distinguished from an intention as an explanation of an act and not a description of it."[19] This view is appealing because it lends itself to a theory about why intention but not motive is material to liability. According to this theory, criminal statutes simply describe unlawful conduct. A complete description of conduct includes not only the defendant's *actus reus*, but also his *mens rea* or intention. Trying to kill is a different action than merely pointing a gun in a victim's direction and shooting, even though the physical, behavioral, external components of these actions may be identical. By contrast, this theory continues, motives are *not* included in complete descriptions of conduct. Two actions might be tokens of the same type although explained by different motives. Trying to kill for money is not a different action than trying to kill for spite. Therefore intention, but not motive, is material to criminal liability.

This theory could be challenged at its foundation. Why should the criminal law merely describe illegal conduct? It must be conceded that many factors that are relevant to a defendant's blameworthiness are excluded from a description of his conduct (when the scope of a description is confined to his *actus reus* and his intention). Why should these factors be pertinent only to sentencing, and not to liability? A deeper justification is required to support treating variables that *describe* conduct as relevant only to liability, while treating variables that *explain* conduct as material only to punishment. Surely it is insufficient to simply reply without supporting argument that liability is "action-directed," while punishment is "person-directed." Theories of liability and theories of sentencing each seem to contain assessments of actions as well as of persons,[20] insofar as evaluations of actions and of persons can be clearly distinguished in the first place. Until this "deeper justification" is produced in detail, judgment about this sketch of a theory should be withheld.

Moreover, the claim that intentions describe while motives explain cannot be assessed without sophisticated theories of descriptions and explanations, and no criminal theorist has yet produced them. In the absence of a theory, there is no obvious fact of the matter that settles whether a proposition qualifies as a description or as an explanation of conduct. Depending upon our purposes in raising the inquiry, a proposition might count as either descriptive or explanatory. The end that a person believes will be achieved by his action might either describe or explain it. In this light, reconsider Gross's example about the rich/poor man who is concerned about the motives/intentions of his ugly/beautiful daughter's suitor. If the father is concerned about the suitor's interest in his daughter, either her physical attraction or her wealth seems to qualify as an explanation. But her beauty or money might just as well describe the nature of the suitor's interest. Why is Gross so confident that the plan of the suitor to marry the ugly but rich daughter explains his interest, while the plan of the suitor to seduce the poor but beautiful daughter describes his interest? Gross may be correct in his supposition, but his view cannot be evaluated in the absence of a theory of descriptions and explanations.

Hall's thesis hardly qualifies as an important claim if no conceivable instance of liability could possibly contravene it.

Consider the example of *State v. Warshow*,[21] in which the defendant was convicted of trespassing. Each of the following propositions about his conduct is true. The defendant was:

(a) sitting;
(b) demonstrating;
(c) protesting the opening of a nuclear power plant; and
(d) calling attention to the hazards of nuclear energy.

The orthodox theory of criminal liability would probably label (a) as descriptive, and (b), (c), and (d) as explanatory. The information in addition to (a) that is supplied by (b), (c), and (d) pertains neither to the defendant's *actus reus* nor to his *mens rea* or intention, and thus explains but does not describe his conduct. But these labels seem arbitrary and unfounded. Surely the defendant himself would stress that (a) is inadequate to describe *what* he was doing. He would insist that he was performing a *different action* from that of a defendant who was sitting for altogether different reasons, for example, because he was tired, or paid by a rival power company to cause disruption. There is no obvious reason to insist that the defendant must be incorrect in his insistence.

If the distinction between description and explanation is relative to a purpose, what purpose is operative in the criminal law? Typically, the objective in collecting information about the defendant's conduct is to decide whether he is liable, that is, whether he has committed an offense without justification or excuse. Thus the question of whether motive is relevant or irrelevant to the criminal law depends upon whether the elements of any offenses contain motives, or whether the availability of any justifications or excuses depends upon motives. There is no shortcut to answering this question without examining particular offenses, and attending to theories of justifications and excuses.[22] But what *is* the truth about motives? I believe that the correct account is a hybrid of the two kinds of theories sketched above, and represents something of a compromise between them. This view denies that motives are always a kind of intention, or that they never are. According to this account, some motives are intentions while others are not. Some actions are initiated by further intentions, while others are initiated by reasons, or other mental states. Motives might thus be understood as a "polymorphous collection of action initiators."[23] A somewhat more detailed analysis that might be acceptable to both those who emphasize the similarities and those who emphasize the differences between motives and intentions has been defended by Paul Grice. According to Grice, to have a motive for an action is to believe that some end will be furthered by performing it, and to want or desire to further that end.[24]

Whatever the differences between intentions and motives, there is an important connection between them. If Grice's account is accurate, an action that lacks a motive would be performed without the belief that some desired end would be furthered by performing it. These actions would be purposeless, and it is doubtful that *any* intentional action is purposeless in this sense. Thus it might be said that a person P intentionally performs action x only if P acts on a motive for x-ing. A motive for x-ing must provide some rationale, perhaps very weak, for x-ing. If there were no motive for P's x-ing, x would not be intentional. If these claims are correct,[25] Hall's thesis must again be reinterpreted. *Whether* the defendant has a motive *must* be relevant to liability if the criminal law is to remain interested in intention. The conclusion that a defendant lacked a motive altogether entails that he acted unintentionally, and surely *this* finding is material to liability. Hall must be understood to assert that what is irrelevant to liability is not *whether* the defendant has a motive, but *what* his motive is.

The Relevance of Motive

I do not pretend to have resolved the question of what motives are, or precisely how they might be differentiated from intentions. Nonetheless, I believe Hall's thesis can be shown to be false according to any of the above accounts of motives. Any uncertainty about the relevance of motives does not derive from philosophical confusion about the concept of motive, but rather from substantive moral ambivalence. In this section I will defend this claim by indicating four respects in which it is likely that motives are relevant to criminal liability.

The first of four ways in which motives are material has been described above. Motives (or so-called "specific intentions") are incorporated as elements into the descriptions of a number of existing offenses. Textbooks contain several illustrations of these offenses.[26] They are defined in terms of some end that a defendant wants to further, and believes will be promoted by his action. Whether the "further end" included in these offenses is an explanation or description of the defendant's conduct is immaterial; on any (noncircular) account of motives, the existence of these offenses provides good reason to reject Hall's thesis. Since commentators have long noted the difficulty of reconciling these offenses with Hall's thesis, I will not dwell upon them here. Instead, I will describe three additional (and less obvious) respects in which motives are relevant.

As indicated above, if motives can be shown to be material to whether a defendant has (a) committed a criminal offense (b) without justification or (c) without excuse, their relevance to liability will have been demonstrated. In fact, I believe that motives are sometimes material to *each* of these three determinations. First, I will indicate how a consideration of motives helps to identify whether conduct should be construed as an *act* that transgresses a criminal statute, rather than as an *omission* that does not. Second, I will argue that a defendant may be justified in committing an offense only if he acts with the proper motive. Finally, I will discuss how an evaluation of motives limits the availability of a number of excusing conditions. Despite the apparent significance of motives in each of these three additional respects, criminal theory continues to suffer from the pretense that motives are unimportant.

Acts versus Omissions

Criminal liability does not arise unless the defendant violates a legal duty. Consider the application of this requirement to liability for homicide. In cases in which the defendant's conduct causes death by a positive action, the requirement of a duty owed by the defendant to his victim is always satisfied. Each person owes a duty to all other persons not to cause death by a positive action. But when the defendant's conduct consists in an omission, the existence of a duty becomes problematic. The criminal law has delineated carefully defined circumstances in which persons owe duties to others not to cause death by omission.[27] Thus a defendant who causes death is much more likely to escape liability if he can succeed in convincing the court that his conduct should be characterized as an omission rather than as a positive action.

Unfortunately, the distinction between positive actions and omissions is anything but clear. Perhaps cases of beneficent euthanasia provide the best examples of uncertainty. Is the discontinuance of aid to a terminal patient a positive action or an omission? Reasonable arguments can be made on both sides. The conscientious attempts of commentators to apply an analytical distinction between positive actions and omissions to cases of beneficent euthanasia sometimes yield bizarre results. Depending upon the details of how aid is discontinued, liability is made to depend on subtle distinctions that have no clear significance. Is the withdrawal of the tube of a drip feed that keeps a person alive a positive action? Is the failure to replace an emptied bag an omission?[28] It seems preposterous that liability for homicide would turn on such questions.[29]

As a result of this predicament, the distinction between positive actions and omissions is frequently gerrymandered to achieve desired outcomes.[30] It is doubtful that existing law could ever allow the cessation of aid if all cases of euthanasia consisted of positive actions. Thus those commentators who would permit some instances of euthanasia have been well advised to describe such conduct as an omission. They do not reason that "liability should not arise because this conduct is an omission," but rather "this conduct is an omission because liability should not arise." The contrast between positive actions and omissions is not invoked to *support* the judgment that liability is unjust; it is applied *after* this judgment is reached on independent, unarticulated grounds.

This strategy is objectionable. The integrity of legal reasoning suffers from "arguing backwards." It is disingenuous to invoke a distinction in support of a decision if that decision is reached on grounds having nothing whatever to do with the distinction. The distinction between positive actions and omissions contributes nothing to the analysis in many of these cases. The factor that *really* explains these decisions is hidden from critical scrutiny.

Clearly, motive is one of the most significant factors in explaining why commentators are willing to categorize many cases of euthanasia as omissions rather than as positive actions. Typically, the motive of the physician and the patient's family is to relieve suffering. But if the physician had a bad motive for discontinuing aid to a terminal patient, for example, if he were paid to allow the patient's relatives to collect an early inheritance, there would be no hesitation to describe his conduct as a positive action. The doctor would be a murderer, even though the *effect* of his decision upon the patient -- relief from suffering -- would be identical to that achieved by a good motive.

Expressed in terms of Grice's analysis, the practitioner of beneficent euthanasia is motivated to prevent suffering, inasmuch as he wants or desires to prevent suffering, and believes that euthanasia will further that end. But Grice's account need not be invoked to support the claim that motives are used to draw the distinction between positive actions and omissions. The relevance

The distinction between positive actions and omissions is frequently gerrymandered to achieve desired outcomes.

of motive does not depend upon whether one accepts Williams's account, according to which all motives are ulterior intentions, or Gross's account, according to which no motive is an intention, or some hybrid of the two. If Williams is correct, the physician is motivated to prevent suffering, although this motive is now described as an ulterior intention. And if Gross is correct, the physician still is motivated to prevent suffering, although this motive does not describe his action, but rather explains it. The important point is that motive is material notwithstanding these philosophical differences. Any reluctance to acknowledge the significance of motives does not stem from unclarity about the concept of motive, but rather from substantive moral qualms about the permissibility of euthanasia.

If the criminal law is to avoid injustice, health care professionals who practice beneficent euthanasia will evade liability *somehow*. At present, courts are usually spared the charade of manipulating the distinction between positive actions and omissions because prosecutors exercise their discretion not to bring charges. This "solution," of course, is unprincipled. Doctors should not be forced to entrust their fate to acts of prosecutorial grace. Clearly, a better approach is available. Our moral judgments about whether and to what extent euthanasia is impermissible attach extraordinary significance to the physician's motive, and there is good reason for the criminal law to do likewise. There is nothing improper about allowing liability in such cases to depend largely upon motive. The unwillingness of theorists to identify motive as the crucial variable in order to help distinguish permissible from impermissible euthanasia can be explained only by the powerful grip Hall's thesis holds upon them. I hope to help loosen this grip. A theory of criminal liability would have less need to embrace fictions, engage in backwards reasoning, rely upon prosecutorial discretion, and risk injustice if the real basis for allowing beneficent euthanasia were openly acknowledged.

Justifications and Proper Motives

Under what conditions is a defendant justified in apparently committing a criminal offense?[31] Answers to this question require a theory of justification as a criminal law defense category. A comprehensive theory should provide a plausible view about the relevance of *mistakes* to the availability of a justification. Mistakes typically exculpate, but the apparent significance of motives arises from those relatively rare cases in which mistakes might be said to have an *inculpatory* effect. Can a defendant invoke a justification for his apparent criminal conduct if he was unaware at the time of his conduct of the circumstances that gave rise to the justification? Suppose, for example, that Smith assaults Jones without being aware of any justificatory circumstances. He is ignorant that Jones is about to destroy his most cherished possession, a bust of his aunt, and can be prevented only by the use of force. Had Smith been aware of Jones's effort, there would be no question that his assault would be justifiable under the law that allows the use of (non-deadly) force in the protection of property. May he invoke this justification as a defense if he becomes aware of Jones's plan subsequent to his assault?

The guilt or innocence of a defendant can depend upon how this hypothetical is resolved. But deeper theoretical questions are at stake as well, for the ultimate issue is how the structure of criminal offenses is to be conceptualized. It is important to determine whether the elements that comprise the definitions of distinct offenses must be differentiated from the absence of justifications for committing those offenses. It is clear that a defendant is not liable if he is mistaken in his belief about the presence of an element in the definition of a given offense. Suppose, for example, that a defendant believes he is stealing the property of another. If in fact the property belongs to him, he cannot be liable for theft, regardless of his belief. This result follows from an application of the principle of legality, *nulla poena sine lege*. Simply expressed, the defendant is not violating a criminal law, whatever his intentions. The difficult issue is whether the same analysis applies to mistakes about justifications. Should the absence of justification (for example, that an assault is not in self-defense) be understood as an element (perhaps an "implicit element") in the definition of a given offense? If so, a defendant may invoke a justification even if he was unaware of its existence at the time of his conduct: if a justificatory condition exists in fact, the defendant is not violating a criminal law. But if the absence of justification should not be understood as an element in the definition of a given offense, so that the word "lege" in the principle of legality does not encompass the absence of justifications, it is arguable that the defendant may not invoke a justification he discovers subsequent to his conduct.

A defendant is not liable if he is mistaken in his belief about the presence of an element in the definition of a given offense.

George Fletcher maintains that defendants can invoke a justification only if they act with "justificatory intent."[32] What does this mean? Surprisingly, Fletcher does not provide a detailed elaboration. This much is clear: the absence of belief in a fact that would otherwise serve as a justification implies the absence of a justificatory intent. When so expressed, Fletcher's claim is that a defendant cannot be justified in apparently committing an offense unless he is aware of those facts in which the justification consists. This conclusion can be challenged, but seems to yield a plausible solution in the Jones/Smith hypothetical.[33]

If Fletcher's position is accepted thus far, the next difficult issue is whether mere belief in the existence of a justification is *sufficient* to comprise a "justificatory intent." If belief alone sufficed, Fletcher would probably speak of a "justificatory belief" rather than a "justificatory intent." The question of whether an additional condition is necessary becomes crucial if the above hypothetical is altered so that Smith's ignorance of those facts in which the justification consists plays no role in his conduct. Suppose that Smith planned to assault Jones all along. Suppose further that the following counterfactual is true. Had Smith been aware of

Jones's plan to destroy his bust, he would have reasoned, "How fortunate! Now I can escape liability for assaulting Jones, and, if I am really lucky, get rid of that awful reminder of my aunt at the same time!" This revised hypothetical does not involve a case in which Smith, were he cognizant of the facts, would have *two* sufficient reasons for assaulting Jones.[34] In my example, Smith does not care about his bust at all, and has only one reason to assault Jones upon discovering that his property is about to be destroyed. Should the defense of use of force in the protection of property be available to Smith under these circumstances?[35]

It is hard to understand why mere belief should have a bearing on liability unless it influences conduct.[36] Why should a mistake about a justification make a difference to the defendant's liability if he would have acted exactly as he did whether or not he had made that mistake? Perhaps Fletcher's position should be reinterpreted as follows: A defendant cannot be justified in committing an offense unless he (a) believes those facts in which the justification consists, and (b) acts because of those beliefs.

It seems clear that condition (b) refers to the defendant's motive.[37] Expressed in terms of Grice's analysis, the defense is unavailable to Smith unless he wants or desires to protect his property, and believes that assaulting Jones will further that end. Once again, however, the relevance of motive is established by any competing account of motives as well. The philosophical questions of whether the reference to motive in condition (b) is to an ulterior intention or a desire, or whether motives describe or explain, are immaterial to the argument that confirms their relevance to liability. The defendant cannot be justified if he lacks the proper motive for apparently committing a criminal offense, whatever the deep truth about the nature of motives. Any reluctance to accept this conclusion is based upon substantive disagreements about whether the defendant should be held liable or acquitted in these kinds of cases, and not upon conceptual doubts about the correct analysis of motives.

It is hard to understand why mere belief should have a bearing on liability unless it influences conduct.

If the argument has been accepted to this point, the relevance of motive to a theory of justification and thus to criminal liability has been established. But it is interesting to pursue the analysis one step further, and inquire whether condition (a) is necessary. Alter the hypothetical once again so that Smith is *not* mistaken at the time he assaults Jones; he knows Jones is about to destroy his property, but he would have assaulted Jones even if he had not known this. Is there good reason why the claim "actors may avail themselves of justifications only if they act with justificatory intent" should apply only when a mistake is made? Presumably defendants may lack a "justificatory intent" even when they are *not* mistaken. If so, this position does not appear to be about the relevance of *mistake* to liability at all. The important question is not whether the defendant holds any false beliefs. More simply, Smith cannot plead the defense of use of force in the protection of property unless he had the proper motive for assaulting Jones. If other justifications in the criminal law conform to a similar pattern of analysis, the relevance of motive to criminal liability is clear.

The Availability of Excusing Conditions

Most (recognized as well as controversial) excusing conditions -- intoxication, immaturity, insanity, hypnotism, brainwashing, chromosomal abnormality, and the like -- are named after the disabilities that cause illegal but excused conduct. *Why* should these conditions excuse? Answers to this question require a theory of excuse as a criminal law defense category.

Many of these disabilities give rise to an excuse because they result in nonvoluntary behavior.[38] When is conduct sufficiently nonvoluntary for it to be excused? There is no simple, single answer to this question. Conduct need not be *totally* nonvoluntary, as in a spasm or reflex reaction, before an excuse should be recognized. Conduct that is completely nonvoluntary may not require an excuse; arguably, it does not involve an *actus reus*. The test to determine whether conduct should be exempt from criminal liability on grounds of nonvoluntariness is normative: in light of the circumstances, *should* the defendant have been expected to conform his conduct to law?[39]

It is clear that one factor weighs heavily against, and perhaps defeats altogether, the defendant's allegation that his illegal act should be excused because of nonvoluntariness. This factor is *deliberation*. Suppose a court is initially inclined to excuse a kleptomaniac who provides evidence that he was unable to effectively resist his urge to steal. The court should be prepared to reconsider its judgment upon discovering that the defendant yielded to his inclination only after learning that kleptomaniacs are frequently excused.[40] Illegal conduct that would not have been performed but for the expectation of acquittal seems calculating and controlled. The defendant's reliance on the availability of an excuse is at odds with his claim that his conduct was nonvoluntary.[41]

The same analysis applies to each of the many defenses that depend upon nonvoluntariness. Consider the defense of provocation, which typically reduces the grade of homicide from murder to manslaughter. The most obvious requirement of this defense is that the defendant himself must have been provoked; a defendant is not eligible for this defense simply because the external circumstances were sufficient to provoke a reasonable

The motive *of the defendant is crucial to the availability of those excusing conditions that are based upon nonvoluntariness.*

person. In many jurisdictions, the defendant must actually "lose control," a condition that is reinforced by the requirement that a "cooling-off" period cannot have elapsed between the provocative event and the killing. What factors determine whether a defendant was genuinely provoked? Again, a complete answer to this question is complex and controversial. But it should be clear that an admission by the defendant that his killing was preceded by deliberation, performed in expectation of acquittal (from a charge of murder) undermines his allegation that he lost control. The defense cannot be used as a strategic instrument to allow defendants to accomplish results that are the products of calculation.

These examples illustrate that the *motive* of the defendant is crucial to the availability of those excusing conditions that are based upon nonvoluntariness. Those excusing conditions should be extended only to defendants whose motive for acting is (roughly) the immediate gratification that is experienced by succumbing to inclination. In other words, a defendant must *not* have acted from given motives if a nonvoluntariness defense is to be clearly acceptable. If the alleged kleptomaniac or provoked killer relied upon his belief that he would escape liability for his crimes, and would not have acted but for this belief, it is doubtful that he can be said to have lost control or to have acted nonvoluntarily.

It may be important to distinguish an extreme from a moderate version of the claim that deliberation is at odds with nonvoluntariness. According to the extreme version, deliberation defeats an allegation of nonvoluntariness altogether. Expressed in terms of Grice's analysis -- or, alternatively, in a vocabulary more amenable to Williams or Gross -- a defendant should be convicted if he believed he could escape liability for his offense, wanted or desired to do so, and would not have acted but for this combination of beliefs, wants, and desires. According to the moderate version, deliberation does not conclusively defeat an allegation of nonvoluntariness. The fact that the defendant would not have committed the offense but for this combination of beliefs, wants, and desires does not (as with the extreme version) conclusively preclude the availability of a defense that depends upon nonvoluntariness, but merely provides good reason not to allow that defense. Fortunately, it is not necessary for present purposes to decide whether the extreme or moderate version should be preferred, for either confirms the importance of motives to a theory of excuses and thus to criminal liability.

Conclusion

If my position on the significance of motives to criminal liability is accepted, there is much important work that remains to be done. I hope it will not be objected that I have not undertaken that difficult work here. I have not been so ambitious as to attempt to identify the best or the worst motives, or to describe the several conditions under which motives *should* be relevant to criminal liability. In the context of euthanasia, for example, it must be decided what requirements the physician must satisfy in addition to good motive before he should have a defense to homicide. Must there be uncontroverted medical evidence that no cure is forthcoming? Must the patient consent? How severely must the patient be suffering before beneficent euthanasia may be practiced without liability? I have not sought to answer these questions, but theorists of the substantive criminal law rarely *ask* them. (They are, of course, frequently debated by moral philosophers as well as by sentencing authorities.) There is an understandable reluctance to open Pandora's Box by acknowledging the relevance of motives, but criminal theory pays an even higher price by neglecting them. Finally, I hope to have shown that theorists need not be entirely confident about their analysis of the nature of motives before they can begin to address these difficult issues.

NOTES

I would like to thank Brian McLaughlin, Harold Rubinstein, and the referees of *Criminal Justice Ethics* for their helpful contributions.

1 J. HALL, GENERAL PRINCIPLES OF CRIMINAL LAW 88 (2d ed. 1960). I offer no hypothesis about why Hall's thesis is so widely accepted among criminal theorists.

2 "The basis for . . . assuming a clear distinction between excusing conditions, which operate to relieve a criminal defendant from liability entirely, and mitigating excuses, which are taken into account by way of sentencing discretion . . . is rarely articulated, and when it is, seems unconvincing." Wasik, *Partial Excuses in the Criminal Law*, 45 MOD. L. REV. 516 (1982).

3 *See* Note, *The Cultural Defense in the Criminal Law*, 99 HARV. L. REV. 1293 (1986).

4 *See* Tonry, *Criminal Law: The Missing Element in Sentencing Reform*, 35 VAND. L. REV. 607 (1982).

5 *See* the discussion in A. ASHWORTH, SENTENCING AND PENAL POLICY 81-91 (1983).

6 Federal criminal civil rights statutes -- 18 U.S.A. Sec. 241 and 242 -- are typically used to prosecute criminal conduct motivated by racial prejudice. The reference to racial motive, however, is included to establish federal jurisdiction, and thus may not reflect a judgment that racially motivated crimes are more culpable than non-racially motivated crimes.

7 *See* Hall's ground for rejecting Salmond's definition: "[T]he criticism of Salmond's usage is based upon . . . countless decisions holding that motive is not a material element of a crime." *Supra* note 1, at 85, n. 67.

8 H. GROSS, A THEORY OF CRIMINAL JUSTICE 111 (1979). Gross attributes this example to "a philosopher," but neglects to identify him.

9 *See* Sistare, *Agent Motives and the Criminal Law*, 13 SOC. THEORY & PRAC. 303 (1987).

10 G. WILLIAMS, CRIMINAL LAW: THE GENERAL PART 48 (2d ed. 1961). *See also* J. SALMOND, JURISPRUDENCE 397 (7th ed. 1924).

11 G. WILLIAMS, *id.*

12 G. WILLIAMS, *supra* note 10, n. 2.

13 Yet Williams insists that the distinction is significant. *See* text accompanying *infra* note 15.

14 *See* Hitchler, *Motive as an Essential Element of Crime*, 35 DICK L. REV. 105 (1930-1931).

15 *Supra* note 10, at 49.

16 *See* W. LAFAVE & A. SCOTT, CRIMINAL LAW 206 (1972). .

17 *See* D. HUSAK, PHILOSOPHY OF CRIMINAL LAW (1987), for a discussion of how the *actus reus, mens rea*, causation, and harm requirements have been "defended" by being interpreted as tautologies.

18 Notice that according to Williams's kind of account, according to which motives are a kind of intention, it is difficult (or impossible) to defend the view that intentions are descriptions while motives are explanations. If intentions describe, and motives are a kind of intention, then presumably motives describe as well.

19 *Supra* note 8, at 111.

20 *See* Von Hirsch, *Desert and Previous Convictions in Sentencing*, 65 U. MINN. L. REV. 591 (1981).

21 410 A.2d 1000 (1979).

22 *See* Part III.

23 *See* Sistare, *supra* note 9, at 306. The chief difficulty with this view is to identify those "action-initiators" that are not motives.

24 *See* P. Grice, *Motive and Reason*, in PRACTICAL REASONING 168 (J. Raz ed. 1978).

25 I believe these claims are widely accepted among philosophers. Disagreement surrounds the nature of practical reasoning and whether the notion of "acting on" a motive must be understood causally.

26 In light of these offenses, Sistare remarks, "If there is a real ground for dispute here, it seems to be a question of how many exceptions remake the rule." *Supra* note 9, at 316.

27 *See Jones v. U.S.*, 308 F.2d 307 (1962).

28 *See* Beynon, *Doctors as Murderers*, CRIM. L. REV.. (1982).

29 *See* J.C. SMITH & B. HOGAN, CRIMINAL LAW 44 (5th ed. 1983).

30 *See* the analysis in Fletcher, *Prolonging Life: Some Legal Considerations*, 42 WASH. L. REV. 999 (1967). The influence of this analysis in case law is illustrated by *Barber v. Superior Court of Los Angeles County*, 195 Cal. Rptr. 484 (1983).

31 It is unclear whether a defendant whose conduct is justified actually commits a criminal offense. *See* D. HUSAK,, *supra* note 17, at 190-92.

32 G. FLETCHER, RETHINKING CRIMINAL LAW 557 (1978).

33 But *see* Robinson, *A Theory of Justification: Societal Harm as*

a Prerequisite for Criminal Liability, 23 UCLA L. REV. 261 (1975).

34 Thus my hypothetical does not involve overdetermination. In my original hypothetical, were Smith aware of Jones's plan, he probably would have two sufficient motives for assault. Presumably, if either of the defendant's motives for assault falls under a justification, the defense should be available. But some requirements for the use of justifications are more stringent. A few commentators refer to the defendant's "dominant motivation." *See* W. LAFAVE & F. SCOTT, *supra* note 16, at 207. California requires that some such defenses be available only if the defendant acts "under the influence of such fears alone." *See* CAL. PENAL CODE, Sec. 198 (1970).

35 I do not discuss the formidable problems of evidence that are involved in resolving these hypotheticals about the inculpatory effect of mistakes.

36 LaFave and Scott endorse the puzzling view that the availability of a justification is dependent upon "objective facts," but immediately contradict this conclusion by adding: "This does not mean, of course, that the defense can be manufactured after the event by resort to facts not known to the actor when he engaged in the conduct." *Supra* note 16, at 206-07.

37 Robinson describes "justificatory intent" not as motive but "purpose." *See* P. ROBINSON, 2 CRIMINAL LAW DEFENSES 17, n. 7 (1982).

38 There is a great deal of debate among commentators about how many excusing conditions involve nonvoluntary behavior. Robinson contends that a condition does not excuse unless "the act constituting the offense is not the product of a meaningful choice." *Id.*, at 223, n.1.

39 *See* the insightful discussion of voluntariness as a "variable concept" in J. FEINBERG, HARM TO SELF 117-24 (1986).

40 Some commentators tentatively suggest that excusing conditions not be publicized, so that resolve to comply with the law is not weakened. See Dan-Cohen, *Decision Rules and Conduct Rules: On Acoustic Separation in Criminal Law*, 97 HARV. L. Rev. 625 (1984).

41 See Fletcher, *Paradoxes in Legal Thought*, 85 COL. L. REV. 1263, 1283 (1985).

Part IV
Defences, Justifications and Excuses

[9]

A THEORY OF JUSTIFICATION: SOCIETAL HARM AS A PREREQUISITE FOR CRIMINAL LIABILITY

Paul H. Robinson*

I. Introduction: The Requirement of Societal Harm

All would agree that the criminal law seeks to prevent harmful results rather than to punish evil intent that produces no harm. Justice Holmes suggested that "the aim of the law is not to punish sins, but to prevent certain external results."[1] LaFave and Scott similarly claim that "[t]he broad purposes of the criminal law are, of course, to make people do what society regards as desirable and to prevent them from doing what society considers to be undesirable."[2] If the criminal law is extended to punish bad intent alone or the mere possibility of harmful conduct, it goes beyond its accepted role, appears unfair and overreaching, and ultimately loses its credibility and integrity.[3]

If one views deterrence as the proper function of the criminal law, a harm requirement is appropriate. To the extent that the criminal law punishes nonharmful conduct, it weakens the stigma and deterrent effect of criminal conviction for harmful conduct. If a defendant who has caused no harm feels that he is punished unjustifiably, rehabilitative efforts will be hampered. Indeed, one may ask: If no harm has been caused, what harm will be deterred by punishment, and what harm-causing characteristic will be rehabili-

---

* B.S. 1970, Rensselaer Polytechnic Institute; J.D. 1973, UCLA School of Law; LL.M. 1974, Harvard Law School. Attorney, United States Department of Justice, Criminal Division, Legislation and Special Projects Section. The views expressed in this Article do not necessarily represent the views of the United States Department of Justice.

I am indebted to Professor George P. Fletcher of UCLA Law School for his intellectual contributions and moral support during the development and preparation of this Article. As is clear from his reply article, however, his support of my efforts cannot necessarily be taken as support for my ideas.

1 Commonwealth v. Kennedy, 170 Mass. 18, 20, 48 N.E. 770, 777 (1897).

2 W. LaFave & A. Scott, Handbook on Criminal Law 21 (1972) [hereinafter cited as LaFave & Scott].

3 This danger is reflected in the existence of such controversies as those concerning preventive detention, decriminalization of prostitution, marijuana, gambling, private sexual acts, and regulatory offenses.

tated? If one believes that the role of the criminal law is to provide retribution, a harm requirement is also proper; in the absence of harm there is nothing for which to seek retribution. Edward Livingston suggests that "[m]oral guilt must be united to injury in order to justify punishment."[4] The consistency of a requirement of harm with these fundamental purposes of the criminal law is reflected in the fact that harm has, from the earliest of civilized times, been treated as a de facto requirement. In ancient Israel where murder was a recognized societal harm but assault was not,[5] the victim's death was a prerequisite to imposition of any criminal sanctions,[6] even if the attacker struck the blow with intent to kill.

If the criminal law is limited in operation to situations involving a harm of some sort,[7] then an act found to be beneficial, or at

---

[4] 1 THE COMPLETE WORKS OF EDWARD LIVINGSTON ON CRIMINAL JURISPRUDENCE 235 (1873) [hereinafter cited as LIVINGSTON].

[5] A. PHILLIPS, ANCIENT ISRAEL'S CRIMINAL LAW 87 (1970). *Exodus* 21:18, 19 (King James) reads:

> And if men strive together, and one smite another with a stone, or with *his* fist, nad he die not, but keepeth *his* bed:
>
> If he rise again, and walk abroad upon his staff, then shall he that smote *him* be quit: only he shall pay *for* the loss of this time, and shall cause *him* to be htoroughly healed.

[6]
> Exodus 21:18f confirms that even if there is both intent and the requisite blow, this is immaterial as far as criminal law is concerned, unless the victim dies. If he is saved by the skill of the doctor, the case is one of assault.

PHILLIPS, *supra* note 5, at 87.

[7] The term "harm" as used here has its common meaning "physical or mental damage," "an act or instance of injury," or a "detriment or loss to a person." WEBSTER'S THIRD NEW INTERNATIONAL DICTIONARY 1034 (1971). The concept of "societal harm" as used in this Article is similarly defined by these attributes—damage, injury, detriment, and loss—and includes not only harm done to individuals but also damage to the society or a part of it. Thus societal harm includes injury to an individual, a group, an institution, or a society. It may be to human beings directly, or indirectly through harm to the property or relationships of persons.

The concept of societal harm has an admittedly controversial fringe. It is currently debated, for example, whether gambling or private sexual acts cause societal harm. Some may claim that this concept of societal harm is so vague and amorphous as to be meaningless, but in fact the concept has a straight-forward and distinct meaning. For example, one could argue to a legislature that homosexual acts do not constitute a societal harm and should not be prohibited. One argues this by making and trying to document the claim that homosexual acts do not damage or injure society. It is not necessary to repudiate the requirement of societal harm to support legalization of homosexual acts.

Some acts will be neutral, causing neither a societal harm nor a societal benefit; and many acts will have both harmful and beneficial results. If an act causes more harm than benefit it is natural to look on the act as being harmful. This, of course, reflects an orientation toward the ultimate rather than an intermediate harm. The universal acceptance of such an orientation is reflected in the general acceptance by all of some limited principle of justification. Our willingness to forgo punishment for a killing reasonably done in self-defense, for example, illustrates our orientation toward the end result, not an intermediate result alone.

The nature of a neutral act merits special mention. It, like all other acts, must be either criminal or noncriminal. Because the standard for noncriminality has

least not harmful, should be of no concern to the criminal law. As Macaulay explains:

> When an act is of such a description that it would be better that it should not be done, it is quite proper to look at the motives and intentions of the doer, for the purpose of deciding whether he shall be punished or not. But when an act which is really useful to society, an act of a sort which it is desirable to encourage, has been done, it is absurd to inquire into the motives of the doer, for the purpose of punishing him if it shall appear that his motives were bad.[8]

Views of what is societally harmful may differ from time to time and from society to society. This occurs because, first, views of what is considered an injury may differ. Rape in one society may be an honor in another. Second, conduct which causes harm at one time or in one society may not cause harm in another. Broadcasting a wide range radio signal is a societal harm in the twentieth century but would not have been in the nineteenth. Similarly, the extent of the injury—the seriousness of the harm—may change, as in horsestealing. Third, the level of scientific achievement may affect the ability of society to detect injury. Failure to pasteurize milk could not have been seen as criminal before the germ theory of disease was understood.

Creation of a risk of harm is not necessarily a harm in itself. But acts which create only a risk of harm may in fact cause another harm. Swinging a fist at a person may not injure him as intended, but it may cause an apprehension of injury that is itself a harm. The possession of burglary tools, while only creating a risk of a burgla-

---

been set as the absence of harm rather than the presence of a benefit, it follows that a neutral act would then be noncriminal. Note, however, that objective symmetry is not necessarily neutrality. For example, in the case of two shipwreck survivors clinging to a plank that can support only one, the societal harm of one death seems at first to be identical to another; thus if one pushed the other off to save his own life, it would be a neutral and hence noncriminal act. But it may well be that the required pushing prevents the act from being truly neutral. It might be contended, for example, that the use, and approval, of aggression in any situation tends to cause aggression by other persons, and does in fact result in clearly harmful results. Thus the aggression of one survivor toward the other would render the act harmful, rather than neutral, and hence criminal.

For an enlightening examination of the concept of harm and its role in criminal law, see J. HALL, GENERAL PRINCIPLES OF CRIMINAL LAW 213-46 (2d ed. 1960) [hereinafter cited as HALL]. Hall concludes, "[H]arm, in sum, is the fulcrum between criminal conduct and the punitive sanction; and the elucidation of these interrelationships is a principal task of penal theory." *Id.* at 213.

[8] 7 THE WORKS OF LORD MACAULAY 552-53 (H. Trevelyan ed. 1866). The passage continues:

> If A. kills Z. it is proper to inquire whether the killing was malicious; for killing is *primâ facie* a bad act. But if A. saves Z.'s life, no tribunal inquires whether A. did so from good feeling, or from malice to some person who was bound to pay Z. an annuity; for it is better that human life should be saved from malice than not at all.

Id.

ry, may cause in addition a separate harm in itself. The possession of such tools may support a system for producing and distributing tools which *are* used for burglaries. There are, however, other risks of harm that do not cause harm in themselves. For example, no harm results from a person shaking his fist at a rain cloud honestly expecting to cause the destruction of the world. If one adopts the theory that dangerous but nonharmful conduct should be punished, then why not punish one who shakes his fist at a rain cloud, since he has shown his dangerous intentions? Or why not punish a man for having sexual intercourse with a twenty-two year old woman he reasonably believed to be under sixteen, since such conduct is similarly dangerous? We do not do so because the harm requirement has not been met. Just as our common law tradition prevents punishment of evil thoughts or of potentially dangerous people, so too does it prohibit criminal liability for acts that create only the possibility of harm. Even criminal negligence, which is ostensibly punishment for creating a risk of harm, is punished only when the risk of harm has actually resulted in a harm.[9]

In many cases, rational men can disagree about whether a harm has occurred. It has been suggested, for example, that inchoate offenses such as conspiracy, solicitation, and attempt are by definition crimes from which no ultimate harm results—in other words, punishment is imposed for intending to do harm or for creating a risk of harm.[10] I will contend, however, that the inchoate offenses do not punish bad intent evidenced by overt acts, but rather punish conduct which is harmful to society in a way apart from the harm which might have resulted had the actor's intent been fulfilled.[11] The harm is intangible in character, and society is its object. Inchoate offenses not only create a risk of harm, they are harms in themselves. Thus the debate surrounding inchoate offenses does not focus on whether a harm shall be required, but on whether the harm from inchoate offenses is substantial enough to merit prohibition and punishment by the criminal law.

Whether a particular societal harm is sufficient to justify criminal punishment can cause considerable debate, as evidenced by the extensive and long-lived concern over the impossible attempt problem.[12] Some have concluded that an impossible attempt

[9] The felony-murder rule, for example, punishes only felons who actually cause a death, not those who create the identical risk of such a death.

[10] *See, e.g.*, LA FAVE & SCOTT, *supra* note 2, at 9.

[11] *See, e.g.*, HALL, *supra* note 7, at 217-20. *See* notes 12-25 & accompanying text *infra*.

[12] Impossible attempts should be distinguished from the traditional attempt paradigm. In the latter, the actor can only be convicted of attempting to commit a substantive offense because his actions did not go far enough toward committing

does not cause societal harm sufficient for punishment. In *People v. Jaffe*[13] the defendant believed he was purchasing stolen cloth. Unknown to him, the police had discovered the theft and returned the stolen cloth, but continued the prearranged delivery to Jaffe in an attempt to apprehend the fence. The cloth Jaffe bought was not in fact stolen, and the court refused to convict.[14] A number of other cases have demonstrated a similar judgment that an impossible attempt, even with the requisite guilty intent, does not produce sufficient harm to warrant criminal liability.[15] One commentator supporting this view has concluded that "the act of attempt is not in itself harmful to the state. The crime is a mere shadow of the attempted offense."[16] Another states that "[n]either society, nor any private person, has been injured by [an attempt]. There is no damage, therefore, to redress."[17]

Other courts and commentators, however, have concluded that an impossible attempt does generate sufficient harm to warrant criminal liability. In *People v. Siu*[18] the defendant purchased what he believed was heroin. The seller was a police officer who had substituted sugar for the heroin seized earlier. The court concluded that it was sufficient that Siu believed he was purchasing heroin and went through all the necessary motions to make the purchase. Supporting this view Edward Livington has said, "every attempt, although it fail . . . of itself, is an injury."[19] Other writers have described criminal attempts as causing "a disturbance of the social order,"[20] "a sufficient social harm to be deemed criminal,"[21] "a

---

the substantive offense. For example, he might have been caught lighting a fuse on dynamite sticks planted under a building. An impossible attempt is an entirely different situation in that the substantive offense not only was not committed, but *could not* have been committed, even if the actor had gone through all the motions. For example, if the "dynamite sticks" were, unbeknownst to the actor, only wooden sticks, he might still be prosecuted for an attempt, even though the substantive offense was impossible.

13 185 N.Y. 497, 78 N.E. 169 (1906).

14 The court's opinion, however, attempted to use traditional concepts by reasoning that, to be convicted of receiving stolen property, Jaffe had to *know* the property was stolen and since the cloth was not stolen, no man could have that knowledge. *Id.* at 501, 78 N.E. at 170.

15 *See* Wilson v. State, 85 Miss. 687, 690, 38 So. 46, 47 (1905); People v. Teal, 196 N.Y. 372, 377, 89 N.E. 1086, 1087 (1909); Rex v. Osborn, 84 J.P. 63 (1919).

16 Beale, *Criminal Attempts*, 16 HARV. L. REV. 491 (1903).

17 1 F. WHARTON, CRIMINAL LAW 307 (12th ed. 1932). This statement, however, does not appear in later editions.

18 126 Cal. App. 2d 41, 271 P.2d 575 (1954). *See also* Faustina v. Superior Court, 174 Cal. App. 2d 830, 345 P.2d 543 (1959) (noting and disapproving *Jaffe*); People v. Rojas, 55 Cal. 2d 252, 358 P.2d 921, 10 Cal. Rptr. 465 (1961) (approving *Faustina*).

19 1 LIVINGSTON, *supra* note 4, at 235.

20 J. MAY, LAW OF CRIMES 191 (4th ed. K. Sears & H. Weihofen 1938).

21 Hitchler, *Criminal Attempts*, 43 DICK. L. REV. 211 (1939).

substantial but incomplete impairment of some interest,"[22] "a societal harm,"[23] and "a community disturbance."[24] The controversy over impossible attempts demonstrates the law's concern that harm be present whenever criminal liability is imposed.[25]

The issue whether a harm is sufficient to support criminal liability need not be endlessly disputed. It can for practical purposes be authoritatively decided by a legislature. But if the legislature fails to determine whether particular conduct causes sufficient societal harm, or if the legislature cannot make this decision—either because the situation cannot reasonably be anticipated or because the circumstances relevant to the decision are so numerous or varied that case-by-case decisions are necessary—the courts must undertake the determination. The question whether harm has occurred may appropriately be resolved in the same way as any other question of fact. The vehicle for raising such a question, as suggested in the next Part, is the defense of justification. The factors which are pertinent to such a determination have been discussed here; other factors which are mistakenly treated as pertinent are discussed in Part IV.

II. The Role of Justification

A society's need for a public statement of the conduct deemed impermissible and for guidance in determining whether given conduct has violated those standards often gives rise to a written criminal code. No such code, however, can accurately prescribe the correct conduct in all situations; it can only provide an approximation of society's intuitive judgments. This limitation may be attributed to a number of factors: First, in attempting to provide for the infinite variety of factual situations, a code must necessarily make generalizations which are subject to exceptions; second, and perhaps more important, human moral judgments may

---

[22] Strahorn, *The Effect of Impossibility on Criminal Attempts*, 78 U. PA. L. REV. 962, 970 (1930).

[23] Curran, *Criminal and Non-Criminal Attempts* (pts. 1-2), 13 GEO. L.J. 185, 316 (1930-1931).

[24] 1 J. BISHOP, CRIMINAL LAW 530 (9th ed. 1923).

[25] The issue of the sufficiency of societal harm to justify criminal liability can also be seen in the considerable debate over whether the criminal law should be restricted to preventing an individual from harming others or whether it might properly be used to prevent a person from harming himself. *See* J. MILL, ON LIBERTY (1863); J. STEPHEN, LIBERTY, EQUALITY, FRATERNITY (2d ed. 1874). The debate generally centers on whether the criminal law should be used to enforce morality. *See* P. DEVLIN, THE ENFORCEMENT OF MORALS (1965); H.L.A. HART, LAW, LIBERTY AND MORALITY (1963). Neither side would suggest that the criminal law may punish without a harm. Rather, they differ only on whether immoral conduct is a sufficient harm.

well be too complex to be represented by a set of rules, or at least any set now available.[26]

The imperfect correspondence between acts which are intuitively felt to be impermissible and acts defined as impermissible by a written penal code produces two groups of inaccurate results: Some undesirable acts are not prohibited by the code (*e.g.*, few codes prohibit eating the flesh of dead humans);[27] and some desirable acts are prohibited (*e.g.*, burning a field without permission in order to create a firebreak which will protect a town). The first category produces many interesting difficulties, often centering on what constitutes sufficient notice of criminal conduct, and the demands of a "higher" unwritten code of conduct. The concern of this Article, however, is with the second category.

It is contended here that the role of the principle of justification is to compensate for the limitations of a written code reflected in this second group of inaccurate results—to provide an exculpating exception for acts that are prohibited by the written code but nonetheless are proper because of justifying circumstances not accounted for in it.[28] Under this theory, the principle of justification is in a sense similar to a penal code: Both serve to limit the jurisdiction of the criminal law to acts deemed undesirable, or, more precisely, to consequences deemed harmful. The penal code identifies conduct that society normally considers harmful; the principle of justification further screens out those cases where, due to the special circumstances of the situation, no harm has in fact occurred.[29]

---

[26] Sir James Stephen suggests:

> It is just possible to imagine cases in which the expediency of breaking the law is so overwhelmingly great that people may be justified in breaking it; but these cases cannot be defined beforehand.

2 J. Stephen, A History of the Criminal Law of England 109 (1883).

[27] Punishment for an undesirable act not specifically prohibited by the code is generally forbidden under the maxim *nullum crimen sine lege.*

[28] As Serjeant Pollard expressed it in the case of Peniger v. Forgossa, 75 Eng. Rep. 1 (1550), one of the first cases formally recognizing the defense of necessity:

> [I]n every law there are some things which when they happen a man may break the words of the law, and yet not break the law itself; and such things are exempted out of the penalty of the law, and the law privileges them although they are done against the letter of it, for breaking the words of the law is not breaking the law, so as the intent of the law is not broken. . . . [I]t is a common proverb, *Quod necessitas non habet legem.*

Id. at 29-30.

[29] The theory of justification presented here is in a sense the reverse side of strict liability and objective criminality: That is, a man may be convicted of a crime because of harm he has caused, notwithstanding his failure to intend to cause such harm; conversely, a man may be free from criminal liability if he intended to commit a crime yet committed no harm. While in the former case his behavior did not meet the objective standard of conduct society had set down, in the latter case it did.

To a limited extent, this concept of justification is currently reflected in the criminal law. The killing of another human being is normally a form of manslaughter or murder, yet the killing of a bank robber who is resisting lawful arrest with lethal force is justifiable homicide. Society's need to apprehend robbers, to protect its police, and to deter other robbers from using lethal force to resist arrest make the killing—on balance—more beneficial than harmful, and it should therefore be legal.[30] Many commentators agree that the absence of ultimate harm is at least a factor in permitting a defense of justification.[31] However, apparently no writer agrees that the presence or absence of societal harm is alone determinative of the justification issue.[32]

---

30 Some writers, however, contend that the basis for a defense of justification is not that there is on balance an absence of harm, but an absence of the *mens rea* necessary to convict the actor. *See, e.g.*, W. CLARK & W. MARSHALL, A TREATISE ON THE LAW OF CRIMES 462 (7th ed. 1967). But to be consistent, these writers must either exclude from the operation of the principle those offenses requiring a specific intent or assume that an element of every offense is a general intent to do something criminal. No commentator appears to have approved the first alternative. Indeed, such a theory does not correspond to any accepted meaning of the justification principle. The second alternative proves too much. The requirement of a general criminal intent would prevent criminal liability from being founded on theories of strict liability, criminal negligence, or even recklessness. It would require, at the very least, a purposeful or knowing state of mind, no matter how harmful the act. This view is inconsistent with our intuitive judgments of which acts, coupled with which states of mind, warrant punishment.

31 Justin Miller, for example, observes:

> [T]hese [justified] acts are ones, as regard which, upon balancing all considerations of public policy, it seems desirable that they should be encouraged and commended even though in each case some individual may be injured or the result may be otherwise not wholly to be desired.

J. MILLER, HANDBOOK OF CRIMINAL LAW 189 (1934). LaFave and Scott specifically note:

> The rationale of the necessity defense is not that a person, when faced with the pressure of circumstances of nature, lacks the mental element which the crime in question requires. Rather, it is this reason of public policy: the law ought to promote the achievement of higher values at the expense of lesser values, and sometimes the greater good for society will be accomplished by violating the literal language of the criminal law.

LAFAVE & SCOTT, *supra* note 2, at 382. Similarly, Jerome Hall points out that:

> [w]hat is common in these [justification] situations is that no crime was committed because there were special circumstances which made the commission of the injury in question . . . a 'privilege.' . . .
>
> . . . The accused has done something which, under the special conditions, is not a penal harm. . . .

HALL, *supra* note 7, at 232-33. Hall defines "penal harm" in a way different from "societal harm" as defined here, in that "penal harm" will have occurred, for example, even if an act is beneficial, if the actor did not have knowledge of the justifying circumstances. *Id.* at 233. Hall specifically rejects a concept in which "justification can be established solely by reference to the external situation." *Id.* This would presumably include the theory of justification presented here.

32 Though justification is often considered a "defense" (*see, e.g.*, MODEL PENAL CODE § 3.01(1) (Proposed Official Draft 1962)), it is more properly viewed as an "element" of an offense in the sense that no crime can be said to

III. THE PROCESS AND EFFECT OF MIXING JUSTIFICATION AND EXCUSE

The essence of the question of justification should be whether harm has occurred. Thus, as Macaulay suggests, actor-oriented considerations such as motive are not pertinent to the analysis.[33] Yet such considerations have been introduced; in all probability they have been derived from the other general principle of exculpation, excuse. Accordingly, to understand the principle of justification one must appreciate its contrast to the principle of excuse, as well as the process by which the two principles have been mixed.

A. *The Distinction*

The theoretical distinction between justification and excuse is well established.[34] Justified behavior is correct behavior and therefore is not only tolerated but encouraged. In determining whether given conduct is justified, the focus is upon the *act*, not the

---

have occurred if the act is justified or, in other words, *unless* the act was *non*-justified. Although non-justification may conceptually be an element of each offense, it may be procedurally necessary to give the defendant the burden of coming forward with evidence of justification, or of at least raising the issue. On the other hand, one might argue that the state should be required to make a prima facie case that a legislatively recognized harm has resulted.

33 7 THE WORKS OF LORD MACAULAY (T. Trevelyan ed. 1866).

34 In the case of 'justification' what is done is regarded as something which the law does not condemn, or even welcomes.[16] [note 16: "In 1811 Mr. Purcell of Co. Cork, a septuagenarian, was knighted for killing four burglars with a carving knife." Kenny, *Outlines of Criminal Law*, 5th edn., p.103, n.3.] But where the killing (e.g. accidental) is excused criminal responsibility is excluded on a different footing. What has been done is something which is deplored, but the psychological state of the agent when he did it exemplified one or more of a variety of conditions which are held to rule out the public condemnation and punishment of individuals.

H.L.A. HART, PUNISHMENT AND RESPONSIBILITY 13-14 (1968).

"Justification" is defined as:

> The action of justifying or showing something to be just, right, or proper; vindication of oneself or another; exculpation. . . .
> *Law*. a. The showing or maintaining in court that one had sufficient reason for doing that which he is called to answer. . . .

5 THE OXFORD ENGLISH DICTIONARY 643 (1933). In contrast, "excuse" is defined as:

> I. To offer, or serve as, an exculpation for.
> 1. *trans.* To offer an apology for.
> a. To attempt to clear (a person) wholly or partially from blame, without denying or justifying his imputed action.
> . . . .
> b. To seek or extenuate or remove the blame of (an acknowledged fault).
> . . . .
> II. To accept an excuse for or from.
> 6. . . . .
> a. To accept a plea in exculpation of (a person); to judge leniently on the ground of extenuating circumstances.

3 THE OXFORD ENGLISH DICTIONARY 391 (1933).

actor; hence, a finding of justification is a finding that the act was justified. Traditional examples of justification include necessity, defense of others, actions in an official capacity, and some cases of self-defense. Excuse, on the other hand, focuses on the actor, rather than the act. A successful defense of excuse represents a legal conclusion that although the act was wrong, liability is inappropriate because some characteristic of the actor vitiates society's desire to punish him. Insanity, duress, infancy, mistake, and some forms of self-defense are typical examples of excuse.

Justification and excuse are serial rather than alternative determinations. One asks whether an actor should be excused only after one has determined that the act was not justified. If the act were justified, there would of course be nothing to excuse.

B. *The Process of Mixing Justification and Excuse*

At early common law, the distinction between justification and excuse was not only theoretically clear but of crucial practical importance. A person with a defense of justification was acquitted "as if the finding had been that he did not do the killing,"[35] while a person with a defense of excuse was given a sentence identical to what he or she would have received without the defense—death and forfeiture of all goods. The excused defendant could, however, escape execution if pardoned by the Crown.[36] While pardons may originally have been special occurrences,[37] they were granted with increasing regularity until the chancellor issued them as a matter of course without consulting the monarch;[38] but a defendant was still held in custody, and later under bail, until the pardon was granted.[39] During this period of institutionalization of the pardon, a defendant's goods were still forfeited.[40] This practice too was gradually abandoned and the excused defendant was given a "writ of restitution of his goods" in addition to a pardon.[41] Throughout this evolution of the punishment for an excused defendant, a justified act resulted in complete acquittal.[42]

---

[35] R. PERKINS, CRIMINAL LAW 1001 (2d ed. 1969) [hereinafter cited as PERKINS].

[36] *Id.* at 1001 n.56.

[37] *Id.* at 1001 n.58.

[38] *Id.* at 1001 n.59.

[39] *Id.* at 1001 n.61.

[40] *Id.* at 1001 n.60.

[41] 4 W. BLACKSTONE, COMMENTARIES *188. It was not until 1838 that forfeiture was abolished by statute. 9 Geo. 4, c. 13, § 10 (1838).

[42] The historical distinction between justification and excuse is practically and theoretically identical to the distinction used here and by other writers. *See, e.g.*, H.L.A. HART, *supra* note 34, at 13-14. However, the defenses categorized under the respective principles differ slightly from the common law usage. Self-defense, for example, is under certain circumstances considered a form of justifica-

The early common law distinction between justification and excuse exists today only in theory.[43] For example, one writer, commenting on self-defense, explains:

> [T]he distinction between justifiable and excusable self-defense was, at one time, one of considerable importance. Moreover, it is still occasionally referred to in the cases and the two are still separately classified in the texts. However, so far as present day law is concerned, the distinction is one without a difference. . . . The terms are generally used synonymously and interchangeably.[44]

The remainder of this Article will explore the problems created by mixing justification and excuse.[45]

---

tion. But at early common law it appears to have been considered an excuse. *See, e.g.*, 4 W. BLACKSTONE, COMMENTARIES *187. It has been suggested that at a still earlier period self-defense was neither a justification nor an excuse. 2 F. POLLOCK & F. MAITLAND, THE HISTORY OF ENGLISH LAW 476 (2d ed. 1898); Ames, *Law and Morals*, 22 HARV. L. REV. 97 (1908); Beale, *Retreat from a Murderous Assault*, 16 HARV. L. REV. 567 (1903).

43 Some practical vestiges remain, however. In California Penal Code sections 195, 196, and 197, for example, excusable homicide is described as that caused by an unfortunate accident, while justifiable homicide is that which might be considered necessary, privileged, or desirable under the circumstances. *See* CAL. PENAL CODE §§ 195-97 (West 1970). This is consistent with Blackstone's statement of the distinction between excusable and justifiable homicide.

> In these instances of *justifiable* homicide, it may be observed that the slayer is in no kind of fault whatsoever, not even in the minutest degree; and is therefore to be totally acquitted and discharged, with commendation rather than blame. But that is not quite the case in *excusable* homicide, the very name whereof imports some fault, some error, or omission; so trivial however, that the law excuses it from the guilt of felony, though in strictness it judges it deserving of . . . punishment.

4 W. BLACKSTONE, COMMENTARIES *182.

44 J. MILLER, *supra* note 31, at 199. Miller also notes that, "the distinction between justifiable and excusable homicide is unimportant in the law of to-day." *Id.* at 255. Jerome Hall considers the distinction "fallacious and misleading when . . . applied as notions of substantive penal theory." HALL, *supra* note 7, at 233. And in a recent criminal law hornbook the defenses of "ignorance or mistake," "entrapment," "duress," "necessity," "public duty," "domestic authority," "self-defense," "defense of another," "defense of property," "law enforcement," and "consent, conduct, or condonation by victim" are presented in that order, in a single chapter entitled "Justification and Excuse," and without any attempt at classifying the various defenses as one or the other. LAFAVE & SCOTT, *supra* note 2, at 356. *See also* GA. CODE § 26-1011 (1933), *as amended*, § 26-901 (1972): "There being no rational distinction between excusable and justifiable homicide, it shall no longer exist."

It might be argued that the gradual elimination of the penalty in the case of excuse was a conscious effort to reject the justification-excuse distinction. But the fact that, even after the abolition of a difference in penalty, the common law retained for two centuries a working conceptual distinction, would seem to refute this contention.

45 In addition to the specific inequities discussed in notes 46-52 and accompanying text *infra*, the merger of justification and excuse creates a more general difficulty for the criminal justice system. The determination by a court that a defendant is excused, when in fact his conduct is justified, condemns conduct that the legal system should encourage. As people find that some excused conduct seems wrong (that which should be excused) and other excused

C. *The Effect of Mixing Justification and Excuse*

1. The Use of Defensive Force to Repel an Attacker

The propriety of using defensive force to repel an attack cannot be properly determined without reviving the distinction between justification and excuse. If an attack, an act normally prohibited, is justified, as in the case of a lawful arrest, then defensive force should not be approved. But if the attack is only excused, defensive force should be deemed justified.[46] The present

---

conduct appears correct (that which should be justified), the condemnation of improper conduct by excuse is weakened. Thus all justification or excuse cases will necessarily serve less of a deterrent function, since the conduct sought to be deterred is confused with the conduct sought to be encouraged. This confusion is also likely to create a general feeling of judicial inconsistency, thus seriously affecting the credibility and integrity of the courts in all of their workings. This confusion is not only a problem for the public; the same conflict is necessarily felt by every judge who tries to reach a just conclusion. A judge may hesitate to exculpate a defendant whom he believes should be excused, since he does not want others to conclude that the defendant's actions were proper. In a system where the concepts of justification and excuse are well-distinguished, this would not be a problem; the condemning character of a grant of excuse would be clear.

The famous case of United States v. Holmes, 26 F. Cas. 360 (No. 15,382) (C.C.E.D. Pa. 1842), not only illustrates the problem, but also some of the creative, though makeshift, solutions to which the courts have resorted. Eight seamen and 32 passengers were adrift in a life boat following a shipwreck. The crowded quarters, rough seas, and need for constant bailing caused the passengers to panic. Eighteen passengers were jettisoned before a rescue ship arrived. The grand jury refused to return a murder indictment against Holmes, one of the crew who assisted in the jettison. He was ultimately charged with manslaughter, convicted, and sentenced to six months' imprisonment and fined $20. Shortly thereafter the penalty was remitted. While the initial conviction demonstrated the court's condemnation of the act, the subsequent remittance seemed to exculpate the defendant. This quick step, which only seems to operate in cases of great notoriety, is not an adequate substitute for a clear justification-excuse distinction.

The minimal punishment initially assigned to Holmes demonstrates another form of compensation, the "pardoning power of juries." *See* United States v. Moylan, 417 F.2d 1002 (4th Cir. 1969), *cert. denied*, 397 U.S. 910 (1970). The unstructured nature of this power makes it a possible substitute for justification or excuse principles; in other words, it can be used in any situation in which the law does not appear to provide an intuitively "just" result. But the perverseness of this solution can be seen in the fact that although this is an acknowledged power of juries, even after request of defense counsel, the court may refuse to tell the jury that it has such authority. *Id.* This position was explained as necessary to avoid encouraging jury "lawlessness"—apparently with reference to the jury's failure to follow legal rules which are in present form admittedly inadequate to do justice. Acknowledgement of a "jury pardon" power is an acknowledgement that general principles of justification and excuse are needed to temper the present criminal law. The treatment of the "jury pardon" power parallels the similarly confused and distorted treatment of justification and excuse. *See also* Beale, *Justification for Injury*, 41 HARV. L. REV. 553 (1928); Radbruch, *Jurisprudence in the Criminal Law*, 18 J. COMP. LEG. & INT'L L. (3d ser.) 212, 218-19 (1936).

46 In certain situations, it is not entirely clear what the proper result should be. There is some dispute, for example, as to whether defensive force should be permitted against an insane assailant whose acts are excused but not justified. The

system protects some justified acts by specifying situations, such as lawful arrest, in which one may not use defensive force.[47] But by implication it is lawful to use defensive force in all other instances. It is suggested here that any justified attack—not just those specified by statute—should be free from defensive force. Failure to recognize a general principle of justification would, of course, prevent implementation of this rule.

Suppose that a forest fire is raging toward a town, and that the only possibility of stopping it is to start another fire in an adjacent field to create a firebreak.[48] Starting the second fire is a societally desirable, and thus justifiable, act. A person may or may not have an obligation himself to burn the field and save the town, but if burning the field is justifiable, it would be inconsistent to conclude that a person may lawfully prevent it. This is not to say that anyone who prevents the burning should be punished; if he was insane, or ignorant of the justified nature of the act, he might be excused. But only one of the acts can be justified, and the criminal code should require the nonjustified act to yield to the justified.[49]

Since present law condones the use of defensive force to repel a justified attack, it is legal for a person to prevent the burning of the field. This is true even if he has no excuse, such as insanity or ignorance of the danger to the town. This anomaly occurs because, using the approach of selective exceptions, one cannot define every situation in which a defense of justification is appropriate. What is needed is a general rule stating that it is illegal to prevent a justified act; such a rule follows from recognition of the general concept of justification.

---

proper result, it is contended here, should be to allow the use of defensive force. This situation is analogous to the case where *X* is assaulted by *Y* who in turn is acting under duress applied by *Z*. In the duress situation, though *Y* may be excused for his attack on *X*, *X* is still justified in using defensive force against *Y* (assuming, of course, that *X* cannot shoot *Z*). Even though the case of the insane assailant is analogous in theory, some may intuitively feel that defensive force is not permissible against an insane attacker. But this hesitation may be attributed simply to our justice system's requirement of a volitional act and the fact that many people consider the actions of an insane man more akin to an act of nature. Consider a related problem: May *X*, his life endangered by a man suffering an epileptic seizure, use deadly force to defend himself? This is the issue of volitional act, not the distinction between justification and excuse. *Cf.* Fletcher, *Proportionality and the Psychotic Aggressor: A Vignette in Comparative Criminal Theory*, 8 ISRAEL L. REV. 367 (1973).

[47] *See, e.g.*, CAL. PENAL CODE § 148 (West 1970).

[48] *Cf.* CAL. JOINT LEGISLATIVE COMM. FOR REVISION OF THE PENAL CODE, THE CRIMINAL CODE § 610, Comment (Staff Draft 1971) [hereinafter cited as PROPOSED CAL. CRIM. CODE].

[49] This also demonstrates the universal character of a justified act. Since justification is dependent not on the actor but only on the act, an act which is justifiable when performed by one actor is necessarily justifiable when performed by any actor.

2. The Propriety of Third-Party Assistance

The problem of third-party assistance is similar to the question of defensive force. The controlling question is whether the principal act is justified. If an act is justified, the conduct of anyone assisting in the act should also be justified. But if an actor is excused, the excuse should appropriately be limited to him and should not extend to others.[50] If *X* robs a bank because he is insane, *Y*, his accomplice, is not shielded by *X*'s insanity. Unfortunately, the individualized character of excuse is often applied to justification because of confusion in current legal theory; it is currently no defense that the actions of the principal, identical to the defendant's, are deemed justified.[51] It is possible, then, that the acts of one person will be found justified, while the identical acts of another will not.[52]

---

50 The excuse of one actor has been held to shield both when the crime, like conspiracy, requires an intent of both actors. *See* Regle v. State, 9 Md. App. 346, 264 A.2d 119 (1970). In *Regle* the court concluded that the insanity of one defendant exculpated a co-defendant because the latter could not have had a joint intent with a person who could have no criminal intent at all. An alternative—and perhaps more satisfying—analysis is that the case simply involved an impossible attempt to conspire.

51 Thus the present system might, in the raging fire example, consider one actor justified in burning the field yet still consider a companion unjustified in assisting in the identical act. Such erroneous results are not always apparent. They only become visible when it is known whether a principal actor is exculpated under a theory of justification or excuse, information not available under the current system. The corollary, of course, is that without knowing whether or not the principal was exculpated under a theory of justification, it is impossible to determine whether the universality of justification should be applied.

52 Another practical problem which arises upon dissolution of the justification-excuse distinction, but one which under current law has little significance, is that of treatment. When the criminal justice system concludes that a person's act is justified, it is suggesting that the act was correct by the normative standards of society. The question of treatment is never considered. Since the act was "correct," the actor cannot be said to have manifested any deviance or abnormality. It is possible that an abnormal person could have done this normal, justified act; but since his abnormality was not manifested in the act he would not be subject to treatment under the criminal system, although he might properly be given treatment under some civil system.

When an act is judged unjustified, the individual may still escape punishment if it can be shown that he qualified for an excuse. When a person asks to be excused he admits that his action was not justified, was incorrect, but claims that he acted because of certain personal weaknesses, not of an evil nature, and thus, that he should not be punished. As Professor Fletcher suggests, this might be personified as "I couldn't help myself," or "I didn't mean to do it." Fletcher, *The Individualization of Excusing Conditions*, 47 S. Cal. L. Rev. 1269 (1974). The focus here has shifted from the act to the actor. When justification and excuse are merged it is no longer possible to determine which of the persons exculpated are persons whose behavior was criminal and caused by an abnormality and which are persons whose behavior was in fact laudable. This in turn prevents identification of persons who may require treatment.

It is assumed here that the successful plea of an excuse should lead to some sort of treatment. Since the defendant has claimed that he acted in an incorrect

IV. ACTOR-ORIENTED CONSIDERATIONS INTRODUCED INTO THE PRINCIPLE OF JUSTIFICATION

The preceding Part demonstrated the inconsistencies created by the improper merger of justification and excuse. This Part will independently establish that the principle of justification should not contain actor-oriented considerations, such as prior fault, motive, belief, and knowledge,[53] not simply because they are more properly associated with the principle of excuse, but also because their use generates results which are illogical and inconsistent with fundamental principles of criminal liability.

A. *Prior Fault as a Bar to Justification*

Justification statutes typically deny the defense of justification to a defendant who has created the necessity for the justified act. For example, section 610 of the Proposed California Criminal Code entitled "Justification; generally," provides in part, "A person is justified in conduct which would otherwise constitute an offense when such conduct is . . . necessary to avoid [certain enumerated

way because of an abnormality in his character, it does not seem unreasonable for society to demand that this abnormality be corrected in order to avoid a similar harm in the future. Prevention of recurrence of the incorrect behavior is automatic in many excuse situations. In the case of mistake of fact, the defendant usually discovers his mistake immediately, thus preventing recurrence. In the case of mistake of law (if accepted as an excuse, a minority position) the trial is the treatment. The abnormality is the defendant's ignorance as to certain laws. In cases of duress and necessity the society may be content to allow the abnormalities to continue in the belief that they will rarely produce harm because of the infrequency of such situations. If the excuse is insanity, a successful plea should lead to immediate psychiatric treatment. But when a defendant is excused under present law, he is neither punished nor treated. Although the exact causal relationship between the absence of mandatory treatment and the demise of the justification-excuse distinction is not known, movement toward treatment of the excused defendant will be hampered by the absence of the justification-excuse distinction.

53 Other typical statutory restrictions include requirements that the act be "*immediately* necessary," that it avoid an "*imminent* public *disaster*" or "*serious* bodily injury to a person" or "*serious* damage to property." *See, e.g.*, PROPOSED CAL. CRIM. CODE, *supra* note 48, § 610(b) (emphasis added); MODEL PENAL CODE § 3.04 (Proposed Official Draft 1962) (emphasis added). While these modifications are not theoretically inconsistent with the principle of justification, unlike those discussed in this Part, they are artificial limitations on the operation of the principle. There is no conceptually sound basis for excluding the principle from situations in which the threat is not "imminent" or "serious" in nature as long as the act is necessary to prevent a greater harm, a societal harm. Such restrictions may be tolerated, however, as simply an a priori balance of pertinent factors, a balance to which each citizen is bound.

> [In order to balance harms in a particular case], [t]he issue of competing values must not have been foreclosed by a deliberate legislative choice, as when the law has dealt explicitly with the specific situation that presents the choice of evils or a legislative purpose to exclude the justification claimed otherwise appears.

MODEL PENAL CODE § 3.02, Comment 1(b) (Tent. Draft No. 8, 1961).

harms] which [are] about to occur *through no fault of the actor* . . . ."[54] Though a prior fault restriction might be appropriate for an excuse provision, and indeed is found in a number of excuse situations,[55] such a restriction is inconsistent with the concept of justification. The prior acts of an actor cannot negate the social desirability of the act, which is the essence of the principle of justification. The prior fault may still be charged against the actor, of course, if it is itself illegal.

Suppose *D* is negligent or reckless in having a defective muffler on his camper, and sparks from his muffler start a forest fire. He would normally be justified in burning a field to serve as a firebreak to save the town from the forest fire.[56] But under the Proposed California Criminal Code, for example, he would be guilty of arson were he to burn the field; his initial negligence would bar the defense of justification. If he made no effort to

---

[54] PROPOSED CAL. CRIM. CODE, *supra* note 48, § 610 (emphasis added). New York law provides:

Justification; generally

> [C]onduct which would otherwise constitute an offense is justifiable and not criminal when:
>
> . . . .
>
> 2. Such conduct is necessary . . . by reason of a situation *occasioned or developed through no fault of the actor*, and which is of such gravity that, according to ordinary standards of intelligence and morality, the desirability and urgency of avoiding the injury sought to be prevented by the statute defining the offense in issue.

N.Y. PENAL LAW § 35.05 (McKinney 1965) (emphasis added). Similar provisions exist in other statutes. *See, e.g.*, WIS. STAT. ANN. § 939.47 (1958), *quoted in* note 60 *infra*.

The Model Penal Code provides a somewhat more sophisticated restriction:

> *When the actor was reckless or negligent in bringing about the situation requiring a choice of harms or evils* or in appraising the necessity for his conduct, the justification afforded by this Section is unavailable in a prosecution for any offense for which recklessness or negligence, as the case may be, suffices to establish culpability.

MODEL PENAL CODE § 3.02(2) (Proposed Official Draft 1962) (emphasis added). The Proposed California Criminal Code would apparently bar the justification defense if the actor had even negligently caused the situation, no matter what the offense for which the defendant was being prosecuted. The Model Penal Code provides that if an actor was reckless or negligent in bringing about the situation, then the justification defense is not available in a prosecution for an offense for which recklessness or negligence suffices to establish culpability. *Id.* While both statutory restrictions are theoretically indefensible and likely to cause very real inequities, the Proposed California Criminal Code is certainly the more insensitive of the two.

[55] For example, intoxication may at times provide an excuse, analogous to insanity; but there is authority which denies the excuse in some cases of voluntary intoxication, under the theory that the actor has in some way "caused" the occurrence of the situation in which he acted in an incorrect manner because of his intoxication and for which he now seeks to be excused. *See, e.g.*, LAFAVE & SCOTT, *supra* note 2, at 341-42; MODEL PENAL CODE § 2.08(2) (Proposed Official Draft 1962).

[56] *See* Cope v. Sharpe (No. 2), [1912] 1 K.B. 496, where it was held justifiable to burn a strip of heather to prevent a fire from spreading.

save the town, he could not be charged with arson even for the original fire, since the Proposed Code has no negligent or reckless form of arson.[57] The law clearly urges him to let the town burn. This anomaly occurs because *D*'s initial fault in starting the forest fire is erroneously applied to his justified act of intentionally burning the field to save the town.

The Model Penal Code would hold *D* liable for burning the field only if arson could be committed negligently or recklessly.[58] Yet even the Model Penal Code's view is inappropriate since it is in society's interest to encourage *D* to burn the field and save the town even if he started the forest fire intentionally.

The prior fault bar to justification is even more clearly shown to be irrational in the situation where someone other than *D*, the person with the defective muffler, assists *D* in burning the field. In such a case, the second person would not be punished since he could assert the justification defense. Such a result would be new to the common law tradition. It would be difficult to explain why the criminal law should encourage one person to burn the field and save the town while discouraging another, or why it should punish one person for such an act but not another.[59]

More difficult cases arise when the necessity or other justifying situation is not simply the result of an actor's prior fault, but of a grand scheme in which the actor committed the prior act specifically to create justifying circumstances of which he could then take advantage. Consider the following: *D* starts a forest fire knowing that it will threaten the town and create justifying circumstances which will permit him to burn his enemy's field. In such cases, the defendant should be liable for acts committed under the justifying circumstances. *D* should be liable not only for the forest fire, but for the direct consequences which he intended or risked. Whether he burns his enemy's field or a passerby does so, he should be responsible. Liability should be imposed, however, not because the defendant's prior fault vitiates the defense of justification, but because the prior unjustified act directly caused the justifying circumstances *and* the subsequent justified act. The basis of liability is the first, unjustified act, not the second, justified act. Despite the previous circumstances, society would want him, or someone, to burn the field and save the town. Even though the actor with a "grand scheme" is subject to greater liability than one who is

---

57 *See, e.g.*, PROPOSED CAL. CRIM. CODE, *supra* note 48, § 1076.

58 *See* note 54 *supra*.

59 Consider also the case where a passerby had begun burning the field to save the community. If he needed additional help and called upon another person, would it be rational to suggest that of the two actors working side by side, one is justified and the other is not?

merely negligent, the law would still encourage him to burn the field once the fire is started. If he does not, the town will be destroyed as a result of his initial unjustified act, and he might then be liable for homicide as well as arson.

B. *Mistaken Belief as a Basis for Justification*

Many jurisdictions provide a defense of justification if the defendant "reasonably believed" his conduct was justified, even though in fact it was not. The Model Penal Code's provision is representative: "Conduct *which the actor believes* to be necessary to avoid a harm or evil to himself or to another is justifiable . . . ."[60] This rule is endorsed by most commentators. LaFave and Scott, for example, explain:

> An honest (and, doubtless, reasonable) belief in the necessity of [one's] action is all that is required . . . so that [one] has the defense [of justification] even if, unknown to him, the situation did not in fact call for the drastic action taken. Thus if *A* kills *B* reasonably believing it to be necessary to save *C* and *D*, he is not guilty of murder even though, unknown to *A*, *C* and *D* could have been rescued without the necessity of killing *B*.[61]

Here again an actor-oriented factor is introduced into the justification defense: the actor's belief. As noted before, such factors are erroneously adopted from the doctrine of excuse.[62] If a person reasonably, but mistakenly, believes his acts are justified, the proper legal determination is that the act was not justified or socially

---

[60] MODEL PENAL CODE § 3.02(1) (Proposed Official Draft 1962) (emphasis added). A comparable Wisconsin statute provides:

> Pressure of natural physical forces which causes the actor *reasonably to believe* that his act is the only means of preventing imminent public disaster, or imminent death or great bodily harm to himself or another and which causes him so to act, is a defense to a prosecution for any crime based on that act except that if the prosecution is for murder the degree of the crime is reduced to manslaughter.

WIS. STAT. ANN. § 939.47 (1958) (emphasis added). Illinois has a similar provision:

> Conduct which would otherwise be an offense is justifiable by reason of necessity if the accused was without blame in occasioning or developing the situation and *reasonably believed* such conduct was necessary to avoid a public or private injury greater than the injury which might reasonably result from his own conduct.

ILL. ANN. STAT. ch. 38, § 7-13 (Smith-Hurd 1972) (emphasis added). While the comparable New York statute contains no reference to the actor's belief (N.Y. PENAL LAW § 35.05 (McKinney 1965), *quoted in* note 54 *supra*), some writers claim that such a "belief" restriction can be implied. *See, e.g.*, LAFAVE & SCOTT, *supra* note 2, at 386 n.35.

[61] LAFAVE & SCOTT, *supra* note 2, at 386 (footnote omitted).

[62] Mistaken belief is like other traditional excuses such as duress or insanity; it has been viewed as generating a form of involuntary conduct. "Those things, then, are thought involuntary, which take place under compulsion or owing to ignorance." THE NICOMACHEAN ETHICS OF ARISTOTLE, BOOK III, ch. I, at 48 (Ross transl. 1954).

desirable, but since the actor made a reasonable mistake he should be excused. For example, if the actor burns a field with the mistaken belief that a raging fire is threatening the town, the proper result would be to excuse him. Such mistakes of fact are traditional grounds for excuse.[63]

C. *Bad Motive and Lack of Knowledge of Justifying Circumstances as Bars to Justification*

1. Bad Motive

Bad motive is another common bar to the defense of justification. In *Laws v. State*,[64] for example, a Texas statute provided that it was justifiable homicide to kill a person burglarizing one's house at night. The defendant was convicted of murder for killing such a burglar, despite the statute, because the jury was persuaded that the defendant's primary motivation was malice toward the burglar. The court explained, "[I]t is not the intention of the statute to justify *murder*. Such a construction of the statute would to our minds be unreasonable and exceedingly dangerous."[65]

Three observations are in order concerning *Laws* and related cases. First, all concern the weakest case for justification, self-defense. In self-defense, society does not encourage the resulting death, as it does in necessity situations, but merely tolerates it; no benefit occurs, rather the defender is permitted to take the life of the attacker in order to save his own. Thus in self-defense cases the courts are more inclined to improperly consider any bad motives of the actor. Indeed, it has been observed, erroneously however, that:

> [A]ll justifications will fall into one or the other of these two classes; the first where the objects sought for are so important that motive must be ignored, the second where the objects are not so important but that the presence of ill-will may turn the scale.[66]

---

[63] Whether the actor will in fact be excused for his mistake depends on the nature of the mistake, his own personal characteristics, and other individual circumstances. *See, e.g.*, MODEL PENAL CODE § 2.04 (Proposed Official Draft 1962).

[64] 26 Tex. Crim. 643, 10 S.W. 220 (1888).

[65] *Id.* at 655, 10 S.W. at 221 (emphasis in original). Similar conclusions have been reached in other cases. In Lyons v. People, 137 Ill. 602, 27 N.E. 677 (1891), the defendant, a member of the gang that had previously killed a relative of the deceased, was denied the defense of justification though the deceased attacked him, because the jury believed he had killed the deceased out of malice. The defendant in Wortham v. State, 70 Ga. 336 (1883), was denied a defense when he shot the deceased after being struck by him with a stick; again the jury believed the defendant acted out of vengeance and not self-defense. *Accord*, People v. Williams, 32 Cal. 280 (1867); Josey v. United States, 135 F.2d 809 (D.C. Cir. 1943). *See also* Garcia v. State, 91 Tex. Crim. 9, 237 S.W. 279, 281 (1922).

[66] Note, *Effect of Bad Motive in the Law of Torts*, 26 HARV. L. REV. 740, 741 (1913).

Second, bad motive on the part of the defender may call into question his need to have injured the attacker;[67] that is, bad motive may be evidence that the injuring response was not in fact justified. Such a determination is uniquely difficult in self-defense cases. In the firebreak case, by comparison, the need for the response is obvious. The actions of the judges and the juries in self-defense cases may be only a misarticulation: They say that the defendant's act was unjustified because of his malice when they mean that his response was unreasonable and thus not justified.

The third point to be made concerning these cases is that they are contradicted by a number of decisions reaching opposite results under similar circumstances. For example, in *Golden v. State*[68] the court explained:

> Whenever the circumstances of the killing would not amount to murder, the proof even of express malice will not make it so. One may harbor the most intense hatred toward another; he may court an opportunity to take his life; may rejoice while he is imbruing his hands in his heart's blood; and yet, if, to save his own life, the facts showed that he was fully justified in slaying his adversary, his malice shall not be taken into the account. This principle is too plain to need amplification.[69]

Although bad motive may bar a defendant's defense of excuse,[70] it should not preclude the defense of justification, which focuses on the act and not on the actor's motive. This position has been expressed most eloquently by Macaulay:

> If A. sets on fire a quantity of cotton belonging to Z., it is proper to inquire whether A. acted maliciously; for the destruction of valuable property by fire is *primâ facie* a bad act. But if Z.'s cotton is burning, and A. puts it out, no tri-

---

[67] *See* LaFave & Scott, *supra* note 2, at 206 n.22.

[68] 25 Ga. 527 (1858).

[69] *Id.* at 532. Other cases have reached similar conclusions. *See, e.g.*, Giblan v. National Amalgamated Labourers' Union, [1903] 2 K.B. 600 (1902); Allen v. Flood, [1898] A.C. 1 (P.C. 1897). A number of related cases making the same point involve the more extreme situation where the defendant not only acts out of malice, but is unaware of justifying circumstances. *See* notes 86-88 & accompanying text *infra*.

[70] Inherent in the existence of a motive is the attribution of knowledgeable free will. An actor may be excused if he was insane, if he acted upon reasonably mistaken facts, or if he acted under duress; but an act stemming from a defendant's bad motive will tend to preclude these possibilities, and will therefore generally bar an excuse. Bad motive may also operate to bar an excuse in a more subtle way. In Regina v. Prince, L.R. 2 Cr. Cas. Res. 154 (1875), for example, Prince was charged with taking an unmarried girl of under 16 from her father. He was denied a defense of mistake of fact even though he reasonably believed that the girl was eighteen, because the court believed that taking a girl of eighteen was an immoral, though not illegal, act. As one writer suggests, "[A] defense of mistake rests ultimately on the defendant's being able to say that he has observed the community ethic, and this Prince could not do." P. Brett, An Inquiry into Criminal Guilt 148-49 (1963). Any act upon bad motive would of course fail to meet this requirement.

> bunal inquires whether A. did so from good feeling or from malice to some other dealer in cotton, who, if Z.'s stock had been destroyed, would have been a great gainer; for the saving of valuable property from destruction is an act which it is desirable to encourage, and it is better that such property should be saved from bad motives than that it should be suffered to perish.[71]

Most commentators who have considered the question disagree and suggest that bad motive should vitiate the defense of justification. Perkins explains:

> Suppose a grave felony is about to be committed under such circumstances that the killing of the offender to prevent the crime would be justified by law. At that very moment he is shot and killed. If the slayer was prompted by the impulse to promote the social security by preventing the felony he is guilty of no offense. If he had no such impulse but merely acted upon the urge to satisfy an old grudge by killing a personal enemy, he is guilty of murder. The intent is the same in either case, to kill the person. The difference between innocence and guilt lies in the motive which prompted this intent.[72]

But in the same discussion he acknowledges that an executioner who carries out the sentence of a competent court is guilty of no crime even if his motivation is not to serve society but "to satisfy an old grudge by killing a personal enemy." Perkins concludes that carrying out the mandate is the "only legally recognized motive for his act,"[73] although he does not explain why.

The executioner exception made by Perkins may reveal that his view on the effect of bad motive is due to the confusion between the evidentiary and conceptual impact of bad motive noted above. In an execution there is no doubt as to the justified nature of the killing as there is in the self-defense situation, where bad motive may cause the defendant to kill an attacker when killing is not in fact necessary. To be consistent, Perkins must agree that bad motive has no pertinence if the need for the defensive killing in the self-defense situation—its justifiable nature—is as well established as the justified nature of an execution.[74]

---

[71] 7 The Works of Lord Macaulay 553 (H. Trevelyan ed. 1866). Lord Macaulay was advocating that truth be an absolute defense to defamation in the Indian Penal Code. The passage goes on:

> Since, then, no act ought to be made punishable on account of malicious intention, unless it be in itself an act of a kind which it is desirable to prevent, it follows that malice is not a test which can with propriety be used for the purpose of determining what true imputations on character ought to be punished, and what true imputations on character ought not to be punished; for the throwing of true imputations on character is not *primâ facie* a pernicious act.

Id.

[72] Perkins, *A Rationale of Mens Rea*, 52 Harv. L. Rev. 905, 923 (1939) (footnote omitted); Perkins, *supra* note 35, at 832.

[73] Perkins, *supra* note 35, at 833.

[74] Hitchler makes a point similar to Perkins':

The pertinence of bad motive is analyzed in a manner similar to that employed to examine prior fault. Consider the following: A passerby sees a forest fire and begins to burn an adjacent field to save the town. He finds, however, that he cannot do it in time without assistance. A second passerby is an old enemy of the owner of the field who would burn the field simply to injure the owner rather than to save the town. Should the law prevent this person from acting by convicting him of arson?[75] Is it rational to convict the second man of arson and not the first, even though they work side by side? Finally, if the passerby helps, should the law convict him of a crime when in the final analysis not only was no harm done but society was in fact benefited? If the justified act benefits society, it should be performed no matter what the motive and, further, if no harm has occurred, then the act is not a proper concern of the law.[76]

> The lawfulness of the killing in these cases depends upon the motive with which it was done, i.e., to prevent a felony or defend oneself. It follows therefore that though all the external circumstances exist which would justify one in killing to prevent a felony or in self-defense, he would be guilty of murder if he killed solely for revenge and not with the motive to prevent the commission of a felony or to save life.

Hitchler, *Motive As An Essential Element of Crime*, 35 DICK. L. REV. 105, 114 (1931) (footnote omitted). Both Hitchler and Perkins agree that their view of motive as a determinative factor is an exception to the general rule that motive is normally irrelevant. *Id.*; PERKINS, *supra* note 35, at 833.

[75] Failure to exculpate those who commit justified acts may create the potential for unjust results. In cases such as Laws v. State, 26 Tex. Crim. 643, 10 S.W. 220 (1888), for example, it might encourage prospective burglars to break into the houses of people who already hate them, since those persons may not be privileged to assault the burglar. *See* text accompanying notes 64-65 *supra*.

[76] One modern authority would agree with this position, at least in part:

> There is, however, at least one good reason to resist characterizing the defenses, such as necessity and self-defense, as instances in which a good motive serves a defense. Such a characterization leads to analytical difficulties, for it suggests that these defenses are available only if the actor, in each case, had as his primary inducement the objective recognized as lawful by the defense. Although this position has sometimes been taken, the better view is that the law is not concerned with motive once facts supporting the defense have been established. Thus, when a person authorized to carry out a death sentence does so, he is acting lawfully whether he pursues his duties with regret, joy, or indifference. Similarly, when an individual finds himself in a position where the law grants him the right to kill another in his own defense, it makes no difference whether his dominant motive is other than self-preservation.

LAFAVE & SCOTT, *supra* note 2, at 206-07 (footnotes omitted). But the writers continue:

> This does not mean, of course, that the defense can be manufactured after the event by resort to facts not known to the actor when he engaged in the conduct. Thus, in the prison-break illustration described earlier, the defendant would not have a defense if he escaped from prison and then later learned, to his pleasant surprise, that when he left it was on fire and that he would have been burned to death had he remained.

Id. at 207 (footnote omitted). Apparently their position is that while bad motive will not bar a defense of justification, lack of knowledge of the justifying circumstances will. *See* text accompanying notes 77-80 *infra*.

2. Lack of Knowledge of Justifying Circumstances

The inappropriateness of granting a defense of justification, rather than excuse, to a defendant who honestly but erroneously believed his conduct was justified has already been considered. This Part will examine the converse situation: when a defendant believes his conduct is not justified because he is unaware of circumstances which in fact render his conduct beneficial to society. Such situations are analytically similar to instances where the defendant acts because of bad motive; in both cases, an act intended to be harmful results in a benefit to society which would otherwise have provided the actor with a recognized defense of justification. And in many instances the fact that the defendant lacked knowledge of the justifying circumstances may compel an inference that he acted out of bad motive.

Of the commentators who have considered this situation, almost all have concluded that a defense of justification should not be available.[77] LaFave and Scott, for example, explain:

> To have the defense of necessity, the defendant must have acted with the intention of avoiding the greater harm. Actual necessity, without the intention is not enough. If *A* kills his enemy *B* for revenge, and he later learns to his happy surprise that by killing *B* he saved the lives of *C* and *D*, *A* has no defense to murder. In other words, he must believe that his act is necessary to avoid the greater harm.[78]

They provide no authority or further explanation for this conclusion, however.[79] And interestingly enough, while they would deny a defense of justification to a defendant who lacked knowledge of justifying circumstances, they would not deny the defense to one who acted out of bad motive.[80]

---

77 Even these writers might exculpate an unknowingly justified actor, but on a theory of excuse. For example, an actor might burn a field reasonably but mistakenly believing it to be his own, and save the town from an approaching fire about which he knew nothing.

78 LAFAVE & SCOTT, *supra* note 2, at 386 (footnote omitted). *See also id.* at 207 n.25.

79 They do refer the reader to "§ 29, supra, for a discussion of motive in criminal law." *Id.* at 386 n.31. Their discussion in this earlier section has been reviewed in note 76 *supra.*

80 Perkins, also without explanation, denies the defense to those acting in ignorance. PERKINS, *supra* note 35, at 832 n.37. This is at least more consistent than LaFave and Scott. Perkins may believe that bad motive may be inferred from ignorance or justifying circumstances, and thus that the two must be treated similarly. This is not necessarily true. Suppose *A*, ignorant of an onrushing fire, burns the field of his neighbor under the mistaken belief that he is burning his own field. Inadvertently, *A* saves the town. Although *A* had no knowledge of the justifying circumstances, it cannot be said that he acted out of bad motive.

Beale's view of the effect of ignorance on the justification defense is similar to Perkins', but more fully explained:

A number of cases support the views of these commentators. In the best known, *The Queen v. Dadson*,[81] the defendant was a police officer who, in order to prevent an escape, shot a person whom he had just arrested for stealing wood. Such killings were ordinarily permitted only to prevent the escape of a felon. While the offense for which the person had been arrested would not normally have been a felony, the fact that the arrestee had previously been convicted, a fact unknown to Dadson, made it a felony. Dadson was convicted and punished for the shooting.[82]

It is argued here, however, that *Dadson* and related cases have been decided incorrectly; the justification defense should be available even to defendants who lack knowledge of the justifying circumstances. One's mental state simply cannot convert otherwise harmless conduct into a crime,[83] and it is irrational to claim that of two actors working side by side to burn the field to save the city, the one who knows of the fire is justified, while the one who is innocently helping his friend is not justified.[84] More funda-

> Justification, then, is a legal power to act offensively. The power is the power to act, not the right to cause the result. Though the result would be desirable, it is not justified unless the defendant's personal action was done in exercise of the power.

Beale, *Justification for Injury*, 41 HARV. L. REV. 553 (1928). Characterization of justification as a "power" (or "privilege" as many writers suggest) granted to the defendant sharply contrasts with this Article's position of justification as a limitation on the criminal law.

81 169 Eng. Rep. 407 (1850).

82 An American case, People v. Burt, 51 Mich. 199, 16 N.W. 378 (1883), makes a similar point: "Where the life of an actual felon is taken by one who does not know or believe his guilt, such slaying is murder." *Id.* at 202, 16 N.W. at 379. A similar result was reached in Collett v. Commonwealth, 296 Ky. 267, 176 S.W.2d 893 (1943), where the court concluded that "[the defendant] cannot be excused from his wilful malicious act by a showing of circumstances of which he was unaware." *Id.* at 273, 176 S.W.2d at 896. The allusion to *excusing* the defendant, instead of justifying, is revealing. Part III of this Article attempted to show how the introduction of the actor-oriented factors discussed in this Part was due to a confusion and mixture of the principles of justification and excuse. The language in *Collett* appears to bear this out. *See also* Trogdon v. State, 133 Ind. 1, 8, 32 N.E. 725, 727 (1892) (defendant was denied a defense of self-defense because he was not aware of the actual danger to himself when he killed the deceased); Strang v. Russell, 24 N.Z.L.R. 916, 922 (1905) (defendant rowed upon a lagoon to which the plaintiff claimed title in order to contest that title. Defendant was fined £1 for trespass when it was determined that plaintiff did have title, even though it was also found that defendant had a license to enter of which he was not aware).

A fairly recent discussion of the same point is contained in People v. Taylor, 3 Cal. 3d 578, 592, 477 P.2d 131, 140, 91 Cal. Rptr. 275, 284 (1970) (Peters, J., dissenting), where a dissent noted that if it was fortuitous whether a situation in fact turned out to be justified, then the justifying circumstances must be logically irrelevant to his culpability. The writer would agree with this statement, but would go on to note that culpability, without a resulting harm, is an insufficient basis for conviction of a crime.

83 PERKINS, *supra* note 35, at 236, *citing* State v. Holder, 81 N.C. 527 (1879); Sentell v. New Orleans & C.R. Co., 166 U.S. 698, 701 (1897).

84 The argument concerning the desirability of having a justified act done, even with bad motive for example, is obviously inapplicable here since the actor who does not know of the justifying circumstances cannot be encouraged to act

mentally, since no harm has occurred, the incident should be of no concern to the criminal law.[85]

This position is supported by a number of cases. For example, *Regina v. Clarke*,[86] decided one hundred years after *Dadson*, reached a contrary result on similar facts. Clarke was arrested for loitering with intent to commit a felony. He was deemed a "suspected person," as required for that offense, because of his previous convictions. Yet at the time of his arrest the police officers had been unaware of his previous convictions. His conviction was upheld because "knowledge [of the previous convictions] on the part of the police is irrelevant and certainly not essential."[87] Analogous tort cases are found in the area of malicious prosecution. It is generally held that the bad faith initiation of prosecution is not tortious if the person who is the object of the prosecution is found guilty, even if the person responsible for prosecution had no knowledge of the plaintiff's guilt when he initiated the suit.[88] It is

---

accordingly, for any reason. In other words, in the case of lack of knowledge, the conduct-modifying function of law is irrelevant; only the punishment-for-past conduct function is applicable.

[85] One writer, Glanville Williams, would apparently agree with this position. He notes: "Where . . . the objective situation is one that the law actively wishes to promote, it cannot be turned into a crime by *mens rea*." G. WILLIAMS, CRIMINAL LAW: THE GENERAL PART § 12, at 23 (2d ed. 1961). He goes on to criticize the leading case on point, The Queen v. Dadson, 169 Eng. Rep. 407 (1850), and makes a point similar to the one presented here:

> The point of interest here is that the rule hardly accords with the requirement of an *actus reus*. In *Dadson* the arrester had *mens rea*, for he intended to arrest the other and on the facts as he knew them the arrest was unlawful. But common sense would suggest that the arrest was nevertheless not criminal, because there was no *actus reus*.

G. WILLIAMS, *supra* § 12, at 24. *See* note 81 & accompanying text *supra*.

Another English commentator analyzing impossible attempts appears to agree with Williams. *See* Smith, *Two Problems in Criminal Attempts*, 70 HARV. L. REV. 422, 445 (1957). Williams defines "*actus reus*" as the "whole situation forbidden by law with the exception of the mental element . . . ." G. WILLIAMS, *supra* § 12, at 22. Although Williams fails to explain the "common sense" of his conclusion, his position on this point appears to support at least in part the theory proposed here.

Williams' theory would support the one presented here entirely except that he exempts from application of his definition of *actus reus* the case of attempt. He would admit that attempts are an exception because the *actus reus* of attempt must include the actor's intent. Thus, presumably the presence or absence of intent might affect the applicability of a justification defense to a charge of attempt. In contrast, it is proposed here that no such exception need be made, that attempt, like any other offense, may have a justification defense available if no harm occurs, without regard to an actor's intent.

[86] [1950] 1 K.B. 523.

[87] *Id.* at 530. *See also* The Abby, 165 Eng. Rep. 765 (1804) (action against a ship for violating a prohibition of entering an enemy port dismissed even though the ship's officials learned only after arriving that the enemy port had been captured by friendly forces).

[88] Mooney v. Mull, 216 N.C. 410, 5 S.E.2d 122 (1939); Newton v. Weaver, 13 R.I. 616 (1882); W. PROSSER, HANDBOOK ON THE LAW OF TORTS 840 (4th ed. 1971).

conceded here, however, that a beneficial act done with no knowledge of the justifying circumstances or for bad motive arguably gives rise to an intangible harm similar to that associated with impossible attempts. The differences of opinion over criminal liability for impossible attempts are also applicable to the no-knowledge and bad motive situations. If wrongful intent combined with an act that fails to prove harmful does not suffice for criminal liability for impossible attempts, neither should it here since the intentions, acts, and results are analogous. If it is sufficient for impossible attempts, so would it be here. But note that when punished, such conduct is punished as an "attempt," a special classification of crime for punishing the intangible harm stemming from acts done upon a bad intent but which do not result in the harm expected.

One must conclude, then, that conduct based on bad motive or on ignorance of justifying circumstances may only be punished—if at all—as an attempt to commit the ultimate act. In the firebreak case, if the actor does not know of the threatening forest fire or knows but acts out of bad motive, he may be punished at most for attempted arson.[89] Again it can be seen that the defense of justification should remain available in every situation for which no resulting harm can be demonstrated, regardless of any actor-oriented considerations such as prior fault, motive, belief, or knowledge.[90]

V. CONCLUSION

This Article has presented a new theory of the principle of justification in which justification compensates for the inherent limitations of a written criminal code. It excludes from the jurisdiction of the criminal law those cases where a defendant engages in conduct which the code prohibits, but which, because of special circumstances, does not in fact harm society or its members and

---

89 Although his reasoning might differ somewhat, Glanville Williams would apparently agree to this in certain circumstances. *See* G. WILLIAMS, *supra* note 85, at 27.

90 While one may properly argue that an intangible yet sufficient harm exists in the impossible attempt and unknowingly justified situations to support conviction for a crime of attempt, no such argument is available in the prior fault and bad motive situations. Nor are the previous conclusions concerning mistaken belief affected. No such extensions have been made for prior fault or bad motive. Nowhere in the criminal law has prior fault plus otherwise legal activity, or bad motive plus otherwise legal activity, yet been made a crime. Note, however, that preventive detention statutes do approach it, in the case of prior fault. And many, according to one commentator, may wish it in the case of bad motive. J. AMES, LECTURES ON LEGAL HISTORY 438 (1913).

which therefore should not be prohibited or punished. Inherent in this theory of justification is the view that harm is a prerequisite to criminal liability. As a penal code prohibits only harmful acts, so does justification, in refining the application of the code, exculpate nonharmful acts.

The proposed role of justification as a corrective device for the penal code, and the application of that device to require a societal harm, are admittedly inconsistent with today's common use of actor-oriented factors in the justification determination. The use of such factors, however, undermines the purpose of the penal code and the principle of justification to prohibit certain acts (sometimes defined in terms of the result they cause, sometimes only as the acts themselves) and to punish those who commit such acts without excuse. With regard to the requirement of societal harm, it is similarly clear that the use of such factors would be inconsistent with the claim that justification should depend on the presence or absence of a societal harm, since harm is a characteristic of the act, not the actor.

A theoretical analysis entirely independent of the proposed theory demonstrates that the actor-oriented considerations which have been introduced into the principle of justification—prior fault, belief, motive, and knowledge—cause results inconsistent with fundamental legal principles, while the proposed theory does not. The contradiction between the proposed theory and actor-oriented considerations thus lends the theory independent support. Adoption of a general theory of justification in the form proposed would eliminate the incongruous results caused by actor-oriented factors introduced through mixing justification and excuse, and would provide a more accurate and comprehensive method of defining prohibited conduct within the framework of a written code system.

[10]

The Gist of Excuses

John Gardner

It is often said that the criminal law judges actions, not character. That is true, but misleading. It is true that, barring certain exceptional and troubling examples, crimes are actions, and being a crime is therefore a property of actions.[1] Nevertheless, the criminality of an action frequently falls to be determined, in part, according to *standards of character*—according to standards of courage, carefulness, honesty, self-discipline, diligence, humanity, good will, and so forth. Nobody can be a thief in English law, for instance, unless she acts dishonestly.[2] There is, to be sure, a difference between asking whether the accused acted dishonestly, and asking whether she is dishonest. She is dishonest if and only if she tends to act dishonestly. In other words, judging a person dishonest has a diachronic aspect which judging an action dishonest lacks. But apart from this diachronic aspect, the standard by which we judge a person dishonest is exactly the same standard as that by which we judge an action dishonest. It is a standard of character, a standard which bears not only on what is done, but also on the spirit in which and reason for which it is done. The mere fact that I did something that a dishonest person might do—for example, pocketed someone else's cash without asking—does not entail that I am dishonest, and nor, by the same token, does it entail that I acted dishonestly. If I pocketed the cash to save the owner from an embarrassing revelation, or as part of a complex practical joke, or in the belief that the cash was left out for me, or even just absent-mindedly, then pocketing the cash was, other things

[1] The exceptional and troubling examples I have in mind are examples of status crimes such as those in *R* v *Larsonneur* (1933) 24 Cr App Rep 74 and *Robinson* v *California* 370 US 660, 82 S Ct 1417, 8 L Ed 758 (1966). Crimes of possession are on the borderline between action crimes and status crimes, and present some but not all of the same problems. Michael Moore thinks that crimes of omission are also troubling exceptions: MS Moore, *Act and Crime* (1994), 22–34. I do not share this view and when I speak of actions in the text I always mean to include omissions.

[2] Theft Act 1968, s 1.

being equal,[3] not a dishonest action any more than it was the action of a dishonest person. It may have been meddlesome, or puerile, or presumptuous, or thoughtless. But those judgments invoke quite different standards of character, depending on quite different configurations of reason and spirit, from the dishonesty standard specified for the identification of a thief in English law.

This example shows that, sometimes, standards of character figure in the criminal law because they are built into the definitions of particular criminal offences, i.e. they are part of what makes an action wrongful in the eyes of the criminal law. They also figure separately, however, in many of the criminal law's *excusatory* doctrines. Now a link between character and excuse has often been forged by those interested in the philosophical foundations of the criminal law. On one familiar view, sometimes called the 'Humean' view, we should grant an excuse to somebody in respect of what he did if and only if what he did was no manifestation of his character.[4] This view proceeds from the sound thought that excuses matter because a person's excused actions do not reflect badly on him—do not show him, personally, in a bad light. That being so, the thinking goes, an excuse must be something that blocks the path from an adverse judgment about an action to a correspondingly adverse judgment about the person whose action it is. The action is cowardly, say, but since this person does not otherwise tend towards cowardly actions, she herself is no coward. Her cowardly action is 'out of character'. And that, according to the Humean view, is the gist of excuses. But there is a good deal of confusion in this line of thought. For there is no such thing as a cowardly action which does not show its agent in a cowardly light. It is true that a cowardly light may be a rather unflattering light; as I accepted already, one cowardly action does not make a coward. But an unflattering light is not the same as a false light. In my cowardly action, by definition, I manifest at least the *beginnings* of a cowardly tendency, the *stirrings* of cowardice. By 'manifest' here I do not mean that my cowardly action is mere evidence of some condition called cowardice hidden within me, evidence which may ultimately be discounted for want of

[3] I say 'other things being equal' only to anticipate the objections: (1) that many people have mixed motives; and (2) that even without mixed motives pocketing cash to save someone from embarrassment might be dishonest under another description, e.g. as a concealment of the truth.

[4] P Helm, 'Hume on Exculpation', *Philosophy* 42 (1967), 268; MD Bayles, 'Character, Purpose, and Criminal Responsibility', *Law and Philosophy* 1 (1982), 5. That Hume is truly committed to this view is doubted by J Bricke in 'Hume, Freedom to Act, and Personal Evaluation', *History of Philosophy Quarterly* 5 (1988), 141.

corroboration. Cowards are no more and no less than people who tend to perform cowardly actions. Their cowardly actions add up to *constitute*, not to evidence, their cowardice.[5] Thus even if this cowardly action is my first, and is quite unprecedented, it necessarily counts constitutively and not merely evidentially against me whenever, thereafter, the question arises of whether I am a coward. And that is exactly what it means to say that my cowardly actions show me in a cowardly light. It follows that the Humean view unravels. If my excused actions do not show me in a cowardly light, they cannot, after all, be cowardly actions. That they are excused cannot therefore block the path from the judgment that I did something cowardly to the judgment that I am a coward. The excuse must intervene earlier to forestall the original judgment that this was a cowardly action. Supporters of the Humean view may object that this makes no sense, since if my action was not cowardly after all then I scarcely need to make an excuse for it. What have I left to excuse? But that question betrays another confusion. I need to make an excuse for my action because it is wrongful. As criminal lawyers are usually the first to point out, the wrongfulness of an action is not comprehensively or invariably dictated by character standards. That point holds both in the law and outside the law. Even morally speaking, it is perfectly possible for actions to be admirable at the same time as wrongful, i.e. to be things that should not have been done, whether prima facie or all things considered, but which cast the person who did them in a favourable light.[6] *A fortiori* there can be things that should not have been done, whether prima facie or all things considered, but which do not cast the person who did them in an *un*favourable light, but at worst an indifferent light. And that is precisely the equilibrium which a valid excuse, whether inside or outside the law, establishes.

So the gist of an excuse is not that the action was 'out of character', in the sense of being a departure from what we have come to expect from

[5] Michael Moore rejects this 'dispositional' conception of character on the ground that it 'doesn't say much about the person whose character it is': MS Moore, 'Choice, Character, and Excuse', *Social Philosophy and Policy* 7 (1990), 29 at 42. But that is no objection. By definition, whatever view of character is sound says as much about the person, in the dimension of character, as there is to be said. Moore's worry cannot be that the dispositional conception doesn't say enough about the person, but rather that it portrays the person to be, in at least one dimension, a less substantial entity than he imagined it to be. And that is not surprising, since the person is a less substantial entity than most people imagine it to be.

[6] For argument, see M Slote, *Goods and Virtues* (1983), 77–107; D Parfit, *Reasons and Persons* (1984), 31–35; M Stocker, *Plural and Conflicting Values* (1990), 37–50.

the person whose action it is.[7] Quite the contrary, in fact. The gist of an excuse, as I will try to explain, is precisely that the person with the excuse lived up to our expectations. On first encounter, this claim may give the misleading impression that people's wrongful actions are excused so long as they continue to live up to the character standards that they have always lived up to, however appalling. One may have an image of someone excusing themselves by saying: 'I've always been spiteful and malicious, so how did you expect me to behave?' Being spiteful and malicious is, of course, no excuse for anything. Pointing to the spite and malice in one's wrongful actions is asserting, not denying, that these actions cast one in a bad light. So the question, for excusatory purposes, is obviously not whether the person claiming the excuse lived up to expectations in the predictive sense of being true to form or true to type or even true to our disappointing experience of human beings in general. The question is whether that person lived up to expectations in the *normative* sense. Did she manifest as much resilience, or loyalty, or thoroughness, or presence of mind as a person in her situation should have manifested? In the face of terrible threats, for example, did this person show as much fortitude as someone in his situation could properly be asked to show? In the face of constant taunts, did this person exhibit as much self-restraint as we have a right to demand of someone in her situation? The character standards which are relevant to these and other excuses are not the standards of our own characters, nor even the standards of most people's characters, but rather the standards to which our characters should, minimally, conform.

This word 'minimally' here may lead one to suppose that we are talking of uniform normative expectations—that the same basic standard of self-restraint or fortitude is the excusatory standard for all of us. But that is not so. Different people are subject to different normative expectations when their excuses are assessed. Imagine, for example, a young and inexperienced soldier operating a checkpoint in some troubled frontier zone, who has been warned that the intelligence services expect such a checkpoint to come under terrorist attack today. Already on edge, he misinterprets some motorist's actions—he thinks she was going for a

[7] That a person acted 'out of character' may, if accompanied by the appropriate sense of guilt or remorse, be a reason for forgiving her or showing her mercy, things which criminal courts often do at the sentencing stage of the criminal trial. But those whose actions are excused do not need any forgiveness or mercy, so this issue need not be explored here. For exploration of this and several related issues, see JG Murphy and J Hampton, *Forgiveness and Mercy* (1988).

gun, say, when she was only reaching for her car documents—and kills her with one panic-stricken shot.[8] There are various aspects of this situation which may attract our attention when we think about the soldier's possible excuses for this (as we will assume) wrongful killing. One is that he is young and inexperienced. There is a view of excuses, sometimes (mistakenly) labelled 'Kantian', according to which the standards of character applicable to an excuse are relativized to the *capacities* of the person claiming the excuse.[9] The soldier in our example does not react with the kind of level-headedness which some soldiers might have exhibited. But being young and inexperienced, the thinking goes, he may not have been *capable* of that more mature degree of level-headedness. One has to imagine how working in this troubled frontier zone, under constant tension and at constant risk, might have affected one so young and new to the job, and how his capacity for keeping a level head might have been affected by this. This is not the same, adherents of the 'Kantian' view would stress, as relying on mere predictions of how our soldier will stand up under pressure. Our soldier's excuse is not validated by the standards of level-headedness which he tends to live up to, so that he can excuse himself by saying: 'I've always been a bit of a panicker, so what did you expect?' Rather, the assumption in the so-called 'Kantian' view is that people may have in principle the capacity—the inner resources, if you like—to live up to standards of character higher than those which they do live up to. It is that capacity, thought to vary from person to person and indeed possibly within one person from one phase of her life to the next, which places a cap on our normative expectations of people when we come to consider their excuses. Thus whether the terrorist threat which was imagined to be posed by the motorist in our example excuses

[8] The scenario is loosely based on that in *R* v *Clegg* [1995] 1 All ER 334, where the legal issue was the availability of an excusatory defence to murder for those, particularly soldiers, who kill in mistaken or excessive self-defence. In that case, the victim of the shooting was complicitous in venal wrongdoing. This, together with the political context (the sectarian conflict in Northern Ireland), created distractions which I have stripped out of my own example.

[9] MD Bayles, 'Character, Purpose, and Criminal Responsibility', above n 4; N Lacey, *State Punishment: Political Principles and Community Values* (1988), 63. That Kant did not and could not have subscribed to any such view is apparent from the following passage in *The Doctrine of Virtue* (trans Gregor, (1964) at 66: 'We must not determine ethical duties according to our estimate of man's power to fulfil the [moral] law; on the contrary we must estimate man's power by the standard of the law, which commands categorically. Hence we must appraise this power on the basis of our rational knowledge of what men should be in keeping with the Idea of Humanity, not on the basis of our empirical knowledge of men as they are.'

what our soldier did depends, among other things, on whether, in shooting her dead, he showed as much level-headedness as he was capable of showing in the circumstances.

The supposed relationship between a virtue and the capacity for it needs a good deal of explanation if this view is to make sense. True, just because we are human beings, every one of us has the capacity to *develop* new virtues by learning to recognize different rationally-significant features of situations and respond to them in our actions by acting, in a suitably positive spirit, on the reasons they give. But that is not the capacity that the so-called 'Kantian' view is concerned with. It is not concerned with a capacity I might have at time (t) to develop virtues by time (t+1), but with a capacity I might have at time (t) to act more virtuously at time (t) than I do in fact act at time (t). Could there be any such capacity? That people *do* act 'out of character', and sometimes for better rather than for worse, cannot be doubted. Someone who never showed any heroic tendency in her life may, in some extreme situation, perform an act of great courage. And if she does do so, then necessarily she *can*. The real question is what sense it makes to think of this 'can' as the 'can' of capacity rather than merely the 'can' of possibility. Given the march of technology, I may one day enjoy the possibility of flying to the moon. But I will never enjoy the *capacity* to fly to the moon, because the fact that I can fly to the moon will never be owed to anything *about me*. Instead, my flying to the moon will exploit the capacities of others, e.g. engineers and spaceship commanders. They are the ones with the array of qualities—in this case, skills as well as virtues—that will get me to the moon.[10] Now courage is undoubtedly one of those qualities. Being courageous means that one has capacities that one would not otherwise have, such as the capacity to be a spaceship commander. That is because courage gives one the capacity to act courageously, and spaceship commanders, among others, need that capacity to be fit for their job. The question we are facing here is whether someone who is *not* courageous may nonetheless have that same capacity to act courageously. I must admit to finding the whole idea baffling. The reason is that I cannot see how someone with that capacity could fail to have the corresponding tendency. Someone may say that he understands the world just as the

[10] This is perhaps a suitable place to make clear, for the sake of completeness, that some excuses invoke technical standards rather than standards of character. Although these excuses differ in certain ways from those under discussion here, their gist mirrors that of the excuses under discussion here: that the person who has them lived up to expectations in respect of her skill.

courageous person understands it, and yet somehow does not manage, by and large, to put this understanding into practice. His inclination towards self-preservation often gets the better of him. To which my reply would be that in that case he is kidding himself if he thinks he understands the world just as the courageous person understands it. For a person who sees the world through genuinely courageous eyes, there is nothing to 'manage', no question of putting anything 'into practice', no room for any motivational obstruction between understanding why a situation calls for courage and acting courageously. If one sees the world through genuinely courageous eyes one does not see danger to oneself the way that more cowardly people see it, as a threat, but rather as a challenge, something which, up to a point, one inclines towards rather than away from. Up to that point, one therefore has no inclination to overcome, no will-power to exercise. One looks with bewilderment upon those who hold back and say they're too scared to act. How, one asks oneself, can they so comprehensively miss the point? And how, to return our question, can such people ever be thought to have a *capacity* for courage when, in their actions, they manifest nothing at all of the courageous mentality—when they admittedly do not share in the spirit of the courageous person, and therefore cannot be seeing the world as the courageous person sees it? Perhaps, like most people, they have the capacity to learn to be more courageous by being faced with fearful situations which put the trivial fears of their lives to date in perspective. Or perhaps one day they will simply act courageously, quite out of character—we human beings have an unpredictable side to us. But the idea that right now, as they shrink back, some of these people might already have the capacity for courage—that idea makes no sense. Right now, these people have no relationship to courage except a palpable lack of it. It follows that the standard of courage which they must show if they are to benefit from an excuse cannot be the standard of their own extant capacity for it. Because, in spite of what adherents of the so-called 'Kantian' view say, that standard does reduce straightforwardly to the standard of purely predictive expectation, the standard of character which those making the excuse already meet. That is because the extent of someone's capacity for courageous action at time (*t*) is no more and no less than the extent of her courage at time (*t*). Apart from that courage, there is no further something about her, at time (*t*), which can intelligibly be described as a capacity for acting courageously at that time. There is, in respect of truly courageous action, no further variety of 'inner resources' anyone could ever intelligibly be said to have.

Now it may be said that level-headedness, the virtue which is at stake in the case of our young soldier, differs from courage in precisely this respect. It may be said that it belongs, alongside self-discipline and self-restraint, to a family of virtues characterized by motivational conflict. On this view the spirit of level-headedness is not the positive I-can-cope-with-this, I-just-look-danger-in-the-eye spirit of the courageous, but an unstable teeth-gritted, whatever-I-do-I-must-stay-calm sense of apprehension and self-doubt. The level-headed person has a strong inclination to act in a panicky way, the story goes, which he controls only by sheer will-power. Therefore, apart from the question of whether our soldier is sufficiently level-headed, there is also the question of whether he has sufficient will-power, i.e. a sufficient capacity, to be any more level-headed than he is in such a situation. Personally, I doubt whether the virtue of level-headedness belongs to any such family of virtues or comprises any of these features, which strike me as the features of someone who is very far from level-headed. In fact, I think this is the non-level-headed person's stilted view of what life as a level-headed person might be like. But even if level-headedness were like this, those who rely on this fact when defending the so-called 'Kantian' view of excuses merely expose that view to deeper doubts in the process. They may rely on the fact that our soldier had limited will-power to suggest that our expectations of him in the dimension of level-headedness should be limited. But then they instantly face the question of why our expectations of him *in the dimension of will-power itself* should not exceed the standards which he currently meets in that dimension. Why, having been denied the excuse 'I've always been a bit of a panicker, so what did you expect?' should he nevertheless be granted the excuse 'I've always had a bit of a problem with will-power, so what did you expect?' Is there something about lack of will-power such that it doesn't show people in a bad light in the way that lack of courage or lack of level-headedness does?

Not for the real Kant, and not for the rest of us. If it makes any sense to say that our soldier was as level-headed as he was capable of being, as distinct from merely being as level-headed as he was, then it is always a possible answer to his purported excuse that *he simply should have had a greater capacity for level-headedness.* And when we ask 'by what standards should his capacity have been greater?', our excusatory focus naturally switches from the fact that he was young and inexperienced to the fact that he was a soldier in a troubled frontier zone. Why, of course—he should have had the capacity that a soldier in a troubled frontier zone should have had. His excuse, when he wrongly shoots the motorist, should be structured by normative expectations which are in turn structured by his role as a soldier. A soldier should be more level-headed than most (and therefore, if that really is something different, needs a greater capacity for level-headedness than most), because coping with tension and threats and emergencies is the soldier's stock-in-trade. A soldier who tends to panic is unfit to be a soldier. It is true, of course, that a junior soldier may not properly be expected to meet quite the same standards of level-headedness as, say, his platoon sergeant, and a rookie junior soldier perhaps *a fortiori*. But this has nothing to do with any capacity or incapacity the rookie soldier may have, at this early stage, to meet the higher standards of level-headedness which will later be expected of him. It has to do with the fact that the role of a soldier changes with rank and with training. The process of learning to be a soldier is partly the process of learning to be more level-headed that one might otherwise have been, of learning to see how the world looks without the clouding presence of panic. Thus not even all soldiers, let alone all people, are subject to exactly the same normative expectations so far as their level-headedness is concerned. But, nevertheless, for each soldier and for each person the relevant normative expectations, *including expectations of capacity itself*, vary not according to capacity but according to role. Someone who tries to excuse her betrayals of her friends in the face of threats or other pressures to betray has his excuses judged by the standards of loyalty applicable to friendship, and if she is incapable of such loyalty (or, in my plainer terms, if she is not loyal enough) then that only goes to show that she is unfit for friendship, unfit to call herself a friend. A mountaineer who tries to excuse his cutting of the ropes between himself and his colleague when the link puts him in danger, even though the cutting of it may put his colleague in comparable danger, has his excuses judged by the standards of dependability befitting mountaineers, and if there is something about him which means that he cannot be that dependable (or, in my plainer terms, if he is not dependable enough) then that confirms, rather than denies, that he is unfit to join a mountaineering expedition.

Those still in the thrall of the supposedly 'Kantian' view of excuses are bound to balk at the implication, in this alternative and broadly Aristotelian view of mine, of an automatic correlation between being unfit for the role one occupies and being shown in a bad light. Doesn't this depend, they are sure to ask, on the soundness of the earlier claim that we all have the capacity to *develop* virtues and skills which would make us fit for the lives we lead, so that those who do not are being caught by some fallback doctrine of prior fault?[11] If it turned out that somebody could *never have become* fit to be a soldier, or a friend, or a mountaineer, then would it still be true that her unfitness to be one reflects badly upon her now that she is one? These questions comprehensively—I would say almost wilfully—miss the point. That our actions exhibit our unfitness for the role we are occupying, or more broadly the life we are leading, is just what it *means* for our actions to reflect badly on us. As I have just been trying to convey, there is no further question of whether our unfitness, in turn, reflects badly on us. There are, fundamentally, two closely related things that matter about our relationship with the life we lead, and the roles which go to make it up. The first is that we do not fail in those roles, that we do not do things which people in those roles should not do—that we do not betray our friends, trip up our fellow athletes, misdiagnose our patients' ailments. The second is that we are fit for those roles, that we have the qualities (the virtues, skills, and tastes, as well as the physical and mental constitution) which people in those roles should have—that we are loyal friends, fair minded (as well as powerful) athletes, thorough (as well as expert) doctors. As my list of examples brings out, our fitness regulates, up to a point, our prospect of failure. That we have the right qualities for our role contributes to our not doing the wrong thing, either constitutively (where the wrong thing is partly defined in terms of standards of character, skill, etc.) or at any rate instrumentally (where meeting a relevant standard of character, skill, etc. makes our doing the wrong thing less likely). Nevertheless, fitness and the avoidance of failure do not inevitably go hand-in-hand. I already mentioned the possibility of admirable wrongdoing—of actions which should not have been done but which reflect favourably on the person who did them. Such actions—the thoughtful act which back-fires and causes offence, the act of solicitousness for one's children which only brings out the worst in them—yield examples of failure in spite of fitness. Conversely, there are examples of unfitness without failure—police officers who treat suspects properly but are grudging about it, athletes who never cheat but only

[11] Many people describe the Aristotelian view as depending on this, which shows only that they have preoccupations quite different from Aristotle's own. See e.g. EL Pincoffs, 'Legal Responsibility and Moral Character', *Wayne Law Review* 19 (1973), 905; MS Moore, 'Choice, Character, and Excuse', above n 5, at 45–46. Aristotle did hold that all people have the capacity to develop virtues and skills, but the importance of the point was not, in his mind, that if it were the case that they never had this capacity they would be excused, or in some other way exonnerated, in respect of their later vicious actions. That these are vicious actions is enough *automatically* to pre-empt any such excuse, however the viciousness may have arisen: Aristotle, *Nicomachean Ethics*, 1113^{b}3–22.

because they fear disqualification. But in all this the question of whether and how one's actions reflect upon one *just is* the question of whether they point to one's fitness or unfitness for whatever role one is occupying, for whatever life one is leading. So valid excuses, which prevent one's wrong actions from reflecting badly upon one, cannot conceivably invoke standards of character (or for that matter standards of skill or taste or physical or intellectual fitness) which fall short of the standards of fitness for the role in which, by doing the wrong thing, one failed. In particular, those standards cannot be capped according to the capacities (be they past, present, or even future) of the person to whom the excuse is supposed to apply. For such incapacity, far from militating against unfitness, is a mode of unfitness in its own right.

Now of course there are some people whose incapacity goes very deep—taking them, in some or all of what they do, beyond the realm in which talk of the occupation of roles and the application of the standards of fitness for those roles makes any sense. Of these people we say that they are not responsible for their actions. One of the biggest sources of confusion in the study of excuses lies in the thought that those who make excuses are thereby denying their responsibility for their actions.[12] This thought is nourished by one of the many ambiguities of the word 'responsible'.[13] In one sense, being responsible for what was done means bearing the adverse normative consequences of its having been done. Many people who make excuses, for example those who make them in a criminal court, are denying that they should bear responsibility in this sense. But they are not denying their responsibility in a second sense, which is normally, and certainly in any legitimate criminal court, a precondition of responsibility in the first sense. By making excuses people are, on the contrary, *asserting* their responsibility in this second sense. For being responsible in this sense—being responsible for our actions—is none other than being in that condition in which our actions are amenable, in principle, to justification and excuse.[14] Justifications and excuses are available only to those whose

[12] Among many examples: JL Austin, 'A Plea for Excuses' in Austin, *Philosophical Papers* (1961), 123 at 124; E D'Arcy, *Human Acts* (1965), 85; George Fletcher, *Basic Concepts of Legal Thought* (1996), 104–105.

[13] The classic taxonomy of different senses of this word is HLA Hart, 'Varieties of Responsibility', *Law Quarterly Review* 83 (1967), 346. The two senses I am about to distinguish correspond, respectively, to Hart's 'liability responsibility' and his 'capacity responsibility', although his definitions depart from mine at certain points.

[14] And in which, I should add for the sake of completeness, we are also in a fit state to *offer* justification or excuse. When the question arises of whether we are responsible for our actions, attention must be paid to our condition at two separate stages—first at the

actions have intelligible rational explanations, i.e. whose actions properly reflected reasons for action that they took themselves to have, and this is the basic condition of our responsibility for our actions.[15] It is met by our young soldier, who, even in his panic, took himself to be facing a terrorist who was going for a gun, and who shot her in what he incorrectly took to be an act of self-defence. It is similarly met by those who commit wrongs under duress or provocation. They believe the threats or taunts they are facing to be reasons for them to do as they do, and they intelligibly, even if quite mistakenly, do what they do for those reasons. It is sometimes hinted that this element of rational intelligibility is all that it takes to ground an excuse. If only we can *make sense of* what someone did in the light of the reasons she took herself to have for doing it, then can't we by that token excuse her for doing it? The answer is that, of course, we can't, because even when we have made sense of the reasons on which someone acted, on any credible view we still have to *assess* her reasons, as well as the spirit in which she acted, according to the applicable standards of character. But the focus on making sense of people's actions in the light of their reasons rightly brings to the surface the important point that those whose reasoning *can't* be made sense of in this way, whether because of profound mental illness or infancy or sleepwalking or (on some interpretations of it) post-hypnotic suggestion, are not responsible for their actions and therefore need no excuses for what they do. And of course this means that there is a sense in which one very specific and deep-seated incapacity—namely the incapacity to reason intelligibly through to action—can place a cap on the standards of character by which one is judged when one makes an excuse. It places that cap by extinguishing the need for one to rely on excuses altogether. But it does not follow that when one does need to rely on excuses, one can enjoy an analogous cap based on one's *other* incapacities. For the analogy is false, since now one is not denying one's responsibility for one's actions, but asserting it instead.

Even once one has understood this contrast between denials of responsibility and excuses, it is easy to underestimate its importance. Criminal lawyers, in particular, tend to be fixated with responsibility in the first

time of the action which is under scrutiny, and secondly at the time of its evaluation, e.g. when the case comes to court. The basic idea of responsibility (also known as accountability) is the etymologically undemanding one of an ability to respond to accusations, being in a position to account for one's actions: JR Lucas, *Responsibility* (1993), 5–12.

[15] I have tried to explain justifications, and their relationship to excuses, in J Gardner, 'Justifications and Reasons' in ATH Smith and AP Simester (eds), *Harm and Culpability* (1996) (reprinted as Chapter 5 in this volume).

sense I mentioned, and tend to take it for granted that any doctrine that serves to acquit the accused, and therefore to avert the adverse normative consequences of her action, is as good as any other so far as the accused is concerned. I have always found this an astonishing assumption, which implies that nobody who is tried in the criminal courts has, or even deserves to have, any self-respect. Self-respect is an attitude which everyone ought to have if they deserve it, and which, moreover, everyone ought to deserve. The self-respecting person aspires to live up to the proper standards for success in and fitness for the life she leads, and holds herself out to be judged by those standards. It follows that it is part of the nature of self-respect that a self-respecting person wants to be able to give an intelligible rational account of herself, to be able to show that her actions were the actions of someone who aspired to live up to the proper standards for success in her life and fitness to lead it.[16] She wants it to be the case that her actions were not truly wrongful, or if they were wrongful, that they were at any rate justified, or if they were not justified, that they were at any rate excused. A denial of responsibility rules all of this out, and that is, accordingly, the line of defence which counts as an admission of defeat for any self-respecting person.

The point can be nicely illustrated by comparing the defences of provocation and diminished responsibility which are found side-by-side in the modern English legislation on homicide, and both of which, if successfully pleaded, have the effect of substituting a manslaughter conviction for a murder conviction.[17] To those who have complained of deficiencies in the provocation defence, which is quite tightly circumscribed, it is sometimes said that they could always rely on the more loosely drawn diminished responsibility defence instead. If your long history as a victim of domestic violence was not allowed to affect the assessment of how gravely you had been provoked by your violent partner when you killed him, well why not say instead that your 'battered woman syndrome' left you with diminished responsibility for your actions?[18] After all, it surely comes to the same thing in the end. But it does not come to the same thing at all.[19] The whole point of the diminished responsibility defence

[16] In this explanation, I have been influenced by S Darwall, 'Two Kinds of Respect', *Ethics* 88 (1977), 36 and J Raz, 'Liberating Duties', *Law and Philosophy* 8 (1989), 3.

[17] Homicide Act 1957, ss 2 and 3.

[18] See e.g. *R* v *Thornton* [1992] 1 All ER 306 at 315–316, *per* Beldam LJ. The label 'battered woman syndrome' was coined in L Walker, *The Battered Woman Syndrome* (1984) and is now frequently used in English-speaking courts.

[19] The following point has been made many times before although its broader implications for the relationship between excuses and responsibility have rarely been

is that it depends on the *unreasonableness* of the defendant's reactions, i.e. their unamenability to intelligible rational explanation. 'Why would anyone have done that? It makes no sense. It must be some pathological condition, some kind of "battered woman syndrome".' The whole point of the provocation defence, on the other hand, is that it depends on the *reasonableness* of the provoked person's reaction to the provocation. 'I can see why she did it; she did it because she could see no other escape.' 'I can see why she did it; she did it because she needed to save some vestige of her dignity before he destroyed it utterly.' 'I can see why she did it; she did it for the sake of the children, whom she thought would be the next target.' Of course, intelligible rational explanations like this will not automatically be *sufficient* to make the provocation plea successful—that depends on whether they also meet the relevant normative expectations—but they are certainly *necessary*. Nobody can have a provocation defence without them, but, equally, they cannot have a diminished responsibility defence with them. Faced with the choice, any self-respecting defendant would rather be able to give a intelligible account of herself in rational terms. She would also rather be judged, in the light of that account, by the proper standards of character, skill, taste, etc. for the life she leads, not by some standard manipulated to take account of some claimed weakness in her, which only brands her constitutionally unfit for the life she leads, an incapable and pathetic specimen. Any self-respecting person would rather have a provocation defence, in other words, that properly takes account of the scale of the provocation she was subjected to but judges her reactions to that provocation by the proper standards of character applicable to all, as opposed to falling back on a diminished responsibility defence and conceding that those standards of character do not apply to her in the first place.

I said 'applicable to all'; but surely, if I am true to my own Aristotelian account of excuses, I must mean 'applicable to people in her role'? And what, for these purposes, *is* her role? By exactly which standards of character should the law of provocation, through its reasonableness test, be judging her? Certainly not by the standards of character which determine fitness for being a victim of domestic violence. Since nobody should be a victim of domestic violence, there is no self-respect in living up to any standards of fitness for this role. Nor in living up to standards of fitness

appreciated. See e.g. P Crocker, 'The Meaning of Equality for Battered Women Who Kill Men in Self-Defense', *Harvard Women's Law Journal* 8 (1985), 121 or A Norrie, *Crime Reason and History* (1993), 254.

for being a killer, by the same token. The standards of fitness for being a parent? A partner? An airline pilot or gas installer (if that is what she also happens to be)? A citizen? The problem seems to be that the broadly Aristotelian view of excuses is role-based, but the modern criminal law is not. Surely we come before the modern criminal law, or if we take all this talk of 'equality before the law' seriously we are at any rate supposed to come before it, stripped of our roles, and so subject to the same rules and principles irrespective of the particular kind of life we lead?[20] Actually that is far from true when we look at the criminal law as a whole. A large and ever growing body of criminal law today is what academic commentators call 'regulatory' criminal law, criminal law that applies to us only in our roles as shopkeepers, householders, social security claimants, witnesses, motorists, parents, waste-disposal contractors, and so forth, and purports to judge our actions, *inter alia*, by standards of character specifically befitting these roles.[21] But the law of homicide is not part of the regulatory criminal law in this sense. Like the law of theft and the law of assault, it applies to us all, whatever furrows we may plough in life. So shouldn't the standards of character applicable to it, including those which govern the availability of excuses in it, be uniform? And if so, the question remains, what exactly should they be? My own view is that there is no fundamental objection to making excusatory standards vary, even in the law of homicide, according to the standards applicable to roles which the defendant occupies when he kills. If he kills while on duty and armed as a police officer, then there is no fundamental objection to judging him by the standards of courage, level-headedness and self-restraint applicable specifically to police officers. But I agree that the problem is more difficult when we are dealing with people who kill while occupying a role (such as that of robber or slave), the internal standards of which should not be supported by law because the role should not exist, or a role (such as that of lover or friend), the internal standards of which should be supported by law but do not include any relevant standards (e.g. have nothing specifically to say about level-headedness or courage). The criminal law then seems to have only two options. One is the *lowest common denominator* option. It holds people only to the minimum standards of character needed to lead *any* kind of worthwhile life. The

[20] See e.g. M Sandel, 'The Political Theory of the Procedural Republic' in AC Hutchinson and Patrick Monahan (eds), *The Rule of Law: Ideal or Ideology?* (1987), 85.

[21] Some textbook writers confuse 'regulatory' crime in this sense with *less serious* crime. For a welcome corrective, see N Lacey, C Wells and D Meure, *Reconstructing Criminal Law* (1990), especially at 233–256.

other is the *overarching role* option. It holds that, whatever other roles we may have in life, we also have the distinct role of being human beings, which itself sets basic standards of character. The former option, however, turns out to be a non-starter as soon as one realizes that there can be no common denominator across the various roles we occupy, except to the extent that there is an overarching role of being a human being. Every virtue, every skill, every taste is such that some roles make no specific demand for it, unless, as it turns out, they must incidentally make that demand just by virtue of being human roles. It follows that the lowest common denominator option collapses into the overarching role option. And that leaves the criminal law with the problem of setting distinctive standards of character (and other standards of fitness) for that overarching role, reopening that age-old intractable question of what it means to be human.

Of course this is not the place to tackle this question. Suffice it to say that it need not remain quite as intractable for the criminal law as it does for moral philosophers. For the law has a function not only in supporting but also in *establishing* the proper standards of character (as well as the other standards) for the roles it governs. That the regulatory criminal law does this is neither open to doubt nor, in general, a source of much moral anxiety. The measure of attentiveness required of drivers, the measure of probity required of company directors, the measure of truthfulness required of witnesses; these and many other standards of character are settled directly by doctrines of the regulatory criminal law. In some cases the roles themselves are creations of law, so that the law has no alternative but to set the applicable standards until the roles start to take on a life of their own. But even when roles do acquire a life of their own, and also when they are not creations of law in the first place, the law often has a role in settling which of various competing applicable standards will be the appropriate standard for the role. There comes a point at which, as between these competing standards, it matters less which of them becomes the standard for the role than that the standard for the role is authoritatively settled to allow us to have uniform expectations of each other when we are in that role. This is, of course, the classic 'co-ordination' argument for legal regulation.[22] It applies no less to standards of character than to other standards supported and enforced by law. And, if it is true that the non-regulatory criminal law is concerned with us in our overarching role as human beings, it applies no less to the

[22] See J Finnis, 'Law as Co-ordination', *Ratio Juris* 2 (1989), 97.

non-regulatory criminal law than to the regulatory criminal law. There is no reason to assume that the standards for this overarching role of ours are more determinately settled in advance of the law's intervention than they are for the less overarching roles of electrician or spouse or lawyer. Again, there may be a variety of competing defensible standards for failure and fitness as a human being *simpliciter*, and at a certain point in the competition it may be less important which one of them wins than that we have a clear winner to rely upon in forging our expectations of each other. The basic standard of honesty which people should show is not merely captured but *set* by the law of fraud and theft, and the setting of that basic standard by law rather than by, say, the person whose honesty is at issue is justified by the co-ordinating power of the law. Likewise, the law on duress and provocation, which settles which of a variety of possible and otherwise defensible minimum standards for courage and self-control we have a right to expect of each other, making that the true applicable minimum standard thanks to the extra value which comes of co-ordinating our expectations of each other to a uniform standard. To the extent that there is any real force in demands for 'equality before the law', that force comes of this consideration coupled with the consideration I adduced in the previous paragraph.[23] It comes of the instrumental value of uniform standards in resolving co-ordination problems coupled with the intrinsic value of granting self-respecting people what, as self-respecting people, they want—namely to be judged by the proper standards which apply to their role, be that their role as golfers or parents or guests or engineers or merely as people. And both of these considerations militate strongly against placing a capacity-based cap on the level at which the standards of character applicable to particular defendant's excuses are set.

It may be objected that the fact that this is the authoritative voice of the law speaking also introduces a major countervailing consideration. Surely, under the doctrine of the rule of law, it is crucial that people who are subject to the law's authority can be guided by the law, so that they can deliberately steer their lives round it and avoid the disruption

[23] I should say that I find the label 'equality' misleading in this setting, as in so many others. I find it more perspicuous to frame the demand as a demand that courts be faithful to their role as administrators of justice. I have explored some of the other implications of this role in J Gardner, 'The Purity and Priority of Private Law', *University of Toronto Law Journal* 46 (1996), 459 and in J Gardner, 'Crime: in Proportion and in Perspective' in AJ Ashworth and M Wasik (eds), *Fundamentals of Sentencing Theory* (1998) (reprinted as Chapter 11 in this volume).

of the law's adverse normative consequences? Doesn't it follow that a law which sets standards to which self-respecting people may well aspire but which they have no capacity to reach is in violation of the rule of law?[24] Yes and no. The consideration is a powerful one so far as the definitions of criminal offences are concerned. These should be such that everyone can be guided by them, and therefore should be such that everyone has the capacity to avoid violating them.[25] Although it can often be achieved in other ways, it is possible that this can sometimes be achieved only by individuating the standards of the offence definition, including its character standards, to the reduced capacities of the accused. If my Aristotelian understanding of character is correct, this solution comes to much the same thing as eliminating character standards from that offence definition altogether. So this rule of law argument may help to explain the Anglo-American criminal lawyer's traditional reluctance to employ character standards in the definitions of criminal offences.[26] But the same consideration does not apply to the definitions of criminal *excuses*, which are not supposed to provide any guidance to those whose actions may fall foul of the criminal law.[27] To attempt to benefit from a legal excuse by being guided by it is to forfeit that excuse. One is under duress, from the legal point of view, only if one's fear of the threats one is subject to was rationally adequate, in one's own eyes as well as according to the applicable standards of character, for one to commit the wrong one committed. Accordingly, if in evaluating those threats one also takes account of the likelihood that one will benefit from the legal excuse of duress when one gives into them, one's excuse is thereby lost. It is thus

[24] This was the essence of HLA Hart's famous defence of a capacity-capped doctrine of excuse in the criminal law: Hart, 'Legal Responsibility and Excuses' in Hart, *Punishment and Responsibility* (1968), 28 at 46–47. It is unclear whether Hart had a view about the gist of excuses outside the criminal law context, and if so how that view was related to his rule of law argument for the recognition of capacity-capped excuses in that context.

[25] I have considered some aspects of this requirement in more detail in J Gardner, 'Rationality and the Rule of Law in Offences Against the Person', *Cambridge Law Journal* 53 (1994), 502 (Chapter 2 in this volume).

[26] Consider the furore among the major academic textbook writers in England after the decision in *R* v *Caldwell* [1981] 1 All ER 961, which held an accused to capacity-independent standards in respect of recklessness. JC Smith and B Hogan, *Criminal Law* (5th edn, 1983), 52–58; G Williams, 'Recklessness Redefined', *Cambridge Law Journal* 40 (1981), 252.

[27] This distinction provides the key to answering Alan Norrie's important question: 'If doing justice to individuals involves recognising their motives in acting in the duress situation, why does the law not recognise their motives in all those other contexts in which crimes are committed?' (A Norrie, *Crime Reason and History*, above n 19, 166).

no objection to the law's definition of the excuse of duress that there are some people, their capacity for courage lacking, who cannot be guided by that definition. The same is necessarily true for everyone, irrespective of their capacity for courage; those with the lower capacity labour under no special disadvantage so far as the guiding power of the law is concerned. It follows that a capacity-based cap on the standards of character used in legal excuses cannot be justified along the rule of law lines, any more than it can be justified along any of the other lines we have been considering. Contrary to popular myth, the gist of an excuse, even in the criminal law, is not that one had no capacity to conform, in one's actions, to the standards of character which were demanded of one. On the contrary, as I have tried to explain, the gist of an excuse is that one lived up to those standards.

[11]

THE PERPLEXING BORDERS OF JUSTIFICATION AND EXCUSE

Kent Greenawalt *

INTRODUCTION

Most reasons why otherwise criminal acts, such as *A*'s intentional shooting of *B*, may be noncriminal fall roughly into the categories of justification and excuse.[1] If *A*'s claim is that what he did was fully warranted—he shot *B* to stop *B* from killing other people—*A* offers a justification; if *A* acknowledges he acted wrongfully but claims he was not to blame—he was too disturbed mentally to be responsible for his behavior—he offers an excuse.

Anglo-American law and scholarly writings about that law recognize a distinction between these two sorts of claims,[2] but generally do not do so in any systematic way. For example, a moderately close examination reveals that particular defenses such as self-defense and duress reach instances of both justification and excuse. No very precise theory is advanced to distinguish between justifications and excuses, and most scholars and reformers evince little concern over this sloppy state of affairs.

Crying in the wilderness, however, are a few possibly prophetic voices,

---

* Cardozo Professor of Jurisprudence, Columbia University School of Law. B.A. 1958, Swarthmore College; B. Phil. 1960, Oxford University; L.L.B. 1963, Columbia University. This paper was prepared for the German-Angloamerican Workshop on Basic Problems in Criminal Theory that met in Freiburg, West Germany in July 1984. It is in part a response to a paper that George Fletcher, one of the two conference organizers, had prepared, which is to be published in the March 1985 issue of the *Harvard Law Review*. The paper has benefited significantly from criticisms made by participants at the workshop and from very helpful comments made by my colleague Harold Edgar on an earlier draft.

1. Paul Robinson suggests three categories of defenses in addition to justifications and excuses. Of those, failure of proof defenses and offense modification defenses relate to the basic elements of the offense as defined. See Robinson, Criminal Law Defenses: A Systematic Analysis, 82 Colum. L. Rev. 199, 203 (1982). What Robinson calls nonexculpatory public policy defenses, such as statutes of limitations, however, are genuine exceptions to the idea that *all* defenses constitute justifications or excuses. See generally, id. at 229-32. These defenses are "not based on a lack of culpability of the defendant. They are purely public policy arguments." Id. at 230. I do not consider such defenses in this Article.

2. See Model Penal Code art. 3 (Proposed Official Draft 1962) (Justification); id. art. 4 (Responsibility); id. §§ 2.08-2.10 (Intoxication, Duress, Military Orders); W. LaFave & A. Scott, Jr., Handbook on Criminal Law 268-413 (1972).

Though the Model Penal Code was reformative in many of its efforts to rationalize the criminal law, most of its crucial provisions have been followed in enough jurisdictions so that they now represent major themes in the law of the United States. Since the aims of this Article are mainly theoretical, I frequently cite provisions of the Model Penal Code without attempting to trace their acceptance in particular jurisdictions.

among which the loudest and most eloquent is George Fletcher's.[3] He tells us that in distinguishing justification from excuse our own practices and level of understanding compare unfavorably with those of legal systems in the civil law tradition, and that this failing correlates with deeper and more pervasive attitudes, such as "flat" thinking and legal positivism.[4] He proposes techniques for common law jurisdictions to remedy their present inadequacies in dealing with justification and excuse. The linkage of these inadequacies to more comprehensive attitudes, however, may dampen hope that much improvement on this narrow subject will precede broader enlightenment.

This Article's central theme is that Anglo-American criminal law should not attempt to distinguish between justification and excuse in a fully systematic way. I explore three possible bases for drawing the distinction: (1) a distinction between warranted and wrongful conduct; (2) a division between general and individual claims; and (3) a distinction based on the rights of others. I show why none of these bases yields a clear and simple criterion for categorization. The difficulty rests largely on the conceptual fuzziness of the terms "justification" and "excuse" in ordinary usage and on the uneasy quality of many of the moral judgments that underlie decisions that behavior should not be treated as criminal. Beyond these conceptual difficulties, there are features of the criminal process, notably the general verdict rendered by lay jurors in criminal trials, that would impede implementation in individual cases of any system that distinguishes fully between justification and excuse. Though I sketch some of the broader implications of my comments on justification and excuse, I do not pursue in depth what they signify about the openness of natural language, the appropriate relationship between the criminal law and moral judgment, and the nature of practical moral judgment itself.

Although I emphasize borderline problems, I firmly believe that the basic distinctions between justification and excuse are important in the law. My thesis does not deny any of the following propositions: that the distinction between justification and excuse is a fundamental one for moral judgment; that there is value in the law reflecting fundamental moral categories, including, when it is clear, the distinction between justification and excuse; that scholarly attention to the distinction in analysis and criticism of the

---

3. See, e.g., G. Fletcher, Rethinking Criminal Law 759-875 (1978); Fletcher, The Right and the Reasonable, 98 Harv. L. Rev. (forthcoming March 1985) [hereinafter cited as Fletcher, Right & Reasonable]; Fletcher, The Individualization of Excusing Conditions, 47 S. Cal. L. Rev. 1269 (1974) [hereinafter cited as Fletcher, Excusing Conditions]; Fletcher, Should Intolerable Prison Conditions Generate a Justification or an Excuse for Escape?, 26 U.C.L.A. L. Rev. 1355 (1979) [hereinafter cited as Fletcher, Prison Conditions]. Other observers have also argued strongly for a clearer differentiation. See Robinson, supra note 1, at 291; Note, Justification: The Impact of the Model Penal Code on Statutory Reform, 75 Colum. L. Rev. 914, 960-61 (1975).

4. Professor Fletcher makes these points explicitly in Fletcher, Right & Reasonable, supra note 3, at pts. I & II; and in G. Fletcher, supra note 3, at 768.

criminal law can be fruitful;[5] that in most circumstances when justification and excuse are plainly distinguishable, questions of justification have a kind of natural priority over questions of excuse.[6]

My thesis is modest in other senses. Its acceptance does not require one to take a position on the proper role of objective and subjective factors in the determination of criminal liability, on the disagreement between retributivists and utilitarians over the reasons for punishment, or on the general jurisprudential questions that divide legal positivists, natural lawyers, and those who conceive the rich fabric of the created law and its underlying rationales as providing answers to all legal questions.[7]

Before I proceed to defend my thesis in relation to proposals for rigorous distinctions between justification and excuse, I need to say a little bit more about the basic lines on which such distinctions may be drawn, about the possible aims of a program to induce greater systematization, and about the levels at which such a program might be carried out.

A. *Distinctions*

When one focuses on paradigm cases, the difference between justification and excuse is pretty straightforward. For example, a driver of a fire engine rushing to a fire is justified in exceeding the speed limit. Even with sirens wailing, the speeding engine may raise slightly the danger of a traffic accident, but the risks of harm are greater if time is lost getting to the fire. The driver's behavior is not wrongful; it is warranted. Members of society expect, indeed hope, that other persons placed in the same position will act similarly. In contrast, a worker who is experiencing extreme distress at home and who, in a fit of uncontrollable rage, strikes a blameless fellow

5. Indeed, I think a scholar may usefully apply a particular moral philosophy and precise conceptual apparatus to categorize every imaginable case as justification or excuse, though I do not believe the law itself should attempt to do so.

6. The idea of natural priority is that one determines whether behavior is justified before one considers whether it is excused. Generally it is desirable to decide what behavior is wrongful before one decides what excuses for that behavior will be accepted, and often it will be impossible to evaluate claims of excuse without attending to the precise behavior that is sought to be excused. The natural priority of justification is not, however, absolute. When an actor is a psychotic who has behaved like a "wild beast," someone applying the law might recognize the presence of an excuse-like defense before examining the wrongfulness of the particular act.

7. Though my basic thesis is compatible with any plausible version of these various views, I do not undertake the extensive analysis required to support that position. I do not deny that one's positions on these broader issues might incline one to accept my thesis more or less easily.

My presentation does proceed on the assumption that academic constructions of underlying principles are not a *part* of the law, a position that is accepted almost universally in common law jurisdictions. My major points would be unaffected by rejection of this view, but some of them would need to be formulated differently, in terms of the limits to which statutes and judicial opinions should go. A similar reformulation might be needed if the law were understood to incorporate all the soundest principles on which present statutes and decisions might be rationalized, see R. Dworkin, Taking Rights Seriously (1977), since these ideal principles might include some systematic differentiation between justification and excuse.

employee is not justified in doing so, but his emotional state might constitute a total or partial excuse. His act was wrong, he and others hope it will not be replicated; but he was not fully responsible and is less blameworthy than someone else who performs a similar act.

Some of the typical features of justification and excuse may be generalized in the following way.[8] Justified action is warranted action; similar actions could properly be performed by others; such actions should not be interfered with by those capable of stopping them; and such actions may be assisted by those in a position to render aid. If action is excused, the actor is relieved of blame but others may not properly perform similar actions; interference with such actions is appropriate; and assistance of such actions is wrongful.

Though these respective features of justification and excuse often coalesce, they do not always do so. Their imperfect correlation raises the question of what is—or should be—regarded as the central distinction between justification and excuse in ordinary legal discourse.[9] That question underlies some disputes over whether particular defenses are justifications or excuses. A resolution of this issue is necessary to evaluate any program to introduce more rigor into the law's treatment of justification and excuse. The virtues and drawbacks of drawing the line in terms of one set of opposing features might be quite different from those of drawing the line in terms of another.

I evaluate two major alternatives: that the crucial distinction is between warranted and unwarranted action and that the crucial distinction lies—or should lie—in terms of rights of resistance and assistance. I more briefly consider the possibility that the central ground of distinction is that justifications are general or objective, while excuses are individual or subjective.

B. *Aims*

Systematic distinctions between justifications and excuses might be recommended to further two objectives: (1) producing authoritative determinations of whether persons escaping liability have presented justifications or only excuses and (2) achieving theoretical clarity in the criminal law. The first, more ambitious, goal cannot be fully realized in any system that relies upon a general verdict by lay jurors for tried cases. When only a single ground of acquittal is presented, a not guilty verdict will reveal the ground of the jury's judgment,[10] but if jurors who return a verdict have been

8. See G. Fletcher, supra note 3, at 760–61; Eser, Justification and Excuse, 24 Am. J. Comp. L. 621, 622–23 (1976).

9. One might, of course, take the position that no one distinction can be central, and that in drawing the line between justification and excuse one must have regard to multiple factors. Many of the objections I raise to a fully systematic differentiation in the law would apply if one tried to employ some complicated multifactor criterion. Moreover, the claimed benefits of analytical clarity would be diminished were such a complex approach used.

10. This proposition is not precisely accurate given the jury's ability to acquit despite its

presented with claims amounting to justifications and excuses, the legal system will have produced no authoritative determination *why* liability is not imposed. In most American jurisdictions, a jury that acquits on the ground of mental disease must say that it is doing so, its specific verdict providing the basis for civil commitment; but this practice is not followed for most other excuses or for justifications.

The general verdict is not an inextricable feature of lay juries, and a critic might object to that device since it provides the community with incomplete guidance as to how to regard an acquitted defendant.[11] Were juries asked to indicate their precise reasons for acquittal, the great majority of cases might yield authoritative determinations about justifications and excuses, failure occurring only when jurors agreed upon acquittal and differed in their reasons.

This hypothetical system would carry costs. Although providing authoritative determinations, the special verdict has disadvantages, most notably the elimination of the latitude the general verdict affords jurors to exercise leniency by overriding strict legal instructions. The introduction of specific verdicts, or specific findings, for a broad range of cases would encounter considerable resistance and might well be regarded as unconstitutional in the United States.[12] Short of this radical shift in how juries operate, authoritative determination of justification and excuse in particular cases can be achieved only to a limited extent.

The general verdict is hardly a complete answer to the call for greater rigor in the classification of criminal law defenses,[13] however, for precision can serve other objectives. The educative force of a criminal code may be furthered by a labelling of justifications and excuses that promotes in citizens proper views about how to make difficult choices and how to regard the behavior of others.[14] Clarity in distinctions can enhance understanding of the criminal law and its purposes among those who think about that subject, and can help lay the groundwork for intelligent reform. Although the boundaries of grounds of defenses should be determined in light of all

---

finding that a defendant is guilty under the law. A jury might, for example, decide that a proffered justification does not correspond with the facts but acquit because for some reason outside the law it does not want to impose liability.

11. Cf. Robinson, supra note 1, at 245-47 (suggesting the desirability of more specific verdicts for claims of justification and excuse).

12. See United States v. Spock, 416 F.2d. 165, 180-83 (1st Cir. 1969). In that case the court held that the use of special findings was prejudicial error. It relied on its supervisory power and made reference to the particular inappropriateness of special findings in a sensitive first amendment case, but much of its language casts doubt on the constitutionality of special verdicts or special findings in ordinary criminal cases.

13. It is relevant here that only a very small percentage of criminal charges are actually disposed of by jury trial.

14. Clarity about what behavior the law declines to punish may sometimes conflict with the law's aim of affecting the conduct of ordinary citizens. See Dan-Cohen, Decision Rules and Conduct Rules: On Acoustic Separation in Criminal Law, 97 Harv. L. Rev. 625, 630-41 (1984). I do not explore whether clarity about the distinction between justifications and excuses could ever be similarly counterproductive.

relevant considerations, not dictated by abstract legal definitions of justification and excuse, exploration of the nature of justification and excuse still may affect perceptions about what the overall scope of defenses should be.[15] Finally, conceptual clarity and comprehensiveness may be worth striving after for their own sake. Although I acknowledge the genuine virtues of clarification of what counts as a justification and what counts as an excuse, I shall show why pursuit of that objective within the law becomes, after a certain point, misconceived or unwise.

C. *Levels*

Clarity about justification and excuse can be introduced at different levels; and clarifications at one level may be promising even if clarifications at some other level are not. At the most obvious level, each specific defense in a criminal code could be either a justification or an excuse. In that event, jury instructions would sharply distinguish between the two kinds of defenses even if the resulting general verdicts did not plainly indicate the grounds of acquittal. At another level, the criminal code could provide a general definitional distinction between justification and excuse; such a distinction might coexist with more specific formulations of defenses, such as duress, that covered both justification and excuse. Whether judges would use these definitional sections to instruct jurors could be resolved either way. The third level at which clear distinctions might be achieved would be in authoritative judicial opinions. Appellate judges might build systematic theories about justification and excuse from the rough materials of the criminal code, from more general principles of law, and from prevailing moral conceptions. A judicially constructed theory that won acceptance would form a part of the law though not found directly in any criminal statute. Finally, the job of theory building might be done by scholars rather than judges.[16] In the Anglo-American tradition, scholarly constructions would not become a part of the law unless they won legislative or judicial acceptance, but they might nevertheless have explanatory power about the implicit values of the law and inform discussions of legal reform.

Given my own view that the blurred edges of the basic concepts and the diversity of moral judgments underlie the crucial restrictions on complete distinctions between justifications and excuses, I do not think at this stage of our legal and cultural development that achieving such distinctions is a sound aim for the law itself. But scholars explaining the law have greater freedom to adopt definitions and moral positions that deviate from

---

15. Indeed, the accomplishment of specific reforms could actually be the motivating force behind a proposal for clarification (or the adoption of a vocabulary more sympathetic to the reform). I do not address that possible basis for systematic clarification, since the main advocates of such clarification have not relied on it.

16. Given the present state of interest and understanding in the United States, one cannot realistically expect busy judges resolving particular cases to develop full blown distinctions between justifications and excuses; such a development would be likely to take place only if preceded by more intensive scholarly endeavors.

common understandings than that properly assumed by those who make the law. Moreover, insofar as systematic clarification contributes to intelligent reform of the law, that illumination does not require embodiment of every subtle distinction in the criminal law itself. Thus, my reservations about systematic clarification within the law do not apply to scholarly endeavors to distinguish rigorously between justification and excuse.[17]

I. Warranted and Unwarranted Behavior

From the perspective of ordinary English language, the central characteristic of justified action is that it is warranted, not wrongful.[18] Whatever may be true about analagous words in other languages, "justified" is most definitely not a special legal term.[19] In discussions of ethics, justified action is morally proper action. "Justification" is also used in relation to the reasons one puts forward for one's choices; an action is "justified" in this sense when one has defended it with sound arguments. An essentially similar sense is employed when people speak of opinion writing as a process of legal justification. In epistemology, reference is made to "justified" belief—that is, a well-founded belief about facts. What joins these various senses is the idea that to be justified is to have sound, good reasons for what one does or believes. An inquiry into whether a person's acts or beliefs are justified is not centrally about what other people may do in respect to that person. Although the conclusion that someone is justified often bears importantly on judgments about the permissible actions of others, those judgments are analytically separate from the initial conclusion.

If the law's central distinction between justification and excuse is to follow ordinary usage, it will be drawn in terms of warranted and unwarranted behavior. That, indeed, is the central distinction in existing American law insofar as one can be discerned; and exploration of the desirability of greater precision sensibly begins with it.

A. *Troubling Borderlines*

The major barriers to precise classification along this line lie in two uncertain borderlines between justified and excused action and in divergences of moral evaluations of why actors should escape criminal convic-

17. Interestingly, the Penal Code of the Federal Republic of Germany is not generally more systematic in distinguishing justification from excuse than the Model Penal Code. As I learned at the Freiburg Workshop on Basic Problems in Criminal Theory, the efforts to formulate complete and categorized distinctions arise in scholarly writings, which themselves disagree on critical points. If German law is viewed as having attained a much richer division of justification from excuse than American law, the attainment is in these scholarly endeavors, which are more ambitious in this respect and have a higher status in the legal community than American scholarly efforts.

18. As George Fletcher puts it, "A justification speaks to the rightness of the act; an excuse, to whether the actor is accountable for a concededly wrongful act." G. Fletcher, supra note 3, at 759; accord Eser, supra note 8, at 629.

19. Hall, Comment on Justification and Excuse, 24 Am. J. Comp. L. 638, 639 (1976) ("'Justification' and 'excuse' . . . have long been parts of everyday speech.").

tion. The price of much greater rigor in the law would be to press concepts beyond their natural capacity, to generate avoidable disagreements or submerge controversies with misleading labels, and, likely, to complicate the tasks of jurors.

1. *Permissible Acts that are Less than Ideal.* — If *A* performs the morally best possible act in the circumstances, he is morally justified. If he performs an act that is wrongful, he is not justified, though he may have an excuse. Regrettably, these two categories do not necessarily exhaust acts that are subject to moral evaluation.

An act may be thought to be morally permissible even though it is not the best possible among the available alternatives. A person may act in a manner that reflects what most people would do or that in some sense is "within his rights,"[20] although a different response would be morally preferable. For example, after Bruce betrays Al's confidence, Al refuses to speak to Bruce. One may acknowledge that Al's anger and hostile response are "natural" and that Al has not wronged Bruce, while at the same time believing that Al would have acted in a morally preferable way if he had forgiven Bruce.[21] How are we to summarize such an evaluation? Blaming Al may not be appropriate; his claim that his response was normal and consonant with Bruce's wrong is not really an excuse. Yet we may feel uncomfortable about calling Al's behavior *justified.* What we have, in fact, is a claim in defense of action that may not fit smoothly into either of the two categories.

The perplexity here not only concerns the common problem of classifying situations at the edges of competing categories; it goes much deeper, raising fundamental questions about the exercise of moral evaluation. People who accept some version of perfectionist ethics—for example, that a person should always act to promote the greatest happiness or should always act with loving concern—will tend to view Al's claim as an excuse. All of us fall short of what we should do and Al's yielding to his natural emotional feeling, though an instance of ordinary human shortcoming, is not a justification for what he has done. On the other hand, people who believe that ethical "oughts" mainly concern duties involving minimal requisites for behavior toward others, will tend to regard Al's claim as justificatory, bringing his actions within the wide range of morally permitted behavior.[22] Innumerable other examples raise similar questions about evaluation, but the most pervasive instances involve the pursuit of one's own interests at the expense of the greater interests of others.[23] Ordinary social morality and

20. I am speaking here of some loose sense of moral rights, not of legal rights.

21. Al's forgiveness of Bruce might be considered a supererogatory act, not something Al "ought" to do but something that it would be appropriate to praise him for doing if he did it. See D. Heyd, Supererogation 154–64 (1982).

22. Suggestions that when conduct is justified, the benefits of it necessarily outweigh the harms, see Robinson, supra note 1, at 203, are shown by this example to involve serious oversimplification.

23. For a broad discussion of how our moral sense falls short of a rigorous utilitarian

moralities focused on narrow rights and duties leave considerable scope for egoistic behavior that versions of perfectionist ethics deem unjustified.

Members of liberal societies have widely differing views about these fundamental questions of ethics. That much is obvious. What may be less obvious are the ways in which variant perspectives can combine in the same individuals. Many persons who accept a version of perfectionist ethics intellectually and who may feel emotionally committed to such ethics in their "best" moments nonetheless revert to a more minimal, less demanding approach as they struggle through their daily existence.[24] Lest such examples be dismissed as involving simple failures to live up to ideals, we need also to recognize that the two kinds of moral views can be joined in a coherent set of beliefs. A person might think that basic social relations should be grounded in a minimalist morality that concedes large areas of autonomy.[25] On this view, what people in society can reasonably expect and demand of each other would appropriately be defined in terms of broad individual rights. The same person might also believe that he and others should be guided in their actions by a perfectionist ethic, say, of loving concern, and that for some purposes evaluation of other people in light of such an ethic is appropriate.[26] If someone with these views tried to be very precise, he might say something like this about Al's behavior: "From the standpoint of what Bruce and society could fairly expect of Al, what Al did was justified; from the standpoint of the perfectionist standards that should guide us all, he was only excused."[27]

The criminal law does not demand ideal behavior from people. Basic definitions of criminal behavior leave untouched many actions that fall below even modestly rigorous standards of moral acceptability, and privileges to engage in otherwise criminal acts also make concessions to the realities of human nature.

Permissions to use physical force in self-defense are an example. Even when a person knows he can retreat safely and fears no damage to his property, he may use deadly force rather than retreat from his home in the face of an assailant who threatens his life, and in many jurisdictions he can use

---

perfectionism that demands that we always do the best possible act, see S. Scheffler, The Rejection of Consequentialism (1982).

24. I believe that many seriously religious persons roughly fit this description.

25. See, e.g., G. Fletcher, supra note 3, at 770, 860.

26. My emphasis here is on the application of such a morality to the acts of others and as a basis of judgments about those acts. Perfectionist principles are sometimes aspirations individuals accept only for themselves, but often they are not. Since the minimalist morality governing social relations might admit of praise for generous acts that go beyond the required minimum, the shift in perspective to the perfectionist ethic will produce a shift in judgment only if one uses terms like "ought not" and "blame" for acts permissible under the minimalist morality.

27. Some Christian accounts would not even concede that Al's action was excused, treating it rather as a sin for which he stands in need of forgiveness. The idea of "justification by faith" represents the understanding that we are all subject to condemnation according to our actions alone; our conduct is neither justified nor excused.

deadly force rather than retreat from a public place as well. Many people would say that safe retreat is morally more commendable than attempting to take an enraged assailant's life. A legal privilege not to retreat might be supported on the ground that those defending their rights have a basic moral right not to retreat, or that nonretreat deters future aggressions,[28] or that factfinders are incapable of judging when retreat would clearly be safe, or that the law should accommodate the outraged feelings of victims of aggression.

Imagine that a jurisdiction in which the rule of retreat for dwellings is being considered believes that precise classification of justifications and excuses is an important objective of the criminal code. One member of the legislative drafting committee thinks refusal to retreat is positively desirable, deterring aggression and symbolizing the sacredness of dwellings. The second thinks that refusal to retreat is morally less desirable than retreat, when retreat can be carried out safely, but that refusal to retreat is within the range of morally permissible responses. A third member thinks refusal to retreat is decidedly wrong and doubts whether a person aware that retreat would be safe has even a moral excuse for using deadly force instead; yet this member is hesitant to impose his moral conviction and demand behavior many people find unnatural, and he is also skeptical of the capacity of jurors to determine when someone knows he can retreat safely. Each legislator agrees that criminal liability should not be imposed on people who decline to retreat from their homes; the first plainly thinks failure to retreat is justified, the second regards it as justified only in the broad sense of morally permitted, the third thinks that the actor who declines to retreat when he knows he can do so safely has only an excuse, an excuse based on common human weakness and administrative difficulties. If the legislators believed that the law had to label precisely what constituted an excuse and what constituted a justification, they would somehow have to iron out that troublesome issue in respect to retreat. On the other hand, if the law's approach to that distinction does not purport to be rigorous, they would not need to worry too much about whether the privilege received one label or another, or indeed received either label. In this instance, since the general privilege to use deadly force in self-defense is a justification, any provision for retreat could be handled most conveniently within that category.

At the very least, resolution between justification and excuse would be likely to take a lot of time and energy. Whatever decision was made, a powerful minority view would be submerged by the law's choice, and if the dominant or centrist position is that of the second legislator, namely that failure to retreat is morally permissible but less commendable than retreat, either label would fail even to reflect fairly the prevailing view, unless justifications were very carefully defined to include all morally permitted acts.

What effects would the exercise in classification produce? Let us sup-

28. Eser, supra note 8, at 632, notes the individualistic and social function grounds of self-defense.

pose that the law labels failure to retreat justified if the home dweller is in danger, but only excused if he could retreat safely. Whether or not retreat would have been safe, the jury in an actual case should acquit if the other requisites of self-defense are made out; so the general verdict will not reveal the jury's judgment about this matter. Knowing all this in advance, should the judge permit evidence and argument about the safety of retreat? That seems highly doubtful. Juries have had a hard enough time sifting through everything that is directly relevant to what they must decide; cluttering trials with evidence that is irrelevant to what they must decide is not a good idea. If evidence and argument about the safety of retreat were not admitted, the law would be left then with a legally authoritative pronouncement having no bearing on the conduct of actual criminal trials.[29]

The payoff of such precise labelling might appear so meagre that legislative cynicism would set in. The purported seriousness of fine distinctions in the law between justification and excuse might continue to hold sway among legal scholars, but drafters would concentrate on more crucial problems.

The other side of the coin is the positive benefit from the law's lack of rigor. Drafters can sensibly attend to what matters most without worrying too much about labels, and observers can acknowledge the conflicting perspectives that may yield acceptance of a particular defense. In that event, aspects of privileges, such as the retreat aspect of self-defense, can simply be dealt with in sections appropriate for the main privilege, without inordinate worry about whether particular circumstances turn what would ordinarily be a justification into what is *only* an excuse.

2. *"Mistakes" in Judgment.* — People often engage in conduct that would be justified if the actual facts were precisely as they believed them to be, but would not be justified if the actual facts had been fully comprehended. How should such acts be characterized?[30] Does that depend on

29. I do not mean to deny that such a pronouncement could retain some educative and clarificatory value even if it does not affect actual trials.

30. A similar question arises if the conduct would be wrongful on the facts as the actor perceived them, but would be justified if all the actual facts had been fully comprehended. Sam shoots Victor because Victor's enemy has paid him $10,000 to do so; completely unknown to Sam, Victor is just about to detonate a bomb that will kill scores of people at the moment Sam kills him. In this context, the conceptual issue is not whether Sam's shooting of Victor is justified or excused, but whether it is justified (because desirable) or wrongful and unexcused (because the product of aims and appraisals that involve no excuse from blame).

I do not address this question in the body of the essay, since most modern American statutes, endorsed by George Fletcher, see G. Fletcher, supra note 3, at 557, 559–60, 564–65, do require a subjective belief in justification for the defense to succeed. Paul Robinson, however, argues strongly for a totally objective approach to justification, cites authority for that proposition, and construes statutory formulations that include belief as not requiring that one have a subjective belief in justifying circumstances. See 2 P. Robinson, Criminal Law Defenses § 122 (1984).

In contrast to many questions of labelling concerning persons who have mistaken beliefs in justification (who may be free of liability altogether whether called justified or excused), the decision about characterization of Sam's act directly affects what he is guilty of and his

whether the factual mistake involves some fault of the actor? If, as I contend, the act based on a faultless mistake of fact should be regarded as justified by the law, should the law try to distinguish the faultless misperception from one that is faulty but will still relieve the actor from liability?

I begin with a situation in which from the standpoint of all existing human knowledge an action appears to be desirable, but unforeseeable consequences make it turn out to be undesirable.

> Employing the most advanced techniques for predicting wind patterns, Roger decides that a fire in a national forest that threatens human lives can be halted only by carefully burning out a section of the forest that is in the path of the fire. That section is burned on Roger's orders; shortly thereafter the wind shifts in a wholly unexpected way that halts the forest fire before it reaches the burned section.

We may hesitate to classify a situation like this simply as an instance of justification or excuse,[31] and our natural language is rich enough to convey the reasons for our hesitation. We may say, "the risk Roger took was justified," or, somewhat more precisely, "the actor, but not the act, was justified," or more precisely yet, "Roger's choice and action were justified, but what they actually produced turned out fortuitously not to be justified." Such language conveys succinctly our evaluation of what has transpired.[32]

Despite the difference between this situation and paradigm examples of justification, that the law should treat Roger's defense as one of justifica-

---

potential liability. If his act is justified, he has committed only attempted murder; if it is not justified he has committed murder. Whether Sam was careful or careless in failing to realize what Victor was about to do is irrelevant. If he thought he was killing Victor without any semblance of justification, the degree of his diligence in his reaching that conclusion would not bear on his blameworthiness.

Conceptually we can distinguish five major positions on mistakes about justifying circumstances: (1) that the actual circumstances control; (2) that the circumstances believed by the actor control; (3) that circumstances reasonably believed by the actor control; (4) that the act must be justified under *both* the actual and the believed circumstances; (5) that the act may be justified under either the actual or the believed circumstances.

31. The problem here closely parallels the preliminary concern in judging the morality of actions: whether the reasonable perceptions of the actor or the actual facts are to govern. Depending on which perspective one adopted, for example, one might say that what Roger did was a proper action from a utilitarian point of view or that it was not.

32. Lest it be thought that because this example involves unforeseeable consequences after the conduct, it does not involve factual mistake, let me state the assumption implicit in the text: that if the actor had complete knowledge of the present circumstances and complete knowledge of general causal relationships, he would have been able to predict these presently unforeseeable consequences. The example thus rests on the general idea that future natural events are "determined" by present conditions. Since in the example the unexpected consequences do not rest on an exercise of human will, the example does not require determinist assumptions about human choices.

The force of the example would not be altered by an assumption that Roger's critical judgment more directly involved a present state of facts, for example, the dampness of the wood in a remote section of the forest. Imagine that Roger makes the best possible judgment about that and concludes that a fire break is needed; but two days earlier a highly localized

tion seems plain, at least if the law's crucial distinction is to be between warranted and wrongful action.[33] In respect to Roger's behavior, society would expect and hope that a similar actor with a similar set of available facts would make the same choice. And society's view of the morality of the manner in which he acted, its moral judgment about him, should not be affected by the unfortunate outcome. Roger is not asking to be relieved of responsibility for his choice because of some personal inadequacy like mental disturbance; rather, he has acted as the most competent practitioner in his field would have acted.[34]

When a mistake about the facts results from conscious indifference to relevant information or from inadequate care or effort in acquiring information, and the misperception produces an act that would clearly have been wrong had the perceivable facts been understood, then the actor's fault has contributed to the act. Should the actor offer his factual assumptions as the reasons behind his act, he would be offering an excuse—one that might not wholly eliminate his moral blameworthiness, but might be sufficient to preclude legal liability or reduce its gravity.

Some intermediate cases are less simple to classify. Suppose that Roger is dealing with a situation that requires a quick on-the-spot choice. He makes a choice that is the best possible under the circumstances, but one that could correctly have been seen as wrong in advance by experts using sophisticated weather-predicting equipment. Whatever else the law may allow, certainly any choice that is the best that could be expected in the circumstances must be regarded as justified.

A more troublesome question is how much the inherent talents and training of the particular person making the choice should count. Suppose Roger is careful and conscientious, but he makes what turns out to be the

---

and unreported storm had dropped so much rain on the intervening part of the forest that the fire stops short of the break.

Another straightforward instance of mistaken appraisal concerning existing facts is when a policeman with probable cause arrests a person who is innocent. See, e.g., infra note 77 and accompanying text.

33. My view about this stands in opposition to suggestions by those who propose rigorous distinctions between justification and excuse that acts that would be wrong if all the true facts had been known are never justified, only excused. See Fletcher, Right & Reasonable, supra note 3, at pt. III; Robinson, supra note 1, at 224, 239; Note, supra note 3, at 918; cf. G. Fletcher, supra note 3, at 762–68 (Model Penal Code, in permitting factual mistakes to give rise to justification, supports the supposed paradox that two actors in conflict could both be justified).

34. At a higher level of subtlety this position might be contested. It might be argued that if people are regarded as excused rather than justified when things turn out badly, actors generally will be more careful, and that such labelling will somehow better satisfy the feelings of those who are injured by fortuitously unfortunate acts. The plausibility of this position may well vary among different classes of actions and the optimal labelling for moral judgment would not necessarily coincide with the optimal labelling for legal judgment. In any event, those who have argued that claims resting on factual mistakes can only be claims of excuse, see supra note 33, have yet to put forward any such complex theory of moral judgment; rather, they seem to believe that their position is self-evident.

wrong choice because he is less skilled or experienced than most other forest rangers with such responsibilities. His actions are the best that could be expected of him but are not the best that could be expected of the average ranger. Given the law's inability to make infinite gradations in skill and experience, it should not label the behavior in a manner that will encourage emulation. This consideration points in favor of calling Roger's factual misperception an excuse. How society should regard him is less clear. In a sense his choice has rested on a personal inadequacy, but one that does not involve the carelessness or diminished responsibility associated with typical excuses. I shall not try to resolve this particular borderline problem, which relates to the more general issue of how far legal elements of justification and excuse should be cast in objective or subjective terms.

Yet another intermediate case is a choice based on a factual perception that is reasonable, but is not the very best of which the person was capable. Is the reasonableness of a perception enough to make an act based on it justified, or would the possibility of a yet more accurate perception leave the actor with only an excuse?

However these cases are treated, the crucial point for our purposes is that were the law to attempt precise categorization, some actions grounded in factual mistake should be viewed as justified, others as only excused. The critical question is whether for cases in which the criminal law is to relieve actors of liability in either event, it should try to distinguish justifications from excuses. Suppose that negligently setting a forest fire is not a crime and that ordering a fire with a negligent belief in justifying circumstances is also not a crime.[35] To exonerate Roger of possible liability, a jury would have to decide that he sincerely believed that the justifying circumstances existed and saw no need to check further.[36] The jury would not need to decide if he was reasonable or negligent in forming his belief. As indicated already in respect to retreat, there are good reasons for not burdening jurors with instructions and evidence that do not touch issues they necessarily have to determine.[37] Including provisions covering negligent belief about

35. The Model Penal Code systematically correlates the standards of culpability for possible justifying circumstances, such as negligent belief, to the standards of culpability for the underlying offense. See Model Penal Code § 3.09(2) (Proposed Official Draft 1962). In some jurisdictions a belief in justifying circumstances does not relieve one of liability unless the belief is reasonable. I do not discuss here the possible arguments for treating action based on a negligent belief in justifying circumstances more severely than action based on a negligent belief that no legally cognizable harm will be caused.

36. An awareness that he should check further might amount to recklessness, see Model Penal Code § 2.02(2)(c) (Proposed Official Draft 1962), making him liable if recklessly starting a fire is criminal. If only intentionally starting a fire were criminal, Roger's honest belief in justifying circumstances would be a defense even if he had been consciously reckless in forming that belief.

37. In one important respect, however, the evidentiary setting here is likely to be different than in the retreat example. See supra text accompanying notes 28-29. If the prosecution tries to prove that Roger knew that the justifying circumstances did not exist or was reckless as to the possibility, a part of its evidence is likely to be that a belief in justifying circumstances would have been highly unreasonable. The jury would then have before it

justifying circumstances in criminal code sections that reach true belief and faultless mistaken belief makes considerable practical sense.

A further illustration of how the common law system works strengthens this conclusion. Sue shoots at what she thinks is a deer but the object turns out to be another hunter who is hit in the arm. Sam shoots in the arm a person he wrongly believes is trying to shoot someone else. Each instance presents a potential question whether the factual misperception was negligent or reasonable. Whether Sam's misperception was reasonable or negligent will determine whether his conduct was justified or excused. In either case, no criminal liability will be imposed. If the commission of assault requires an intentional or reckless wounding, Sue's is not, in *present* legal terminology, a case of justification or excuse since the basic elements of the crime have not been made out.[38] Whatever evidence has been introduced at her trial, the jury is instructed that she simply has not committed assault unless she has been at least reckless. When the basic elements of a crime are not satisfied, Anglo-American law does not concern itself with whether the actor has displayed *some* moral failing or even acted in a way giving rise to tort liability.[39] In a moral sense, the same question about justification or excuse—whether a factual misperception is negligent or reasonable—that arises in Sam's case also arises in Sue's. If the law really should be precise and label as excuses all negligent beliefs about justifying circumstances, then it should also label as excuses negligent perceptions about likely harm to legally protected interests. The logic of a program for systematic clarification of justification and excuse thus reaches how primary bases of liability are treated as well. Conversely, if it is acceptable not to resolve the reasonableness of a mistaken perception that negates a required intention or recklessness concerning the basic elements of an offense, then the absence of resolution for mistaken perceptions about justifying circumstances is also acceptable. That the present approach to primary bases of liability is so widely perceived as unobjectionable supports the view that the law need not always differentiate between reasonable and unreasonable beliefs about justification.

---

evidence bearing on negligence even if negligence were not directly an issue. But the jury would not need to sift and resolve that evidence if it was convinced that Roger was fully persuaded that he needed to order the fire.

38. The Model Penal Code makes negligence a basis for liability when one wounds with a gun. See Model Penal Code § 211.1(1)(b) (Proposed Official Draft 1962). Under such a provision, the line between negligent and reasonable action is crucial to liability. For injuries not inflicted with deadly weapons, recklessness is the lowest level of culpability. Id. § 211.1(1).

39. If a country's tort law generally made negligent action a sufficient basis for recovery, but not a sufficient basis for imposing criminal liability, *and* criminal actions and tort actions were not discrete, then in cases of potential criminal liability involving a victim with a potential tort recovery, fact-finders would need to decide if mistakes were negligent. In such a system, asking fact-finders to distinguish reasonable from unreasonable actions would not impose unnecessary burdens.

B. *Simplicity of Categorization and Duress*

I have suggested in connection with retreat and factual misconceptions about justifying circumstances that simplicity in categorization is a virtue. That point has broader relevance, even when the moral status of variant actions is fairly clear. The crucial inquiry for the Anglo-American defense of duress falls along a line different from that dividing justification and excuse. Under the Model Penal Code, a person has the defense if he was coerced to commit criminal conduct by force or a threat of force that "a person of reasonable firmness in his situation would have been unable to resist."[40]

Though coerced persons are often rendered incapable of making rational judgments, the defense need not depend on one's inability to make a sensible choice. Someone who is fully rational can be coerced if the threatened harm is so great that he is no longer "free" to choose that harm. If Fred remains completely cool while he steals a diamond in response to a credible threat that three strangers will be killed if he refuses, his action falls within the defense. Here, Fred's choice is the best under the circumstances and is morally justified. If threats that incapacitated his judgment led Fred to sacrifice greater interests for lesser ones, duress would be offered as an excuse.[41]

The traditional defense of duress thus covers some behavior that is justified and other behavior that is only excused. In some jurisdictions, the general justification, or lesser evils, defense has historically been considered applicable only when natural events presented a choice between evils. Were Fred's theft committed someplace where that limitation is still accepted, his defense would have to depend on duress.[42] In other jurisdictions, the general justification defense is not so restricted, and Fred could make claims both of general justification and duress, the two defenses overlapping in their content.[43] Yet another possibility would be to prune the duress defense so that it reaches only unjustified responses to threats, leaving the general justification defense to cover all justified responses to threats.[44]

Were one to pursue the aim of clear distinction between justification and excuse, the last course would appear to be the best. Yet the difference between it and the course actually followed by the Model Penal Code and

40. Model Penal Code § 2.09(1) (Proposed Official Draft 1962).

41. When threats lead people to make understandable choices favoring family interest over the equal or more powerful interests of strangers, the moral appraisal is more doubtful, but the law properly regards such choices as only excused, not justified.

42. Were his theft clearly a response to a serious threat to kill three people, no prosecution would be brought, but one can imagine charges if the prosecutor disbelieved his story.

43. E.g., Model Penal Code § 2.09(4) (Proposed Official Draft 1962); see Hall, supra note 21, at 640.

44. See Eser, supra note 8, at 622 (discussing German Penal Code). The German law sensibly permits a defense of excuse for some responses that fall short of being justified to exigent natural circumstances. The Model Penal Code's failure to provide such a defense for "natural threats" as well as human threats is unsupported by any persuasive rationale.

many modern American jurisdictions,[45] is not great, since that course also indicates that submission to threats is sometimes justified and sometimes excused. Whether the defenses are overlapping or alternative, a general verdict will fail to reveal the basis for the jury's judgment if it has considered both defenses.[46] While the expansion of general justification purchases some increase in clarity without undue complexity, and thus is to be preferred to the practice of relegating all threat claims exclusively to the duress defense, having a single unified defense of duress that reaches justifications and excuses hardly constitutes a breach of any fundamental principle of what a criminal code should look like.[47]

C. *Overarching Principles of Justification and Excuse in a Criminal Code*

Instead of introducing sharp distinctions between justification and excuse in the definition of specific defenses, a jurisdiction might adopt general and abstract definitions of justification and excuse that would cut across specific defenses that themselves did not sharply distinguish the two general grounds of defense. Such abstract definitions might be developed by judges, but it is hard to imagine isolated cases in which judges would need to develop a full blown theory of justification and excuse. Moreover, incremental development that would also be consistent and systematic does not seem likely, especially in the present climate of relative undevelopment of theories of justification and excuse. Thus, I shall address the possibility of abstract definitions in the context of a criminal code.

Definitions designed to capture common understandings about justification and excuse would be too vague to resolve troublesome borderline cases. On the other hand, definitions precise enough to work clean distinctions between justified and excused actions would have to employ a sense of the terms that was partly creative. Since such definitions would provide no important guidance to juries resolving cases, the aim of such definitions would be to serve clarifying and educative functions.

Their possible value would depend on what exactly was "clarified" and what the basis of the clarification was. We have difficulty articulating our moral evaluation when action is based on a perfectly reasonable factual misperception, but sifting out the actual elements of the evaluation is rather simple. A legal categorization of such actions as justified or excused would not alter the evaluation or increase our understanding of it. The character

45. See Model Penal Code §§ 2.09(1), 2.09(4), 3.02(1) (Proposed Official Draft 1962).

46. In some jurisdictions, e.g., N.Y. Penal Law § 35.05(2) (McKinney 1975), the judge must decide whether a claim of fact satisfies the defense of general justification. In trials in those jurisdictions, a judicial determination about the "balance of evils" may take that defense out of the case. But if the judge instructs that certain facts, if believed, would satisfy the defense, the jury verdict still might not reveal whether it found those facts or only some other facts that would amount to duress. For example, a defendant who aided a robbery testified that someone threatened to bomb a whole occupied building if he refused, but others testified that the only threat was that he would be badly beaten if he refused.

47. Cf. Robinson, supra note 1, at 240 ("[A] single defense should have a single classification.").

of other behavior, such as a failure to retreat safely, is subject to genuine dispute. For such behavior, a sharp classification by the law might achieve a resolution affecting to some degree how people would regard the behavior in the future, but the resolving definitions could not remain faithful to the complexity and diversity of a society's moral views.

There is a further problem with any legal "clarification." By selecting some crucial factors for examination, the law is bound to exclude others that will appear of moral relevance in some circumstances. Any definition of legal justification that is more specific than an open-ended reference to morally relevant factors is virtually certain to treat as justified some instances in which special factors would make the act only excused, at best, from a moral point of view (e.g., refusing to retreat when the aggressor is an angered spouse). The law's current lack of clarity itself may help foster the healthy notion that legal categorization does not determine moral appraisal.

If one conceives the criminal law as a proper and important medium for transmitting correct moral views to a confused public, despite certain inevitable variations between the optimal moral and optimal legal judgments, then departing from conventional understanding and existing moral consensus in defining justification and excuse will not be worrisome. One's opinions on how far the law should depart from conventional morality are likely to reflect a bundle of complex views about the role of law and the nature of moral understanding. Very roughly, we can put at one extreme the views that fundamental moral truth is discoverable by reason, that the proper dispositions of specific moral questions can be derived from abstract principles, and that the law should implement those dispositions. The other extreme set of views is that the law should reflect a community's present values and that moral understanding is not reducible to abstract principles but is eked out in not always comprehensible ways in the collective life of a culture.[48] Few people accept either extreme undiluted; but those who so adamantly argue that justifications and excuses must be sharply distinguished may be closer to the first view than those who are skeptical about that program. Drafters should have more room to implement enlightened moral perspectives when differentiating between justification and excuse for nonpunishable actions than when contemplating punishment for actions that many in the community believe are warranted. Nevertheless, I am dubious that the draftsman's sharp abstract categorization of justification and excuse is likely to improve on the present, more complicated understandings and to educate citizens in a constructive way.

While conceding that some value might derive from more strenuous efforts to distinguish warranted action from wrongful but excused action, I have argued that many, though not all, attempts to attain greater precision

48. This sentence fails to distinguish the relativist view that there is no such thing as moral truth that transcends particular cultures from the nonrelativist view that such a moral truth exists but cannot be grasped by reasoned analysis and abstract principles. For the particular purpose here, the distinction does not seem important.

in the law itself would be counterproductive in light of the overall aims of a system of criminal law. Though many of the comments made thus far also bear on distinctions between justification and excuse drawn along different lines, a closer examination of those distinctions is required for a judgment about their advisability. I turn now to that task.

II. Justifications as Objective and General; Excuses as Subjective and Individual

Justifications typically arise out of the nature of the actor's situation, excuses out of the actor's personal characteristics.[49] Though this basic distinction works when one compares claims like self-defense and mental irresponsibility, it hardly serves as a general explanation for the crucial differences between justification and excuse. Legal categories drawn exclusively on this basis would not correlate completely with what is regarded as the important moral difference between a justification and an excuse.

What does it mean to say that excuses are individual and justifications general?[50] Roughly, the idea is that an excuse does not reach others who perform similar acts, but a valid justification would apply to anyone else in similar conditions. Exactly what this contrast amounts to is somewhat cloudy. In the broad sense of "universalizability" common to discussions of moral philosophy, excuses as well as justifications are general: all persons with similar mental disturbances committing similar acts would have a similar excuse based on mental illness. The point must be that excuses, but not justifications, are based on personal characteristics or subjective attributes.[51] But, however the distinction is understood, its fit with the distinction between justification and excuse is less than perfect.

Some justifications depend upon the social role of the actor or his relation to a person affected by the act. Police and parents, for example, have special authorizations to use physical force when others may not.[52] Traditionally, relatives of potential victims had greater rights than strangers to intervene against aggressors,[53] though the movement now is to eliminate this distinction.[54] If "the situation" is defined broadly enough, it may include roles and relational characteristics; so perhaps their relevance to justi-

49. See G. Fletcher, supra note 3, at 761-62; Note, supra note 3, at 916, 960.

50. Insofar as the distinction refers to the rights of others to prevent or assist, it is discussed in the next section.

51. See Fletcher, Excusing Conditions, supra note 3.

52. E.g.,Model Penal Code, §§3.03, 3.07, 3.08 (Proposed Official Draft 1962).

53. Id. §3.05; W. LaFave & A. Scott, Jr., supra note 2, at 397 (1972).

54. Model Penal Code § 3.05(1) (Proposed Official Draft 1962). The relative's greater knowledge of background circumstances and of the character of one party to a struggle may still lead to his being justified in acting in a way that would not be proper for a stranger just coming upon the scene.

In other branches of law, including evidentiary privileges not to testify, see 2 J. Weinstein, Weinstein's Evidence §§ 505.01-.06 (1982) (husband-wife testimonial privilege), family relationships remain more directly critical.

fication is not at odds with the idea that justifications are general and objective.

One subjective characteristic of the actor is crucial, however, for justification in both ordinary usage and in the law: his belief in the presence of justifying circumstances.[55] If, unknown to Sue, David has begun to draw a gun to shoot her a split second before she shoots him, Sue's claim of self-defense is unavailing. Although the objective situation warranted her shooting in self-defense, Sue lacks that justification because she was unaware of the relevant facts when she shot.

A more complicated point involves judgments about justification that depend on the moral perspectives of the actor. A nonpacifist might say, "A person who believes that all killing is wrong is justified in not submitting to a draft." The nonpacifist regards refusal to submit as mistaken because he believes pacifism, from which refusal follows, is mistaken. Yet in another sense the nonpacifist thinks refusal is warranted because he believes people should act upon their firm convictions of what is morally right.[56] Claims based on peculiar moral views are not generally part of criminal law justifications,[57] but American law does recognize claims relating to exemption from military service under a special statutory privilege.[58] In addition, the Constitution has been interpreted to confer similar privileges in certain circumstances, such as exempting from forced jury duty those who have a conscientious objection to such service.[59] Though the law does not label these privileges either justifications or excuses, justification comes closer in my view.

Some excuses include features that are not individual and subjective. A person may be blamed morally for giving way to threats if the vast majority of people would have had the strength to resist. In most jurisdictions the duress defense has an objective component, formulated in the Model Penal

---

55. E.g., Model Penal Code § 3.04(1) (Proposed Official Draft 1962); G. Fletcher, supra note 3, at 768; Note, supra note 3, at 917-18. Though this is the prevailing view, there are dissenters. See 2 P. Robinson, supra note 30, § 122. One who rejects the relevance of the actor's state of mind can plausibly maintain that justifications are exclusively objective. My rejection of this position is based on the sense that justification in law should correlate more closely with moral appraisal.

56. The outsider judging the actor is likely to take this position only if the actor's moral views fall within a certain range of acceptability. He will not say, "A Nazi is justified in trying to kill Jews."

57. However, whether a parental use of force is justified might in some circumstances turn on the parent's moral views. A parent who thought physical punishment helpful for the development of a child might have a justification that would be absent for a parent in objectively identical circumstances who believed that striking his child served no constructive purpose but struck him anyway out of irritation.

58. See 50 U.S.C. app. § 456(j) (1976). Previously this privilege applied mainly to people otherwise subject to the draft. Now, it governs applications by people presently serving in the military to be released from their commitment. See 32 C.F.R. §§ 75.1-.11 (1984).

59. See In re Jenison, 267 Minn. 136, 125 N.W.2d 588 (1963) (decided after the Supreme Court, 375 U.S. 14, vacated and remanded the Minnesota Supreme Court's initial decision).

Code as whether a "person of reasonable firmness" would have yielded.[60] Since one kind of situation in which this objective component matters is when a person is so overwhelmed that he makes a choice that would be indefensible for a cool and rational actor, the objective element obviously applies to duress as an excuse as well as to duress as a justification.

Although some excuses may now have an objective component, perhaps they are misconceived, because excuses *should* be exclusively individual and subjective. Such an argument might be mounted, but if it rested on wooden application of abstract bases of categorization, it would lack persuasiveness; and closer scrutiny reveals that whether duress should have an objective component is not intuitively obvious.

Whether a wholly subjective test for blame is practically comprehensible when a person has yielded to fear and committed an undesirable act is subject to some doubt.[61] Suppose that Fred has given in to a threat that is not great enough to make most people do what he did. If Fred has yielded because he cares less about doing the harm than most people, then he is blameworthy; if the threat has greater power over him, perhaps he is not; but can these two questions be separated? Unless Fred has some peculiarity,[62] does it make sense to speak of the strength of the threat as to him apart from his relative desire to avoid the harmful act? And assuming that the two inquiries can be separated, is it clear that moral blame is inappropriate if an actor is abnormally susceptible to threats? That susceptibility may reflect some moral failure; in any event, blaming Fred may help him and others become more resistant to threats.[63]

Even if one opts to resolve these troubling questions by sticking to a

60. Model Penal Code § 2.09(1) (Proposed Official Draft 1962). Similar in this respect is the principle of mitigation (which might be viewed as a partial excuse or as a complete excuse from murder per se) that reduces intentional homicide from murder to manslaughter when the actor has suffered a provocation that most people would find extremely upsetting.

61. I use the word "practically" because for me the doubts concern standards of *human* judgment. The idea that divine judgment might be wholly individual is one that seems clearly comprehensible, and, if that is comprehensible, the possibility that human judgment could be similar is also comprehensible on some theoretical level. The issue from my perspective is whether this possibility is practically significant given human limitations.

62. Such a distinction plainly does make sense if some traumatic childhood experience or phobia makes a particular threat much more disturbing to Fred than it would be to other people.

63. Professor Fletcher makes the interesting point that when a duress claim is denied, a court may actually find the claim of duress in the next similar case more appealing, because the actor is aware that he will not escape legal penalties. See Fletcher, Excusing Conditions, supra note 3, at 1304. A similar point applies in respect to some claims of justification, the actor's assumption that he would not escape liability helping to demonstrate the urgency of the situation and the necessity of the steps he took.

Both points rest, of course, on an assumption that subsequent actors are aware of how cases have been decided, an assumption that is more plausible in some contexts than others. If one danger of duress and justification defenses is that awareness of their availability will encourage others not to perform legal duties when they should, there may be reason, as Meir Dan-Cohen has suggested, not to inform the public very precisely about the scope of exemptions from liability and to curtail defenses when the affected population, for example, prison-

wholly subjective standard for moral blame, the law's use of objective elements in excuses cannot be declared wrong in principle. The law must concern itself with judgments that strangers (members of a jury) are capable of making. Absent strong evidence that a particular actor is highly idiosyncratic, a jury must be largely guided by intuitive judgments about the resistability of threats, inferring a great deal about the actor's reactions from the normal reactions of most people. Those who develop the legal standard might reasonably conclude that instructing the jury to apply a completely subjective standard would make the jury's task too difficult, introduce too much uncertainty in application, provide some incentive for fraudulent efforts to establish that actors have inordinate susceptibility to threat or insult, and reduce the constraints on people who are strongly tempted to yield to powerful emotions. Whether such reasons for having objective elements are convincing may be debatable; but an abstract premise that excuses are individual and subjective would certainly not be adequate to dispose of them.

The discussion in this section has shown that although the distinction between justification and excuse may correlate substantially with the distinction between bases for relief from liability that are general and objective and bases that are individual and subjective, the latter distinction is not, and cannot reasonably be made, the central method for dividing justifications from excuses.

III. Distinguishing Justification and Excuse by Appropriateness of Defense, Intervention, and Support

A final possibility is that the crucial line between justification and excuse concerns the rights of others.[64] The idea is that a justified act may be supported but not stopped, whereas an excused act may be stopped, by its victim or an intervenor, but not supported.

What may be said on behalf of this line? First, as I have suggested earlier, if one began with some very rough categorization between justifications and excuses, the claimed consequences in terms of the rights of others would correlate pretty well with the respective designations. Second, this distinction is sharper and practically more significant than the distinction between warranted and unwarranted action. It is practically more significant because actual legal consequences would turn on the characterization of the defense as a justification or excuse; these legal consequences would not directly concern the law's treatment of the actor who offers the defense, but they would make a difference for the actual or possible actions of others. The distinction is sharp-edged because it admits of no gray area of uncer-

ers thinking about escape, is likely to learn of their scope. See Dan-Cohen, supra note 14, at 637-48.

64. This apparently is the distinction that George Fletcher would make the operative one. G. Fletcher, supra note 3, at 760-61, 830, 859; Fletcher, Prison Conditions, supra note 3, at 1357-58; see also Robinson, supra note 1, at 274-75 (lawful resistance or interference should be allowed for excused aggression, but never for justified aggression).

tainty of the sort that would exist between warranted and wrongful action; either others have a right to prevent an act or they do not. Third, the distinction appears to fit well with the idea that real justifications depend on accurate assessment of the facts; persons who know that their rights are being impaired because of the mistaken perceptions of others are generally allowed to defend those rights.

Despite these reasons in favor of a distinction drawn in terms of the rights of others, an effort to reform the law in this direction would be misguided, both because the distinction deviates from what is most fundamental about judgments of justification and excuse, and because it unravels. Rights of defense, intervention and support do not always correlate with each other or with the actual facts in the manner supposed. How the law should handle the intervention of others is too complicated a matter to be determined by initial characterization of a defense as a justification or excuse, and were that labeling to await careful judgment about intervention, legislatures or courts would be pushed to resolve immensely troublesome hypothetical issues that might never arise.

A. *The Rights of Others And the Basic Moral Distinction*

I have suggested that the central distinction between justification and excuse involves the difference between warranted actions and unwarranted actions for which the actor is not to blame, and concerns the moral appraisals these sorts of actions call forth. The rights of others is an inadequate substitute for this distinction. A well-known New York case illustrates the appeal of a distinction based on the difference between warranted and wrongful action and provides a useful context in which to contrast it with a "rights of others" approach.

> Young came upon two middle-aged men beating and struggling with a youth. Reasonably believing the youth was being unlawfully assaulted, Young went to his rescue, pulling on or punching at the seeming assailants. They turned out to be plain clothes detectives trying to make an arrest for disorderly conduct. One of them suffered a broken leg in the struggle.

Young's conviction for criminal assault was upheld by New York's highest court;[65] but the present New York statute privileges such behavior.[66] Actions like Young's should not be the subject of criminal liability, but the question here is whether they should be labelled justified or excused. Young is to be praised, not blamed, for what he did, and members of society would wish that others faced with similar situations requiring instant judgment would act as Young did.[67] A moral assessment of Young's

65. People v. Young, 11 N.Y.2d 274, 183 N.E.2d 319, 229 N.Y.S.2d 1 (1962), rev'g, 12 A.D.2d 262, 210 N.Y.S.2d 358 (1961). *Young* is commented upon in Recent Developments—Intervener Held Liable for Assault Despite Reasonable Belief That His Conduct Protected Another From Unlawful Harm, 63 Colum. L. Rev. 160 (1963).

66. N.Y. Penal Law § 35.15 (McKinney 1975).

67. There is an argument that Young should have been more careful in figuring out

act would treat it as justified. Yet the detectives were undoubtedly warranted in trying to fend off Young's intervention. They acted lawfully, even prior to identifying themselves, in resisting his acts.[68] If justification precludes a right of defense, then Young was only excused, not justified. This example shows how exclusive focus on the rights of others would blunt the clarity of the basic moral difference between justification and excuse.

Temporary escapes from jail to avoid serious harm at the hands of fellow prisoners illustrate the same point. The relevant law in the United States is somewhat unsettled, but let us suppose that the rule is that escaping confinement is privileged if one has a well-grounded fear of serious injury and if one intends to surrender at the earliest opportunity.[69] Does a prisoner who escapes under these circumstances have a justification or only an excuse? If the threat to the prisoner is great enough, say immediate loss of life, his choice to escape may be the best possible under the circumstances, yet the guards are not acting unlawfully in trying to stop him. By a right of intervention standard, the prisoner does not have a justification but only an excuse; and that indeed is the conclusion that George Fletcher has urged strongly for these situations.[70]

May guards always intervene when prisoners attempt to escape confinement? Presumably not. If a jail catches fire and guards are aware of that fact and orderly exit is no longer possible, we should expect guards not to use force to prevent prisoners from running out of the building. What distinguishes this situation from the escape to avoid a threat is that the relevant external facts and the prisoner's likely intent not to escape permanently are much more capable of appraisal by prison guards. The sensible rules about what prison guards should be allowed to do and told to do rest heavily on an assessment of such considerations; but these are remote from

---

what was going on before he got involved. Further, in some societies, discouraging intervention by strangers who know they are not fully acquainted with all possibly relevant facts might be defensible, even to the extent of making them strictly liable for mistakes. Cf. Dan-Cohen, supra note 14, at 643–45 (analyzing "the vagaries of the 'act at your own peril' rule"). The sentence in the text rests on the implicit undefended assumptions that New York City does not constitute such a society, and that Young had no opportunity to be more careful *and* save the apparent victim.

68. They could resist even if they realized that Young's intervention was justified, given the facts as he reasonably understood them. Though this conclusion seems obvious, deriving it from controlling statutes may not always be simple. See, e.g., Model Penal Code § 3.11(1) (Proposed Official Draft 1962) (definition of unlawful force to which one can respond), discussed and criticized in G. Fletcher, supra note 3, at 763–66; Robinson, supra note 1, at 276–77.

69. See United States v. Bailey, 444 U.S. 394 (1980). As Justice Blackmun points out in dissent, a requirement that the escapee turn himself in even if he reasonably believes that he will continue to be subject to the same danger does not fit very well with the rationale of the defense. Id. at 426–27 (Blackmun, J., dissenting). No doubt one reason why courts are hesitant to be generous here is because of worries about the effects on other prisoners who learn that escape can sometimes be privileged. See Dan-Cohen, supra note 14, at 641–42; Greenawalt, Conflicts of Law and Morality—Institutions of Amelioration, 67 Va. L. Rev. 177, 196–97 (1981).

70. Fletcher, Prison Conditions, supra note 3, at 1359.

appraisal of the prisoner's actions in light of the facts available to him. To be guided exclusively by appropriate guard response and to label the prisoner escaping fire as justified and the the prisoner escaping threatened assault as only excused would be odd.

B. *The Absence of a Comprehensive Sharp-Edged Distinction*

Another reason why attempts to develop systematic distinctions between justification and excuse in terms of the rights of others are misguided is because no single sharp-edged distinction is capable of both capturing the rights of others and conforming with the facts as they actually exist rather than with how they are reasonably perceived.

Part of the force behind a search for such a distinction lies in the claimed anomaly of saying, as does the prevailing American approach, that both the prisoner's attempted escape and the guard's intervention may be justified. George Fletcher offers as an alternative what he calls the incompatibility thesis "that it is logically impossible for both sides in a conflict to be justified."[71] Support for this thesis is found in the oddity of speaking of both sides as justified. Such oddity as there is derives in large part from the general difficulty of talking about justification or excuse when action rests on a well-founded but mistaken view of the facts. I have already suggested, with the forest fire example,[72] that natural language is rich enough for people to differentiate between the justification of an actor's behavior and whether the consequences of that behavior turn out to be justified; and natural language can perform the same function with cases like Young's and prison escapes.

One argument against the view that behavior based on a mistake about facts can be justified is that when things turn out badly for innocent individuals, actors will feel remorse. The presence of this guilt-related emotion is taken as a sign that one can only be offering an excuse, rather than a justification.[73] This argument underestimates the complexity of our moral practices. We learn to feel guilt over causing certain kinds of consequences, and we cannot turn off these feelings on the unusual occasions when our actions causing the consequences are warranted. Moreover, the social life of the community may benefit in the long run from the presence of those feelings since they lead people to consider very carefully acts likely to produce the consequences. Feelings of remorse are quite compatible with claims that an action is justified.[74]

Interestingly, when people are in the regular business of making impor-

71. Fletcher, Right & Reasonable, supra note 3, at pt. III; see G. Fletcher, supra note 3, at 767; Fletcher, Prison Conditions, supra note 3, at 1360.

72. See supra text accompanying notes 30–34.

73. Fletcher, Prison Conditions, supra note 3, at 1363.

74. Indeed, even a sense of duty to apologize may be compatible with such claims. If I break an important promise in order to save a life, I may have a social duty to offer some kind of apology to the harmed promisee, but my failure to fulfill the promise was my moral duty and therefore justifiable.

tant judgments on incomplete facts, as are doctors, generals, and police officers, we do not expect, or wish, them to feel remorse every time things turn out badly. Continual remorse would cripple their effectiveness in a way that simple regret at the turn of events does not.

In supposing that justifications are present only if acts would be warranted upon the actual facts and only if no conflicting justification exists, Professor Fletcher links talk about justification with talk about whether a person has a right to perform the act he does.[75] My own sense of the English language is that saying "*A* had a right" connotes somewhat more strongly the absence of conflicting right and consonance with a true view of the facts than does "*A*'s act was justified." Careful focus on rights, however, reveals that rights are not always consonant with the true facts.

Fletcher has used "putative" self-defense as an illustration of the view said to be embodied in continental law that a use of force engendered by a mistaken view of the facts cannot be justified, only excused.[76] Although he concentrates on self-defense, I understand his claim to have much broader applicability; yet its extension to some other circumstances shows its weakness and reveals that its plausibility for self-defense has something to do with the peculiar character of that use of force.

I shall approach the problem somewhat obliquely but in a manner whose relevance will soon be evident.

> Powerful evidence exists that Megan committed a murder. The prosecutor presents the evidence to a judge, who determines that probable cause exists of her guilt and issues a warrant for her arrest. A police officer executes the warrant. Were all the true facts known, Megan's innocence would also be known, but those facts are unavailable to the relevant governmental actors when the officer proceeds to arrest her.

Under American law, the officer, exercising a valid warrant, has a *right* to arrest Megan, using force or a threat of force that would otherwise be criminal. Megan has no right to resist although *she knows* she is the victim of mistaken identification and is wholly innocent. The same conclusion applies if the officer arrives on the scene of a just-committed murder and arrests Megan upon reasonable grounds for thinking she committed the crime.[77] Thus even when the police officer proceeds without an authorizing legal document and makes an on-the-spot factual judgment that proves to

75. Fletcher, Right & Reasonable, supra note 3, at pt. III; Fletcher, Prison Conditions, supra note 3, at 1358.

76. Fletcher, Right & Reasonable, supra note 3, at pt. III; accord G. Fletcher, supra note 3, at 762-68. The Freiburg Conference revealed that German scholars themselves disagreed about the status of acts based on faultless mistakes of fact.

77. What is a topic of dispute is whether Megan is privileged to resist if she is the victim of an illegal arrest, that is, one not based on probable cause. Most jurisdictions adopt the position (mistaken in my view) that she cannot resist even then. Such a case is, in a way of speaking, the counterside of those in which both sides are justified. In this case, the police officer's arrest of Megan is not warranted and may be the basis of a tort action or even criminal penalties, but any resistance to the arrest is made criminal.

be wrong, the officer has a right to act as he does and the "innocent" object of those acts has no right to resist. Barring some complex and blatant distortion of common usage, one must conclude that existing law, sensible law, does give *rights* to use force that are not congruent with what would exist under the true facts completely understood.

Some readers may be tempted to dispose of this example by saying that it is not relevant because the law's standard here is *probable cause*, and that probable cause exists. That would be to miss the point. The point is that the standard reflects a view that the overall aims of the law are served by making rights to use physical force turn on a reasonable official view of probable facts given the limited facts currently available. There is no *logical* reason why the law could not similarly deal with putative self-defense, giving rights to those who correctly conclude that they have probable cause to think they are being attacked and denying any right to resist to the seeming attackers. That such a rule would be foolish I do not doubt, because ordinary people are not educated to exercise refined judgment, because seeming attackers will not usually instantly understand why others think they are attacking, and most emphatically, because submission to putative self-defense is likely to result in much more permanent damage than submission to arrest by someone who is plainly a police officer. But saying that a possible rule would be foolish is quite different from saying that it would offend some logic about rights.

Another way of avoiding the force of the arrest example would be to claim that it concerns official functions, and that when persons perform official functions, such as beginning procedures to determine guilt, they are justified in acting on a reasonable appraisal of the facts. But would not a uniformed policeman who intervened to stop a fight also be performing an official function? And might not private citizens trying to stop assaults and make private arrests also be performing a kind of public responsibility spread among citizens? These inquiries show that no neat conceptual distinction exists between the policeman's arrest and Young's intervention, to stop a perceived assault. If the law provides that the policeman's force may not be resisted but Young's may, the difference lies not in logic but in sound policy judgment.

The law may include some other instances in which persons must yield to adversaries with a mistaken view of the facts, although they would have a right of self-defense against similar adversaries who understood the facts completely. Under the Model Penal Code's attempt to work out sensible accommodations in much more detail than most statutory formulations, a person who knows he has a right to possess property may not use force to resist force used by a present possessor of the property if he also knows that the present possessor acts under a claim of right.[78] The rights to use force to

78. See Model Penal Code § 3.04(2)(a)(ii) (Proposed Official Draft 1962). This is so even though the present possessor's claim of right might be based on an erroneous view of the facts. The present possessor's force may be resisted if it is not backed by a claim of right.

retake property and to defend against a retaking are also sometimes dependent on one's belief whether an adversary has a claim of right.[79]

Even when the mistake concerns whether one person is a threat to another, we can think of at least one fantastic self-defense case not involving officials in which the apparent aggressor almost certainly may not use deadly force against someone mistakenly acting in self-defense.[80] Imagine that David, wishing to die as an apparent victim, has cleverly set things up so that Vicki will think David is trying to shoot her and will shoot him in return. As Vicki begins to draw her weapon, David suddenly decides he would like to live. Since he has intentionally created Vicki's misperception, he should not now be able to use deadly force to defend himself from a threat produced by that misperception. In this instance, at least, a right to use defensive force does not stem from David's knowledge of the true facts.

What could a stranger aware of all the true facts permissibly do in this situation? Unless David does try to defend himself, the stranger may not aid Vicki by shooting David, since he knows that David does not pose an actual threat; yet the stranger may not save David by shooting Vicki, since he knows that David has intentionally caused Vicki's misperception and that if one life is to be lost it should be David's. If classification of Vicki's act turned on the right of a fully informed "victim" to resist, the act would be justified, though not justified by the true facts. If the classification of Vicki's act turned on the right of an informed stranger to assist her, she would only be excused.

Another bizarre case demonstrates that even when a person has a justification based on all the relevant facts, a stranger's intervention to stop his justified act may be proper. John attacks Mike with a knife; Mike justifiably draws his own knife, and each raises his arm to strike. Both are very weak. Arnold, who is extremely strong, is capable of grabbing John and Mike by their wrists and forcing each to drop his knife. Certainly that action, which will adequately protect Mike's interests,[81] is morally preferable to stopping John's attack and permitting Mike's response to continue; and any decent legal system would privilege Arnold's use of moderate force against Mike.[82]

How might a defender of the view that justification always correlates with a right against interference respond to this example? He might claim that at the moment Arnold starts to intervene, Mike's act ceases to be justifiable, because he no longer has to hurt John to defend his interests. Transforming a movement of the arm that begins as a justified striking with a knife into an excusable striking when unexpected intervention occurs seems artificial. In any event, characterization as excuse does not alter the conclu-

79. See id. § 3.06(1)(b)(ii); id. § 3.06(3)(c).

80. See New York Penal Law § 35.15 (McKinney 1975), which apparently provides for this outcome, although the statutory language indicates that this situation was not envisaged.

81. John will be subject to tort and criminal liability for his initial assault.

82. I put the point this way because deriving that answer from the language of existing statutory schemes will not always be simple.

sion that an act undertaken justifiably may be stopped. Could it be argued that Mike's act was only excusable from the start, because if he had known that Arnold would intervene, no use of his knife would have been justified?[83] This argument is flawed at the outset by the faulty premise that justification must always be congruent with what one could do given all the true facts. Even were that premise accepted, the argument would not meet every contingency. For instance, Arnold might be a friend of John's who would not intervene if he thought John was in no danger.[84] In that event, Mike's response is actually necessary to stimulate Arnold's intervention.

C. *Excuses and the Rights of Others*

I now turn briefly to excuses to broaden the argument that the rights of others do not correlate perfectly with the distinction between justification and excuse. Although the law is not very clear on most relevant situations, it very well might in some circumstances condition a right to resist on the absence of a known excuse. If I would otherwise be killed, I may use deadly force against an aggressor who is insane or subject to duress; but perhaps I should be required to retreat if I know I can do so safely and I also know that the "aggressor" is not responsible.[85] One possible position about this issue is that the aggressor's excuse simply cannot affect one's right to resist. If that position does not depend on administrative simplicity, it must rest either on unsupported conceptual dogmatism or on a rights centered moral theory that is certainty disputed and is in my view highly implausible.[86] The second position is that rights of resistance can be affected. The third, middle position, assents to the practical consequences of the second position while clinging to the conceptual baggage of the first. It asserts that one has a right to resist regardless of the aggressor's known excuse but that resistance would be "an abuse of right" and therefore wrongful, possibly giving rise to civil damages or criminal penalties. Whether or not the third view enjoys any inherent conceptual superiority over the second, both recognize that *properly exercisable rights* can be affected by excuses as well as by justifications.[87]

---

83. It would not be justified because it would involve greater force than that necessary to stop John.

84. If so, why when Arnold does intervene does he protect both John and Mike? Others watching the fight are aware that John is the aggressor and Arnold's intervention on his side will subject Arnold to criminal liability he is not willing to risk.

85. George Fletcher indicates that German law imposes a duty to retreat from aggressors who are insane, but not from aggressors who are responsible. G. Fletcher, supra note 3, at 865-66.

86. Most American jurisdictions do not require retreat from one's dwelling, even when the aggressor is a member of the same household. Does anyone think that a person has a moral right not to retreat when he knows he can do so safely and he also knows that the aggressor is a member of his family who is temporarily deranged? I briefly discuss the moral underpinnings of possible distinctions in rights of response to guilty and innocent aggressors in Greenawalt, Violence—Legal Justification and Moral Appraisal, 32 Emory L.J. 437, 449-56 (1983).

87. This problem is closely related to the issue of proportionate defense—whether one

D. *The Inadequacy of the Rights of Others As a Guide to Classification*

I have pointed out that justification and excuse would be unable to capture the kind of moral judgment that seems appropriate for the actor if they were identified by reference to the rights of others. For this reason alone, I would oppose the effort to transmute the ordinary significance of these terms in an effort to achieve legal clarity. I have also argued that the rights of others do not always depend on the true facts and may be combined in ways that a simple distinction between justification and excuse could not accommodate.

These complexities suggest further grave difficulties with any program to systemize justifications and excuses in terms of the rights of others. Suppose that drafters began such a program with a common sense classification of justifications and excuses and let exercisable rights of interference and support flow strictly from that, justifications always allowing support and barring defense and interference, excuses barring support and allowing defense and interference. The resulting law would then simply be insensitive to all the variations in circumstance that should be deemed relevant. Crude definition would be doing the work that should be done by open and careful examination of what the rights of others should be in different contexts. For some people, the fruit of such an examination might be the conclusion that correlations between interference and excuse and between noninterference and justification should be very high. Such persons might emphasize rights to be free of aggression, giving little importance to the responsibility of the aggressors. The point here is that the possible grounds for such a conclusion need to be explicated and defended on their own merits, not unthinkingly derived from a prior classification.

Alternatively, drafters could address questions of interference first and then let those answers determine whether a reason for exoneration will be considered a justification or an excuse. For example, if drafters decide that guards may permissibly try to prevent all threat-motivated escapes, such escapes could only be excused, not justified. It is highly doubtful whether attempts to carry out this program would actually produce greater clarity about the law.[88] Drafters would have to develop a terminology and conceptual apparatus to deal with mistaken perceptions of fact and with situations in which the possibilities regarding support and resistance do not correlate in the usual ways. In addition, actions that appear very similar from the actor's point of view might be labelled differently because of opportunities to acquire knowledge available to those who might resist. Thus, one instance of escape might be labelled justified, because guards could eas-

---

can employ very grave force if that is the only way to stop a small wrong, such as the theft of an apple. In that context, Professor Eser has written that "it is of minor significance" whether one talks of " 'abuse' . . . or simply (and more honestly) . . . [of] 'proportionate' defense." Eser, supra note 8, at 633.

88. If enough situations were worked through, there might be more clarity about results for the highly trained lawyer; certainly the complexity of delineations would reduce the educative clarity for ordinary citizens.

ily perceive its basis, while another was only excused because they could not.

The most serious flaw in this approach may be that it puts the cart before the horse. It would require the initial resolution of immensely complex problems about the rights of outsiders before drafters were in a position to lay down the most basic defenses to liability. For many scholars following the common law tradition, an attempt to resolve all of a set of variations—the great majority of which are based on events that may never take place—would be misconceived.

Conclusion

Neither the rights of others nor any difference between general and individual claims provides an adequate basis for distinguishing between justifications and excuses. Rather, the central distinction between justification and excuse is between warranted action and unwarranted action for which the actor is not to blame. Although the law's failure to be as precise as it might in reflecting this distinction is partially due to correctible inattention or indifference, much of the imprecision is a consequence of the troubling borderlines of the two concepts, of legal rules that compromise disagreements about substantive morality, and of canons of convenience that support placing similar factual situations under the same rubric in order to focus the jury's efforts on the questions crucial to liability and nonliability.

Achieving greater clarity between justification and excuse is a laudatory goal, deserving the serious attention of scholars. I want to reemphasize this point, because my lengthy discussion of borderline problems may tend to obscure both my conviction that the basic distinction between justification and excuse is very important for moral and legal thought, and my hope that this essay will contribute to understanding some of the complexities of that distinction. A fully comprehensive system *could* divide up all instances of justification and excuse, but it could do so only by distorting of ordinary concepts or by employing some complicated subcategories reflecting significant policy judgments.[89] A program to achieve that objective is not an appropriate one for Anglo-American penal law.

89. I have in mind such conclusions as that a police officer's arrest of a suspect on probable cause will be deemed warranted and not subject to resistance even if the person arrested is innocent and knows himself to be so. See supra note 77 and accompanying text.

[12]

Self-Defense

JUDITH JARVIS THOMSON

I

Before we take a close look at it, we may think of self-defense as morally transparent. What could be clearer than that morality permits a person to save his or her life against threats to it?

But what if in order to save one's life one has to kill another person? In some cases that is obviously permissible. In a case I will call Villainous Aggressor, you are standing in a meadow, innocently minding your own business, and a truck suddenly heads toward you. You try to sidestep the truck, but it turns as you turn. Now you can see the driver: he is a man you know has long hated you. What to do? You cannot outrun the truck. Fortunately, this is not pure nightmare: you just happen to have an antitank gun with you, and can blow up the truck. Of course, if you do this you will kill the driver, but that does not matter: it is morally permissible for you to blow up the truck, driver and all, in defense of your life.

It is probably not necessary to stress *here*—though the point is important for our purposes—that you do not merely have an excuse for blowing up the truck, you are morally permitted to do so. Suppose Peter killed Paul. For it to be the case that Peter merely has an excuse for killing Paul is for it to be the case that though he ought not have done so, and acted wrongly in doing so, still he is not as much at fault for doing so as he would have been had he not had the excuse, and, if his excuse is not merely mitigating but completely exculpating, then he is not at fault at all for doing so. But blowing up the truck in Villainous Aggressor is not something you ought not do. We cannot plausibly say that you ought not

An early version of this article was presented at the University of Arizona Philosophy Colloquium; I am grateful to those present for their comments. A number of people made helpful comments on a later draft: I am particularly grateful to Jonathan Bennett, Bruce Ackerman, and the Editors of *Philosophy & Public Affairs*.

blow up the truck, but will only be in a measure at fault, or in no measure at fault, for doing so: you simply *may* blow up the truck. Morality permits it.

But why may you blow up the truck? The following answer suggests itself: the driver is villainously aggressing against you, and will thereby kill you unless you stop him—and, moreover, you can stop him only by blowing up the truck. That second clause is important. Suppose you had two ways by which you could stop him. One, blow up the truck with your antitank gun, or two, wave your antitank gun and shout, "Stop, or I'll blow up the truck!" If you do not actually need to blow up the truck, if you really could stop him by merely threatening to blow up the truck, then that is what you ought to do. It would be wrong to kill even a villainous aggressor when you do not need to do so.

So the driver is villainously aggressing against you, and will thereby kill you unless you stop him, and you can stop him only by blowing up the truck. Why not say that *that* premise explains why you may proceed? I suggest that it is in at least one way stronger than it need have been.

II

For let us look at a second hypothetical case, which is like the first except in this respect: the driver is entirely without fault for what he is doing. How can that be, given that he is chasing you around the meadow in a truck, trying to run you down? Well, let's suppose some villain had just injected him with a drug that made him go temporarily crazy. It is not his fault that he is going to kill you if you do not blow up the truck, he is not villainously aggressing against you; but he is aggressing against you, and he will in fact kill you if you do not blow up the truck. Does morality permit you to blow up the truck? *I* think it does: I think self-defense permissible in this case—which I will call Innocent Aggressor—just as in the case I called Villainous Aggressor.[1]

1. Innocent Aggressor is modeled on George P. Fletcher's splendid hypothetical case in "Proportionality and the Psychotic Aggressor," *Israel Law Review* 8 (1973): 367–90: "Imagine that your companion in an elevator goes berserk and attacks you with a knife. . . ."

I will everywhere be using "innocent" to mean free of fault. But it might pay to take note here of another use of "innocent"—sometimes "technically innocent"—under which it means "not harming": see G.E.M. Anscombe, "Mr. Truman's Degree," reprinted in her

But I suspect that some people would say that while self-defense is permissible in Villainous Aggressor it is merely excusable in Innocent Aggressor. Should we agree with them? By hypothesis, the driver in Villainous Aggressor is villainously aggressing against you and the driver in Innocent Aggressor is not; but how exactly could that difference be thought to show that while it is permissible for you to proceed in Villainous Aggressor, it is merely excusable for you to proceed in Innocent Aggressor?

Perhaps it will be thought that the point is this: the villainous driver is less worthy (less good) than the fault-free driver. But the fault-free driver too might be a not particularly worthy person. His being fault-free in Innocent Aggressor consists only in his being free of fault for the particular aggression that he is currently committing.

Alternatively, perhaps it will be thought that the point is this: the villainous driver deserves punishment for his aggression, whereas the fault-free driver does not. But who are you, private person that you are, to be dishing out punishment to the villainous for the things that they do? And anyway, what makes it permissible for you to blow up the truck in Villainous Aggressor is not the fact that the driver in that case deserves punishment for what he is doing, or else it would be permissible for you to blow up the truck even if you do not need to do so to save your life.

Moreover, to say that self-defense is merely excusable in Innocent Aggressor is to say that although you would not be at fault for blowing up the truck in that case, you ought not blow it up, you act wrongly if you do. I think that cannot be right. (I think it an excessively high-minded conception of the requirements of morality.)

It might help also if I stress that I am not saying here that the fault of an aggressor is nowhere relevant to the question what you may do to defend yourself. I say here only that it is not relevant when what is in question is his life for yours. What if we lower the cost to you? I should think that fault is also irrelevant when the aggressor would otherwise blind you, or cut off your legs: the aggressor's fault or lack of fault has no bearing on whether you may kill the aggressor to defend your eyes or legs. (Death is worse than blindness or being without legs, but other

Collected Philosophical Papers (Oxford: Basil Blackwell, 1981), 3:7. The driver in Innocent Aggressor is not innocent in that sense of the term.

things being equal, morality does not require submission to such an aggressor, even if he is without fault.) I should think, more generally, that the same holds whenever the aggressor would otherwise cause you very grave bodily harm. Similarly if we go to the other extreme and imagine the prospective cost to you is minimal. If the aggressor would otherwise take your wallet or hat, then you may not kill the aggressor to defend yourself, whether or not the aggressor is at fault for his aggression. (That it is a villain who will otherwise take your wallet or hat is not sufficient reason to kill him to protect it.) There is room for argument, however, at places between these extremes of very grave bodily harm on the one hand, and loss of wallet or hat on the other hand. Suppose an aggressor will take, not both your legs, but only your left foot unless you kill him. Here the aggressor's fault or lack of fault may well be thought to make a difference: thus it may be thought that you may kill him to defend your left foot against his aggression if he is at fault but not if he is without fault. I leave this open. (I also leave open what should be said in cases in which it is not certain that the aggressor will cause you a harm if you do not kill him but only more or less probable that he will.) What *I* think is clear in any event is that if the aggressor will (certainly) take your life unless you kill him, then his being or not being at fault for his aggression is irrelevant to the question whether you may kill him.

But as I said, I suspect that some people would say that self-defense is merely excusable in Innocent Aggressor—or at least would feel uncomfortable about saying that it is permissible. I have a hypothesis as to what is at work in anyone of whom this is true, and will come back to it later.

Suppose, however, that we are in agreement that morality permits blowing up the truck in Innocent Aggressor as in Villainous Aggressor, so that you do not in either case merely have an excuse for proceeding. Then we are in agreement that the fault of the driver in Villainous Aggressor does no moral work in making it permissible for you to proceed in that case. But then the premise we looked at, by appeal to which it might be thought possible to explain why you may proceed in Villainous Aggressor, was stronger than it need have been. (I fancy we overrate the role of fault in many areas of moral theory; further examples will turn up shortly.)[2]

2. I think we also misinterpret the role played by fault. See, e.g., my "Morality and Bad Luck," *Metaphilosophy* 20 (1989): 203–21.

Then why may you blow up the truck in the two cases? Why not just say this: the drivers are aggressing against you—in the one case villainously, in the other case without fault—and will thereby kill you unless you stop them, and you can stop them only by blowing up the trucks, and *that* premise explains why you may proceed.

But isn't this premise, too, stronger than it need have been?

III

In a third hypothetical case—which I will call Innocent Threat—you are lying in the sun on your deck.[3] Up in the cliff-top park above your house, a fat man is sitting on a bench, eating a picnic lunch. A villain now pushes the fat man off the cliff down toward you. If you do nothing, the fat man will fall on you, and be safe. But he is *very* fat, so if he falls on you, he will squash you flat and thereby kill you. What alternative do you have? Well, you only have time to shift the position of your awning; if you do this, the fat man will be deflected away from you. But deflecting him away from you will be deflecting him past the edge of the deck down onto the road below. Does morality permit you to shift the awning? I think it does.

As I said in the preceding section, I suspect that some people would say that while self-defense is permissible in Villainous Aggressor it is merely excusable in Innocent Aggressor; I suspect that even more people would say that self-defense is merely excusable in Innocent Threat. Why so? The innocent aggressor, though without fault, is at least aggressing against you; the fat man is not only without fault, he is not doing anything at all—he is merely *falling* toward you.

I think that difference makes no moral difference, and thus that it is permissible for you to proceed in Innocent Threat just as in Villainous Aggressor and Innocent Aggressor. I have a hypothesis as to what is at work in those who think otherwise, and will come back to it later.

Suppose we are in agreement that morality permits proceeding in Innocent Threat just as in Villainous Aggressor and Innocent Aggressor, so that you do not in any of these cases merely have an excuse for proceeding. Then we are in agreement that the aggression of the drivers in

3. Similar cases have been discussed by others, but unless I am mistaken, the first to draw moral philosophers' attention to them was Robert Nozick, in *Anarchy, State, and Utopia* (New York: Basic Books, 1974), pp. 34–35.

Villainous Aggressor and Innocent Aggressor does no moral work in making it permissible for you to proceed in those cases. But then the premise we looked at, by appeal to which it might be thought possible to explain why you may proceed in those cases, was stronger than it need have been.

How to weaken it? The premise says: the drivers in Villainous Aggressor and Innocent Aggressor are aggressing against you and will thereby kill you unless you stop them, and you can stop them only by blowing up the trucks. It follows that the drivers in those two cases will kill you unless you kill them. Can we say of the fat man in Innocent Threat that he too will kill you if you do not kill him? If so, then it is plausible to think that what is at work in this third case is the same as what is at work in the first two: that is, it is plausible to think we can explain the permissibility of proceeding in all three cases by appeal to the fact that in all three, the man you kill if you proceed *will otherwise kill you.*

It might be replied, however, that this is not true of the fat man in Innocent Threat. I said earlier that if he falls on you, he will squash you flat and thereby kill you, but is it really right to say that if he falls on you he will *kill* you? It might be said that while an event consisting in his fall on you will kill you, *he* will not have killed you. After all, he will not have aggressed against you, he will merely have fallen on you.

If we are moved by that idea, then we will think that the premise should not be weakened in the way I just pointed to. Perhaps, then, we will have the following thought: even if it is not true of all three—the two drivers and the fat man—that they will otherwise kill you, they are anyway all threats to your life, threats to your life that you can defend against only by killing them. And perhaps we will think *that* is what the premise should be weakened to.

I think that we should not be moved by that idea. Is it really to be thought that Y kills X only if Y aggresses against X? Suppose a piano and a safe fell off a roof, and we know that one fell on Alfred, and that the event that consisted in its fall on him killed him. We might ask, "Which killed Alfred, the piano or the safe?" The correct answer might be, "The piano," despite the fact that pianos commit no acts of aggression. ("Which of these bullets killed Kennedy?" asks the museum curator of the bullets just donated to the museum by the police. "That one," say the police, pointing to one in particular. And they might be right.) Indeed, I should think that if an event that consists in the fall of Y on X kills X, then it follows that Y killed X, whatever Y may be.

Moreover, the suggested alternative weakening of the premise is not self-explanatory. What exactly is it for one thing to be a threat to the life of another? The two drivers will kill you if you do not kill them, and perhaps that clearly enough marks them as in some appropriate sense threats to your life. If we say it is not true of the fat man that he will kill you if you do not kill him, then what exactly does he have in common with the two drivers that is supposed to mark him too as in that same sense a threat to your life?

So I suggest we reject both the idea and the suggested alternative weakening of the premise; I suggest we say that, like the drivers in Villainous Aggressor and Innocent Aggressor, the fat man in Innocent Threat will kill you if you do not kill him. There is no need to be confused: we need merely remember about the fat man that, though he will kill you if you do not kill him, he will not have killed you by an act of aggression. If we agree to this, and I will assume we do, then we can say that in all three cases, the person you kill if you proceed *will otherwise kill you*.

And then if we are in agreement that morality permits proceeding in all three cases, why not say it is that premise that explains why?

Well, it will not do. I think we are helped to get at what is missing if we attend first to some cases in which the premise is false.

IV

The three cases we have been looking at are cases in which I think it permissible for you to kill a person in defense of your life; I will therefore call them Yes cases. It is perfectly plain, on any view, that there are No cases, cases in which it is impermissible for you to kill a person in defense of your life. Three classes are of particular interest.

In the first place there are Substitution-of-a-Bystander cases. In a case I will call Trolley, a villain has started a trolley down a track toward you. You cannot stop the trolley, but you can deflect it. Unfortunately, the only path onto which you can deflect it will take it onto a bystander who cannot get off the path in time. (I intend this allusion to the Trolley Problem, and will return to it briefly later.) I take it to be plain that you may not proceed. If you proceed, you will be making a bystander be a substitute victim; hence the name of the class.

A second class of cases might be called Use-of-a-Bystander cases. A villain has started a trolley down a track toward you, and the only way you have of defending yourself is to shoot a bystander who stands on a footpath over the track: he is sufficiently heavy to crush the trolley's rooftop mechanism when he falls onto it, which will thereby stop the trolley. In this case too it is plain that you may not proceed. To proceed would be to use a bystander as a piece of equipment; hence the name of the class.

The mark of a Use-of-a-Bystander case is that you need the bystander you would have to kill if you are to defend your life. In a Use-of-a-Bystander case, if the bystander goes miraculously out of existence just before you act, then there is no way at all in which you can defend yourself. That is not true in Substitution-of-a-Bystander cases such as Trolley. But there are cases that fall into both classes, as, for example, where you defend yourself against a villain's gunfire by grabbing a bystander and using him as a shield so that he is shot instead of you. That case is both a Substitution-of-a-Bystander case and a Use-of-a-Bystander case.

A third class of cases I will call (for want of a better name) Riding-Roughshod-over-a-Bystander cases. A villain is shooting at you, and your only defense is to run. But your only path to safety lies across a bridge that will hold only one person, and there is already a man on it; if you rush onto the bridge, he will be toppled off it into the valley below. In this case too it is plain that you may not proceed. If you proceed, you do not make a bystander be a substitute victim, so it is not a Substitution-of-a-Bystander case. If you proceed, you do not use a bystander as a piece of equipment, so it is not a Use-of-a-Bystander case. What you do if you proceed is to "ride roughshod" over a bystander; hence the name of the class.

Proceeding in some of these cases is worse than proceeding in others. Here is another Use-of-a-Bystander case, which I will call Starvation. Some villains throw you in a dungeon, and leave you there, without food, for several weeks. Not surprisingly, you are by now very hungry. To tempt you, and thereby increase your misery, the villains now introduce a plump baby into the dungeon. They remove the baby for feeding periodically, so that *it* is at no risk of starvation. But you are. May you eat the baby? Of course not. It would presumably be far worse to eat the baby in

Starvation, which is a Use-of-a-Bystander case, than it would be to turn the trolley in Trolley, which is a Substitution-of-a-Bystander case. If, in the press of fear, you turned the trolley in Trolley, then we might think this, though wrongful, nevertheless more or less excusable. If, in the press of pain and fear, you ate the baby in Starvation, that would be both wrongful and in no measure excusable.[4] But proceeding in Use-of-a-Bystander cases is not everywhere worse than proceeding in Substitution-of-a-Bystander cases and Riding-Roughshod-over-a-Bystander cases. Suppose you are a subway track workman. A subway is headed toward you. (1) There is a small alcove in the wall near you, but there is another workman already in it. You can pull him out into the path of the subway and get into the alcove yourself. This is a Substitution-of-a-Bystander case. (2) There is a small alcove in the wall near you, but there is another workman already in it. You can force your way into the alcove, thereby crushing him to death. This is a Riding-Roughshod-over-a-Bystander case. (3) There is no alcove, but there is another workman with you on the track. You can shove him into the path of the subway, which will stop it. This is a Use-of-a-Bystander case. I do not think that there is any difference in the degree of moral badness of your proceeding according as we supply ending (1), (2), or (3) to the story that begins with a subway headed toward you.

Why, after all, should it have been thought that the fact that you *need* the person you would have to kill in order to defend yourself makes it worse for you to proceed than it would have been had you not needed the person? If I am right in thinking that is the mark of a Use-of-a-Bystander case, then *using* a person does not in general have the special moral taint that has been ascribed to it. Appeals to the notion "respect for persons" will certainly not suffice to make out this special moral taint. After all, if one proceeds in a Substitution-of-a-Bystander case (a Substitution-of-a-Bystander case that is not also a Use-of-a-Bystander case) or in a Riding-Roughshod-over-a-Bystander case, one behaves as if the person one kills were not there at all—surely no less a display of lack of respect for persons.[5]

4. Or so I think. Some people think it was in a measure excusable (though of course wrongful) for the sailors to eat the cabin boy in Regina v. Dudley & Stephens 14 Q.B. 273 (1884). Perhaps what is at work in those people is the thought that it was likely that all, including the cabin boy, would otherwise die. Even so. . . .

5. I am indebted to Jonathan Bennett here.

Let us go back. Cases of these three kinds are No cases. And in all of them our premise is false: it is not true in any of them that the person you have to kill to save your life *will otherwise kill you*. Indeed, that person is, as I have everywhere put it, a bystander.

V

Is it everywhere impermissible to kill a bystander in defense of one's life? Consider a case that is often discussed in the literature on the Doctrine of Double Effect. In Strategic Bomber, the villainous Bads have invaded noble country Good, and a Good pilot has been ordered to bomb a munitions factory in Bad. Unfortunately, the factory is so situated that if the pilot bombs the factory, some nearby Bad civilians will be killed—let us imagine them to be children, in a nearby children's hospital. Doesn't morality permit the pilot to proceed all the same? But the children are mere bystanders.

In the literature on the Doctrine of Double Effect, Strategic Bomber is often contrasted with Terror Bomber, in which the Good pilot is ordered to bomb, not a Bad munitions factory, but a Bad children's hospital—the point of having him do this is to terrorize the Bad population and thereby get them to sue for peace with the Goods. Friends of the doctrine say it is clear that while the pilot may proceed in Strategic Bomber, he may not proceed in Terror Bomber, and they claim that the Doctrine of Double Effect explains this moral difference between the cases.

Very roughly, the Doctrine of Double Effect says that we may do what will cause a bad outcome in order to cause a good outcome if and only if (1) the good is in appropriate proportion to the bad *and* (2) we do not intend the bad outcome as our means to the good outcome. Thus, for example, the doctrine yields that the Good pilot in Strategic Bomber may bomb the Bad munitions factory in order to cause the Goods to win the war (good outcome), despite the fact that he will thereby cause the deaths of some children (bad outcome), if while he foresees that he will cause the deaths of the children, their deaths are not intended by him as a means to causing the Goods to win the war. By contrast, the doctrine yields that the Good pilot in Terror Bomber may not bomb Bad children in order to cause the Goods to win the war (good outcome) if *he* would be causing the children's deaths (bad outcome) as a means to causing terror and thereby causing the Goods to win the war. Many people take it to be an attractive feature of this doctrine that it supplies an explanation of the moral difference between the cases.

Much of the literature on the Doctrine of Double Effect consists, on the one hand, in efforts to make it precise in a way that does not make it yield morally implausible results in other pairs of cases to which it is applied, and on the other hand, in efforts to explain why the distinction to which it draws our attention—that between foreseen and intended effects—is morally relevant.[6]

It is a very odd idea, however, that a person's intentions play a role in fixing what he may or may not do. What I have in mind comes out as follows. Suppose a pilot comes to us with a request for advice: "See, we're at war with a villainous country called Bad, and my superiors have ordered me to drop some bombs at Placetown in Bad. Now there's a munitions factory at Placetown, but there's a children's hospital there too. Is it permissible for me to drop the bombs?" And suppose we make the following reply: "Well, it all depends on what your intentions would be in dropping the bombs. If you would be intending to destroy the munitions factory and thereby win the war, merely foreseeing, though not intending, the deaths of the children, then yes, you may drop the bombs. On the other hand, if you would be intending to destroy the children and thereby terrorize the Bads and thereby win the war, merely foreseeing, though not intending, the destruction of the munitions factory, then no, you may not drop the bombs." What a queer performance this would be! Can anyone really think that the pilot should decide whether he may drop the bombs by looking inward for the intention with which he would be dropping them if he dropped them?[7]

Here is Alfred, whose wife is dying, and whose death he wishes to hasten. He buys a certain stuff, thinking it a poison and intending to give it to his wife to hasten her death. Unbeknownst to him, that stuff is the only existing cure for what ails his wife. Is it permissible for Alfred to give it to her? Surely yes. We cannot plausibly think that the fact that if he gives it to her he will give it to her to kill her means that he may not

6. A recent example is Warren S. Quinn, "Actions, Intentions, and Consequences: The Doctrine of Double Effect," *Philosophy & Public Affairs* 18, no. 4 (Fall 1989): 334–51.

7. Jonathan Bennett's criticism of the Doctrine of Double Effect in *Morality and Consequences*, The Tanner Lectures on Human Values III (Salt Lake City: University of Utah Press, 1981) focuses on its friends' use of the notion 'intention', but he also points on pp. 96–98 to the oddity I point to here, as well as to the ideas that issue in two theses I will shortly propose for adoption.

give it to her. (How could *his* having a bad intention make it impermissible for him to do what *she* needs for life?)

The badness of Alfred's intention may incline some people to want to say that while it is permissible for Alfred to give-his-wife-the-stuff, it is impermissible for Alfred to give-his-wife-the-stuff-to-kill-her. (And compare: while it is permissible for the pilot to drop-the-bombs, it is impermissible for the pilot to drop-the-bombs-to-cause-terror.) It would of course be odd to say to Alfred, "You may give your wife the stuff, but you may not give it to her to kill her"; but that it would be odd to say a thing is compatible with the thing's being true. A puzzle lurks here, however. Some people believe that the conjunction of "If X were to do alpha then X would in fact do beta" and "X may not do beta" entails "X may not do alpha." Now by hypothesis, if Alfred were to give-his-wife-the-stuff, he would in fact give-his-wife-the-stuff-to-kill-her. So on that view, if we say that Alfred may not give-his-wife-the-stuff-to-kill-her, we are committed to saying that Alfred may not give-his-wife-the-stuff. I think that view is mistaken, but I take no stand on it here.[8] I here suggest only that *if* we accept it, then we must also accept that Alfred may give-his-wife-the-stuff-to-kill-her. For whatever else we say, we must accept that Alfred may give-his-wife-the-stuff. After all, she needs it for life.

I suggest, quite generally, that we should accept

> *The Irrelevance-of-Intention-to-Permissibility Thesis*: It is irrelevant to the question whether X may do alpha what intention X would do alpha with if he or she did it.

Thus in particular, it is irrelevant to the question whether Alfred may give-his-wife-the-stuff what intention he will do it with if he does it. (Indeed, it is also irrelevant to the question whether Alfred may give-his-wife-the-stuff-to-kill-her what intention he will do *that* with if he does it—thus, for example, whether he will give-his-wife-the-stuff-to-kill-her to inherit her estate or to get her early entry into heaven or what you will.)

There is a more general thesis in the offing here that I think we should also accept—indeed, it is the truth of this more general thesis that explains the truth of the less general thesis. If Alfred gives the stuff to his

8. A recent discussion of a cousin of this issue is Michael J. Zimmerman's "Where Did I Go Wrong?" *Philosophical Studies* 59 (1990): 55–77.

wife he will give it to her to kill her. His giving her the stuff to kill her would be his giving it to her with a bad intention, and he will therefore be gravely at fault if he gives it to her with this intention. But that he will be at fault if he gives it to her with this intention does not mean that he may not give it to her.

The point I make here is simply the other side of a coin we took note of earlier. I drew attention to the fact that a man may be without fault though he does something wrongful; what we take note of here is that a man may be at fault though he does something that is not wrongful. (Supposing that the fact that a man would be at fault in doing a thing fixes that it is impermissible for him to do it is yet another example of our overrating of the role of fault in morality.) In short, I think we should accept a thesis that incorporates both sides of this coin, namely,

> *The Irrelevance-of-Fault-to-Permissibility Thesis*: It is irrelevant to the question whether X may do alpha whether X would be at fault in doing it.

And the truth of this more general thesis explains the truth of the less general thesis, for if fault is irrelevant to permissibility, then so also is intention. If it is irrelevant to the question whether Alfred may give the stuff to his wife whether Alfred would be at fault if he did it, then it must also be irrelevant to this question what intention he would give her the stuff with if he gave it to her. Alfred's intention is of moral interest only via its being the case that he will be at fault if he acts on it, and therefore his intention has no bearing on the permissibility of his acting if his being at fault itself has no such bearing.

But what matters for our purposes is only the Irrelevance-of-Intention-to-Permissibility Thesis, for if that thesis is true, then an agent's intending or merely foreseeing an effect of his or her action is irrelevant to the question whether he or she may proceed with it, and the Doctrine of Double Effect collapses.[9] (Not because the doctrine is in need of a yet

9. I should add, however, that this is so only if the doctrine is interpreted in the way I indicated. There are other ways of interpreting it. One possibility is to construe the doctrine as concerned, not with intendings, but with sheer causal order; I ignored this possibility in the text above, since I think it pretty obvious that the doctrine so construed has no future at all. A second possibility is to construe the doctrine as concerned with intendings all right, but not with permissibility, rather with fault. I think it possible to interpret G.E.M. Anscombe's remarks on the distinction between foreseen and intended consequences in her article "Modern Moral Philosophy" in this way: she there speaks of the distinction as bear-

more subtle characterization of the relevant intendings, but because it is a product of a misassessment of the role of intendings in morality.)[10] A fortiori, the doctrine cannot be appealed to to explain the moral difference between Strategic Bomber and Terror Bomber.

VI

What should we think of Strategic Bomber? I think it a murkier case than has usually been thought. I said that the children whom the pilot would kill are mere bystanders. But then why isn't this a No case, a No case falling into the class of Riding-Roughshod-over-a-Bystander cases?

In Trolley, a villain has started a trolley toward you. You can save yourself only if you deflect the trolley, but there is a bystander on the only path you can deflect it onto, and you therefore may not proceed. Consider a variant on Trolley, which I will call Trolley-Preemption. In this case you cannot deflect the trolley at all, you can only fire your antitank gun at it. But there is a bystander standing next to the trolley track, and if you fire your antitank gun, you will blow up the bystander along with the trolley. Can anyone plausibly think it impermissible to deflect the trolley in Trolley but permissible to blow it up in Trolley-Preemption? Hardly. Trolley is a No case falling into the class of Substitution-of-a-Bystander cases; surely Trolley-Preemption is also a No case, but one that falls instead into the class of Riding-Roughshod-over-a-Bystander cases.

But Trolley-Preemption is Strategic Bomber without the war between

ing on "responsibility" and "credit." ("Modern Moral Philosophy" is reprinted in her *Collected Philosophical Papers*, vol. 3.) But so construed, the doctrine does not—by hypothesis it does not—have anything to say about permissibility, which is our topic here.

10. I suspect that this misassessment is made only by those who misassess the role of fault in morality, for I suspect that you would think intendings relevant to permissibility only if you thought fault is. But why do people think fault is? There must be something deep behind this idea, since it is so common, and not merely among friends of the Doctrine of Double Effect. Perhaps what is at work in at least some people who harbor this idea is an inward-looking, stoic conception of the limits of morality. If you think morality is wholly a matter of what makes a person be good or bad—if you suppose it is wholly a set of instructions for being virtuous and not being vicious—then it would be no surprise if you thought that one is in breach of morality only if one does a thing the doing of which marks one as so far a bad person, i.e., a thing one is at fault or to blame for doing. (I think this conception of morality could be described as a kind of moral solipsism.) It is a good question what could make morality true if it goes beyond these limits; but perhaps no better than the question what could make it true even if it does not.

the Goods and the Bads: Strategic Bomber differs from Trolley-Preemption only in that the pilot's proceeding in Strategic Bomber is part of a larger process in which the noble Goods are defending themselves in a war being waged against them by the villainous Bads. If we think it permissible for the pilot to proceed in Strategic Bomber, but impermissible for you to proceed in Trolley-Preemption, then we must grant that that is because there is a war on in Strategic Bomber.

How does the fact that there is a war on in Strategic Bomber do the moral work of making it permissible for the pilot to proceed? At least partly, I am sure, by virtue of making it the case that the (long-range) stakes are higher than we have been told about in being told about those children in the hospital next door to the munitions factory.

Not just anything goes in wartime, of course. The fact that it is villains who, in the course of fighting an unjust war against your side, have so arranged things that you can save your life only by killing a person does not by itself make it permissible to kill the person. For example, it would not be permissible for you to eat the baby in Starvation even in mid-war. Moreover, most people think it impermissible for the pilot to proceed in Terror Bomber. (But why, exactly? Suppose a Good pilot bombed a place in Bad that contained both a munitions factory and a children's hospital, and that the Bads therefore sued for peace—not because of the loss of the munitions factory, but because of the loss of the children: the bombing terrorized the Bads, bringing home to them what war was going to have in store for them. It can hardly be thought that the fact that the causal route to the Goods' winning the war passed through Bad terror, rather than through Bad lack of munitions, shows that it was impermissible for the pilot to drop his bombs. It is of course large-scale terror bombing of enemy cities that people have in mind when they think of Terror Bomber; but why exactly is that wrongful? Well, is it always wrongful? Must it be? Perhaps the point is that it mostly is wrongful, or even that it in fact always is wrongful, in that it mostly is, or even in fact always is, unnecessary for the accomplishing of any morally acceptable wartime purpose—which leaves open that it is, or anyway might be, permissible when it is necessary for the accomplishing of a morally acceptable wartime purpose.[11] If that is correct, however, then terror bombing

11. This is the view taken by Michael Walzer in *Just and Unjust Wars* (New York: Basic Books, 1977), chap. 16. It seems to me very attractive.

is not in moral principle different from strategic or tactical bombing, for they too are wrongful when unnecessary for the accomplishing of a morally acceptable wartime purpose.)

I will have to bypass as too hard the question how the fact of war affects questions about self-defense. Let us take ourselves to have before us only the question what it is and is not permissible to do by way of self-defense in private life, when the episode is not part of a continuing process whose stakes are higher. That means we here bypass the question what makes it permissible for the pilot to drop his bombs in Strategic Bomber, and impermissible (if it is) for him to do so in Terror Bomber.

VII

I had asked at the beginning of Section V whether it is everywhere impermissible to kill a bystander in defense of one's life. We looked in Sections V and VI at a putative countercase to the idea that it is, namely, Strategic Bomber, and I have suggested that the permissibility of proceeding in that case is due to the fact of the war between the Goods and the Bads. Is it everywhere in private life impermissible to kill a bystander in defense of one's life? In the cases we looked at in Sections I through IV, what is in question is one life for one: yours and that of a person Y whom you have to kill if you are to save your life. We will look briefly in Section X at cases in which several lives would be saved by the killing of Y; let us consider here only cases in which what is in question is one life for one. I suggest that in all such cases, it is impermissible for X to kill Y if Y is a bystander.

But what exactly are bystanders, and why should it be thought that they are morally protected in this way?

A person is a bystander relative to a particular situation. Suppose Y is in no way causally involved in X's being at risk of death. That seems intuitively to be a sufficient condition for Y's being a bystander to the situation that consists in X's being at risk of death.

Is this condition necessary as well as sufficient? Ordinary use of the word "bystander" gives no precise directive. Perhaps we would regard Y as a bystander to the situation that consists in X's being at risk of death even if Y is in *some* way causally involved in it, so long as Y's causal involvement in it is in one or another respect minimal. No matter for our purposes. Two things are enough for us. First, if Y is in no way causally involved in the situation that consists in X's being at risk of death, then Y is clearly a bystander to it. And second, if Y is causally involved in it, and not minimally so—as, for example, when it is Y himself or herself who is about to kill X—then Y is clearly not a bystander to it.

Then it suggests itself that we can explain as follows why bystanders are morally protected in cases in which what is in question is one life for one. Other things being equal, every person Y has a right against X that X not kill Y. That is vague, for what are those other things that may or may not be equal? But we do know about some of those other things. Suppose that X is at risk of death. Suppose also that Y is clearly a bystander to X's being at risk of death. Then the fact that X can save himself only by killing Y does *not* make other things be unequal, and thus does *not* make Y lack the right.

Might something else make Y lack the right? By hypothesis, we are considering only cases in which what is in question is one life for one, so that there are no other people whose life or limb is relevant.

Might something override Y's right? The fact that X can save himself only by killing Y no more overrides Y's right than it makes Y lack the right. I will in fact ignore the possibility of overridings since in all of the cases we are considering there is no better reason to think Y's right is overridden than there is to think Y lacks the right.

It seems to me very plausible then to think that, given that Y is clearly a bystander to the situation that consists in X's being at risk of death, Y has a right that X not kill Y, and that *that* is why X may not kill Y.

Consider, for example, the No cases we looked at in Section IV. You are at risk of death in all of those cases, and can save your life only by killing a bystander. Given that they are bystanders, the fact that you can save your life only by killing them does not make other things be unequal: it does not make them lack rights against you that you not kill them. Nor does anything else make them lack these rights. Then we can surely say that

(1) In the circumstances, he has a right that you not kill him

is true of each of them. If so, then a fortiori you may not kill them. Indeed, if these ideas are correct, we have an explanation of why you may not.

It is certainly arguable that others besides bystanders are morally protected in this way. I leave that open.

Let us now look at the two drivers in Villainous Aggressor and Innocent Aggressor, and the fat man in Innocent Threat. *They* are clearly not bystanders, so there is not that reason to think (1) true of each of them.

I have left open that others besides bystanders are morally protected in the way we are looking at, so perhaps there is some other reason to think (1) true of each of them?

Quite to the contrary, there is reason to think (1) false of them. As I said, other things being equal, every person Y has a right against X that X not kill Y. So in particular, other things being equal, *you* have rights against each of them that they not kill you. Suppose, in fact, that

(2) In the circumstances, you have a right that he not kill you

is true of each of them. If so, then surely

(3) If he kills you, he will violate your right that he not kill you

is also true of each of them. But given that

(4) If you do not kill him, he will kill you

is also true of each of them, it surely follows that (1) is *not* true of any of them. That is, it follows that they lack rights that you not kill them. A fortiori, you may kill them. Indeed, if these ideas are correct, then we have an explanation of why you may.

I spelled all this out in detail in order that it be clear exactly where the shoe pinches.

The shoe fits well in Villainous Aggressor: we have no trouble regarding (2) and therefore (3) as true of the villainous driver, and we have no trouble regarding him as therefore lacking a right that you not kill him—he has, as we say, forfeited that right. But what of the driver of Innocent Aggressor? *He* is without fault, and we are accustomed to thinking of violation of rights as requiring fault in the violator.

But I suggest that the shoe stretches a bit with further wear, for there are good reasons to think we should not take fault to be required for a violation of a right. To begin with, the villainous driver in Villainous Aggressor has no right to kill you, and surely it is also true of the fault-free driver in Innocent Aggressor that *he* has no right to kill you. In Hohfeldian terms, neither of the two drivers has a privilege of killing you. For them to lack the privilege of killing you, however, is for you to have rights (Hohfeldian claims) that they not do so, rights they will infringe if they succeed in killing you. So it really does seem right to think that (2) is true of the fault-free driver as well as of the villainous driver.

What of (3)? Well, given that (2) is true of the fault-free driver, you have a right that he not kill you. Can it be thought that morality all the same permits him to kill you? Can it be thought morally permissible for him to do so? No doubt the fault-free driver—unlike the villainous driver—will have an excuse, a very good excuse, a completely exculpating excuse, if he runs you down; but these considerations suggest that he has no more than an excuse. If so, then he really does, however faultlessly, violate a right of yours if he kills you.

Can we conclude that (1) is therefore not true of the fault-free driver? Perhaps we will feel reluctant to say that the fault-free driver *forfeits* his right by virtue of being about to violate your right. Some people, I think, take it that forfeiting a right by definition requires fault. No matter. What is in question is not whether the innocent aggressor forfeits his right but whether he lacks it. And once we agree that he is about to violate your right—and that you can prevent this only by killing him—it seems right to conclude that he no longer has a right that you not kill him.

Still, there are bound to be some people who would resist these ideas: "No violation of a right without fault," they would say. In particular, since the driver in Innocent Aggressor is free of fault, he will not violate a right of yours if you do not stop him, and he therefore does not cease to possess a right by virtue of doing what he does. But do these people then think it all the same permissible for you to kill the fault-free driver? How *could* they think this? I said in Section II that some people would insist that self-defense is merely excusable in Innocent Aggressor, and that I have a hypothesis as to what is at work in anyone of whom this is true. The hypothesis is precisely that they think the fault-free driver will violate no right of yours if you do not stop him, and therefore does not cease to possess a right by virtue of doing what he does. It would certainly be no wonder if a person who thought this also thought it merely excusable in you to blow up the truck in Innocent Aggressor. Moved by the considerations that suggest that fault is not required for violation of a right, *I* think it permissible for you to proceed. Others, as I say, may insist that fault is required. It constitutes confirmation of the account of self-defense I offered if they conclude that self-defense is not permissible, and is merely excusable, in Innocent Aggressor.

Does the shoe stretch far enough to accommodate Innocent Threat as well? The fat man in that case is not only not at fault, he *does* nothing at all—he merely falls toward you. How can anyone say that (3) is true of him? I think there are good reasons in general to say that agency is no more required for violating a right than fault is, and good reasons therefore to say that (3) is true of the fat man, and therefore that (1) is not true of him.[12] No matter, if those who say "No violation of rights without agency" *also* say it is not permissible, but merely excusable, for you to proceed in Innocent Threat. I said in Section III that some people would insist that self-defense is merely excusable in Innocent Threat, and that I have a hypothesis as to what is at work in anyone of whom this is true. The hypothesis is precisely that they think the fat man will violate no right of yours if you do not stop him, and therefore does not cease to possess a right by virtue of falling toward you. It would certainly be no wonder if a person who thought this also thought it merely excusable in you to shift your awning. Moved by the considerations that suggest that agency is not required for violation of a right, *I* think it permissible for you to proceed. It constitutes confirmation of the account of self-defense I offered if those who think agency is required for violation of rights draw the conclusion that self-defense is not permissible, and is merely excusable, in Innocent Threat.

In short, I suggest that what makes it permissible for you to kill the two drivers and the fat man is the fact that they will otherwise violate your rights that they not kill you, and therefore lack rights that you not kill them.[13] Some people may say there is no such fact in the case of

12. Frances Kamm draws attention to the fact that if the falling fat man could alter his own direction of fall, then morality would call for his doing so, even at some considerable cost to himself—*he* is required to absorb a larger cost to prevent his landing on you than would be required of a third-party bystander who could prevent the fat man's landing on you. (But she expresses doubt as to how large a cost: minor injury is one thing, death arguably quite another.) See her "The Insanity Defense and Innocent Threats," *Criminal Justice Ethics* 6 (1987): 61–76, esp. pp. 63–67. The moral phenomenon she draws attention to is easily explained if we suppose that the fat man will violate a right of yours if he lands on you. (Kamm herself uses the terminology of "duty," and may well have in mind the correlative of a Hohfeldian claim.)

13. I stress that what makes it permissible for you to kill them is the fact that they will otherwise violate your rights *that they not kill you*. That is a very stringent right. So is the right violated in rape, for example. But it would not be permissible for you to kill a man just on the ground that he will otherwise violate your right that he not take your wallet or your hat. Some of the lawyers whose views are analyzed by Fletcher (in "Proportionality and the Psychotic Aggressor") think an appeal to rights violation is required to justify self-defense, and then seem to have had trouble understanding how there can be a 'proportion-

either the fault-free driver or the fat man; some (probably more) people may say there is no such fact at least in the case of the fat man. All is well for the account of self-defense I offered if the first group are also content to say that it is impermissible (though excusable) for you to proceed in Innocent Aggressor and Innocent Threat, and the second group to say this at least of your proceeding in Innocent Threat.

VIII

I hope it will have been noticed that the account I just offered of why you may proceed in Villainous Aggressor, Innocent Aggressor, and Innocent Threat is not the same as the account we had reached at the end of Section III. We were there considering the possibility of explaining why you may proceed in those cases by appeal to the premise "They will otherwise kill you." The account I just offered includes that premise, but adds something, namely, that if they kill you they will violate your right that they not do so. That is a significant addition.

And it—or something that does a comparable job—is necessary, for it just is not sufficient to justify your killing a person that that person will otherwise kill you.[14]

ality' requirement on self-defense; but it is curious that they should have had this trouble, since a proportionality requirement flows very naturally out of the fact that some rights are more stringent than others, a fact that any plausible theory of rights must accommodate. (Perhaps their having this trouble issues from their assuming that all rights are 'absolute', an assumption that would thereby be shown to have had bad effects in law as well as in philosophy.)

14. G.E.M. Anscombe believes that one may not directly kill the innocent, even in self-defense, but that the non-innocent are another matter. In *Mr. Truman's Degree*, she defines "innocent" as "non-harming"; see note 1. That might incline us to think she believes "They will otherwise kill you" to be sufficient to justify your killing them. But in a later paper she defines "innocent" as follows: "What is required, for the people attacked to be non-innocent in the relevant sense, is that they should themselves be engaged in an objectively unjust proceeding which the attacker has the right to make his concern; or—the commonest case—should be unjustly attacking him. Then he can attack them with a view to stopping them. . . ." See G.E.M. Anscombe, "War and Murder," reprinted in her *Collected Philosophical Papers* 3:51–61. If it is this latter that she all along had in mind as the non-innocence required in Y if X is to kill Y in defense of X's life, then she at no time believed "They will otherwise kill you" sufficient to justify your killing them: she all along believed that justifying that conclusion requires something more, here expressed as the requirement that they be "engaged in an objectively unjust proceeding." One way of interpreting that phrase is as requiring what I have offered, namely, that they be about to violate your rights; but however it is construed, the shoe will pinch in the same places—if it is to justify

Perhaps this will come out most vividly if we consider fighting back, a topic that any account of self-defense must in any case address itself to. Consider Villainous Aggressor, for example. You have an antitank gun, and it is permissible for you to blow up the truck. What if the villainous driver has his own antitank gun, and can use it on you so that you cannot use your antitank gun on him? Is it permissible for him to do this? I should think it obviously impermissible for him to do this, even if it is the case (since he will in fact continue to drive toward you in his truck) that you will shoot him unless he shoots you.

Why may the villainous driver not fight back in self-defense? We have an answer if we accept the account of self-defense that I offered in the preceding section. Suppose you are Alice, and that he shoots, and later says, "It was a matter of self-defense, your honor; after all, Alice was going to kill me unless I killed her." Self-defense? How so? Suppose he says, "Look, your honor, it might have been thought that

(1′) In the circumstances, Alice had a right that I not kill her

is true. But it is not true. For

(2′) In the circumstances, I had a right that Alice not kill me,

and therefore

(3′) If Alice killed me she would violate my right that she not kill me

are true. But

(4′) If I did not kill her, she was going to kill me

is also true. It follows that (1′) is not true. It follows that it was permissible for me to kill her." This is a bad joke. (2′) is false, for he had ceased to have the right by virtue of driving toward you in the truck.

Is fighting back permissible in Innocent Aggressor and Innocent Threat? I think not, but that is because I think the same holds of the fault-free driver and the fat man as holds of the villainous driver, namely, that they too lack rights that you not kill them. Others may disagree. It would be a further confirmation of the account of self-defense I offered if those who think the fault-free driver and the fat man do have rights that you not kill them also think it permissible for them to fight back.

your proceeding in Innocent Aggressor and Innocent Threat as well as in Villainous Aggressor. (I suspect that the role of that "objectively" is precisely to stretch the shoe.)

In short, I suggest that the permissibility of X's killing Y in self-defense goes hand in hand with the impermissibility of Y's fighting back, and that both phenomena have a common source.

I am of course assuming it to be obvious that the villainous driver may not fight back. I suspect that some would take a Hobbesian line here: on their view, all bets are off when a person will otherwise kill you. Thus they would say that the premise "Y will otherwise kill X" really is sufficient for the conclusion that X may kill Y, so that even the villainous driver may fight back. But why stop there? Why not go on to say more generally that all bets are off when you will otherwise *die*, and thus that the premise "X will otherwise die" is sufficient for the conclusion that X may kill Y? That, alas, yields that you may eat the baby in Starvation. It is hard to see what rationale could be offered for stopping this slide into moral absurdity, and that should make us suspicious of what inclined us to want to start it. In any case, I am assuming that we do not want to start it.

IX

All of the cases we have been looking at are cases in which the situation you find yourself in was ultimately caused by a villain. All of them (except, I suppose, Villainous Aggressor) have variants in which no villain is involved at all. Thus, for example, we might imagine a case in which the fat man in Innocent Threat was caused to fall toward you, not by a villain, but instead by a sudden strong gust of wind. Does the presence or absence of a villain make a difference? I should think not. That it is a villain as opposed to nature (or as opposed to someone without fault) who made it be the case that you have to kill a person to save your life does not by itself work in support of its being the case that you may proceed—or in support of its being the case that you may not.

But there are two other kinds of variants on those cases that are worth stopping over.

In the first place there are what might be called Third-Party cases, in which what is in question is not self-defense, but other-defense: cases in which you cannot save yourself but some third party can. So, for example, let us imagine that you have no antitank gun in Villainous Aggressor, but a third party does; then what we have is a Third-Party case, and our question is whether the third party may use *his* antitank gun to save *your* life, and if so, why. Similar variants are available for all of the cases we have been looking at.

Self- and other-defense are not exactly two sides of one coin, but they are nevertheless close to it. I say they are not exactly two sides of one coin in light of considerations of autonomy. Suppose that X can defend himself or herself against an attack by Y and that a third party Z can also defend X against the attack by Y. In some such cases, Z ought to refrain from proceeding in that defending X would constitute "barging in," meddling, interfering. Indeed, Z's defending X might constitute "barging in" even when X cannot defend himself against the attack by Y—we do think that people should be left to fight their own battles, even at the cost of losing some. (Some, but decidedly not all. We draw a line well before a potential victim's life is at stake.)

Considerations of autonomy apart, however, I think it very plausible to suppose that the permissibility of X's killing Y in self-defense goes hand in hand with the permissibility of Z's killing Y in defense of X, and that both phenomena have a common source. So all three phenomena—the permissibility of X's killing Y in self-defense, the impermissibility of Y's fighting back, and the permissibility of Z's killing Y in defense of X—go hand in hand and have a common source.

And I take it to be a further confirmation of the account of self-defense I offered if anyone who thinks the fault-free driver and the fat man have rights that you not kill them also thinks they have rights that a third party not kill them, and thus that it is impermissible for the third party to intervene in your defense.

Some people may say, "But the driver in Innocent Aggressor and the fat man in Innocent Threat are without fault!" Of course they are without fault. But why should that bar third-party action if it does not bar first-party action?

Some people may ask, "Who is the third party to choose who shall live as between two who are equally without fault?" You and the driver are both without fault in Innocent Aggressor; you and the fat man are both without fault in Innocent Threat. But why should that bar third-party choice if it does not bar first-party choice?

In addition, it should be remembered that if the driver in Innocent Aggressor and the fat man in Innocent Threat are about to violate your rights, then they are not merely people who are without fault. Not that the third party must intervene: I should think he may prefer to do nothing at all. (Just as you may prefer to do nothing at all.) If, on the other hand, they are not about to violate your rights, then it is impermissible for the third party to intervene—just as it is impermissible for you to do so.

The account of self-defense that I gave in Section VII may of course be incorrect. But if the facts in Innocent Aggressor and Innocent Threat did not in *some* way make it permissible for the third party to intervene in your favor, how *could* they make it permissible for you to intervene in your own favor?

One kind of answer that has been offered is this: what makes it permissible for you to kill the driver in Innocent Aggressor and the fat man in Innocent Threat is the fact that you have an "agent-relative permission" to do so, a permission that the third party lacks. The idea is that X (and only X) is permitted to kill Y when Y will otherwise kill X, since it is X (and only X) whom Y will otherwise kill.[15] But that cannot be right.

In the first place, not just anything goes in self-defense: we have no across-the-board agent-relative permission to kill others to save our lives. (You certainly may not eat the baby in Starvation.) Could it be said that we have an agent-relative permission to kill another to save our lives but that the permission is limited to cases in which the other will otherwise kill us? What is supposed to be the rationale for this limit? If agent-relativity is what is crucial (Me! Me! I'm the one at risk!), why *isn't* the permission an across-the-board permission? (Compare my comments in the preceding section about the Hobbesian idea that all bets are off when Y will kill X unless X kills Y.)

Moreover, if the agent-relative permission is limited in this way, why *isn't* there a comparable limited third-party-centered permission? Is it just to be taken, flatly, as a datum, that while I have a permission to kill a person who will otherwise kill me, a third party lacks a permission to kill a person who will otherwise kill me?

Most important, it just is not acceptable to say that a person may do to save his own life something that it would not be permissible for him or her to do to save the life of another—considerations of the other's autonomy apart—for whatever I may do to save my own life I may surely do to save the life of someone I love.

15. Nancy Davis offers this kind of answer in regard to a similar case in "Abortion and Self-Defense," *Philosophy & Public Affairs* 13, no. 3 (Summer 1984): 175–207. As her title indicates, she brings out the bearing of these issues on the problem of abortion.

Well, on some views of the agent-relative permission it extends to defending those I love as well as to defending myself. (After all, those I love are those *I* love, so that it's still Me! Me! that is crucial.) But do we really wish to have it that a man's being rather a bore is going to make him later be undefendable in circumstances in which he would have been defendable had he only been charming enough to be loved?

No doubt X may have an excuse for doing something to save his or her own life that it was wrongful in X to do to save it, when a third party who saved X's life in those circumstances would have acted not merely wrongly but also inexcusably. (Just as X may have an excuse for doing something wrongful to save his or her child's life, when a third party who saved X's child's life in those circumstances would have acted not merely wrongly but also inexcusably.) So far as I can see, this is the only *fact* that lies behind appeals to agent-relative permission here. And it does not come to much.[16] For having an excuse for doing something wrongful is just that: doing something wrongful, though having an excuse for doing it. But our question was whether it is permissible (and not merely excusable) for you to proceed in these cases.

In short, it is not because of the personal fact of your special relation to those who will kill you in those cases, it is not because they will otherwise kill *you*, that you may proceed; it is because of the entirely impersonal fact that they will *otherwise violate your rights that they not kill you* that you may proceed. But that impersonal fact may be acted on by a third party as well as by you.

X

A second interesting kind of variant on these cases is what we get when we imagine that what is in question is not self-defense but other-defense, and moreover, not merely other-defense but other-defense of more than one. So, for example, let us imagine that the villain in Villainous Aggres-

16. I should perhaps make clear that I am not saying that appeals to agent-relative permissions are unsuccessful everywhere in moral theory. For example, they certainly do seem to have a role to play in cases that involve only the distribution of benefits, i.e., in cases of the kind discussed by John M. Taurek in "Should the Numbers Count?" *Philosophy & Public Affairs* 6, no. 4 (Summer 1977): 293–316.

sor is driving toward five, not one, and that none of the five has an antitank gun. Is it permissible for a third party to use his antitank gun to save the five? Yes. If it is permissible for a third party to use his antitank gun to save only one, it is surely permissible for him to do so to save five. Similarly for similar variants on Innocent Aggressor and Innocent Threat. Let us call these Third-Party Different Number cases.

What is of interest here are the Third-Party Different Number variants on the No cases we surveyed in Section IV. In Trolley, a villain has started a trolley down a track toward you. You cannot stop the trolley, but you can deflect it. Unfortunately, the only path onto which you can deflect it will take it onto a bystander. It is impermissible for you to deflect the trolley. In a Third-Party variant on this case, you cannot do anything at all to save yourself, but a third party can save you—*he* can deflect the trolley onto the bystander. Given that it is impermissible for you to deflect the trolley in Trolley, the thesis of the preceding section tells us it is also impermissible for the third party to deflect the trolley in the Third-Party variant of Trolley. That consequence of the thesis is surely welcome. But now consider a Third-Party Different Number variant of Trolley in which the third party will save five if he deflects the trolley.[17] In *this* case it would be permissible for the third party to deflect the trolley: the third party's turning the trolley here would yield a net saving of four lives. Well, not just anything is permissible on the ground that it yields a net saving of four lives (supplying five who are starving with knives, forks, and the neighbors' baby obviously will not do), and what has come to be known as the Trolley Problem is the problem of explaining why it is permissible to do what would yield this net saving of lives—when it is.

I do not address that problem here, except to draw attention to the fact that a satisfactory solution to it must make clear why altering the numbers makes a difference. That is, it is *not* permissible for the third party to proceed in a variant on Trolley in which only one will be saved; it *is* permissible for the third party to proceed if five instead of one will be saved. The answer to the question why it is permissible to proceed when five will be saved had better be sensitive to the numbers: it had better

17. The case comes, of course, from Philippa Foot's "The Problem of Abortion and the Doctrine of the Double Effect," reprinted in her *Virtues and Vices* (Oxford: Basil Blackwell, 1978), pp. 19–32.

explain why it matters that five instead of one will be saved.[18] It is not enough to say *just*, "Well, five is four more than one"; we need an account of why adding the four makes a difference. Solutions to the Trolley Problem that focus on the means the agent uses to save those he saves do not, and I think cannot, answer to this need.

18. I mention with some diffidence that the solution to this problem offered in my *The Realm of Rights* (Cambridge, Mass.: Harvard University Press, 1990) *is* sensitive to the numbers, for what that solution focuses on is the increased probability of advantage secured for all six by a decision made in advance to turn the trolley when it later comes to threaten five and can be turned onto a sixth.

For what it is worth, however, I should mention that my discussion of self-defense here departs from that of chap. 14 of that book: I now think I was mistaken about some of the cases discussed there.

[13]

THE BASIS OF MORAL LIABILITY TO DEFENSIVE KILLING

Jeff McMahan
Rutgers University

There may be circumstances in which it is morally justifiable intentionally to kill a person who is morally innocent, threatens no one, rationally wishes not to die, and does not consent to be killed. Although the killing would wrong the victim, it might be justified by the necessity of averting some disaster that would otherwise occur. In other instances of permissible killing, however, the justification appeals to more than consequences. It may appeal to the claim that the person to be killed has acted in such a way that to kill him would neither wrong him nor violate his rights, even if he has not consented to be killed or to be subjected to the risk of being killed. In these cases, I will say that the person is *liable* to be killed. Although I borrow the notion of liability from legal theory, and although much of what I say will be informed by the literature on liability in both tort law and criminal law, my concern in this article is with moral rather than legal liability.

Liability is different from desert. The claim that someone deserves to be killed implies that there is a reason to kill her even if it is possible for no one to be killed; but the claim that someone is liable to be killed has no such implication. Liability is the broader notion: desert implies liability but liability does not imply desert. Thus, if a person deserves to be killed, it follows that he is liable to be killed, but he can be liable to be killed without deserving to be killed. My focus will be on forms of liability that do not involve desert; I will not consider punitive or retributive killing. My focus will instead be primarily on liability to *defensive* killing, though I will also consider whether there can be liability to killing that preserves life but is not strictly defensive because the person to be killed is not the cause of the threat to be averted. Liability, of course, also extends to forms of harmful treatment other than killing, but for simplicity of exposition I will focus on moral liability to be killed. Much of what I will say, however, can be generalized to other forms of harming.

The question I will address is: "What is the basis of liability to killing?" Or, more precisely: "What must a person who does not deserve to die have done to make it the case that he would not be wronged by being killed?" I will examine two widely held accounts of the basis of liability to defensive killing before sketching the outlines of what I think is the most promising account.

The Rights-Based Account

The *Rights-Based Account* holds that what makes a person liable to defensive killing is that he will otherwise violate a right that is sufficiently stringent for killing to be a proportionate means of prevention.[1] According to its most original and influential exponent, Judith Jarvis Thomson, this account offers a justification for self-defensive killing in cases that pose problems for other accounts. It explains, for example, how it can be permissible to kill an "innocent threat," a moral agent who through voluntary action poses an unjust threat but is not culpable for doing so. Here is an example.

> The identical twin brother of a notorious murderer is driving during a stormy night in a remote area when his car breaks down. Unaware that his brother has recently escaped from prison and is thought to be hiding in this same area, he knocks on the door of the nearest house, seeking to phone for help. On opening the door, the armed and frightened resident mistakes the harmless twin for the murderer and lunges at him with a knife.

Assuming that this is the only way to save his own life, may the twin kill the resident? Most people believe that he would be justified in doing so, even if the resident is acting reasonably in the circumstances and thus is fully excused for the threat he poses to the twin. And the Rights-Based Account provides an explanation of why the twin would be justified: because the resident would otherwise violate the twin's right not to be killed, the resident lacks a right not to be killed by him. In short, the resident makes himself liable to be killed.

Another type of case that is even more problematic for many accounts of self-defense involves a "nonresponsible threat," a person who poses an unjust threat without being in any way responsible for doing so. Here is Thomson's example.

> A fat man is enjoying a picnic on a cliff directly above the deck on which you are lying with your leg in traction. Suddenly a villain pushes him off the cliff. If he lands on you he will kill you; but he will survive because you will cushion his fall. You cannot move aside but can save yourself by hoisting your sun umbrella and impaling him on it.[2]

Again, most people believe that you would be justified in killing the fat man. And again the Rights-Based Account offers an explanation, which is that, because the fat man will otherwise violate your right not to be killed, he lacks a right not to be killed by you. He too is liable.

Some have argued that it is not true that the fat man will violate your right if you do not kill him, since only a morally responsible agent can violate a right. Even on Thomson's own account, for a person to have a right is just for others to be morally constrained in certain ways.[3] And just as a falling boulder or a charging tiger cannot be morally constrained and therefore cannot violate a right, so also a person cannot be morally constrained except in the exercise of responsible agency. Since the fat man cannot be morally constrained from having his body used by someone else against his will, he does not threaten your right when his body is hurled at you.

This does not, of course, show that the Rights-Based Account is wrong. It if is correct that the fat man would not violate your right, all this shows is that the Rights-Based Account does not, after all, have the intuitively appealing implication that nonresponsible threats may be liable to defensive killing.

Here is another case that challenges the Rights-Based Account. It is familiar from discussions of the Doctrine of Double Effect.

> A tactical bomber fighting in a just war has been ordered to bomb a military facility located on the border of the enemy country. He knows that if he bombs the factory, the explosion will kill innocent civilians living just across the border in a neutral country. But this would be a side effect of his action and would be proportionate to the contribution that the destruction of the facility would make to the achievement of the just cause. As he approaches, the civilians learn of his mission. They cannot flee in time but they have access to an anti-aircraft gun.

The traditional question is how the tactical bomber can be justified in bombing the facility when it would not be justifiable for a terror bomber to drop a bomb in the same spot, producing the same effects, with the *intention* of killing the civilians. My question is different. Assuming that the tactical bomber would be morally justified in dropping his bomb, would the civilians be justified in shooting him down in self-defense?

To explain why this case challenges the Rights-Based Account, I need to distinguish two ways of acting against a right. When one is morally justified in doing what another has a right that one not do, one *infringes* her right. When one acts without justification in doing what another has a right that one not do, one *violates* her right.[4] Because the tactical bomber acts with justification, he will merely infringe the civilians' rights. The usual assumption is that one does not lose one's rights by virtue of morally justified action. If that is right, the tactical bomber retains his right not to be killed even though he will otherwise infringe the civilians' rights. According to the Rights-Based Account, therefore, the civilians may not kill him in self-defense.

But this is hard to believe—unless, perhaps, his mission is so important that they are morally required to sacrifice themselves for the sake of its success. Can the Rights-Based Account accommodate the common intuition that the civilians may kill the tactical bomber in self-defense? It cannot be claimed that his right is overridden by morally weightier considerations; for the stipulation that his act would be proportionate entails that the failure of his mission, which would be a consequence of their killing him, would be worse from an impartial perspective than their being killed. Perhaps then, contrary to the common assumption, one may lose rights by threatening to infringe rights. If so, then the fact that the tactical bomber will otherwise infringe their right not to be killed means that he lacks a right not to be killed by them—that is, he makes himself liable to be killed by them.

But this too is hard to believe. For if he has lost his right not to be killed by them, it seems that he can have no right of self-defense against them. Yet intuitively it seems that, just as it is permissible for the civilians to kill the tactical bomber in self-defense, it is also permissible for the tactical bomber preemptively to kill the civilians in self-defense. It is, however, hard to see how the Rights-Based Account can explain this apparent symmetry. How can each party have a right to kill the other while at the same time lacking a right not to be killed by the other? How can one be justified in killing someone to prevent him from doing what he has a right to do?

The case of the tactical bomber is a problem not only for the Rights-Based Account but for other accounts as well. I will return to it at the end of the paper. For the moment I will consider another widely held account of the basis of liability to defensive killing.

The Culpability Account

According to Thomson, the violation of a right is a matter of what one person causes to happen to another. It does not require culpability, responsibility, or even agency on the part of the violator. Thus both innocent and nonresponsible threats may violate rights. Although they may be fully excused, they are nevertheless liable to necessary and proportionate defensive action. Yet Thomson acknowledges that some people believe that culpability on the part of the agent is necessary for the violation of a right, and that even more believe that responsible agency is necessary. The latter believe that nonresponsible threats cannot violate rights and thus are not liable to defensive killing, while the former believe that this is true of both nonresponsible *and* innocent threats.

Some theorists have developed accounts of liability to defensive killing that focus on issues of responsibility and culpability for unjust threats. An unjust threat is a threat of harm that would wrong the victim—harm to which the victim is not morally liable. The *Culpability Account* of liability holds that the criterion of liability is culpability for an unjust threat.[5] There is a narrow version of this account that assigns liability only for culpably *posing* an unjust threat, while a broader version assigns liability for culpable *responsibility* for an unjust threat. According to the broader version, a person may be liable to killing now if that is necessary to avert an unjust threat for which he is responsible through past culpable action, even if he is now no part of the threat. I will assume that the Culpability Account takes this broader form.

It is possible that the Culpability Account is equivalent to a version of the Rights-Based Account that assumes that culpability is necessary for the violation of a right. Like the Rights-Based Account, this account has trouble with the case of the tactical bomber, since it implies that, because the tactical bomber does not act culpably, he does not make himself liable and thus, presumably, may not be attacked in self-defense by the civilians. But I will put these issues aside in order to focus on a different problem for the idea that culpability is the basis of liability. Consider a case of attempted murder.[6]

> A villain, fully intending to kill you, points his gun at you and slowly begins to squeeze the trigger. You and he both reasonably believe that the gun is loaded but in fact it is not. You have just enough time to kill him with your concealed derringer before he pulls the trigger.

Most people believe that you are justified in killing him, for he is culpably attempting to kill you and you reasonably believe that he will succeed unless you kill him first. It is not, moreover, obvious that you will wrong him if you kill him. Yet he in fact poses no threat to you. He is not culpably responsible for a threat to your life. He does not, therefore, satisfy the Culpability Account's criterion of liability.

There are several options. One is to retain the Culpability Account's criterion of liability—culpability for an unjust threat—and conjoin it with an objective account of justification. On this view, because objectively the villain poses no threat to you, he is not liable and you cannot claim necessity as a justification. Your killing him would therefore be objectively unjustified, though it would be fully excused because it would be reasonable given your epistemic limitations.

A second option is to retain the Culpability Account's criterion of liability but conjoin it with a subjective account of justification, according to which justification depends not the objective nature of the relation between you and the villain but on what you believe or reasonably believe about that relation. On this view, the villain is not liable but because you believe, or reasonably believe, that he *is* liable and that killing him is necessary for self-defense, your killing him would be justified.

A third option is to modify the criterion of liability. Intuitively this may seem to be a case in which the villain is liable to defensive killing. Because he is culpably *attempting* to kill you, it does not seem that you would wrong him if you were to kill him, given that you reasonably believe that killing him is necessary for self-defense and that he is culpably responsible for putting you in a situation in which you have to act on that belief. It seems, in short, that the villain's culpability for the attempt on your life is sufficient for liability even though there is in fact no threat for which he is responsible.[7]

Suppose we accept that a person can be liable to be killed by you in self-defense either if he is culpably responsible for an unjust threat to your life or if he is culpably making an unjust attempt on your life. We may still believe that your killing the villain in the case of the culpable attempt is unjustified (though excused). For the villain's liability is not a sufficient justification for killing him if killing him would be pointless because he is in fact harmless. It would, after all, clearly be unjustified for you to kill him if you *knew* that his gun was unloaded, and it is not clear how your lack of morally relevant knowledge can establish a justification where otherwise there would be none. (This is one of the oddities of the subjective account of justification: that it makes mistake of fact a ground of moral justification rather than excuse.)

It seems, however, that there can be cases in which a person can be liable for a culpable attempt on your life and in which your killing him could be justified even when you *know* that he poses no threat to you. These are cases in which the kind of threat the person is attempting to pose arises from a different source and can be averted only by killing the person who is making the attempt. Here is an example.

> Aware that a villain plans to kill you, you begin to carry a gun. On one occasion you have the opportunity to empty the bullets from his gun and you do so. Immediately thereafter, he confronts you in an alley and tries to fire. As he continues to pull the trigger in frustration, you see that a second villain is preparing to shoot you from behind a narrow basement window (it is a tough neighborhood). Unable to flee in time and also unable to fire with accuracy through the tiny window, you can save yourself only by shooting the first villain, causing him to slump in front of the window, thereby blocking the second villain's line of fire.

According to the Culpability Account's revised criterion of liability—culpability for an unjust threat *or* culpability for an unjust *attempt*—the first villain is liable to be killed by you because he is making a culpable attempt on your life. You know that this villain is harmless but your killing him would not be pointless, for it is necessary to prevent yourself from being killed by the second villain. My intuition, which is not shared by everyone, is that you would be justified in killing the first villain. Because he is culpably attempting to pose the same threat you in fact face from another agent, it is difficult to accept that you would wrong him by killing him in order to avert that threat.

Perhaps another case may push us even further.

> All of the details are the same as in the previous case except that the second villain is preparing to shoot not you but another innocent person who has appeared in the alley. You can prevent the second villain from killing this innocent person only by killing the first villain, thereby causing him to drop to the ground and block the window.

Again, my intuition is that you would be justified in killing the first villain. My sense that he would not be wronged by being killed by you is slightly weaker in this case than in the previous case, but even in this case I doubt that he has any persuasive ground for complaint.

In short, I suspect that liability to defensive killing can extend beyond culpability for an unjust threat. But once liability becomes detached from threat, various questions arise. One is: "Culpability for what?" These cases suggest, at least to many people, that we should accept an extended criterion of liability to defensive killing that recognizes liability for culpable attempts. But why stop there? It seems arbitrary to draw the line at attempts. Suppose that in the initial case involving the second villain, the first villain follows you into the alley with the intention of killing you but decides to check his gun before firing. Just as the second villain appears at the window, the first villain discovers that his gun is empty. As in the original case, the only way you can prevent the second villain from killing you is to kill the first villain, who not only poses no threat but also now makes no attempt to kill you—though he would kill you if he could. My sense is that his merely discovering that an attempt would be futile cannot make the difference between his being liable and his not being liable.

But is it plausible to suppose that a person can be liable to be killed simply because he *would* unjustly kill an innocent person if he could? And if we accept this as a basis of liability, should we stop here or go further? What about someone who now intends to kill an innocent person in the future? Does it make a difference whether he is actively preparing for the killing? (These questions are crucial to understanding the permissibility of preventive defense.) What about someone who intends to kill an innocent person *if* certain conditions obtain? Does it matter how likely it is that the conditions will obtain?

Other possibilities are suggested by further variations of the case involving the threatening villain behind the basement window. What if the person who might be killed in order to block this villain's fire is not now attempting to harm you but made an attempt on your life earlier in the day? Or a month ago? What if, instead, he made an attempt on someone else's life a year ago? What if he is not now attempting to kill anyone but is a murderer who was never punished? Or a murderer who has been punished but remains unrepentant? What if, though harmless, he is simply a thoroughly nasty person?

Clearly we must draw a line before we reach this final possibility. I find it plausible that the person who is culpably but futilely attempting to kill you would not, in our first three cases, be wronged if you were to kill him. But once liability is divorced from culpability for an actual threat, I do not know where to draw a principled line at which culpability ceases to be a basis of liability.

There is another problem. If, as the Culpability Account originally asserted, liability to defensive killing arises only from culpability for an unjust threat, that implicitly limits the purpose for which the liable person may be killed to the elimination of the threat. But if liability is divorced from responsibility for an actual threat, it is an open question for what purposes a person who is liable to be killed may justifiably be killed. This problem is illustrated by the case in which the purpose of killing the first villain is not to defend the person he is attempting to kill but to defend a different person from a different threat. But there are other possibilities. We might, for example, kill those who are liable for culpable attempts in order to use their organs for transplantation. It is unclear, however, whether there is a stable, principled line between this unappealing suggestion and the view that it is permissible to kill the first villain to prevent an innocent bystander from being killed by the second villain.

The cases I have considered thus far pose the question whether certain forms of culpability are sufficient for liability. But one point on which the Culpability Account is firm is that culpability is *necessary* for liability. It thus denies that either innocent or nonresponsible threats can be liable to defensive killing. Many people will regard this as a sufficient basis for rejecting the account. For most people agree with Thomson that it can be permissible to kill innocent and nonresponsible threats in self-defense.

I disagree. I think that there is no moral basis for holding nonresponsible threats liable.[8] And it is possible that there is no basis for holding certain innocent threats liable. But *some* innocent threats *are* liable. In other words, culpability is not necessary for liability. Here is an example of liability without culpability.

> A person keeps his car well maintained and always drives cautiously and alertly. On one occasion, however, freak circumstances cause the car to go out of control. It has veered in the direction of a pedestrian whom it will kill unless she blows it up by using one of the explosive devices with which pedestrians in philosophical examples are typically equipped.

This conscientious driver is an example of one type of innocent threat, which I call an "inadvertent threat." The pedestrian has done nothing to make herself liable to be killed but the driver will kill her unless he is himself killed first. Yet he is in no way culpable. The unjust threat he poses is not the result of wrongful intent, recklessness, or negligence; it is the result of sheer bad luck. On what basis, then, may he be said to be liable?

What makes him liable is that, as a morally responsible agent, he voluntarily chose to set a couple of tons of steel rolling as a means of pursuing his ends, knowing that this would involve a tiny risk that he would lose control of this dangerous object that he had set in motion, thereby imperiling the lives of the innocent. It is important to notice that the claim here is not that he is liable because he alone had the chance to avoid the tragic conflict between himself and the pedestrian. For the pedestrian could have avoided it as well by simply staying at home. The claim is, rather, that the driver is liable because he voluntarily engaged in a risk-imposing activity and is responsible for the consequences when the risks he imposed eventuate in harms.

Admittedly, what I am citing as the relevant difference between the driver and the pedestrian is of comparatively slight moral significance. But given that the costs of the driver's voluntarily engaging in a risk-imposing activity cannot be divided, it is fair that he should suffer them all rather than impose them all on the pedestrian. Yet because he is not culpable for the threat of unjust harm he poses, it might be reasonable to demand that the pedestrian share the costs with him if that were possible. If, for example, the pedestrian could defend her life in a way that would inflict nonlethal harm on the driver but also allow his action to inflict a nonlethal injury on her, she might, particularly if the harm she would suffer would not be severe, be obliged to suffer this harm rather than kill the driver. To kill him when this alternative is available might indeed be to wrong him. (Note that this assumes that liability and proportionality in self-defense are interrelated.)

The Responsibility Account

The case of the conscientious driver suggests an alternative account of the basis of liability. According to what I will call the *Responsibility Account*, the criterion of liability to defensive killing is moral responsibility, through action that lacks objective justification, for a threat of unjust harm to others, where a harm is unjust if it is one to which the victim is not liable and to which she has not consented. For convenience, I will sometimes abbreviate this to "responsibility for an unjust threat." The conscientious driver satisfies this criterion because he is a morally responsible agent who has acted voluntarily in a way that foreseeably imposed risks on others and now threatens the pedestrian with unjust harm. And he acts without objective justification because, although he may act reasonably given his epistemic limitations, it is not justifiable to drive a car that is in fact going to go out of control. Yet he is in no way culpable for the threat he poses. The epistemic constraints under which he acts are fully exculpating.

The Responsibility Account treats liability as a matter of degree. Responsibility for an unjust threat can vary in degree, and liability varies concomitantly. A person's liability is therefore greater when his action is culpable, and the degree of his liability varies with the degree of his culpability. The degree of a person's liability is manifest in the severity of what may be done to him without wronging him—that is, in the stringency of the proportionality requirement.

It may be instructive to compare liability to defensive action to liability in tort law. Just as we may think of liability in torts as a matter of corrective justice, or justice in the distribution of harm ex post, so we may think of liability to defensive action as a matter of preventive justice, or justice in the distribution of harm ex ante. According to the Culpability Account, liability to defensive action corresponds to fault liability in torts. But the Responsibility Account treats liability to defensive action as strict, as in the case of the conscientious driver. It says to all people who engage in socially permitted risk-imposing activities such as driving: "You know that if you drive you impose a very small risk on other innocent people. If you choose to drive, the consequences are your responsibility unless others also contribute to the outcome through their own risk-imposing activities. You will be liable to defensive action even if you satisfy the relevant standards of due care."

It is, perhaps, significant that there is no account of liability in torts that corresponds to the Rights-Based Account as it is usually understood, for example by Thomson. Suppose the fat man who is pushed off a cliff actually lands on you but merely breaks your leg rather than killing you. There is no conception of strict liability that is strict enough to hold him liable for damages.

It is also true, however, that if the conscientious driver were merely to injure the pedestrian rather than kill her, he too would escape liability in tort law. His act would not be among those that tort law subjects to a standard of strict liability. More generally, the range of injurious acts for which tort law holds people strictly liable is narrower than the range of threatening acts for which the Responsibility Account holds people liable to defensive action. I believe, however, that tort law would correspond more closely to our sense of corrective justice if it were to hold the conscientious driver liable. Yet the provisions of tort law have to be formulated to take account not only of considerations of justice but also of consequences. If people like the conscientious driver were held strictly liable ex post, that might help to deter people from driving for frivolous reasons, which would be desirable, but it might also have undesirable effects as well. I cannot pursue these issues here.[9]

I believe that some version of the Responsibility Account will turn out to be the best account of liability to defensive killing. Like the other accounts, however, the Responsibility Account, at least in the form in which I have stated it, faces a battery of objections. In the remainder of this article I will review some of these objections and suggest some initial responses.

Suppose that the only way you can prevent yourself from being killed by a culpable attacker is to kill his mother. If you do kill her, can you then claim that she was liable to be killed because, as a morally responsible agent, she voluntarily chose to engage in an activity (having a child) that had a tiny probability of resulting in an unjust threat and that this made her responsible for the threat you faced from her son?[10] Obviously not. But it is less obvious what the right explanation is of why the mother is not liable.

One explanation is that the woman's act of having a child is causally too remote for her to be responsible for the threat he poses. It might be argued that just as tort law insists that a person must have been the "proximate" cause of harm to another in order to be liable to repair that harm, so a person must be the proximate cause of an unjust threat to another in order to be liable to defensive killing. This seems, however, to be too strong a requirement. Suppose that a wholly innocent person is about to be tortured as a terrorist suspect under newly adopted rules that wrongfully permit certain forms of torture during interrogation. She cannot defend herself against the person who will actually conduct the torture but, through a remarkable mechanism known only to those who devise philosophical examples, she can prevent the torture by inflicting a proportionate harm on an official who provided sophistical arguments for the legal permissibility of the new rules, thereby making it possible to implement them. This official seems responsible for the practice of torture in a way that makes him liable to defensive action. He would not be wronged if this woman were to inflict a proportionate harm on him as a necessary means of avoiding torture that she would not have faced were it not for his action. Yet the action that makes him liable is causally remote from the unjust threat the woman faces. The torturer, not the official, is the proximate cause of that threat. Still, it seems that the causal connections are of the right sort for the transmission of moral responsibility. I will not try to determine what sorts of causal connection are the right sorts. But it seems that the official's causal role in implementing the policy of torture is part of the cause of the torturer's action and that this makes him responsible to a significant degree for what the torturer does. By contrast, the mother's action in causing her child to exist does not in anything like the same way cause his subsequent acts and does not make her to any degree responsible for them.

Not only are there some who, like the official, are liable for an unjust threat without being its proximate cause; there are also some who are the proximate cause of an unjust threat but are not liable. This is true, for example, of the falling fat man. But it also seems true of some innocent threats who might seem to be liable under the Responsibility Account as I have stated it. In earlier work, I assumed that the only instances in which a person can be altogether lacking in responsibility for harm he causes are those in which he causes harm independently of his responsible agency. I therefore assumed that whenever a morally responsible agent causes harm through his own voluntary action, he is to some degree responsible for it, even if he is fully excused for causing it because of some excusing condition or simple bad luck.[11] But I now believe that this was a mistake. Here is an example that shows why.

> A villain has secretly tampered with a man's cell phone in such a way that if the man presses the "send" button, he will detonate a bomb to which you have been tied by this same villain. The villain has trussed you up so that you cannot escape or alert the man with the cell phone to your plight. But the villain has given you a weapon with which you can kill the man with the cell phone.

Suppose the cell phone operator has pressed in a number and is about to press the send button. He now inadvertently poses an unjust threat to you—that is, a threat to which you are in no way liable. He is, moreover, a morally responsible agent whose pressing the button would be a free, voluntary act. But, even though he is the proximate cause of the threat to you, he seems in no way responsible for that threat. Consequently, he seems no more liable than the falling fat man. It is possible that you could be justified in killing him, but you could not plausibly claim that he had made himself liable to be killed.

In our earlier example, the killer's mother could reasonably have foreseen that there was a very small probability that if she had a child he would become a murderer. But in that case there was not the right sort of causal connection between her having a child and that child's later posing an unjust threat to transmit responsibility for that threat back to her. In the example of the cell phone operator, there is certainly the right sort of causal connection between the man's action and the unjust threat you face. The necessary ingredient of responsibility that is missing in this case is foreseeability.

There is, of course, a problem about how probable a threat or harm must be in order to count as foreseeable. I cannot address that problem here; for present purposes I will sidestep it by simply invoking the notion of a "risk-imposing activity"—that is, an activity of a type that is known or can be seen to impose a risk of significant harm on others, even if the probability is comparatively low, as it is in the case of driving. I will assume that it is a condition of responsibility for an unjust threat that the action that gave rise to the threat either was of a risk-imposing type or was such that in the circumstances the agent ought to have foreseen that it carried a non-negligible risk of causing a significant unjust harm.

While the conscientious driver and the cell phone operator are both the inadvertent but proximate cause of an unjust threat, only the driver is engaged in a risk-imposing activity. Pressing a button on a cell phone is not the kind of act that typically carries any risk to others, however slight. This is why the cell phone operator cannot be held responsible or therefore liable for the harm his pressing the button would cause. (Having a child is also not a risk-imposing activity, but this is not because it is not a type of activity that leads ultimately to risks to others. It is because any subsequent risks or harms cannot be traced in the right way back to the activity itself.)

In short, the cell phone operator is not liable to defensive killing according to the Responsibility Account because he fails to meet one of the conditions of moral responsibility—the foreseeability condition—for the unjust threat he poses. Although he is a morally responsible agent who acts voluntarily and without objective justification (since his pressing the send button is objectively unjustified), he is nevertheless, like the falling fat man, a nonresponsible threat.

I find it a virtue of the Responsibility Account that it identifies a basis for attributing liability to the conscientious driver. Intuitively, however, it seems to matter what his reason is for driving. On considering the example, we naturally assume that this person is driving for one of the self-interested reasons for which people typically drive: to go to the store, to get to work, or whatever. But some people, such as ambulance drivers, drive for more important reasons—reasons for which other people reasonably want them to drive despite the risks they impose. If we imagine a variant of the case of the conscientious driver involving an ambulance driver on the way to the scene of an accident, we are likely to question whether his voluntarily engaging in this risk-imposing activity can make him liable to defensive killing by the pedestrian when the ambulance goes out of control.

It is tempting to suppose that the ambulance driver's action is justified in a more robust sense than the action of the conscientious person who drives for reasons of self-interest and that this blocks an attribution to him of liability. But objectively neither driver is justified. For in each case, however faultless or even meritorious the driver may be, there is an objective description of what he will do unless he is killed—killing an innocent pedestrian—under which it is clear that his action is unjustified. (I am assuming that getting to the accident site is not sufficiently important to make it justifiable for the ambulance driver knowingly to kill a pedestrian if that were necessary to get there.)

This, of course, presupposes an objective account of justification. But even a subjective account of justification is unlikely to be able to distinguish between the two drivers in a way that supports an attribution of liability to the self-interested driver but denies that attribution to the ambulance driver. For any plausible subjective account that implies that the ambulance driver's action is justified will have the same implication for the conscientious driver's self-interested action, given how low the antecedent subjective probability of his car's going out of control was.

Suppose, however, that we were to find a plausible basis for claiming that, while the conscientious driver is liable for having chosen to engage in a risk-imposing activity, the ambulance driver's *reason* for engaging in that same activity shields him from liability in the same circumstances, even if his action is objectively unjustified. We would still face a line-drawing problem. For people's reasons for engaging in a risk-imposing activity such as driving lie along a spectrum from culpable to morally neutral to praiseworthy. If we claim that the ambulance driver's reason for driving blocks an attribution of liability to him, what should we say about a person who drives to take his child to the doctor? Or to take his sick dog to the vet? Or to present a paper on liability to defensive killing at a philosophy colloquium? There does not seem to be any point at which a principled line can be drawn between liable and not liable on the spectrum of cases between the conscientious driver and the ambulance driver. (And even if we could find such a point, identifying it would be largely irrelevant to matters of practice, since in cases of self-defense, and particularly cases of defense against inadvertent threats, agents tend to have little or no reliable information about the reasons for which those who pose an unjust threat have acted.)

It may seem that the ambulance driver is similar to the tactical bomber in that both unintentionally threaten the innocent as a side effect of engaging in morally desirable action. According to the Responsibility Account, however, they are quite different, for the tactical bomber acts with objective justification while the ambulance driver does not. This fact about the tactical bomber may, indeed, enable the Responsibility Account to deal in an intuitively satisfactory way with the problem the tactical bomber poses.

In the case of the tactical bomber, the civilians are not liable. The tactical bomber will therefore wrong them if he drops his bomb. Yet he acts with objective moral justification. And, according to the Responsibility Account, justification defeats liability: one is liable to defensive killing by virtue of responsibility for an unjust threat only if one acts without justification. This seems intuitively plausible; for it is hard to see how one's moral immunity to being killed could be compromised merely by one's acting in a way that is morally justified.

As I noted earlier, however, it seems intuitively that the civilians are permitted to kill the tactical bomber in self-defense. How can that be if he is not liable? I suggest that people are permitted a necessary and proportionate defense against being wronged either by unjustified *or justified* action. People are not morally required, or at least not always, simply to submit to being wronged by another's morally justified action. They are, at least sometimes, morally permitted to resist. This is a special form of justification for killing; it does not appeal either to liability on the part of the victim or to the overriding moral importance of avoiding disastrous consequences.

It is essential to this form of justification that it applies only to those who would otherwise be wronged by morally justified action. A person who acts with justification to threaten another with harm to which the other is morally liable does not threaten to wrong that other person. There can be no permissible defense against harm to which one is morally liable.

Because the tactical bomber's justified action would wrong the civilians, they are permitted a proportionate defense. And killing him would be proportionate. But because he is not morally liable to be killed by them, they will wrong him if they kill him in self-defense. He too, therefore, is permitted a proportionate defense against their permissible defensive action. He is justified in killing them in preemptive self-defense.

This reasoning establishes the intuitive moral parity between the tactical bomber and the civilians. Neither party to the conflict is liable to be killed by the other, but each is justified in killing the other in self-defense.

This reasoning is also compatible with the plausible view that third parties are not, other things being equal, permitted to intervene. Although the fact that each party threatens to wrong the other seems to provide a ground for third party intervention, that is canceled by the fact that each party also acts with justification.

This understanding of the case of the tactical bomber can, it seems, also be stated in the language of rights. The civilians have a right not to be killed. Because the tactical bomber acts with justification, his killing them would not violate but would infringe their rights. But people are permitted a necessary and proportionate defense of their rights against both violation *and infringement* (though perhaps what is proportionate to prevent violation may be disproportionate as a means of preventing infringement). Hence the civilians are permitted to kill the tactical bomber in self-defense. In doing so, however, they would infringe his right not to be killed by them. For while it is true that one may lose rights by threatening to violate rights, one does not lose rights by threatening to infringe rights. For one cannot lose rights merely by acting in a way that is morally justified. Thus, because the tactical bomber would merely infringe the rights of the civilians by killing them, he retains his own right not to be killed by them. It is therefore permissible for him to defend his right against infringement by killing them in preemptive self-defense. In short, he is justified in dropping his bomb, though that would infringe the rights of the civilians; they are justified in killing him to prevent him from infringing their rights; but their killing him would infringe his rights; hence he is also justified in killing them to prevent them from infringing his right not to be killed. Moreover, disinterested third parties may not intervene on behalf of either party to the conflict; for while they may, and sometimes must, prevent the *violation* of a right, they may not prevent the infringement of a right, since they must not kill a person in order to prevent him from engaging in morally justified action.

Only those whose rights would be infringed may do that; others must remain neutral.

The ease of translation here suggests the possibility of formulating a variant of the Rights-Based Account that is equivalent, or at least extensionally equivalent, to the Responsibility Account. We may, perhaps, think of the Rights-Based Account as developed by Thomson as only one way of filling out a formal structure that may yield a rather different theory when filled out with substantive assumptions different from those made by Thomson. Among these assumptions are that the conditions for the violation or infringement of a right are the same as the conditions of moral responsibility for an unjust harm and that it is permissible to resist the infringement as well as the violation of one's rights (though the proportionality restriction may be more stringent in the former case than in the latter). But while it is possible that all that I say may be translatable without loss into the idiom of rights, I will not investigate this possibility further here.

One worry that may arise is that the explanation I have given of why the civilians are justified in killing the tactical bomber in self-defense also applies to the potential victims of the falling fat man and the cell phone operator. If the civilians may kill the tactical bomber to prevent him from wronging them, why is it not similarly permissible for you to kill the falling fat man and the cell phone operator in order to prevent them from wronging you? Admittedly, there are many civilians and only one tactical bomber, whereas the exchange of lives in the other two cases would be one for one. But this consideration is offset by the fact that the tactical bomber, but not the fat man or the cell phone operator, poses an unjust threat through action that is objectively justified. In short, while the tactical bomber will wrong his victims with justification, both the fat man and the cell phone operator will wrong you *without justification*. Why may you not kill them?

The answer is that they will not in fact wrong you. Whether you are *wronged* is not a matter only of what happens to you. It also depends on facts about agency and responsibility. A falling boulder or a charging tiger may harm you but not wrong you. Moral responsibility is a precondition of wronging, and neither the fat man nor the cell phone operator satisfies the conditions of moral responsibility for the unjust threat he poses. The threat posed by the fat man is not a product of his responsible agency, while the threat posed by the cell phone operator cannot be foreseen by him—that is, he cannot know that he poses that threat. (Expressed in the language of rights, the claim here is that neither the fat man nor the cell phone operator will either violate or infringe your right not to be killed. Both violation and infringement of rights require moral responsibility. Indeed, infringement, as I understand it, refers to action that is morally justified. And the fat man, for example, is not justified in falling on you. Involuntarily falling is neither justified nor unjustified.)

In short, the tactical bomber, the fat man, and the cell phone operator all fail to meet the Responsibility Account's conditions of liability. But the tactical bomber does meet the account's conditions of responsibility; thus, his action will wrong the civilians. The reason he is released from liability is that he acts with justification. The fat man and the cell phone operator, by contrast, are not released from liability because they act with justification. The reason they are not liable is that they fail to meet the conditions of moral responsibility; and this means that though they act without justification, they will not wrong you even if they kill you.

Because they are not liable, all three—the tactical bomber, the fat man, and the cell phone operator—would be wronged by being killed. But at least in the circumstances as described, only the tactical bomber may permissibly be wronged. Acting with justification does not, it seems, afford the same degree of immunity as lack of moral responsibility.

Recall now three other cases we have discussed. The resident in the case of the identical twin, the conscientious driver, and the ambulance driver all seem to meet the conditions of responsibility for the unjust threats they pose. All will violate their victim's right not to be killed. For none acts with objective justification. It seems that all three are liable to defensive killing according to the Responsibility Account. (Perhaps implausibly in the view of most people, the one who may come closest to avoiding liability, according to the Responsibility Account, is the resident. For we can imagine that story in ways in which it would be virtually impossible for him to know, in the time in which it is reasonable for him to act, that the threat he poses is unjust. Even so, we may think it a relevant difference between him and the cell phone operator that he at least knows that he poses a threat, and thus is responsible for ensuring that it is not an unjust threat.)

It is, perhaps, tempting to think that these last three cases should be treated in the way I have suggested that we treat the case of the tactical bomber. Consider, for example, the conscientious driver. I have argued that he is liable by virtue of having chosen to engage in a risk-imposing activity. But this, it might be argued, is too flimsy a basis for a claim of liability. For many of the normal activities of life are risk-imposing, and it would be absurd to assign liability to people for simply living their lives in normal ways. Even just going out in public imposes risks of serious harm on others. One may, for example, be an asymptomatic carrier of a flu virus, which might prove fatal to a very young or very elderly person whom one might expose to it. (This, unlike the possibility of one's cell phone being secretly transformed into a detonator, is a possibility of which one is, or ought to be, aware.)

This suggestion is likely to be urged by a proponent of the Culpability Account, who claims that fault is necessary for liability. To be liable, on this view, one must depart in certain specific ways from the norms of ordinary social life. The defender of this view could argue, moreover, that the denial that the conscientious driver is liable does not entail that the pedestrian must allow herself to be killed—that is, that she may not kill in self-defense. For my own discussion of the tactical bomber concedes that there are justifications for killing that appeal to neither the victim's liability nor the necessity of averting a catastrophe. Why cannot we say that the pedestrian may kill the conscientious driver in self-defense simply because the conscientious driver will otherwise wrong her, or violate her rights, and that the conscientious driver, being free of liability because he is not culpable, is likewise permitted to kill the pedestrian in preemptive self-defense?

The problem is that this sort of resolution does not seem to be available in the conflict between the conscientious driver and the pedestrian. The case of the tactical bomber is special: what absolves him of liability is that he acts with objective justification. But this is not true of the conscientious driver. Even if he acts reasonably, he has no positive moral justification for doing what will kill the pedestrian. Since he will therefore *violate* the pedestrian's right not to be killed, it is unclear how he could be free of liability. Is it because he fails to meet the conditions of moral responsibility? No, because he clearly does meet those conditions. There is, moreover, a relevant difference between him and the pedestrian, which is that he chose to act in a way that exposed the pedestrian to a risk of serious harm whereas the pedestrian imposes no comparable risk on him. I believe, therefore, that it would be unjust if the conscientious driver, having chosen to do what exposed the pedestrian to risk, were then to kill her preemptively to prevent her from defending herself from the harm that he would otherwise, and without justification, cause her.

I continue to believe, therefore, that the Responsibility Account's implications for the case of the conscientious driver are more plausible than those of the Culpability Account. I do not, however, point to this in triumph, for this is not the kind of case against which we can usefully test a theory's implications. It is a case about which most of us have only weak or doubtful intuitions, and thus is precisely the sort of case for which we need guidance from a theory.

In criticizing the Culpability Account, I suggested that it seems plausible to regard those engaged in culpable attempts as liable to defensive action, even though they would otherwise cause no harm. If this is an objection to the Culpability Account, it is equally an objection to the Responsibility Account, which also insists on causation as a condition of liability. (The problem of attempts arises only in cases in which the Responsibility Account coincides with the Culpability Account—namely, cases involving culpable responsibility for an attempt to cause an unjust harm.)

In my earlier discussion of culpable attempts, I left the line-drawing problem unresolved. I will conclude by offering a brief argument in favor of retaining causation as a condition of liability. The argument appeals, not to attempts, but to a variant of the case of the conscientious driver. Suppose that when the driver's car goes out of control, it threatens another driver rather than a pedestrian. In this case, the imposition of risk has been reciprocal. Both drivers made the same choice to expose others to risk. But only one, through moral bad luck, now threatens unjust harm to the other. Most people are willing to allow that moral luck may affect liability and thus believe that only the driver who poses an unjust threat is liable. Most people, I think, would agree that the driver who is threatened would be justified in acting in self-defense but that the threatening driver would not be justified in acting to preempt the other's defensive action. If that is right, the mere imposition of risk—or, in the case of attempts, mere culpability—is not sufficient for liability in the absence of causation. Causal responsibility for an unjust threat is a necessary condition of liability to defensive killing.[12]

Notes

1. This view is developed and defended in Judith Jarvis Thomson's important article, "Self-Defense," *Philosophy and Public Affairs* 20 (1991): 283–310. Thomson uses the term "innocent aggressor" to refer to what I call an innocent threat. What she refers to as an innocent threat is what I call a nonresponsible threat.
2. Thomson, p. 287. In the story as she tells it, you can use your awning to deflect him past the edge of the deck onto the road below. Since there are accounts of the distinction between killing and letting die that would classify your deflecting him as allowing him to die rather than killing him, I have altered the example in a way that makes your act an uncontroversial instance of killing.
3. Judith Jarvis Thomson, *The Realm of Rights* (Cambridge, MA: Harvard University Press, 1990), p. 77.
4. I draw this distinction differently from the way Thomson does. Ibid., p. 122.
5. One question I will not pursue is whether a person may be liable for being culpably responsible for a threat that is not unjust because the victim is liable to that threat. There are two relevant types of case. In one, a case of "unknown justification," an agent poses a threat to which the potential victim is in fact liable though the agent acts on a wrongful reason in ignorance of the reasons that could justify his action. In the other, a case of "ostensible justification," an agent poses a threat to which the potential victim is liable but does so for a wrongful reason on the pretense of acting on the basis of the justifying reason. In these cases, it is controversial not only whether the agent is justified but also whether the potential victim has a right of self-defense.
6. Some parts of this section draw on my "Self-Defense and Culpability," forthcoming in *Law and Philosophy*. That paper comments on an account of the right of self-defense advanced by Kimberly Kessler Ferzan in "Justifying Self-Defense," which is also forthcoming in *Law and Philosophy* and from which I have learned a great deal.
7. This is the view defended by Ferzan in "Justifying Self-Defense.".

8. I argue for this in *The Ethics of Killing: Problems at the Margins of Life* (New York: Oxford University Press, 2002), pp. 398–411.
9. For relevant discussion, see Steven Shavell, "Strict Liability versus Negligence," *Journal of Legal Studies* 9 (1980): 1–25; and Douglas Husak, "Vehicles and Crashes: Why is this Moral Issue Overlooked?," *Social Theory and Practice* 30 (2004): 351–70.
10. I owe this objection to Kai Draper.
11. See *The Ethics of Killing*, pp. 401–5.
12. For perceptive written comments on an earlier draft, I am grateful to Shawn Bayern, Ruth Chang, Kimberly Kessler Ferzan, Peter Vallentyne, and Alec Walen. I am also indebted to Judith Jarvis Thomson for comments on an earlier manuscript from which this article draws. For exceptionally stimulating discussion, I am grateful to Larry Alexander, Allen Buchanan, Agnieszka Jaworska, Sanford Kadish, Shelly Kagan, Frances Kamm, Christopher Kutz, William McMahan, Eric Rakowski, Larry Temkin, Eric Wampler, and, especially, Samuel Scheffler.

Part V
Attempts

[14]

Impossibility in Criminal Attempts—Legality and the Legal Process

Arnold N. Enker*

Problems of criminal attempts have exerted a fascination for legal scholars far beyond their significance in terms of the number of litigated cases which actually pose difficult issues. Probably the largest volume of legal writing has dealt with what seems to be the most intractable problem of all, namely, impossibility, factual and legal.[1] Perhaps one reason we have not yet laid the dragon to rest is that we have used the wrong analytic weapons. Attempt, together with legal and factual impossibility, too often have been viewed solely as problems of mens rea.[2] The major thesis of this article is that when the issue of impossibility is approached as an aspect of the broader problem of understanding the role of the criminal act in the statutory definition of substantive crime, the doctrine of impossibility becomes a useful tool in forwarding legal analysis.

I. INTRODUCTION

Some words of definition are necessary. For convenience of usage the following terms shall be used as indicated: *Act*—the defendant's physical bodily movements; *Circumstances* or *attendant circumstances*—the external, objective situation which the substantive law may require be present in addition to the defendant's act before he can be convicted of the substantive crime; *Conduct*—the act combined with the circumstances regarded by the substantive law as relevant; *Consequences* or *result*—an additional occurrence caused by the defendant's act.[3]

A few examples of the application of such terminology will be helpful. The crime of possession of stolen goods contains among its elements an act, namely, possession of goods. It also

---

* Professor, University of Minnesota Law School.

1. Two recent revivals of the issue are Elkind, *Impossibility in Criminal Attempts: A Theorist's Headache*, 54 VA. L. REV. 20 (1968), and Hughes, *One Further Footnote on Attempting the Impossible*, 42 N.Y.U.L. REV. 1005 (1967). Professor Hughes' effort is a more significant contribution than its title suggests.

2. *But see* Smith, *Two Problems in Criminal Attempts*, 70 HARV. L. REV. 422, 447-48 (1957); Smith, *Two Problems in Criminal Attempts Re-Examined-II*, 1962 CRIM. L. REV. (Eng.) 212.

3. The terminology is not original. *See* Smith, *supra* note 2; MODEL PENAL CODE § 2.02, comment at 124 (Tent. Draft No. 4, 1955).

contains an attendant circumstance, that the goods possessed be stolen. For the defendant to be guilty of the substantive crime both elements—the act and the circumstance—must be present, but the defendant's act need not cause any additional consequence or result. His act of possession combined with the circumstance that the goods possessed are stolen constitute all the objective elements of the crime.

The crime of smuggling requires the act of bringing goods into the country without paying a duty and the circumstance that customs duty be due on the goods. Again, defendant's act need not cause any additional result.

For murder, although some act by the defendant is ordinarily required—non-acts or omissions will occasionally suffice—no specific act is defined in the statute as being an element of the offense. Nor are there any attendant circumstances which must be present to constitute the substantive crime. To be guilty of murder the defendant must do an act, any act, that causes the forbidden result—the death of a human being.[4]

Admittedly, these classifications are not airtight. Murder could be defined as an act of killing or as requiring the presence of the circumstance of a living person. There are a variety of acts which could constitute a taking for purposes of theft or possession in the crime of possession of stolen goods. Nonetheless, their application to most cases is substantially free of difficulty. And since their proposed use in this article is not as a definitional basis for the application of different legal rules but as analytic tools or aids to disclose problems not always apparent in the cases, they appear useful.

The most typical group of attempt cases involves the situation in which the accused has not committed the act required by the substantive crime: he has not penetrated his intended rape victim, he has not taken the money from his robbery victim, or he has not attained possession of the goods whose possession was forbidden. Of course, since he has not committed the forbidden act, he cannot be convicted of the substantive crime. The issue of his possible guilt for attempting to commit the substantive crime usually turns on whether his acts have gone beyond the point of innocence, called preparation.

Occasionally, one of these cases will present a problem of

4. There must also be a mens rea, but we are here concerned with describing the components of the elements of these crimes other than mens rea.

impossibility. It was impossible for the defendant to penetrate his intended rape victim because he is impotent. Or it was impossible for the defendant to take the money from the robbery victim or from the person whose pocket he picked because the victim had no money at the time. If still thought of in terms of impossibility, these cases are called "factual impossibility," which is no longer regarded as a defense.

A second group of cases presents the situation in which the defendant's failure to bring about the forbidden result—the death of the intended victim, the destruction of the fetus—is what precludes conviction for the substantive crime. If the defendant has not done the last act thought necessary to cause the forbidden result, a prosecution for attempt once again will usually raise a preparation-attempt issue. If he has done that last act or one very close to it, but the circumstances are such that the apparent likelihood of success was remote or nonexistent, the issue of factual impossibility will again be raised. Occasionally, in extreme cases, it may be treated as properly raised and will succeed as a defense. I shall later examine the need for two separate doctrines, preparation-attempt and factual impossibility, and the role played by the latter doctrine.

The final group of cases presents the most controversial situation, that in which the defendant has committed the forbidden act in its narrow sense—he has forcefully penetrated his intended rape victim, or he has secured possession of the forbidden goods—but one of the external elements of the substantive crime, what I have earlier called an attendant circumstance, is absent: the woman was his wife, or the goods were not in fact stolen. Again, of course, the defendant cannot be convicted of violating the substantive crime since one of its elements, this time a circumstance, is absent from the case.

The last category describes the most famous "impossibility" cases. For example, in *Jaffe*[5] the defendant committed the act of receiving the goods, but the circumstance that they be stolen was absent; in the "case" of Lady Eldon,[6] the "defendant" committed the act of bringing the goods into the country and did not pay any duty, but the circumstance that the goods be dutiable was absent; in *Wilson*,[7] the defendant committed the act

5. People v. Jaffe, 185 N.Y. 497, 78 N.E. 169 (1906).

6. 1 F. Wharton, Criminal Law § 225, at 304 n.9 (12th ed. 1932). *See also* M. Paulsen & S. Kadish, Criminal Law and Its Processes 480-86 (1962).

7. Wilson v. State, 85 Miss. 687, 38 So. 46 (1905).

of altering the figures on the check, but the circumstance of materiality was absent; and in *Teal*,[8] the defendant committed the acts of taking an oath and testifying, one attendant circumstance, falsity, was present, but again the substantive offense was not committed because the circumstance of materiality was absent.

In these cases, it is claimed by most contemporary writers, if the evidence establishes that when the defendant committed the act he believed that the missing circumstance was present, he should be guilty of attempting to commit the substantive crime.[9] The policy grounds supporting this position are well known and do not require elaboration. Stated concisely, the defendant's mens rea is the same as that of a guilty person. By committing the proscribed act he has demonstrated his readiness to carry out his illegal venture, and therefore he has shown himself to be as deserving of conviction and as in need of correctional handling as the guilty defendant who does the act under the proscribed circumstances.[10] The Model Penal Code takes this position. Section 5.01(1) provides:

> A person is guilty of an attempt to commit a crime if, acting with the kind of culpability otherwise required for commission of the crime, he:
>
> (a) purposely engages in conduct which would constitute the crime if the attendant circumstances were as he believes them to be; or
>
> (b) when causing a particular result is an element of the crime, does or omits to do anything with the purpose of causing or with the belief that it will cause such result without further conduct on his part; or
>
> (c) purposely does or omits to do anything which, under the circumstances as he believes them to be, is an act or omission constituting a substantial step in a course of conduct planned to culminate in his commission of the crime.

As the draftsmen indicate in their comments to this section, these provisions eliminate the defense of impossibility by making the actor's liability turn on his purpose considered in the light of his beliefs concerning the attendant situation rather than the

8. People v. Teal, 196 N.Y. 372, 89 N.E. 1086 (1909).

9. J. Hall, General Principles of Criminal Law 594-99 (2d ed. 1960) [hereinafter cited as Hall]; G. Williams, Criminal Law, The General Part 635-37, 646-51, (2d ed. 1961) [hereinafter cited as Williams]. Recent legislation is consistent with this trend. *See, e.g.*, Wechsler, Jones, & Korn, *The Treatment of Inchoate Crimes in the Model Penal Code of the American Law Institute: Attempt, Solicitation and Conspiracy*, 61 Colum. L. Rev. 571, 579 nn.25-30 (1961) (references cited); Minn. Stat. § 609.17(2) (1967); N.Y. Penal Law § 110.10 (McKinney 1967).

10. M. Paulsen & S. Kadish, *supra* note 6, at 483.

actual facts surrounding his act.[11]

As a matter of convenient terminology, in this article the issue raised in this third group of cases will be called "legal impossibility." Some would prefer to call these cases "factual impossibility" just as those in groups 1 and 2, and to reserve legal impossibility for those cases in which the defendant's mistake concerns not the presence or absence of a circumstance in the defined crime but the presence or absence of any crime at all. To use the *Jaffe* example, these writers would say that if Jaffe possessed stolen goods believing his conduct to be a crime, but the statute declaring it a crime had been repealed the day before, Jaffe would not be guilty of attempting to commit the crime of possession of stolen goods because of the doctrine of legal impossibility.[12]

Of course, it does not particularly matter what it is called so long as we all understand clearly what we are talking about. Yet it does seem strange that a system that places so much stress on procedural legality should require a special, obscure and dimly understood doctrine to deal with such an elementary problem.[13] But more important than this aesthetic consideration, to restrict the term legal impossibility to this narrow class of cases leaves the single term factual impossibility the duty of doing service for all three groups of cases described above. Since, as I shall attempt to demonstrate, the cases in our controversial last group raise some problems that are significantly different from those present in the other two groups, they deserve to be given their own identity. And since these unique problems are problems of substantive legality in the criminal process, the

---

11. Wechsler, Jones, & Korn, *supra* note 9, at 585.

12. HALL at 586-87; WILLIAMS at 633-35; Hughes, *supra* note 1, at 1006-07. The classification is no doubt influenced by the authors' desires to reconcile their views of the proper result in these cases with the traditional learning that legal impossibility acquits while factual impossibility is not a defense. The categories, then, are merely descriptive of the desired results. They do not further analysis of the underlying problems.

13. Williams asserts, correctly, that:

> [*i*]*t should need no demonstration* that a person who commits or attempts to commit what is not a crime in law cannot be convicted of attempting to commit a crime, and it makes no difference that he thinks it is a crime.

WILLIAMS at 633 (emphasis added). Hall is equally insistent that to make such conduct a criminal attempt would violate the principle of legality. HALL at 586. The reader should consider the obvious problems that would be involved in determining the offense to be charged in the indictment or the sentence applicable to this attempt. *Cf.* Hughes, *supra* note 1, at 1016.

term legal impossibility seems an appropriate description for the problems raised by *Jaffe*, Lady Eldon, et al.

II. LEGALITY AND CRIMINAL ACT

Legality requires that the forbidden conduct be defined in advance. This is in part so that the citizen will receive advance guidance as to what conduct is forbidden. But it is well recognized that the requirement of advance definition also serves to control the discretion, and thereby minimize the bias, of those officers of the criminal process who make decisions affecting the defendant.[14]

The defendant's intent, his purpose, his belief or knowledge as regards external facts often may all be inferred from character and reputation. They can easily become the subject of credibility contests concerning statements and admissions allegedly made. The outcome of these contests will be influenced by the trier's assessment of the defendant's reputation. To the extent that these issues are permitted to become the determining issues in criminal trials, justice is likely to be too greatly influenced by such factors as the defendant's popularity or unpopularity in the community, his associations which accomplice testimony is likely to show to be damaging even if the accomplices are lying, and his prior convictions received into evidence ostensibly to prove his intent or motive or identity.

By requiring the presence of specified objective conduct defined in advance, the law limits the powers of police to arrest "undesirable persons" and controls the jury's power to speculate as to the defendant's intent. There must first be evidence of specific conduct. Acts extend beyond the actor. They often generate consequences and they have a degree of visibility, all of which make it more difficult to lie about them. The issues seem more precise and controlled, less speculative and inferential, when one is arguing whether the defendant committed the acts charged than when the issue is his state of mind.[15]

---

14. *See* Musser v. Utah, 333 U.S. 95, 97 (1948); H. PACKER, THE LIMITS OF THE CRIMINAL SANCTION 79-80 (1968); WILLIAMS at 605-06; Amsterdam, *Federal Constitutional Restrictions on the Punishment of Crimes of Status, Crimes of General Obnoxiousness, Crimes of Displeasing Police Officers, and the Like*, 3 CRIM. L. BULL. 205, 216-17, 220-24 (1967); Note, *Due Process Requirements of Definiteness in Statutes*, 62 HARV. L. REV. 77-78 (1948); Note, *The Void-for-Vagueness Doctrine in the Supreme Court*, 109 U. PA. L. REV. 67 (1960).

15. This is, of course, at the core of the objections to status crimes. *See* Robinson v. California, 370 U.S. 660 (1962).

The degree to which the objective conduct elements of the crime are defined in advance vary from case to case. Thus, for example, robbery is a crime in which the objective requirements are relatively precisely set forth; there must be a taking of goods belonging to another, accompanied by force or the threat thereof. No matter how anti-social or in need of rehabilitation a particular defendant may be regarded, he cannot be convicted of robbery unless it is established that he engaged in the specific conduct defined in advance by the law. We can move across a spectrum of statutory crimes and find crimes in which the objective conduct elements of the offense are less precisely set forth in advance.

An extreme case of dispensing with the requirement that the crime encompass specific conduct defined in advance is the crime of conspiracy. Theoretically, conspiracy does contain a predefined act, agreement. But actually the "agreement" requirement has little independent significance. Parallel conduct[16] and spontaneous momentary collaboration for a single incident without prior consultation or planning[17] have been held to constitute agreements for purposes of the conspiracy concept so that the agreement requirement may contain no more delimitation than the knowing mutually related activity of two or more persons. Perhaps more significantly, rarely is the act of agreement proved by direct evidence. Judges commonly warn juries not to expect such proof in view of the secret nature of most conspiracies. The agreement is "proved" by inference from the acts of the alleged conspirators. But this means that in reality there is no pre-specified objective act, circumstance or consequence which must be established before one can be convicted of conspiracy. Any course of conduct from which the jury may infer an "agreement" will do. With such latitude given to uncontrolled inference, the danger of ad hoc judgment based on the trier's biases concerning the defendants rapidly

16. From all accounts the issue seems squarely presented in the prosecution of Dr. Spock in the disturbing context of free speech. Compare the discussion at pages 689-90, *infra*. The large-scale federal narcotics prosecutions are a good example of the limited independent significance of the requirement of an agreement. *E.g.*, United States v. Bentvena, 319 F.2d 916 (2d Cir.), *cert. denied*, 375 U.S. 940 (1963); United States v. Aviles, 274 F.2d 179 (2d Cir.), *cert. denied*, 362 U.S. 974 (1960); United States v. Bruno, 105 F.2d 921 (2d Cir. 1939). A fairly extreme example is United States v. Stromberg, 268 F.2d 256 (2d Cir.), *cert. denied*, 361 U.S. 863 (1959). *But see* United States v. Bufalino, 285 F.2d 408 (2d Cir. 1960).

17. See the materials contained in M. PAULSEN & S. KADISH, *supra* note 6, at 519-23.

increases.[18] It is no wonder that conspiracy is feared by those concerned with preserving legality.

Murder seems to be between the extremes of robbery and conspiracy. The only non-mens rea element of the offense of murder is causing death. The statutes ordinarily do not set forth in advance any specific act of the defendant or any set of external circumstances as an essential element of the offense. Any act done by the defendant will furnish a basis for conviction if that act caused death. Theoretically, this situation, as in the case of conspiracy, might be thought to present dangers of after-the-fact biased judgment imposing guilt on unpopular defendants. Since no particular act is required, and mens rea can be proved by confessions, testimony of unreliable informers, or proof of prior crimes, there may be great potential for biased prosecutor selection of cases for prosecution and prejudiced jury reliance on such relatively unreliable evidence.

But this theoretical danger is largely offset by the remaining requirements that the defendant cause and intend to cause the victim's death. First, it is rare that people in our society cause the death of others or become involved in circumstances creating such suspicion so that the opportunity for biased prosecution presented by the lack of a defined act can be expected to be extremely low. Second, while the murder statute does not limit itself to any specifically described conduct, the requirement of causation limits the acts that can be a basis for prosecution. To use two extreme examples, if the defendant had intoned mystic incantations or placed sugar in the deceased's tea immediately before the deceased's death, a jury doubtless would not be permitted to speculate concerning the defendant's mens rea because there would be no evidence that the defendant in fact caused the death. The requirement of causation, then, overcomes the absence of a defined act by limiting prosecution to those cases in which the defendant's acts bear an objective "teleological relationship"[19] to the death in the case.[20] Finally,

---

18. For an example, see pages 705-06, *infra*.

19. The phrase is Jerome Hall's. *See* HALL at 195-98. Compare the following Biblical verses defining the objective elements of murder:

> Anyone, however, who strikes another with an iron object so that death results is a murderer; the murderer must be put to death. If he struck him with a stone *tool* [literally—"a stone of the hand"] *that could cause death*, and death resulted, he is a murderer; the murderer must be put to death. Similarly, if the object with which he struck him was a wooden *tool* [literally—"a wood of the hand"] *that could cause death*, and death resulted, he is a murderer; the murderer must be put to death.

the requirement of intent ordinarily requires evidence of purposive conduct, of the kind of conduct one would expect from someone who deliberately kills as distinguished from an apparently accidental killing.

III. ATTEMPT—THE NEED FOR LEGISLATIVE DELEGATION TO THE COURTS, THE PROBLEM OF LEGALITY, AND THE TECHNIQUE OF ANALOGY AS A SOLUTION

Attempt is a crime in which no precise act requirement is defined in advance. By definition, attempt involves a situation in which at least one of the objective elements of the substantive crime was lacking. That, after all, is the reason the defendant is not guilty of the substantive crime. The problem in attempt is to define what objective elements may be dispensed with and which, if any, are necessary to constitute the crime.

Probably the most common attempt case is that in which the defendant has not committed the act, as narrowly defined, required for the substantive crime. He has engaged "in a course

---

Numbers 35:16-18, in THE TORAH, THE FIVE BOOKS OF MOSES 318 (Jew. Publ. Soc. transl., 1962) (emphasis added).

Commenting on additional elements contained in the second and third verses, the Talmud, B Sanhedrin 76b, explains that the Bible does not fix an objective measure for an iron object because any iron object is capable of piercing the body, thereby causing death. The Babylonian Talmud, 2 Sanhedrin 519 (Soncino trans. 1935).

20. This analysis suggests some of the reasons our law hesitates to punish omissions. Since it is the element of causation that introduces neutrality and objectivity into the proceedings by insisting upon an objective or apparent causal relationship between the act and the death, omissions—which cannot themselves cause death, but do so only in conjunction with external circumstances—do not provide an objective limit to prosecutable cases. To establish such an objective limit we must define the relationship between the defendant's failure to act and the external circumstances. But just as the acts which may cause death are so varied that they cannot be defined in advance, so too the situations in which a passive person "cooperates with" external circumstances to bring about death are too varied to be defined in advance. A substitute the legal system has found for the undefinable pattern of relationships between omissions and death-causing acts is the defined patterns of relationships between the passive party and the deceased—*e.g.*, parent-child, doctor-patient, husband-wife—expressed in the notion of duty. These duty relationships are more susceptible of definition than the act relationships, although even here there are severe limits.

The old argument that omissions cannot "cause" death does, then, express an insight, however inadequately. Omissions do pose special legality problems apart from problems of proving the mens rea. *But see* HALL at 194-98, 208.

of conduct planned to culminate in"[21] the forbidden act, but he was stopped short of culmination. The robber was overcome before he took the money, the rapist was stopped before he penetrated the woman, or the "fence" was arrested before he acquired possession of the stolen goods.

These cases can cover a broad spectrum of possible acts beginning with the defendant's very first act in the planned illegal "course of conduct" and ending with the very last act short of that act which constitutes the substantive crime. For well known reasons, we are unwilling to regard every single act along this spectrum adequate for an attempt. Our problem, then, is to define the point along this spectrum at which the act requirement for the crime of attempt is satisfied. But because of the infinite variations in fact patterns that may occur short of the consummated substantive crime, it is usually impossible for the legislature to state in advance which acts or group of acts should be classified as attempts and which should not. The only technique available is a broad legislative delegation of power to the courts to extend the policies underlying the substantive crimes to individual cases of attempt.

Because attempt is a relational crime—it is defined in relation to the statutorily defined substantive crime allegedly attempted—there is available a judicial technique for deciding individual cases, namely the technique of analogy. Cases arising along the preparation-attempt spectrum are handled in terms of their similarities to and differences from the substantive crime attempted, and in terms of analogy to previously decided or hypothetical attempt cases.[22] In deciding, the court weighs several factors, principally: whether the act at issue is sufficiently close to the substantive crime or close enough to potential irreparable harm so as to preclude any further postponement of official intervention; whether the defendant's conduct has progressed to the point that one may be reasonably certain that he is firmly committed to a specific illegal venture rather than merely contemplating the possible future commission of a crime; and whether the act is sufficiently unambiguous to demonstrate the actor's illegal intent.

In light of our earlier discussion of the relationship between legality and the requirements that the act element of the crime be defined in advance, prosecution for attempt contains potential

21. Model Penal Code § 5.01(1)(c) (Proposed Official Draft, 1962).

22. *See* Arnold, *Criminal Attempts—The Rise and Fall of an Abstraction*, 40 YALE L.J. 53 (1930).

for arbitrary ex post facto judgments. But in large measure this danger is mitigated by the following factors: (1) The requirement that the defendant intend to commit the substantive crime: while recklessness or negligence may be adequate for certain substantive crimes, they are not adequate for attempts. This has the effect of limiting the acts which can be held to be attempts to those which appear to be intentionally directed toward the acts defined in the substantive crime, or toward bringing about the illegal result, a process similar to that noted above in the case of murder.[23] (2) The requirement that the act evidence commitment to the criminal venture and corroborate the mens rea: to the extent that this requirement is preserved it prevents the conviction of persons engaged in innocent acts on the basis of a mens rea proved through speculative inferences, unreliable forms of testimony and/or past criminal conduct. (3) The use of the technique of analogy whereby the decision in each case must be rationalized in comparison with other more or less similar cases which presumably were decided neutrally. (4) Finally, the alternative to running the risk of occasional erroneous or arbitrary judgment is to prosecute only those attempts which can be carefully defined in advance, a rather intolerable option at least in the case of the more serious crimes.

Though it does not ordinarily occur to us, our legal system could have adopted a completely different technique for distinguishing culpable attempts from those which are not culpable but are rather, in the conventional terminology, preparations. It would have been possible to eliminate the preparation-attempt dichotomy, thereby eliminating any notion of particular indispensable acts, and simply approach each case in terms of whether the evidence at hand is sufficient to prove the necessary

23. Because negligence is a far less defined criterion of fault than intent, liability for negligently caused homicide increases the risk of biased judgment. See the illuminating collection of materials relating to the *Welansky* case [316 Mass. 383, 55 N.E.2d 902 (1944)] in R. DONNELLY, J. GOLDSTEIN & R. SCHWARTZ, CRIMINAL LAW 587-600 (1962). If negligence were a basis for attempt liability, we would have a crime requiring no particular act or circumstance, no consequence, and no defined mens rea. The crime would be acting in a way that unreasonably risks someone's life. And, apart from the lack of definition in such a crime, the jury would be asked to evaluate the harmful tendencies of conduct that did not result in harm. If we are to have such a crime, at least the penalties should be very light. It would not do, for example, to treat certain negligent conduct as attempted manslaughter. *See* MODEL PENAL CODE § 201.11 (Tent. Draft No. 9, 1959) (reckless conduct a misdemeanor); Wechsler, *The Challenge of a Model Penal Code*, 65 HARV. L. REV. 1097, 1106-07 (1952).

intent, encompassing intent and commitment to the venture, or will.[24] But even the Model Penal Code resolution of the issue does not rely solely on the sufficiency of the evidence to prove intent and will. It, too, requires that the act itself be "a substantial step" toward completion of the crime and that the act corroborate "the actor's criminal purpose."[25]

There are several reasons justifying our reluctance to substitute a sufficiency-of-the-evidence test for the act requirement. Degrees of commitment vary so that we would again lack an objective criterion in cases falling short of consummation. Accomplice testimony and alleged confessions would ordinarily meet the sufficiency hurdles so that this would be an inadequate technique for controlling the jury unless corroboration standards were tightened.[26] Defendants with prior criminal records for similar crimes would be particularly vulnerable under such an approach.[27] And the technique of analogy would be considerably less significant, possibly resulting in less judicial objectivity.

To summarize, then, the determination of a rule for these cases is necessarily delegated by the legislature to the court. The court must then define the objective conduct essential to a conviction for attempt on a case-by-case basis by employing the judicial technique of analogy.

IV. LEGAL IMPOSSIBILITY

A. The Act and Proof of Mens Rea

The preparation-attempt-substantive-crime continuum presents a workable model for the identification and solution of the problems posed by those attempts in which the defendant has not yet committed the act element of the substantive crime. But let us turn to that group of cases which raises the issue we have called legal impossibility.

Consider the now infamous Lady Eldon.

> Lady Eldon, when traveling with her husband on the Continent, bought what she supposed to be a quantity of French lace, which she hid, concealing it from Lord Eldon in one of the pock-

---

24. The thought has occurred to Dr. Glanville Williams. *See* Williams, *Police Control of Intending Criminals*, 1955 Crim. L. Rev. (Eng.) 66, 69.

25. Model Penal Code §§ 5.01(1)(c), (2) (Proposed Official Draft, 1962).

26. *See* page 709, *infra*.

27. See the examples discussed at pages 690-91, *infra*.

> ets of the coach. The package was brought to light by a custom officer at Dover. The lace turned out to be an English manufactured article of little value and, of course, not subject to duty. Lady Eldon had bought it at a price vastly above its value, believing it to be genuine, intending to smuggle it into England.[28]

Lady Eldon has committed the forbidden act—importing the lace and not paying duty—but a circumstance is missing—the goods are not dutiable. Preparation-attempt is clearly an irrelevant dichtomy to this case. Having done the act, the defendant has clearly gone beyond the stage of preparation. Yet some of the same concerns that required us to develop that dichotomy in the first group of cases, and caused us to hold acts of preparation inadequate for conviction, may be present in these legal impossibility cases as well. If so, we are in need of a new analytic tool to help identify and solve these problems in this context. The doctrine of legal impossibility may be that tool.

The argument that Lady Eldon should be convicted of attempted smuggling is that having gone beyond preparatory acts to the point where she has committed the very act defined by the crime—importing the lace—it is clear that she is fully committed to her illegal escapade. Only the accidental absence of an external circumstance required by the statute—that the imported goods be dutiable—precludes liability for the substantive crime. Since she thought the goods were dutiable, intended to avoid paying the duty, and did all the acts that would have supported substantive liability had the facts been as she thought, she should be guilty of an attempt.

But, we are entitled to ask, if Lady Eldon's handkerchief really is cheap linen, how do we know that she thought it was expensive dutiable lace? The facts state that she "hid" the lace, "concealing" it in a pocket, but those are loaded words that assume the very thing at issue, namely that she sought to avoid a duty she mistakenly believed due. Where there are present two objective factors—lace subject to import duty and an act of concealment—the coincidence of an objective motive to smuggle and conduct consistent with that motive and supportive of that goal is fair ground for the conclusion that Lady Eldon in fact intended to avoid paying the duty. If we remove the objective existence of the motive, the evidentiary basis for the conclusion that she intended to evade a duty believed due is correspondingly weakened.

An even more questionable assumption of Wharton's hypo-

28. 1 F. WHARTON, *supra* note 6.

thetical is that the term "concealing" has as objective a meaning as Wharton gives it. Objectively all one can say is that Lady Eldon placed the handkerchief in the seat pocket. To say that she "concealed" it there is to assume that she intended to hide something, to avoid paying a duty believed due, the very motive which must be proved. Once this is recognized, the probative relationship between the circumstance of dutiability and intent to avoid the duty can be made clearer.[29]

Suppose, instead of placing the handkerchief in the seat pocket, as in Wharton's hypothetical, Lady Eldon had simply kept it in her purse and had not declared it in her customs declaration. We all know that customs inspectors almost never examine the arriving traveler's person. Had the handkerchief been dutiable, Lady Eldon would have been under a duty to declare it and her failure to declare it would have been an objective act of concealment corroborating any other proof of intent to avoid the duty. Thus, a returning tourist who wears his new Swiss watch on his wrist as he enters the country presumably "clandestinely introduces"[30] that watch into the country if he does not declare it. If, however, the goods are not in fact dutiable, failure to declare them is of no significance. The elimination of the circumstantial element that the goods in fact be subject to duty not only eliminates the objective basis for positing a motive to conceal the goods but it also deprives us of a simple and convenient reference point for evaluating the "clandestine" character of the defendant's act.

In the situation, then, where Lady Eldon keeps the handkerchief in her purse, we have no objective basis for concluding either that she has a motive to smuggle or that she acted clandestinely. Of course, one can suppose a case in which the lace is placed in the false bottom of Lady Eldon's suitcase. The evidence of mens rea would be quite strong. But if Lady Eldon could be convicted of attempted smuggling under the facts of Wharton's hypothetical or in the case of the false bottomed suitcase even though the goods are not in fact dutiable, she can also

29. Hughes, *supra* note 1, at 1024-26, recently trod a somewhat different path to the same argument.

30. This is one of the operative terms of the federal smuggling statute. 18 U.S.C. § 545 (1964). Note that the statute permits an inference of guilt from possession of such goods. The inference clearly would have no rational basis in an attempt prosecution where the goods were in fact legally in the country but the defendant allegedly thought there were unimportable or dutiable. *See* Sherman v. United States, 268 F. 516 (5th Cir. 1920); United States v. Lot of Jewelry, 26 F. Cas. 994 (No. 15,626) (C.C.S.D.N.Y. 1875).

be convicted of attempted smuggling when she keeps them in her purse, for we have dispensed with the need to establish dutiability as an element of the crime. To convict Lady Eldon in either case is to substitute a sufficiency-of-the-evidence-to-prove-intent test for an indispensable objective element of the crime, an approach our law rejects in the preparation-attempt cases.

Let us apply a similar analysis to another famous legal impossibility case, *People v. Jaffe*.[31] It will be recalled that in that case a thief had in his possession certain goods stolen from their true owner and had arranged to deliver them to defendant Jaffe. Before Jaffe actually came into possession of the goods the thief was arrested by the police and the goods were recovered. Having decided to cooperate with the police who wanted to catch Jaffe, the thief, with the consent of the owner of the goods and under police surveillance, delivered the goods to Jaffe as arranged. Jaffe was then arrested with the goods in his possession. Jaffe was charged in two presumably alternative counts with possession of stolen goods and attempted possession of stolen goods. The court held that Jaffe was not guilty of possession of stolen goods because the elements of that crime include the requirement that the goods possessed be stolen in fact, whereas at the time they were delivered into Jaffe's possession they had been recovered and hence were not stolen goods. It also held him not guilty of attempt. Disregarding the court's often criticized and rather mechanical line of reasoning, let us consider the attempt issue afresh.

Those who would eliminate the defense of legal impossibility from the legal lexicon and would convict Jaffe of attempted possession of stolen goods because he thought they were stolen presumably would convict any other defendant of the same crime with respect to goods that had never been stolen if it could be proved that the defendant thought they were stolen. Having dispensed with the need for establishing the circumstance that the goods are stolen, they must permit this result if there is evidence of guilty belief. Assume two cases in which the sole direct evidence of the defendant's alleged belief that the goods are stolen is a confession or the testimony of an informer or an accomplice. In one case the goods possessed are in fact stolen; in the other they are not. It is reasonably clear that most of us would rest easier with a conviction in the first case than in the second although we might have a difficult time articulating rea-

31. 185 N.Y. 497, 78 N.E. 169 (1906).

sons for this distinction. Some of the reasons for this distinction are explored below,[32] but it may also be that possession of stolen goods furnishes some evidence of belief that they are stolen while, clearly, possession of goods not in fact stolen furnishes no reason to believe that the defendant thought they were stolen.

This requires some elaboration. Concededly, the probative relationship between the fact that the goods are stolen and the possessor's knowledge that they are stolen differs from the probative relationship between, say, the fact that certain goods are machine guns or narcotics and the possessor's knowledge of their nature. Ordinarily, knowledge that goods are within one's possession carries with it knowledge of their physical nature. Where the defendant is proved to have had in his possession certain objects, say, narcotics, it seems reasonable to conclude that he knew the physical nature of those objects and to cast on him the risk of conviction if he does not adduce some evidence to dispel this normal inference.[33] It is clear, then, that to convict someone of attempted possession of narcotics for possessing non-narcotic goods which he allegedly believed were narcotics would be to redefine the crime of possession of narcotics to eliminate an objective element that had major evidentiary significance and to increase the risk of mistaken conclusions that the defendant believed the goods were narcotics.

The change is less clear in the case of possession of stolen goods. Physical possession of goods does not readily carry with it knowledge of their non-physical qualities, such as where they were made, who made them or whether they were stolen. But there is a change. Where the defendant is proved to have possessed goods recently stolen, the law permits the jury to infer that he knew they were stolen.[34] Although the stolen quality of the goods is not apparent upon observation, there is a rational basis for this inference.[35] In the first place there exists, or is believed to exist, a significant statistical correlation between possession of recently stolen goods and knowledge of the fact that they have been stolen. If we can say that in a given percentage of the cases the possessor knows the goods are stolen, then possession of stolen goods is probative of knowledge that

32. *See* pages 687-92, *infra*.

33. *See, e.g.*, Yee Hem v. United States, 268 U.S. 178 (1925).

34. 1 F. WHARTON, CRIMINAL EVIDENCE § 191, at 199 (11th ed. 1935); 9 J. WIGMORE, EVIDENCE § 2513 (3d ed. 1940).

35. While the literature considers the scope and effect of this presumption, there is a remarkable dearth of discussion of its rational basis.

the good are stolen at least in the sense that proof of possession of such goods makes it more likely that the defendant knew the goods were stolen than if there is no proof of possession.[36] What is more important for our purposes, however, is that whatever the statistical relation between possession and knowledge may be, the percentage of persons possessing unstolen goods who believe the goods are stolen is clearly much lower.[37]

Moreover, stolen goods normally enter the stream of commerce through illegal channels. If the goods have been recently stolen, the illegal channel through which they entered commerce is relatively proximate to the defendant's source of the goods and it is not unreasonable to draw inferences adverse to the defendant when he does not identify his source so that the channels of distribution may be traced back. Since goods not in fact stolen never entered the market through illegal channels, little or nothing is accomplished by forcing the defendant to explain his acquisition of the goods, particularly when it is recalled that creating presumptions which force a defendant to explain his conduct raises due process and fifth amendment problems.[38]

---

36. C. McCormick, Evidence § 152, at 317-19 (1954); 1 F. Wharton, Criminal Evidence § 224 (11th ed. 1935).

37. J. Maguire, Evidence of Guilt § 2.09, at 99 (1959), points out that the presumption arises after the corpus delicti has been established. A recent decision of the Supreme Court of Israel, discussed in Feller, *The Application of Presumptions to the Derivative Forms of an Offence*, 3 Israel L. Rev. 562 (1968), held that the statutory presumption of illegality arising from the possession of foreign currency did not apply when the defendant, apparently much to his surprise, was found possessing counterfeit foreign currency. The court thereby avoided discussion of the attempt issues. The author of the article criticizing the decision is certainly wrong in asserting broadly that "where a certain presumption has been introduced with regard to a specific offence, it applies not only to the completed offence but to all forms of criminal conduct derived therefrom [*e.g.*, attempt, solicitation]," *id.* at 569, or that "there are as a rule no grounds for distinguishing [with respect to presumptions] between attempts where it is impossible to complete the intended offence, because of the absence of a circumstance relevant to its commission, and attempts where the conduct constituting the offence is not in fact completed." *Id.* at 568. Where the rational basis for the presumption is rooted in the presence of one or more of the circumstantial elements required for the substantive offense, application of the presumption in the absence of the objective element would be arbitrary. When the defendant commits the forbidden act and the required circumstance is present, there may be a rational basis for a "presumption" that he knew the circumstance was present. But when the circumstance is absent, mere performance of the act (possession of goods, importing goods, etc.) furnishes by itself no basis for a presumption that the defendant thought the circumstance present. *See also* note 30, *supra*.

38. *See* J. Maguire, *supra* note 37, § 209, at 98-100; *cf.* United States v. Grainey, 380 U.S. 63, 71, 74 (1965) (dissenting opinions).

This analysis indicates that the elimination of the objective elements of the crime, such as that the goods possessed were in fact narcotics or were in fact stolen, creates new problems of proving the relevant mens rea just as the elimination of the requirement that the goods be in fact dutiable made proof of intent to evade the duty more problematic.

This is not to say merely that it makes it more difficult to prove the crime. If that were the sole problem, it could still be insufficient ground to argue against eliminating these elements, for we might still wish to convict those against whom we have adequate evidence. The point is, however, that by eliminating these objective elements we create newly defined crimes in which we replace the statutorily defined fixed reference points for judging the defendant's mens rea with an open-ended sufficiency-of-the-evidence test which may include the less reliable forms of evidence such as questionable admissions, the testimony of informers and accomplices, and proof of prior convictions.

The draftsmen of the Model Penal Code have argued that while eliminating legal impossibility as a defense, the Code adequately takes care of these problems by its separate provision requiring that the defendant's act corroborate his mens rea.[39] But the Model Penal Code's requirement that the act corroborate the mens rea applies only to cases in the preparation-attempt continuum. Cases such as *Jaffe* and Lady Eldon are covered by a separate provision which provides that where the defendant does any act which would constitute a crime under the circumstances as he thought them to be, he is guilty of an attempt. The corroboration requirement of section 5.01(2) does not apply to this section.[40] Perhaps the draftsmen assumed that doing the act defined in the substantive crime will always supply at least as much corroboration of mens rea as is present in the substantive crime itself. If so, what they have failed to see is that the act in its narrow sense of the defendant's physical movements can be perfectly innocent in itself—possession of goods, bringing goods

39. Wechsler, Jones, & Korn, *supra* note 9, at 584.

40. Impossibility cases are dealt with in paragraphs (1)(a) (what we have called factual impossibility) and (1)(b) (what we have called legal impossibility) of § 5.01. Paragraph (1)(c) deals with attempt-preparation cases. The corroboration requirement is contained in the first sentence of § 5.01(2) which is limited to defining the term "substantial step" under paragraph (1)(c). Indeed, paragraphs (1)(a) and (1)(b) do not require a "substantial step." And while some impossibility cases will fit under § (1)(c), the requirement of substantiality is judged there, too, by reference to "the circumstances as [the defendant] believes them to be . . ."

into the country—and that what gives the act character as corroborative of mens rea is often the objective element or the attendant circumstances that the goods possessed are in fact stolen, or that the goods brought into the country are in fact dutiable, or that the goods possessed are in fact narcotics.

B. Legal Impossibility: A Problem for the Court or the Legislature?

As we have seen, in all three cases—Lady Eldon, *Jaffe*, possession of narcotics—elimination of the objective circumstance required by the definition of the substantive crime would remove a stable focal point in the proof of the mens rea. Ultimately, of course, the issue to be decided is whether the costs outweigh the gains, whether the number of "dangerous" Lady Eldons and Jaffes whom we would like to convict but cannot because of the impossibility defense justifies such a loosening of the definition of the offenses as results from the elimination of legal impossibility from the lawyer's brief. But we are not yet ready to decide that issue. At this point it is appropriate to ask which agency of the community ought to resolve that question, the court or the legislature.

If the court is to resolve this problem, what techniques of judicial decision-making are available to aid it? It was indicated earlier that in the preparation-attempt cases the court looks to the statute defining the substantive crime and to other cases along the spectrum extending from commencement to completion of the criminal act and applies analogy as a tool in deciding whether to extend guilt to the attempt. But analogy is not a very useful technique in the Lady Eldon or *Jaffe* cases. There is no spectrum of numerous cases of varying degrees of similarity to the substantive crime. Vary the facts as we may, no Lady Eldon case will approach the substantive crime. We can speak of the defendant coming ever closer to the act of importing the lace, but we cannot speak of a series of cases in which the goods are ever more dutiable. We can, of course, construct a series of cases in each of which the proof of Lady Eldon's belief that the goods are dutiable becomes stronger but nothing in this group of cases helps the court decide analogically whether and when it should dispense with the objective element of the offense and allow to be substituted in its stead proof that defendant thought it existed. Similarly, one cannot speak of *Jaffe* and other such cases in which the goods are not in fact stolen as being more or less similar to the substantive crime.

One recent study of the problem suggests that such a comparison can be made. In an article largely in accord with the views here offered, Professor Graham Hughes talks of the court "matching [the defendant's] conduct with a model of success in completing the crime."[41] But notice the shift. In the preparation-attempt cases, where the defendant did not commit the required act, the attempt formula using the technique of analogy compares the defendant's acts to the act set forth in the statute defining the substantive crime. In these impossibility cases, where a required circumstance is missing, the proposal would compare the defendant's conduct not with the statutorily defined conduct but with an undefined "model of success." Nor is the notion of a "model of success" very helpful in deciding these cases. The "model of success" for the crime of possessing stolen goods is really nothing more than the simple act of possession. But this merely returns us to the problems already considered. If the "model" be broadened to include purchase at a low price and conversations between the thief and the fence, it becomes in effect a sufficiency-of-the-evidence-of-intent test in different garb, particularly since this evidence will most often come from the thief. So, too, in the case of smuggling where the "model of success" is importing goods clandestinely. But, as shown, the term "clandestinely" derives its relatively clear meaning from the fact that the goods are dutiable. Here perhaps the model can be broadened to include clearcut acts of concealment such as the rare case of the false bottomed suitcase. It is no longer clear, however, whether Lady Eldon should be convicted, that is, whether the presence of an inexpensive handkerchief in the seat cushion fits a "model of success" for smuggling. Abandonment of the defense of legal impossibility, then, cuts the court adrift by severing the ties between the actus reus of attempt and that of the substantive crime attempted, at the same time furnishing the court no new tools for deciding individual cases.

Further, the substantive smuggling statute not only furnishes a court no basis for concluding that Lady Eldon should be convicted of attempted smuggling, but the inclusion in the substantive statute of the objective element that the goods be subject to duty at least suggests that the legislature may not want to dispense with this element of the offense for any case. After all, it would have been equally simple for the legislature to have drafted the substantive smuggling statute in terms of importing goods believed to be dutiable rather than in terms of

41. Hughes, *supra* note 1, at 1030-34.

goods in fact dutiable. So, too, in drafting the substantive statute involved in *Jaffe*, nothing prevented the legislature from defining the crime as the possession of goods in the belief that they are stolen without also requiring that they be in fact stolen. As earlier suggested, a crucial factor justifying legislative delegation of the power to define the act element of attempts in the preparation-attempt cases was the inability of the legislature to provide for the infinitely varying acts in advance. In the case of the circumstantial elements of the crimes here considered—whether the goods are in fact dutiable, are stolen, or are narcotics—the legislature is perfectly capable of deciding in advance whether or not to require the particular element. There is no need to delegate that power to the courts under the attempt rubric.[42]

It may be helpful at this point to consider one additional legal impossibility case, *People v. Teal*.[43] The defendant had solicited false testimony to an alleged act of adultery in connection with a divorce proceeding. Since the solicited testimony related to an act other than that alleged in the divorce complaint, the court concluded that the testimony was immaterial. Materiality being one of the elements—an attendant circumstance in the terminology of this article—required by the substantive statute, defendant could not be convicted of subornation of perjury. She was, however, convicted in the lower court of attempted subornation of perjury, apparently on the ground that she thought the testimony was material. Her conviction was reversed on appeal by a divided court.

The draftsmen of the Model Penal Code provisions which dispense with the doctrine of impossibility question the decision on the ground that "rather than engaging in an exercise in futility, defendant sought to induce false testimony which he [*sic*] thought would be material."[44] The trouble with this argument is that the inference or assumption is equally true of just about every other case in which the false testimony is immaterial, yet the legislature required that the testimony in fact be material, not that the defendant think it is material. If the argument is accepted, what the legislature sought to exclude from

42. It seems reasonably clear that the real issue in *Jaffe* is whether once stolen goods now recovered are "stolen" within the meaning of the statute defining the substantive crime. This issue should be resolved in the context of that count of the indictment charging the substantive offense, not in an attempt context.

43. 196 N.Y. 372, 89 N.E. 1086 (1909).

44. Wechsler, Jones, & Korn, *supra* note 9, at 579 n.32.

the substantive crime, by imposing the requirement of materiality, the court would reintroduce by convicting the defendant of attempt.

The point is not merely that the legislature should be understood to have expressed a policy that persons who testify falsely to immaterial matters should not be convicted of crime. This might be challenged; after all, in the preparation-attempt cases we did not regard the legislative inclusion of an act requirement in the substantive crime as a declaration of policy inconsistent with the conviction for attempt of some persons who do not commit the otherwise required act. But in those cases the legislature was incapable of defining all the required acts in advance; it had no choice but to define the modal crime, leaving other cases to the courts under the attempt rubric. Here the legislature is perfectly capable of declaring a contrary view for *Teal* and every other case in which the false testimony is immaterial simply by striking the word material from the substantive crime. Here there is no need to leave matters in an undefined state and delegate decision of the issue to the court.

Indeed, there are policy grounds for taking the substantive statute at face value and limiting guilt to cases in which the testimony is material. One such ground again concerns the relationship between the circumstance, this time materiality, and proof of the mens rea. One is much more readily, and more reasonably, led to the inference that the falsification is deliberate when it concerns a material matter than when it is immaterial.[45]

We may, therefore, characterize the issue presented by legal

45. The Model Penal Code definition of perjury, § 208.20(1), retains the requirement of materiality. The draftsmen offer other reasons. Model Penal Code § 208.20, comment at 104-05 (Tent. Draft No. 6, 1957). Nonmaterial false testimony is covered by the separate substantive crime of false swearing, in § 208.21. *See id.* at 103. It appears that the real objection to *Teal* was the court's narrow definition of materiality. *See id.* at 105-06. This certainly is no basis for invoking the attempt doctrine. *Cf.* note 42, *supra.* It is not entirely clear whether "the attendant circumstances as [the defendant] believes them to be," Model Penal Code § 5.01(1)(a), include the circumstance of materiality or circumstances such as those from which the draftsmen inferred Mrs. Teal's belief that the testimony was material. Their criticism of the decision implies an affirmative answer. If so, in addition to the false swearing statute, Mrs. Teal could be convicted of attempted perjury, and, punishment for attempt being the same as for the substantive offense attempted, *id.* § 5.05(1), there turns out to be no difference between material and nonmaterial false testimony except that nonmaterial false testimony can be prosecuted as a felony or a misdemeanor. This seems an awkward way to construct a penal code, to say the least.

impossibility thus: the legislature has defined the substantive crime to require the presence of a particular circumstance; there is no reason why—for cases in which that circumstance is absent but the defendant allegedly thinks it is present—the legislature should delegate to the courts the power or the duty to decide whether that circumstance may be dispensed with; if the legislature were to delegate the issue to the courts—or the courts were to assume it—the courts would have no analytic tools for deciding the issue; delegation to the court of the power to define the elements of a crime after the act raises serious issues of legality, particularly when such analytic tools are lacking; and there are in any event good policy reasons favoring retention of the circumstance as an element of the crime.

It is not the burden of this article to argue that the legislature must preserve the objective element of the crime in all instances. The point is that the defense of legal impossibility is a device which enables the court to return the ball to the legislature to resolve for each crime separately what are its appropriate objective elements and which objective elements may be safely dispensed with. And if, as suggested above, the significance of the objective element may vary from crime to crime, there is reason for the legislature to make discriminating choices to retain the objective element in certain crimes and eliminate it in others rather than deal with the issue in the attempt context which has the unfortunate tendency to generalize its results indiscriminately across the entire spectrum of crimes.[46]

The problem of legal impossibility, in the final analysis, is not really an attempt problem at all. It is rather a problem of the proper definition of the objective elements of specific crimes, a peculiarly legislative task.

C. The Act Requirement and the Restriction of Official Power

We have seen that the objective elements of certain crimes, including both acts and circumstances, serve as something more than merely evidence of resolution, of will to act, but also introduce an element of neutrality into the criminal decision-making process by restricting prosecution to those cases in which the defendant's conduct furnishes objective evidence of the illegality of his will and by furnishing a fixed reference point to aid us in determining how far to extend attempts. These ob-

46. *Cf.* Arnold, *supra* note 22.

jective elements serve a perhaps even more important function in setting an objective limit to those situations and persons that can become the objects of official assertions of control. The requirement that the defendant's acts be themselves unlawful, rather than commonplace and permitted, establishes a formidable barrier between the organs of state and private citizens.

Professor H. L. A. Hart has made a similar point with respect to the mens rea elements of criminal offenses. Among the virtues of a system of criminal law that recognizes the absence of mens rea as a defense, Hart lists, "[f]irst, we maximize the individual's power to predict the likelihood that the sanctions of the criminal law will be applied to him."[47] It is the function of the criminal law to promote the security and well being of members of society by securing for them a high measure of protection from harmful acts. But since society achieves such protection by inflicting harm on those who would commit such acts, it must take care not to offset this gain in security by unduly increasing the risks that persons will be subjected to official harm unpredictably. Acts can occur accidentally, but the state of mind that accompanies one's acts is entirely within the individual's control. Thus, by recognizing mens rea as an indispensable element of crimes, we substantially increase the individual's power to control his freedom from punishment.

But it would be shortsighted to think that only the mens rea element serves this function. Mens rea is within one's control but, as already seen, it is not subject to direct proof. More importantly, perhaps, it is not subject to direct refutation either. It is the subject of inference and speculation. The act requirement with its relative fixedness, its greater visibility and difficulty of fabrication, serves to provide additional security and predictability by limiting the scope of the criminal law to those who have engaged in conduct that is itself objectively forbidden and objectively verifiable. Security from officially imposed harm comes not only from the knowledge that one's thoughts are pure but that one's acts are similarly pure. So long as a citizen does not engage in forbidden conduct, he has little need to worry about possible erroneous official conclusions about his guilty mind.

In his Jerusalem lectures, replying to Lady Barbara Wootton's proposals to eliminate mens rea as an element of the offense

47. Hart, *Legal Responsibility and Excuses*, in DETERMINISM AND FREEDOM IN THE AGE OF MODERN SCIENCE 99 (S. Hook ed. 1965).

and treat it as a matter relevant solely to the choice of an appropriate disposition of the offender,[48] Professor Hart warned us that:

> In a system in which proof of *mens rea* is no longer a necessary condition for conviction, the occasions for official interferences with our lives and for compulsion will be vastly increased. Take, for example, the notion of a criminal assault. If the doctrine of *mens rea* were swept away, every blow, even if it was apparent to a policeman that it was purely accidental or merely careless and therefore not, according to the present law, a criminal assault, would be a matter for investigation under the new scheme, since the possibilities of a curable or treatable condition would have to be investigated and the condition if serious treated by medical or penal methods. No doubt under the new dispensation, as at present, prosecuting authorities would use their common sense; but very considerable discretionary powers would have to be entrusted to them to sift from the mass the cases worth investigation as possible candidates for therapeutic or penal treatment. No one could view this kind of expansion of police powers with equanimity, for with it will come great uncertainty for the individual: official interferences with his life will be more frequent but he will be less able to predict their incidence if any accidental or careless blow may be an occasion for them.[49]

Similarly, the objective elements of the crime—those definitional elements of the crime relating to conduct as distinguished from the mens rea—serve to identify and limit those cases which are to be the objects of prosecutional and judicial interest. The police, of course, when informed that someone is planning a crime, must take steps to investigate the matter before any criminal acts have been committed; they must ordinarily seek to prevent the crime, or at least catch the culprit while committing it. But the exercise of prosecutional and judicial discretion to investigate the existence of mens rea and invoke the severe penal sanctions regarded as punishment should ordinarily be limited to those cases in which the alleged mens rea accompanies objectively defined illegal conduct.

Ordinarily, then, the criminal act itself, as distinguished from the act with its accompanying mens rea, should set off the actor from the rest of society. The act should be unique rather than so commonplace that it is engaged in by persons not in violation of the law. In the case of uncompleted conduct, this is a key factor that distinguishes preparation from attempt.[50]

48. B. Wootton, Crime and the Criminal Law (1963).

49. H. Hart, The Morality of the Criminal Law 26 (1964).

50. See the well-known case of People v. Rizzo, 246 N.Y. 334, 158 N.E. 888 (1927), in which the court, although convinced that the defendants intended to commit a robbery, held that the acts of driving about in search of the victim were insufficient to constitute an attempt. Un-

It is interesting in this regard to examine the following statutory definition of those guilty of criminal syndicalism:

> Any person who shall . . . have in his possession or control anything with intent to destroy life or property, in the pursuance or furtherance of any of the doctrines of criminal syndicalism as defined in this chapter . . . .[51]

The statute provides punishment of one to 25 years in prison and/or a fine of $1000 to $10,000. The vice in this statute, aggravated of course by its setting in the context of protected speech, is that the only act required by the statute is the possession of "anything." Since everyone possesses some "thing," everyone has committed the proscribed act. The prosecution can bring anyone within this statute if it can persuade a jury that he possesses the necessary mens rea. And since mens rea may be proved by prior acts as well as by the defendant's statements and expressions of belief, the opportunities for biased prosecution are great.[52] In such a context, the right to jury trial is not likely to be significant protection from official bias.

One context in which similar problems have arisen is that

---

doubtedly the court was influenced by the fact that the defendant's acts objectively were the ordinary acts of innumerable innocent persons. *But see* page 707, *infra.*

51. S.D. Code § 13.0801 (1939).

52. Consider the following recently enacted federal statute:

> Whoever travels in interstate or foreign commerce . . . with intent—
> (A) to incite a riot; or
> (B) to organize, promote, encourage, participate in, or carry on a riot; or
> (C) to commit any act of violence in furtherance of a riot; or
> (D) to aid or abet any person in inciting or participating in or carrying on a riot or committing any act of violence in furtherance of a riot;
>
> and who either during the course of any such travel . . . or thereafter performs or attempts to perform any other overt act for any purpose specified in subparagraph (A), (B), (C), or (D) of this paragraph—
>
> Shall be fined not more than $10,000, or imprisoned not more than five years, or both.

Civil Rights Act of 1968, ch. 102, § 2101(a), 82 Stat. 73. Considering the fact that almost all of our unpopular "agitators" frequently travel in interstate commerce in connection with their activities, the statute does not contain any significant act requirement. The requirement of some "other overt act" will not be very meaningful unless the courts interpret it to require an act closely related to and evidencing one of the listed illicit purposes. Compare the rule in treason cases that the overt act must show that defendant gave aid and comfort to the enemy, Cramer v. United States, 325 U.S. 1 (1945), with the much more relaxed rule in conspiracy cases that any overt act will do, no matter how commonplace and innocent, so long as it can be proved by other evidence to have been a step in the furtherance of the conspiracy. *E.g.*, Carlson v. United States, 187 F.2d 366 (10th Cir.), *cert. denied*, 341 U.S. 940 (1951).

relating to the possession of burglar's tools. Most such tools are capable of innocent as well as illegal use. The broader the definition of the category of implements encompassed by the statute, the greater the danger that persons not intent on committing buglaries may be convicted. Persons with prior burglary convictions and co-called "professional burglars" are in a particularly exposed position since the determination of intent to use the implements is likely to be based, in large measure at least, on the evidence of prior convictions or alleged professionality.

People v. Taylor[53] illustrates the point well. Taylor was in possession of tools that could be used to commit a burglary, and while walking in an area where several burglaries had recently occurred he was arrested for possession with intent to break and enter. His testimony—that he used these tools on a temporary job from which he was returning at the time of his arrest, and that he had sought to leave the tools at the place but had been dissuaded by the lady of the house—was corroborated by the persons for whom he did the work. Nonetheless Taylor was convicted. Prosecution evidence, in addition to the ambiguous act of possession, included a conviction for burglary some 17 years earlier and recent irregular employment. On appeal, the Supreme Court of Illinois held the evidence of intent insufficient, discounting the earlier conviction because of the long lapse of intervening time. Taylor was eventually protected by the Illinois Supreme Court. Defendants have fared less well in such cases before the Michigan Supreme Court.[54] And one may question what would have been Taylor's fortune if his burglary conviction had been of recent vintage. Even then, in each of these situations the statute did not encompass the possession of anything and everything as does the syndicalism statute quoted above.

Considered in this light, the defense of legal impossibility takes on still further meaning. In the case of Lady Eldon, for example, if the substantive crime is defined to include as an element of the offense the fact that the goods were subject to duty, the more limited group of acts of importing dutiable goods is separated from the mass of acts of bringing goods into the coun-

53. 410 Ill. 469, 102 N.E.2d 529 (1951); *see* 30 CHI.-KENT L. REV. 278 (1952).

54. *See* People v. Howard, 73 Mich. 10, 40 N.W. 789 (1888); *accord*, People v. Jefferson, 161 Mich. 621, 126 N.W. 829 (1910). *Compare* State v. Ingram, 237 N.C. 197, 74 S.E.2d 532 (1953), *with* McQuirter v. State, 36 Ala. App. 707, 63 So. 2d 388 (1953).

try and official intervention is limited to the narrower class. If we were to eliminate the element of dutiability from the offense, the criminal act would become simply the importation of any article. All travelers would be potentially subject to prosecution and conviction under the statute, their only protection being review of the sufficiency of the evidence of mens rea. And, as discussed above, while broadening the class of persons and acts potentially subject to this criminal provision, we would be eliminating the objective basis for evaluating the mens rea, the one remaining means of distinguishing those to be punished.

In the case of *Jaffe*, elimination of the requirement that the goods in fact be stolen would redefine the act element of the crime to the mere possession of goods. But as indicated above in connection with the syndicalism statute, everyone in our society possesses goods. Under this redefined crime, everyone may now become the subject of official control if the authorities can gather a minimum of evidence relating to mens rea. And, again, we have simultaneously eliminated a crucial objective factor in the proof of that mens rea.

The point is still clearer in the case of possession of narcotics. If possession of any innocuous substance in the belief that the substance is heroin is an attempt to possess narcotics, everyone who possesses any substance may be convicted of that crime without the extremely probative objective basis for evaluating the sole remaining significant factor, the mens rea.

The narcotics case illustrates an additional point. Suppose there existed a rare substance similar in appearance to heroin. If the crime of attempted possession were limited to possession of this substance we might still preserve both an objective basis for our conclusion as to the existence of mens rea and an objective limit to those persons subject to prosecution. In other words the narcotics case offers an opportunity for drawing a line short of possession of *any* goods in the belief that they are narcotics by limiting criminality to the act of possessing certain specified goods in such a belief. This is not true of the *Jaffe* case, however. Whereas some goods could more readily be confused with heroin than others, any goods could reasonably be thought to be stolen, there being nothing in their physical nature that reflects the possessor's belief, or mens rea.

This again suggests that the problem of legal impossibility is in reality a problem of the proper definition of the act element of the offense. It also reinforces the thought that there is no single solution which cuts across all substantive crimes, but rather that the definition of each crime presents an opportunity for discriminating legislative judgment.

Tested in this light, the Model Penal Code provisions may once again be shortsighted. Not only have the draftsmen assumed that a single across-the-board solution to the problem is proper, but they actually deprive the court of any vehicle to control the jury in individual cases. In a preparation-attempt case, the court exercises such power in its determination whether the act is "a substantial step" toward consummation of the crime. But where the defendant has done the act absent an attendant circumstance, no other objective element need be established. All that is necessary is a showing that the defendant thought the circumstance was present, judicial control being limited to review of the sufficiency of the evidence.[55]

This approach is surprising in light of the Model Penal Code's considerable sensitivity to this problem in the preparation-attempt context. In formulating specific instances of conduct that go beyond preparation the Code specifies:

> possession of materials to be employed in the commission of the crime, *which are specially designed for such unlawful use or which can serve no lawful purpose of the actor under the circumstances.*[56]

Another section defines the separate crime of possessing instruments of crime more broadly as possession of instruments "commonly used for criminal purposes . . . under circumstances which do not negative unlawful purpose."[57] This provision still does not reach the breadth of across-the-board elimination of objective circumstances as results from the elimination of the notion of impossibility. Moreover, this latter offense is only a misdemeanor.[58]

All of this illustrates once again the preferability of legislative handling of these situations, with its greater flexibility and capacity for a discrete approach, rather than the use of the

---

55. Under the Model Penal Code provision a person who testifies to the truth can be convicted of attempted perjury on proof that he thought his testimony was false. Or one who has intercourse with a girl over the age of consent can be convicted on proof that he believed her to be under age. And a soldier performing his duties could be convicted of attempted treason on proof that he incorrectly thought he was performing them for the enemy. *But see* Respublica v. Malin, 1 U.S. (1 Dall.) 33 (1778).

56. MODEL PENAL CODE § 5.01(2)(e) (Proposed Official Draft, 1962) (emphasis added). *See also id.* § 5.01(2)(f).

57. *Id.* § 5.06(1)(b).

58. For discussion of these considerations see AMERICAN LAW INSTITUTE, MODEL PENAL CODE, Council Draft #29, at 131-32 (1961).

judicial technique of attempt with its necessarily generalizing tendencies.[59]

If we are correct in our analysis up to this point two conclusions emerge. First, in the absence of statutory treatment of the problem, retention of the defense of legal impossibility is an appropriate judicial device to shift or leave to the legislature the burden of defining the actus reus of the crime. Secondly, the doctrine says something significant to the legislature as well, namely, that it is not forced to choose between the extreme alternatives of always or never basing criminality on mistaken belief of objective facts. The legislature has the freedom, indeed the duty, to consider separately as to each offense category the needs of law enforcement and the dangers of drafting the substantive criminal provisions broadly to encompass too many people.

D. Attempt and the Notion of Harm

One of the least developed of the general concepts of Anglo-American criminal law is the notion of harm and its role in the definition of crime.[60] Although it is sometimes stated that harm is essential to criminal conduct,[61] and there are a few cases which suggest that there are some constitutional limits to the legislature's power to forbid harmless conduct,[62] there has been very little exploration of what does and what does not constitute harm.[63]

To add to the confusion, it has frequently been asserted that the punishment of attempts is an exception to the principle that conduct which does no harm is not criminal.[64] The supporting argument is that since attempt necessarily involves a failure to commit the harmful act or cause the harm forbidden by the substantive crime, it follows that no harm has been done.

59. For other such illustrations, see notes 23 & 45, *supra*, and page 707, *infra*.

60. Mueller, *Criminal Theory: An Appraisal of Jerome Hall's "Studies in Jurisprudence and Criminal Theory,"* 34 Ind. L.J. 206, 220 (1959).

61. Hall at 213; R. Perkins, Criminal Law 7 (1957).

62. *E.g.*, Benton v. United States, 232 F.2d 341 (D.C. Cir. 1956); State v. Birdsell, 235 La. 396, 104 So. 2d 148 (1958); People v. Munoz, 9 N.Y.2d 51, 172 N.E.2d 535, 211 N.Y.S.2d 146 (1961); People v. Bunis, 9 N.Y.2d 1, 172 N.E.2d 273, 210 N.Y.2d 505 (1961).

63. *See* Hall at 212-46; Eser, *The Principle of "Harm" in the Concept of Crime: A Comparative Analysis of the Criminally Protected Legal Interests*, 4 Duquesne U.L. Rev. 345 (1966).

64. The leading quotations are collected in Morris, *Punishment for Thoughts*, 49 The Monist 342, 354 n.14 (1965).

Punishment for attempt, then, is really punishment for a mens rea. The act of the attempt, this view continues, is not harmful; it is relevant merely as evidence of the firmness of defendant's resolve to commit the crime and hence furnishes reason to believe that the defendant will commit the crime on some future occasion. If this argument is correct, it follows that the extension of criminal liability for attempt to cases traditionally held not to involve criminality due to the defense of impossibility is not a departure from accepted notions regarding the relevance of harm to attempts.

On the other hand, others assert that the conduct prosecuted in attempts does constitute harm. They would argue that it does not follow that no harm has occurred simply because the harm sought to be prevented by the substantive statute has been avoided. The conduct denominated an attempt did create a risk that harm would result and that alone is a harm that justifies punishment. Each attempt carries with it a risk that the ultimate harm sought to be prevented will occur, so that an increase in the number of attempts means an increase in the number of cases in which the attempt will succeed.[65]

The latter view does remind us of an important difference between the types of harm, or risks, involved in ordinary attempts—those fitting the preparation-attempt formula—and those raising the issue of legal impossibility. In ordinary attempts the risk is that the defendant will cause the harm by the very activity for which he is being prosecuted. In the legal impossibility cases, since the goods Lady Eldon sought to smuggle were not subject to duty and the false testimony solicited by Mrs. Teal was immaterial, there was no risk that the harm sought to be prevented by the substantive statute would in fact occur.[66] The risk is, rather, that if not prosecuted successfully now the defendant may repeat his conduct and cause the harm on some future occasion.

This distinction supports the position taken earlier that analogy is a useful technique in the one group of cases but not in the other. One can speak of the degree to which conduct on

65. HALL at 217-18, 591-94; Morris, *supra* note 64, at 359; Strahorn, *The Effect of Impossibility on Criminal Attempts*, 78 U. PA. L. REV. 962 (1930).

66. If the harm sought to be prevented—obstruction of the proceedings—was risked in *Teal*, then the court was merely wrong in declaring the testimony immaterial. But, that is a problem of the correct interpretation of the substantive statute; it is not an attempt issue. *Cf.* notes 42 & 45, *supra*.

a specific occasion risks certain harm and can compare the risk of harm with the harm itself. It is far more difficult to make such a comparison in the case of conduct that does not risk the harm it is being compared with, but which is only predictive of future harmful conduct.

There is another way to describe this difference which avoids the definitional controversy whether risk of harm is harm. In the ordinary attempt cases, since the defendant's conduct risks harm we wish to prevent, we cannot wait until he is completed and then prosecute him for the substantive crime. It is this need to stop the defendant before he commits the criminal act that prevents us from prosecuting him for the substantive crime and forces us to fall back upon the crime of attempt with its undefined act element. There is no reasonable alternative.

Legal impossibility cases, however, pose no risk of harm requiring intervention before the defendant completes his acts. If the defendant's conduct does not violate the statute defining the substantive crime, it is not because we had to intervene before he had a chance to commit the crime. It is because the statute as drafted does not cover this conduct. There is, then, a reasonable alternative to applying undefined attempt concepts to this defendant. Attend to the statute defining the substantive crime. As indicated above, that is the more appropriate place to consider the issue.

This distinction between the risk of harm in ordinary attempt cases and legal impossibility cases suggests still another matter. We have certainly not yet thought through the implications of this shift from the criminal act as an act that we wish to prevent to one that we have no particular interest in preventing but consider significant solely because of its evidentiary capacity to identify persons likely to commit future anti-social acts.[67] I shall not explore the moral aspects of the question except to note that there is a difficult moral issue involved in

67. It is conceded that the proposal to eliminate the defense of legal impossibility is quite different from the notion that prediction of future criminality based on the defendant's social environment and childhood conduct be made a basis for isolation from the community and curative or preventive efforts. In the legal impossibility case the defendant has or is assumed to have a specific mens rea of a defined crime and has acted pursuant to that mens rea. In other predictive situations, there is as yet neither the specific mens rea nor evidence of readiness to act on it. In the impossibility cases we are predicting a future repetition of the act as the defendant assumedly understood it, a less far reaching prediction. This is in part what makes the rejection of the defense plausible. But it is still a departure from traditional views, the unexplored implications of which are being considered in the text.

punishing a person solely for having acted with harmful intent when he has neither caused nor risked any harm. Actually, the goal in such cases would not be punishment but rather rehabilitative and preventive treatment. Still, it is one thing to subject one who has merited punishment to coercive, rehabilitative and preventive measures. It is quite another matter to impose such harm on a person who has not earned punishment.[68]

This shift in the function of the act has implications for the administration of justice as well. Where acts are defined in terms of that conduct which society regards as harmful and seeks to prevent, law enforcement officials have a strong duty and motive to prevent criminal conduct. The community has an equally strong claim upon these officials not to encourage such conduct, or in the parlance of entrapment cases, not to create crimes. If the act, however, is itself harmless but is significant because of its predictive relevance, not only is there no motive or ethical claim upon law enforcement officers not to encourage the commission of such acts, but the encouragement of such conduct seems to be a logical follow through. After all, our goal now is to identify those who will in the future be dangerous and we can do so without encouraging harmful or wrong conduct but by encouraging perfectly harmless conduct.[69]

Indeed, it may well be that absence of harm is one of the reasons entrapment is a recurring problem in certain crimes more than others. Because of the risks of harm, it would be rare

68. Our present system functions on a dual level. It convicts people largely on the basis of wrongful conduct, while at the sentencing stage there is greater emphasis on future-oriented goals. For a discussion of the tensions that arise from this dualism, see Silving, *"Rule of Law" in Criminal Justice*, in ESSAYS IN CRIMINAL SCIENCE 77 (G. Mueller ed. 1961). Although perhaps not a logically "neat" package, this dualism may be a reasonable accommodation of the different interests at stake—protection against overly broad definitions of criminal conduct and punishment that is disproportionate to the seriousness of the crime, and recognition of the interest in shaping our sentencing policies toward rational future-oriented social goals. The elimination of legal impossibility as a defense may be logically neat but it may also overlook the need to accommodate interests other than crime prevention.

Much of recent discussion of the criminal law has considered the dangers involved in completely severing correctional treatment from the notions of punishment and responsibility. *E.g.*, H. HART, PUNISHMENT AND THE ELIMINATION OF RESPONSIBILITY (1962); Allen, *Criminal Justice, Legal Values and the Rehabilitative Ideal*, 50 J. CRIM. L.C. & P.S. 226 (1959); Hart, *Prolegomenon to the Principles of Punishment*, in 1959-1960 PROCEEDINGS OF THE ARISTOTELIAN SOCIETY 1; Lewis, *The Humanitarian Theory of Punishment*, 6 RES JUDICATAE 224 (1953); Morris, *Persons and Punishment*, 52 THE MONIST 475 (1968).

69. Morris, *supra* note 64, at 349.

that an officer would seek to entrap a suspect into committing a homicide or an armed robbery. But since the officer sees no harm done when he buys heroin from a dealer—indeed some good is done since the heroin is withdrawn from circulation—entrapment is a common practice in such cases.[70] The policies considered here are not uniquely relevant to attempts. Certainly we should be equally careful about defining substantive crimes to cover conduct we do not wish to prevent. The point is that the doctrine of legal impossibility alerts us to the presence of that very issue every time we seek to extend attempts to cover cases in which a required circumstantial element of the substantive crime is missing.

None of the foregoing is intended to suggest that our legal system never punishes harmless acts. Sometimes an act, itself harmless, may appear so similar to a harmful act that the legislature may reasonably conclude that administrative considerations warrant forbidding the harmless act as well. This judgment is particularly acceptable when there is no strong social interest in encouraging or even allowing the harmless act. The example of the substance that appeared similar to heroin could fit this situation. Assuming there was no strong countervailing reason to permit the distribution of this commodity, it would be reasonable for the legislature to forbid its possession in order to prevent those prosecuted for possessing heroin from asserting in defense that they thought they were possessing Brand X. This would be a sort of prophylactic rule, a "fence about the law."[71] But once again, this is a uniquely legislative judgment. It is the kind of judgment that should be made separately for each crime rather than in the attempt context with its generalizing tendencies.

Thus, once again, we find that "legal impossibility" can be a useful term to alert us to certain dangers in overextending criminality and to encompass a group of cases more appropriate to legislative than judicial decision-making.

V. FACTUAL IMPOSSIBILITY

Thus far, we have considered the notion of legal impossibility. Let us now consider again the same matters treated above, this time in the context of so-called factual impossibility.

70. The relationship between entrapment and impossibility is further explored in section VI, *infra*.

71. The BABYLONIAN TALMUD, *Mishnah Aboth*, ch. 1, mishnah 1 (1935).

To use two common hypotheticals, suppose defendant *A* pours sugar in another's tea believing that the sugar is deadly poison, and defendant *B* pours an inadequate quantity of poison into the tea, both intending to kill the victim. Both cases would be thought of as posing factual impossibility issues although some writers would say that case A presents an issue of absolute impossibility which would constitute a defense whereas the act of defendant *B* was only relatively impossible, which is no defense.[72]

Approaching the two cases in accordance with our previous analysis, case A seems to pose many of the same problems as are posed by the "mere preparation" and legal impossibility cases. Although we assumed that defendant intended to kill his victim, that intent is not evidenced by defendant's conduct. The objective facts are simply that defendant *A* placed sugar in the person's tea. From the perspective of the criminal act's function of restricting the scope of official power, again *A*'s act of putting sugar in the tea is a perfectly commonplace act that in no way distinguishes him from any other person. And finally, *A*'s act is objectively harmless. In this posture, if the case would fit the preparation-attempt formula, a court would almost certainly call defendant's act "mere preparation" and acquit him.

Case B, however, is completely different. Although the quantity of poison was insufficient to kill the intended victim, it certainly does furnish some objective evidentiary basis for evaluating *B*'s intent. While the evidence of intent to kill is less clear than it would have been had the dose been sufficient, that is usually a problem in unsuccessful attempts. What is more significant is that the evidence of intent is certainly clearer than it was in case A. So too, *B*'s act is not an act that people ordinarily engage in so that making this act criminal would still preserve a discriminate and reasonable basis for identifying those activities which warrant official intervention. And finally, *B*'s act, though not risking the precise harm sought to be prevented by the homicide statute, does risk bodily injury.

We can posit any number of hypothetical cases along a scale ranging from case A through case B to violation of the substantive statute. Note, then, that as distinguished from the cases of legal impossibility, analogy is once again useful. While avoiding the definitional swamp of relative and absolute impos-

72. *See* Commonwealth v. Kennedy, 170 Mass. 18, 48 N.E. 770 (1897); WILLIAMS at 623, 642-48.

sibility, we have discovered a tool for making appropriate distinctions between different cases quite similar to the distinctions we sought to make by use of the preparation-attempt formula.

Further, again unlike the legal impossibility cases, the legislature must delegate discretion over this group of cases to the courts. We noted above[73] that the crime of homicide differs from most crimes in that its actus reus is not defined in terms of specific forbidden acts but in terms of bringing about a specified result, death. Thus, to convict someone of murder, the only indispensable objective fact the prosecution must prove is the death. Any act causing that death will do. We also noted, however, that the requirements of causation and intent served to limit prosecution for murder to those acts which can cause death and which appear reasonably calculated to do so. In a prosecution for attempted murder, that one indispensable fact—death—is dispensed with, and with it goes, of course, the requirement of causation. The actus reus of a crime limited to no particular act and which does not require the causation of any particular result can hardly be defined in advance by the legislature.

The only remaining objective limit to prosecution is the requirement that the defendant's conduct *appear* capable of producing death. How much appearance is necessary the court decides by the process of analogy. At the one end is the substantive crime and its requirements, conduct that causes death. At the other end, firmly rooted by the notion of factual impossibility, is that probably hypothetical odd-ball case in which the defendant's conduct carries no risk of death. Between the two sits the court judging the case before it. Just as the preparation-attempt formula provides the court with a framework for deciding one group of attempt cases, factual impossibility alerts the court to the presence of identical problems in a different group of cases and helps to solve them.

Law professors occasionally delight in debunking the idea of factual impossibility by pointing out to their students that when defendant fires a pistol and misses his victim's head by one inch, under all the circumstances, including the precise manner in which defendant aimed the pistol, it was factually impossible for defendant to kill the intended victim. In other words, every attempt being a failure, success is factually impossible in every attempt.[74] This is largely true but irrelevant. One of the interesting aspects of the analysis of the role of factual impossibility

73. *See* pages 672-73, *supra*.
74. *Cf.* J. BISHOP, CRIMINAL LAW § 738 (9th ed. 1923).

offered here is that calling this case one of factual impossibility would in no way change the result. Alerted to the problems, the court should nonetheless conclude that the case is objectively so similar to one in which the victim was hit and killed by the bullet that the defendant should be convicted of attempted murder. Actually, of course, the case is so nearly identical to a successful killing that we do not even pause to ask such questions. The point of the analysis is that even if we did, we would reach the same result.

Similarly, it no longer matters if we call the famous old pick-pocketing cases factual impossibility because there was no money in the victim's pocket. The defendant's act of placing his hand in someone else's pocket sufficiently satisfies the act requirements set forth so that it can be prosecuted as an attempt.

One may ask at this point: If the two doctrines—preparation-attempt and factual impossibility—serve identical purposes, what is the need for two separate doctrines? A likely explanation is that the preparation-attempt formula is linguistically inadequate to alert us to the presence of these problems in those cases called factual impossibility. From a linguistic point of view it is difficult to picture either case A or B as one of preparation rather than attempt. In each case the defendant has done every act he intended to do. Since it is linguistically inappropriate for us to call *A*'s act mere acts of preparation, if we were to apply the preparation-attempt formulation we would probably readily call *A*'s acts an attempt and never discover that in terms of its hidden problems it is more like an act of preparation. The factual impossibility formulation furnishes an additional warning device for cases in which the language of the preparation-attempt formulation is an inadequate shorthand to identify the problem.

There is, then, one important difference between what has here been called factual impossibility and legal impossibility. Legal impossibility—the absence of one of the circumstances required for the substantive crime as defined by the legislature—prevails as a defense in the cases thus far considered because such circumstances can never be more or less present. In cases of factual impossibility, however, the objective possibility of success can vary and the court must make a separate judgment as to each particular case.

It was earlier observed that it will not always be clear whether a particular case presents an issue of factual or legal impossibility. The line between acts, circumstances and consequences is not very certain. For that reason, courts should approach these notions, not as rigid conceptual categories yielding inevitable results, but as analytic tools.

United States v. Thomas[75] is an excellent illustration of this point. In that case several young sailors had spent an evening bar-hopping. One of the sailors was dancing with a girl at a bar when she collapsed in his arms. The three decided to drive her home. In the car, thinking she was merely unconscious, they had sexual intercourse with her. Actually, she was dead at the time. Thomas was acquitted of rape because the girl was dead, but was convicted of attempted rape. The issue on appeal was whether impossibility was a defense under these facts.

The requirement that, in order to constitute a rape, the girl be alive at the time of the acts of intercourse can be categorized either as a circumstance or as part of the definition of the act element of the offense. Defendant's own physical acts are the same regardless of whether the girl is dead or alive. Her state is external to his acts and could be called a circumstance. On the other hand, his acts take on a completely different meaning and significance if she is dead or alive, so that it is sensible to talk of the act as different. Indeed, most would consider it grotesque to regard the question whether the girl is dead or alive as an external element separate from the defendant's act.

If we go beyond the labels and consider the underlying considerations explored in this article, it is not very difficult to conclude that the court was correct in convicting the defendant of attempted rape. His conduct is objectively unique, thereby distinguishing him from other persons for prosecution. And the conduct corroborates the alleged mens rea. The only other reasonable explanation of Thomas' conduct was that he was engaging in an act of necrophelia, under the circumstances a less plausible inference than the inference that he thought the girl was alive. The one argument in favor of acquittal is that the legislature could have defined rape as encompassing intercourse with the body of a dead woman thought by the defendant to be alive. But that would be carrying the argument to grotesque extremes. The presence of objectively unique conduct that evidences the mens rea is sufficient to overcome this suggestion.

Thus, it turns out that legal and factual impossibility need not be sharply defined categories. Cases can arise or can be hypothesized in which it is difficult to distinguish the two. But

75. 13 U.S.C.M.A. 278, 32 C.M.R. 278 (1962).

for the most part they point to two readily identifiable groups of cases and alert us to the special problems present in each. If we approach these concepts thoughtfully, we should not have much difficulty dealing with those cases which cannot be so neatly categorized.

VI. IMPOSSIBILITY, ENTRAPMENT AND NEUTRAL LAW ENFORCEMENT

It was suggested earlier that there are points of intersection between the defense of impossibility and official entrapment.[76] In their commentary to the Model Penal Code's elimination of the impossibility defense, the draftsmen argue that the Code adequately deals with the entrapment issue elsewhere.[77] Actually, however, the Code's entrapment provisions are limited to one aspect of the entrapment problem, namely, officially induced attempts to persuade the defendant to commit a crime.[78] But entrapment is in reality part of a much broader problem of police surveillance and law enforcement selection bias.[79]

If, as suggested above, we view the act requirement as introducing an element of neutrality in law enforcement by establishing objective external criteria to identify the class of cases that calls for official investigation and intervention, entrapment may be seen as the use of investigative techniques that undermine such neutrality. If the citizen maximizes his area of freedom from official scrutiny by taking care not to engage in the specified forbidden conduct, entrapment is an official manipulation of the act element of the offense that undercuts the citizen's ability to preserve his freedom from such scrutiny. Because the decision to put the citizen to the test is made before the illegal act has been committed, the uncontrolled use of entrapment techniques would undercut the act requirement's limitation on the persons subject to investigation.

The problem is even more significant today with the increased emphasis on intelligence gathering. At the risk of some exaggeration, we might posit two models of investigation. Traditionally, the emphasis was on the investigation of crimes rather than criminals. A crime had been committed and the

76. *See* pages 697-98, *supra*.

77. Wechsler, Jones, & Korn, *The Treatment of Inchoate Crimes in the Model Penal Code of the American Law Institute: Attempt, Solicitation and Conspiracy*, 61 COLUM. L. REV. 571, 584 (1961).

78. MODEL PENAL CODE § 2.13 (Proposed Official Draft 1962).

79. *See generally* Note, *Judicial Control of Secret Agents*, 76 YALE L.J. 994 (1967).

officials sought its perpetrator. Not having made up their minds in advance as to the identity of the person they sought, the direction of the investigation was undetermined; it was controlled to a significant degree by the objective facts developed.[80] More recently, in part the result of efforts to combat organized crime, there has been a greater emphasis on the investigation of individuals and the search for crimes for which the chosen individuals can be prosecuted.

Under the "crime" model, the facts of the crime determined to a degree the persons on whom official suspicion focused, whereas under the "criminal" system no such element of neutrality is introduced. The disagreement in the Supreme Court whether the appropriate criteria for the control of entrapment should be based solely on the entrapping officer's conduct or should include some reference to whether the defendant is "otherwise innocent" or "predisposed" to commit the crime[81] may be understood as reflecting disagreement over the proper balance between the "crime" and the "criminal" models.

Of course, under the "criminal" model the officials must still produce evidence sufficient to convict. But many of our constitutional protections are based on the assumption that the crime model of prosecution will prevail. Double jeopardy retains its meaningfulness as a protection against harassment when a specific crime is the object of attention. It becomes a very limited protection when the government decides that *X* is dangerous to society and invests enormous resources to research his entire life to seek prosecutable actions. The recent series of Hoffa prosecutions is a case in point. Without judging the merits of the cases, it is clear that the double jeopardy clause, even applying a broad "same-transaction" test, would have been inadequate to protect Hoffa from repeated prosecution until his ability to resist effectively was worn down.

Both models of investigation operate within a legal system that presumes innocence and requires proof of guilt to the satisfaction of a jury. But in the "crime" model, the presumption of

80. Problems of bias did begin to enter the picture at the point at which the facts began to focus suspicion on a particular suspect whom the police would interrogate to elicit facts to fit an already fixed theory of the case. This formed a component of the police interrogation problem, *see* Gallegos v. Nebraska, 342 U.S. 71-73 (1951) (concurring opinion of Jackson & Frankfurter, JJ.), and explains in part the relevance of the "focus" test in Escobedo v. Illinois, 378 U.S. 478 (1964).

81. Sherman v. United States, 356 U.S. 369 (1958); Sorrells v. United States, 287 U.S. 435 (1932).

innocence takes on added meaning from the fact that the prosecutor will weigh the evidence carefully before deciding to prosecute. Prosecutional screening will eliminate cases in which the evidence, though sufficient to go to the jury, is weak or is based on witnesses of doubtful credibility. And in cases that pass such screening the jury, having no bias against the defendant, may still find reasonable doubt. These protections do not function so well in the "criminal" model. The law enforcement authorities make up their minds about the defendant before the evidence is developed, and being engaged in a search for a case that can be "made," the prosecutor will not screen out potential cases based on doubtful witnesses. And the jury, having been conditioned by the authorities for years to believe that X is a Mafia leader or a labor racketeer, is far more likely to believe the doubtful witness or draw the questionable inference against the defendant.[82]

Entrapment, then, is merely a part of the problem of law enforcement activities such an intelligence gathering, surveillance, eavesdropping, undercover work and the use of informers in which official decisions to investigate and prosecute individuals are based on judgments of character rather than in a context controlled by objective fact or other criteria to be tested in court.[83] The effectiveness of the trial process as a control over prosecutional decisions is seriously weakened in the "criminal" model.

These problems reach their height in prosecutions for conspiracy,[84] since conspiracy has no specified, predefined act requirement.[85] Moreover, because of the division of labor which conspiracies can devise, only some of the conspirators need engage in conduct that is objectively illegal or at least visibly re-

82. The writer recalls the income tax prosecution of a major figure in the financial world of Wall Street in which one of the jurors, after the defendant was acquitted, commented, "you had enough evidence to convict Frank Costello but not ———." Compare the Appalachian case, United States v. Bufalino, 285 F.2d 408 (2d Cir. 1960).

83. It is not suggested that for the above reasons all of these practices must be forbidden. Some of them are useful and necessary techniques which, because of their dangers, require control. Whether such control should be judicial through use of the fourth amendment, or administrative, or something else, is of course far beyond the scope of this article. *Cf.* Enker, *Controls on Electronic Eavesdropping—A Basic Distinction*, 2 ISRAEL L. REV. 461 (1967).

84. Similar problems arise in the administration of plea bargaining as a result of statutes imposing mandatory minimum sentences. *See* Enker, *Perspectives on Plea Bargaining*, in THE PRESIDENT'S COMM'N ON LAW ENFORCEMENT AND THE ADMINISTRATION OF JUSTICE, TASK FORCE REPORT: THE COURTS 108, 109-10 (1967).

85. *See* pages 671-72, *supra*.

lated to other illegal conduct. Defendants may be brought into the conspiracy on the basis of commonplace acts that bear no apparent or objective relationship to the other participants' acts.

I have observed at least one successful prosecution of defendants identified as major Mafia figures which illustrates these points. As to some defendants, the evidence established relatively visible and clearly criminal acts of possession and distribution of narcotics. It was corroborated by agent surveillance and the seizure of narcotics by law enforcement officers. The main defendant, an alleged high level Mafia boss, was convicted on uncorroborated testimony that he attended a secret basement meeting at which the distribution of these narcotics was discussed. This sole witness who testified to this meeting was of highly doubtful credibility: he had a series of convictions; was facing a state narcotics charge; had lied before the grand jury, and had testified before the grand jury that he had never met the defendant; then that he had met him once; and, finally, shortly before the indictment was filed, that this alleged basement meeting had occurred. Indeed, the story of the basement meeting came forward only after months of interrogation during which the prosecutor several times inquired whether the defendant was involved. By the time the witness implicated the defendant, it must have become perfectly clear to him that the Government was anxious for a case against that defendant. There is no way of knowing at this point whether the witness made up the story to satisfy the prosecutor. Instead of the facts leading to the defendant, in this case the prosecutor's prejudgment of the defendant may have developed the facts. The prosecution's decision to accept this testimony was most certainly influenced by the fact that it had been "after" this defendant for years. One can only speculate as to the impact on the jury of years of adverse newspaper publicity concerning the defendant and his alleged Mafia activities. And credibility being an issue for the jury, the defendant got nowhere on appeal. He was sentenced to serve a 15 year sentence in a federal penitentiary.

Perhaps the risks must be run in the case of conspiracies. These are the dangers that must be encountered if we are to prosecute successfully those who organize and stay in the background of criminal conspiracies. In these instances, objectively innocuous acts of low visibility, difficult to prove or disprove, can be highly dangerous, and perhaps a case can be made for defining the crime so broadly even though it eliminates the protections usually afforded by more careful definition of the criminal act.

But no case has been made for the need to extend these problems to the attempt area. There is no peculiar danger across the board in attempts that requires dispensing with relatively precise act definitions that limit the offense to acts objectively illegal. Only in limited situations can such a case of need be made. Attempted robbery is a good example. Here we cannot wait to intervene until the defendant draws his gun in a crowded bank.[86] Presumably this justifies the federal statute making it a crime "to enter any bank . . . with intent to commit in such bank . . . any felony affecting such bank . . . ."[87] But this illustrates once again the need and the opportunity for particularized legislative consideration of such problems rather than across the board elimination of the requirement of a meaningful act.

VII. AN ALTERNATE PROPOSAL

Several persons who examined an early draft of this article suggested that the problems considered herein could be solved by requiring evidence corroborating the defendant's mens rea. If we can limit prosecution of impossibility cases to those in which there exists satisfactory and reliable evidence of the mens rea, we need not be terribly concerned that the defendant's act does not itself corroborate his mens rea or that it is so commonplace that it does not single him out for investigation. In effect, the proposal states: Assuming everything stated in this article is correct, the elimination of the entire actus reus can be compensated for by tinkering with the sufficiency-of-the-evidence test for these cases. A requirement of corroboration would furnish judges with a legal handle for greater control of the jury.

A corroboration requirement will not always solve the court's problem. In *Teal*, for example, there was little need for special evidence corroborating defendant's knowledge that the testimony was false. Corroboration of the defendant's belief that the testimony was material would not have been very significant either. The assumption or inference that defendant thought the false testimony material was fair enough; but it was equally applicable to all cases. The real problem facing the court was whether to override the legislative requirement of materiality. Corroboration would not have helped decide that issue.

86. *But see* People v. Rizzo, 246 N.Y. 334, 158 N.E. 888 (1927).
87. 18 U.S.C. § 2113(a) (1964).

Nor is it certain that corroboration is an adequate substitute for the fixedness and neutrality of a requirement that a designated circumstance exist as a predicate of guilt. Decisions on the sufficiency of the corroboration may retain a considerable ad hoc character. The proposal has the merit of enabling the judge to assert greater control over the jury, but it does not meet the need to insulate the local trial judge from pressure and bias.[88] In any event, the legislatures have not enacted such a corroboration requirement. And strict corroboration requirements are not always looked upon with favor.[89] Under the cir-

---

88. This point, indeed, the point of this entire article—that fixed act definitions are vital protection for the accused—is illustrated by two recent Minnesota prosecutions. State *ex rel.* Webber v. Tahash, 277 Minn. 302, 152 N.W.2d 497 (1967); State v. Webber, 266 Minn. 224, 123 N.W.2d 193 (1963). Both prosecutions of Webber arose in the same county in rural Minnesota. The first prosecution was for robbery. The "victim," a farmer, came to town early in the afternoon and spent most of the day drinking. He met defendant and another man—a co-defendant—at a bar, and sometime after 11 p.m. they left by car "to have a good time." Upon arriving at a farmsite after their car had become stuck, the "victim" and the co-defendant walked across a yard while the defendant remained at the car. According to the victim, "something struck me and I went down." He later returned to the car where he and the defendant unsuccessfully attempted to move it. When complaining to the sheriff that he had been robbed, he stated that he had begun the day with $100 and had paid about $20 to have the car towed and to have his wounds taken care of. He still had some $43 on his person after the "robbery." There was no evidence that any of the "victim's" money was found in the possession of the defendant or the co-defendant. The evidence also clearly established that the "victim" was intoxicated when he reported the "robbery" to the sheriff. On these facts, defendant, who had four prior felony convictions, was convicted of robbery and sentenced to life imprisonment. His conviction was reversed by the Minnesota Supreme Court.

The second case arose in September, 1964, just about one year after the Supreme Court's reversal. Apparently, or allegedly, Webber broke into a farmer's tool shed and stole some copper wire which, after burning off some of the insulation, he sold as salvage copper for $37. Theft of goods valued at less than $100 is a misdemeanor in Minnesota carrying a maximum prison sentence of 90 days. MINN. STAT. § 609.52 subd. 3(5) (1967). Webber was charged with burglary, convicted and sentenced to five years in prison. In habeas corpus proceedings during 1966 and 1967 this second conviction was quashed on the ground that MINN. STAT. § 609.58 subd. 1(2) (1967) requires as an element of the crime of burglary that the "building" burglarized be "suitable for affording shelter for human beings," a requirement that the testimony of the owner of the tool shed demonstrated was clearly absent.

Both cases involved crimes with relatively specific objective elements which furnished the basis for appellate review. Such review would have been much more difficult in the absence of these requirements.

89. *See* 7 J. WIGMORE, EVIDENCE § 2057 (3d ed. 1940). There is no requirement of corroboration of accomplice testimony in the federal

cumstances, the judiciary may be justified in taking the position that the decision whether to substitute corroboration for actus reus belongs with the legislature.

It is also necessary to explore further precisely what is meant by corroboration in this context. Consider again the *Jaffe* case. Corroboration of the defendant's belief that the goods are stolen will often take the form of testimony concerning discussions of that fact and testimony of an unusually low sales price. Suppose this evidence comes entirely from the testimony of a thief. As indicated earlier, there may be valid reasons for allowing a conviction on the basis of this testimony when the goods involved are actually stolen, but those reasons disappear when the goods are only believed to have been stolen. Presumably, then, we are talking about a different type or higher degree of corroboration, a type not required for conviction of the substantive crime.[90] This would, then, entail something more than merely extending the requirement that the defendant's act be "substantial"—to use the Model Penal Code terminology for preparation-attempt cases—to all other attempts. For, having eliminated all objective conduct requirements, we are now forced to consider the quality of the evidence in terms of the reliability of the witnesses, a frame of reference not present in the substantive crime.

At this point we need not consider further whether the proposal has merit. For the proposal, so understood, validates the thesis of this article. The doctrine of impossibility has proved its significance in that it has alerted us to the need for special considerations and additional protections for a particular group of cases. In fact, if we accept the proposition that we are talking about different types of corroboration, then we have to retain the notion of impossibility or create some equivalent concept to help identify which cases need which type of corroboration.

courts. *E.g.*, Moody v. United States, 376 F.2d 525 (9th Cir. 1967); United States v. Marks, 368 F.2d 566 (2d Cir. 1966), *cert. denied*, 386 U.S. 933 (1967). For an extremely interesting case in which the court declined to require corroboration in a prosecution for violating the federal crime of entering a federally insured bank with intent to commit a felony therein, in effect an attempt crime, see page 707, *supra*, see United States v. Audett, 265 F.2d 837, 846-47 (9th Cir. 1959).

90. J. Hall, Theft, Law and Society 174-89 (2d ed. 1952), describes how the difficulty of obtaining proof against "fences" led to the elimination of evidentiary protections such as the requirement of corroboration. It sounds strange to hear the resurrection of corroboration suggested in this context. And if adopted, the experience suggests it may be so effective that nothing is gained in terms of additional convictions.

VIII. CONCLUSION

It has been said that elimination of the defense of impossibility accomplishes the goal of treating similar cases alike.[91] What is similar depends, of course, on the policies one pursues and the factors considered relevant for comparison. To those who would eliminate impossibility as a defense, the defendant's illegal purpose, his mens rea, is the relevant factor. Hopefully it has been demonstrated that the more traditional view was not the result of obtuseness or perversity, but was based on a belief that the defendant's conduct as well as his mens rea were to be considered in drawing the comparison. If we do include the conduct in the comparison, we find that those cases resulting in acquittal due to the impossibility doctrine no longer appear very similar to the cases that result in conviction.

The important contribution of Wharton, Hall, and Williams was their telling demonstration that the problem of impossibility was not at all a problem of logic. Perhaps, in their concentration on this issue, they overlooked the fact that there remained some serious policy determinations to be made. It is here that it might be well to remember the admonition that total law enforcement is not the goal of a democratic society which acknowledges the need to accomodate interests other than crime prevention.[92] This admonition applies to the definition of substantive crimes no less than to the formulation of rules governing the investigation and prosecution of crime.

---

91. Wechsler, Jones & Korn, *supra* note 77, at 572-73.

92. Schwartz, *On Current Proposals to Legalize Wire Tapping*, 103 U. PA. L. REV. 157-58 (1954).

[15]

The Punishment That Leaves Something to Chance

DAVID LEWIS

I

We are accustomed to punish criminal attempts much more severely if they succeed than if they fail. We are also accustomed to wonder why. It is hard to find any rationale for our leniency toward the unsuccessful. Leniency toward aborted attempts, or mere preparation, might be easier to understand. (And whether easy or hard, it is not my present topic.) But what sense can we make of leniency toward a completed attempt—one that puts a victim at risk of harm, and fails only by luck to do actual harm?

Dee takes a shot at his enemy, and so does Dum. They both want to kill; they both try, and we may suppose they try equally hard. Both act out of malice, without any shred of justification or excuse. Both give us reason to fear that they might be ready to kill in the future. The only difference is that Dee hits and Dum misses. So Dee has killed, he is guilty of murder, and we put him to death.[1] Dum has not killed, he is guilty only of attempted murder, and he gets a short prison sentence.

Why? Dee and Dum were equally wicked in their desires. They were equally uninhibited in pursuing their wicked desires. Insofar as the wicked deserve to be punished, they deserve it equally. Their conduct was equally dangerous: they inflicted equal risks of death on their re-

This article arose out of discussion of a lecture by Judith Thomson about the guilt of successful and unsuccessful attempters. I am grateful for comments by John Broome, Stephanie Lewis, T. M. Scanlon, Thomas Schelling, and Jonathan Suzman; by the Editors of *Philosophy & Public Affairs*; and by audiences at Monash University, the Australian National University, and the Russellian Society (Sydney).

1. I do not wish to enter the debate about whether the traditional death penalty is ever justified. If you think not, substitute throughout whatever you think is the correct maximum penalty; my argument will go through almost without change.

spective victims. Insofar as those who act dangerously deserve to be punished, again they deserve it equally. Maybe Dee's act was worse than Dum's act, just because of Dee's success; but it is not the act that suffers punishment, it is the agent. Likewise, if we want to express our abhorrence of wickedness or of dangerous conduct, either exemplar of what we abhor is fit to star in the drama of crime and punishment. Further, Dee and Dum have equally engaged in conduct we want to prevent by deterrence. For we prevent successful attempts by preventing attempts generally. We cannot deter success separately from deterring attempts, since attempters make no separate choice about whether to succeed. Further, Dee and Dum have equally shown us that we might all be safer if we defended ourselves against them; and one function of punishment (at any rate if it is death, imprisonment, or transportation) is to get dangerous criminals off the streets before they do more harm. So how does their different luck in hitting or missing make any difference to considerations of desert, expression, deterrence, or defense? How can it be just, on any credible theory of just punishment, to punish them differently?

Here is one rationale for our peculiar practice. If the gods see innocent blood shed, they will be angry; if they are angry, none of us will be safe until they are propitiated; and to propitiate the gods, we must shed guilty blood. Whereas if by luck no innocent blood is shed, the gods will not be angered just by the sight of unsuccessful wickedness, so there will be no need of propitiation.—This rationale would make sense, if its premises were true. And if we put "the public" or "the victim's kin" for "the gods" throughout it still makes sense; and that way, maybe the premises are true, at least sometimes and to some extent. But this rationale does nothing at all to defend our practice *as just*. If our practice is unjust, then the ways of the gods (or the public, or the kin) are unjust, although if the powers that be want to see injustice done, it might be prudent to ignore justice and do their bidding.

A purely conservative rationale is open to the same complaint. Maybe it is a good idea to stay with the practice we have learned how to operate, lest a reform cause unexpected problems. Maybe it is good for people to see the law go on working as they are accustomed to expect it to. Maybe a reform would convey unintended and disruptive messages: as it might be, that we have decided to take murder less seriously than we used to. These considerations may be excellent reasons why it is prudent to leave well enough alone, and condone whatever injustice there may be in our present practice. They do nothing at all to defend our practice as just.

Another rationale concerns the deterrence of second attempts. If at first you don't succeed, and if success would bring no extra punishment, then you have nothing left to lose if you try, try again. "If exactly the same penalty is prescribed for successes as for attempts, there will be every reason to make sure that one is successful."[2] It cannot hurt to have some deterrence left after deterrence has failed. Maybe the experience of having tried once will make the criminal more deterrable than he was at first.—But why is this any reason for punishing successful attempts more severely? It might as well just be a reason for punishing two attempts more severely than one, which we could do regardless of success. If each separate attempt is punished, and if one share of punishment is not so bad that a second share would be no worse, then we have some deterrence against second attempts.

Another rationale sees punishment purely as a deterrent, and assumes that we will have deterrence enough if we make sure that crime never pays. If so, there is no justification for any more penal harm than it takes to offset the gains from a crime. Then a failed attempt needs no punishment: there are no gains to be offset, so even if unpunished it still doesn't pay.—I reply that in the first place, this system of minimum deterrence seems likely to dissuade only the most calculating of criminals. In the second place, punishment is not just a deterrent. I myself might not insist on retribution per se, but certainly the expressive and defensive functions of punishment are not to be lightly forsaken.

Another rationale invokes the idea of "moral luck."[3] Strange to say, it can happen by luck alone that one person ends up more wicked than another. Perhaps that is why the successful attempter, by luck alone, ends up deserving more severe punishment?—I rely, first, that to some extent this suggestion merely names our problem. We ask how Dee can deserve more severe punishment just because his shot hits the mark.

2. John Kleinig, *Punishment and Desert* (The Hague: Martinus Nijhoff, 1973), p. 132. Kleinig does not take this to afford an adequate justification.

3. See Thomas Nagel, "Moral Luck," *Proceedings of the Aristotelian Society*, supp. vol. 50 (1976): 141, repr. in Nagel, *Mortal Questions* (Cambridge: Cambridge University Press, 1979), p. 29. Nagel distinguishes, as he should, between the "moral luck" of the attempter and the different sort of moral luck that makes some genuine difference to how one is and how one acts.

Call that "moral luck" if you will; then we have been asking all along how this sort of moral luck is possible. But, second, it may be misleading to speak of the moral luck of the attempter, since it may tend to conflate this case with something quite different. The most intelligible cases of moral luck are those in which the lucky and the unlucky alike are disposed to become wicked if tempted, and only the unlucky are tempted. But then, however alike they may have been originally, the lucky and the unlucky do end up different in how they are and in how they act. Not so for the luck of hitting or missing. It makes no difference to how the lucky and the unlucky are, and no difference to how they act.[4]

Finally, another rationale invokes the difference between wholehearted and halfhearted attempts.[5] Both are bad, but wholehearted attempts are worse. A wholehearted attempt involves more careful planning, more precautions against failure, more effort, more persistence, and perhaps repeated tries. *Ceteris paribus*, a wholehearted attempt evinces more wickedness—stronger wicked desires, or less inhibition about pursuing them. *Ceteris paribus*, a wholehearted attempt is more dangerous. It is more likely to succeed; it subjects the victim, knowingly and wrongfully, to a greater risk. Therefore it is more urgently in need of prevention by deterrence. *Ceteris paribus*, the perpetrator of a wholehearted attempt is more of a proven danger to us all, so it is more urgent to get him off the streets. So from every standpoint—desert, expression, deterrence, defense—it makes good sense to punish attempts more severely when they are wholehearted. Now, since wholehearted attempts

4. The luck of hitting and missing does make a difference to how their actions of shooting may be described: Dee's is a killing, Dum's is not. Dee's causes harm and thereby invades the victim's rights in a way that Dum's does not. (Dee invades the victim's right not to be harmed, as well as his right not to be endangered; Dum invades only the latter right.) But this is no difference in how they act, since the description of an action in terms of what it causes is an extrinsic description. The actions themselves, events that are finished when the agent has done his part, do not differ in any intrinsic way.

You might protest that a killing is not over when the killer has done his part; it is a more prolonged event that ends with the death of the victim; so there is, after all, an intrinsic difference between Dee's action of killing and Dum's action of shooting and missing.—No; an action of killing is different from the prolonged event of someone's getting killed, even though "the killing" can denote either one.

5. See Lawrence C. Becker, "Criminal Attempt and the Theory of the Law of Crimes," *Philosophy & Public Affairs* 3, no. 3 (Spring 1974): 288. Becker does not take this to afford an adequate justification.

are more likely to succeed, success is some evidence that the attempt was wholehearted. Punishing success, then, is a rough and ready way of punishing wholeheartedness.

I grant that it is just to punish wholehearted attempts more severely—or better, since "heartedness" admits of degrees, to proportion the punishment to the heartedness of the attempt. And I grant that in so doing we may take the probability of success—in other words, the risk inflicted on the victim—as our measure of heartedness. That means not proportioning the punishment simply to the offender's wickedness, because two equally wicked attempters may not be equally likely to succeed. One may be more dangerous than the other because he has the advantage in skill or resources or information or opportunity. Then if we proportion punishment to heartedness measured by risk, we may punish one attempter more severely not because he was more wicked, but because his conduct was more dangerous. From a purely retributive standpoint, wickedness might seem the more appropriate measure; but from the expressive standpoint, we may prefer to dramatize our abhorrence not of wickedness per se but of dangerous wickedness; and from the standpoint of deterrence or defense, clearly it is dangerous conduct that matters.

So far, so good; but I protest that it is unjust to punish success as a rough and ready way of punishing wholeheartedness. It's just too rough and ready. Success is some evidence of wholeheartedness, sure enough. But it is very unreliable evidence: the wholehearted attempt may very well be thwarted, the half- or quarterhearted attempt may succeed. And we can have other evidence that bears as much or more on whether the attempt was wholehearted. If what we really want is to punish wholeheartedness, we have no business heeding only one unreliable fragment of the total evidence, and then treating that fragment as if it were conclusive. Suppose we had reason—*good* reason—to think that on average the old tend to be more wholehearted than the young in their criminal attempts. Suppose even that we could infer wholeheartedness from age somewhat more reliably than we can infer it from success. Then if we punished attempters more severely in proportion to their age, that would be another rough and ready way of punishing wholeheartedness. *Ex hypothesi*, it would be less rough and ready than what we do in punishing success. It would still fall far short of our standards of justice.

II

In what follows, I shall propose a new rationale. *I do not say that it works.* I do say that the new rationale works better than the old ones. It makes at least a prima facie case that our peculiar practice is just, and I do not see any decisive rebuttal. All the same, I think that the prima facie case is probably not good enough, and probably there is no adequate justification for punishing attempts more severely when they succeed.

Our present practice amounts to a disguised form of *penal lottery*—a punishment that leaves something to chance. Seen thus, it *does* in some sense punish all attempts alike, regardless of success. It is no less just, and no more just, than an undisguised penal lottery would be. Probably any penal lottery is seriously unjust, but it is none too easy to explain why.

By a penal lottery, I mean a system of punishment in which the convicted criminal is subjected to a risk of punitive harm. If he wins the lottery, he escapes the harm. If he loses, he does not. A pure penal lottery is one in which the winners suffer no harm at all; an impure penal lottery is one in which winners and losers alike suffer some harm, but the losers suffer more harm. It is a mixture: part of the punishment is certain harm, part is the penal lottery.

An overt penal lottery is one in which the punishment is announced explicitly as a risk—there might be ways of dramatizing the fact, such as a drawing of straws on the steps of the gallows. A covert penal lottery is one in which the punishment is not announced as a risk, but it is common knowledge that it brings risk with it. (A covert lottery must presumably be impure.)

A historical example of an overt penal lottery is the decimation of a regiment as punishment for mutiny. Each soldier is punished for his part in the mutiny by a one-in-ten risk of being put to death. It is a fairly pure penal lottery, but not entirely pure: the terror of waiting to see who must die is part of the punishment, and this part falls with certainty on all the mutineers alike.

Covert and impure penal lotteries are commonplace in our own time. If one drawback of prison is that it is a place where one is exposed to capricious violence, or to a serious risk of catching AIDS,[6] then a prison

6. See A. Hough and D. M. Schwartz, "AIDS and Prisons," in *Meeting the Challenge: Papers of the First National Conference on AIDS*, ed. Adam Carr (Canberra: Australian Government Publishing Service, 1986), pp. 171–80.

sentence is in part a penal lottery. If the gulag is noted for its abysmal standards of occupational health and safety, then a sentence of forced labor is in part a penal lottery.

III

What do we think, and what should we think, of penal lotteries? Specifically, what should we think of a penal lottery, with death for the losers, as the punishment for all attempts at murder, regardless of success? Successful or not, the essence of the crime is to subject the victim, knowingly and wrongfully, to a serious risk of death. The proposed punishment is to be subjected to a like risk of death.

We need a standard of comparison. Our present system of leniency toward the unsuccessful is too problematic to make a good standard, so let us instead compare the penal lottery with a hypothetical reformed system. How does the lottery compare with a system that punishes all attempts regardless of success, by the certain harm of a moderate prison term? A moderate term, because if we punished successful and unsuccessful attempts alike, we would presumably set the punishment somewhere between our present severe punishment of the one and our lenient punishment of the other. (Let the prison be a safe one, so that in the comparison case we have no trace of a penal lottery.) Both for the lottery and for the comparison case, I shall assume that we punish regardless of success. In the one case, success per se makes no difference to the odds; in the other case, no difference to the time in prison. This is not to say that every convicted criminal gets the very same sentence. Other factors might still make a difference. In particular, heartedness (measured by the risk inflicted) could make a difference, and success could make a difference to the extent that it is part of our evidence about heartedness.

Now, how do the two alternatives compare?

The penal lottery may have some practical advantages. It gets the case over and done with quickly. It is not a crime school. A prison costs a lot more than a gallows plus a supply of long and short straws.[7]

(Likewise a prison with adequate protection against random brutality by guards and fellow inmates costs more than a prison without. So it

7. This point would disappear if something less cheap and quick than death were the penalty for losers of the lottery.

seems that we have already been attracted by the economy of a system that has at least some covert admixture of lottery.)

Like a prison term (or fines, or flogging) and unlike the death penalty *simpliciter*, the penal lottery can be graduated as finely as we like. When we take the crime to be worse, we provide fewer long straws to go with the fatal short straws. In particular, that is how we can provide a more severe punishment for the more wholehearted attempt that subjected the victim to a greater risk.

From the standpoint of dramatizing our abhorrence of wicked and dangerous conduct, a penal lottery seems at least as good as a prison sentence. Making the punishment fit the crime, Mikado-fashion, is *poetic* justice. The point we want to dramatize, both to the criminal and to the public, is that what we think of the crime is just like what the criminal thinks of his punishment. If it's a risk for a risk, how can anybody miss the point?

From the standpoint of deterrence, there is no doubt that we are sometimes well deterred by the prospect of risk.[8] It happens every time we wait to cross the street. It is an empirical question how effective a deterrent the penal lottery might be. Compared with the alternative punishment of a certain harm, such as a moderate prison term, the lottery might give us more deterrence for a given amount of penal harm, or it might give us less. Whether it gives us more or less might depend a lot on the details of how the two systems operate. If the lottery gave us more, that would make it preferable from the standpoint of deterrence.

(We often hear about evidence that certainty is more deterring than severity. But to the extent that this evidence pertains only to the uncertainty of getting caught, getting convicted, and serving the full sentence, it is scarcely relevant. The criminal might think of escaping punishment as a game of skill—his skill, or perhaps his lawyer's. For all we know, a risk of losing a game of chance might be much more deterring than an equal risk of losing a game of skill.)

From the standpoint of defense, the penal lottery gets some dangerous criminals off the streets forever, while others go free at once. Moderate

8. See Thomas C. Schelling, "The Threat That Leaves Something to Chance," in his book *The Strategy of Conflict* (Cambridge: Harvard University Press, 1960). Schelling does not discuss penal lotteries as such, but much of his discussion carries over. What does not carry over, or not much, is his discussion of chancy threats as a way to gain credibility when one has strong reason not to fulfill one's threat.

prison terms would let all go free after a longer time, some of them perhaps reformed and some of them hardened and embittered. It is another empirical question which alternative is the more effective system of defense. Again, the answer may depend greatly on the details of the two systems, and on much else that we cannot easily find out.[9]

IV

So far we have abundant uncertainties, but no clear-cut case against the penal lottery. If anything, the balance may be tipping in its favor. So let us turn finally to the standpoint of desert. Here it is a bit hard to know what to make of the penal lottery. If the court has done its job correctly, then all who are sentenced to face the same lottery, with the same odds, are equally guilty of equally grave crimes. They deserve equal treatment. Do they get it?—Yes and no.

Yes. We treat them alike because we subject them all to the very same penal lottery, with the very same odds. And when the lots are drawn, we treat them alike again, because we follow the same predetermined contingency plan—death for losers, freedom for winners—for all of them alike.

> *No.* Some of them are put to death, some are set free, and what could be more unequal than that?

Yes. Their fates are unequal, of course. But that is not our doing. They are treated unequally by Fortune, not by us.

> *No.* But it is we who hand them over to the inequity of Fortune. We are Fortune's accomplices.

Yes. Everyone is exposed to the inequity of Fortune, in ever so many ways. However nice it may be to undo some of these inequities, we do not ordinarily think of this as part of what is required for equal treatment.

> *No.* It's one thing not to go out of our way to undo the inequities of Fortune; it's another thing to go out of our way to increase them.

9. This question would have to be reconsidered if something other than death were the maximum penalty, and so the penalty for losers of the lottery. It would remain an empirical question, and probably a difficult one, which is the more effective system of defense.

Yes. We do that too, and think it not at all contrary to equal treatment. When we hire astronauts, or soldiers or sailors or firemen or police, we knowingly subject these people to more of the inequities of Fortune than are found in ordinary life.

No. But the astronauts are volunteers . . .

Yes. . . . and so are the criminals, when they commit the crimes for which they know they must face the lottery. The soldiers, however, sometimes are not.

No. Start over. We agreed that the winners and losers deserve equal punishment. That is because they are equally guilty. Then they deserve to suffer equally. But they do not.

Yes. They do not suffer equally; but if they deserve to, that is not our affair. We seldom think that equal punishment means making sure of equal suffering. Does the cheerful man get a longer prison sentence than the equally guilty morose man, to make sure of equal suffering? If one convict gets lung cancer in prison, do we see to it that the rest who are equally guilty suffer equally? When we punish equally, what we equalize is not the suffering itself. What we equalize is our contribution to expected suffering.

No. This all seems like grim sophistry. Surely, equal treatment has to mean more than just treating people so that *some* common description of what we are doing will apply to them all alike.

Yes. True. But we have made up our minds already, in other connections, that lotteries count as equal treatment, or near enough. When we have an indivisible benefit or burden to hand out (or even one that is divisible at a significant cost) we are very well content to resort to a lottery. We are satisfied that all who have equal chances are getting equal treatment—and not in some queer philosophers' sense, but in the sense that matters to justice.

It seems to me that "Yes" is winning this argument, but that truth and justice are still somehow on the side of "No." The next move, dear reader, is up to you. I shall leave it unsettled whether a penal lottery would be just. I shall move on to my second task, which is to show that our present practice amounts to a covert penal lottery. If the penal lottery is just, so is our present practice. If not, not.

63 *The Punishment That Leaves Something to Chance*

V

To show that they do not matter, I shall introduce the differences between an overt penal lottery and our present practice one at a time, by running through a sequence of cases. I claim that at no step is there any significant difference of justice between one case and the next. Such differences as there are will be practical advantages only, and will come out much in favor of our present practice.

Case 1 is the overt penal lottery as we have imagined it already, with one added stipulation, as follows. We will proportion the punishment to the heartedness of the attempt, as measured by the risk of death[10] the criminal knowingly and wrongfully inflicted on the victim. We will do this by sentencing the criminal to a risk equal to the one he inflicted on the victim. If the criminal subjected his victim to an 80 percent risk of death, he shall draw his straw from a bundle of eight short and two long; whereas if he halfheartedly subjected the victim to a mere 40 percent risk, he shall draw from four short and six long; and in this way his punishment shall fit his crime. Therefore the court's task is not limited to ascertaining whether the defendant did knowingly and wrongfully subject the victim to a risk of death; also the court must ascertain how much of a risk it was.

Case 2 is like Case 1, except that we skip the dramatic ceremony on the steps of the gallows and draw straws ahead of time. In fact, we have the drawing even before the trial. It is not the defendant himself who draws, but the Public Drawer. The Drawer is sworn to secrecy; he reveals the outcome only when and if the defendant has been found guilty and sentenced to the lottery. If the defendant is acquitted and the drawing turns out to have been idle, no harm done. Since it is not known ahead of time whether the sentence will be eight and two, four and six, or what, the Drawer must make not one but many drawings ahead of time. He reveals the one, if any, that turns out to be called for.

Case 3 is like Case 2, except without the secrecy. The Drawer announces at once whether the defendant will win or lose in case he is

10. I note a complication once and for all, but I shall ignore it in what follows. The relevant risk is not really the victim's risk of death, but rather the risk of being killed—that is, of dying a death which is caused, perhaps probabilistically, and in the appropriate insensitive fashion, by the criminal's act. Likewise for the criminal's risk in the penal lottery. (On probabilistic and insensitive causation, see my *Philosophical Papers*, vol. II [New York: Oxford University Press, 1986], pp. 175–88.)

found guilty and sentenced. (Or rather, whether he will win or lose if he is sentenced to eight and two, whether he will win or lose if he is sentenced to four and six, and so on.) This means that the suspense in the courtroom is higher on some occasions than others. But that need not matter, provided that the court can stick conscientiously to the task of ascertaining whether the defendant did knowingly and wrongfully subject the victim to risk, and if so how much risk. It is by declaring that a criminal deserves the lottery that the court expresses society's abhorrence of the crime. So the court's task is still worth doing, even when it is a foregone conclusion that the defendant will win the lottery if sentenced (as might happen if he had won all the alternative draws). But the trial may seem idle, and the expression of abhorrence may fall flat, when it is known all along that, come what may, the defendant will never face the lottery and lose.

Case 4 is like Case 3, except that we make the penal lottery less pure. Losers of the penal lottery get death, as before; winners get a short prison sentence. Therefore it is certain that every criminal who is sentenced to the lottery will suffer at least some penal harm. Thus we make sure that the trial and the sentence will be taken seriously even when it is a foregone conclusion that the defendant, if sentenced, will win the lottery.

Case 1 also was significantly impure. If the draw is held at the last minute, on the very steps of the gallows, then every criminal who is sentenced to face the lottery must spend a period of time—days? weeks? years?—in fear and trembling, and imprisoned, waiting to learn whether he will win or lose. This period of terror is a certain harm that falls on winners and losers alike. Case 2 very nearly eliminates the impurity, since there is no reason why the Drawer should not reveal the outcome very soon after the criminal is sentenced. Case 3 eliminates it entirely. (In every case, a defendant must spend a period in fear as he waits to learn whether he will be convicted. But this harm cannot count as penal, because it falls equally on the guilty and the innocent, on those who will be convicted and those who will be acquitted.) Case 4 restores impurity, to whatever extent we see fit, but in a different form.

Case 5 is like Case 4, except that the straws are replaced by a different chance device for determining the outcome of the lottery. The Public Drawer conducts an exact reenactment of the crime. If the victim in the reenactment dies, then the criminal loses the lottery. If it is a good reenactment, the risk to the original victim equals the risk to the new victim in the reenactment, which in turn equals the risk that the criminal will lose the lottery; and so, as desired, we punish a risk by an equal risk.

If the outcome of the lottery is to be settled before the trial, as in Cases 2, 3, and 4, then it will be necessary for the Drawer to conduct not just one but several reenactments. He will entertain all reasonable alternative hypotheses about exactly how the crime might have happened—exactly what the defendant might have done by way of knowingly and wrongfully inflicting risk on the victim. He will conduct one reenactment for each hypothesis. The court's task changes. If the court finds the defendant guilty of knowingly and wrongfully inflicting a risk of death, it is no longer required also to measure the amount of risk. Nobody need ever figure out whether it was 80 percent, 40 percent, or what. Instead, the court is required to ascertain which hypothesis about exactly how the crime happened is correct. Thereby the court chooses which of all the hypothetical reenactments is the one that determines whether the criminal wins or loses his lottery. If the court finds that the criminal took careful aim, then the chosen reenactment will be one in which the criminal's stand-in also took careful aim, whereas if the court finds that the criminal halfheartedly fired in the victim's general direction, the chosen reenactment will be one in which the stand-in did likewise. So the criminal will be more likely to lose his lottery in the first case than in the second.

The drawbacks of a lottery by reenactment are plain to see. Soon we shall find the remedy. But first, let us look at the advantages of a lottery by reenactment over a lottery by drawing straws. We have already noted that with straws, the court had to measure how much risk the criminal inflicted, whereas with reenactments, the court has only to ascertain exactly how the crime happened. Both tasks look well-nigh impossible. But the second must be easier, because the first task consists of the second plus more besides. The only way for the court to measure the risk would be to ascertain just what happened, and then find out just how much risk results from such happenings.

Another advantage of reenactments over straws appears when we try to be more careful about what we mean by "amount of risk." Is it (1) an "objective chance"? Or is it (2) a reasonable degree of belief for a hypothetical observer who knows the situation in as much minute detail as feasible instruments could permit? Or is it (3) a reasonable degree of belief for someone who knows just as much about the details of the situation as the criminal did? Or is it (4) the criminal's actual degree of belief, however unreasonable that might have been? It would be nice not to have to decide. But if we want to match the criminal's risk in a lottery by straws to the victim's risk, then we must decide. Not so for a lottery by reenactment. If the reenactment is perfect, we automatically match the amount of risk in all four senses. Even if the reenactment is imperfect, at least we can assure ourselves of match in senses (3) and (4). It may or may not be feasible to get assured match in senses (1) and (2), depending on the details of what happened. (If it turns out that the criminal left a bomb hooked up to a quantum randomizer, it will be comparatively easy. If he committed his crime in a more commonplace way, it will be much harder.) But whenever it is hard to get assured match in senses (1) and (2), it will be harder still to measure the risk and get assured match in a lottery by straws. So however the crime happened, and whatever sense of match we want, we do at least as well by reenactment as by straws, and sometimes we do better.

Case 6 is like Case 5, except that enactment replaces *re*enactment. We use the original crime, so to speak, as its own perfect reenactment. If the criminal is sentenced to face the lottery, then if his victim dies, he loses his lottery and he dies too, whereas if the victim lives, the criminal wins, and he gets only the short prison sentence. It does not matter when the lottery takes place, provided only that it is not settled so soon that the criminal may know its outcome before he decides whether to commit his crime.

The advantages are many: we need no Drawer to do the work; we need not find volunteers to be the stand-in victims in all the hypothetical reenactments; the "reenactment" is automatically perfect, matching the risk in all four senses; we spare the court the difficult task of ascertaining exactly how the crime happened. If we want to give a risk for a risk, and if we want to match risks in any but a very approximate and uncertain fashion, the lottery by enactment is not only the easy way, it is the only remotely feasible way.

The drawback is confusion. When a criminal is sentenced to face the lottery by straws, nobody will think him more guilty or more wicked just because his straw is short. And when a criminal is sentenced to face the lottery by reenactment, nobody will think him more guilty just because the stand-in victim dies.[11] But if he is sentenced to the lottery by enactment, then one and the same event plays a double role: if his victim dies, that death is at once the main harm done by his crime and also the way of losing his lottery. If we are not careful, we are apt to misunderstand. We may think that the successful attempter suffers a worse fate because he is more guilty when he does a worse harm, rather than because he loses his lottery. But it is not so: his success is irrelevant to his guilt, his wickedness, his desert, and his sentence to face the lottery—exactly as the shortness of his straw would have been, had he been sentenced to the lottery by straws.

VI

I submit that our present practice is exactly Case 6: punishment for attempts regardless of success, a penal lottery by enactment, impurity to help us take the affair seriously even when the lottery is won, and the inevitable confusion. We may not understand our practice as a penal lottery—confused as we are, we have trouble understanding it at all—but, so understood, it does make a good deal of sense. It is another question whether it is really just. Most likely it isn't, but I don't understand why not.

11. If it were known that the victim's risk was fifty-fifty, or if we did not care about matching risks, we could just as well reverse the lottery by enactment: the criminal loses if the victim lives, wins if the victim dies. Certainly nobody will think the criminal is more guilty if the victim *lives*.

Part VI
The Justification of Punishment

[16]

THE EXPRESSIVE FUNCTION OF PUNISHMENT

Joel Feinberg

It might well appear to a moral philosopher absorbed in the classical literature of his discipline, or to a moralist sensitive to injustice and suffering, that recent philosophical discussions of the problem of punishment have somehow missed the point of his interest. Recent influential articles[1] have quite sensibly distinguished between questions of definition and justification, between justifying general rules and particular decisions, between moral and legal guilt. So much is all to the good. When these articles go on to *define* 'punishment', however, it seems to many that they leave out of their ken altogether the very element that makes punishment theoretically puzzling and morally disquieting. Punishment is defined, in effect, as the infliction of hard treatment by an authority on a person for his prior failing in some respect (usually an infraction of a rule or command).[2] There may be a very general sense of the word 'punishment' which is well expressed by this definition; but even if that is so, we can distinguish

---

1 See especially the following: A. Flew, "The Justification of Punishment," *Philosophy,* 29 (1954), 291-307; S. I Benn, "An Approach to the Problems of Punishment," *Philosophy,* 33 (1958), 325-341; and H. L. A. Hart, "Prolegomenon to the Principles of Punishment," *Proceedings of the Aristotelian Society,* 60 (1959-60), 1-26.

2 Hart and Benn both borrow Flew's definition. In Hart's paraphrase, punishment "(i) . . . must involve pain or other consequences normally considered unpleasant. (ii) It must be for an offense against legal rules. (iii) It must be of an actual or supposed offender for his offense. (iv) It must be intentionally administered by human beings other than the offender. (v) It must be imposed and administered by an authority constituted by a legal system against which the offense is committed." (*op. cit.,* p. 4.)

a narrower, more emphatic sense that slips through its meshes. Imprisonment at hard labor for committing a felony is a clear case of punishment in the emphatic sense; but I think we would be less willing to apply that term to parking tickets, offside penalties, sackings, flunkings, and disqualifications. Examples of the latter sort I propose to call *penalties* (merely), so that I may inquire further what distinguishes punishment, in the strict and narrow sense that interests the moralist, from other kinds of penalties.[3]

One method of answering this question is to focus one's attention on the class of nonpunitive penalties in an effort to discover some clearly identifiable characteristic common to them all, and absent from all punishments, on which the distinction between the two might be grounded. The hypotheses yielded by this approach, however, are not likely to survive close scrutiny. One might conclude, for example, that mere penalties are less severe than punishments, but although this is generally true, it is not necessarily and universally so. Again we might be tempted to interpret

---

3 The distinction between punishments and penalties was first called to my attention by Dr. Anita Fritz of the University of Connecticut. Similar distinctions in different terminologies have been made by many. Pollock and Maitland speak of 'true afflictive punishments' as opposed to outlawry, private vengeance, fine, and emendation. (*History of English Law*, 2d ed., II, pp. 451 ff.) The phrase 'afflictive punishment' was invented by Bentham (*Rationale of Punishment*, London, 1830): "These [corporal] punishments are almost always attended with a portion of ignominy, and this does not always increase with the organic pain, but principally depends upon the condition [social class] of the offender." (p. 83). James Stephen says of legal punishment that it "should always connote . . . moral infamy." (*History of the Criminal Law*, II, p. 171.) Lasswell and Donnelly distinguish 'condemnation sanctions' and 'other deprivations'. ("The Continuing Debate over Responsibility: An Introduction to Isolating the Condemnation Sanction," *Yale Law Journal*, 68, 1959.) The traditional common law distinction is between 'infamous' and 'noninfamous' crimes and punishments. Conviction of an 'infamous crime' rendered a person liable to such postpunitive civil disabilities as incompetence to be a witness.

penalties as mere 'price-tags' attached to certain types of behavior that are generally undesirable, so that only those with especially strong motivation will be willing to pay the price.[4] So, for example, deliberate efforts on the part of some western states to keep roads from urban centers to wilderness areas few in number and poor in quality are essentially no different from various parking fines and football penalties. In each case a certain kind of conduct is discouraged without being absolutely prohibited: Anyone who desires strongly enough to get to the wilderness (or park overtime, or interfere with a pass) may do so provided he is willing to pay the penalty (price). On this view penalties are, in effect, licensing fees, different from other purchased permits in that the price is often paid afterward rather than in advance. Since a similar interpretation of punishments seems implausible, it might be alleged that this is the basis of the distinction between penalties and punishments. However, while a great number of penalties can, no doubt, plausibly be treated as retroactive license fees, this is hardly true of all of them. It is certainly not true, for example, of most demotions, firings, and flunkings, that they are 'prices' paid for some already consumed benefit; and even parking fines are sanctions for rules "meant to be taken seriously as . . . standard[s] of behavior,"[5] and thus are more than mere public parking fees.

Rather than look for a characteristic common and

---

[4] That even punishments proper are to be interpreted as taxes on certain kinds of conduct is a view often associated with O. W. Holmes, Jr. For an excellent discussion of Holmes's fluctuations of this question see Mark De Wolfe Howe, *Justice Holmes, The Proving Years* (Cambridge, Mass., 1963), pp. 74-80. See also Lon Fuller, *The Morality of Law* (New Haven, 1964), Chap. II, part 7, and H. L. A. Hart, *The Concept of Law* (Oxford, 1961), p. 39, for illuminating comparisons and contrasts of punishment and taxation.

[5] H. L. A. Hart, *loc. cit.*

peculiar to the penalties on which to ground the distinction between penalties and punishments, we would be better advised, I think, to cast our attention to the examples of punishments. Both penalties and punishments are authoritative deprivations for failures; but apart from these common features, penalties have a miscellaneous character, whereas punishments have an important additional characteristic in common. That characteristic, or specific difference, I shall argue, is a certain expressive function: Punishment is a conventional device for the expression of attitudes of resentment and indignation, and of judgments of disapproval and reprobation, either on the part of the punishing authority himself or of those "in whose name" the punishment is inflicted. Punishment, in short, has a *symbolic significance* largely missing from other kinds of penalties.

The reprobative symbolism of punishment and its character as 'hard treatment', while never separate in reality, must be carefully distinguished for purposes of analysis. Reprobation is itself painful, whether or not it is accompanied by further 'hard treatment'; and hard treatment, such as fine or imprisonment, because of its conventional symbolism, can itself be reprobatory; but still we can conceive of ritualistic condemnation unaccompanied by any *further* hard treatment, and of inflictions and deprivations which, because of different symbolic conventions, have no reprobative force. It will be my thesis in this essay that (1) both the hard treatment aspect of punishment and its reprobative function must be part of the *definition* of legal punishment; and (2) each of these aspects raises its own kind of question about the *justification* of legal punishment as a general practice. I shall argue that some of the jobs punishment does, and some of the conceptual problems it raises, cannot be intelligibly described unless (1) is true; and that the incoherence of a familiar form of the retributive theory results from failure to appreciate the force of (2).

I. *Punishment as Condemnation*

That the expression of the community's condemnation is an essential ingredient in legal punishment is widely acknowledged by legal writers. Henry M. Hart, for example, gives eloquent emphasis to the point:

> What distinguishes a criminal from a civil sanction and all that distinguishes it, it is ventured, is the judgment of community condemnation which accompanies . . . its imposition. As Professor Gardner wrote not long ago, in a distinct but cognate connection:
>
> 'The essence of punishment for moral delinquency lies in the criminal conviction itself. One may lose more money on the stock market than in a court-room; a prisoner of war camp may well provide a harsher environment than a state prison; death on the field of battle has the same physical characteristics as death by sentence of law. It is the expression of the community's hatred, fear, or contempt for the convict which alone characterizes physical hardship as punishment.'
>
> If this is what a 'criminal' penalty is, then we can say readily enough what a 'crime' is. . . . It is conduct which, if duly shown to have taken place, will incur a formal and solemn pronouncement of the moral condemnation of the community. . . . Indeed the condemnation plus the added [unpleasant physical] consequences may well be considered, compendiously, as constituting the punishment.[6]

Professor Hart's compendious definition needs qualification in one respect. The moral condemnation and the

[6] Henry M. Hart, "The Aims of the Criminal Law," *Law and Contemporary Problems,* 23 (1958), II, A, 4.

'unpleasant consequences' that he rightly identifies as essential elements of punishment are not as distinct and separate as he suggests. It is not always the case that the convicted prisoner is first solemnly condemned and then subjected to unpleasant physical treatment. It would be more accurate in many cases to say that the unpleasant treatment itself expresses the condemnation, and that this expressive aspect of his incarceration is precisely the element by reason of which it is properly characterized as punishment and not mere penalty. The administrator who regretfully suspends the license of a conscientious but accident-prone driver can inflict a deprivation without any scolding, express or implied; but the reckless motorist who is sent to prison for six months is thereby inevitably subject to shame and ignominy—the very walls of his cell condemn him and his record becomes a stigma.

To say that the very physical treatment itself expresses condemnation is to say simply that certain forms of hard treatment have become the conventional symbols of public reprobation. This is neither more nor less paradoxical than to say that certain words have become conventional vehicles in our language for the expression of certain attitudes, or that champagne is the alcoholic beverage traditionally used in celebration of great events, or that black is the color of mourning. Moreover, particular kinds of punishment are often used to express quite specific attitudes (loosely speaking, this is part of their 'meaning'); note the differences, for example, between beheading a nobleman and hanging a yeoman, burning a heretic and hanging a traitor, hanging an enemy soldier and executing him by firing squad.

It is much easier to show that punishment has a symbolic significance than to say exactly what it is that punishment expresses. At its best, in civilized and democratic countries, punishment surely expresses the community's strong *disapproval* of what the criminal did. Indeed it can be said that punishment expresses the *judgment* (as distinct from any emotion) of the community that what the criminal did was wrong. I think it is fair to say of our community, however, that punishment generally expresses more than judgments of disapproval; it is also a symbolic way of getting back at the criminal, of expressing a kind of vindictive resentment. To any reader who has in fact spent time in a prison, I venture to say, even Professor Gardner's strong terms—'hatred, fear, or contempt for the convict'—will not seem too strong an account of what imprisonment is universally taken to express. Not only does the criminal feel the naked hostility of his guards and the outside world—that would be fierce enough—but that hostility is self-righteous as well. His punishment bears the aspect of legitimized vengefulness; hence there is much truth in J. F. Stephen's celebrated remark that "The criminal law stands to the passion of revenge in much the same relation as marriage to the sexual appetite."[7]

If we reserve the less dramatic term 'resentment' for the various vengeful attitudes, and the term 'reprobation' for the stern judgment of disapproval, then perhaps we can characterize *condemnation* (or denunciation) as a kind of fusing of resentment and reprobation. That these two elements are generally to be found in legal punishment was well understood by the authors of the Report of the Royal Commission on Capital Punishment:

> Discussion of the principle of *retribution* is apt to be confused because the word is not always used in the same sense. Some-

[7] *General View of the Criminal Law of England,* First ed. (London, 1863), p. 99.

times it is intended to mean vengeance, sometimes reprobation. In the first sense the idea is that of satisfaction by the State of a wronged individual's desire to be avenged; in the second it is that of the State's *marking its disapproval* of the breaking of its laws by a punishment proportionate to the gravity of the offense [my italics].[8]

II. *Some Derivative Symbolic Functions of Punishment*

The relation of the expressive function of punishment to its various central purposes is not always easy to trace. Symbolic public condemnation added to deprivation may help or hinder deterrence, reform, and rehabilitation—the evidence is not clear. On the other hand, there are other functions of punishment, often lost sight of in the preoccupation with deterrence and reform, that presuppose the expressive function and would be impossible without it.

1. *Authoritative Disavowal.* Consider the standard international practice of demanding that a nation whose agent has unlawfully violated the complaining nation's rights should punish the offending agent. For example, suppose that an airplane of nation *A* fires on an airplane of nation *B* while the latter is flying over international waters. Very likely high authorities in nation *B* will send a note of protest to their counterparts in nation *A* demanding, among other things, that the transgressive pilot be punished. Punishing the pilot is an emphatic, dramatic, and well understood way of *condemning* and thereby *disavowing* his act. It tells the world that the pilot had no right to do what he did, that he was on his own in doing it, that his government does not condone that sort of thing. It testifies thereby to government *A*'s recognition of the violated rights

[8] (London, 1953), pp. 17-18.

of government *B* in the affected area, and therefore to the wrongfulness of the pilot's act. Failure to punish the pilot tells the world that government *A* does not consider him to have been personally at fault. That in turn is to claim responsibility for the act, which in effect labels that act as an 'instrument of deliberate national policy', and therefore an act of war. In that case either formal hostilities or humiliating loss of face by one side or the other almost certainly follows. None of this makes any sense without the well understood reprobative symbolism of punishment. In quite parallel ways punishment enables employers to disavow the acts of their employees (though not civil liability for those acts), and fathers the destructive acts of their sons.

2. *Symbolic Non-Acquiescence: 'Speaking in the Name of the People'*. The symbolic function of punishment also explains why even those sophisticated persons who abjure resentment of criminals and look with small favor generally on the penal law are likely to demand that certain kinds of conduct be punished when or if the law lets them go by. In the state of Texas, so-called 'paramour killings' are regarded by the law as not merely mitigated, but completely justifiable.[9] Many humanitarians, I believe, will feel quite spontaneously that a great injustice is done when such killings are left unpunished. The sense of violated justice, moreover, might be distinct and unaccompanied by any frustrated *schaden-freude* toward the killer, lust for blood

[9] The Texas Penal Code (Art. 1220) states: "Homicide is justifiable when committed by the husband upon one taken in the act of adultery with the wife, provided the killing takes place before the parties to the act have separated. Such circumstances cannot justify a homicide when it appears that there has been on the part of the husband, any connivance in or assent to the adulterous connection." New Mexico and Utah have similar statutes. For some striking descriptions of perfectly legal paramour killings in Texas, see John Bainbridge, *The Super-Americans* (Garden City, 1961), pp. 238 ff.

or vengeance, or metaphysical concern lest the universe stay 'out of joint'. The demand for punishment in cases of this sort may instead represent the feeling that paramour killings deserve to be *condemned,* that the law in condoning, even approving of them, speaks for all citizens in expressing a wholly inappropriate attitude toward them. For, in effect, the law expresses the judgment of the 'people of Texas', in whose name it speaks, that the vindictive satisfaction in the mind of a cuckolded husband is a thing of greater value than the very life of his wife's lover. The demand that paramour killings be punished may simply be the demand that this lopsided value judgment be withdrawn and that the state *go on record* against paramour killings, and the law *testify to the recognition* that such killings are wrongful. Punishment no doubt would also help deter killers. This too is a desideratum and a closely related one, but it is not to be identified with reprobation; for deterrence might be achieved by a dozen other techniques, from simple penalties and forfeitures to exhortation and propaganda; but effective public denunciation and, through it, symbolic non-acquiescence in the crime, seem virtually to require punishment.

This symbolic function of punishment was given great emphasis by Kant, who, characteristically, proceeded to exaggerate its importance. Even if a desert island community were to disband, Kant argued, its members should first execute the last murderer left in its jails, "for otherwise they might all be regarded as participators in the [unpunished] murder. . . ."[10] This Kantian idea that in failing to punish wicked acts society endorses them and thus becomes *particeps criminis* does seem to reflect, however dimly, some-

10 *The Philosophy of Law,* trans. W. Hastie (Edinburgh, 1887), p. 198.

thing embedded in common sense. A similar notion underlies whatever is intelligible in the widespread notion that all citizens share the responsibility for political atrocities. Insofar as there is a coherent argument behind the extravagant distributions of guilt made by existentialists and other literary figures, it can be reconstructed in some such way as this: To whatever extent a political act is done 'in one's name', to that extent one is responsible for it. A citizen can avoid responsibility in advance by explicitly disowning the government as his spokesman, or after the fact through open protest, resistance, and so on. Otherwise, by 'acquiescing' in what is done in one's name, one incurs the responsibility for it. The root notion here is a kind of 'power of attorney' a government has for its citizens.

3. *Vindication of the Law.* Sometimes the state goes on record through its statutes, in a way that might well please a conscientious citizen in whose name it speaks, but then through official evasion and unreliable enforcement, gives rise to doubts that the law really means what it says. It is murder in Mississippi, as elsewhere, for a white man intentionally to kill a Negro; but if grand juries refuse to issue indictments or if trial juries refuse to convict, and this is well understood by most citizens, then it is in a purely formal and empty sense indeed that killings of Negroes by whites are illegal in Mississippi. Yet the law stays on the books, to give ever-less-convincing lip service to a noble moral judgment. A statute honored mainly in the breach begins to lose its character as law, unless, as we say, it is *vindicated* (emphatically reaffirmed); and clearly the way to do this (indeed the only way) is to punish those who violate it.

Similarly, *punitive damages,* so-called, are sometimes awarded the plaintiff in a civil action, as a supplement to compensation for his injuries. What more dramatic way of vindicating his violated right can be imagined than to have a court thus forcibly condemn its violation through the symbolic machinery of punishment?

4. *Absolution of Others.* When something scandalous has occurred and it is clear that the wrongdoer must be one of a small number of suspects, then the state, by punishing one of these parties, thereby relieves the others of suspicion, and informally absolves them of blame. Moreover, quite often the absolution of an accuser hangs as much in the balance at a criminal trial as the inculpation of the accused. A good example of this can be found in James Gould Cozzens's novel, *By Love Possessed.* A young girl, after an evening of illicit sexual activity with her boy friend, is found out by her bullying mother, who then insists that she clear her name by bringing criminal charges against the boy. He used physical force, the girl charges; she freely consented, he replies. If the jury finds him guilty of rape, it will by the same token absolve her from (moral) guilt; and her reputation as well as his rides on the outcome. Could not the state do this job without punishment? Perhaps, but when it speaks by punishing, its message is loud, and sure of getting across.

III. *The Constitutional Problem of Defining Legal Punishment*

A philosophical theory of punishment that, through inadequate definition, leaves out the condemnatory function, not only will disappoint the moralist and the traditional moral philosopher; it will seem offensively irrelevant as well to the constitutional lawyer, whose vital concern with punishment is both conceptual, and therefore genuinely philosophical, and practically urgent. The distinction between punishment and mere penalties is a familiar one in the criminal law, where theorists have long engaged in what Jerome Hall calls "dubious dogmatics distinguishing 'civil penalties' from punitive sanctions, and 'public wrongs' from crimes."[11] Our courts now regard it as true (by definition) that all criminal statutes are punitive (merely labeling an act a crime does not make it one unless sanctions are specified); but to the converse question whether all statutes specifying sanctions are *criminal* statutes, the courts are reluctant to give an affirmative reply. There are now a great number of statutes that permit 'unpleasant consequences' to be inflicted on persons and yet are surely not criminal statutes—tax bills, for example, are aimed at regulating, not forbidding, certain types of activity. How to classify borderline cases as either 'regulative' or 'punitive' is not merely an idle conceptual riddle; it very quickly draws the courts into questions of great constitutional import. There are elaborate constitutional safeguards for persons faced with the prospect of punishment; but these do not, or need not, apply when the threatened hard treatment merely 'regulates an activity'.

The 1960 Supreme Court case of Flemming *v.* Nestor[12] is a dramatic (and shocking) example of how a man's fate can depend on whether a government-inflicted deprivation is interpreted as a 'regulative' or 'punitive' sanction. Nestor had immigrated to the United States from Bulgaria in 1913, and in 1955 became eligible for old-age benefits under the Social Security Act. In 1956, however, he was deported in accordance with the Immigration and Nation-

---

11 *General Principles of Criminal Law,* 2d ed. (Indianapolis, 1960), p. 328, hereafter cited as GPCL.

12 Flemming *v.* Nestor 80 S. Ct. 1367 (1960).

ality Act, for having been a member of the Communist Party from 1933 to 1939. This was a hard fate for a man who had been in America for forty-three years and who was no longer a Communist; but at least he would have his social security benefits to support him in his exiled old age. Or so he thought. Section 202 of the amended Social Security Act, however,

> provides for the termination of old-age, survivor, and disability insurance benefits payable to . . . an alien individual who, after September 1, 1954 (the date of enactment of the section) is deported under the Immigration and Nationality Act on any one of certain specified grounds, including past membership in the Communist Party.[13]

Accordingly, Nestor was informed that his benefits would cease.

Nestor then brought suit in a District Court for a reversal of the administrative decision. The court found in his favor and held §202 of the Social Security Act unconstitutional, on the grounds that

> termination of [Nestor's] benefits amounts to punishing him without a judicial trial, that [it] constitutes the imposition of punishment by legislative act rendering §202 a bill of attainder; and that the punishment exacted is imposed for past conduct not unlawful when engaged in, thereby violating the constitutional prohibition on *ex post facto* laws.[14]

The Secretary of Health, Education, and Welfare, Mr. Flemming, then appealed this decision to the Supreme Court.

It was essential to the argument of the District Court that the termination of old-age benefits under §202 was

---

[13] *Ibid.*, p. 1370.

[14] *Ibid.*, p. 1374 (Interspersed citations omitted).

in fact punishment, for if it were properly classified as nonpunitive deprivation, then none of the cited constitutional guarantees was relevant. The constitution, for example, does not forbid all retroactive laws, but only those providing punishment. (Retroactive tax laws may also be hard and unfair, but they are not unconstitutional.) The question before the Supreme Court then was whether the hardship imposed by §202 was punishment. Did this not bring the Court face to face with the properly philosophical question 'What is punishment?' and is it not clear that under the usual definition that fails to distinguish punishment from mere penalties, this particular judicial problem could not even arise?

The fate of the appellee Nestor can be recounted briefly. The five man majority of the court held that he had not been punished—this despite Mr. Justice Brennan's eloquent characterization of him in a dissenting opinion as "an aging man deprived of the means with which to live after being separated from his family and exiled to live among strangers in a land he quit forty-seven years ago."[15] Mr. Justice Harlan, writing for the majority, argued that the termination of benefits, like the deportation itself, was the exercise of the plenary power of Congress incident to the regulation of an activity.

> Similarly, the setting by a State of qualifications for the practice of medicine, and their modification from time to time, is an incident of the State's power to protect the health and safety of its citizens, and its decision to bar from practice persons who commit or have committed a felony is taken as evidencing an intent to exercise that regulatory power, and not a purpose to add to the punishment of ex-felons.[16]

---

[15] *Ibid.*, p. 1385.

[16] *Ibid.*, pp. 1375-6.

Mr. Justice Brennan, on the other hand, argued that it is impossible to think of any purpose the provision in question could possibly serve except to "strike" at "aliens deported for conduct displeasing to the lawmakers."[17]

Surely Justice Brennan seems right in finding in the sanction the expression of Congressional reprobation, and therefore 'punitive intent'; but the sanction itself (in Justice Harlan's words, "the mere denial of a noncontractual governmental benefit"[18]) was not a conventional vehicle for the expression of censure, being wholly outside the apparatus of the criminal law. It therefore lacked the reprobative symbolism essential to punishment generally, and was thus, in its hybrid character, able to generate confusion and judicial disagreement. It was as if Congress had 'condemned' a certain class of persons privately in stage whispers, rather than by pinning the infamous label of criminal on them and letting that symbol do the condemning in an open and public way. Congress without question "intended" to punish a certain class of aliens and did indeed select sanctions of appropriate severity for that use; but the deprivation they selected was not of an appropriate kind to perform the function of public condemnation. A father who 'punishes' his son for a displeasing act the father had not thought to forbid in advance, by sneaking up on him from behind and then throwing him bodily across the room against the wall, would be in much the same position as the legislators of the amended Social Security Act, especially if he then denied to the son that his physical assault on him had had any 'punitive intent', asserting that it was a mere exercise of his paternal prerogative to

17 *Ibid.*, p. 1387.

18 *Ibid.*, p. 1376.

rearrange the household furnishings and other objects in his own living room. This would be to tarnish the paternal authority and infect all later genuine punishments with hollow hypocrisy. This also happens when legislators go outside the criminal law to do the criminal law's job.

In 1961 the New York State Legislature passed the so-called "Subversive Drivers Act" requiring "suspension and revocation of the driver's license of anyone who has been convicted, under the Smith Act, of advocating the overthrow of the Federal government." *The Reporter* magazine[19] quoted the sponsor of the bill as admitting that it was aimed primarily at one person, Communist Benjamin Davis, who had only recently won a court fight to regain his driver's license after his five year term in prison. *The Reporter* estimated that at most a "few dozen" people would be kept from driving by the new legislation. Was this punishment? Not at all, said the bill's sponsor, Assemblyman Paul Taylor. The legislature was simply exercising its right to regulate automobile traffic in the interest of public safety:

> Driving licenses, Assemblyman Taylor explained . . . are not a 'right' but a 'valuable privilege.' The Smith Act Communists, after all, were convicted of advocating the overthrow of the government by force, violence, or assassination. ('They always leave out the assassination,' he remarked. 'I like to put it in.') Anyone who was convicted under such an act had to be 'a person pretty well dedicated to a certain point of view,' the assemblyman continued, and anyone with that particular point of view 'can't be concerned about the rights of others.' Being concerned about the rights of others, he concluded, 'is a prerequisite of being a good driver.'[20]

---

19 *The Reporter* (May 11, 1961), p. 14.

20 *Loc. cit.*

This shows how transparent can be the effort to mask punitive intent. The Smith Act ex-convicts were treated with such severity and in such circumstances that no non-punitive legislative purpose could *plausibly* be maintained; yet that *kind* of treatment (quite apart from its severity) lacks the reprobative symbolism essential to clear public denunciation. After all, aged, crippled, and blind persons are also deprived of their licenses, so it is not *necessarily* the case that reprobation attaches to that kind of sanction. And so victims of a cruel law understandably claim that they have been punished, and retroactively at that. Yet strictly speaking they have not been *punished;* they have been treated much worse.

IV. *The Problem of Strict Criminal Liability*

The distinction between punishments and mere penalties, and the essentially reprobative function of the former, can also help clarify the controversy among writers on the criminal law about the propriety of so-called 'strict liability offenses'—offenses for the conviction of which there need be no showing of 'fault' or 'culpability' on the part of the accused. If it can be shown that he committed an act proscribed by statute then he is guilty irrespective of whether he had justification or excuse for what he did. Perhaps the most familiar examples come from the traffic laws: Leaving a car parked beyond the permitted time in a restricted zone is automatically to violate the law, and penalties will be imposed however good the excuse. Many strict liability statutes do not even require an overt act; these proscribe not certain conduct but certain *results*. Some make mere unconscious possession of contraband, firearms, or narcotics a crime, others the sale of misbranded articles or impure foods. The liability for so-called 'public welfare offenses' may seem especially severe:

> . . . with rare exceptions, it became definitely established that *mens rea* is not essential in the public welfare offenses, indeed that even a very high degree of care is irrelevant. Thus a seller of cattle feed was convicted of violating a statute forbidding misrepresentation of the percentage of oil in the product, despite the fact that he had employed a reputable chemist to make the analysis and had even understated the chemist's findings.[21]

The rationale of strict liability in public welfare statutes is that violation of the public interest is more likely to be prevented by unconditional liability than by liability that can be defeated by some kind of excuse; that even though liability without 'fault' is severe, it is one of the known risks incurred by businessmen; and that besides, the sanctions are *only fines,* hence not really 'punitive' in character. On the other hand, strict liability to *imprisonment* (or 'punishment proper') "has been held by many to be incompatible with the basic requirements of our Anglo-American, and indeed, any civilized jurisprudence."[22] Why should this be? In both kinds of case, defendants may have sanctions inflicted upon them even though they are acknowledged to be without fault; and the difference cannot be simply that imprisonment is always and necessarily a greater hurt than fine, for this is not always so. Rather, the reason why strict liability to imprisonment (punishment) is so much more repugnant to our sense of justice than is strict liability to fine (penalty) is simply that imprisonment in modern times has taken on the symbolism of public reprobation. In the words of Justice Brandeis, "It is . . . im-

21 Jerome Hall, GPCL, p. 329.

22 Richard A. Wasserstrom, "Strict Liability in the Criminal Law," *Stanford Law Review,* 12 (1960), p. 730.

prisonment in a penitentiary, which now renders a crime infamous."[23] We are familiar with the practice of penalizing persons for 'offenses' they could not help. It happens every day in football games, business firms, traffic courts, and the like. But there is something very odd and offensive in *punishing* people for admittedly faultless conduct; for not only is it arbitrary and cruel to *condemn* someone for something he did (admittedly) without fault, it is also self-defeating and irrational.

Though their abundant proliferation[24] is a relatively recent phenomenon, statutory offenses with nonpunitive sanctions have long been familiar to legal commentators, and long a source of uneasiness to them. This is "indicated by the persistent search for an appropriate label, such as 'public torts,' 'public welfare offenses,' 'prohibitory laws,' 'prohibited acts,' 'regulatory offenses,' 'police regulations,' 'administrative misdemeanors,' 'quasi-crimes,' or 'civil offenses.' "[25] These represent alternatives to the unacceptable categorization of traffic infractions, inadvertent violations of commercial regulations, and the like, as *crimes,* their perpetrators as *criminals,* and their penalties as *punishments.* The drafters of the new Model Penal Code have defined a class of infractions of penal law forming no part

---

23 United States v. Moreland, 258 U.S. 433, 447-48. Quoted in Hall, GPCL, p. 327.

24 "A depth study of Wisconsin statutes in 1956 revealed that of 1113 statutes creating criminal offenses [punishable by fine, imprisonment, or both] which were in force in 1953, no less than 660 used language in the definitions of the offenses which omitted all reference to a mental element, and which therefore, under the canons of construction which have come to govern these matters, left it open to the courts to impose strict liability if they saw fit." Colin Howard, "Not Proven," *Adelaide Law Review,* 1 (1962), 274. The study cited is: Remington, Robinson and Zick, "Liability Without Fault Criminal Statutes," *Wisconsin Law Review* (1956), 625, 636.

25 Rollin M. Perkins, *Criminal Law* (Brooklyn, 1957), pp. 701-2.

of the substantive criminal law. These they call 'violations', and their sanctions 'civil penalties'.

> *Section 1.04. Classes of Crimes: Violations*
>
> (1) An offense defined by this code or by any other statute of this State, for which a sentence of [death or of] imprisonment is authorized, constitutes a crime. Crimes are classified as felonies, misdemeanors, or petty misdemeanors.
>
> [(2), (3), (4) define felonies, misdemeanors, and petty misdemeanors.]
>
> (5) An offense defined by this Code or by any other statute of this State constitutes a violation if it is so designated in this Code or in the law defining the offense or if no other sentence than a fine, or fine and forfeiture or other civil penalty is authorized upon conviction or if it is defined by a statute other than this Code which now provides that the offense shall not constitute a crime. A violation does not constitute a crime and conviction of a violation shall not give rise to any disability or legal disadvantage based on conviction of a criminal offense.[26]

Since violations, unlike crimes, carry no social stigma, it is often argued that there is no serious injustice if, in the interest of quick and effective law enforcement, violators are held unconditionally liable. This line of argument is persuasive when we consider only parking and minor traffic violations, illegal sales of various kinds, and violations of health and safety codes, where the penalties serve as warnings and the fines are light. But the argument loses all cogency when the 'civil penalties' are severe—heavy fines, forfeitures of property, removal from office, suspension of a license, withholding of an important 'benefit', and the like. The condemnation of the faultless may be the most flagrant injustice, but the good natured, noncondemnatory infliction of severe hardship on the innocent is little better.

---

[26] American Law Institute, *Model Penal Code, Proposed Official Draft* (Philadelphia, 1962).

It is useful to distinguish violations and civil penalties from crimes and punishments; but it does not follow that the safeguards of culpability requirements and due process which justice demands for the latter are always irrelevant encumbrances to the former. Two things are morally wrong: (1) to condemn a faultless man while inflicting pain or deprivation on him however slight (unjust punishment); and (2) to inflict unnecessary and severe suffering on a faultless man even in the absence of condemnation (unjust civil penalty). To exact a two dollar fine from a hapless violator for overtime parking, however, even though he could not possibly have helped it, is to do neither of these things.

V. *Justifying Legal Punishment: Letting the Punishment Fit the Crime*

Public condemnation, whether avowed through the stigmatizing symbolism of punishment or unavowed but clearly discernible (mere 'punitive intent'), can greatly magnify the suffering caused by its attendant mode of hard treatment. Samuel Butler keenly appreciated the difference between reprobative hard treatment (punishment) and the same treatment sans reprobation:

> . . . we should hate a single flogging given in the way of mere punishment more than the amputation of a limb, if it were kindly and courteously performed from a wish to help us out of our difficulty, and with the full consciousness on the part of the doctor that it was only by an accident of constitution that he was not in the like plight himself. So the Erewhonians take a flogging once a week, and a diet of bread and water for two or three months together, whenever their straightener recommends it.[27]

[27] *Erewhon* (London, 1901), Chapter 10.

Even floggings and imposed fastings do not constitute punishments, then, where social conventions are such that they do not express public censure (what Butler called 'scouting'); and as therapeutic treatments simply, rather than punishments, they are easier to take.

Yet floggings and fastings do hurt, and far more than is justified by their Erewhonian (therapeutic) objectives. The same is true of our own State Mental Hospitals where criminal psychopaths are often sent for 'rehabilitation': Solitary confinement may not hurt *quite* so much when called 'the quiet room', or the forced support of heavy fire extinguishers when called 'hydrotherapy';[28] but their infliction on patients can be so cruel (whether or not their quasi-medical names mask punitive intent) as to demand justification.

Hard treatment and symbolic condemnation, then, are not only both necessary to an adequate definition of 'punishment'; each also poses a special problem for the justification of punishment. The reprobative symbolism of punishment is subject to attack not only as an independent source of suffering but as the vehicle of undeserved responsive attitudes and unfair judgments of blame. One kind of skeptic, granting that penalties are needed if legal rules are to be enforced, and also that society would be impossible without general and predictable obedience to such rules, might nevertheless question the need to add condemnation to the penalizing of violators. Hard treatment of violators, he might grant, is an unhappy necessity, but reprobation of the offender is offensively self-righteous and cruel; adding gratuitous insult to necessary injury can serve no useful

[28] These two examples are cited by Francis A. Allen in "Criminal Justice, Legal Values and the Rehabilitative Ideal," *Journal of Criminal Law, Criminology and Police Science*, 50 (1959), 229.

purpose. A partial answer to this kind of skeptic has already been given. The condemnatory aspect of punishment does serve a socially useful purpose: It is precisely the element in punishment that makes possible the performance of such symbolic functions as disavowal, non-acquiescence, vindication, and absolution.

Another kind of skeptic might readily grant that the reprobative symbolism of punishment is necessary to and justified by these various derivative functions. Indeed, he may even add deterrence to the list, for condemnation is likely to make it clear where it would not otherwise be so that a penalty is not a mere price-tag. Granting that point, however, this kind of skeptic would have us consider whether the ends that justify public condemnation of criminal conduct might not be achieved equally well by means of less painful symbolic machinery. There was a time, after all, when the gallows and the rack were the leading clear symbols of shame and ignominy. Now we condemn felons to penal servitude as the way of rendering their crimes infamous. Could not the job be done still more economically? Isn't there a way to stigmatize without inflicting any further (pointless) pain to the body, to family, to creative capacity?

One can imagine an elaborate public ritual, exploiting the trustiest devices of religion and mystery, music and drama, to express in the most solemn way the community's condemnation of a criminal for his dastardly deed. Such a ritual might condemn so very emphatically that there could be no doubt of its genuineness, thus rendering symbolically superfluous any further hard physical treatment. Such a device would preserve the condemnatory function of punishment while dispensing with its usual physical forms—incarceration and corporal mistreatment. Perhaps this is only idle fantasy; perhaps there is more to it. The question is surely open. The only point I wish to make here is one about the nature of the question. The problem of justifying punishment, when it takes this form, may really be that of justifying our particular symbols of infamy.

Whatever the form of skeptical challenge to the institution of punishment, however, there is one traditional answer to it that seems to me to be incoherent. I refer to that form of the Retributive Theory which mentions neither condemnation nor vengeance, but insists instead that the ultimate justifying purpose of punishment is to match off moral gravity and pain, to give each offender exactly that amount of pain the evil of his offense calls for, on the alleged principle of justice that the wicked should suffer pain in exact proportion to their turpitude.

I will only mention in passing the familiar and potent objections to this view.[29] The innocent presumably deserve *not* to suffer just as the guilty are supposed to deserve to suffer; yet it is impossible to hurt an evil man without imposing suffering on those who love or depend on him. Deciding the right amount of suffering to inflict in a given case would require an assessment of the character of the offender as manifested through his whole life, and also his total lifelong balance of pleasure and pain, an obvious impossibility. Moreover, justice would probably demand the abandonment of general rules in the interests of individuation of punishment since there will inevitably be inequalities of moral guilt in the commission of the same crime, and inequalities of suffering from the same punish-

---

29 For more convincing statements of these arguments, see *iter alia:* W. D. Ross, *The Right and the Good* (Oxford, 1930), pp. 56-65; J. D. Mabbott, "Punishment," *Mind,* 49 (1939); A. C. Ewing, *The Morality of Punishment* (London, 1929), Chap. 1; and F. Dostoevsky, *The House of the Dead.*

ment. If not dispensed with, however, general rules must list all crimes in the order of their moral gravity, all punishments in the order of their severity, and the matchings between the two scales. But the moral gravity scale would have to list motives and purposes, not simply types of overt acts, for a given crime can be committed from any kind of 'mental state', and its 'moral gravity' in a given case surely must depend in part on its accompanying motive. Condign punishment then would have to match suffering to motive (desire, belief, etc.), not to dangerousness or to amount of harm done. Hence some petty larcenies would be punished more severely than some murders. It is not likely we should wish to give power to judges and juries to make such difficult moral judgments. Worse than this, the judgments required are not merely 'difficult', they are in principle impossible. It may seem 'self-evident' to some moralists that the passionate impulsive killer, for example, deserves less suffering for his wickedness than the scheming deliberate killer; but if the question of comparative *dangerousness* is left out of mind, reasonable men not only can but will disagree in their appraisals of comparative blameworthiness, and there appears no rational way of resolving the issue.[30] Certainly, there is no rational way of demonstrating that one deserves exactly twice or three-eighths or twelve-ninths as much suffering as the other; yet on some forms, at least, of this theory, the amount of suffering inflicted for any two crimes should stand in exact proportion to the 'amounts' of wickedness in the criminals.

For all that, however, the pain-fitting-wickedness version of the retributive theory does erect its edifice of moral

[30] Cf. Jerome Michael and Herbert Wechsler, *Criminal Law and its Administration* (Chicago, 1940), "Note on Deliberation and Character," pp. 170-2.

superstition on a foundation in moral common sense, for justice *does* require that in some (other) sense "the punishment fit the crime." What justice requires is that the *condemnatory aspect* of the punishment suit the crime, that the crime be of a kind that is truly worthy of reprobation. Further, the degree of disapproval expressed by the punishment should 'fit' the crime only in the unproblematic sense that the more serious crimes should receive stronger disapproval than the less serious ones, the seriousness of the crime being determined by the amount of harm it generally causes and the degree to which people are disposed to commit it. That is quite another thing than requiring that the hard treatment component, considered apart from its symbolic function, should 'fit' the moral quality of a specific criminal act, assessed quite independently of its relation to social harm. Given our conventions, of course, condemnation is expressed by hard treatment, and the degree of harshness of the latter expresses the degree of reprobation of the former; still this should not blind us to the fact that it is social disapproval and its appropriate expression that should fit the crime, and not hard treatment (pain) as such. Pain should match guilt only insofar as its infliction is the symbolic vehicle of public condemnation.

JOEL FEINBERG

PRINCETON UNIVERSITY

[17]

The retributive idea

JEAN HAMPTON

> "One day, a serf-boy, a little boy of eight, threw a stone in play and hurt the paw of the General's favourite hound. 'Why is my favourite dog lame?' He was told that the boy had thrown a stone at it and hurt his paw. 'Oh, so it's you, is it?' said the General looking him up and down. 'Take him!' They took him. They took him away from his mother, and he spent the night in the lock-up. Early next morning the General, in full dress, went out hunting. He mounted his horse, surrounded by his hangers-on, his whips, and his huntsmen, all mounted. His house-serfs were all mustered to teach them a lesson, and in front of them all stood the child's mother. The boy was brought out of the lock-up. It was a bleak, cold, misty autumn day, a perfect day for hunting. The General ordered the boy to be undressed. The little boy was stripped naked. He shivered, panic-stricken and not daring to utter a sound. 'Make him run!' ordered the General, 'Run, run!' the whips shouted at him. The boy ran. 'Sick him!' bawled the General, and set the whole pack of borzoi hounds on him. They hunted the child down before the eyes of his mother, and the hounds tore him to pieces. . . . Well, what was one to do with [the General]? . . . "
>
> "Shoot him!" Alyosha said softly.
>
> Fyodor Dostoevsky, *The Brothers Karamazov*

Jeffrie Murphy's qualified defense of retributive hatred prompts me to reconsider my categorization of the "hateful" emotions. I argued in Chapter 2 that there is more than one variety of hatred, two of which - spiteful and malicious hatred - I contended were self-defeating, and another of which - moral hatred - I defended. Murphy suggests, in response, that there is a variety of hatred that I missed: like moral hatred this con-attitude involves opposition to a wrongdoer and his cause on moral grounds, but like malicious or spiteful hatred, it involves the desire either to hurt the wrongdoer or to see him suffer. Murphy names this emotion "retributive hatred." Is it true, as Murphy claims, that this is a distinctive and legitimate (albeit somewhat dangerous) form of hatred?

I. PROBLEMS WITH RETRIBUTION

For some readers, the existence of this emotion as a distinct and morally acceptable response to wrongdoing will seem obvious. Other readers, however, will be troubled by and suspicious of it: is there a justifiable reason, they wonder, why a victim who purportedly experiences such hate wants to see the wrongdoer suffer?

In Chapter 2 I offered explanations of why haters desire suffering for those they hate. Malicious and spiteful haters desire the suffering either to effect or to vindicate their sense of what their relative standings on a competitive ranking ladder should be. And any attempt by the moral hater to inflict pain on the one he hates is a means of securing victory over the hated one and his immoral cause. But if Murphy is right that there is a retributive hatred that is distinct from both of these responses, then neither of these reasons explains the appeal of the hated one's suffering for the person experiencing this emotion.

Murphy proposes both to explain and to justify this appeal by attributing to retributive haters the desire to see the hated one suffer for retributive reasons. But what are these reasons? Advocates of retribution typically answer that there is no *telos*, or goal, behind the suffering retributivists want: it is simply desired because it is supposed to be "fitting" or "suitable" or "right." And in response to queries about *why* suffering is suitable for wrongdoers, retributivists typically insist that this question has no answer. It is supposed to be bedrock intuition that, at the very least, those who are not guilty ought not to suffer pain, and more positively, that those who are guilty deserve to suffer in proportion to the pain they have caused. J. L. Mackie claims that such ideas have for us an "immediate, underived moral appeal or moral authority."[1] And like Kant and Hegel, Mackie contends that "if we did not feel that there was such a positive retributivist reason for imposing a penalty, we should not feel that even sound arguments in terms of deterrence or reformation or any similar future benefit would make it morally right to inflict suffering or deprivation on the criminal."[2]

Those suspicious of retribution are generally unpersuaded by this kind of defense. Presumably they are the people who either do not find this firm "bedrock intuition" inside themselves or are suspicious of its authority and thus cannot be convinced by an unanalyzed appeal to it.[3] Accordingly, some retributivists have attempted to make sense of the supposed fittingness of inflicting suffering on a wrongdoer, with dubious results. For example, Nozick proposes that the punishment represents a kind of "linkage" between the criminal and "right values."[4] But why is inflicting pain on someone a way of effecting this linkage? Why isn't the infliction of a pleasurable experience for the sake of the crime just as good a way of linking the wrongdoer with these right values? If Nozick explains the linkage of pain with crime by saying that the pain is necessary to convey to the criminal that his actions

1 J. L. Mackie, "Morality and the Retributive Emotions," *Criminal Justice Ethics*, (1982), pp. 3–9.
2 Ibid., p. 4.
3 Mackie himself admits that there does not seem to be any readily understandable way of making sense of this idea and, as I will discuss later, proposes an evolutionary – and merely explanatory – derivation of retribution as a sentiment. See pp. 3–4.
4 Robert Nozick, *Philosophical Explanations* (Cambridge, Mass.: Harvard University Press, 1981), p. 374.

were wrong, then he has answered the question but lost his retributive theory, putting forward instead a variation of the theory justifying punishment as moral education.[5] Other philosophers, such as Hegel, speak of punishment as a way of annulling or cancelling the crime, and hence "deserved" for that reason.[6] But although these words have a nice metaphorical ring to them, it is hard to see how they can be given a literal force that will explain the retributivist's concept of desert. As Mackie notes, punishment cannot eliminate crimes in any literal sense, because future events never cause past events not to have happened.[7]

A different defense of retribution has been advocated by Herbert Morris, and although attracted to it in earlier writings, Murphy has recently come to question it.[8] On this view, retribution is characterized in terms of *distributive justice*. Laws are understood as constraints on behavior which society finds collectively beneficial; individuals who break those laws for individually rational reasons are subverting the system for private gain in a way that makes them similar to free riders (i.e., people who derive gain from a collective good without paying for that good). Punishment of these free riders is a way to "even up the score": the legal system takes away, by means of pain, the benefit these individuals derived from their lawbreaking.

5 See Herbert Morris, "The Paternalistic Theory of Punishment," in *Punishment and Rehabilitation*, ed. J. Murphy (Belmont, Calif.: Wadsworth, 1985); and Jean Hampton, "The Moral Education Theory of Punishment," *Philosophy and Public Affairs*, Summer 1984, pp. 245-73.

6 See his *Philosophy of Right*, ed. T. M. Knox (Oxford: Oxford University Press, 1976).

7 See Mackie, p. 4. Both Mackie and Herbert Fingarette (the latter in "Punishment and Suffering," *Proceedings of the American Philosophical Association*, 1977) review a variety of retributivist arguments in defense of the idea that wrongdoers deserve to suffer, all of which appear to come up short. Each also makes a positive proposal of his own. I consider Mackie's later in this chapter and Fingarette's in note 20.

8 See Herbert Morris, "Persons and Punishment," in Murphy, *Punishment and Rehabilitation*. Murphy discusses this paper and his new worries about it in note 10 to Chapter 3.

But what is this benefit? If it is the monetary gain from the crime, then compensation of the victim would be sufficient to take away the wrongdoer's benefit. Yet the retributivist would desire punishment over and above any compensation provided by, say, a thief to her victim. And on this view it would make no sense to punish unsuccessful offenders.

So perhaps the criminal's benefit which the punishment is supposed to take away is the elevation of utility that comes from being able to break off the restraints of society and pursue one's own good. On this view, a thief must be punished even after she has been made to compensate her victim, in order to take from her the advantage that comes from the lawbreaking itself. One immediate problem with this position is that because all lawbreakers have benefited in the same way and (it seems) to the same extent by throwing off the restraints of law, the position seems to require that all lawbreakers receive the same punishment. To avoid this problem, an advocate of the position would have to develop a theory that explains how those who break gravely important laws derive more benefit from so doing that those who violate less serious laws, so that the former deserve more punishment than the latter.

Suppose for the sake of argument that such a theory could be developed.[9] While there are some crimes which this position, supplemented by such a theory, might be thought to suit, such as thefts, embezzlements and property crimes generally, other crimes make the position look uncomfortably strange - even repulsive. Consider the crime of rape. Are we to understand that the reason we punish rapists is that we believe they derived a benefit from being able to rape (which is greater than that gained by those who merely steal cars or speed on the highway) that we wish *we* could have but which we prevent ourselves from enjoying because we believe such conduct, when performed on a widespread basis, is collectively disadvantageous? Or consider murder: do we envy the

9 See George Sher, *Desert* (Princeton, N.J.: Princeton University Press, 1987), which tries to do this.

murderer his freedom to satisfy his desires through killing, and punish him merely because we seek to take from him the advantage of being unrestrained in pursuit of his murderous desires, where that restraint is one we would willingly throw off but for our recognition that retaining it is mutually advantageous? Such suggestions seem ridiculous. The idea that punishment is simply the taking away of the *advantages* which rapists or murderers have by virtue of being unrestrained presupposes that we accept that their actions (or the consequences of the actions) are, at least in certain circumstances, inherently desirable and rational, and that we object to them only because, if performed by everyone, they would be collectively harmful. Hence it is a theory presupposing a position on the nature of criminal law and criminal acts which is (to use a phrase of Murphy's) too "creepy" to be right.[10]

But perhaps we can make it less creepy.[11] Suppose we say, not that the criminal gets an advantage from his crime, but that when he commits a crime he isn't paying the *cost* we are paying when we obey the law. Again, this makes him, in a different way, a free rider, because he enjoys the benefits of our cost paying while not paying them himself. But once again, although this theory may explain, in part, the nature of our condemnation of those who violate various sorts of property or tax laws, it does a poor job of accounting for condemnation of those who violate persons. If I refrain from murdering you, am I really imposing a cost on myself for the sake of creating a collectively advantageous social order? If I become angry at you for murdering, is my anger solely or even primarily about the fact that you haven't paid the cost I've paid but enjoyed the fact that I and others have paid it? Once again, such a view seems incorrect.

But the fact that it is incorrect teaches us something important: this theory of retribution fails in a fully adequate way to

10 J. Murphy, "The Justice of Economics," *Philosophical Topics*, 14 (Fall 1986), p. 206.

11 This more plausible line was suggested to me by Richard Gale.

link our condemnation of a wrongdoer *to that which makes his conduct wrong.*[12] The *right* theory of retribution is one that will be able to connect retributive punishment with the immorality of the conduct being punished.

Does Mackie's theory of retribution successfully link assessments of immorality with the retributive response? Mackie believes retribution is a *feeling* which has evolved in our species and which is much like the "bite back" response I briefly mentioned in Chapter 2. Even as dogs may bite and cats may scratch those who attack them, human beings, according to Mackie, feel the emotional urge to "hit" those who hurt them. Such "hitting" is unreasoned and unreasoning – it is instinctive in just the way that a snarl or a bite following a harm is instinctive in other mammals. So we snap at relatives, verbally spar with colleagues, and some of us even physically attack those who have hurt us. Mackie argues that this emotional response exists within us because it encourages cooperation among human beings by introducing a negative sanction for non-cooperation, so that it has been selected for and refined in our highly social species. Hence, this response is not something one engages in so that one might deter exploiters in the future; instead it is an instinct for attack following a harm engaged in for *no* reason, but which has been implanted in one as a member of the human species because of its deterring consequences. The instinct itself isn't teleological, but its existence in the human being is explained by the fact that it furthers this creature's efforts at survival.

Mackie found this style of explanation of retribution appealing insofar as it fits with advocates' defense of it as foundational while also making teleological sense of it. Appealing though it is, I would argue that this approach to retribution is at best incomplete. Mackie's theory implicitly denies to retribution any cognitive content. (Note that his

12 Except perhaps for property crimes. The free-rider explanation might provide at least part of the reason why these sorts of actions are immoral, accounting for the plausibility of the theory when it is applied to them.

referring to it as a 'sentiment' presupposes a non-cognitivist approach to the emotions, with which both Murphy and I disagree.) But cognitive content is precisely what those who defend retribution must understand the response to have if retribution is to *justify* the infliction of harm on wrongdoers. A primitive urge, which is all the bite-back response could be in other mammals, cannot by itself justify anything.[13] Mackie himself realizes this, and thereby justifies the harm his retributive sentiment calls for by appealing to the evolutionary advantages of the sentiment's existence in human beings; for Mackie *the sentiment itself* doesn't justify the harm. Yet traditional retributivists have insisted that retribution is an idea which does have justificatory force in and of itself: that wrongdoers deserve to suffer is supposed to be a good *reason* for inflicting harm on them.

Mackie's analysis also seems to provide us with too simple a characterization of the victim's state of mind. Consider Franny, the rape victim in John Irving's *The Hotel New Hampshire* (discussed by Murphy in note 7 to Chapter 3). Franny was an angry woman, and there might well have been something primitive and unreasoned about her anger. But she is also described as someone who, after satisfying her desire to harm the gang leader rapist, finally achieved *peace* by doing so. Now successful accomplishment of what instinct demands brings with it what we might call 'relief' (e.g., after sexual intercourse or a good meal), but 'peace' seems to describe a mental as well as a physical contentment. Franny badly *wanted* something which the harm to the gang leader could effect; once that harm was inflicted by her she got what she badly wanted, and this is the kind of situation in which people find themselves "at peace." Proponents of

13 Mackie himself believes this, and he argues that the retributive sentiment in human beings would have to be explained by making reference to its development in a social context. But he never explains how the sentiment's role in a society helps us to understand the sentiment in a more full-bodied way, or how it helps us to differentiate it from mere strike-back responses in more primitive creatures (some of whom, e.g., primates, are also social animals).

retribution would say Franny saw the suffering as "deserved," wanted it for that reason and achieved satisfaction and contentment after delivering it. But this notion of "desert" seems to be a cognitive element in Franny's emotional state. Mackie provides us with no explanation of what it is. So while I believe Mackie is probably right that there is a natural instinct for harming that frequently accompanies (although need not accompany) our attempts to inflict pain on those who wrong us, I would also argue that he is not correct to think that this is *all* retribution is. The concept of retributive desert has once again escaped analysis.

It is partly because retributivists have been at a loss to explain their notion of desert that I, along with others,[14] have proposed that retribution may be nothing more than revenge. Perhaps the retributivist's *lex talionis*, his "eye for an eye, tooth for a tooth" conception of punishment, is just a restatement of the kind of vengeance which victims frequently want. The wrongdoer inflicts one pain; the victim (or the society which represents him) reciprocates with a second. Aren't both parties simply engaged in a kind of competitive struggle for standing, in which harm is taken either to effect or to prove a diminishment of the other's position relative to one's own, a diminishment in which one glories?

Some of Murphy's examples encourage this dark thought. Consider his discussion of Ruth (in note 20 to Chapter 3) from Fay Weldon's novel *The Life and Loves of a She-Devil*, whose wish to get even with her former husband and his new wife drives her to extraordinary lengths until she successfully brings them low. Here is a woman whose demand for "justice" seems in fact to be a demand for a competitive victory over those she wants to diminish, and that is precisely the strategy of the malicious hater.

But Murphy describes other victims, whose interest in harming their assailants does not seem, at least at first

14 See my "Moral Education Theory of Punishment." And note that the Supreme Court justices' decision in *Furman v. Georgia* characterized retribution as "naked vengeance" arising from a need of our "baser selves" (408 U.S. 238, 1972: see pp. 304 and 345).

glance, spiteful or malicious. As discussed earlier, there is Franny, the character in Irving's *Hotel New Hampshire* who can achieve peace after suffering the trauma of gang rape only by causing harm to the gang's leader. And there are the real-life victims of the Camelback rapist; they vigorously campaigned for his receiving the maximum sentence allowed by law, outraged at the thought that his punishment should be anything short of severe, given what he had done to them. Murphy chides those who would criticize these women for such feelings, contending that, given what the rapist did to them, their demand that he suffer great pain is "natural, fitting, and proper."

Certainly we can sympathize with these women, and share their outrage at the rapist's deed. And we may experience the same sort of outrage if we dwell on personal experiences in which others have badly wronged us. But people who angrily insist on intense suffering for their wrongdoers do not strike us as *noble* or in any way exceptionally meritorious (in contrast, for example, to people who, like Jesus, "forgive from the cross"). Perhaps the only reason we are reluctant to criticize these victims for their hatred is because we believe they are already experiencing too much pain to make it right to inflict any more. Moreover, when Murphy describes what Franny wants when she experiences what he takes to be the retributive emotion, he uses the word 'revenge' (Chapter 3, note 7), suggesting once again that her emotion is in fact malicious hatred, which merits moral criticism.

Proponents of retribution maintain, in the face of such doubts, that there can be something profoundly ignoble, even despicable, about someone who would block or deny the retributivist response following at least *some* crimes. Consider the story told by Ivan to his brother Alyosha in *The Brothers Karamazov*, quoted at the beginning of this chapter. How could even the most loving Christian saint resist the thought that a man who would set dogs on an innocent child and force his mother to watch the boy being torn to pieces should die? Turning the other cheek towards such a monster seems villainous.

The retributive idea

Does Christianity insist on such villainy? One might well think so if one notes the many passages in which Jesus is hostile to the *lex talionis*:

> You have learned that they were told, "Eye for eye, tooth for tooth." But what I tell you is this: Do not set yourself against the man who wrongs you. . . . You have heard that they were told "Love your neighbor, hate your enemy." But what I tell you is this: Love your enemy and pray for your persecutors: only so can you be children of your heavenly father, who makes the sun rise on the good and the bad alike, and sends the rain on the honest and dishonest. (Matt. 5:38–9, 43–5)

The sunshine and the rain are for us all because God loves us as his children. Surely, if we are to follow the Lord's example, we must not strive to hurt those who are his beloved children, and our own spiritual brothers and sisters, no matter what they do to us.

Yet this may be far too saccharine a portrait of Christianity's requirements, given other actions and teachings of Jesus. There is the famous incident in which he angrily overthrows the tables of the moneychangers in the temple of Jerusalem (Matt. 21:12–13); there are his ruthless judgements of the scribes and Pharisees: "Woe unto you, scribes and Pharisees, hypocrites! For ye are like unto white-washed sepulchres, which outwardly appear beautiful, but inwardly are full of dead men's bones; and of all uncleanness" (Matt. 23:27);[15] and there is his invocation of hell: "Ye serpents, ye offspring of vipers [said to the Pharisees], how shall ye escape the judgement of hell?" (Matt. 23: 33). Jesus sounds here like an angry Old Testament prophet, and doesn't that anger presuppose the judgement that these people are wicked and deserve to suffer, at least the fire of his words,

15 He also warns the people: "Beware of the scribes, who desire to walk in long robes, and to have salutations in the marketplaces, and chief seats in the synagogues, and chief places at feasts; they that devour widows' houses and for a pretence make long prayers; these shall receive greater condemnation" (Mark 12:38–40).

and maybe even the fires of hell? (See, e.g., Luke 13:1–5 or Matt. 5:29–30.)

How do we reconcile Jesus' retributive-sounding anger with his attacks on the *lex talionis*, his insistence on loving one's enemies and his encouragement of forgiveness? Perhaps we cannot. Perhaps Jesus' teachings are informed by the claims both of love and of justice, the latter prompting an anger which he cannot deny but which he is afraid to recommend or approve because it violates what love requires.

And perhaps Jesus' dilemma is also our dilemma: even though we value and encourage love towards our fellow human beings, prompting us to forgive them when they wrong us, we also seem to respect the idea that the guilty deserve to pay in pain for the wrongs they cause others, a thought generally encased in an anger that drives out love. There does not seem to be any easy way to reconcile these two responses to wrongdoing, nor is it easy to give either response up. Yet they coexist uneasily within us.

II. MAKING SENSE OF THE RETRIBUTIVE IDEA

The preceding section showed the problems one faces if one wants to endorse the idea of retribution. They are problems that I have decided to take on, insofar as examples of criminals such as Dostoevsky's General seem to make the retributive idea virtually irresistible. But to endorse retribution, I must satisfy myself that it makes sense as a legitimation of harm, and is importantly different from the vengefulness that emanates from malice. Even more ambitiously, I believe I must argue, *contra* Murphy, that *retribution is not a form of hatred at all*, so that (as Jesus may have been trying to say) the claims of love need not be violated by the claims of justice, or vice versa. This is not an easy task. As we have seen, the project of "making sense" of retribution in order to show how it is different from revenge has been attempted before and is notoriously difficult to pull off. Explanations of retribution either miss the mark entirely or else presuppose the very idea they try to explain, perhaps because, as Mackie says, people are "so firmly wedded to retributivist thinking that they find it difficult to confront the task of justifying retribution from cold, without implicitly assuming what they are setting out to explain."[16] Moreover, advocates of retribution who are convinced it is a bedrock intuition will believe I am foolish to try to analyze it; a foundational moral idea cannot be broken into pieces, nor can it be explained by something more fundamental.

I do not believe retribution is foundational. Instead I believe it gets its irresistible character by being the conjunction of two basic ideas mandating the harm of the wrongdoer as a means to an end. (I will not, as Murphy did, merely suppose that those who have the retributive sentiment desire to inflict retributive suffering on their wrongdoers; I will attempt to show two ways in which that retributive suffering is desirable.) Those who believe deeply that retribution is deontological may well object to my teleological reduction of it; as I noted earlier, retributivists have been loath to admit that retributive punishment has any goal in sight. But revenge itself seemed goalless before its strategic character was uncovered. So might there also be a hidden goal in a victim's call for retribution?

I will argue that there is. To put it metaphorically (but in a way that I hope is evocative), I will argue that those who want retribution want to inflict suffering that is taken to be the victim's value "striking back" and in this way proving itself. But why must a victim's value strike back by means of pain? And how does painful retaliation constitute vindication of the victim's worth? Just like Nozick, I must explain why pain effects a linkage between the criminal and what is true about a victim's value.

But before pursuing this idea, let me point out that because I will understand retribution as a communication about the wrongdoer's value, my analysis of it presupposes a theory of

16 Mackie, "Morality and the Retributive Emotions," p. 6.

human worth. As I said in Chapter 2, there are a variety of such theories, and what *kinds* of punishment a retributivist will recommend depends upon which theory she accepts (although the *point* of the retributive punishment will be the same, no matter what theory of human worth is presupposed).[17] For now, let me illustrate the theory using a Kantian theory of human worth, which makes people intrinsically, objectively and equally valuable. Aside from the fact that I believe this is the theory retribution ought to presuppose, I will also maintain that it is the theory its advocates generally do presuppose.

Retributive idea 1: punishment as a defeat. Those who wrong others, on the definition developed in Chapter 2, objectively demean them. They incorrectly believe or else fail to realize that others' value rules out the treatment their actions have accorded the others, and they incorrectly believe or implicitly assume that their own value is high enough to make this treatment permissible. So, implicit in their wrongdoings is a message about their value relative to that of their victims.

Now consider again a wrongdoer we discussed in Chapter 2, the neighborhood bully, whose *raison d'être* is to establish his superiority over those he beats up. A child who has been victimized by this bully and who desires in turn to beat him up may be neither spiteful nor malicious: rather than try to elevate himself by defeating the bully, he may simply want to establish that the bully is not elevated above him - or, indeed, above anyone. The child therefore aims to *defeat* the bully, and the defeat is supposed to be proof that the bully is not the "lord" he has claimed to be. I take this child to be characteristic of someone who desires retributive punishment.

Readers of Chapter 2 should recognize the child's action as

17 However, although I am not able to develop this idea here, I doubt that those who hold an instrumental theory of human worth can make use of it to ground any kind of retributive response.

an attempt at diminishment in the first sense defined there, that is, an attempt to diminish the wrongdoer's sense of his own value. Such diminishment was not itself taken to be a wrong in that chapter; it was only deemed a wrong if a wrongdoer's value was taken to preclude it so that it could be considered demeaning treatment. But the child's attempt at diminishment is aimed at conveying what the child takes to be the truth about how valuable the bully is relative to himself and to others. And I will argue that it is *not* demeaning to accord someone treatment designed to represent the *truth* about his value relative to others (assuming, of course, that it really does represent the truth).

However, the child is after more than diminishment in this sense. A retributivist's commitment to punishment is not merely a commitment to taking hubristic wrongdoers down a peg or two;[18] it is also a commitment to asserting moral truth in the face of its denial. If I have value equal to that of my assailant, then that must be made manifest after I have been victimized. By victimizing me, the wrongdoer has declared himself elevated with respect to me, acting as a superior who is permitted to use me for his purposes. A false moral claim has been made. Moral reality has been denied. The retributivist demands that the false claim be corrected. The lord must be humbled to show that he isn't the lord of the victim. If I cause the wrongdoer to suffer in proportion to my suffering at his hands, his elevation over me is denied, and moral reality is reaffirmed. I master the purported master, showing that he is my peer.

So I am proposing that retributive punishment is the defeat of the wrongdoer at the hands of the victim (either directly or indirectly through an agent of the victim's, e.g., the state) that symbolizes the correct relative value of wrongdoer and victim.[19] It is a symbol that is conceptually

18 Iakovos Vasiliou has suggested to me that it may be possible to link this analysis of retribution to the Greek concept of hubris.

19 In what follows, I speak of there being victims of crimes, but I do not point out the way in which every member of a society can be considered a victim of some sorts of wrongdoings (e.g., felonies). Were this

required to reaffirm a victim's equal worth in the face of a challenge to it. Thus the punishment has a *telos*, but the *telos* is not so much to produce good as it is to establish goodness.[20]

How does the infliction of pain constitute such a symbol? The answer is that pain conveys defeat - so that if defeat could be accomplished in some other way, presumably the child would be just as likely to use it as he would to use pain. But *any non-painful method*, so long as it was still a method for *defeating* the wrongdoer, *would still count as punishment*. Indeed, if one considers the wide variety of experiences which count as punishment in our society but which are not inherently painful (e.g., requiring public service), one realizes that what makes any experience the suffering of punishment is not the objective painfulness of the experience, but the fact that it is one the wrongdoer is *made* to suffer and one which represents his *submission* to the punisher. To use a phrase of Fingarette's, punishment is an experience designed to "humble the will" of the person who committed the wrongdoing.[21] And such humbling is generally disliked and found to be painful, perhaps explaining why punishment is so often confused with the infliction of pain. A better synonym for 'punishment,' according to Fingarette,[22] is the infliction of *suffering* (some meanings of 'suffer,' according to the *OED*, being "endure," "submit," "be subjected to") so that "in the respect that we suffer, we experience what we do not will, or in a stronger sense, we experience what is *against* our will." But I propose that the most general and accurate definition of 'punishment' is:

> the experience of defeat at the hands of the victim (either directly or indirectly through a legal authority).

idea to be incorporated into the discussion, wrongdoers would have to "pay" not only for what they did to particular people but also for what they did to all of us.

20 I am indebted to Richard Gale for this way of putting things, and for pressing me about many of the ideas in this section.

21 See Fingarette, "Punishment and Suffering."

22 Ibid., p. 510.

The retributive idea

If punishment is understood in this way, it appears morally problematic not only insofar as it may involve the infliction of pain but, more important, because it *always* involves the attempt to master another human being. I want to argue, however, that such mastery is morally wrong, that is, demeaning, *only* when it aims to establish something false about the relative value of the one claiming it (i.e., the one we call *wrong*) and of his victim; it is not morally wrong if the point of the mastery is to deny the wrongdoer's false claim to superiority and to assert the victim's equal value.[23]

But exactly how does punishment make this assertion? Consider that retributivists typically endorse the *lex talionis* as a punishment formula, or (as I would reinterpret it) as a formula for determining the extent to which the wrongdoer must be mastered. That formula calls for a wrongdoer to suffer something like what his victim suffered, and as Murphy notes, it is frequently mocked by those who point out that delivering to the criminal what he delivered to the victim can

23 This defense of retribution sounds, in some respects, like Fingarette's, but it is worthwhile pointing out the difference between the two accounts. Like Fingarette, I see punishment as the experience of submission, of being dominated. But Fingarette justifies punishment *only* by a legal institution. And the point of its infliction is to make the wrongdoer recognize that he is required not to defy the law's imperatives, that is, in order to see that the law (and not he himself) is "boss." This justification of retribution succeeds only as long as the law is a legitimate institution, and Fingarette offers no such justification for it. He also offers no justification of the punishment practices of non-legal institutions such as schools and families. So at best his is only a partial explanation of retributive thinking, that is, such thinking in legal contexts. Moreover, Fingarette's account is a strikingly nonmoral explanation of the retributive idea, one which he believes is necessary if the law is not to be confused with morality. But surely retributivists such as Kant have taken retribution to be a deeply moral notion - perhaps even part of the bedrock of moral thought. To offer a non-moral explanation of it seems, therefore, to misrepresent the idea fundamentally. I am inclined to think his account might be right as part of the reason a legal system punishes, but wrong as an account of retribution. My account of retribution tries to explain its moral core, a core which I believe a variety of institutions, including the law as well as families and universities, make use of in pursuing both moral and non-moral objectives.

be impossible or ridiculous or both in many instances. But the punishment formula does not seem quite so silly if it is interpreted as calling *only* for proportionality between crime and punishment. To inflict on a wrongdoer something comparable to what he inflicted on the victim is to master him in the way that he mastered the victim. The score is even. Whatever mastery he can claim, she can also claim. If her victimization is taken as evidence of her inferiority relative to the wrongdoer, then his defeat at her hands negates that evidence. Hence the *lex talionis* calls for a wrongdoer to be subjugated in a way that symbolizes his being the victim's equal. The punishment is a second act of mastery that denies the lordship asserted in the first act of mastery.

A critic might query this analysis by worrying that even if retributive punishment is one way to achieve this end, it might not be the only way or even the best way. And if there is another way to reassert the victim's value that is as good as, or better than, the punitive method, then why shouldn't the retributivist permit or prefer that method, and suspend the punishment of the wrongdoer - something a "hard-core" retributivist would presumably never want to do?

But I contend that punishment is uniquely suited to the vindication of the victim's relative worth, so that no other method purporting to achieve vindication could be preferred to it.[24] Suppose we gave a victim a ticker-tape parade after the crime to express our commitment to his value. Still the fact that he had been mastered by the wrongdoer would stand. He would have lost to her, and no matter how much the community might contend that he was not her inferior, the loss counts as evidence that he is. Hence *the victim wants*

24 But consider the fact that Martin Luther King, Jr., is acknowledged as the great champion of the rights (and thus the value) of blacks, and yet he never inflicted punishment. Strategies such as civil disobedience might be almost as effective (maybe even as effective), in certain circumstances, as punitive defenses of worth. Still, one wonders whether King and others chose their non-violent method of fighting criminality because the superior, punitive method was denied them.

the evidence nullified.[25] And punishment is the best way to do that. The wrongdoer can't take her crime to have established or to have revealed her superiority if the victim is able to do to her what she did to him. The punishment is therefore a second act of mastery that negates the evidence of superiority implicit in the wrongdoer's original act.

What is the retributivist's motive for wanting to reaffirm the equal worth of wrongdoer and victim?

His retributive motive should not be confused with a variety of non-retributive motives he might have. For example, he might see the communication as having desirable deterring effects both for the criminal and for the larger society. Or he may believe that it can morally educate the criminal and the society, on the grounds that the wrongdoer's loss to his victim (or to that victim's societal representative) will force both parties to reassess their relative value.[26] He may also desire to inflict punishment in order to benefit the victim,

25 The evidence is neither made to vanish by punishment nor made never to have existed. Instead it is explained away. Copernicus didn't make the evidence of the sun's literally rising vanish, but he did nullify it in the sense that he showed it wasn't really evidence for that conclusion. Similarly, punishment undercuts the probative force of the evidence of his superiority provided by the wrongdoer's action. I am indebted to Richard Healey for helping me to clarify this point.

26 Non-malicious victors will wish wrongdoers to conclude not that "this victim (or his government representative) is now my superior because he can force me to submit to his will" but, rather, that "I am not more valuable than anyone else, and my loss to this person is a sign of that fact" or, as children generally put it, that "I'm not better than anyone else." Moreover, if the wrongdoer is defeated because he hurt you, then he is aware of a cost to future transgressions that will make him (and others) less likely to commit them in the future. He is also aware that the *fact* that you have a protective response makes you someone he has to "take into account" in his calculations about how to achieve his goals. You aren't a "nobody" he can "walk all over." This is not to say that the punishment will make him respect you in the right way, to the extent that you deserve. But it may well make him "fear" you to some extent, and for a person seeking some acknowledgement of her worth, this is at least a start. As I argue in "The Moral Education Theory of Punishment," it may have more sophisticated educative effects on the criminal.

who may feel a resentment or hatred that is fed by a fear that the crime has revealed her as or made her lower. (A major reason why Franny was so pleased at being able to harm the gang leader may be that the harming confirmed in her own mind that those who raped her were not her superiors.) Perhaps some of the impatience felt by victims towards people, such as myself, who have advocated punishment as a way of morally educating criminals stems from the fact that we have tended to see the suffering as helpful only to the one who did the harming or to society members tempted to do what he did, and thus have ignored the very real help to the victim's injured self-esteem which she can and should get from the defeat of her assailant.

But the *retributive* motive for inflicting suffering is to annul or counter the appearance of the wrongdoer's superiority and thus affirm the victim's real value.[27] So even in a situation where neither the wrongdoer nor society will either listen to or believe the message about the victim's worth which the "punitive defeat" is meant to carry, and where the victim doesn't need to hear (or will not believe) that message in order to allay any personal fears of diminishment, the retributivist will insist on the infliction of punishment insofar as it is a way of "striking a blow for morality" or (to use a phrase of C. S. Lewis's) a way to "plant the flag"[28] of morality. Recall that an adequate theory of retribution would show how it was a response to what was immoral about the wrongdoer's action. This is precisely what the present theory tries to do. If punishment symbolizes the reassertion of the victim's value, it is desired by one who is responding to and rejects the denial of that value by the criminal's action (where

27 So punishment is expressive. See Joel Feinberg, "The Expressive Function of Punishment," *Doing and Deserving* (Princeton, N.J.: Princeton University Press, 1970).

28 C. S. Lewis, *The Problem of Pain* (New York: Macmillan, 1944), p. 45. Quoted by Robert Nozick in his *Philosophical Explanations*, p. 718 n. 80. The complete passage is: "It plants the flag of truth within the citadel of a rebel soul." So expanded, it sounds a bit too educative to be a purely retributive sentiment.

that denial is what makes the action immoral). And one's commitment to that value can motivate one to carry out that reassertion even when one is quite sure that the defiance will persist despite the message.

This reassertion may be what Hegel meant when he spoke of the way punishment "annuls the crime." Of course it can't annul the act itself, but *it can annul the false evidence seemingly provided by the wrongdoing of the relative worth of the victim and the wrongdoer.* Or to put it another way, it can annul the message, sent by the crime, that they are not equal in value.

We might also use this approach to retribution to explain Kant's famous concern to punish criminals even when the society of which they are members is about to disband:

> Even if a civil society were to dissolve itself by common agreement of all its members (for example if the people inhabiting an island decided to separate and disperse themselves around the world), the last murderer remaining in prison must first be executed, so that everyone will duly receive what his actions are worth and so that the bloodguilt thereof will not be fixed on the people because they failed to insist on carrying out the punishment; for if they fail to do so, they may be regarded as accomplices in this public violation of legal justice.[29]

I agree with Kant that we would be accomplices in the crime if we failed to punish its perpetrator, because we would be condoning the evidence it gave us of the relative worth of victim and offender, or to put it another way, because we would be acquiescing in the message it sent about the victim's inferiority. Kant takes it as fundamental that to be committed to morality is to be committed to asserting and defending it no matter what the consequences. Hence it is morally required that we send an annulling message after a crime so that the victim's value receives its proper defense.

These last remarks should make it clear that this analysis of retribution presents it as something other than a justification of punishment designed to convey a moral lesson to the

29 Immanuel Kant, *The Metaphysical Elements of Justice*, trans. John Ladd (Indianapolis: Bobbs-Merrill, 1965), p. 102.

wrongdoer or to society. Indeed, it may be that *part of what it is to view an action as immoral is to have the desire to reassert the victim's value through punishment*.[30] But having made this proposal, I want to argue that such an assertion makes sense (and appears justifiable) only if people are at least *able* to understand the symbolic significance of the punishment, albeit perhaps unwilling to do so. Imagine Kant's island suddenly hit by toxic fumes which mentally disable all but one person; would that person still believe he would be the accomplice of the one responsible if he desisted from punishing her? Wouldn't the punishment of an individual who can neither remember the crime nor understand what the punishment is about, in a community of people who are no better able than she to comprehend either, seem a meaningless cruelty? My point is that even if retributivists insist that their main reason for reasserting value through punishment is not to effect moral education but to utter moral truth whether or not anyone bothers to listen, in fact one would bother to utter it only in a world where the truth can be comprehended. So the retributivist is concerned with 'education' in an attenuated sense of the word insofar as he wants the moral truth to be heard, but is not intent on successful persuasion or criminal reform; he wants to annul the criminal's message and reassert the moral truth, but does not perceive punishment as a certain cure for immorality.

We have set the stage for another question: should one punish a wrongdoer who is unable to understand the assertion behind the punishment even if the rest of society is able to comprehend it? This question has contemporary relevance to those disturbed by some people's enthusiasm for the punishment of Nazi war criminals who are now senile, and who ramble and drool through their trials. Here too I think a retributivist who appreciates what retributive punishment is for would refrain from inflicting it. Such punishment is sup-

30 Perhaps the conceptual linkage between the judgement of an action as immoral and its punishment exists only if there is a certain kind of practice or conception of morality in society.

posed to be a defeat; but if a wrongdoer has changed so that he has lost considerable rationality and now cannot understand that he is defeated or why that defeat has occurred, then the man who was able to, and who did, defy the facts of others' value no longer exists. Now it was that agent who implicitly claimed superiority over the victim through his action. He is therefore the one who must be defeated. But he is gone, and in his place is an individual whose value as a human being without agency may be problematic to assess. The time for punishment is passed, just as surely as if the wrongdoer had died.

Do these remarks raise problems for the retributive punishment of reformed criminals? No; one would think so only if one mistook retributive punishment for moral education. But retribution isn't about making a criminal better; it is about denying a false claim of relative value. The reformed and penitent murderer (who retains the capacity to understand what he has done) is still (for moral purposes) the same person who committed the murder, because he retains the agency which produced the murder (i.e., he is still an agent who chose to perform this act). Thus he is the one who implicitly claimed superiority over the victim through the crime, and he remains the one who must be levelled in order to negate the evidence of superiority provided by the crime. If he is truly penitent, he may be just as interested in seeing that claim denied as the family of the victim. It is not uncommon for remorseful wrongdoers to seek out punishment, seeing it as a way of making up for what they did to their victims. On my theory, "making it up to them" means, "voluntarily undergoing an experience which symbolizes that one is *not* as great in value, relative to them, as one's wrongdoing made it appear." (This is not to say that there are no problems surrounding the retributive punishment of reformed wrongdoers, as I shall discuss in the final section of this chapter.)

Let us return to the retributivist's punishment formula. As I said, the retributivist's endorsement of the *lex talionis* is the insistence on proportionality between crime and punishment. The more severe the offense, the more severe the punishment is supposed to be. But this makes sense if punishment is a defeat for the wrongdoer in the name of the victim which is intended to express the victim's value. The more severe the punishment, the more he is being brought low; and how low we want to bring a criminal depends on the extent to which his actions symbolize his superiority and lordship over the one he hurt. The higher wrongdoers believe themselves to be (and thus the more grievously they wrong others), the harder and farther they must fall if the moral reality of the parties' relative value is to be properly represented. So the increasing harshness of punishment symbolizes the increasing severity of the violation of the valuable entity. The value will "strike back" more severely against more severe transgressions of it.

Thus if the Camelback rapist, who used his victims for his own satisfaction as if they were his slaves, were to receive a light sentence, this would be a small defeat for him. What he has done to them turns out to be vastly more than what they are able (either directly or through their legal representatives) to do to him, a fact that seems to symbolize his persistent superiority over them despite his having been sentenced. So he has gotten away with something: he has gotten away with a claim of relative superiority. Society has failed to annul that claim successfully. And the fact that it is not annulled can brutalize the rapist's victim more thoroughly than his original attacks did.

Of course, it "brutalizes" them only if one takes it that they are right to claim they are his equals. Sexist or racist or caste-based societies might insist that some victims are not the equals of their assailants, so that the assault is either not wrong in the first place (for example, a slave owner in the American South could not be understood to have raped any of his slaves) or not as wrong as the victim might try to argue (a society might contend that the wife beater deserves a mild rebuke, but not a jail term). On the other hand, such a society would view an inferior's assault of a superior as worse than the latter's assault of the former, so that the inferior's assault should receive punishment that causes more suffering than the crime committed, not only to counter the evidence of the wrongdoer's relative superiority, but also to provide evidence of his relative inferiority. So to the extent that a retributivist does not hold an egalitarian theory of human worth, he will not endorse the *lex talionis* as the appropriate punishment formula. How much a wrongdoer must be defeated depends on what one believes the relative worth of victim and offender to be. Still, it is interesting that retribution is normally identified with the *lex talionis*, showing, I think, how thoroughly infected that theory of punishment is with an egalitarian theory of our value.

Our discussion of the retributivist's formula is still not complete: a good retributivist generally wants limits placed on punishment sentences. Moreover, the retributivist would prefer that these limits come not from *outside* his theory (so that without modification by external moral considerations the theory would be taken to endorse, say, torturing torturers) but from *within* the theory (so that the theory itself has the resources to rule out torture, no matter what the wrongdoer has done). Retributivists have, however, generally despaired of being able to do this. They have instead tended to devise what seems to be morally required external criteria for drawing the line between permissible and impermissible punishment. Thus Murphy speaks in Chapter 3 of "intrinsically immoral" actions which one's "inherent moral decency" won't permit one to perform as punishments, and he uses the Constitution's phrase 'cruel and unusual' to try to pick out those punishments which are prohibited. But these phrases are not precise either in picking out or in explaining what counts as illicit treatment.

I want to propose that we might be able to set the limits of retributive punishment by using the internal resources of the theory as I have interpreted it, assuming a Kantian theory of human worth. Consider that on my analysis, genuinely non-malicious retributivists have as the aim behind the infliction of suffering not the vengeful diminishment of the criminal to a bestial level but the vindication of the victim's value. This aim means that the punisher must not do anything that could be interpreted as an attempt not merely to deny wrongdoers' claim to superiority but also to *degrade* them, that is, cause them in some way to lose value. Sometimes a crime is ghastly in the way it portrays the victim as vastly lower than the criminal or in the way it seems to reduce him almost to a bestial level, for example, mutilation, torture, enslavement. The *lex talionis* would license doing the same thing to the wrongdoer as a way of making the equal status of the victim manifest. But to one who is committed to the idea that the wrongdoer has an intrinsic value that is equal to the value of others, such treatment can be hard, if not impossible, to stomach. One cannot see the punishment as reasserting the moral facts if it involves doing something to the wrongdoer that either makes him or represents him to be degraded below the level of human beings generally. Of course, the next question to be asked is, Why isn't *every* punishment in violation of those facts insofar as it is an attempt to master a human being whose value is supposed to be intrinsic, permanent (for as long as he remains a human being) and equal to that of others? Retributivists can reply that there are methods of mastery that deny the criminal's claim to lordship and that may be severe if the criminal has gravely mistreated his victim, but which are nonetheless not so harsh that they are identical either to the treatments which are considered permissible only for entities far less valuable than human beings or to treatments which actually make them less valuable. Being made to pay a fine or perform a public service or suffer confinement (under humane conditions) is to experience subjugation and defeat, but (at least arguably) none of these is appropriate only for something subhuman, nor do they make one subhuman. On the other hand, having an eye gouged out, having acid thrown in one's face, losing fingers, being tortured – these are treatments one would refuse to consider permissible for animals, much less humans, and which may damage people so as to cause them (at least to appear) to lose value. So the retributivist who is committed to reasserting moral truth must beware that her way of reasserting it does not implicitly deny for the criminal what it seeks to establish for the victim. Or alternatively, if the retributivist wants to establish the relative equality of victim and offender, he does not want to treat the offender in such a way that her value as a human being is denied. (So I would argue that one reason why capital punishment is controversial is that it is simply not clear whether execution does deny value.)

The *lex talionis* therefore cannot, by itself, be the appropriate punishment formula for the sophisticated retributivist, because there is no upper limit to the amount of pain it would require a wrongdoer to suffer for his crime, other than "what he did to his victim" - a limit that could well be far too high. A more accurate retributivist formula would call for comparability of punishments with crimes within certain limits that reflect the value of the wrongdoer, and a policy towards constructing punishments that would give the best expression possible of the value of the person hurt by the wrongdoer subject to these limits. To strike a blow for morality and thus for the idea that all human beings have great value, the victim must make sure that she fights in a way that recognizes the wrongdoer's very real value; she must, to use Kant's phrase, defeat him in such a way that she continues to "respect humanity in his person."

If this analysis of retribution is right, we can understand why retribution and revenge are importantly different, but nonetheless easily confused. The vengeful hater does not respect but aims to diminish the worth of the offender (either by representing it as lower or by making it lower) in order to elevate herself, a strategy that I have argued is self-defeating. The retributivist, on the other hand, aims to defeat the wrongdoer in order to annul the evidence provided by the crime of his relative superiority. The retributivist is interested in asserting moral truth; hence he is always mindful of, and respectful towards, the value of his wrongdoer. Indeed, the retributivist who accepts an egalitarian theory of worth has *no* interest in doing anything to *change* the value of either the wrongdoer or the victim. Instead, he is interested in using his domination to deny the wrongdoer's prior claim of superiority. Although he is like some avengers, namely, those who want to reveal wrongdoers to be lower than the crime makes them appear, nonetheless, he wants them diminished to a level that is correct and equal to the level of their victims. Nor is there anything self-defeating about his project: he is not using a competitive victory to elevate the victim; instead, he is using the victory to symbolize the equality in value and rank of victim and wrongdoer. Even a retributivist who accepts a hierarchical theory of human worth is uninterested in winning over the wrongdoer in order to elevate the victim. Instead he wishes to master the criminal so as to deny her prior claim to a higher place in the hierarchy, relative to the victim, than she in fact occupies. Again, there is nothing self-defeating about the retributivist's goal: he is using a competitive victory to deny an incorrect claim about relative rank.

But having isolated the difference between retribution and revenge, we can appreciate how close the two responses are (so that many victims may slide, unaware, back and forth between them). Both responses involve the desire to inflict pain as a way of mastering another, and both see such mastery as making a point about the relative value of offender and victim. But the point each wants to make is different. The vengeful hater masters the offender either to make the offender low in rank in order to elevate herself or to reveal the offender as low in rank and thereby reveal herself as higher, where the mastery is supposed to be competitive proof of superiority. Alas, this elevation is actually defeated rather than achieved by her diminishment of the offender. The retributivist, on the other hand, wants incorrect evidence of superiority denied and the victim's value reaffirmed. The punitive mastery of the wrongdoer is perceived not as a competitive victory that elevates the victim but, rather, as a denial of the wrongdoer's claim to elevation over (or relative to) the victim.

Retributive idea 2: punishment as vindicating value through protection. The preceding argument was an attempt to explain a way in which the wrongdoer could be "linked up with right values," and his crime "annulled," by inflicting punishment on him. The key idea in that argument was that punishment was the experience of defeat, designed to humble the wrongdoer and thus express his real worth relative to the victim. However, there is another way to make the connection between right values and pain. This connection can be made only when, for various reasons, *society* rather than the victim is responsible for carrying out punishment of wrongdoers.

No matter how else punishment is justified, its role as a deterrent is a primary reason why societies inflict it on criminals. The way it works to deter crime is not dissimilar to the way nature affords protection to many plants and animals. Consider the lowly nettle. To the naked eye, this plant has no obvious protection against damage. There are no visible thorns, it grows in readily accessible places rather than only on hard-to-reach crags or in deep ravines, and it is ubiquitous in summer. Yet anyone who touches it once is loath to do so again, because a chemical secretion from fine hairs on the leaves reacts with human skin to produce a prickly, burning sensation for several minutes. The nettle therefore enjoys a protective defense against human beings. It is a protection that does not stop someone from touching or damaging it (in the way that being encased in impenetrable glass would do); instead it is a protection that "strikes back" after human interference with the plant, thereby deterring future interference.

Punishment is analogous to a nettle's sting. The threat of suffering punishment is like the nettle's protective chemical secretion: a transgression activates an unpleasant experience such that future transgressions are deterred. Human beings, as I have already discussed, have an instinctive bite-back response which (as Mackie notes) may have evolved in us because of its desirable deterrent consequences. But reason as well as instinct directs us to harm wrongdoers in order to deter future crimes.

As retributivists are fond of pointing out, this can't be the whole story behind punishment, because victims see the punishment not only as a protection against the future but also as an appropriate response to the past, one that is *deserved* because of what was done. I now want to propose a second source of the retributivist's notion of desert, one that is *derived from* punishment's role as a deterrent but is quite different from deterrence.

Why should human beings have any kind of protection from attack, provided either by legal machinery or through social censure or ostracism? Clearly each of us has some ability to react against a transgressor, and some of us enjoy significant abilities in this area. But others of us, for instance, the newborn, the aged, the sick or the just plain weak, do not. One way to understand our practices of punishment is to see them as a societal attempt to deliver for each victim a protective "sting" against a transgressor which he may be ill-prepared or unable to deliver for himself.

But why should society want to afford each of us this protection? The answer to this question depends upon what theory of human worth one holds. One may believe that our worth derives from our ability to be of use to our fellows, so that society ought to protect each of us to the extent that we are instrumentally valuable to it. Or one may believe with Kant that human beings enjoy an equal and intrinsic worth, so that society should protect us equally. But whatever one's theory of human worth is, I am suggesting that societal punishment practices should be seen as created and designed to protect it. If society knew how to encase those it values in a substance that would protect them from all damage, it would surely do so (assuming it could afford to do so). But since no such protection is possible, it protects us in the way nettles are protected - by means of a kind of sting that is felt after a transgression and is intended to deter future transgressions.

Societies also have limited resources. How should they use these resources to punish wrongdoers? In particular, should all human beings be accorded the same protection? If there are some who are more valuable than most, shouldn't society protect them by a legally or socially created sting that is more severe than usual, and which is thus a better deterrent? And if there are people who are less valuable than others, shouldn't society protect them by a legally or socially created sting that is less severe than usual, thereby deterring less effectively? Not only are these grades of protection possible, but they exist in virtually every legal system that has ever been created, either officially or unofficially. I have already discussed the way in which racist, sexist or caste-based societies declare that some kinds of human beings are worth more than others; in these societies the punishment for those who injure the less valuable people is lighter than for those who injure the more valuable people. Statistics exist which support the view that killing a white man in the United States has historically been punished more severely than killing a black man.[31] Certain crimes against women by men in this and other societies have been lightly punished, and even condoned, for instance, rape or wife beating. One also sees differences in treatment in response to social status; the rich and powerful enjoy a more thorough and surer defense of their persons than do prostitutes, drug addicts and ghetto dwellers.

Accordingly, how society reacts to one's victimization can be seen by one as an indication of *how valuable* society takes one to be, which in turn can be viewed as an indication of how valuable one really is. This point is essential to understanding a societal component of the retributive idea. Of course a victim wants her assailant punished insofar as that punishment is one form of her defense against future crime. But she also wants her assailant punished by society in a way that is properly expressive of what she takes her value to be. *If legal punishment is a protection of one's value, then its infliction on a wrongdoer is a reflection of that value.* Because society's punishment protects those who are valuable, people who long for a high valuation may come to demand punishment, not only because they want this legal protection, but also

31 Hugo Bedau (ed.), *The Death Penalty in America*, 3rd ed. (Oxford: Oxford University Press, 1982); see the discussion of racial discrimination in the application of the death penalty in articles by Wolfgang and Reidel and by Bowers and Pace.

because they want the expression of what the legal protection symbolizes. (Witness a man who wants a high salary not only because he desires great wealth but also because he desires what great wealth in his profession symbolizes, e.g., career success, or great prowess on the job.)

Victims of criminals such as the Camelback rapist worry that if society allows the wrongdoer to suffer no painful consequences as a result of his action, he (and others) may conclude that the ones against whom he transgressed are not valuable enough for society to construct a significant protective barrier that exacts a (deterring) cost from one who would transgress it. So another idea behind victims' insistence that their wrongdoers shouldn't be allowed to "get away with it" is that society shouldn't allow the wrongdoers or the society to conclude, because of little or no protective response, that they were right to believe the victims lacked value relative to them. The rage felt by San Francisco's gay community after the light sentence given to Dan White, the murderer of Harvey Milk, was surely connected with their belief that the jury did not regard this homosexual as of sufficiently high value to punish his murderer severely. In their eyes the murderer *did* get away with something, namely, with the idea that as a white, male heterosexual he was of more value than Milk.[32]

So now we have two ways to link the infliction of suffering after a wrongdoing to the expression of the victim's worth. Both arguments attempt to capture and explain Nozick's intuition that retributive punishment is a way to link up a wrongdoer with right values and Hegel's idea that punishment in some sense "annuls" the crime. Earlier I expressed puzzlement over why *pain* was required to effect such a link-

32 But I do not endorse this reading of the light sentence. Given that Mayor Moscone (a heterosexual) was murdered along with Milk, the jury cannot be taken to have made a statement about homosexuals with its verdict, and its members were probably confused by a morally problematic California law on diminished capacity that obscured their good sense.

age or annul the crime. But as I said in discussing the first idea, punishment is not so much the infliction of pain as it is the infliction of a *defeat* that annuls the wrongdoer's claim of superiority, which such non-painful experiences as community service can deliver, just as well as pain (although because pain is commonly seen to represent defeat, it is a useful medium to symbolize the idea that the wrongdoer is not one's superior). And as I said in discussing the second idea, pain, or more generally, a humbling defeat which prideful wrongdoers will intensely dislike, can deter the commission of a crime against someone (or even something) having value; and the victim can come to see the value which the humbling defeat is meant to protect as symbolically expressed through the protection.

The Greeks talked of the Furies pursuing wrongdoers, torturing them for what they did. Each of us hopes that something like the Furies will doggedly pursue those who wrong us. Retributive punishment is our name for the Furies, and at a fundamental level it is punishment we desire because we see it, for the two reasons discussed in this section, as our *value* striking back at those who harmed us, and thus confirming that we *are* valuable, that their actions were indeed wrong and that we must be treated with respect.

[18]

Expression, Penance and Reform

R.A. Duff

And some, we know, when they by wilful act
a single human life have wrongly taken,
pass sentence on themselves, confess the fact,
and, to atone for it, with soul unshaken
kneel at the feet of Justice, and, for faith
broken with all mankind solicit death.

William Wordsworth,
Sonnets upon the Punishment of Death, III

It is not enough that wrong-doers be justly punished.
They must if possible judge and condemn themselves.

P Aynault, *L'Ordre,*
Formalité et Instruction Judiciaire, I.1, ch. 14

I INTRODUCTORY

The criminal law and the criminal trial are, like moral criticism, communicative enterprises which seek the assent and the participation of those whom they address: the law seeks the allegiance of the citizen as a rational moral agent, by appealing to the relevant moral reasons which justify its demands; the trial seeks to engage the defendant in a rational dialogue about the justice of the charge which she faces, and to persuade her – if that charge is proved against her – to accept and make her own the condemnation which her conviction expresses. Laws and trials respect the citizen as an autonomous agent: they aim to guide her conduct by offering her relevant reasons for action. But we have not yet shown that punishment can accord the same respect to the citizen; that its purposes are continuous with those of the criminal law and the criminal trial; or that it too seeks the offender's assent and participation.

A consequentialist account portrays punishment as a manipulative technique for promoting certain further ends: it might (given certain non-consequentialist constraints on our pursuit of those ends) portray punishment as a mode of rational deterrence which has some regard for the citizen as a rational agent; but such a system still manipulates those whose obedience it tries to secure by the threat of punishment, since it imposes on them irrelevant prudential reasons for obedience. The kind of retributivist account which I discussed in the last chapter avoids the charge of manipulation, since it does not portray punishment as an attempt to modify conduct: but its appeal to the criminal's 'rational will' fails to reconcile the imposition of punishment with a respect for his autonomy; and its account of the relationship between crime and punishment (of why punishment is an appropriate response to crime) depends on an unpersuasive picture of the nature of crime.

I turn now to a very different conception of punishment, according to which punishment does express our respect and concern for the criminal as a rational moral agent, and has a justifying purpose which is continuous with those of the criminal trial and of moral blame. This conception is retributivist, in that it makes the relationship between past crime and present punishment central to the meaning and justification of punishment, but it differs from other kinds of retributivist account in ascribing a forward-looking purpose to punishment. This is not, however, a consequentialist purpose (such as that of preventing crime, or bringing the criminal's conduct into external conformity with the law) to which punishment is contingently related as a means: the purpose of punishment, like that of moral blame, is logically rather than contingently related to the 'means' by which it is to be achieved; and the very nature of that purpose requires that it be achieved by bringing offenders to suffer for their offences.

We begin with the familiar idea that punishment has an essentially *expressive* meaning; it aims to communicate something to the criminal. The nature and purpose of this communicative endeavour is then explained by portraying punishment as a kind of *penance* which aims to secure and to express the criminal's repentance of his wrong-doing; and thus as a process of *reform* (or self-reform) through which the criminal can attain or regain a proper concern for the law and his proper place in the community. But to talk thus of punishment as a reformative endeavour is not to suggest that it is a contingently efficient means towards a further and independently identifiable end: for the kind of reform at which punishment aims can be achieved only through the kind of suffering which punishment aims to impose on, or to induce in, the criminal.

Ideas of this kind have been a persistent, if not always prominent, feature of discussions of punishment. They promise to show that punishment must seek the assent and the participation of the person punished; and that it expresses our concern, not merely for some further social benefit or for the restoration of an abstract balance of benefits and burdens, but for the criminal's own good as a rational moral agent and as a member of a moral community.

Two recent writers have made interesting moves in this direction. Lucas, who once argued that we must understand punishment in essentially deterrent terms, now wants to place more emphasis on its retributive, communicative and penitential purposes.[1] Morris, on the other hand, once argued that punishment could restore an abstract and 'rule-established balance of benefits and burdens', but could not restore those 'close relationships defined by feelings and attitudes' which are essential to our personal and social lives, and which wrong-doing disrupts. More recently, however, he has canvassed a 'paternalistic' theory of punishment which makes a concern for the criminal's moral well-being, and for her relationships with her fellows, central to its meaning.[2] My task in what follows is to see what sense we can make of punishment in such terms as these.

2 PUNISHMENT AS EXPRESSIVE

It is often said that punishment has an expressive or communicative purpose: but what is expressed, by whom, and to whom?[3]

Punishment, we may say, expresses condemnation: it denounces and formally disapproves the criminal's act; it disavows that act as one which is not to be tolerated or condoned.[4] This condemnation is expressed by those who officially decree and impose the punishment, which is supposedly imposed on behalf of the whole community: it expresses that condemnation in which all members of the

1 J R Lucas, 'Or Else' (for the earlier account, discussed in ch. 6(3)–(5) above); *Freedom and Grace* p. xii, and *On Justice* ch. 6 for the new account.

2 H Morris, 'Persons and Punishment' (for the earlier account, discussed in ch. 8 above); 'Guilt and Suffering' (from which the quotations are taken); and 'A Paternalistic Theory of Punishment' for the new account. Compare also R Nozick, *Philosophical Explanations* 4.3; J Hampton, 'The Moral Education Theory of Punishment'.

3 See A J Skillen, 'How to Say Things with Walls'.

4 See, among others, J Feinberg, 'The Expressive Function of Punishment'; J F Stephen, *A History of the Criminal Law of England* vol. 2, ch. 17, and *Liberty, Equality, Fraternity* 152; Lucas, *On Justice* ch. 6; Morris, 'A Paternalistic Theory of Punishment'; Lord Denning, quoted in the *Report of the Royal Commission on Capital Punishment* para. 53; H.M Hart, 'Criminal Punishment as Public Condemnation'; J Charvet, 'Criticism and Punishment'; A von Hirsch, *Doing Justice: The Choice of Punishments*; W Moberly, *The Ethics of Punishment* chs. 5, 8; N Morris, *The Future of Imprisonment* 78–9. For criticisms, see S I Benn, 'An Approach to the Problems of Punishment'; H L A Hart, *Law, Liberty and Morality* 60–9; Skillen, 'How to Say Things with Walls'; N Walker, 'Punishing, Denouncing, or Reducing Crime', and 'The Ultimate Justification'.

community should share when they contemplate the crime. Though this condemnation is expressed to the criminal himself, punishment may also communicate to the public at large (and especially to potential criminals) a reminder of the wrongness of the criminal's conduct, and to the victims of crime an authoritative disavowal of such conduct.[5] But if we are to avoid the charge that in punishing a criminal we are simply using him as a means to some communicative purpose which is directed at others, its essential expressive aim must be that of communicating to the criminal himself a proper condemnation of his crime.

How can punishment (the infliction of suffering) express such condemnation? The particular kinds of punishment which a penal system imposes may be determined in part by convention: but it is not a matter of convention that we should express condemnation or disapproval to a person by a communicative act which is meant to make her suffer. The infliction of suffering *need* not have such an expressive meaning; and we can express a formal disapproval of someone's criminal wrong-doing simply by the words which constitute a criminal conviction: but the further punitive measures which are then imposed on a criminal can also express condemnation; and since that condemnation is itself meant to pain her, it could not be expressed through measures which are meant to please her.

Why should we think it important to express this condemnation to the criminal? If we care for the law, and regard its requirements as important; if we care about crime, as a breach of the law and a wrong done to others: we may simply need to express this concern – for no *further* purpose, and for no other reason than that to remain silent in the face of crime would be to betray the values which the law expresses, and to which we are committed. We may also hope, however, to bring the criminal to recognise the wrongness of his past conduct, and to modify his future conduct accordingly; and to remind others of the importance of the law's requirements. But this persuasive purpose is not a further end to which expressive punishments are related as an instrumental technique: for such punishments aim not merely to prevent crime, but to bring people to see and to understand the wrongness of such conduct; and it is not merely a matter of contingent efficiency that we can achieve *that* end by communicating to them our condemnation of such conduct.[6]

Our actual motives for condemning the moral or criminal

[5] Feinberg, 'The Expressive Function of Punishment'.

[6] See ch. 2(3) above.

wrong-doings of others are no doubt often far less admirable than those suggested here: an envious resentment of those who do what we ourselves are tempted to do; a self-righteous desire to assert our own moral superiority; the satisfaction of finding a scapegoat. But we are talking now of what punishment *ought* to be; of the motives and reasons which would provide a justificatory explanation of punishment. If our actual motives are not such that the punishments which we impose or approve do express a proper condemnation of criminal conduct, we must criticise ourselves for not punishing as we should: but the prevalence of such improper motives does not preclude us from identifying the motives which *would* inform a properly justified system of expressive punishments.

Rewards, like punishments, serve an expressive purpose; and just as the law's formal punishments can be compared with our informal responses to moral wrong-doing, so public and formal rewards can be compared with private expressions of gratitude or admiration. If I want to express my gratitude for someone's help or support, or my admiration for what she has done, I might simply thank or praise her: but I might also, in order to express my feelings more adequately, give her a present, or do her some service. The primary purpose of such expressive actions is not (unless they are corrupt) instrumental: it is to express to her the thanks or admiration which are due to her for what she has done; and though they may also serve and be intended to encourage such conduct, they aim to do so by appealing to the relevant reasons which make that conduct admirable, not by providing an irrelevant prudential reason for repeating it. Expressions of gratitude and admiration, whether verbal or material, are related to the past conduct for which thanks or praise are due, and to the future conduct which they may encourage, as moral blame is related to the past conduct which is blamed and to the future modification of conduct which it may secure: both express an appropriate response to past conduct; both thus also provide relevant reasons for future conduct.

The same is true of public expressions of gratitude and admiration. A community may give public thanks and praise to its benefactors, servants and heroes: these may be simply expressed in some public and formal commendation – a speech or a formal vote of thanks; or they may be given a more tangible form in a symbolic or material reward – a medal, a title, a pension, or exemption from some duty or burden. Such rewards, whether symbolic or material, express the gratitude or admiration which their recipient deserves for what she has done. They may also serve and be intended to encourage such conduct by the person rewarded or by others: but if they are not to be corrupt they must do this by appealing to the relevant reasons which make that conduct deserving of thanks or praise, not by adding to them an irrelevant prudential reason (the prospect of material benefit) for engaging in such conduct.[7]

An account of punishment as a communicative enterprise satisfies the desiderata noted at the start of this chapter. Punishment is now continuous in its meaning and purpose with the criminal trial and the criminal law: it seeks to communicate to the offender that judgment on, and that condemnation of, his conduct which his trial has justified and which his conviction also expresses; to bring him to accept that judgment, to condemn himself, and to modify his future conduct accordingly; and thus to persuade him not merely to *obey* the law, but to *accept* its justified demands and judgments. Punishment, like moral blame, respects and addresses the criminal as a rational moral agent: it seeks his understanding and his assent; it aims to bring him to repent his crime, and to reform himself, by communicating to him the reasons which justify our condemnation of his conduct. A system of criminal law and punishment can now be seen as a unitary enterprise of dialogue and judgment in which law-abiding citizens, defendants and convicted offenders are all called to participate. Our reasons for maintaining such a system of law have to do with the prevention of crime and the good of the community, but we do not simply use citizens or criminals as means to these ends: the law addresses all the citizens as rational moral agents, seeking their assent and their understanding; and punishment is part of that continuing dialogue with the criminal through which the law aims to guide his conduct by appealing to relevant reasons.

Such an account also shows how punishment embodies the condemnatory dimension of the criminal law; it distinguishes a system of punishment from a system of deterrent taxation, and from a licensing system which sets a price on certain activities. Some have suggested, however, that not all the sanctions which the criminal law might impose have, or should have, this kind of expressive meaning. We must distinguish *punishments* properly speaking from mere *penalties* which aim to discourage certain kinds of conduct, but do not condemn them; so we should perhaps narrow the scope of the strictly *criminal* law, and create a new category of administrative or regulatory prescriptions, breaches of which (though they attract

[7] On rewards, see Feinberg, 'The Expressive Function of Punishment'; Moberly, *The Ethics of Punishment* ch. 6; P Winch, 'Ethical Reward and Punishment'.

a penalty) will not properly count as *crimes*.[8] But such a distinction between 'punishments' and 'penalties' raises serious problems.

How, firstly, is the distinction to be drawn? Should we say, for instance, that expressive punishments are appropriate to *mala in se*, which are the central and proper concern of the criminal law; while administrative penalties are more appropriate to *mala prohibita*? But many *mala prohibita* should be seen as wrongs, insofar as they involve the breach of laws which protect the interests, safety or convenience of others; insofar as they are either themselves dangerous or troublesome acts, or take unfair advantage of the law-abiding self-restraint of others (and if they do not involve either of these kinds of wrong, why should they be prohibited?): so why should not the relatively modest sanctions which may be attached to them express a relatively restrained condemnation of them as wrongs? More generally, if the law's requirements are justified, there are good and relevant moral reasons for its prescriptions and proscriptions: a citizen who wilfully or negligently breaks the law then acts wrongly, even if that wrong is not a very serious one; and she can properly be condemned by her conviction and by her punishment. Our existing laws might in fact define as guilty some who are innocent of any such genuine wrong – whose conduct should not be condemned: but this is a fault in those laws themselves, and suggests that such people should not be penalised at all, not that they should suffer a penalty rather than a punishment which condemns them.

How, secondly, are such penalties to be understood? They should not be seen simply as taxes, even if this is how some offenders do see them: for they are attached to legal *prohibitions*. But if we instead portray, and justify, them as deterrents; and if we admit, as I have argued, that a system of deterrent sanctions is manipulative: we seem to be saying that the law may use manipulative means to prevent such relatively minor infractions, but may not do so to prevent more serious kinds of crime – which is surely bizarre.[9]

I will not pursue these problems here: my present concern is with the claim that the sanctions which are imposed on conduct which is properly defined as criminal are to be understood and justified as expressive punishments; and there is a familiar and apparently devastating objection to any such claim.

[8] Feinberg ('The Expressive Function of Punishment') and Lucas (*On Justice* ch. 6) both distinguish 'punishments' from 'penalties': see also Walker, 'Punishing, Denouncing or Reducing Crime'; R M Jackson, *Enforcing the Law* ch. 2; and J Feinberg, *Harm to Others* 242.

[9] One who thinks that expressive punishments themselves also serve as deterrents will not see this as a problem; see text at n. 14 below.

3 EXPRESSIVE PUNISHMENTS AND HARD TREATMENT

Why, we must ask, should we express our condemnation of the criminal's wrong-doing through the kinds of 'hard treatment' (such as imprisonment) which are typically imposed as punishments by legal systems like our own?[10] Hard treatment *can* serve this expressive purpose; and the fact that our actual punishments may not succeed in communicating the appropriate message to those on whom they are imposed might show only that they are inadequate to their proper purpose (and that they properly leave the criminal free to close his mind to them) – not that they cannot in principle serve this purpose. Nor would it be enough, if punishments are to serve this purpose, merely to pretend to impose them.[11] That would hardly impress the offenders towards whom they are primarily directed; and a legal system which is to respect its citizens cannot properly set out to deceive them. But why should we choose this method of expression?

We can imagine a criminal process which ends with the formal verdict of the court – the offender is convicted (and thus condemned) and then released; or a system of purely symbolic punishments which, unlike hard treatment, cause suffering to the offender only insofar as they communicate a condemnation of her conduct.[12] Criminal convictions and symbolic punishments aim to communicate the condemnation which it is, on this account, the central purpose of punishment to communicate: why then should punishment take the form of hard treatment; why is *this* the most appropriate mode of communication?

It may be said that only thus will we *effectively* communicate our condemnation to the criminal; or that formal convictions and purely symbolic punishments do not *adequately* express the appropriate response to her wrong-doing.[13] To which it may be replied that what this actually reveals is the need to relate the expressive purpose of punishment to a consequentialist account of punishment as a means of reducing crime, or to a retributivist account of punishment as the infliction of deserved suffering; that punishment's

[10] On 'hard treatment' see Feinberg, 'The Expressive Function of Punishment'.

[11] See Walker, 'Punishing, Denouncing, or Reducing Crime'; 'The Ultimate Justification'.

[12] See ch. 5 above; also I Dilman, *Morality and the Inner Life* 71–2; Feinberg, 'The Expressive Function of Punishment'.

[13] See Lucas, *On Justice* 132–6; Moberly, *The Ethics of Punishment* 140–2.

expressive function can be no more than an aspect of one of these primary functions.

Some who portray punishment as expressive have taken this route. Feinberg, for instance, while insisting that we can understand punishment only if we recognise its expressive function, is equally insistent that we need to justify the use of hard treatment as our preferred mode of expression; and his reference to 'the relation of the expressive function of punishment to its various central purposes' (which he takes to include deterrence, reform and rehabilitation) suggest that the use of hard treatment is to be justified by reference to these 'central purposes'.[14] A consequentialist who wishes to justify punishment in primarily deterrent terms could thus argue that hard treatment serves both to express our condemnation of the criminal's conduct, which might itself dissuade some potential criminals, and to provide a more effective prudential deterrent for those who are insufficiently impressed by mere condemnation. And a retributivist could argue that hard treatment serves both to express our justified condemnation and to exact from the criminal the debt of suffering which he owes to his fellow-citizens.

Indeed, there is surely some tension between the claim that the *primary* purpose of punishment is expressive and the use of hard treatment as the primary method of punishment. For if the primary purpose of punishment is to communicate to the criminal our condemnation of her conduct, the suffering which punishment is meant to cause her must, like that which moral blame aims to induce in a moral wrong-doer, be the pain of recognised guilt. She should understand that, and why, she is being condemned, and make that condemnation her own; she should be pained not merely by the fact that she is condemned, but by the fact that she deserves to be condemned – by her own guilt. The pain which expressive punishments aim to inflict or induce – the pain which wrong-doers deserve to suffer – must be mediated by the criminal's own understanding of the condemnation which they express.[15]

Now purely symbolic punishments fit this picture. We may know that some criminals will in fact be pained by such punishments, if at all, only insofar as they generate further and independently undesirable consequences, such as the loss of job opportunities or the hostility of others; and the prudential incentives for obedience to the law which such further consequences may

[14] Feinberg, 'The Expressive Function of Punishment' 101.

[15] See ch. 2(5) above; Dilman, *Morality and the Inner Life* 71–2; Winch, 'Ethical Reward and Punishment'.

offer opens the way to a manipulative use of symbolic punishments as deterrents. Their essential and proper purpose, however, is not to provide such prudential deterrents to crime, but to bring the criminal to recognise the wrongfulness of her past conduct; to induce the kind of pain which flows from an understanding of the condemnation which they express.

But matters are surely quite different when punishment takes the form of hard treatment: for the suffering which such punishments most obviously and directly cause is independent of their communicative meaning. My understanding of the expressive meaning of my imprisonment (of its character as punishment) will, of course, alter both my understanding of that imprisonment and the nature of the suffering which it causes me: whether I think my punishment just or unjust, I will experience it differently from someone who sees it merely as coercive detention.[16] But imprisonment and the like are painful independently of any expressive meaning which they may have: so is this not liable to distract the offender from their expressive meaning, rather than reinforcing it? And must we not now suspect that the reason for imposing hard treatment on criminals is not to ensure that they suffer the pain of condemnation and remorse, but rather to supplement that pain (in case the criminal does not come to feel it as he should) by some further pain which is to serve as a deterrent or as retribution? If this suspicion is well-founded, however, we can no longer claim that the primary purpose of such punishments is expressive.

Rewards raise a similar problem. If a reward is purely symbolic (a medal or a title, for instance) we can plausibly say that its primary purpose is expressive: it aims to please the recipient by expressing to her our gratitude or admiration; the pleasure which it aims to induce is the pleasure of being justly praised for what one has done; it focuses our and her attention – where it should be focused – on the worth of the action which is rewarded, and offers an appropriate and relevant incentive for performing such actions. Once we give a reward a material content which can be valued or desired independently of its communicative purpose, however, we create the danger that it will be used or received in the wrong spirit, and the suspicion that we replace the purely symbolic by the material in order to provide a bribe – an irrelevant prudential reason for action. (Even symbolic rewards can of course be used or received corruptly, as bribes, if attention is focused on such further benefits as they may bring, or on the pleasure of being praised rather than on the

[16] A point emphasised by Winch in 'Ethical Reward and Punishment'.

justice of the praise; but they are then used or received improperly.) If we offer a financial reward for some noble action, or express our gratitude through some material gift, we may distract attention from the reward's expressive purpose; and we must suspect that our motive is not merely to express our gratitude or admiration – that such rewards are, in intention or in fact, corrupting (we must of course distinguish rewards from repayments; my comments here are not directed against attempts to reimburse a benefactor for such costs as she incurred in helping me).

But yet – this *need* not be the case with a material reward: it *can* be offered and received as nothing other than an expression of gratitude or admiration; my intention in offering it may be simply that this will provide a more persuasive token of my feelings, and that it should be received in just this spirit.[17] So could we not still insist that punishment, even when it takes the form of hard treatment, can and should have a purely or primarily expressive purpose?

We should of course be more worried by the imposition of painful punishments than by the offering of pleasing rewards. We may feel too that in a more perfect world rewards would not take such a material form: perhaps the feeling that rewards should take a material form still reflects a corrupt belief that I should benefit materially from my good deeds (that virtue is not its own reward).[18] But the crucial question now is this. What sense can we make of the claim that hard treatment makes our condemnatory communication more effective, other than that it adds a prudential deterrent which is not provided by formal convictions or by purely symbolic punishments; that it aims not only to bring the criminal to recognise and repent his wrong-doing, but to offer him a prudential deterrent against repeating it? Or what sense can we make of the claim that hard treatment expresses more adequately the condemnation which crime warrants, other than that it also imposes some *further* suffering which the criminal supposedly deserves? For without an adequate answer to this question we cannot justify punishments which involve hard treatment by claiming that their primary or essential purpose is expressive.

The central problem here concerns the relationship between the pain or suffering involved in hard treatment and the kind of pain which expressive punishment is meant to induce in the criminal.

[17] Compare Lucas, *On Justice* 133.

[18] Compare Moberly, *The Ethics of Punishment* 158ff; S Kierkegaard, *Purity of Heart* ch. 4.

Consider, for instance, the suggestion that punishment serves to impose on the criminal the pain of remorse which she ought to impose on herself: we must inflict hard treatment on criminals who are not adequately pained by remorse in order to ensure that they still suffer the pain which they ought to suffer.[19] The trouble with this suggestion is that the pain which the criminal ought to suffer cannot be identified independently, as a contingent effect, of her remorseful recognition of her own wrong-doing; it takes its meaning and its identity from that recognition. But it follows from this that hard treatment *cannot* by itself inflict the pain which the criminal ought to suffer: for the pain which hard treatment inflicts on an unrepentant criminal is unrelated to any such remorseful recognition of guilt.

Or consider the suggestion that punishment serves to express our disapproval 'in a universal currency, capable of being appreciated by any and every man, no matter what his values are'. A criminal who 'is insensitive to the values of society, and is concerned only with his own interests', will not heed the condemnation which a conviction expresses, or 'acknowledge that what he has done was wrong': but by inflicting hard and unwelcome punitive treatment on him we can at least ensure that he will 'be forced to see that [what he has done] was from his point of view a mistake'. Punishment 'translates the disesteem of society into the value system of the recalcitrant individual'.[20] But how can this 'translation' preserve the meaning of that which it purports to translate? If I am dealing with a wrong-doer whose culture conventionally expresses condemnation by hand-clapping, I can communicate my condemnation to her by clapping my hands, thus translating it into a language which she will understand. She, however, receives and understands my clapping as a condemnation; we have yet to show how a punishment which the criminal receives and perceives merely as a coercive and unwelcome hindrance to her own interests can communicate to her the condemnation which we aim to express. Should we not rather say that in this case our condemnation has been translated out of existence?

Could we perhaps say that such punishments aim to bring home to the criminal the nature and implications of his crime? Punishment might be seen, for example, as a forcible exercise in universalising: we bring home to him the injury he has done to others, in fact rather than merely in imagination, by imposing on him what he

[19] See R J Lemos, 'A Defence of Retributivism'.

[20] Lucas, *On Justice* 133–4, 147.

will perceive as injurious to himself; by forcibly reminding him how he dislikes having his own interests injured, we try to get him to see more clearly the wrongness of injuring the interests of others. This need not involve a crude application of the Lex Talionis – an attempt to do to him something of the same material kind as that which he did to others: apart from the impracticality and inhumanity of many such attempts, the use of extreme violence or torture, for instance, against one who has treated others in this way would not address him as a moral agent whose *understanding* is to be engaged.[21] What we should impose on him, however, is a hindrance or injury proportionate to that which he inflicted on others.

This rather crude picture of punishment as an attempt to get the criminal to universalise his prescriptions is hardly satisfying: most criminals do not, after all, need to be reminded of what it is like to have their own interests hindered; and such an account implies an abstract conception of crime, as consisting essentially in some hindrance or injury to the interests of others which we can match or represent by a hindrance to the criminal's own interests, which is itself open to objection.[22] But this suggestion, and the two previous ones, point us in the right direction: they lead us to look beyond the simple claim that punishment serves to express condemnation, and to ask more carefully about both the content and the purpose of the communicative enterprise which punishment is meant to be. We need a richer and more subtle account of what punishment is meant to communicate to the criminal (a better understanding of the nature and implications of his crime); of why it should be so important to communicate this (because we hope that this will bring the criminal to repent his crime and thus enable him to restore those relationships which his crime threatened to injure or destroy); and of the part which hard treatment can properly play in this communicative and reformative endeavour (it serves as a penance which the criminal should ideally come to will for himself).

The material for this more adequate account of punishment as an essentially expressive or communicative enterprise has already been provided, in part, in my discussion of moral blame.[23] The central elements of the account can best be clarified by a further discussion of the idea of penance, and of the meaning of a formal system of penances in its familiar context of a religious community.

[21] See J G Murphy, 'Cruel and Unusual Punishments' 233–4.

[22] Compare ch. 8(2) above.

[23] See especially ch. 2(5)–(7) above.

4 PENANCE AND SELF-PUNISHMENT

I have talked already of penance as a kind of self-imposed punishment: some onerous task or painful deprivation which I undertake or accept because of the wrong which I have done. My penance expresses my recognition, my understanding and my repentance of my wrong-doing to God, whose will I have ignored and whose mercy I now seek; to those whom I have wronged, whose forgiveness I now seek; to the community whose values I have flouted, to which I wish to restore myself. Expressive penance stands to apology and confession as expressive punishment stands to a criminal conviction. In undertaking a penance I both own and disown my sin: I own it as mine – as a wrong which I have done; but I disown it as an act which I now condemn and repent.

But why should I express my repentance in this way, by imposing hard treatment on myself, rather than directly by apology and confession, or by a purely symbolic act? Is it simply, as Lucas suggests, because such a penance provides a persuasive proof of my sincerity – a 'disavowal of the values which the crime manifested, expressed in a way so costly that its sincerity cannot be impugned'?[24] This may be part of the reason: but there is more to a penance than the forceful expression of an already complete repentance.

A penance can assist and strengthen my repentant understanding of what I have done: it forces me to contemplate my sin, and the values I have flouted, rather than being distracted by the other interests and concerns which usually fill my life, and provides a focus and stimulus for my penitent attention. But my attention is not simply focused on my past sin: penance looks to the present, since I must realise that my sin was not merely the aberrant act of a past and separate self, but the manifestation of a vice which is still part of me; and it looks to the future, since it is through my penance that I hope to reform myself and restore my relationships with those from whom my sin has sundered me.

A sincere repentance of my wrong-doing involves a sincere desire to reform myself. I recognise and am distressed by the harm which I have done to others. I see that I have harmed myself, by injuring my relationships with others – by separating myself from God or the Good; from those whom I have directly wronged; from other members of the community whose values I have betrayed; and from myself as someone who truly desires good rather than evil. For I re-

[24] Lucas, *On Justice* 133.

alise that my true well-being (and thus the proper object of my desires) lies, not in those material or egoistical goods to which my wrong-doing showed me to be attached, but in a life lived in accordance with the values which I have betrayed, and within a moral community united by shared values and shared concerns for each other. Penance can help to focus my attention on this task of self-reform; it can solicit the assistance and the good will of others in this task, by expressing to them my repentant desire to disavow the wrong which I have done, and my determination to reform and restore myself. I might talk of trying to *purify* myself by a penance which helps to direct my attention away from the selfish and material concerns which led me to sin, towards the Good which I desire; or of *expiating* or *atoning* for my sin by a penance which imposes on me, in painful and material form, a kind of suffering which symbolically represents (and thus expresses my repentance of) the harm I have done to others and to myself.[25]

Penance, as self-imposed suffering which expresses and assists repentance, aims to reconcile the penitent wrong-doer with others and with herself. The particular form which my penance takes can express my understanding of the character of my sin, and of the nature of the Good from which it has separated me. A sin against God may be atoned for in private prayer and meditation; a wrong against another person, or against the community, may be expiated by some task which benefits that person or the community (although we must distinguish penance from restitution, the same task can serve both purposes); I may express my recognition of the way in which I have betrayed or injured my relationships with others by withdrawing into a penitential solitude. A penance will often involve depriving myself of some material or non-moral good (money, comfort, or some ordinary kind of pleasure or enjoyment): this can express my awareness of, and my concern for, the greater importance of the moral good which my wrong-doing implicitly denied; and my recognition that I should not be able to enjoy my ordinary pursuits and pleasures until I have considered and repented my sin.

A penance may be a private act which I conceive and undertake for myself: but it may have a more formal and institutional context, such as that of a church or religious community; and it may in that context be something which is required of me, or even imposed on me, by others. In the simplest kind of case I make my confession to a priest who, in virtue of the authority vested in him by God and by

[25] Compare Dilman, *Morality and the Inner Life* ch. 5; Morris, 'Guilt and Suffering'.

the church, specifies an appropriate penance for me. Both confession and penance are required of me, not merely suggested to me, by the church of which I am a member, and by God to whom I owe obedience and repentance: but there need be no human sanction against failure to perform the penance – no attempt to impose it on me against my will. If I fail to perform it, I might suffer the criticism of my priest or my fellows – but they might instead stay silent, believing it to be a matter between me and God. I might be told that I should not take part in the worship of the church until I have performed the penance – but it might also be left entirely up to me to make my confession, perform my penance, and exclude myself meanwhile from the services in which I should not take part.

But a failure to perform the penance which is appropriate must make a difference to my relationship with God: if my sin has separated me from God; if a penance is the proper way to seek His mercy and restore myself to Him; then a failure to perform the penance must preserve my separation from him. And since the church is a community of believers, bound together by their love of God and by their spiritual relationship to each other in God, my impenitent sinfulness must also injure my relationship with the church and with my fellows in the church: it separates me not just from God but from them. The church may thus naturally (though not inevitably) express such an understanding of the implications of my sin by excluding me from its services, from its holy places, or even from contact and communion with its members. So we find, in the history of the Christian church, detailed rules for such matters: rules requiring confession and penance before communion can be taken, and threatening excommunication against persistent, serious and unrepentant sinners; rules for the 'binding and loosing' of sinners, which specify the periods of exclusion (a physical exclusion from the church which symbolised the sinner's separation from God and from the community of the church) appropriate for different sins, and the penances which must be undertaken or undergone if the sinner was to be restored to communion with God and with the church.[26]

There was a continuing controversy within the Christian church about whether any sin was so serious that it required permanent excommunication; or whether any penitent, however serious his sin, should be offered a way back to communion with God and with the church. But it is clear that the church's response to most, if not

[26] On the history and meaning of penance, see especially J T McNeill, *A History of the Cure of Souls*; K Rahner, *Theological Investigations* vol. 2, 135–74, vol. 10, 125–49.

to all, sins was not simply one of expulsion. The sinner must be excluded (he had by his sin excluded himself) from full participation in the life and worship of the church: but he must be allowed, encouraged and helped to restore himself, through penance, to a full communion with God and with the church; he was still to be treated and cared for as a member of the community.

Excommunication, like penance, is a kind of punishment – it could indeed be seen as part of the penitential process on which a sinner must embark; and the fear of excommunication would provide a powerful incentive to refrain from sin and to undertake penance. But neither excommunication nor penance are penalties which the church *attaches* to sin, either as prudential deterrents or as inflicting some further deserved suffering on the sinner. For such punishments are already implicit in his sin: in excommunicating him the church is recognising, and giving formal effect and expression to, the way in which he has by his sin *separated himself* from God and the church; in requiring a penance of him the church is showing him that this is what he must do to restore himself. Nor are such punishments to be seen merely as prudential deterrents: the potential sinner should indeed fear excommunication and the need to undergo penance – and this fear should dissuade him from sin; but what he should fear is the sin itself, whose nature and implications are represented in his excommunication and penance. He should fear the separation from God and his fellows which his sin itself entails; and it should be that fear (which itself expresses his love of God and his awareness that his own good lies in communion with God and the church) which deters him from sin and makes him welcome his penance as the way back to fellowship with God and man.

Such punishments as these would not, ideally, be coercive. For, ideally, a sinner will voluntarily make her confession, realising the importance of this for her relationship with God and for her own well-being; come to see for herself, with the help of her priest, the nature and implications of her sin; exclude herself from communion until she has undertaken an appropriate penance in the appropriate spirit; undertake that penance, and solicit readmission to the fellowship of the church. Nor does the church coerce her merely by *requiring* her to exclude herself from its services and to undertake a penance: for the satisfaction of these requirements could be left entirely up to her. But sinners will not always thus voluntarily obey the church's rules and requirements; and the church might then begin to *impose* them, by force, on recalcitrant sinners.

It might begin by forcibly excluding from its services an unrepentant sinner who refuses to exclude herself: but this need not be a kind of coercion which fails to respect the sinner's autonomy or her will. So long as the church can justify to the sinner its claim that she has by her sin made herself unfit or ineligible for participation in its services, in forcibly excluding her from those services it is simply defending itself against her unjustified intrusion. Such exclusions are, even if backed up by force, comparable to the loss of trust or friendship which a moral wrong-doer may suffer.

But what if the church goes further than this, and seeks to *impose* a penance on the sinner? The sinner would ideally undertake the penance for herself, because she sees that, and why, it is necessary. Or she might undertake it, not because she already understands and repents her sin, but because she is told that she should undertake it and hopes that, through the penance, she will come to a better understanding and a more genuine repentance of her sin. She still undertakes the penance voluntarily, because she accepts the authority of the church which requires it of her; because she has some understanding both of her sin and of the meaning of the penance; and because, even though she is at the moment disinclined to do penance, she believes that it is necessary if she is to restore herself to the community through a proper understanding and repentance of her sin. Suppose, however, that she refuses to undertake the penance which is prescribed for her; and that she is then forcibly subjected to solitary confinement, to a diet of bread and water, or even to physical beatings: could this be justified as an attempt to force her to undergo the penance which she ought to undertake for herself – and as an attempt which still expresses a proper concern and respect for her as a moral agent?

If such coercive measures are to be justified in these terms, several conditions must be satisfied. First, the sinner must be seen as a member of the church community – a community united by shared beliefs and values, within which her true spiritual well-being is to be found. Second, her sin must be seen to separate her from that community, and thus to be injurious to her: by flouting, and thus implicitly denying, the values which give the community its identity she has broken the bonds which tie her to the community and to God; she has separated herself from her own good. Third, in subjecting her to such coercive treatment (rather than, for instance, simply expelling her from the community) the aim must be not merely to inflict suffering on her, but to bring her, through her suffering, to understand and repent her sin; to accept her penance; and thus to restore herself to full communion with God and her fellows. Fourth, the coercion to which she is subjected must therefore aim to secure her understanding and her assent: if it is to be or become the penance which she needs to undertake, it must be (if not at first, then in the end) mediated by her own understanding and acceptance of its necessity.

This last point is crucial. If a penance is to have its proper meaning, it must be understood and willed as a penance by the sinner herself: if it is initially imposed on her against her express will, it can achieve its proper purpose only if she comes, through her subjection to it, to accept it for herself – to impose it on herself. For an outward penance must express an inward repentance: what is required of the sinner is not merely that she undergo some visible deprivation or suffering, or observe certain external forms, but that she do this in a proper spirit of penitential remorse. The imposition of suffering on an unrepentant or unwilling sinner can be justified in these penitential terms only if it addresses her as a moral agent who can and should come to understand and repent her own sin, and will her own penance: for only then can it become a *penance*.

Now I do not claim that the actual treatment of sinners by the Christian church has always fitted this model. Churches are as prone to abuse their power as any other human institution; and the history of the Christian church is littered with coercive practices which cannot plausibly be justified as genuine and caring attempts to bring sinners to a repentant understanding of their sins. I claim only that we have here an *ideal* model of both voluntary and compulsory penance; a model which can be drawn from the doctrines of the church, and against which the actual practices of the church can be critically measured.

We can, I hope, understand the sense of a penance to which a sinner voluntarily submits himself, as a self-imposed punishment through which he can express his repentance and restore himself to the communion from which his sin separated him. We can also, I hope, see how an imposed penance could bring an initially unrepentant sinner to repentance. If the suffering to which he is subjected is imposed on him in the right way and in the right spirit it can bring home to him, as merely verbal or symbolic condemnation would not, the extent and nature of his sin. He is forced to attend to what he has done, by asking why he is being treated thus: he may thus grasp the communicative content of what is done to him; come to see and accept that he has sinned, and see how this penance can (given its expressive meaning) help to restore him; and come in this way to will his own penance as an appropriate stimulus and vehicle for his repentance.

But even if imposed penance can thus become voluntary penance; even if it can communicate to the sinner a better understanding of his sin, and bring him to repentance: is this enough to justify it? Or must we say that it is still a coercive and unwarranted infringement of his autonomy; that the church, while it may properly excommunicate a sinner and require him to undertake a penance, has no right to *force* that penance on him, or *coerce* him into a repentant understanding of his sin; and that in doing so the church is *using* him as a *means* to his own spiritual well-being? To this it may be replied that the idea of respecting the sinner's autonomy has no place in a doctrine of compulsory penance: a church which is ready to coerce its sinners in this way clearly does not regard them as autonomous agents, but as helpless victims of the flesh and the devil who need to be saved from sin and from themselves. An adequate treatment of these issues would require a fuller account of a church's authority over its members; of its proper interest in their spiritual well-being; and of the conception of sin which might inform its treatment of them. I will not offer such an account here, since my primary concern is with a state's right to impose punishments on its citizens; but two further relevant points may be noted.

First, the church may wish to claim that the imposition of penance on a recalcitrant sinner is still in accordance with her own will (it might thus distinguish, for instance, the coercion of a member of the church from the coercion of someone who is not and never has been a member). This claim could be sustained by showing that she joined the community by a voluntary act of allegiance, such as the taking of vows; or that, though she did not join the community voluntarily (being simply born into it), she still wishes to remain a member of it; or perhaps that, despite her present recalcitrance, she retains a fundamental regard for the authority of the church, for the values which define it, and for her membership of it. For in entering or wishing to remain within the church she explicitly or implicitly accepts its rules, and submits herself to its disciplinary procedures. In imposing penance on her against her presently expressed and sinful will, the church can thus claim to be acting in accordance with her authentic will to remain a member of the community and an obedient servant to God. Indeed, if her enforced penance does bring her to repentance she will herself assent to it, as having been in accordance with her true will. She might then say with Paul, 'the good that I would I do not: but the evil which I would not, that I do',[27] and be thankful that she has been saved from sin.

The imposition of penance on a sinner who does not thus accept the authority or values of the church cannot of course be justified in this way: an appeal to what she 'really' wills cannot depend on what she has avowed (or will avow, since she might remain unrepentant) as her will. The church might appeal instead to the good will which is buried within her soul, and which must be freed from the bonds of sin; and such an appeal may have some content – some connection to her actual life and concerns – insofar as she is or was a genuine member of the community of the church. Now no such appeal to the sinner's (actual or supposed) will is by itself sufficient to render the imposition of penance consistent with a respect for her autonomy: when I stopped Jane drinking, I acted in accordance with her previously expressed will; but I still infringed her autonomy.[28] However, and secondly, we may still be able to show that the imposition of penance is consistent with a respect for her autonomy, insofar as it still addresses her as a rational moral agent.

When penance is imposed on her, she is certainly coerced: she is forced to suffer something painful; and this suffering is meant to force her attention onto what should concern her – her own sin and its implications. But she is not, or need not be, *manipulated*, if the penance to which she is subjected still appeals to her understanding and seeks her acceptance of the relevant reasons which justify the claim that she ought to repent her sin and accept her penance. For her imposed penance then still addresses her as a rational moral agent: it seeks to engage and arouse, but not to manipulate or coerce, her understanding and her judgment; it leaves her free to reject the judgment and the understanding which it seeks to communicate to her. If this is the character of her penance, she is not being used merely as a means; nor is that penance related to the repentant understanding which it seeks to arouse as a contingent means to a further end – it is related to that end as moral blame is related to the repentant recognition of guilt at which it aims.[29]

If the imposition of penance is to be justified in such terms as these, it must be justified as a warranted response to the sinner's own wrong-doing – a response which attempts to bring her to see and to accept for herself the nature of what she has done, and the need to undergo penance because of it. If this response is not to be manipulative, its character and content are clearly crucial: the

[27] *Romans* vii.19.

[28] See ch. 8(3) above.

[29] See ch. 2(3) above.

infliction, for instance, of extreme physical suffering, or of certain kinds of extreme psychological pressure, must surely count as an attempt to coerce the sinner's will and consent, rather than as an appeal to her understanding.[30] But my point here is simply this: that the demand that we respect the autonomy of others (which includes the demand that we should not manipulate them) may be interpreted, not as forbidding us to impose any kind of coercion on a person against his will, but as forbidding (particularly and especially) the use of coercive measures which aim to coerce or manipulate his will – measures which do not try to justify themselves to him by appealing to his understanding, and by seeking his rational assent.[31]

The sense and implications of this possibility can best be explained in the context of criminal punishment, to which we must now return.

5 PUNISHMENT, PENANCE AND RECONCILIATION

The idea of penance helps us to understand the sense of a voluntary or self-imposed punishment: a criminal who repents her crime (or who is brought by her trial and conviction to repent it) might request punishment, or accept it willingly, as a penance. Now we could imagine a legal system which required and facilitated, but did not enforce, such penances: its courts would convict offenders, specify appropriate penances for them, and provide suitable facilities for those penances; but it would be left up to the offender to submit herself for her penitential punishment. Even in a just system of law, however, it is unlikely that all offenders would submit thus voluntarily to punishment; and the *imposition* of punishment on recalcitrant offenders is a central feature of legal systems like our own: so we must ask whether such coercive punishments can be explained and justified as compulsory penances.

We may begin with the idea of a society, not simply as a collection of discrete and separate individuals (who could have no *common* good or common concerns), but as a *community* whose laws serve and preserve its common good, and of which the criminal is a member. Now a liberal society must accept and encourage a plurality of individual interests and values: but if it is to exist as a community at all its members must (as a matter of logic, not merely of pragmatic necessity) share a regard for certain central values, and a

30 Compare Murphy, 'Cruel and Unusual Punishments' 233.

31 See also ch. 8(3) above.

concern for each other as members of the community. This is not to say that an analytical or metaphysical inquiry could reveal some unique and univocal set of values which are necessary to the existence of any and every community: but any community must depend on (and is in part defined by) a shared allegiance to *some* core of values; and it is these values which the community's laws must declare and support.[32]

If a community's laws are just, a crime against those laws is injurious to the community. A criminal injures the direct victims of his crime (if there are any); he flouts the duty of care or respect which he owes to them as fellow-members of the community. But he also injures the community itself: he injures its common good by injuring any of its members; he implicitly denies or rejects the values on which the community depends; he damages or destroys his relationships both with those whom he directly injures and with other members of the community, by implicitly denying the values on which those relationships depend.

One who breaks the law in such a community makes himself liable to the criticism and condemnation of his fellows; and this condemnation may be given formal expression through a system of criminal trials and convictions. If his crimes are serious and persistent, the community might even (were this practicable) be justified in expelling him: for, we might say, he has disqualified himself from membership of the community by thus denying the values on which the community itself (and thus his membership of it) depend. But what can justify us in imposing on him a punishment which serves, not as a measure of self-defence against his criminal attack (since it follows his crime); nor simply as an expressive condemnation of his crime (since that is achieved by his conviction); nor as a purely preventive or deterrent measure (since that would deny him the respect which is his due as a rational agent); nor as a penance which he must undergo *if* he wishes to remain in the community (since he is given no choice in the matter); but as a compulsory penance which aims to bring him to repent his crime and thus to reform himself?

What is wrong with expelling a criminal is that it expresses no concern for *him* as a member, albeit a recalcitrant member, of the community; it simply excludes him from the community and its

32 See D N MacCormick, 'Against Moral Disestablishment'; P Winch, 'Nature and Convention': also J Finnis, *Natural Law and Natural Rights* ch. 6; Morris, 'A Paternalistic Theory of Punishment'; P F Strawson, 'Social Morality and Individual Ideal'; H L A Hart, *The Concept of Law* ch. 9.2.

concerns. What is essential to the justification of punishment as compulsory penance is that, by contrast, it expresses a continuing concern for the criminal as a member of the community: he has injured himself, as well as others, by his crime; and his punishment will, if it is administered and received in the appropriate spirit, help him to repair that injury.

But how can we say that the criminal is injured by his crime – especially if, in terms of the interests and values which he actually avows, and which he may share with his immediate friends and colleagues, he is injured by breaking the law only if and because he is punished for it? The claim that he is injured by his crime follows directly from a certain understanding of the wrongfulness of that crime. When Plato or Kierkegaard argue that a wrong-doer is necessarily harmed by his wrong-doing, their claim is not that his wrongful deeds will produce contingent effects which he himself will, in the end, see to be harmful to him; indeed, the sinner who never realises his wretched state is in the most wretched condition of all. Their claim is rather that what matters above all in a person's life – and what *should* matter to him above all – is his relation to the Good: his well-being is to be *defined* in terms of that relation; one who is separated from the Good suffers by that very separation the worst harm which could befall him, whether he realises it or not.[33]

A more modest and secularised version of the Platonic claim would be this. A person can find well-being only within a community which is, necessarily, structured by certain shared values and concerns, and within the kinds of relationship which such a community makes possible. A criminal who flouts the just laws of her community thereby injures herself: she separates herself from the values on which the community and her own well-being depend; she damages or destroys her relationships with other members of the community, and separates herself from them. She may not in fact be made consciously unhappy by her crime (especially if she avoids punishment); she may attain the ends which she actually pursues, and lead the kind of life she enjoys; and her crime may in fact be consistent with her actual relationships with others (she has no concern for those whom she robs or attacks; her family and friends share her criminal attitudes and goals). But this shows only that she, and those with whom she lives, have turned away from the values which should concern them; that they fail or refuse to see how such criminal pursuits are inconsistent with the existence of a

33 See Plato, *Gorgias* and *Republic*; Kierkegaard, *Purity of Heart*: also Dilman, *Morality and the Inner Life* ch. 4; D Z Phillips and H O Mounce, *Moral Practices* chs. 3–4.

community within which any worthwhile human life is possible; and that their relationships are themselves corrupted by false values. If she would only recognise the moral truth about her criminal attitudes and activities, she would see how they are injurious to her true well-being.[34]

The claim that the criminal is harmed by her crime is thus a moral rather than an empirical claim: it concerns the moral implications of her crime for her life as a member of the community, and the moral foundations of that community and the relationships within it, rather than the contingent effects of her crime on herself or on those around her. Note too that this claim concerns the nature and implications of crime in a genuine community, which is held together by bonds of mutual concern and respect for the shared values which are expressed in its just laws. I will have more to say later about the implications of crime in a society which is not thus a genuine community.

A repentant criminal recognises the implications of her crime, and the harm it has done to others and to herself; and she may hope by her penance to express her remorseful understanding of her crime, and to restore her relationships with the rest of the community. She sees her penance as a benefit to herself; and, just as the harm done to her by her crime is internal to the crime, as a matter of its moral implications, so too is the benefit which her penance brings her internal to its moral character as a penance. She might find that others are in fact self-righteously unforgiving; that despite her genuinely penitential remorse they continue to shun or ostracise her as someone who has disqualified herself from membership of the community: but the fault then lies in them and their response to her penance. She is injured by such a response, but she has still benefited in and by her penance: it has reconciled her to the values which should inform her life and her relationships with others, and has thus restored a proper moral basis for those relationships.

If the imposition of punishment on an unrepentant criminal is to be justified as a compulsory penance, it too must claim to reconcile him to the Good and to other members of the community, and thus to benefit him; and this benefit must likewise be internal to his punishment, at least in the sense that it does not depend (or does not depend entirely) on the actual effect of his punishment on *others*. Even if he is now shunned both by his former criminal colleagues

[34] Compare also S Weil, *The Need for Roots*; Morris, 'Guilt and Suffering' and 'A Paternalistic Theory of Punishment'; Finnis, *Natural Law and Natural Rights* 264; A I Melden, *Rights and Persons* 181–4.

and by the self-righteously law-abiding we must be able to say, with Socrates, that it is better for him to have been punished than to have escaped punishment;[35] because he has still been reconciled to the Good. But can this benefit also be independent of his punishment's actual effect on *him*; or does he benefit only if he in fact comes to repent his crime and accept his punishment as a penance?

Hegel's account is instructive here. Punishment serves to annul past crimes –

> The sole positive existence which the injury possesses is that it is the particular will of the criminal. Hence to injure this particular will as a will determinately existent is to annul the crime, which otherwise would have been held valid, and to restore the right.[36]

Crime is a form of coercion which denies its victim's freedom and rights; which thus infringes the right as right: this infringement must be annulled by a punishment which coerces the criminal's own will. But punishment is also the criminal's right: it honours and accords with his implicit will as a rational being.

> Objectively, [punishment] is the reconciliation of the law with itself; by the annulment of the crime the law is restored and its authority is thereby actualized. Subjectively, it is the reconciliation of the criminal with himself, i.e. with the law known by him as his own and as valid for him and his protection: when this law is executed upon him, he himself finds in this process the satisfaction of justice and nothing save his own act.[37]

Punishment reconciles the criminal with himself – as a rational agent who wills the law: but how does it do this? Are we to say, as Hegel seems to imply, that this reconciliation is *necessarily* intrinsic to the very fact of just punishment: that even if he actually sees his punishment as nothing more than a coercive imposition, it necessarily reconciles him with himself; that even if he is unaware of any 'satisfaction' in his punishment, it is a satisfaction which he must find as a rational agent who wills the law?

Now it is true that the satisfaction which penance brings to the penitent, and the reconciliation which it secures, are internal to the penance itself, not contingent effects of it. But it is also true that that satisfaction and that reconciliation involve the penitent's own understanding: he is satisfied and reconciled because the pain of his penance expresses his painful awareness of the wrong he has done. How then can a punishment which the criminal sees merely as co-

[35] Plato, *Gorgias* 472–3, 476–80.
[36] G W F Hegel, *Philosophy of Right* s. 99.
[37] *Ibid.* s. 220.

ercive, which does not involve his own repentant understanding of his wrong-doing (and which thus cannot be a *penance*),[38] reconcile him with himself, or with the Right? To tell him that, whether he realises it or not, his punishment does thus reconcile and satisfy him implies an objectification of his 'real' or rational will, and a discounting of his actual response to his punishment, which is both problematic in itself and inconsistent with the claim that his punishment respects *him*, the actual criminal, as a rational agent.[39]

Perhaps, therefore, we should follow McTaggart's reading of Hegel. The purpose of punishment, like that of a penance which is imposed on a recalcitrant sinner, is to bring the criminal to understand the nature and implications of her crime; to repent that crime; and *thus*, by willing her own punishment as a penance which can expiate her crime, to reconcile herself with the Right and with her community.[40]

Such a conception of punishment as a communicative and reformative endeavour has a long history. It appears in Plato: both in the more practically oriented discussion of *The Laws*, according to which punishment should serve a reformative as well as a deterrent function –

> to bring the criminal and all who witness his punishment in the future to complete renunciation of such criminality, or at least to recover in great part from the dreadful state;[41]

and in the *Gorgias* and *Republic*, in the claim that punishment aims to cure the wrong-doer's soul of its unjust and disordered condition.[42] It is found too in Kierkegaard –

> But if he has done wrong, then he must, if he really wills one thing and sincerely wills the Good, desire to be punished, that the punishment may heal him just as medicine heals the sick;[43]

and in Simone Weil –

> Punishment is solely a method of procuring pure good for men who do not desire it. The art of punishing is the art of awakening in a criminal, by pain or even death, the desire for pure good.[44]

38 See ch. 9(4) above. 39 See ch. 8(3) above.

40 J M E McTaggart, *Studies in Hegelian Cosmology* ch. 5; see also P Bean, *Punishment* 47–53.

41 Plato, *The Laws* XI, 934.

42 I will not pursue the problems of Platonic interpretation here: contrast Dilman, *Morality and the Inner Life* ch. 5, with M M Mackenzie, *Plato on Punishment*.

43 Kierkegaard, *Purity of Heart* 70 (and ch. 5 generally).

44 S Weil, 'Human Personality' 31; see also *The Need for Roots* 20–1. See also F Dostoevsky, *Crime and Punishment* – discussed by Dilman, *Morality and the Inner Life* ch. 5.

We may find elements of such a view in, for instance, the early Quaker view of imprisonment as the appropriate mode of punishment: prison removes the criminal from his corrupting peers, and provides the opportunity for and the stimulus to a reflective self-examination which will induce repentance and self-reform.[45] One could also cite the importance attached in some societies to the condemned man's acceptance of and participation in his own execution: he was urged to confess his crimes, and to play the penitential part assigned to him in the formal process of execution; for this would express his recognition of the justice of his punishment, and enable him to made his peace with God and with man.[46] The condemned prisoner in classical Athens was expected to drink the fatal hemlock himself: not so that he might by committing suicide avoid the pain or indignity of being executed by others; but so that he might participate in, express his consent to, and will his own punishment.[47]

Punishment is, on this conception, communicative, retributive and reformative. It is communicative in that it seeks to communicate to the criminal a proper understanding of his crime: by imposing on him some material injury which can be seen as injurious even through the eyes of egoistical self-interest, we hope to represent, and to force on his attention, the harm he has done both to others and to himself; by imprisonment, which separates him physically from the rest of the community, we give material and symbolic expression to the spiritual separation created by his crime. It is retributive in that it is a response to his past crime whose meaning lies in the judgment on, and the condemnation of, that crime which it seeks to communicate; and whose aim is to bring the criminal to suffer the pain of remorse which he ought to feel when he considers his crime. And it is reformative in that it aims to bring the criminal, through his understanding of his crime and his punishment, to repent his crime; to accept his punishment as an appropriate vehicle for his repentance; and thus to reform himself – to reconcile himself to the values which his crime denied and to the community to which he belongs.

This is the proper punitive purpose of hard treatment – a purpose which would not be so well served by purely formal convictions or symbolic punishments. It serves in part to make our communicative

45 See Morris, *The Future of Imprisonment* 4–5.

46 See, for instance, M Foucault, *Discipline and Punish* 38–45; also ch. 1(1) above.

47 See Plato, *Phaedo*; R F Holland, 'Suicide'; R A Duff, 'Socratic Suicide?'.

endeavour more effective, forcing the criminal's attention onto the implications of his crime; he cannot ignore it as easily as he can ignore or forget a conviction or a purely symbolic punishment. But it should serve too – if it is successful – as a penance which the criminal comes to will for himself: the pain or suffering which begins as a coercive attempt to attract and direct the unrepentant criminal's attention should become the penitential pain which the repentant criminal accepts for himself.

We must be clear about the meaning of this claim that punishment serves a reformative purpose. The claim is not simply that punishments such as imprisonment provide, as a side-effect, the opportunity for some further reformative treatment; but rather that punishment itself, as punishment, should reform the criminal.[48] Nor is the claim that punishment is an *efficient technique* for bringing about some desirable change in the criminal's attitudes and conduct, to be compared with other psychological or physiological techniques for manipulating attitudes and behaviour as an instrumental means towards some independently identifiable further end. The claim that punishment aims at the offender's spiritual reform is quite different from, for instance, the claim that criminals are mentally disordered individuals who need psychiatric treatment; or that the proper purpose of punishment is the efficient modification of the criminal's behavioural patterns.[49]

It is true that some, like Plato and Kierkegaard, talk of punishment as an attempt to *cure* the criminal's soul of its spiritual *disorder*: but talk of a person's soul is not to be confused with talk of her psychological states; and the cure of souls is not to be confused with the cure or treatment of psychiatric disorders. To say that a criminal is spiritually sick or disordered is to offer a moral comment on the values which do, as contrasted with those which should, inform her life and her relationships with others, not an empirical diagnosis of some impairment in her rational capacities.[50] To say that we need to punish her in order to cure her soul is not to say that we need to subject her to some technique which will efficiently modify her attitudes or conduct, and that punishment is in fact the most efficient available technique for this purpose: it is rather to say that she should, for the sake of her moral well-being, come to understand and repent her wrong-doing; and that punishment is the appropriate

[48] See A C Ewing, *The Morality of Punishment* 73–4.
[49] See Hampton, 'The Moral Education Theory of Punishment'.
[50] See I Dilman, 'Wittgenstein on the Soul'.

stimulus to, vehicle for, and expression of such a repentant understanding. For punishment, like moral blame, is related logically rather than merely contingently to the end at which it aims: it aims at a kind of reform which must involve the criminal's repentant understanding of her past crime; and it is that understanding which punishment, as a communicative and penitential enterprise, aims to arouse and express.

This is not to say that punishment (if justly and properly administered) must of logical necessity achieve its purpose – that its end is in *that* sense internal to it: punishment may in fact fail to bring a criminal to repent her crime; and it then fails to achieve the end at which it properly aims. Nor is it to say that there are no technical questions involved in the administration of punishment: we must investigate the actual effects on criminals of different kinds and styles of punishment and ask, among other questions, which of them will most efficiently serve their communicative and penitential purposes. But it is not a contingent matter that punishment – the infliction of suffering on an offender for her offence – is the appropriate way of trying to achieve the kind of penitential reform which is its justifying aim: that aim can, of its nature, be achieved only by bringing the offender to suffer for what she has done. If someone suggested, for instance, that we might hope to develop some kind of drug or psycho-surgical technique which would provide a more efficient and less painful method of securing the kind of reformative change at which punishment aims, we would not need to question the empirical plausibility of her suggestion: for the suggestion itself is incoherent. No such technique could, logically, produce the results at which punishment aims: such techniques do not address the criminal, as punishment must address her, as a responsible moral agent who can and should come to understand the moral implications of what she had done; they are not, as punishment must be, attempts to solicit and arouse her repentant understanding of her crime; and the acquisition of such an understanding must of its nature be painful to the criminal.[51]

6 THE RIGHT TO BE PUNISHED

If we understand punishment in these terms, we can see that its purposes are strictly continuous with those of the criminal law and the criminal trial (and with those of moral blame). It addresses the

[51] Compare J Teichman, 'Punishment and Remorse'; Morris, 'A Paternalistic Theory of Punishment'.

criminal as a rational moral agent, seeking his understanding and his assent; it aims to bring him not merely to obey the law, but to accept its requirements as being justified: to recognise the wrongness of what he has done, to make his own the condemnation which his conviction expresses, and to guide his future conduct in the light of the relevant moral reasons which the law, his trial and his punishment all offer him for obeying the law. It treats him not merely as a passive victim or subject *on* whom suffering is to be imposed, but as a moral agent *with* whom we are engaged in a communicative process of argument and persuasion – it seeks his participation, not merely his submission: for its aim is that he should come to make the punishment, and the repentant understanding which it expresses, his own.

A sane offender has a *right* to be punished: a right to be punished rather than be subjected to some kind of manipulative or preventive treatment which would not address him as a rational agent; and a right to be punished rather than be ignored or dismissed, since his punishment expresses a proper response to his crime as the wrongdoing of a responsible moral agent, and a proper concern for his moral well-being as a fellow-member of the community. We owe it to him, as well as to those whom he has injured, to condemn his crime and to try to bring him to repentance and reform. But an offender who is now so disordered that she cannot understand or respond appropriately to her punishment is not fit to be punished. If she *cannot* grasp the communicative character of her punishment as a response to her past offence; or come through her punishment to feel the pain of remorse which it is meant to arouse in her; or come to accept her punishment as an appropriate penance for her past offence: her punishment cannot be justified – it cannot properly count – as a punishment, and becomes instead nothing more than mere coercion. For if punishment is to be more than mere coercion, it must be justified *to* the person on whom it is imposed, as a penance which she should come to accept and will for herself.

This means that an offender who is to be fit to be punished, like a defendant who is to be fit to be tried, must be capable not only of grasping the *fact* that what is being done to her is done because she has broken the law, but also of grasping and responding to its *moral* meaning and purpose as a punishment. She must have the capacity and the potential for the kind of penitential redemption which punishment aims to induce: which means that she must already have some concern, which punishment may reawaken and strengthen, for the values which she has flouted; or at least that she has some moral concerns which would enable her to come, through her punishment, to understand and care for the values which the law embodies. If she is, for instance, a psychopath who cannot understand her punishment as anything more than a coercive imposition which is provoked by her refusal to obey our demands on her, we cannot properly punish her. Nor, I think, can we properly punish an offender who is now suffering from amnesia which covers the time of her offence: for if she is cut off by her amnesia from truly recognising and acknowledging that offence as her own, she cannot be brought by her punishment to repent and disown it.[52]

The justifying purpose of a punishment which is imposed on an as yet unrepentant criminal is to bring him to repent his crime, and to accept his punishment as an appropriate penance for his wrongdoing. A punishment may in fact fail to achieve this purpose; and it is indeed essential to the justification of punishment, as an attempt to persuade rather than to coerce the criminal's will and understanding, that it is thus fallible – that it leaves the criminal free to dissent, and to continue to dissent, from the law and from his punishment.[53] Now the fact that his punishment thus fails to achieve its purpose does not show that the criminal is unfit to be punished, as being *incapable* of coming to understand and accept his punishment. Not all unrepentant criminals (nor even all persistent and unrepentant criminals) are disordered psychopaths: we must recognise the existence both of the unrepentantly immoral criminal, who offers no principled defence of his actions but persists in flouting the law's moral demands, and of the principled rebel, who is determined to resist and oppose the values which the law embodies; the mere fact of such unrepentant criminality is not a sufficient criterion of psychopathic disorder.[54] Nor does the fact that his punishment has failed to persuade him to repent show by itself that we were not justified in punishing him. Though we must ask whether that failure might not have been due to some deficiency in the manner or the spirit in which the punishment was imposed on him, rather than to his own obstinacy, the failure of our attempt to persuade him does not by itself show that the attempt was not justified.

Suppose, however, that we are reasonably sure in advance that a

[52] See chs. 1, 4(6) above; also Moberly, *The Ethics of Punishment* 133–8. Morris claims ('A Paternalistic Theory of Punishment') that the criminal must already care for the values he has flouted: for reasons discussed in R A Duff, 'Psychopathy and Moral Understanding', I think this requirement is too stringent.

[53] See ch. 10(1) below.

[54] See Duff, *op. cit.*

particular criminal will not be persuaded or brought to repentance by his punishment: must we not then admit that we are not, on this account, justified in punishing him? For if the punishment which is now imposed on him against his unrepentant will is not going to accord in the end, as it should, with his repentant will; if it is not going to become a penance (a *self*-punishment) which he accepts for himself; if the suffering which it inflicts on him is not going to become, as it should, the penitential suffering of one who repents his crime: then surely in punishing him we are simply inflicting pointless suffering on him – or perhaps using him as a means to some other purpose.

It must be admitted that punishment brings no benefit to such a criminal:

> while punishment, which God in his wisdom has connected with every transgression, is a Good, there is no denying that it is such a Good only when it is gratefully received, not when it is simply feared as an evil.[55]

Indeed, it might be said that a punishment which fails to secure the criminal's penitential assent cannot, properly speaking, count as a punishment –

> Punishment only takes place where the hardship is accompanied at some time or another, even after it is over, and in retrospect, by a feeling of justice.[56]

But if a criminal never comes, even in retrospect, to see his punishment as anything other than an evil which is imposed on him, how can it be justified? Plato thought that a criminal who is indeed incurable – whose moral condition is such that we cannot hope to restore him, by punishment, to the Good – should either be killed, since he has no hope of well-being, or be punished simply as an example to others.[57] But we are not, I think, forced to accept this view: we can insist that punishment must be a communicative endeavour to bring the criminal to repentance, without thereby being required to exempt from punishment those whom it will not, we believe, bring to repentance; and without thereby being permitted simply to dispose of such people or to use them as means to our social ends.

So long as we believe that a criminal is a rational and responsible agent, who is thus capable of coming to understand and repent his crime, we have no right to treat him as Plato suggests. To kill him,

55 Kierkegaard, *Purity of Heart* 81–2.
56 Weil, *The Need for Roots* 21.
57 Plato, *Gorgias* 512a, 525c; *The Laws* IX, 862c: see Mackenzie, *Plato on Punishment* ch. 11.

or to use him simply as a terrible example to others, or to refuse to punish him, on the grounds that he is beyond redemption, is to give up any respect or hope for him as a moral agent; and this we may not do. The point here is not that we can never have empirically adequate grounds for believing that punishment will not in fact bring a criminal to repentance: it is rather that we can never have *morally* adequate grounds – nothing could count as morally adequate grounds – for treating a person as being beyond redemption. We owe it to every moral agent to treat him as one who can be brought to reform and redeem himself – to keep trying, however vainly, to reach the good that is in him, and to appeal to his capacity for moral understanding and concern. To talk thus of 'the good that is in him' is not to make some psychological claim to the effect that he 'really' cares for the values which he flouts: it is rather to combine the conceptual claim that every moral agent has the capacity or potential for moral development and reform, with the moral claim that we should never give up hope of bringing him to actualise that potential.

This gives further substance to the idea that every responsible criminal has a right to be punished – though it may not be a right which she is keen to claim: but it may also bring to the boil a number of objections to this account of punishment which must have been simmering during this chapter – objections to which I will attend in the next chapter.

The Ideal and the Actual

.. [I]f the state allows its attention to be distracted in the humble task of frightening criminals from crime, by the higher ambition of converting them to virtue, it is likely to fail in both, and so in its fundamental object of diminishing crime.

J M E McTaggart,
Studies in Hegelian Cosmology, ch. V, para. 145

But we have lost all idea of what punishment is. We are not aware that its purpose is to procure good for a man. For us it stops short with the infliction of harm. That is why there is one, and only one, thing in modern society more hideous than crime – namely, repressive justice.... All talk of chastisement, punishment, retribution, or punitive justice nowadays always refers solely to the basest kind of revenge.

S Weil, 'Human Personality', 31–2

In the previous chapter I outlined an ideal account of criminal punishment as a communicative enterprise in which we engage with the criminal. Punishment aims to express to her the condemnation which her crime warrants; to communicate to her a more adequate understanding of the nature and implications of her crime – the injury she has done to others and to herself; to persuade her to repent her crime, and to accept her punishment as a penance through which she can strengthen and express her repentant understanding and restore herself to the community from which her crime threatened to separate her: the proper purpose of punishment, on this view, is that it should become self-punishment – a penance which the criminal accepts and wills for herself.

I have tried to show how punishment – the infliction of suffering on a member of the community who has broken its laws – could ideally serve this communicative, reformative and penitential purpose; not that the actual punishments which criminals suffer in our own legal systems do serve this purpose. I have claimed too that this account of punishment (unlike, for instance, an account of punishment as a deterrent) shows its proper purposes to be continuous with those of the criminal law and the criminal trial; and shows that it expresses a proper concern and respect for the criminal as a fellow-member of the community. But even if we accept that punishment *could* ideally serve such a purpose; that it could, if properly administered and properly received within a just and authentic community, serve as a penance which enables criminals to understand, to repent and to expiate their crimes: such an account must face some serious objections.

Some of these objections concern its practical implications and applications. We must ask what kinds of punishment – what principles of sentencing – it would sanction, and whether these are acceptable. We must ask too whether we could in practice hope to institute and administer a system of criminal punishment which would be justified in these terms – and this question will force us to examine the extent and the implications of the gap between this ideal of just and proper punishment and the actual systems of punishment which we have or could in practice hope to have. I will turn to these issues later in this chapter: but we must first attend to a more fundamental objection, which attacks the ideal account of punishment itself rather than its practical applicability.

I OBJECTIONS AND CLARIFICATIONS

'You have noted already that it is the coercive dimension of punishment – the fact that it is imposed on a criminal against her will – that must most obviously concern anyone who takes seriously the demand that we should respect the autonomy of those with whom we deal: but you have not shown how the imposition of a purportedly communicative, reformative, and penitential punishment on an as yet unrepentant criminal can be consistent with, let alone expressive of, a proper respect for her as an autonomous moral agent. Granted that – *if* her punishment achieves its proper purpose – she will come to accept it for herself: is it not still true that, in imposing punishment on her against her present will, we are improperly coercing her; indeed that we are using her as a means to her own spiritual reform? We have in effect abandoned or compromised any attempt at rational persuasion, and instead use force to achieve our ends – to coerce her will into conformity with the law.

Indeed, punishments which aim at the criminal's moral reform actually constitute a more serious threat to his integrity, and a more serious infringement of his autonomy, than those which simply offer him a prudential deterrent. For a system of deterrent punishments aims simply to persuade the criminal to conform his external conduct to the law's demands: it leaves him free to disobey the law, if he is prepared to pay the price, and to maintain an inward and autonomous dissent from the law and its values. Deterrent punishment

> although unwelcome, is limited and external. It affords him and others a reason for not doing wrong, but does not impinge upon the inner citadels of his soul. We may hope that he will see the error of his ways and repent, but we do not insist.[1]

Reformative punishments, on the other hand, try to beat down the criminal's will – to coerce him, by physical pain or psychological pressure, into accepting the law and the values which it embodies.

Furthermore, by what right does the state take this kind of intrusive interest in the moral well-being of its citizens? It is one thing to say that the state should prescribe and enforce those minimal standards of conduct which are necessary for the survival and stability of a society in which individuals will be able to pursue their own autonomous projects: it is quite another to say that the state has either the right or the duty to impose on its citizens some particular conception of the good, or to coerce them into a state of supposed moral well-being. Should we not admit that the spiritual improvement of the offender, and the expiation or atonement of her crime, are matters which "must be left to the just determination of the supreme being",[2] and limit the state to the more modest and appropriate task of enforcing certain minimal standards of conduct?'

These objections can be met – and the meeting of them will also help to clarify some of the crucial aspects of this account of punishment.

They will not be met simply by claiming that in imposing punishment on a criminal we respect him by acting in accordance with his real or rational will; or that he must, as a criminal, be so corrupted by vice that he can no longer be addressed as a rational and autonomous agent – that he is instead a heteronomous victim of sin who must, for his own sake, be *dragged* back towards the Good.[3] We do, it is true, find language of this kind in some accounts of punishment as moral reform. Plato, for instance, argued that no one

[1] J R Lucas, 'Or Else' 235 (Lucas is contrasting deterrent punishments with purportedly therapeutic treatment); see also T Honderich, *Punishment: The Supposed Justifications* 90–3.

[2] Sir W Blackstone, *Commentaries on the Laws of England* IV. 1; see also N Walker, *Sentencing in a Rational Society* 13.

[3] See ch. 8(3) above.

willingly does evil, since what everyone truly desires is the good: the wicked man commits his crimes from ignorance, in the mistaken belief that they will bring him well-being; in punishing him we try to cure him of his ignorance, and direct him towards what is truly his good – what he truly wants.[4] And Simone Weil says

> Men who are so estranged from the good that they seek to spread evil everywhere can only be reintegrated with the good by having harm inflicted upon them. This must be done until the completely innocent part of their soul [that part which 'is on the deepest level and even in the most corrupt of men ... remains from earliest infancy perfectly intact and totally innocent'] awakens with the surprised cry 'Why am I being hurt?' The innocent part of the criminal's soul must then be fed to make it grow until it becomes able to judge and condemn his past crimes and at last, by the help of grace, to forgive them.[5]

But we should not, I think, read either Plato or Simone Weil as arguing that the criminal is not a responsible agent who should be condemned, as well as pitied, for his crimes; or as claiming, in the way that Murphy claims, that his punishment accords with his real or rational will.

Certainly, on this account of punishment, the criminal is mistaken, and is the victim of his mistake. But his mistake is a moral one: he wills and pursues what is evil rather than what is good, and has a distorted perception of value; his will, his desires, his concerns are misdirected. And it is a 'mistake' for which he is to be blamed, as well as pitied: he has *turned away* from the good; he has *allowed himself* to be seduced into vice; he has *closed his eyes* to what is good – to the interests and needs of others, as well as to his own true good. (This of course presupposes some conception of free will – of sin as a *wilful* falling from grace: but I will not discuss that conception here, save to note that it must, and can, be compatible with the idea of original sin; the idea that we are inherently sinful beings who need help – grace – if we are to be saved.)

We may say that the criminal 'really' wants or wills the good: but we must be clear about the meaning of such a claim, and about its compatibility with the fact that some criminals are whole-heartedly committed to evil ends. If I say of myself, when I have done wrong, that what I did was not what I 'really' wanted or willed; that 'the

[4] See especially Plato, *Gorgias*, and the discussion in I Dilman, *Morality and the Inner Life*; I should make clear that in citing such writers as Plato and Simone Weil I am concerned not so much with providing a historically accurate interpretation of what they meant as with the construction of an acceptable account of criminal punishment.

[5] S Weil, 'Human Personality' 31.

good that I would I do not: but the evil which I would not, that I do';[6] I am indeed claiming that I have an actual concern and regard for the good. But in saying that it is what I really want I am not making a factual or empirical claim about the relative strength of my various desires; I am making a moral claim which expresses my recognition of what I *should* desire and value above all, and *condemning* the desires which led me to sin. So too I may say of another who does wrong that this is not what she really wants; and this will have some factual purchase insofar as we can find in her actual life and actions some concern for others or for the good. Even then, however, my claim is not a factual claim about the actual strength of her desires, but a moral claim about what she *should* care for – about what should be deepest and most important in her life; and this claim rests on a moral conception of human life in the light of which I criticise her actual life and concerns.[7]

Even if the wrong-doer is apparently totally and ruthlessly corrupt, I might still say that there is deep within her a perfectly innocent part of her soul, which we must try to reach; and this again is a moral claim about how we should respond to her. We should never see a person, or give up on her, as being beyond redemption: for to see her as a person – as a being with a soul – is to see her as someone who always has the potential for repentance and redemption. This is in part a conceptual claim about what it is to see someone as a person, and about the concept of the soul: but it embodies a profound moral claim about the kind of attitude which we should have towards others – and towards ourselves.[8]

The claim that the criminal really wills the good, and therefore wills his own punishment as a way of restoring him to the good, thus has its place and its meaning within the moral conception of human life and well-being which informs this account of punishment; it helps to explain the claim that punishment expresses a concern for the criminal himself. But surely, it may now be said, this simply reinforces (rather than meets) the objection that in imposing punishment on a criminal we are improperly coercing him: it shows that we are trying to force on him a particular moral conception, which he may not share, of his good.

[6] *Romans* vii. 19.

[7] Thus the claim that the wrong-doer 'really' desires the good may be compared with the claim that law must serve the common good (ch. 3(5) above), or that punishment must be of the guilty (ch. 6(1) above).

[8] Compare I Dilman, 'Wittgenstein on the Soul'; and Wittgenstein's comment that 'my attitude towards him is an attitude towards a soul. I am not of the *opinion* that he has a soul', *Philosophical Investigations* Part II.iv: on that comment, and the meaning of 'attitude', see P Winch, 'Eine Einstellung zur Seele'.

Now it is easy to see how a purportedly reformative punishment could become an improperly coercive attempt to *beat down* the criminal's will; to coerce him into accepting the attitudes or beliefs which we want him to have, by whatever means may be effective: this indeed is one of the obvious dangers of an attempt to use punishment as a method of moral reform. We should note, however, that if punishment is used in this coercive and manipulative way, it ceases to be a method of moral reform. A process of moral reform must, logically, be mediated by the person's own understanding: its proper aim is that he should come to understand, and therefore to care for and to live by, the appropriate kinds of value; and a process which forces or manipulates his attitudes into conformity with some favoured set of values is not a possible way of achieving *that* end.[9]

But punishment which aims to induce repentance and self-reform need not have such a coercive and manipulative character: it can, and should, be an attempt to arouse and engage – but not to coerce – the criminal's understanding and his will. We try to draw his attention to the nature and implications of his crime; we try to persuade him to recognise and accept the relevant reasons which justify our condemnation of what he has done, and to see and accept his punishment as a penance; and we offer him a particular understanding of his crime and his punishment. But it is up to him to consider, to understand, and to come to accept the message which his punishment thus tries to communicate to him; it is for him to come to repent his crime and accept his punishment; and it is still open to him to refuse to do so. For it is crucial that his punishment, if it is to address him as a rational moral agent, should leave him this freedom to dissent – to remain unpersuaded and unrepentant. We hope and intend that he should come to accept his punishment, and the condemnation which it expresses; but we must leave him free to reject that condemnation, and to regard (and continue to regard) his punishment as nothing more than an unwarranted imposition. We try to reach 'the inner citadels of his soul': but we do not try to break down their gates; we rather try to persuade him to open those gates himself, and leave him free to keep them firmly closed.

This is not to deny or ignore the coercive dimension of punishment: it is imposed on the criminal against her will; she may see it as nothing more than a coercive imposition; the suffering which it causes her may be, as she perceives and receives it, unrelated to any

[9] See ch. 2(2)–(3) above.

repentant recognition of past wrong-doing. But it is to clarify the nature of the coercion which punishment must involve, and to show that punishment can be coercive without being manipulative: we try to make the criminal hear us; but we do not try to force her to believe or accept what we say. Now I could understand someone who claimed that such coercion is still incompatible with a proper respect for the criminal's autonomy and freedom, just as I can understand someone who claims that a proper respect for human life forbids *any* intentional killing, even in defence of oneself or of others: but just as I believe that I may properly kill an assailant to protect my own or others' lives against his wrongful attack, while still respecting and responding to him as an autonomous agent, I also believe that the coercive imposition of punishment on a criminal can be consistent with a respect for her autonomy.[10]

If someone has wronged me or another, I might try to make him hear – though I cannot and should not force him to accept – my criticism: I shout at him; I chase after him as he walks away; I stand in his way as he tries to leave. I force my criticism on his attention, knowing that he will initially perceive it only as an unwelcome and unfriendly intrusion, but hoping and intending that he will come to understand and accept it for what it is. A criminal is forced to attend her trial, in order that she may answer for her wrong-doing, and receive the condemnation which it warrants. She is not forced to answer for her actions, to play any part in her trial, or to accept her conviction – she is free to remain silent, and to reject the verdict and the condemnation which it expresses; but we force her into a position in which she will hear the charges, the trial, and the verdict, in the hope and with the intention that she will respond as she should. The coercion which is necessarily involved in the imposition of punishment is continuous with, though obviously more drastic than, these kinds of coercion; and it can, as they can, be consistent with a respect for the wrong-doer's autonomy. If it is to be thus consistent, punishment must constitute an attempt to pursue the proper aims of a system of law – to persuade the criminal to accept the law's requirements, and her own punishment, by persuading her to accept the relevant reasons which justify those requirements and her punishment; it must address her as a rational agent – it must seek but not try to coerce her consent; and it must be justified to her by reference to what she has herself done – by showing that it expresses a justified condemnation of her wrong-doing, and constitutes a penance which she ought to accept and will for herself.

[10] See ch. 8(3) above.

The constraints set by these conditions on the kinds of punishment which can properly be imposed will be discussed in the next section: but we must first attend more directly to the state's right to punish. For even if we accept that the imposition of punishment can be consistent with a proper respect for the criminal, this does not yet show that the state has the right or the duty to impose such punishments. It may still be objected that in imposing such punishments the state is taking an unwarrantably intrusive interest in the criminal's moral well-being, and is trying to impose on him a particular moral conception of the good. Several points need to be made in reply to this objection.

First, the claim cannot be that the state has no right or duty to impose *any* moral demands on its citizens through the criminal law: for the law must claim to impose obligations which make a moral claim on the citizens' allegiance. The question is not *whether* the state should try to secure the citizens' allegiance and obedience to some set of moral values, but *what* those values should be, and by what methods the state may properly try to secure the citizens' acceptance of them.[11] Should it, in particular, limit itself to declaring the law; to trying suspects and condemning offenders; to imposing purely symbolic punishments, or to requiring but not imposing penitential punishments which involve hard treatment; or may it properly impose such punishments on offenders?

Second, this account of punishment is quite consistent with the view that the criminal law should embody only a restricted and fairly minimal set of moral demands; that it should not aim to promulgate and secure the citizens' allegiance to some complete morality which will guide every aspect of their lives and determine every aspect of their individual or social good. We may say instead that it must, for the most part, be left up to individuals to determine their own values and ends within their own social groups: the proper task of the criminal law is only to identify, and try to secure acceptance of, a more minimal and central set of moral values which are essential to the preservation of the kind of society in which individuals can determine and pursue their own projects and values. This answers the objection that to see criminal punishment as a mode of moral reform is to sanction the extension of the criminal law to cover every kind of immorality:[12] the law's moral and re-

[11] See chs. 3, 9(5) above; D N MacCormick, 'Against Moral Disestablishment'.

[12] See A C Ewing, *The Morality of Punishment* 43; compare J Hampton, 'The Moral Education Theory of Punishment' 218–20.

formative ambitions should be limited to securing the citizens' allegiance to this more minimal set of essential values.

One reason for thus limiting the scope of the criminal law is that we must recognise the extent and the importance of moral diversity and disagreement – the extent to which individuals and groups will differ in their conceptions of the good. A state which is to preserve and respect its citizens' autonomy must leave them free to develop and pursue their own conceptions of the good. There will of course be scope for disagreement even about those moral demands which the criminal law must embody: I do not suppose that we could hope to identify a determinate set of moral demands which everyone must or will agree are necessary, in every detail, to the existence and survival of the community. Any set of determinate criminal laws must therefore take particular – and contestable – moral stands; it will try to impose on the citizen moral demands from which he might rationally dissent. But, thirdly, a system of criminal law and punishment does not try to *force* the citizen to accept the moral demands which it embodies. It should tell him that, and why, he *ought* to accept those demands; it will insist on judging his conduct in the light of those demands; it will condemn him if he flouts them, and might impose on him a punishment which aims to persuade him to accept them: but it must, as I have been arguing, leave him free to dissent from them; it must try to persuade, not to coerce, his will.

If we ask, fourthly, why the state should use coercive punishments to assist the proper ends of the criminal law (why it should, if not for reasons of deterrence or prevention, go beyond a system of formal convictions and purely symbolic punishments), the answer must refer to the duty of care and respect which the state owes to all its citizens – both the law-abiding and the criminal. If the requirements of the criminal law are properly justified, as being essential for the survival, the security and the well-being of the community and its members, it must follow that the state (in the name of and along with the members of the community) has a strenuous duty to make every permissible effort to ensure that they are accepted and obeyed. It owes this duty both to citizens who might be the direct or indirect victims of crime – to protect them from the criminal wrong-doings of others; and to those who would perpetrate crimes – to enable them to remain within or restore themselves to the community within which they must live and find their well-being. I have argued that a system of coercive punishments can still be an appropriate way of pursuing the law's justified ends, which still addresses and respects wrong-doers as rational moral agents; and it is the importance of those ends which justifies the use of such drastic measures.

This is not to say that the *consequential* ends of the law are so important that the state may use any means to pursue them which are consistent with the *side-constraints* imposed by the demand that it should respect the citizens' autonomy. For neither the protection of the citizen against injury at the hands of others, nor the protection of the criminal against the harm which he does to himself are further ends to which punishment is related contingently as an instrumental means. This should, by now, be clear enough of the relation between punishment and the moral reform of the offender:[13] but it is also true of the relation between punishment and the protection of others. It might be tempting to say, for instance, that the law's aim in protecting the law-abiding from criminal harm is simply to reduce the incidence of criminal conduct; and that the requirement that it should do this by means of a system of would-be reformative and penitential punishments (rather than, for instance, by a system of deterrent punishments or purely preventive treatment) reflects not the nature of that end but the further moral constraints to which our pursuit of it is subject: but that would be a distortion. It suggests that the law-abiding citizen, and the community as a whole, could be protected by measures which infringed the autonomy of those who were subjected to them; that, for instance, a system of deterrent or purely preventive punishments might efficiently serve the end of protecting the community, and is precluded only because it would conflict with a quite separate moral demand concerned with the autonomy of those who would be subjected to such punishments. But this distorts the law's proper protective purpose.

The law aims to serve the common good – which is the good of a community of rational and autonomous agents: but legal measures which infringe the autonomy of any of the citizens are therefore themselves injurious to the common good; we cannot simply see them as efficient methods of serving that good which fall foul of some independent moral demand. Nor do such measures infringe the autonomy only of some distinct sub-class of actual or potential criminals. A system of deterrent punishments issues its coercive and manipulative threats against every citizen; a system of preventive punishments makes every citizen liable to preventive detention if she breaks the law: all are threatened, all are injured, by such laws. Indeed, one might question the kind of benefit which a citizen gains if he is saved from criminal harm only by measures which infringe

[13] See ch. 9(5) above.

the autonomy of his actual or potential assailants. Socrates thought it better to suffer injustice than to do it, since doing injustice is the worst harm that can befall a person: so might we not also say that it is better to suffer injustice than to have injustice done on one's behalf; that I am injured if I am saved from being wrongfully killed only by the deliberate killing of an innocent?[14]

I do not deny that we may face difficult dilemmas between the demands of efficient crime-prevention and the demands of autonomy, if we realise that the only efficient way to prevent or reduce serious criminal acts would involve improperly coercing or manipulating actual or potential criminals. My point is rather that we misrepresent those dilemmas if we portray them simply as conflicts between the proper ends of a system of criminal law and certain moral side-constraints to which our pursuit of those ends is subject: for those 'side-constraints' must enter into our understanding of the ends themselves. A system of law which seeks to prevent or reduce crime by measures which infringe the autonomy of its citizens is not pursuing its proper ends by morally improper means: it has abandoned its pursuit of its *proper* ends, by compromising its allegiance to the values which those ends embody.

I will have more to say about these dilemmas in section 3. I have tried so far to show that a system of criminal law which aims to serve the common good, and which is to respect the autonomy of its citizens as being an essential part of that good, can still be justified in imposing punishments on criminals, even when those punishments involve hard treatment. If such punishments aim to persuade the criminal to repent her crime, and to accept her punishment as a penance, they can still respect her autonomy; they can be an appropriate way of pursuing the law's proper aims. But I must now turn to consider some of the implications of this view of punishment for sentencing policy and practice.

Bibliography

Bean P. *Punishment.* Martin Robertson, 1981.

Benn S I. 'An Approach to the Problems of Punishment', (1958), 33 *Philosophy* 325.

Charvet J. 'Criticism and Punishment', (1966), 75 *Mind* 573.

[14] Plato, *Gorgias*; see R Gaita, '"Better One than Ten"'.

Dilman I. 'Wittgenstein on the Soul' in G Vesey (ed.), *Understanding Wittgenstein*, p. 162. MacMillan, 1974.

Dilman I. *Morality and the Inner Life*. MacMillan, 1979.

Dostoyevsky F. *Crime and Punishment*. Trans. C Garnett. J M Dent (Everyman), 1955.

Duff R A. 'Psychopathy and Moral Understanding', (1977), 14 *American Philosophical Quarterly* 189.

Duff R A. 'Socratic Suicide?', (1982/3), 83 *Proceedings of the Aristotelian Society* 17.

Ewing A C. *The Morality of Punishment*. Kegan Paul, 1929.

Feinberg J. 'The Expressive Function of Punishment' in Feinberg, *Doing and Deserving*, p. 95. Princeton University Press, 1970.

Feinberg J. *Harm to Others*. Oxford University Press (New York), 1984.

Finnis J. *Natural Law and Natural Rights*. Oxford University Press, 1980.

Foucault M. *Discipline and Punish: The Birth of the Prison*. Trans. A Sheridan. Allen Lane, 1977.

Gaita R. '"Better One than Ten"' (1982), 5 *Philosophical Investigations* 87.

Hampton J. 'The Moral Education Theory of Punishment', (1984), 13 *Philosophy & Public Affairs* 208.

Hart H L A. *The Concept of Law*. Oxford University Press, 1961.

Hart H L A. *Law, Liberty and Morality*. Random House, 1963.

Hart H M. 'Criminal Punishment as Public Condemnation' in R J Gerber and P D McAnany (eds.), *Contemporary Punishment*, p. 12. University of Notre Dame Press, 1972.

Hegel G W F. *Philosophy of Right*. Trans. T M Knox. Oxford University Press, 1942.

Hirsch A von. *Doing Justice: The Choice of Punishments*. Hill & Wang, 1976.

Holland R F. 'Suicide' in Holland, *Against Empiricism*, p. 143.

Honderich T. *Punishment: The Supposed Justifications*. Revised edition, with postscript. Penguin Books, 1984.

Jackson R M. *Enforcing the Law*. Revised edition. Penguin Books, 1972.

Kierkegaard S. *Purity of Heart is to Will One Thing*. Trans. D Steere. Collins (Fontana), 1961.

Lemos R J. 'A Defence of Retributivism', (1977), 15 *Southern Journal of Philosophy* 53.

Lucas J R. 'Or Else' (1968/9), 69 *Proceedings of the Aristotelian Society* 207. J Rachels (ed.), *Moral Problems*, p. 222. 1st edition. Harper & Row, 1971.

Lucas J R. *Freedom and Grace*. Society for the Propagation of Christian Knowledge, 1976.

Lucas J R. *On Justice*. Oxford University Press, 1980.

MacCormick D N. 'Against Moral Disestablishment' in MacCormick, *Legal Right and Social Democracy*, p. 18. Oxford University Press, 1982.

Mackenzie M M. *Plato on Punishment*. University of California Press, 1981.
McNeill J T. *A History of the Cure of Souls*. Student Christian Movement, 1952.
McTaggart J M E. *Studies in Hegelian Cosmology*. Cambridge University Press, 1901.
Melden A I. *Rights and Persons*. Blackwell, 1977.
Moberly W. *The Ethics of Punishment*. Faber & Faber, 1968.
Morris H. 'Persons and Punishment', (1968), 52 *The Monist* 475. J G Murphy (ed.), *Punishment and Rehabilitation*, p. 40. Wadsworth, 1973.
Morris H. 'Guilt and Suffering' in Morris, *Guilt and Innocence*, p. 89. University of California Press, 1976.
Morris H. 'A Paternalistic Theory of Punishment', (1981), 18 *American Philosophical Quarterly* 263.
Morris N. *The Future of Imprisonment*. University of Chicago Press, 1974.
Murphy J G. 'Cruel and Unusual Punishments' in Murphy, *Retribution, Justice and Therapy*, p. 223.
Nozick R. *Philosophical Explanations*. Oxford University Press, 1981.
Phillips D Z and Mounce H O. *Moral Practices*. Routledge & Kegan Paul, 1969.
Plato. *Republic*. Trans. Lindsay. Dent (Everyman), 1976.
Plato. *Gorgias*. Trans. Helmbold. Bobbs-Merrill, 1952.
Plato. *Apology*, *Phaedo*. Trans. Tredennich, in *The Last Days of Socrates*. 2nd edition. Penguin Books, 1959.
Plato. *The Laws*. Trans. Taylor. Dent (Everyman), 1960.
Rahner K. *Theological Investigations*. Darton Longman & Todd, 1963 (vol. 2), 1973 (vol. 10).
Skillen A J. 'How to Say Things with Walls', (1980), 55 *Philosophy* 509.
Stephen J F. *A History of the Criminal Law of England*. MacMillan, 1883.
Stephen J F. *Liberty, Equality, Fraternity*. Ed. White. Cambridge University Press, 1967.
Strawson P F. 'Social Morality and Individual Ideal', (1961), 36 *Philosophy* 1.
Teichman J. 'Punishment and Remorse' (1973), 48 *Philosophy* 335.
Walker N. *Sentencing in a Rational Society*. Allen Lane, 1969.
Walker N. 'Punishing, Denouncing or Reducing Crime' in Glazebrook (ed.), *Reshaping the Criminal Law*, p. 391.
Walker N. 'The Ultimate Justification' in Tapper (ed.), *Crime, Proof and Punishment*, p. 109.
Weil S. *The Need for Roots*. Trans. Wills. Routledge & Kegan Paul, 1952.
Weil S. 'Human Personality' in Weil, *Selected Essays*, p. 9. Ed. R Rees. Oxford University Press, 1962.
Winch P. 'Nature and Convention' in Winch, *Ethics and Action*, p. 50.
Winch P. 'Ethical Reward and Punishment' in Winch, *Ethics and Action*, p. 210.
Winch P. 'Eine Einstellung zur Seele', (1980/1), 81 *Proceedings of the Aristotelian Society* 1.

[19]

Punishment and Justification

*Mitchell N. Berman**

I. INTRODUCTION

It is sometimes suggested that philosophical discussions of punishment are plagued by radical dissensus. But this is an overstatement. On at least one matter, a consensus approaches unanimity: punishment stands in need of justification. Very often, this principle constitutes the theorist's first premise.

Of course, proposed responses to the need for justification vary widely. Consequentialist accounts variously emphasize deterrence or incapacitation or norm reinforcement. Retributivist theories are even more diverse. But notwithstanding the variation within each broad camp, both approaches face well-known objections. Briefly, consequentialists are thought misguided for denying the intuitive idea that wrongdoers deserve to suffer, while their opposition to scapegoating is condemned as weak and contingent. Retributivists are said to be unable to explain either why wrongdoers deserve to suffer or why it is permissible for a state to inflict suffering even if deserved. They are also deplored as savage or barbaric.

Partly in response to these criticisms, many theorists have expressed a preference for "mixed" or "hybrid" accounts of the justifiability of criminal punishment.[1] The most famous such accounts belonged to John Rawls

* For helpful comments on previous drafts and for profitable conversations, I am grateful to Larry Alexander, Dan Brudney, John Deigh, David Dolinko, Strefan Fauble, Les Green, Tom Green, Mark Greenberg, Don Herzog, Douglas Husak, Larry Sager, Scott Shapiro, and Peter Westen; to two anonymous referees and two anonymous editors for this journal; and to workshop participants at the law schools of Columbia University and the University of Michigan and at the Second Annual International Congress on Law and Philosophy at the National Autonomous University of Mexico. I am indebted to Jeff McMahan for superb and generous editorial assistance.

1. Many scholars have described retributivism as the dominant theory of punishment today. See, generally, Russell L. Christopher, "Deterring Retributivism: The Injustice of 'Just' Punishment," *Northwestern University Law Review* 96 (2002): 843–976, 845–47 and nn. 2–12 (collecting citations to works proclaiming a retributivist renaissance). But, as these declarations usually preface scathing critique, I doubt that pure retributivism enjoys so

and H. L. A. Hart. In Rawls's rule utilitarian picture, legislators justify criminal justice institutions and practices on consequentialist grounds, while judges justify the punishment of individual offenders on the non-consequential ground that he or she violated a legal command.[2] Similarly, Hart described the "general justifying aim" of the institution of punishment as crime reduction but argued that pursuit of this consequentialist goal is constrained by a principle of "retribution in distribution" that permits imposition of punishment only on "an offender for an offense."[3] A popular cousin view to Hart's—famously dubbed "negative" retributivism,[4] but more aptly called "side-constrained consequentialism"[5]—justifies punishment by its good consequences (realized especially through the mechanisms of general and special deterrence, incapacitation, and diverse expressive or communicative functions) but argues that it should be limited by the offender's desert.

But all of these views have been criticized for marginalizing retributivism relative to consequentialism.[6] And efforts to develop hybrid accounts that give consequentialist and retributivist considerations roughly equal weight have in turn been criticized for yoking the different considerations together in an ad hoc manner. Preferable might be an "integrated dualist" account—one that assigns distinct and coequal roles to retributivist and consequentialist reasoning within the theory's structural logic. However, no such account has appeared, and the possibility of such an appearance has been doubted.[7]

This article offers an integrated dualist theory of punishment.[8] In doing so, it assumes that the road to a satisfactory account of punishment's justifiability must start by examining with seriousness the common point of departure already noted—namely, that punishment stands in need of justification. Frequently, theorists expend some effort trying to define punishment. Yet very rarely do they attend explicitly to what

---

much support. See also, e.g., Douglas N. Husak, "Why Punish the Deserving?" *Noûs* 26 (1992): 447–64, 452 ("Almost all philosophers appreciate the need to construct hybrid syntheses of retributive and consequentialist elements").

2. John Rawls, "Two Concepts of Rules," *Philosophical Review* 64 (1955): 3–32.

3. H. L. A. Hart, *Punishment and Responsibility: Essays in the Philosophy of Law* (Oxford: Oxford University Press, 1968), 8–12.

4. J. L. Mackie, "Morality and the Retributive Emotions," *Criminal Justice Ethics* 1 (1982): 3–10, 3.

5. R. A. Duff, *Punishment, Communication, and Community* (Oxford: Oxford University Press 2001), 11.

6. See David Wood, "Retribution, Crime Reduction and the Justification of Punishment," *Oxford Journal of Legal Studies* 22 (2002): 301–21.

7. For the term 'integrated dualism' and the conclusion that it is conceptually unobtainable, see ibid., 316–17.

8. Although the account is dualist, the elements likely to prove most interesting and contentious arise in support of the role I assign retributivism. So the argument can also be viewed as a partial rehabilitation of retributivism.

it means for punishment (or anything else) to be "in need of justification."[9] That is an unfortunate oversight, for, as Hart recognized, "theories of punishment" is an unhappy term because such "theories" "are not theories in any normal sense. . . . On the contrary, . . . [they] are moral *claims* as to what justifies the practice of punishment."[10] More precisely, they are moral claims in response to the proposition that punishment stands in need of justification. If theories of punishment are thus situated ab initio within an argumentative dialectic, one might expect their persuasiveness to depend, in part, on how fully and satisfactorily they understand the proposition to which they aim to respond.

* * *

Human practices, like other phenomena, often encompass a core and a periphery. Section II therefore distinguishes core from peripheral cases of punishment. Roughly, the core involves "correct" cases; peripheral cases involve adjudicative error or the infliction of excessive punishment. Section III then seeks to unearth the logic of justification by addressing two questions: what creates a need of justification, and how can such a need be met? With regard to the former, I argue that for some practice to need justification, considerations must first be identified that place its overall justifiability or permissibility in doubt. I term any such consideration a "demand basis." With regard to the latter, I explain that justification can be supplied by showing either that the putative reason that constitutes a demand basis—that is, that brings forth the need for justification—does not apply or is outweighed by competing considerations. In Razian terms, justification can be supplied by canceling conditions or by overriding reasons.

Together, Sections IV and V seek to justify punishment in light of Section III's analysis of justification. Section IV identifies the demand basis that underlies the proposition that punishment stands in need of justification—namely, that it inflicts suffering—and unpacks it into two discrete claims—that punishment is wrong because of the bad that it causes (pain, suffering, deprivation of liberty) and that punishment is wrong because the intentional infliction of that bad infringes the defendant's rights. Section V then argues that core cases of punishment are justified by cancellation on retributivist grounds and that peripheral cases of punishment are justified by override on consequentialist

9. John Kleinig, *Punishment and Desert* (The Hague: Martinus Nijhoff, 1973), chap. 1, is a notable exception. As he put it, to say that punishment stands in need of justification "is not to say anything very helpful, without first saying something about the notion of justification to see what it is, precisely, that punishment is said to be in need of" (ibid., 1).

10. Hart, *Punishment and Responsibility*, 72.

grounds. More particularly, core cases of punishment are justified because the offender's desert renders the fact that punishment inflicts suffering wholly inert as a reason against it—that is, the offender's suffering is not a bad and no right of his is infringed. In peripheral cases, by contrast, the offender's suffering is a bad and therefore does count as a reason against the punishment. So even if, as I argue, punishment need not be rights infringing even in peripheral cases, peripheral cases can be justified against this demand basis only if the consequential benefits produced by such punishment have overriding weight. Section VI provides a summary and addresses anticipated objections. Section VII is a brief conclusion.

II. PUNISHMENT

What is criminal, or legal, punishment? Philosophers of a generation or two ago attended to the question partly "because some arguments about its justification ha[d] been supposed to rest on how it is defined."[11] Few theorists still believe that. Accordingly, following R. A. Duff, let us understand punishment, loosely, as "something intended to be burdensome or painful, imposed on a (supposed) offender for a (supposed) offense by someone with (supposedly) the authority to do so."[12]

As the parenthetical terms suggest, we might describe punishment as consisting of two subclasses: the central or core case in which the offense, the offender, and the authority are all actual; and the peripheral case in which one or more of the three is merely supposed.[13] I will adopt this approach, with a modest qualification. Let us say that the core case of punishment—symbolically represented as P_c—involves imposition of something painful or burdensome on an actual offender on account of his offense, and only so long as the imposition satisfies some reasonable proportionality constraint, whether of a retributivist or Benthamite variety.

Peripheral cases—P_p for short—involve imposition of punishment on persons who are not wrongdoers, either because no offense occurred or because, although it did, the individual was not responsible for it. I mean "not responsible" broadly, encompassing cases in which the person punished was no party to an offense (e.g., mistaken identity), does not satisfy all offense elements (e.g., mistakes that negate mens rea), possesses a valid justification defense (e.g., self-defense), or lacks moral responsibility (e.g., insanity or infancy). P_p also include cases in which

11. Ted Honderich, *Punishment: The Supposed Justifications* (London: Hutchinson, 1969), 6 n. 4 (citing several of the best known attempts at definition).

12. Duff, *Punishment, Communication, and Community*, xiv–xv.

13. For distinctions broadly along these lines see, e.g., C. L. Ten, *Crime, Guilt, and Punishment* (New York: Clarendon, 1987), 2; and D. J. Galligan, "The Return to Retribution in Penal Theory," in *Crime, Proof and Punishment*, ed. C. F. H. Tapper (London: Butterworths, 1981), 144–71, 152 n. 3.

the imposed punishment violates whatever proportionality principle the theory in question purports to adhere to.

Peripheral cases all involve genuine adjudicative or legislative error. (This is what places them at the margin of the concept as we have it.) But cases also exist in which the state imposes suffering on an individual aware (or strongly suspecting) that he is not responsible. In this category I include the much-discussed cases of scapegoating, as well as cases of plainer evil, as when one or more agents of the state's criminal justice apparatus, moved by animus or desire for personal gain, inflict punishment on someone they believe innocent. I treat these as degenerate cases of punishment and will put them aside.

In short, then, let us treat punishment as the union of core and peripheral cases, thus defined.[14] As peripheral cases all involve mistakes of one form or another, one might be tempted to ignore them and to endeavor merely to justify P_c, perhaps with the caveat that any such justification must adequately account for the inevitable mistakes. But I doubt that all partisans to the debate would accept this strategy. After all, P_p produce at least one very substantial consequentialist benefit—general deterrence. And in the (possibly nontrivial) number of cases in which the wrongfully convicted defendant actually is a bad apple, society realizes the additional consequentialist benefit of incapacitation. For these reasons, some consequentialists will conclude that peripheral cases are justified despite being mistakes.[15] So I doubt that we're entitled to exclude peripheral cases from our justificatory enterprise at the outset. Accordingly, the remainder of this article is premised on the idea that to separately justify P_c and P_p is thereby to justify punishment.

III. JUSTIFICATION

Punishment stands in need of justification. Call this proposition Jn(P). This is true of core and peripheral cases. Thus Jn(P_c) and Jn(P_p). In order to understand how these needs could be satisfied we must be clear about the nature of the need. What, we should wonder, does it

14. This is not to engage in the "definitional stop" rightly criticized by Hart (*Punishment and Responsibility*, 5), for I do not contend that degenerate cases (P_d) fall outside the bounds of 'punishment' by virtue of neutral or natural semantic criteria. Eliminating degenerate cases from the scope of 'punishment' is a stipulation designed to simplify exposition, on the assumption that most commentators agree that P_d is not justifiable. Therefore, allow 'punishment' to stand for only those forms of punishment whose justification is in doubt and that I will try to establish—namely, $P_c + P_p$. But see n. 51 below (problematizing this straightforward carving between peripheral and degenerate cases).

15. To be sure, the same two points—general deterrence and incapacitation—could be made about degenerate cases as well, but few consequentialists are willing to bite that bullet; by whatever means, they strive to establish that degenerate cases are not justifiable.

mean for punishment to require justification? More fundamentally, what does it mean for anything to be in need of justification?

A

Justification can always be given. There is always some sense in offering the reasons that support one's conduct. But while they may always be offered, justifications cannot always be demanded. Customarily, to claim that actual or contemplated conduct, X, is "in need" of justification means that "ordinarily" or "presumptively" one ought not to X, or that there exists apparent or putative reason not to X. That is, our practice of justification is a dialectical one in which the initial argumentative burden rests on those who deny or question justification.

If you believe, contrary to what I have supposed, that every action does need justification, then let us distinguish two concepts. Call the always-applicable need a requirement for "general justification" and the need to justify action in response to articulable doubt a call for "specific justification." The form of justification implicated in debates over criminal punishment is specific. That is why the literature on punishment starts with Jn(Punishment), whereas the literature on, say, chess does not start with the proposition Jn(Chess). We strive to justify punishment in the face of articulable suspicion that the task might not be doable.

It follows from the principle that only the seemingly objectionable must be justified (or from a focus on specific not general justification) that every claim that X is in need of justification stands, implicitly if not always explicitly, for a fuller claim that contains, as well, the consideration that gives rise to the demand—what I will call the "demand basis." The statement that "X is in need of justification" is therefore incomplete. To make explicit what is implicit, we should say that "X is in need of justification, by virtue of y." Let us represent such a demand for justification thus: Jn(X)(y), where Jn(X) means that some practice X is in need of justification and y is the demand basis in virtue of which the need for justification is said to arise.

B

There are at least two ways to meet Jn(X)(y), two ways to answer a demand for justification. More obvious is to supply overriding reason to X. Presumptively one ought not knowingly cause the death of another human being. Knowingly causing another human being's death, we might say, stands in need of justification. However, the need can sometimes be satisfied. Consider the familiar Trolley Problem, in which a runaway trolley will kill five sleeping workers on the main track unless diverted onto a spur on which one worker is sleeping. In this case it is not true that one ought not knowingly cause the death of that one worker by turning the trolley. That is to say, the fact, z, that turning the trolley is necessary to avoid death to a greater number justifies knowingly causing the death of the one. It does so by furnishing a reason to act so as to produce the individual's death that is of greater weight than the reason not to. Consistent with common usage, I will refer to a countervailing reason that is sufficient to defeat an objection and therefore supply justification as an "overriding reason," though it should be understood that this term refers not just to stronger countervailing reasons but also to equally strong or counterbalancing reasons.

But there is a second way in which some fact, z, can render it untrue that, on balance, one ought not to X. In Razian terms, z can constitute a canceling condition. Consider Raz's own example.[16] Presumptively one ought to act in accord with one's promise, say a promise not to X. But if the promisee has freely released the promisor from her promissory obligation, the promise itself no longer constitutes a reason not to X. The release cancels the reason not to X that the promise had created. Whereas necessity supplies the paradigmatic example of an overriding reason, consent supplies the paradigmatic example of a canceling condition. When an action X, prima facie wrongful, is justified by an overriding reason, the demand basis, y, remains a reason to not X. Not so when X is justified by a canceling condition.

C

One might suppose that if X needs justification then a defender of X has not satisfied her justificatory obligation until she shows that X is right, or at least not wrong, all things considered. But the demand for justification does not impose such a broad argumentative burden. Rather, the principle that only the seemingly objectionable must be justified entails that one's justificatory burden is demarcated by the considerations that provoked the demand. That is, when justification is offered in response to a demand, the demand is satisfied if the considerations that brought forth the need for justification are satisfactorily addressed, either by cancellation or by override. Special justifications are "tailored," not all-things-considered. It follows that what appears to be justified might turn out not to be if the skeptic provides new apparent reasons why the action is wrong. Justification for a practice is always provisional, always partial, always a response to a particular demand basis.

Consider an example. My having showered this morning does not normally stand in need of justification, not because I am unable to give reasons to show that my showering was right or morally permissible but because such reasons are not required. Suppose however that there's a

16. Joseph Raz, *Practical Reason and Norms*, 2nd ed. (Princeton, NJ: Princeton University Press, 1990), 27.

drought. Now my having showered may stand in need of justification. The new demand basis is the stronger-than-usual need to conserve water. Suppose further, however, that I had fallen into a patch of poison ivy. In these circumstances, my showering seems justified despite the drought. Yet further challenges, further demand bases, may still arise that may not be answerable. If today is Tisha B'av, a Jewish day of mourning, and I have promised my father, an observant Jew, to observe the applicable religious proscriptions, one of which concerns washing and is binding even at the cost of an annoying rash, then perhaps my having showered was not justified after all.

Suppose that by pointing out my exposure to poison ivy, I have satisfactorily answered the demand to justify my showering during a drought. Must we conclude that I will not have justified my shower until I have answered every possible objection? Must I establish, among other things, that today is not Tisha B'av? To say that I must is to say that all justification must ultimately be general rather than specific. Yet our justificatory practices all overwhelmingly involve specific rather than general justification—that is, justification proceeds by responding to particular demand bases, not by a fruitless attempt to identify and respond to every conceivable objection. And it is obvious why this is so: general justification is impossibly onerous and demanding. Justification must of practical necessity be tailored rather than all-things-considered.

Of course, when we say "X is justified," it sounds like we are asserting a general or all-things-considered justification. On most occasions, however, we should understand this as shorthand for a claim of specific justification: "X is justified against, or notwithstanding, y." We can represent this statement with the notation J(X)(y). Just as Jn(X)(y) means that X stands in need of justification on account of y, J(X)(y) means that X is justified "against y," or that the particular objection y against X is met. J(X)(y) denotes a satisfactorily tailored response to Jn(X)(y).

* * *

We have identified three features concerning the making of, and responding to, demands for justification. First, to demand that an action or practice be justified requires invocation of, or implicit reliance on, reason to believe the action or practice wrongful. A demand for justification depends on a "demand basis." Second, we meet the demand either by overriding the demand basis or by canceling it. Third, if the demand basis is defeated, the demand for justification retains no additional force; it imposes no further obligation on the proponent of a practice. This is not to say that the practice is thereby rendered justified, or even justifiable, all things considered. Maybe it is, maybe not. The more modest (yet significant) upshot is only that the practice no longer stands, embarrassedly, "in need of justification." Indeed, if we generally presume actions to be permissible absent at least an argument fragment to the contrary (as I submit we do), the argumentative burden shifts back to the practice's doubters.

IV. THE DEMAND BASIS: PUNISHMENT INFLICTS SUFFERING

Why is punishment in need of justification? By virtue of what is Jn(P) true? This is not mysterious. As Hart explained, it is "the deliberate imposition of suffering which is the feature needing justification."[17] Indeed, few claims in the philosophy of criminal law are more widely accepted. Theorists routinely observe not merely that "punishment stands in need of justification" but that such justification is needed precisely "because it involves the infliction of pain or other form of unpleasant treatment."[18] As a first pass, then, say that the demand basis supporting Jn(P) is that it inflicts suffering upon the individual punished.

This is not to claim that the fact that punishment causes suffering to the individual punished is the only possible, or even actual, mark against it. Punishment also causes pain and hardship to individuals who care about the individual in question or who depend upon him; it costs money that the state could spend on other projects or leave in the hands of citizens; and it might brutalize or degrade the society that authorizes it, as well as the individuals who inflict it. The list could be expanded. But no doubt several of these considerations that might weigh against punishment count against innumerable other governmental activities, from imposing taxes to building roads, while the claim that punishment is in need of justification is couched in terms that suggest a particular status, character, or urgency. We do not say (merely) that "punishment, like every state practice, demands justification." Rather, as Richard Burgh rightly emphasized: "The moral problem that the having of a legal institution of punishment presents can be stated in one sentence: It involves the deliberate and intentional infliction of suffering. It is in virtue of this that the institution requires justification *in a way that many other political institutions do not*."[19] It is the fact that punishment involves the intentional infliction of suffering that particularly demands justification. The claim that, I observed at the outset, motivates almost the entire philosophical literature on punishment can therefore be reformulated by recasting Jn(P) as Jn(P)(inflicts suffering), read as "Punishment stands in need of justification on account of the fact that it inflicts suffering."

17. Hart, *Punishment and Responsibility*, 2 n. 3.

18. Claire Finkelstein, "Positivism and the Notion of an Offense," *California Law Review* 88 (2000): 335–94, 358. Passages from other philosophers to the same effect can be multiplied almost without end.

19. R. W. Burgh, "Do the Guilty Deserve Punishment?" *Journal of Philosophy* 79 (1982): 193–210, 193.

Yet still more precision is required, however, for we wish to know what about the fact that punishment inflicts suffering constitutes a reason against it. The obvious welfarist answer is that an individual's suffering is a bad state of affairs, one we all have reason not to bring about. This seems right as far as it goes, but it does not go far enough.

Yes, punishment causes suffering. But it does so in a particular way—by "inflicting" it or (if this is not redundant) by "intentionally" or "deliberately" inflicting it. The theorist's frequent recourse to such terms, and the fact that the suffering that supports Jn(P) (inflicts suffering) is particularly the suffering experienced by the person punished, not the suffering experienced indirectly by that person's friends, lovers, or dependents, suggest a revision. We should say that what makes the fact that punishment intentionally inflicts suffering a reason against it is not only that suffering is an intrinsically bad state of affairs but also that the intentional infliction of suffering is an intrinsically wrongful action. And it is wrongful, some say, because it infringes an individual's rights.

Accordingly, we should view the statement represented by Jn(P) (inflicts suffering)—that "punishment stands in need of justification on account of the fact that it inflicts suffering"—as capturing two distinct but related demand bases. Punishment stands in need of justification both on account of the fact that it causes the punished person to suffer and on account of the supposed fact that, by intentionally inflicting suffering, it infringes an individual's rights. For brevity of exposition these discrete facets or construals of the claim Jn(P) (inflicts suffering) can be formalized, respectively, as Jn(P) (suffering) and Jn(P) (infliction).

That punishment inflicts suffering is true in core and peripheral cases alike. Moreover, both facets or construals of this demand basis seem applicable to both cases. So, by starting with the proposition that punishment stands in need of justification on account of the fact that it inflicts suffering and then (*a*) dividing punishment into core and peripheral cases and (*b*) distinguishing two reasons why the infliction of suffering generates a demand for justification, we are left with four distinct demands for justification. Symbolically, Jn(P) (inflicts suffering) breeds, or is shorthand for, (1) Jn(P_c) (suffering), (2) Jn(P_c) (infliction), (3) Jn(P_p) (suffering), and (4) Jn(P_p) (infliction). Each of these four claims requires a response for punishment to be justified against the fact that it inflicts suffering.

V. JUSTIFYING PUNISHMENT AGAINST THE FACT THAT IT INFLICTS SUFFERING

A

Let us start with Jn(P_c) (suffering), read as "core cases of punishment stand in need of justification on account of the fact that they cause the punished person to suffer." It is close to an analytic truth that suffering is experienced as a bad. For hedonists and most other welfarists, accordingly, the experience of suffering is an intrinsic bad. Hence the common supposition that imposition of suffering by means of criminal punishment can be justified only by the presence of overriding reason.[20] But that suffering is always an intrinsic bad is what most retributivists deny. To be sure, precisely what retributivism is or contends is much debated. Still, if contemporary retributivism contains a core claim, it involves reference to an offender's desert.[21]

Still, ambiguities abound. The first, albeit rarely noticed, is whether what offenders deserve is to suffer or to be punished.[22] Although I cannot fully examine the relative merits and demerits of each formulation here, a few words seem necessary. As a justification for punishment, the claim that wrongdoers deserve to suffer runs into the objection that, in principle, the state would be required to adopt what Gertrude Ezorsky called the "whole life" view of criminal desert: the suffering imposed by means of criminal punishment ought to be reduced or wholly eliminated if the individual had already experienced as much suffering in his life as his wrongdoing merited.[23] This unwelcome conclusion might seem to be avoided if what a wrongdoer deserves is to be punished—for if suffering and punishment are distinct concepts, and if what the wrongdoer deserves is the latter, then no amount of the former can affect the propriety of retributive punishment. But this so-

20. See, e.g., Finkelstein, "Positivism and the Notion of an Offense," 358; and Nicola Lacey, *State Punishment: Political Principles and Community Values* (London: Routledge, 1988), 14. Unfortunately, John Kleinig—the theorist who best understood that those who would speak intelligently about justifications for punishment need first seek to understand the nature of justifications—seemed to make this same assumption. "Impositions require justification since they constitute breaches of a basic moral right to be free from such things," he wrote. But this "does not mean that it cannot be overridden in any circumstances" (Kleinig, *Punishment and Desert*, 65). That he thought punishment must be justified by override is not surprising, however, given his mistaken view (mistaken because seeming to overlook that justification can be accomplished by cancellation) that "demands for justification are demands for reasons" (ibid., 2).

21. As John Cottingham ("Varieties of Retribution," *Philosophical Quarterly* 29 [1979]: 238–46) demonstrates, desert has not always been central to views classified as retributivist. But the centrality of desert to contemporary retributivism is widely accepted. See, e.g., Mirko Bagaric and Kumar Amaraskara, "The Errors of Retributivism," *Melbourne University Law Review* 24 (2000): 124–89, 127 (citing commentators).

22. An exception that does recognize the difference (and argues for the former) is Douglas N. Husak, "Retribution in Criminal Theory," *San Diego Law Review* 37 (2000): 959–86, 972–73.

23. See Gertrude Ezorsky, "The Ethics of Punishment," in *Philosophical Perspectives on Punishment*, ed. Gertrude Ezorsky (Albany, NY: SUNY Press, 1972), xi–xxvii, xxii–xxvii; see also W. D. Ross, *The Right and the Good* (1930), reprinted with an introduction by Phillip Stratton-Lake (Oxford: Oxford University Press, 2002), 58–59 (anticipating this objection).

lution confronts other difficulties. The very notion of desert is mysterious and, as we will see, heavily dependent on intuitive judgments of intrinsic plausibility. To many, that wrongdoers deserve to suffer simply seems truer than that they deserve particular treatment from a contingent entity, the state.

I therefore assume, without further defense, a middle position that wrongdoers deserve to suffer on account of their blameworthy wrongdoing. This construal of what wrongdoers deserve escapes the whole-life view of suffering partly but not fully. Pre-offense suffering is strictly irrelevant to the offender's liability to punishment (except insofar as such suffering could, perhaps in cases of extreme childhood abuse, mitigate the individual's blameworthiness). But if the state aims to ensure that punishment not exceed what is deserved, in principle it must reduce the suffering it would otherwise inflict by an amount equal to any nonpenal suffering the offender experienced on account of the wrongdoing. This "on account of" formulation is intended to signal (although I hold to this view tentatively) that nonpenal suffering is relevant to the calculus only when caused by features of the actor's conduct that render it wrongful—vengeance inflicted by his victim, say, but not (to take Scott Shapiro's example) a hernia incurred by the actor's attempt to abscond with heavy goods.

Having addressed this first ambiguity, it remains to address whether deserved suffering is comparative or noncomparative and responsive to legal or moral wrongdoing. Because I conceive it the most plausible version, I will assume that desert, in the most promising retributivist account, is noncomparative and moralistic. In short, I assume that something like the following is true: a person who unjustifiably and inexcusably causes or risks harm to others or to significant social interests deserves to suffer for that choice, and he deserves to suffer in proportion to the extent to which his regard or concern for others falls short of what is properly demanded of him. Call this the "desert claim." It is often thought equivalent to the claim that for offenders to suffer (on account of, and in proportion to, their blameworthy wrongdoing) is an intrinsic good.[24] (For ease of exposition, I will frequently omit the parenthetical qualifications, saying things like "wrongdoers deserve to suffer" and "the suffering of wrongdoers is an intrinsic good." In either case, the qualifications that punishment be on account of and in proportion to blameworthy wrongdoing should be assumed.) By denying that the experience of suffering is ever an intrinsic bad full stop, and

24. See, e.g., Lawrence H. Davis, "They Deserve to Suffer," *Analysis* 32 (1972): 136–40, 136; Michael S. Moore, "Justifying Retributivism," *Israel Law Review* 27 (1993): 15–49, 19–20; and Thomas Hurka, "The Common Structure of Virtue and Desert," *Ethics* 112 (2001): 6–31.

by contending instead that the goodness or badness of the state of affairs in which one suffers is always contextual or relational, proponents of the desert claim maintain that the state of affairs in which offenders experience the suffering they deserve is not bad and that therefore one we lack reason not to bring about.

Such is the nutshell version of the retributivist argument, by cancellation, for $J(P_c)$ (suffering). Historically, however, the desert claim has faced fierce criticism. According to antiretributivists, the proposition that wrongdoers deserve to suffer on account of their blameworthy wrongdoing is mere ipse dixit. But this charge does not stick.

The charge is false because retributivists do not simply assert that the suffering of wrongdoers is an intrinsic good. To start, they rely on actual incidents and thought experiments designed to evoke the case-specific substantive moral judgments that some particular wrongdoer deserves to suffer. John Kleinig, for example, asks us to imagine whether, stripped of consequential considerations, it is a better world in which Nazi war criminals live happily ever after or suffer on account of their atrocities.[25] Elaborating on similar examples of egregiously blameworthy wrongdoing, retributivists like Michael Moore argue that these specific judgments or intuitions can be made most coherent by endorsing the general principle that wrongdoers deserve to suffer.[26]

Furthermore, the critique wrongly implies that we possess resources for resolving questions of this sort that retributivists have failed to employ. As Bentham himself acknowledged, the intrinsic goodness of pleasure and the intrinsic badness of pain are matters to be assumed, not to be proven.[27] To put the point more sharply, then, this particular antiretributivist charge risks hypocrisy. Consider, for example, Herbert Fingarette, who objected in one breath to the retributivist reliance on unanalyzed intuition,[28] while, in the next, declaring it "self-evident" that "retributive punishment is in itself an evil."[29]

Intrinsic goods just are not well suited to full resolution by rational argumentation.[30] Retributivists believe that such suffering is an intrinsic

25. Kleinig, *Punishment and Desert*, 67.

26. Michael S. Moore, "The Moral Worth of Retribution," in *Responsibility, Character, and the Emotions: New Essays in Moral Psychology*, ed. Ferdinand Schoeman (New York: Cambridge University Press, 1987), 179–219.

27. Jeremy Bentham, *The Principles of Morals and Legislation* (1789; reprint, Oxford: Clarendon, 1907), 4.

28. Herbert Fingarette, "Punishment and Suffering," *Proceedings and Addresses of the American Philosophical Association* 50 (1977): 499–525, 503.

29. Ibid., 513.

30. I am speaking of intrinsic goods supposed to be ultimate. One can rationally justify an intrinsic non–ultimate good by showing how it is a constituent component of another intrinsic good, not as a means to its attainment. (I am grateful to Les Green for this point.)

good. Some of their critics believe otherwise. For them, suffering is always an intrinsic bad, making the avoidance of suffering an intrinsic good. In my view, we lack argumentative resources for resolving disputes of this kind, which is why the list of plausible candidates for intrinsic goodness is so long;[31] it is also why appeal to casuistic judgments is unavoidable.[32]

Thirty-odd years ago, Lawrence Davis succinctly adjudged the proposition that there is intrinsic value in wrongdoers' suffering "very likely" "on the grounds (*a*) that there is no convincing argument against it, and (*b*) that inclination to believe it seems very widespread among the people whose moral intuitions constitute the main data we have for settling questions of value."[33] Today's antiretributivists are no closer to mounting a convincing counterargument (beyond relitigating the hard determinist challenge),[34] while the ranks of those expressing such a belief have swelled. We therefore seem entitled to conclude that $J(P_c)$ (suffering), on account of the fact that wrongdoers deserve to suffer.

B

Even if contemporary antiretributivists won't quite concede the desert claim, many do allow that we are entitled not to affirm its negation; we are permitted to remain agnostic. Instead of continuing to tussle over whether wrongdoers deserve to suffer, then, they have increasingly directed their critical fire elsewhere. In particular, they have more strenuously emphasized that the fact that wrongdoers deserve to suffer, even if true, is insufficient to justify punishment. Indeed, one prominent

31. See, e.g., William Frankena, *Ethics*, 2nd ed. (Englewood Cliffs, NJ: Prentice-Hall, 1973), 87–88.

32. That such an appeal is unavoidable does not mean that we can do nothing more than argue about brute intuitions. Think, e.g., of Thomas Hurka's elegant demonstration of the respect in which desert and virtue share a formal or mathematical structure. Still, even Hurka cautions against exaggerating the significance of his modeling, acknowledging that if we accept desert "it will be primarily on the basis of substantive judgments" about the superiority, as against an otherwise identical world, of a world in which the vicious suffer (Hurka, "The Common Structure of Virtue and Desert," 31).

33. Davis, "They Deserve to Suffer," 139.

34. This is not a challenge that I can meet adequately in this space. But I believe that determinism presents a challenge not only for any retributivist response to Jn(P) but—more fundamentally—even to Jn(P) itself. That is because, in my view, determinism threatens not only judgments of responsibility, blameworthiness, or desert but all normative judgments on the ground that the forward-looking judgment "ought to" implies the cogency of the corresponding backward-looking judgment "ought to have." If so, then to the extent that determinism threatens the latter, it threatens the former too. Relatedly, but more generally, given the dialectical structure of demanding and furnishing justification, a justification for punishment need have no "greater," more secure, or more objective metaethical status than does the demand basis to which it responds.

antiretributivist, David Dolinko, deems this "the principal objection" to retributivism.[35]

As wielded by some critics, this objection means only that the fact that punishment brings about the intrinsic good of deserved suffering cannot establish that it is justified all things considered.[36] This is true but not particularly significant given what I have said so far about the structure of debates over the justification of punishment. Retributivists take themselves to be offering a tailored justification for punishment—tailored to the demand basis that punishment inflicts suffering. Unless they become persuaded that they must offer something more, the proposition that the desert claim cannot establish that it is permissible all things considered for the state to inflict the deserved punishment looks more like an observation they are permitted to accept than an objection to which they need respond.

The contention that the desert claim is insufficient to justify state infliction of punishment has more force against the retributivist case if meant to invoke reasons for the insufficiency that are themselves represented by the demand basis that punishment inflicts suffering. If understood in this way, the objection is not a criticism of retributivists for seeking to offer only a tailored justification but rather a charge that the desert claim does not accomplish even this. This is precisely how some proponents of this objection intend it. The desert claim is insufficient to justify punishment, they say, because the intentional infliction of suffering violates the rights of the person punished.[37] And this is essentially to assert what I have termed Jn(P)(infliction). Having divided punishment into core and peripheral cases, we are therefore now poised to address Jn(P_c)(infliction).

Overview of strategies.—Or almost poised. Before attempting to respond to this argument, we should get clearer on just how it runs, for the simple contention that the intentional infliction of suffering violates the rights of the accused is too bald. To see why, consider the familiar distinction between infringing a right and violating it.[38] A right is infringed when it is trenched upon, when the interests that give rise to it are harmed (and when the harm is traceable, in particular ways, to human agency). The infringement therefore gives rise to a demand for

35. David Dolinko, "Some Thoughts about Retributivism," *Ethics* 101 (1991): 537–59, 558. Others who endorse this objection are cited in Christopher, "Deterring Retributivism," 861 n. 85.

36. See, e.g., Husak, "Why Punish the Deserving?"

37. See, e.g., Burgh, "Do the Guilty Deserve Punishment?" 198; and Dolinko, "Some Thoughts about Retributivism," 543, 544, 558, and "Three Mistakes of Retributivism," *UCLA Law Review* 39 (1992): 1624–57, 1629–30.

38. Judith Jarvis Thomson, *The Realm of Rights* (Cambridge, MA: Harvard University Press, 1990), e.g., chap. 4.

justification. If justification is satisfactorily provided, however, the right is not violated. A violation is a wrongful or unjustified infringement.

If we adopt this vocabulary—one that does not commit us to any particular view about the type or weight of considerations that are required to justify the infringement of a right—we would not then say that the fact that wrongdoers deserve to suffer cannot justify punishment because the intentional infliction of suffering violates person's rights (call this "the violation claim"). This would state a conclusion that would be unacceptable to anybody—retributivist or consequentialist—who believes that punishment can be justified. Put another way, the violation claim can be maintained by punishment skeptics but not by (mere) antiretributivists. We should say, instead, that the fact that wrongdoers deserve to suffer cannot itself justify punishment (against the fact that it inflicts suffering) because the intentional infliction of suffering infringes individual rights, or because people have a right against the intentional infliction of suffering even when such suffering is deserved.

Antiretributivists who press this claim think it amenable to consequentialist justifications for punishment (as the violation claim would not be) because consequentialists who concede that there are rights know how to prevent an infringement from becoming a violation—namely, by supplying overriding reasons for engaging in the practice. Although punishment infringes the right against the intentional infliction of suffering, it can produce enough good—most notably by deterring antisocial conduct—as to prevent the infringement from becoming a violation. But the critics think that retributivists are unable to make a similarly plausible move. Even if the suffering of wrongdoers is an intrinsic good (which some critics concede to be plausible), and even if the state may legitimately endeavor to realize this particular good (which they might deem less plausible),[39] the claim that pursuit of this particular good is so important as to justify infringing rights is not plausible at all. After all, that a good is intrinsic does not necessarily make it important as well. So the fact that wrongdoers deserve to suffer, or

39. That this is not a legitimate state interest has been one recurrent theme in the literature. See, e.g., Jeffrie G. Murphy, "Retribution and the State's Interest in Punishment," *Nomos XXVII: Criminal Justice*, ed. J. R. Pennock and J. Chapman (New York: New York University Press, 1985), 156–64. Because I cannot here give the argument the attention it merits, I merely observe that many plausible political theories would deem the pursuit of any good prima facie legitimate. At the same time, many political theories are not consistent with retributivist justifications for punishment. Nothing in this article should be construed, then, either to claim that integrated dualism satisfactorily justifies punishment across the range of possible and actual theories of the role of the state or to deny that a fully adequate justification of punishment must form part of a more complete political theory. Of course, however, the integrated dualism put forth, if attractive, is to that extent an argument against any political theory with which it is incompatible.

that their suffering is an intrinsic good, does not furnish a sufficiently compelling reason to warrant infringing the individual right against the intentional infliction of suffering.

To this important argument, retributivists might seem to have only two possible avenues of reply: to deny that inflicting suffering in core cases of punishment infringes any right held by the wrongdoer; or, while conceding infringement, to maintain that effectuating a state of affairs in which wrongdoers receive the suffering they deserve justifies infringing the wrongdoers' rights, thus establishing that the wrongdoers' rights are not violated. Both types of reply can be discerned in retributivist writings. Moral forfeiture theories adopt the first approach explicitly. Theories that emphasize retributivism as a species of justice are perhaps best understood as adopting the second. After briefly assessing these two familiar retributivist lines of argument and finding them wanting, I will suggest a third alternative. This "right articulation" alternative pursues the ambition of moral forfeiture theories—to show that core cases of punishment need not infringe rights—but without the forfeiture mechanism.

Moral forfeiture.—Forfeiture analysis starts by acknowledging that individuals do generally have a right that others not inflict suffering upon them (along, perhaps, with such other seemingly implicated rights as the right not to be deprived of liberty). Wrongdoers are said to forfeit that right by virtue of their wrongdoing. By eschewing a need to demonstrate that there exists reason of overriding force sufficient to justify infringing a wrongdoer's right that his suffering, albeit deserved, not be inflicted upon him, the forfeiture route to $J(P_c)$ (infliction) proceeds, in essence, by cancellation.

Although superficially appealing, this claim runs into familiar and formidable difficulties, of which two stand out.[40] First, the mechanism by which forfeiture is effected is unclear. Surely A's violation of rights of B does not logically entail that A thereby forfeits any rights of his own. And any suggestion that A has chosen to relinquish any of his rights by offending against B must employ the notion of choice in a stipulated and tendentious sense. So it is not clear how to explain why a wrongdoer forfeits rights beyond either asserting that it is so or conceiving rights as the product of a social contract that includes forfeiture among its terms. Second, it is surprisingly hard to specify just which rights are forfeited and for how long. While it is implausible to suppose that wrongdoers forfeit rights wholesale and for good, arguments for

40. See, e.g., Burgh, "Do the Guilty Deserve Punishment?" 198–202; Warren Quinn, "The Right to Threaten and the Right to Punish," *Philosophy & Public Affairs* 14 (1985): 327–73, 331–34; and Duff, *Punishment, Communication, and Community*, 15–16.

forfeitures more limited in time and scope often appear opportunistic and unsatisfactorily grounded.

Retributive justice.—If the theory of moral forfeiture is unpromising, one might think the better alternative is to concede that punishment infringes wrongdoers' rights while denying that any such infringement amounts to a violation. It is here that purported justifications of punishment that make reference to "retributivist justice" might profitably be situated.

Notice that the retributivist claims endorsed thus far (in Sec. V.A) take two forms that I have treated as roughly equivalent: wrongdoers deserve to suffer and the suffering of wrongdoers is an intrinsic good. In thus offering a retributivist response to Jn(P_c) (suffering), I have not needed to deploy the concept of "retributive justice." The familiar retributivist contention that retributivism is a species of *justice*, not merely a label for a particular view of intrinsic goods—as in, "retributive justice demands that we inflict punishment in accord with an offender's just deserts"—might instead respond to the demand for justification now under consideration, Jn(P_c) (infliction).

The state has an interest in bringing about various goods, where the strength of its interest is proportional to the importance of the good. Those who doubt that the good of a wrongdoer suffering (on account of and in proportion to his blameworthy wrongdoing) provides a reason of sufficient weight, or of the right sort, to render permissible the infringing of a right might think otherwise once justice is introduced as a mediating norm or value. Retributivists can now argue that a wrongdoer's suffering is demanded by justice and therefore that what provides reason of sufficient weight to justify the infringement of a right is (at least in part) the state's obligation to see that justice is done, not (solely) the entailment or particularistic content of that obligation. Or, insofar as rights are conceived in terms of protected reasons,[41] we might suppose that pursuit of the (mere) good that a wrongdoer suffers counts among the possibly countervailing reasons that the right is specifically designed to exclude, whereas the possibility that infringing the right would further justice is a nonexcluded reason. Happily, we need not resolve whether protected reasons do serve in the better conception of the function and structure of rights for our limited purposes of understanding how the concept of retributive justice might be deployed as a response to Jn(P_c) (infliction). Compare the following: Suppose that each of us has a right not to be deprived of property. Taxation infringes that right. But to the extent that a taxation scheme redistributes wealth in accord with the demands of distributive justice, our rights to property have not been

41. See, e.g., Joseph Raz, *Ethics in the Public Domain: Essays in the Morality of Law and Politics* (Oxford: Clarendon, 1994), chaps. 2 and 12.

violated. In short, the pursuit of distributive justice justifies infringement of one's right against the deprivation of property. So, too, perhaps, the pursuit of retributive justice justifies infringing one's right against the intentional infliction of suffering.

This "retributive justice" argument for $J(P_c)$ (infliction), much like the consequentialist approach briefly described a few pages ago, implicitly proceeds by override: the pursuit of justice provides a reason to inflict suffering that outweighs (and is not excluded by) the rights-based reason not to.[42] However it depends, of course, on the proposition that one's suffering on account of one's wrongdoing is a dictate of justice, not merely a good. But whether there is such a thing as "retributive justice" is vigorously contested. If the suffering a wrongdoer deserves is conceived comparatively, then retributive justice might be just a special case of distributive justice: the bad of suffering should be distributed among individuals in proportion to their relative degrees of wrongdoing. But the noncomparative conception of deserved suffering that I find much more faithful to retributive impulses (e.g., it can support the conclusion that Cain deserves to suffer on account of his killing Abel, as the comparative conception seemingly cannot), is not easily assimilated to distributive justice, making the argument I have just sketched on behalf of retributivism dependent upon retributive justice being a genuine and independent form of justice. And that cannot be established by the arguments employed to support the more modest claim that wrongdoers' suffering is an intrinsic good.[43]

42. One might suppose, to the contrary, that the proposition that justice demands the infliction of suffering upon A is incompatible with the proposition that A has a right against that infliction of suffering. On this view, the right in question might be better conceived as the right against the infliction of undeserved suffering, or something of this sort. And if this is so, then the argument sounding in retributive justice works by cancellation, not override. The distributive justice comparison offers reason to doubt, however, that the incompatibility claim is sound. That distributive justice is served by redistributing property from A to B might justify the taking of A's property but does not entail (though is compatible with) the proposition that A lacks a right that his property not be taken.

43. There is a view about the relationship between desert and justice whereby it is analytically true that A's deserving X entails that, all else equal, justice demands that A be given X. See, e.g., Serena Olsaretti, "Introduction: Debating Desert and Justice," in *Desert and Justice*, ed. Serena Olsaretti (Oxford: Oxford University Press, 2003), 8. I do not share this view, but I need not argue against it here. I have thus far treated the desert claim (wrongdoers deserve to suffer) and the intrinsic good claim (it is an intrinsic good for wrongdoers to suffer) as equivalent. But I can deny this equivalence if challenged by those who believe that the desert claim entails the justice claim (justice demands that wrongdoers be made to suffer). My point in the text, then, would be to drive a wedge between the intrinsic good claim—which is all that the argument of Sec. V.A needs—and the desert claim, not between the desert claim and the justice claim. Still, whether my argument will thus far be read as endorsing the intrinsic good claim and eschewing reliance on the desert and justice claims, or as endorsing the intrinsic good and desert claims and

Rearticulating the right.—In any event, a further difficulty confronts the retributive justice approach if that approach is conceived as a way to establish that wrongdoers' rights, albeit infringed, are not violated. There is no consensus regarding precisely what it means to infringe a right justifiably. On a common view, however, the nonviolative infringement of a right (as famously represented by the lost hiker who breaks into a cabin for warmth and shelter, or by *Vincent v. Lake Erie*) still leaves a residue of some sort—paradigmatically, if not exclusively, of compensation. Yet it is not obvious that fully justified cases of punishment do leave a residue; surely the state owes the wrongdoer neither compensation nor apology, for instance. Perhaps, then, moral forfeiture analysis, despite its defects, was on the better track. With forfeiture theorists, that is, we might deny that wrongdoers have a right against the infliction of suffering and hence that P_c necessarily infringes any right. Put another way, we might wish to find other ways to make good on the cancellation approach to $J(P_c)$(infliction) that moral forfeiture theory embodies. The possibility I propose here takes the seemingly more extreme position that nobody has a right against the purposeful infliction of suffering, that there is no such right.

One might worry that such an approach would deny rights *tout court.* For if any rights exist, the right against purposeful infliction of suffering would seem high on the list of plausible candidates. But to deny that there exists a right against the purposeful infliction of suffering is not to assert that there is no right in the vicinity. It's just to claim that this particular formulation gets the right wrong. The right that the infliction of suffering implicates might be more perspicuously rendered as, say, the right to be treated with respect as a person, a right that usually entails (inter alia) that one ought not to be intentionally made to suffer but does not always entail it. The purported right not to be made to suffer states a useful rule of thumb, nothing more.

The route to this position starts from the now-familiar distinction between foundational and derivative rights, where the latter bear a constitutive or causal relation to the former: if A has a (foundational) right, against B, to X, A will also have a (derivative) right, against B, to Y, if Y is a component of X or a necessary means to X. On some accounts, the large panoply of rights recognized in conventional morality issue from a small number of foundational moral rights, perhaps one. As Hillel Steiner explains in a helpful recent summary of the literature, theorists frequently purport to derive the diverse array of commonly recognized moral rights "from one unifying or underlying right entitling

eschewing reliance on the justice claim, nothing in this section purports to disprove the justice claim. It is enough to observe that my retributivist response to $Jn(P_c)$(infliction) does not depend upon the concept of retributive justice but that neither does it rely upon a rejection of the concept.

its holders to be secure in a certain broadly designated personal condition: well-being, autonomy, self-respect, and agency are among those most favored."[44] I offer two modifications. First, and most important, the monistic foundational accounts are too partisan in attributing privileged status to one single aspect of personhood. Second, we should recognize an additional category of derivative rights—rights whose relation to the foundational right is merely conventional and probabilistic. I'll explain.

Reduced to its core, the idea that nourishes belief in the existence of moral rights is that morality must attend to the distinctness of persons—that people's interests not be aggregated in a fashion that fails to accord moral significance to their distinct personhood. As Steiner's summary highlights, accounts that aim to reduce the diversity of rights to a single foundational right advance different and competing views of the particular aspect of personhood most deserving of respect. In contrast, the central thrust of my proposed foundational right to be treated with respect as a person (or—to describe it differently, for I do not mean yet to offer a canonical formulation—the foundational right to moral regard for one's distinct personhood) is to deny any general right answer to the question of which aspect of personhood must be uniquely respected, or of which aspect trumps the others when the normal way to respect various aspects of personhood (well-being, autonomy, etc.) dictate conflicting courses of conduct. Instead, one's right to respect as a person demands that others attend with seriousness to one's distinct personhood, while recognizing that such serious attention and respect can cash out in a number of ways—a number of ways that is finite, but (often) greater than one.

A full defense of this purported right would require its own article. Briefly, though, for this right to figure into a satisfactory retributivist argument, its proponents must, at least, (1) establish that if this is the correct formulation, then it plausibly follows that core cases of punishment need not infringe any right of the offender; and (2) provide reasons to believe that this is the correct formulation, mostly by accounting for other case-specific intuitions.

The claim that inflicting deserved suffering does not, by itself, infringe an individual's right to respect as a person rests on the simple and familiar idea that such infliction respects human autonomy. This is not to endorse the far more robust claim, often advanced,[45] that failing

44. Hillel Steiner, "Moral Rights," in *The Oxford Handbook of Ethical Theory*, ed. David Copp (Oxford: Oxford University Press, 2006), 459–79, 474.

45. See, e.g., Herbert Morris, "Persons and Punishment," *Monist* 52 (1968): 475–501; Duff, *Punishment, Communication, and Community*, chap. 2; and Jeffrie G. Murphy, "Marxism and Retribution," *Philosophy & Public Affairs* 2 (1973): 217–43.

to punish offenders is presumptively inconsistent with the respect and regard they are due and therefore that the state is (defeasibly) obligated to engage in retributive punishment. Rather, to repeat, the claim is that the right to respect as a person, and the correlative duty to treat persons with such respect, often fails to prescribe a uniquely acceptable course of conduct. People have preferences and interests and are also choosing beings. But because personhood is not reducible to preferences, interests, capacity for agency, or anything else, an individual's right to respect as a person does not translate into a right that regard be paid especially to one of these aspects or dimensions of personhood as opposed to another. We might say that the right to respect as a person does not obey the principle of distributivity across the aspects of personhood that are capable of guiding respectful behavior. If A has a contractual right, against B, to receive either an apple or an orange or a banana, it does not follow that any one of the following statements is true: A has a right against B to an apple; A has a right against B to an orange; A has a right against B to a banana. In the same way, the proposed foundational right to respect as a person does not entail that a person has either a right that her preferences be respected or a right that her interests be respected or a right that her capacity for responsible choice be respected. What she has instead (to oversimplify) is a right that her preferences be respected or that her interests be respected or that her capacity for responsible choice be respected, and so forth. Given the underspecificity of the right's entailments, it cannot always prescribe a uniquely correct action when preferences, interests, and deserts (and perhaps additional things of importance to personhood) pull apart or point in different directions.

Because wrongdoers experience suffering as a bad, a usual way to respect them is to not cause them pain. But insofar as they have exercised their wills to violate legitimate interests of others, it is also plausible that causing them to suffer on account of their willing respects them too. Here, as is often the case (but often overlooked), our duties depend upon our motivations.[46] We respect a person's nature as sentient being by refraining from causing her pain. We respect a person's nature as responsible agent by giving her what she deserves by virtue of the exercise of her will. If we are properly motivated, we can do either—not punish because it is painful or punish because it is deserved—and still accord her the respect that she is due. To again invoke the Razian idiom, conformity with the right is a function not only of guiding reasons but of explanatory reasons as well. To inflict suffering on the genuine belief

46. See Steven Sverdlik, "Motive and Rightness," *Ethics* 106 (1996): 327–49 (arguing for the importance of motivations to act evaluations).

that the suffering is deserved need not fail, then, to treat persons with appropriate respect.

Obviously, this is not to contend that any and all infliction of supposedly deserved suffering is rights respecting. Most notably, forms of torture that seek to destroy the offender's dignity and capacity for autonomous action do seem incompatible with respect for personhood. The right rearticulation approach therefore seems better able than the moral forfeiture approach to support the common intuition that inflicting torture does infringe an individual's rights.[47] Even more plainly rights infringing would be infliction of suffering that is not genuinely supposed to be deserved, which supports the widespread judgment that what I earlier termed degenerate cases of punishment are not justified.

This argument, it bears emphasis, seeks to support $J(P_c)$ (infliction) by reasoning fundamentally akin to the canceling condition that supports $J(P_c)$ (suffering). We ordinarily suspect that suffering is a bad, one we have moral reason not to cause. But when that suffering is deserved, it is not a bad. We frequently say that people have a right against the intentional infliction of pain. But such a derivative right is just a common implication of a more abstract and foundational right—the right to be treated with respect as a person.[48] When suffering is believed by a substantial certainty to be deserved,[49] then intentionally inflicting propor-

47. Dolinko identifies only three possible responses that the retributivist can make to the infliction of torture as punishment (as distinct from a means of eliciting information). She could bite the bullet (1) by conceding that state infliction of torture can be morally permissible. Or she could accept that torture is morally impermissible, either (2) by denying that the torture of a person—even an individual who is himself guilty of torturing others—can ever be an intrinsic good or (3) by contending that the wrongdoer's right not to be tortured cannot be forfeited (David Dolinko, "Retributivism, Consequentialism, and the Intrinsic Goodness of Punishment," *Law and Philosophy* 16 [1997]: 507–28, 525–27). I am suggesting a fourth possibility: (4) it is an intrinsic good that a guilty person suffer in proportion to his blameworthiness, and bringing about such suffering does not infringe the guilty person's rights insofar—but only insofar—as the infliction of punishment treats him with the respect for personhood to which he has a right. Unlike response 1, this view can concede that torture (as punishment) is impermissible because it is person-disrespecting; unlike 2, it is not committed to denying that, in extreme cases, the state of affairs in which an individual suffers torture can be an intrinsic good; and unlike 3, it does not depend upon the selective forfeiture of rights.

48. Jeff McMahan objects that, if the often-supposed right against the infliction of pain is merely an implication of the right to be treated with respect as a person, then it would follow—unacceptably—that animals have no right against the infliction of suffering. I am not certain, however, that this conclusion is unacceptable. The suffering of animals can be (as I think it surely is) a bad state of affairs that we have moral reason not to bring about and even to ameliorate, without the animals necessarily possessing any rights.

49. We can see how this position would help support an argument for the "beyond a reasonable doubt" standard of proof, though developing and defending the argument cannot be attempted here. Very briefly, the idea is that a posture of proper respect demands

tional suffering accords the respect due personhood and thus does not amount to a rights infringement that needs further justification. If this is so, then $J(P_c)$(infliction). Given the argument in Section V.A for $J(P_c)$(suffering), we can conclude that $J(P_c)$(inflicts suffering).

C

The right rearticulation approach I have sketched on behalf of retributivists contrasts with moral forfeiture theory in not suggesting that the offender has forfeited any right. The offender has forfeited nothing. Like everyone else, he has a right to be treated with respect as a person. Under this right, however, the particular treatment that one is due is necessarily sensitive to his own conduct. The conditions that make punishment justifiable are thus built into the content of the right; they are not grounds for snatching the right away.

That this articulation of the difference is indeed substantive, not merely semantic, becomes apparent when we shift attention from P_c to P_p and, in particular, from $Jn(P_c)$(infliction) to $Jn(P_p)$(infliction). Plainly, moral forfeiture theories furnish no reply to the latter. An innocent person mistakenly believed to have offended cannot sensibly be taken to have forfeited any moral rights. So if an offender's forfeiture of a right is necessary to justify punishment of actual offenders against the fact that such punishment involves the intentional infliction of suffering, then nothing could justify punishment of nonoffenders against the fact that such punishment involves the intentional infliction of suffering, and we should be forced to conclude that not-$J(P_p)$(infliction), hence not-$J(P_p)$(inflicts suffering).

But the analysis supplied above applies equally to P_p as to P_c. Respect is a quality of persons' attitudes (or attitudes-in-action) toward others. Whether B's conduct toward A honors A's right to respect necessarily depends, then, on relevant beliefs held by B about A. Now, which beliefs are relevant is a complex matter. They cannot include all those mistaken beliefs that, if true, would render the conduct appropriately respectful. (At a minimum, they do not include the mistaken belief that, by virtue of some characteristic, such as being gay, disabled, Jewish, black, female, etc., A is not a holder of this very abstract right.) But they do include mistaken beliefs about brute facts concerning A's conduct, such as whether A did in fact shoot C. If inflicting deserved suffering on an offender is consistent with his right to respect as a person (and does not infringe any other right he has), then inflicting suffering on a putative offender that would be deserved if the putative were actual,

that a decision maker or institution-builder appreciate the gravity of a false positive and thus create procedural protections adequate to substantially reduce that possibility.

likewise is not rights infringing. So $J(P_p)$ (infliction) follows automatically from $J(P_c)$ (infliction).

Now, one might think that an innocent person who has been wrongly punished is owed apology and compensation if and when his innocence is discovered and that this shows that the imposition of punishment does infringe rights in peripheral cases.[50] Yet this is too quick. That the state owes duties of apology and repair does not establish that it must have infringed a right, for positive duties are often triggered by an actor's causal responsibility for bad outcomes, even in the absence of a rights infringement. Consider, for example, the duty to express remorse for injuring someone even nonnegligently and the duty to rescue that arises upon even a nonnegligent creation of the peril. Certainly there are differences between the cases of nonnegligent causation of harm and of intentional punishment. But let's not overstate them: in the cases we have in mind, after all, the state intentionally inflicts punishment but is nonnegligent with respect to the critical fact that the person punished is innocent. Most fundamentally, examples such as these establish that we cannot infer a rights violation from the duty to apologize or compensate.[51]

In any event, no similar move can be made for $J(P_p)$ (suffering). Even conceding that the suffering of a wrongdoer is not a bad (insofar as the suffering is on account of, and in proportion to, his blameworthy

50. I am grateful to Larry Alexander for raising this concern.

51. Kent Greenawalt has pressed upon me the different worry that this account might not apply to cases in which the state knowingly imposes punishment in excess of a defendant's blameworthiness because, in order to protect against false exculpations or for other reasons of administrability, it refuses to extend the sort of defense that the defendant would need to rely upon in order to establish his absent or reduced blameworthiness. Such knowing punishment in excess of desert might be the consequence, e.g., of statutory restrictions on the defenses of necessity, duress, or insanity. More broadly, it might result from the fact that non–capital defendants have not been held constitutionally entitled to introduce any and all evidence that might plausibly mitigate their blameworthiness. Cases of this sort sit at the border between what I have termed peripheral and degenerate cases of punishment. See n. 14 above. I am uncertain how best to think about them. I am partly disposed to think of them as unjustifiable and thus most properly classified as degenerate: if the state can fairly be said to know (a complex question regarding how to attribute beliefs in institutional settings) that the statutory punishment would be in excess of a given defendant's blameworthiness but that the facts that make that so are not legally cognizable, it strikes me as plausible to insist that some state actor (prosecutor or judge) exercise her discretion to dismiss the case or to reduce the sentence, as appropriate. A system that effectively prevents such an exercise of discretion would not, on this view, be morally justifiable. If, in contrast, cases of the sort Greenawalt has in mind are morally justifiable—hence not properly classified as degenerate—then they would comprise a (likely small) subset of peripheral cases in which it is not the case, contrary to what I have concluded in text, that $J(P_p)$ (infliction) follows from $J(P_c)$ (infliction). In these cases, the defendant's right to respect as a person is infringed but possibly not violated.

wrongdoing), the suffering of a person erroneously convicted of criminal wrongdoing is a bad, hence a reason against the infliction of suffering upon him. I have argued that whether conduct infringes a right, and thus whether the existence of the right constitutes a reason against the conduct, can be belief dependent. The right to be treated with respect as a person is an example. In contrast, whether a state of affairs is intrinsically bad or intrinsically good (or intrinsically neutral) is belief independent.[52] Accordingly, Jn(P_p)(suffering) cannot be met by cancellation. If J(P_p)(suffering), the justification must proceed by override in the form of the good consequences that P_p produces.

In order to assess just what those good consequences are, however, we must specify more clearly than we have needed to thus far just what P_p represents. Are we trying to justify specific, individual cases of peripheral punishment, or all cases of peripheral punishment, or something else? A nonarbitrary answer requires that we attend to the reasons for introducing P_p in the first place. It was introduced, along with P_c, as one of two subtypes of "punishment." And what was meant by "punishment" (P) was whatever is usually meant in statements of the form "Punishment stands in need of justification." So what should be meant by P_p depends upon what is meant by P in the statement represented by Jn(P).

I take P in this context to mean something like the ordinary or generic instance of punishment, for the philosophical critique of punishment is not focused on individual cases, or even addressed to some specified aggregation thereof. At the same time, we could not, on pain of committing a definitional stop, reduce the ordinary, generic case to what I have called core cases. For this reason, we focused on the two subtypes, P_c and P_p. Therefore, when we ask whether J(P_p)(suffering), we mean to consider the ordinary or generic case of P_p.

The good consequences of P_p depend upon comparing the state of the world with P_p to the state of the world without. But because P_p represents the ordinary or generic case and because the ordinary or generic case of P_p is not practically severable from the ordinary or generic case of P_c, our task is not to compare the worlds with and without a specific case of P_p. That is, the closest possible world to the actual world that contains P_p is not the world with P_c and without P_p but the world without P. Therefore, the good consequences fairly attributable to P_p are all the good consequences attributable generically to punishment.

If this is so, then the good consequences can include (what I have supposed to be) the good of bringing about a state of affairs in which

52. More precisely (to accommodate non-realist metaethics), whether a given state of affairs is a token of the type that is intrinsically bad (or good or neutral) is belief independent.

deserved suffering obtains. But even if we grant to the retributivist the desert claim, it still would not appear to be sufficient for $J(P_p)$ (suffering) if we are to credit the common judgment that undeserved suffering of the innocent is a bad of greater magnitude than deserved suffering of the guilty is a good. And if so, then if $J(P_p)$ (suffering), that must be by virtue of good consequences beyond the causing of deserved suffering.[53] The frequent conclusion that retributivism cannot justify what I have termed peripheral cases of punishment appears vindicated.[54]

VI. SUMMARY AND OBJECTIONS

According to the analysis put forth thus far, core cases of punishment are justified, against the suffering they inflict, by cancellation. When the person punished is morally responsible for the commission of an offense, then her suffering on account of that offense, and commensurate with her blameworthiness, simply is not a bad. Furthermore, the state's inflicting what it takes to be deserved suffering, for the sake of realizing such desert, does not infringe the offender's rights insofar as such infliction treats the offender with respect as a person. For these two reasons, neither the (mere) causing of suffering nor its purposeful infliction constitute a reason against the practice. In peripheral cases of punishment, the fact that the putative offender experiences suffering does constitute a reason against the practice. In those cases, however, that reason can be overridden by the varied benefits that punishment produces—possibly including, but not plausibly limited to, the intrinsic good of deserved suffering.

All this is to restate the justification for punishment thus far developed. This final part anticipates objections. It does so by summarizing what I consider to be the account's three key features—that it is tailored, dualist, and integrated.

A

First, the justification offered is tailored, or modest, in not purporting to justify criminal punishment all-things-considered. Instead, it responds

53. This is not to assume that a system of punishment necessarily produces benefits that outweigh the suffering of those punished in peripheral cases, let alone that the system of punishment operating today in any Anglo American jurisdiction is in fact consequentially justified against $Jn(P_p)$ (suffering). My point is twofold: first, that the good consequences the system produces must form part of any successful argument for $J(P_p)$ (suffering), and hence for $J(P)$ (inflicts suffering); and second, that those good consequences are not plausibly limited to the (supposed) good of producing the good of deserved suffering. (I am grateful to an anonymous referee for encouraging me to add this clarification.)

54. See, e.g., George Schedler, "Can Retributivists Support Legal Punishment?" *Monist* 63 (1980): 185–98 (arguing that retributivists' inability to justify peripheral cases of punishment renders them unable to justify punishment at all).

narrowly to (both aspects of) what I have identified as the principal or conspicuous demand basis giving rise to the animating proposition that punishment is in need of justification—namely, that punishment constitutes the intentional infliction of suffering. It is not a justification of punishment, full stop; rather, it is a justification of punishment against this particular conjunction of reasons (or putative reasons) against it.

The second feature of the account is that it claims necessary roles for both retributivism and consequentialism. Theories of this sort have attracted various labels—"hybrid" and "mixed," most commonly. But both terms might connote that the account to which they attach are neither one nor the other—neither truly retributivist nor truly consequentialist, but some third possibility. In my view, the instant account is both retributivist and consequentialist: retributivism straightforwardly justifies part of punishment (the core); consequentialism straightforwardly justifies the other part (the periphery). To signify that this account has a both/and, rather than neither/nor, character, I call it "dualist."[55]

Although I might be criticized (wrongly, I think) for offering only a tailored justification of criminal punishment, nobody is likely to disagree with the characterization of this justification as tailored. The claim that my account views retributivist and consequentialist considerations as jointly necessary to provide the most satisfactory (tailored) justification for punishment stands on different footing. That this is even a fair description of the analysis might be questioned.

Cancellation and logical priority.—Here's reason to worry that my reliance on retributivist desert might be superfluous as support for J(P)(inflicts suffering). My analysis has supposed that consequentialist considerations can, by override, support $J(P_p)$(suffering). A fortiori they can support $J(P_c)$(suffering) by override as well. Furthermore, these considerations might prove competent even to justify infringing individual rights, hence to support both $J(P_c)$(infliction) and $J(P_p)$(infliction). Admittedly, to establish this latter claim would require sustained argument, especially given vigorous disagreements among rights theorists regarding the types of considerations that can serve to justify an infringement thereby forestalling a violation. But even assuming that rights infringements cannot be justified by the goods they produce, almost all agree that, under appropriate circumstances, they can be justified by the need to prevent other rights violations. Possibly, then, punishment in core and peripheral cases can be justified against the fact that punishment infringes rights on the consequentialist ground that such infringements are necessary to prevent, via deterrence and incapacitation, future rights violations. Until this possibility is foreclosed, we are not entitled to conclude

55. In favoring this nomenclature, I am in accord with Wood, though he does not offer reasons for his terminological choice.

that retributivism is necessary for J(P)(infliction), in either core or peripheral cases. And because we have already supposed that J(P) (suffering) can be supported consequentially, it would follow that we cannot yet conclude that retributivism is necessary to support J(P) (inflicts suffering) in any respect.

This powerfully important objection throws into sharp relief the crux of the case for retributivism against consequentialism, which is that consequentialism can only justify punishment by override whereas retributivism can claim to justify punishment by cancellation. So retributivists can concede without great sacrifice that the goods that punishment is reasonably thought to achieve can, by providing reasons of substantial weight in favor of the practice, justify punishment (in core and peripheral cases alike) against the fact that punishment causes suffering. And they can even concede, arguendo, that consequentialist override can justify core and peripheral cases against the fact (if true) that punishment infringes rights. In making these seeming concessions, the retributivist is entitled to emphasize that her arguments enjoy conceptual or logical priority because they proceed by cancellation: once the putative reasons not to punish—that it causes the bad of suffering and that it infringes rights—are shown not to be actual reasons in core cases, then we have no need to search for reasons to punish of greater weight; there is nothing to be overridden. So if the desert claim is sound, and if an effort to rearticulate the right claimed to be at issue can succeed, then it is fair to conclude that the best justification for punishment (tailored against the fact that it inflicts suffering) is indeed dualist.

Dualism and desert.—But is the desert claim sound? Admittedly, my account comes closer to assuming than to proving it. My integration of retributivism and consequentialism is thus of a qualified sort: it is conditioned on the proposition that wrongdoers deserve to suffer.

Certainly it would be nicer not to assume the desert claim but to prove it. This, I have suggested, is more than can be hoped for. So take this analysis as a philosophical explanation in the sense advocated by Nozick—less an argument that (integrated) dualism is true than an explanation of how it could be.[56] Even this, it seems to me, is something we should very much want to know. Retributivists and consequentialists have been locked in fierce debate for centuries, philosophers of the first rank appearing on both sides. To insist on a univocal justification, retributivist or consequentialist, is to dismiss entirely its traditional competitor. In light of the champions each view has won over the years, that is something we ought not to do cavalierly. This is not a matter of comity

56. See Robert Nozick, *Philosophical Explanations* (Cambridge, MA: Belknap Press/ Harvard University Press, 1981), 8–18.

or etiquette. Rather, that many serious thinkers have embraced any particular view might reasonably be taken as some (defeasible) evidence that there's something to it. We might therefore want to know the best case that can be made for a dualist account.

Nonetheless, to concede that my dualist justification of punishment assumes the desert claim might provoke the further objection that whether wrongdoers deserve to suffer (or, equivalently, whether the suffering of wrongdoers on account of their wrongdoing is an intrinsic good) is precisely the matter in dispute between retributivists and their critics. If everybody already agrees on what follows if wrongdoers deserve to suffer, then my account is vacuous.

But the precedent of this conditional is false. Even assuming that wrongdoers deserve to suffer, the analysis in Section V.C demonstrates that retributivism cannot by itself justify punishment, full stop, for it cannot support $J(P_p)$ (suffering). Against retributivists, therefore, my account argues that consequentialism is a necessary component of J(P) (inflicts suffering). Moreover, as already explained, many contemporary antiretributivists have argued strenuously that retributivism provides no part of a satisfactory justification for punishment, even assuming arguendo that wrongdoers deserve to suffer, because it cannot explain why it would be permissible for the state to inflict suffering even if deserved. The retributivist argument by cancellation for $J(P_c)$ (infliction) suggested in Section V.B aims to rebut this objection. In sum, I have argued that (pure) retributivists have claimed that more follows from the proposition that wrongdoers deserve to suffer than can be sustained and that (pure) consequentialists have granted to that proposition less than it earns.

B

We can imagine a three-part distinction among retributivist, consequentialist, and dualist approaches sitting atop a taxonomy of theories of punishment. The dualist approaches themselves might then be usefully divided between the structured and the unstructured. Unstructured dualist accounts are purely additive or "mere conjunction" theories. Structured accounts, in contrast, can be further subdivided into the hierarchical and the nonhierarchical. The dualist account presented here is structured yet nonhierarchical. I have called it "integrated." It offers something more analytically precise and satisfying than a claim that consequentialist and retributivist considerations each go some of the distance in justifying criminal punishment but are jointly necessary to provide all the justificatory force required. At the same time, it demonstrates that the two classes of considerations need not perform different types of justificatory functions.

Necessary to this integration was our initial division of punishment into core and peripheral cases. Yet one might say that this is an arbitrary way of dividing the terrain and that we ought instead to accept Hart's division between the general justifying aim of the institution of punishment and principles of distribution of punishment. And, further, one might reasonably doubt that any part of my analysis undermines the common judgment that, once questions are formulated in Hart's fashion, a consequentialist answer to the first seems nearly preordained. For to inquire into the "general justifying aim" of a practice is no longer to ask for only its "moral justification" but to seek its "rational justification" as well (or, possibly, instead).[57] And while the effectuating of retributive justice could fairly count among the practice's rational justifications, it is unclear how, except by fiat, the retributivist can identify realization of this particular consequence as a justifying aim without allowing that the aim is, accordingly, to realize net good consequences generally.[58]

I do not claim that my way of carving the complex phenomenon of punishment is preferable to Hart's. To the contrary, I believe that no single way of analyzing punishment is natural or essential. One test of a proffered analysis is whether it helps illuminate that which might otherwise have lain obscured. The Hartian distinction between justifying the institution of punishment and justifying individual applications of punishment within that institution has the tendency to make retributivism assume, at best, a marginal or secondary role. When punishment is viewed not as the tail end of an institution whose leading edge consists of the threat of punishment but as the dog itself, and when core and peripheral instances are distinguished, it becomes easier to appreciate why retributivists believe both that the desert of those upon whom suffering is inflicted is morally significant and that its significance cannot be adequately grasped by consequentialists who think in institutional terms.

I realize that separately justifying core and peripheral cases of punishment strikes some as an odd way to proceed. As Mark Greenberg put the worry in conversation, we do not separately justify core and peripheral cases of surgery; rather, we justify the practice or institution of surgery by reference to the goods that it produces (in the core cases) with the understanding that those goods must be sufficiently great to outweigh the bads that arise in the predictable (peripheral) cases when the operation goes awry.

Most practices are justified by the good consequences they achieve. Were the distinction between core and peripheral cases of the practice

57. On the distinction, and how it applies to the justification of punishment, see Dolinko, "Some Thoughts about Retributivism," 539–42.

58. See, generally, Dolinko, "Retributivism, Consequentialism, and the Intrinsic Goodness of Punishment."

drawn (as I draw it in the case of punishment) between those cases the practice is aimed at and those which arise by accident or mistake, we can anticipate in advance that the latter will be justified, if at all, on the grounds that the goods aimed at and secured in the core cases are sufficient to outweigh the bads produced as unavoidable byproduct. Such is what we anticipate in the surgery example and also what we discover, making the strategy of dividing the practice into its core and peripheral cases fruitless. In contrast, the strategy of separating core from peripheral cases of punishment proves illuminating, I believe, because and insofar as justification in the core cases proceeds by cancellation instead of by override. Insofar as the considerations that justify the core cases (against the demand bases on which I focus) are not themselves reasons to engage in the practice, they do not spill over, as it were, to justify the peripheral cases, making it necessary that other considerations (reasons) be brought to bear. Furthermore, the peripheral cases of "misfiring" are pretty obviously not justified in the normal situation (e.g., surgery) except as unavoidable consequences of a practice that is justifiable even accounting for these costs. But, as I noted in Section II, that is not uncontroversially so in the case of punishment. In sum, then, while an analytical framework that separates core and peripheral cases of punishment might be no truer than one that separates the general justifying aim of punishment from principles of distribution, it is no less true either.

VII. CONCLUSION

A sympathetic or charitable understanding of contemporary retributivism requires one to recognize that its proponents are rarely purporting to provide an all-things-considered justification of punishment. More often, they are offering a tailored justification against the fact that punishment inflicts suffering and both of its aspects—that it causes the putative bad of suffering and that, by inflicting that suffering, it putatively infringes rights.

I have aimed to show that this is a successful justification on two plausible assumptions: first, that wrongdoers deserve to suffer on account of and in proportion to their blameworthy wrongdoing; and second, that any supposed general individual right against the infliction of suffering is better understood as only a usually sound implication—not a logical entailment—of some more abstract right such as the right to respect as a person. If so, then retributivism succeeds in justifying core cases of punishment (in which the person punished is responsible for the charged offense and receives punishment proportionate to his blameworthiness) against the fact that it inflicts suffering. Consequentialist considerations might provide justification, too, but the retributivist justification enjoys logical priority.

So far so good for retributivism. But retributivism lacks the resources to provide (in addition to an all-things-considered justification for the core cases) even a tailored justification for peripheral cases of punishment—those in which the imposition of punishment rests on a mistake regarding the defendant's responsibility for the offense. So if peripheral cases are to be justified against the fact that punishment inflicts suffering, and if punishment simpliciter is to be justified all things considered, then consequentialist considerations must be relied upon. In this way, a fuller understanding of the logic of justification supports at least the framework for an integrated dualist justification of punishment.

Name Index